Advances in Artificial Intelligence: Models, Optimization, and Machine Learning, 2nd Edition

Advances in Artificial Intelligence: Models, Optimization, and Machine Learning, 2nd Edition

Guest Editors

Florin Leon
Mircea Hulea
Marius Gavrilescu

Basel • Beijing • Wuhan • Barcelona • Belgrade • Novi Sad • Cluj • Manchester

Guest Editors

Florin Leon
Faculty of Automatic Control
and Computer Engineering
"Gheorghe Asachi" Technical
University of Iași
Iași
Romania

Mircea Hulea
Faculty of Automatic Control
and Computer Engineering
"Gheorghe Asachi" Technical
University of Iași
Iași
Romania

Marius Gavrilescu
Faculty of Automatic Control
and Computer Engineering
"Gheorghe Asachi" Technical
University of Iași
Iași
Romania

Editorial Office
MDPI AG
Grosspeteranlage 5
4052 Basel, Switzerland

This is a reprint of the Special Issue, published open access by the journal *Mathematics* (ISSN 2227-7390), freely accessible at: https://www.mdpi.com/si/mathematics/Artif_Intell_II.

For citation purposes, cite each article independently as indicated on the article page online and as indicated below:

Lastname, A.A.; Lastname, B.B. Article Title. *Journal Name* **Year**, *Volume Number*, Page Range.

ISBN 978-3-7258-3473-0 (Hbk)
ISBN 978-3-7258-3474-7 (PDF)
https://doi.org/10.3390/books978-3-7258-3474-7

© 2025 by the authors. Articles in this book are Open Access and distributed under the Creative Commons Attribution (CC BY) license. The book as a whole is distributed by MDPI under the terms and conditions of the Creative Commons Attribution-NonCommercial-NoDerivs (CC BY-NC-ND) license (https://creativecommons.org/licenses/by-nc-nd/4.0/).

Contents

About the Editors vii

Marius Gavrilescu, Sabina-Adriana Floria, Florin Leon and Silvia Curteanu
A Hybrid Competitive Evolutionary Neural Network Optimization Algorithm for a Regression Problem in Chemical Engineering
Reprinted from: *Mathematics* 2022, 10, 3581, https://doi.org/10.3390/math10193581 1

Biyao Wang, Yi Han, Siyu Wang, Di Tian, Mengjiao Cai, Ming Liu, et al.
A Review of Intelligent Connected Vehicle Cooperative Driving Development
Reprinted from: *Mathematics* 2022, 10, 3635, https://doi.org/10.3390/math10193635 30

Petru Cașcaval and Florin Leon
Optimization Methods for Redundancy Allocation in Hybrid Structure Large Binary Systems
Reprinted from: *Mathematics* 2022, 10, 3698, https://doi.org/10.3390/math10193698 61

Zhiyu Ma, Shaowen Yao, Liwen Wu, Song Gao and Yunqi Zhang
Hateful Memes Detection Based on Multi-Task Learning
Reprinted from: *Mathematics* 2022, 10, 4525, https://doi.org/10.3390/math10234525 94

Minghua Wan, Xichen Wang, Hai Tan and Guowei Yang
Manifold Regularized Principal Component Analysis Method Using L2,p-Norm
Reprinted from: *Mathematics* 2022, 10, 4603, https://doi.org/10.3390/math10234603 110

Andreea-Iulia Patachi and Florin Leon
Multiagent Multimodal Trajectory Prediction in Urban Traffic Scenarios Using a Neural Network-Based Solution
Reprinted from: *Mathematics* 2023, 11, 1923, https://doi.org/10.3390/math11081923 127

Yuto Omae
Effects of Exploration Weight and Overtuned Kernel Parameters on Gaussian Process-Based Bayesian Optimization Search Performance
Reprinted from: *Mathematics* 2023, 11, 3067, https://doi.org/10.3390/math11143067 152

Sultan Almotairi, Elsayed Badr, Mustafa Abdul Salam and Hagar Ahmed
Breast Cancer Diagnosis Using a Novel Parallel Support Vector Machine with Harris Hawks Optimization
Reprinted from: *Mathematics* 2023, 11, 3251, https://doi.org/10.3390/math11143251 165

Yahao Hu, Yifei Xie, Tianfeng Wang, Man Chen and Zhisong Pan
Structure-Aware Low-Rank Adaptation for Parameter-Efficient Fine-Tuning
Reprinted from: *Mathematics* 2023, 11, 4317, https://doi.org/10.3390/math11204317 190

Gyunyeop Kim, Joon Yoo and Sangwoo Kang
Efficient Federated Learning with Pre-Trained Large Language Model Using Several Adapter Mechanisms
Reprinted from: *Mathematics* 2023, 11, 4479, https://doi.org/10.3390/math11214479 206

Hari Mohan Rai and Joon Yoo
Analysis of Colorectal and Gastric Cancer Classification: A Mathematical Insight Utilizing Traditional Machine Learning Classifiers
Reprinted from: *Mathematics* 2023, 11, 4937, https://doi.org/10.3390/math11244937 225

Yujing Zhou, Dubo He
Multi-Target Feature Selection with Adaptive Graph Learning and Target Correlations
Reprinted from: *Mathematics* **2024**, *12*, 372, https://doi.org/10.3390/math12030372 . . . . **265**

Nan Ma, Hongqi Li and Hualin Liu
State-Space Compression for Efficient Policy Learning in Crude Oil Scheduling
Reprinted from: *Mathematics* **2024**, *12*, 393, https://doi.org/10.3390/math12030393 . . . . **289**

Eunseok Yoo, Gyunyeop Kim and Sangwoo Kang
Summary-Sentence Level Hierarchical Supervision for Re-Ranking Model of Two-Stage Abstractive Summarization Framework
Reprinted from: *Mathematics* **2024**, *12*, 521, https://doi.org/10.3390/math12040521 . . . . **305**

Esperanza García-Gonzalo, Paulino José García-Nieto, Gregorio Fidalgo Valverde, Pedro Riesgo Fernández, Fernando Sánchez Lasheras and Sergio Luis Suárez Gómez
Hybrid DE-Optimized GPR and NARX/SVR Models for Forecasting Gold Spot Prices: A Case Study of the Global Commodities Market
Reprinted from: *Mathematics* **2024**, *12*, 1039, https://doi.org/10.3390/math12071039 . . . . **322**

Silu He, Jun Cao, Shijuan Gao, Hongyuan Yuan, Zhe Chen and Haifeng Li
Graph Information Vanishing Phenomenon in Implicit Graph Neural Networks
Reprinted from: *Mathematics* **2024**, *12*, 2659, https://doi.org/10.3390/math12172659 . . . . **340**

About the Editors

Florin Leon

Florin Leon, Ph.D., is currently a Full Professor at the Department of Computer Science and Engineering of the "Gheorghe Asachi" University of Iasi, Romania. He received a doctoral degree in computer science from the same university, followed by a postdoctoral fellowship completed in 2007. In 2015, he defended his habilitation thesis. He has authored and co-authored more than 200 journal articles, book chapters, and conference papers and 14 books. He has 1189 citations with an h-index of 16 according to Scopus. He was a member of the guest editorial boards for three journal Special Issues, and he has participated in thirty national and international research projects, four of which were as the principal investigator. His scientific interests include artificial intelligence, machine learning, multiagent systems, and software design. In his research, he used various machine learning techniques for modeling, such as simple, stacked, and deep neural networks; instance-based methods; and large-margin nearest-neighbor regression. He also addressed optimization problems using different types of evolutionary algorithms, quantum-inspired algorithms, and combinations of global and local search methods. Moreover, he studied multi-agent systems with complex behaviors and performed various agent-based simulations. Prof. Leon is currently a member of IEEE Systems, Man and Cybernetics Society: Computational Collective Intelligence Technical Community, and the Romanian Association for Artificial Intelligence.

Mircea Hulea

Mircea Hulea, Ph.D., is currently a Full Professor at the Department of Computer Science and Engineering of the "Gheorghe Asachi" Technical University of Iasi, Romania. He received his M.S. and Ph.D. degrees in Computer Engineering and Automatic Control from the same University in 2004 and 2008, respectively. In this institution, he was also a Postdoctoral Researcher when he worked on the project of biomimetic hardware and software systems and their applications, from 2010 to 2013. Besides this postdoctoral project, he leads two projects in the frameworks of hardware implementation of spiking neural networks, which were the starting point and support for his scientific activity. The scientific results were disseminated in more than 35 papers, which are published with him as the main author, 25 being indexed in the Web of Science. His research interests include brain modeling, artificial intelligence, and humanoid robotics. He is the coordinator of the collaborative research network on spiking neural networks at the host university.

Marius Gavrilescu

Marius Gavrilescu, Ph.D., is an Associate Professor in the Department of Computer Science and Engineering at the "Gheorghe Asachi" Technical University of Iași, Romania. His research focuses on machine learning, including classification and regression models, object recognition, and deep learning architecture, primarily applied to medical image processing and data from natural sciences. He is also involved in computer graphics and data visualization, particularly in the visual representation and rendering of multidimensional medical imaging data, volume graphics, GPU programming, as well as image filtering, enhancement, and analysis of applications in the automotive industry, natural sciences, climatology, and meteorology. Additionally, his work extends to modeling and simulating physical phenomena such as fluid dynamics, collisions, and optical models using ray tracing or path tracing, along with real-time graphics and physics engines.

Article

A Hybrid Competitive Evolutionary Neural Network Optimization Algorithm for a Regression Problem in Chemical Engineering

Marius Gavrilescu [1,*], Sabina-Adriana Floria [1], Florin Leon [1] and Silvia Curteanu [2]

[1] Faculty of Automatic Control and Computer Engineering, "Gheorghe Asachi" Technical University of Iași, 700050 Iași, Romania
[2] Faculty of Chemical Engineering and Environmental Protection, "Gheorghe Asachi" Technical University of Iași, 700050 Iași, Romania
* Correspondence: marius.gavrilescu@academic.tuiasi.ro

Abstract: Neural networks have demonstrated their usefulness for solving complex regression problems in circumstances where alternative methods do not provide satisfactory results. Finding a good neural network model is a time-consuming task that involves searching through a complex multidimensional hyperparameter and weight space in order to find the values that provide optimal convergence. We propose a novel neural network optimizer that leverages the advantages of both an improved evolutionary competitive algorithm and gradient-based backpropagation. The method consists of a modified, hybrid variant of the Imperialist Competitive Algorithm (ICA). We analyze multiple strategies for initialization, assimilation, revolution, and competition, in order to find the combination of ICA steps that provides optimal convergence and enhance the algorithm by incorporating a backpropagation step in the ICA loop, which, together with a self-adaptive hyperparameter adjustment strategy, significantly improves on the original algorithm. The resulting hybrid method is used to optimize a neural network to solve a complex problem in the field of chemical engineering: the synthesis and swelling behavior of the semi- and interpenetrated multicomponent crosslinked structures of hydrogels, with the goal of predicting the yield in a crosslinked polymer and the swelling degree based on several reaction-related input parameters. We show that our approach has better performance than other biologically inspired optimization algorithms and generates regression models capable of making predictions that are better correlated with the desired outputs.

Keywords: evolutionary algorithm; biologically inspired optimization; neural network optimization; imperialist competitive algorithm; regression model

MSC: 68W50

1. Introduction

Natural sciences and their related fields of research are essential for providing key answers to a wide range of real-world problems. Finding such answers nearly always involves an experimental phase, where data is collected by observing real-world phenomena or events, carrying out experiments within chemical and/or physical processes and noting the reaction outcomes, or using various sources and sensor arrays. Such methods generally produce large amounts of complex, multidimensional, and often unstructured data, which are difficult to interpret and make sense of.

In particular, chemical engineering processes present difficulties in modeling for several reasons. Often, the experiments are difficult to perform, being time-, material-, and energy-consuming. The mechanisms of complex processes are either unknown or not fully elucidated, which makes it difficult to apply material or energy balances specific to classic modeling. If mathematical models can be obtained, they are often based on approximations that affect their accuracy; they are complex models that are difficult to solve and, above all,

Citation: Gavrilescu, M.; Floria, S.-A.; Leon, F.; Curteanu, S. A Hybrid Competitive Evolutionary Neural Network Optimization Algorithm for a Regression Problem in Chemical Engineering. *Mathematics* 2022, 10, 3581. https://doi.org/10.3390/math10193581

Academic Editor: José Antonio Sanz

Received: 30 August 2022
Accepted: 27 September 2022
Published: 30 September 2022

Publisher's Note: MDPI stays neutral with regard to jurisdictional claims in published maps and institutional affiliations.

Copyright: © 2022 by the authors. Licensee MDPI, Basel, Switzerland. This article is an open access article distributed under the terms and conditions of the Creative Commons Attribution (CC BY) license (https://creativecommons.org/licenses/by/4.0/).

implement online. Thus, the use of "black box" models represents a beneficial approach for many situations in chemical engineering.

Consequently, a wide diversity of numerical processing methods has emerged over the years, which allow for structuring such data and deducing meaningful information from the underlying values. The end goal of such methods is to generate a mathematical or numerical model that describes the studied phenomenon/reaction/experiment as accurately as the experimental data will allow. It is very common for the task of interpreting experimental data to be reduced to a regression problem, where a relationship should be determined among one or multiple inputs and one or multiple observed outcomes. A frequent solution to such a problem is the development of a regression model that consists of a function that maps the inputs to the outputs, given that the outputs are real values from continuous domains. In instances where the data are of high dimensionality and complexity, a common approach is to search for a regression model by numeric optimization of a regression algorithm's parameters. The choice in terms of an adequate algorithm is a difficult one, as many pitfalls exist given the problematic nature of experimentally gathered data. To this extent, neural networks have consistently proven their usefulness for solving complex problems such as those found in natural sciences. Sufficiently tuned and trained neural networks have demonstrated that they are capable of providing meaningful models of the relationships found within the inputs and outputs of experimental data. Such models allow for the generalization of the underlying phenomenon, given that enough effort was invested in searching for the right parameters that provide optimal convergence.

Neural networks can model complex relationships otherwise not possible with more basic alternatives. However, a neural network-based model requires searching through a complex parameter space in order to determine a set of values for the network hyperparameters and weights that provides the optimal solution for the problem at hand. Finding the right neural network architecture and the optimal weight values is often a tedious and time-consuming task, particularly for complex data sets, which themselves require a complex model to completely characterize them. Neural networks require extensive training, a comprehensive exploration of their hyperparameter space, and extensive validation before the right architecture and weights are found for a particular regression problem. Searching for the optimal neural network-based model is usually divided into two tasks: searching through the hyperparameter space of the network to find its optimal architecture and training the said architecture to find the optimal weight values. The former task, in particular, requires extensive computational resources and takes a lengthy amount of time before an optimal architecture is found, especially if an exhaustive exploration of the hyperparameter space is desired. Traditionally, searching through a neural network hyperspace is carried out using either a grid search or a random search. The former involves separately traversing through each hyperparameter domain by sampling each hyperparameter space axis into a finite number of parameter values and iterating through them in order. For each combination of parameter values, a new candidate model is trained and validated. In the latter case, random parameter values are generated from each corresponding hyperparameter domain, producing a candidate model for each random combination of hyperparameters to also be trained and validated. Ultimately, the model that minimizes the loss function or otherwise meets the desired convergence criterion is chosen. Grid searches are useful for systematically iterating through the hyperparameter space or a relevant portion of it, particularly in cases where an even sampling of the space is desired. A finer sampling of each axis yields mode candidate models and a greater chance of finding the optimal one at the cost of more computational time and power required to validate a greater number of models. Random searches are useful when the hyperparameter space is too vast for a systematic grid search. The number of generated candidate models increases the probability of finding the optimal model; however, there is little guarantee that this will occur within a reasonable search time frame and a certain amount of "luck" is required for a good candidate model to be found. In both scenarios, a significant amount of time is required for a good neural network model to be identified.

For this reason, other search methods have been developed to more efficiently search through vast parameter spaces, of which the most notable are evolutionary algorithms. These are usually inspired by natural evolution, where animal and plant species sustain and propagate based on the "survival of the fittest" principle. Given a certain environment with certain characteristics, out of a population, only the individuals most suited to living in that environment survive and reproduce. Therefore, each generation statistically originates from the fittest individuals from the previous one. The evolution of organisms in the natural environment translates well to the evolution of candidate solutions to a given problem that can be mathematically modeled. A multitude of potential solutions that form a population of individuals is subjected within an evolutionary algorithm to mechanisms that mimic transformations occurring in the natural world, such as reproduction, gene crossover, and mutation. The fittest individuals are the ones who offer better solutions to the problem at hand and they are the ones who statistically propagate throughout the iterations of the evolutionary algorithm. For regression problems, finding the solution is often reduced to a minimization problem, where the optimal solution is the one that minimizes an error/loss/cost function. The fitness of a solution, therefore, translates to a lower error value, with the optimal solution being the one with the highest fitness, i.e., the lowest error value.

Evolutionary algorithms have consistently proven to be capable of solving difficult multidimensional problems due to their ability to efficiently explore vast complex solution spaces [1]. An evolutionary-based approach offers more room for experimenting with various random sampling, mutation, and crossover population combination functionalities, which means that they are highly configurable and customizable to specific problems of high complexity. This means that a carefully customized evolutionary algorithm often succeeds at locating the global minimum within a minimization problem and therefore finding the optimal solution, where alternative methods generally fail. Here we would also like to mention gradient descent-based solutions, which tend to get stuck in local minima and are difficult to use for problems with complex search spaces [2].

Considering the abovementioned context, this paper deals with a problem within the field of chemical engineering—the synthesis of polyacrylamide-based multicomponent hydrogels, with the goal of modeling the yield and swelling degree as functions of the reaction conditions. Consequently, the objective can be formulated as a multivariate regression problem, where we want to find a relationship/correlation between the inputs and the output variables. Despite the relatively small size of the available dataset, this regression problem has proven resilient to simple, commonly used regression methods. Therefore, we resort to finding a regression model based on optimizing a fully connected neural network that offers sufficient flexibility for exploring the complex solution space of our available data. In order to optimize the neural network, we propose an evolutionary algorithm that is based on the popular Imperialist Competitive Algorithm (ICA) [3], which we customize and modify so as to effectively explore the hyperparameter and weight space of the neural network and find the optimal architecture and weight values that should minimize the loss for our regression problem. Customization involves making modifications to the more essential steps of the traditional ICA to improve the convergence results, and, where possible, convergence speed. Furthermore, we combine the modified version of the ICA with a backpropagation-based approach by incorporating partial backpropagation training steps within the iterations of the modified ICA. As we describe in the subsequent sections, such an approach has proven to improve convergence effectiveness and speed and therefore lead to better neural network configurations. We use backpropagation as a boosting mechanism, which is meant to slightly "push" the solutions within an ICA iteration toward the optimum. The resulting hybrid algorithm generates neural network models that minimize the Root Mean Squared Error (RMSE) for our dataset to within an order of magnitude less than alternative algorithms while maintaining decent convergence times. We further improve the proposed approach by incorporating adaptive and self-adaptive strategies within the algorithm pipeline. These strategies form a two-part parameter control mechanism: the parameters of the hybrid ICA are adapted along the iterations of the algorithm using methods that are aimed at improving the convergence results and speed; and along with the adapted phase, we employ a self-adaptive strategy, where the parameters of the algorithm are incorporated into the chromosome of the candidate solutions, in which situation the algorithm searches through its own hyperparameter space while also exploring the solution space of the neural network. This self-adaptive strategy means that the hybrid ICA optimizes itself along with the neural network. Such mechanisms added to the basic ICA have shown to improve the convergence results and speed for our problem, as we detail in the subsequent sections.

Our contributions can be summarized as follows:

- We propose a variant of the ICA with alternative versions of some of its fundamental components. To this extent, we analyzed several versions of assimilation, revolution, and competition in order to find the ones that provide the best convergence for our problem.
- We test several initialization strategies in order to find the one that disperses the initial population as evenly as possible throughout the solution space. This allows us to generate initial populations that offer good coverage while having a relatively small individual count. Furthermore, we employ adaptive and self-adaptive strategies to dynamically tune the hyperparameters of the evolutionary algorithm during its iterations.
- We incorporate a backpropagation-boosting mechanism into the iterations of the modified ICA, where each neural network candidate is slightly steered in the direction of the optimal solution using a gradient-based optimizer. This significantly contributes to improving convergence and to minimizing the RMSE. The resulting combination of the modified evolutionary algorithm and the backpropagation-based optimization forms our hybrid method.

The paper is structured as follows. After the Introduction, Section 2 presents the chemical engineering problem and the underlying mechanisms from which our data set originates, as well as the relevant experimentally determined parameters that constitute the inputs and outputs of our regression model. Section 3 presents the most significant results from related state-of-the-art models, in terms of using evolutionary algorithms for general-purpose problems, optimizing neural networks, and achieving good convergence results for difficult regression problems. In Section 4 we present the modified hybrid ICA and provide detailed descriptions of the steps involved in the ICA iterations, the modifications made to the basic algorithm, the particularities of the hybrid aspect of our method, as well as the adaptive and self-adaptive strategies used for parameter control. In Section 5 we present the results of our work, demonstrate the benefits of our customized version of ICA considering all aspects involved, and provide a comparison to other similar approaches from the related literature in terms of convergence effectiveness and speed. The paper ends with the Conclusions, where we provide a closing discussion related to our method and highlight the limitations and possible future improvements of the algorithm.

2. The Case Study

Multicomponent hydrogels are materials characterized by a high swelling capacity and possess special properties (mechanical, diffusion, and absorption), which make their use in various domains possible —food, cosmetics, the pharmaceutical industry, medicine, tissue engineering, agriculture, electrotechnics, electronics, etc.

For many applications, e.g., controlled-release systems, agrochemical products, multicomponent hydrogels are required to present a high capacity of biodegradation under the action of the biologic fluids or the microorganisms present in the soil. In addition, these materials present selective biodegradability under the action of gastrointestinal juices so they can be used as a covering agent for tablets to protect the active principle, conceal the non-agreeable taste and smell, as well as control the release of the active principle. Three-dimensional networks based on polyacrylamide are used in ophthalmology as mechanical protectors for the iris, retina, and corneal endothelia. These are just a few examples that justify the choice of this process for study through modeling and simulation.

From the point of view of modeling action, a high-molecular-weight polymer system represents complex classes of materials and is very difficult to model. Besides being highly nonlinear, there are a large number of parameters that need to be accurately defined if such systems are to be properly characterized. The relationships between the parameters being modeled and the actual behavior of these variables in the real world must be correlated as precisely as possible. However, in most cases, this is not possible and several approximations and simplifications are often made at various stages. Considering the lack of complete knowledge about the phenomenology of the process, the main reasons why a phenomenological model for the addressed process could not be developed were highlighted.

In some previous papers, we reported the synthesis and swelling behavior of semi- and interpenetrated multicomponent crosslinked structures based on polyacrylamide [4–6]. For this process, the yield in the crosslinked polymer and the swelling degree were determined as a function of the monomer (acrylamide) concentration, initiator concentration, crosslinking agent (formaldehyde) concentration, amount of inclusion polymer (starch, poly(vinyl alcohol) (PVA), gelatin), temperature, and reaction time. The experimental results containing 177 data are given in Curteanu et al. [4].

The results obtained using the previous approaches were encouraging but susceptible to error. Consequently, in the current research, improved methods are proposed for modeling the main property of hydrogels, namely the degree of swelling, along with the efficiency of the process.

Seven input variables were considered: CM (monomer concentration), CI (initiator concentration), CA (crosslinking agent concentration), PI (amount of inclusion polymer), T (temperature), t (reaction time), and type of included polymer codified as 1—no polymer added, 2—starch, 3—PVA, and 4—gelatin. The two outputs were η (yield in the crosslinked polymer) and α (swelling degree). Thus, the neural network modeling established the influence of the initial conditions on the reaction yield and swelling degree.

The predictions of the two outputs are useful in practice because they are related to process efficiency (yield) and they can replace experiments that necessitate a great number of materials and, especially, time (a determination of the swelling degree takes around 20 days).

3. Related Work

Neuroevolution (NE) is a procedure in which an evolutionary algorithm (EA) is used to optimize an artificial neural network and is an alternative to classical training (i.e., gradient-based algorithms). It can also evolve the hyperparameters of neural networks, such as the number of hidden layers, the number of neurons in each layer, biases, and the activation functions. Interestingly, neuroevolutionary methods achieve promising results using simple evolutionary algorithms [7], and proposing new strategies for these simple algorithms can significantly improve the convergence of training a neural network and its prediction performance. Although neuroevolutionary methods are generally computationally expensive, especially in deep learning [8], they are still preferred because they also offer flexibility in choosing the cost function (e.g., reward maximization [9]).

Various studies have been carried out in the literature on small-sized neural networks with fixed topologies in addition to studies that have addressed the evolution of neural network architecture.

Three neural network models, namely Multi-Layer Perceptron (MLP), Recurrent Neural Network (RNN), and Evolutionary Neural Networks (Neuroevolution: MLP-ABC), were used in [10] to predict the output of a photovoltaic panel. The authors used the Artificial Bee Colony (ABC) algorithm to optimize the neural network weights. The experimental results showed that the MLP-ABC model provided the best results.

In [11], four evolutionary algorithms, i.e., Multi-Verse Optimizer (MVO), Moth–flame optimization (MFO), Cuckoo Search (CS), and Particle Swarm Optimization (PSO), were used to train and optimize MLPs. The trained MLPs were then used to navigate an autonomous robot. The authors proposed two strategies for avoiding the local optimum, which were applied to each algorithm. In the first proposed strategy, 20% of the worst solutions were reinitialized at each iteration. The second strategy consisted of a mutation operator that randomly changed the genes of some solutions with a 20% chance. The experimental results showed that MFO had the lowest mean square error value and the fastest convergence speed. Also, MFO had a superior ability to avoid local optimum and good optimization efficiency. PSO, in particular, has seen extensive use for neural architecture search with applications for convolutional neural networks [12,13], deep belief networks [14,15], and autoencoders [16,17]. In most cases, the encoding of the particles only encompassed the hyperparameters of the neural networks, leaving the tuning of the optimal architecture to a more traditional backpropagation-based approach.

In [18], the authors solved an electrical load problem using a 1D convolutional neural network tweaked using a variant of Enhanced Grey Wolf Optimization (EGWO). Like many other evolutionary algorithms, this optimizer draws inspiration from the behavior of an animal in its natural habitat, specifically, the hunting behavior of wolves. The solution candidates were divided into hierarchical categories (such as alpha and beta individuals) and they interacted throughout the solution space via a mathematical model that simulated a pack-like behavior. Aside from the actual optimization, the authors noted the fast convergence of this meta-heuristic model and the low requirements in terms of computational resources.

The Cellular Genetic Algorithm (CGA) was used in [19] to find optimal weights of MLP to classify medical data accurately. The authors proposed a specially designed crossover operator called Damped Crossover (DX) that used information related to the best solution in the current iteration and the stage of the evolutionary process. The DX operator had a greater influence on the changing variables at the beginning of the evolutionary process and a reduced influence at the end of the iterations (i.e., the operator was more accurate at the end of the evolutionary process).

The Biogeography-based Optimization algorithm (BBO) was used in [20] to train the MLP to classify the sonar dataset, a high-dimensional problem. To improve the exploration ability of BBO, the authors used various mutation operators based on Gaussian mutation, Cauchy mutation, and exponential mutation and then proposed a novel mixed mutation strategy called Neighborhood Search Trainer (NST). The NST strategy consisted of a combination of Gaussian, Cauchy, and exponential mutations.

In [21], six neuroevolutionary classification techniques were used for the slope/failure stability assessment problem. The MLP was trained with Ant Colony Optimization (ACO), BBO, Evolutionary Strategy (ES), Genetic Algorithm (GA), Probability-based Incremental Learning (PBIL), and PSO to improve classification accuracy in the stability assessment. The experimental results showed that the MLP trained with the BBO algorithm obtained the best classification accuracy.

Two optimization techniques, i.e., GA and Binary Particle Swarm (BPS) optimization, were used in [22] to improve the predictive power of credit risk scorecards. GA and BPS were used to find the optimal architecture of an MLP along with activation functions, whereas the weights were optimized with the backpropagation algorithm. In terms of predictability, the two optimization techniques outperformed the logistic regression and a default neural network, but GA was more time-consuming than BPS.

In [23], a genetic algorithm was used with the ADAM optimizer to optimize the architecture and parameters of small neural networks. The problem addressed was the compact modeling of MOSFET devices using neural networks. Due to the requirements of requiring a compact model, the optimization problem consisted of finding a neural network of a small size that provided the most accurate answer. The authors used a genetic algorithm to find the optimal topology of the neural network, and ADAM was used to optimize the weights and biases. The architecture of a neural network is defined using blocks of neurons, and how these blocks are connected can lead to partially connected neural networks. By limiting the number of connections between blocks of neurons, the authors minimized the genetic algorithm's search space and improved the network training's convergence speed.

Neuroevolution has also been successfully used in modeling PID controllers [24]. The authors used an MLP neural network with two hidden layers in a closed-loop feedback control to replace a PID controller. The chosen neural network, i.e., the neurocontroller, was subject to unsupervised learning because the optimal behavior of the developed controller was unknown. The training consisted of using a genetic algorithm to optimize the weights and biases of the neurocontroller so that specific closed-loop performance indices were minimized. The experimental results showed that the neurocontroller provided significantly better results than a linear PID controller.

A new algorithm, Evolutionary eXploration of Augmenting Memory Models (EX-AMM), was proposed in [25] to evolve recurrent neural network (RNN) architectures with various cell types to perform the prediction of large-scale, real-world time-series data from the aviation and power industries. The EXAMM algorithm was further used in [26], where a novel speciation strategy based on extinction and repopulation events was proposed (specific strategy for island-based evolutionary algorithms).

Differential evolution (DE) is a popular approach used to optimize the hyperparameters of a wide variety of neural networks. In [27], the authors used a DE algorithm to optimize a pi-sigma neural network. This network drew from traditional MLPs and extended them by incorporating higher-order combinations of the inputs. The authors noted that, although such networks may lead to better solutions for certain complex problems, the added operations also increase the complexity of the network architecture and, consequently, the resulting hyperparameter space. A DE-based approach was, therefore, chosen to optimize the neural network to solve various forecasting problems, with accuracies reported as being higher than those obtained using simpler network structures. In [28], the authors optimized a neural network using differential evolution in order to tackle a lithology identification problem from a geological field. They reported significantly better accuracies compared to more traditional classification algorithms. At the same time, the DE-based approach proved to be able to explore the solution space much more effectively than using a more conventional exhaustive hyperparameter search.

Another category of problems where DE-based optimization is sometimes employed is medical image processing. The authors from [29] presented a technique for medical image fusion using a deep neural network derived from the Inception architecture. Unlike other applications where the objective is to search for the optimal hyperparameters of the network, in this case, a DE algorithm was used to search the feature map space for the best features to be used within the fusion pipeline. In [30], the authors developed a classification model for medical image-based diagnoses using an evolutionary algorithm to optimize the pruning strategy of Generative Adversarial Networks (GAN). Notably, the resulting model offered similar accuracies to the unpruned version, albeit using significantly reduced computational resources. Other significant results in the above-mentioned approaches focused on using DE and/or bio-inspired optimizers for handling global optimization problems [31–33].

Some notable results handled problems involving supply chain management and the related decision-making strategies using multiple exact optimization methods [34–39].

Another form of neural network hyperparameter optimization is cooperative neuroevolution, which has been successfully used in training RNNs for chaotic time-series problems (e.g., signal processing, finance, weather forecasting, etc.) [40,41]. Cooperative neuroevolution is more effective in predicting time-series problems than backpropagation through time [40] or other standard evolutionary algorithms [41]. In this type of optimization, a neural network is decomposed into subcomponents divided into different subpopulations. Initially, the individuals in the created subpopulations do not have fitness because an individual represents only a subcomponent of a neural network. The evaluation of an individual begins with sampling other individuals from the other subpopulations. Afterward, all the chosen individuals are concatenated to reconstruct a neural network and the fitness can be computed.

An increased interest in neuroevolution has also been seen in other fields, such as medicine [42–45], chemistry [46,47], education [48], and games [49,50].

4. Method Description

Our approach focused on finding the optimal neural network architecture and weight values that constitute the best model for describing the aforementioned regression problem. Specifically, the method was intended for searching the combined hyperparameter and parameter spaces of a fully connected neural network to find the best values resulting in the optimal model. For this purpose, we developed an evolutionary algorithm that searched through the network parameter space for the optimal parameter values as quickly and efficiently as possible.

Throughout the paper, we use well-known and understood terminology with regard to the key terms that define the architecture and functionality of a fully connected neural network. The number of hidden layers and the size of each hidden layer in terms of neuron count are hyperparameters, whereas the weights and biases of the network are simply its parameters. We differentiate the hyperparameters of the neural network from the hyperparameters of the evolutionary algorithm, which are the various variables that influence the functionality of the evolutionary method. Among these are the parameters of the various operators applied to the candidate solutions during the iterations of the algorithms, for example, the mutation probability or the assimilation distance.

Our methodology involved combining the hyperparameters and parameters of the neural network into a single network parameter space. Consequently, searching for the optimal neural network involved simultaneously optimizing the architecture of the neural network and its weights and biases, unlike traditional search-train-validate-test approaches, where designing the neural network is a separate task from training it. Therefore, a solution from the perspective of an evolutionary optimizer is a complete set of neural network parameters. The optimal solution, which is the goal of the search, is the set of neural network hyperparameters and parameters that fit the convergence criterion of the problem at hand. In our case, we aimed to find the neural network that minimizes the RMSE of the network predictions from the inputs of the dataset instances and the actual outputs from the same instances. In evolutionary optimization language, a potential solution is encoded as a chromosome containing the full set of neural network parameters, whereas the fitness of an individual with a specific chromosome is the inverse of the RMSE resulting from evaluating the corresponding neural network on the dataset corresponding to the regression problem. Consequently, in our implementation, we considered that the fitter individuals were the ones that generated lower RMSE values, or, in more general terms, that had a lower cost.

Our proposed neural network optimizer was based on the Imperialist Competitive Algorithm, to which we applied multiple modifications intended to improve the convergence results and, where possible, convergence speed. In order to achieve this goal, we implemented alternative versions of the fundamental ICA steps, incorporated a backpropagation boosting mechanism that significantly improved convergence, and added parameter control strategies meant to tweak and optimize the algorithm hyperparameters during execution. We refer to the resulting algorithm as a hybrid of an evolutionary algorithm and backpropagation-based optimization, which leverages the advantages of both approaches to generate a neural network solution that is as close as possible to the optimal one. As we shall illustrate in the subsequent sections, the behavior of this approach is twofold:

- The evolutionary algorithm has the advantage of thoroughly searching through the parameter space of the neural network for a solution that minimizes the RMSE. As we discovered after multiple attempts, the neural network space was sufficiently

complex and had a high-enough dimensionality to make it difficult for the evolutionary algorithm alone to explore it and settle in a global minimum.
- A backpropagation component was incorporated into the evolutionary algorithm's pipeline and significantly contributed to proper convergence. With each iteration, its role was to "steer" the solutions in the direction of the optimum. Essentially, this component involved partially training each neural network solution in a backpropagation manner using gradient-based optimization.

4.1. Neural Network Encoding

As with most evolutionary algorithms, the solutions were represented via a 1D vector of genes forming the solution's chromosome. For our purposes, we required that each neural network candidate be represented in the same manner. We achieved this by re-organizing the parameters and hyperparameters into a "flattened" version of the neural network, where the parameter values were arranged as a one-dimensional array. The resulting two-part chromosome had the following structure:
- A header containing the hyperparameters—the number of hidden layers followed by the hidden layer sizes in order from the input to the output layers.
- A larger body that contained the weights and biases in the same order as found in the neural network layers—first, the flattened weight matrix between the input and first hidden layer, followed by the bias vector of the input layer, followed by the next weight matrix and the corresponding bias vector, and so on.

Note that we used constant-size chromosomes; therefore, the size of each chromosome was the highest possible number of neural network parameters. For networks with fewer parameters than the maximum, the extra values were simply ignored. We found no advantage in using variable-size chromosomes, the only significant difference being a more complex implementation.

The encoding procedure of a neural network is illustrated in Figure 1. The general format of the chromosome shown in Figure 1a is presented for neural networks with a maximum of two hidden layers. The length of the chromosome was set to accommodate the largest possible network with the highest parameter count. For example, if we searched for a network with a maximum of 2 hidden layers and a maximum hidden layer size of 10, considering 7 inputs and 2 outputs, the size of the chromosome would be $3 + 7 \cdot 10 + 10 + 10 \cdot 10 + 10 + 10 \cdot 2 + 2 = 215$, which accommodates a header size of 3 (the number of hidden layers and the size of each hidden layer) and the values of the weights and biases for the maximum-sized network. While searching for the best neural network configuration, we represented any potential network candidate via the maximum-sized chromosome. In cases where the optimal neural network had fewer parameters than the maximum, the "extra" values from the chromosome were simply ignored when reconstituting the corresponding neural network. For example, if the optimal neural network had a single hidden layer, the third value from the chromosome (which represents the size of the second hidden layer) was ignored, despite it being present in the chromosome structure. Likewise, a network with a single hidden layer would have fewer parameters than the maximum count. In this case, only the necessary values for rebuilding the neural network were used and the other trailing ones were ignored. This allowed for the use of constant-sized chromosomes within our evolutionary algorithm, which simplified the implementation to a certain extent. We also experimented with variable-size chromosomes, where each flattened neural network was sized according to the actual number of network parameters. In our experience, there was no noticeable benefit to this approach. Considering that our population was rather small (100 initial solutions), using fixed-size chromosomes did not significantly impact memory use and computational requirements. Conversely, using variable chromosome sizes complicated the implementation, particularly with regard to the adaptive sampling strategy, which is discussed later in this paper. Consequently, the population was formed from fixed-size solutions, where each corresponding chromosome was large enough to store the values of any neural network candidates.

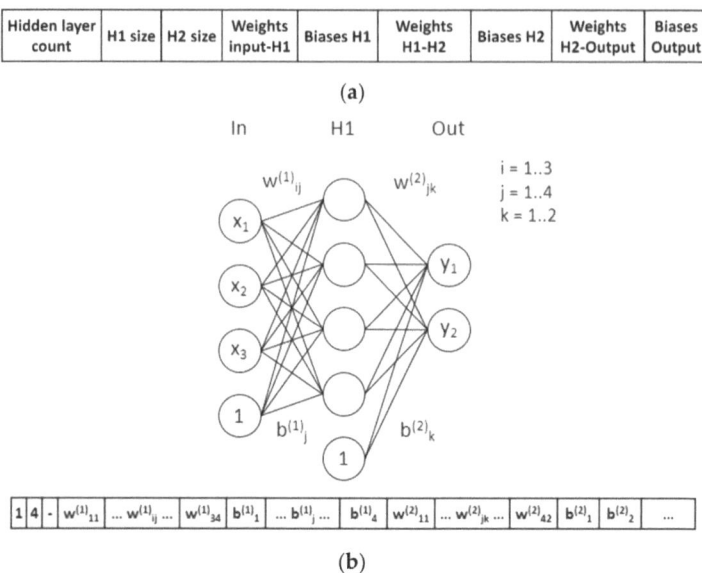

Figure 1. Arranging (flattening) the parameters of a neural network into a 1D array forming a chromosome. The flattening method is illustrated for neural networks with a maximum of two hidden layers but is easily adaptable to larger architectures. (**a**) The general format, regardless of the actual neural network architecture; (**b**) An example of flattening a single hidden layer network into a chromosome.

4.2. The Evolutionary Competitive Algorithm

The evolutionary component of our method was an enhanced version of the Imperialist Competitive Algorithm (ICA), to which we made several modifications and additions in order to improve convergence in our dataset (Figure 2). The main task of the evolutionary algorithm was to explore the parameter space of a fully connected neural network and find a neural network architecture and weight values that come as close as possible to the optimum. Consequently, in the context of the evolutionary algorithm, a solution was a potential neural network configuration, represented by the configuration described in Section 4.1. The optimal solution was the network configuration that minimized the RMSE on our dataset, which could in more general terms be thought of as the *cost* of the solution. Therefore, the evolutionary algorithm searched through the solution space for the minimum-cost solution. The ICA was modeled on the interaction among countries and empires in the course of which the empires compete for dominance. The solutions were considered countries. Some of the solutions were imperialist countries, around which the other countries, known as colonies, formed groups known as empires. Thus, the population was formed from a few of the better solutions, the imperialist countries, which owned the other solutions, the colonies. Each imperialist country competed for the accumulation of as many colonies as possible until there was one dominant empire. Such interaction should ultimately lead to the optimal solution while avoiding the pitfalls of complex, difficult-to-explore solution spaces with multiple local minima. Although it is not the purpose of this paper to describe the ICA in detail, we loosely outline the most significant steps of the classic algorithm:

- As with any evolutionary algorithm, the population is initialized according to a specific sampling policy. Empires and their colonies are also initialized.
- The countries are subjected to an assimilation step, where each empire strengthens its hold on its colonies. Each colony moves closer to its imperialist owner, thereby becoming more similar to it.

- Some of the colonies undergo a revolution step, which is equivalent to a mutation phase.
- Some of the empires undergo a change in leadership. If an imperialist country has a higher cost than one of its colonies, the respective colony becomes the leader of the empire, i.e., the imperialist country and the better colony swap positions.
- The empires compete for dominance. Empire competition can take several forms, but in the simplest case, each empire takes the weakest colony from the weakest empire. This step eventually leads to empires without colonies, which are eliminated (either removed from the population entirely or reverted to a regular colony).
- Once the new empire grouping is established, a convergence criterion is tested. Commonly, the algorithm stops when there is only one empire left. Otherwise, a new iteration begins, involving assimilation, revolution, competition, and all smaller in-between operations.

Our main modifications to the standard ICA loop involved the following three components:

- Alternative initialization, assimilation, revolution, and competition steps. We analyzed several potential versions of these steps and ultimately used the ones that performed the best on our dataset.
- A backpropagation-based boosting step. This involved slightly guiding the solutions of each iteration toward the optimum using a mechanism similar to the backpropagation-based training of a neural network. As such, at each iteration, the weights of each solution were modified via backpropagation to ease convergence toward the optimal weight values.
- An algorithm hyperparameter optimization strategy based on a mixed adaptive/self-adaptive parameter control mechanism.

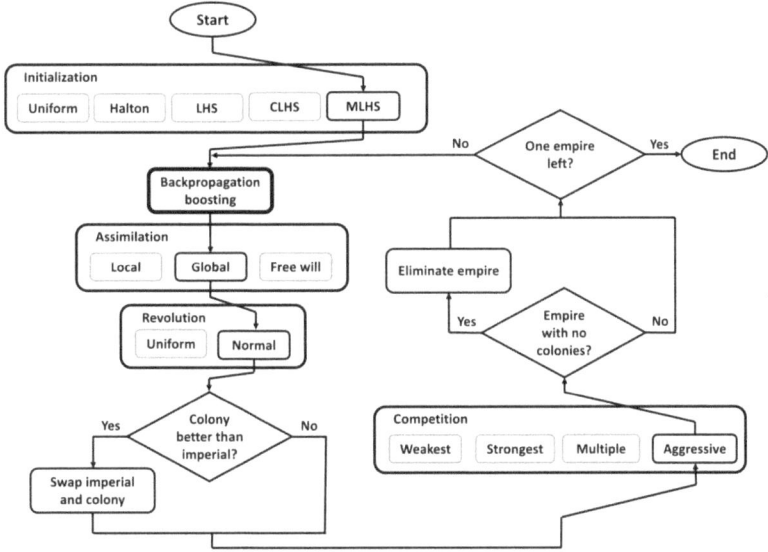

Figure 2. Diagram illustrating the steps of our algorithm: The country population was initialized using Maximin Latin Hypercube Sampling, an approach chosen out of several others. Then, at the start of each ICA iteration, backpropagation boosting was applied in order to steer the solutions toward the optimum. The main loop largely followed the same progression as the traditional ICA; however, the fundamental steps (assimilation, revolution, competition) were chosen out of several possible versions. The choices were made following an analysis to determine the steps that best suited our algorithm in terms of effectiveness, considering the problem described in Section 2.

4.3. Sampling Methods for Population Initialization

In order to improve upon the classic ICA, we analyzed several modified versions of some of the fundamental ICA steps to find the ones that best worked for our purposes. We mainly targeted initialization, revolution, assimilation, and competition methods as candidates for potential improvements.

Initialization is a frequently discussed and disputed aspect of evolutionary algorithms, which are notorious for being overly sensitive to the configuration and distribution of the initial population [51]. The main pitfall with regard to the initialization is the disproportionality between the size of the solution space and the size of the initial solution population. It is desired that the initial population be as representative as possible for its corresponding value-domain. Although, theoretically, a larger population would better cover this space, a practically large initial population would significantly impact performance, not necessarily guaranteeing a better convergence to the optimal solution. In almost all scenarios, the size of the initial population is orders of magnitude smaller than would be required to fully cover the problem space.

Rather than having to rely on large initial populations for the initialization stage, we aimed for small populations where the solutions were spread as evenly as possible throughout the problem space. The most common initialization was carried out using a uniform distribution, which did not generate evenly spread solutions [52]. For this reason, along with uniform generation, we considered several sampling strategies that could potentially generate initial populations with much better coverage of the problem space. By "better coverage" we mean that the initialization relied on a sampling method where the generated samples were spread as evenly as possible throughout their domain so that the generated sample set was as representative as possible of the entire problem space. Such a property is commonly expressed as the discrepancy in the sampling method. A low-discrepancy approach has the property that any number of samples that fall into a certain hypercube is nearly proportional to the measure of the hypercube. Roughly, this means that a low-discrepancy sampling method produces a sample set of almost-even density, whereas a high-discrepancy method has a greater chance of generating samples that are locally grouped, as well as large regions void of samples. Low-discrepancy sampling is a widely discussed topic in related fields [53] and is beyond the scope of this paper. For our purposes, we tested a uniform initialization, as well as several other initialization approaches that are known to rely on low discrepancy sampling:

- Halton sampling, which generates a population from a Halton sequence by applying the radical inverse function to integers expressed in various bases. Halton sequences have been demonstrated to produce low-discrepancy pseudo-random point sets despite generating these points in a fully deterministic manner [54]. Due to the high dimensionality of our solutions, we used a scrambled Halton sequence as our generator, where the actual sequence was built using permutations of the coefficients corresponding to the standard sequence.
- Classic Latin Hypercube sampling (LHS), which spaces the solutions from one another so that no two solutions are found in the same axis-aligned hyperplane within the solution space [55]. In an equivalent 2D space, no two points generated via LHS would be found on the same row or column.
- Centered Latin Hypercube sampling (CLHS): for each generated point, a hypercube may be defined so that each point is centered within its respective hypercube.
- Maximin Latin Hypercube sampling (MLHS), which generates a point set so that, in addition to the standard LHS criterion, the points are further away from each other to maximize the minimum distance among them.

All four non-uniform sampling methods demonstrate low discrepancy and are reasonably capable of generating evenly distributed solutions within the solution space. Figure 3 illustrates this principle for a 2D space, where it can be seen that uniform sampling generally does the poorest job at "filling out" the problem space with the available points, resulting in regions of significantly varying densities (Figure 3a), whereas the other approaches generate points that provide comparatively better coverage of their spaces (Figure 3b–e). In our experience, the low-discrepancy initialization methods were better suited to our approach than standard uniform initialization, although there was little difference among the methods themselves. We did however notice a slight improvement when using MLHS, which we ultimately chose as the default initialization method for our algorithm.

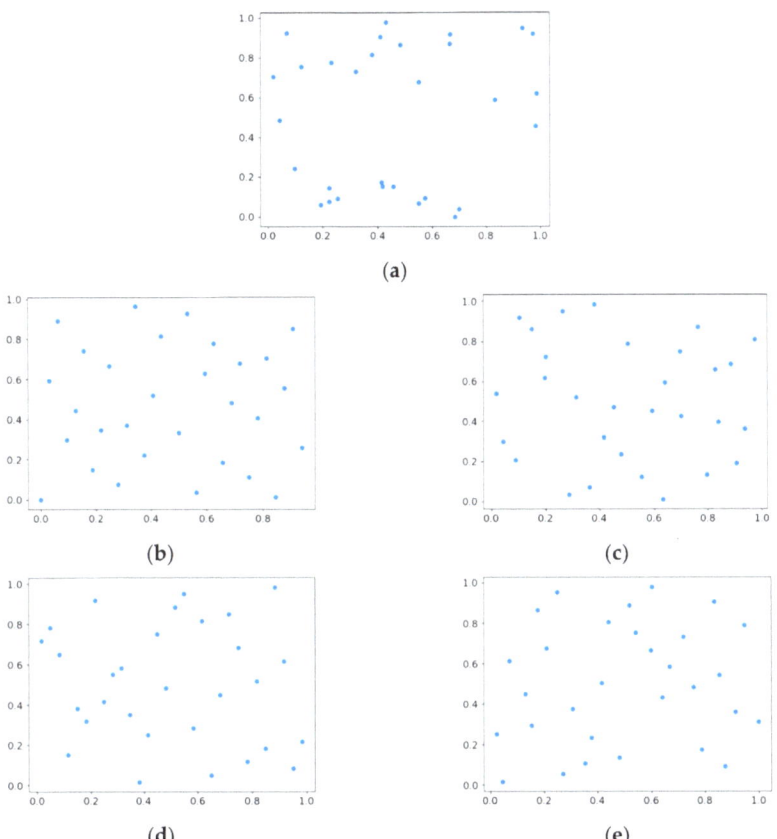

Figure 3. Tested sampling methods exemplified by generating 30 points in a 2D point space: (**a**) uniform sampling; (**b**) Halton sampling; (**c**) Classic Latin Hypercube sampling (LHS); (**d**) Centered Latin Hypercube (CLHS); (**e**) Maximin Latin Hypercube (MLHS). The images illustrate that the more advanced sampling methods (**b**–**e**) generated points that were much more evenly spread out compared to uniform sampling (**a**), i.e., the image plane was much better covered by a relatively small set of points. Thus, using a low-discrepancy sampling method allowed for the generation of sets of relatively few individuals, which were more representative of their corresponding space compared to using simpler sampling approaches.

4.4. Variations of the Fundamental ICA Steps

Although the classic ICA has been proven to perform well for a large number of optimization problems, we analyzed various modified versions of the essential ICA steps in order to find the best ones for our purposes.

Assimilation is a form of mutation in which the colonies are modified so that they are more similar to the imperialist countries. Considering that imperialist countries are constantly maintained to be the best in their respective empires, assimilation is equivalent to moving the solutions toward the fittest local or global one(s). Considering the variables c_i

of any colony from the country population, which is assimilated by a destination imperialist I_{dest}, a new set of variables $c_i{'}$ is obtained by updating the current values c_i using a parameter a_{dist}, which signifies the maximum distance toward the assimilating imperialist, as shown in Equation (1).

$$c_i{'} = c_i + a_{dist} \cdot \mathcal{U}(0,1) \cdot (I_{dest} - c_i) \quad (1)$$

where $\mathcal{U}(0,1)$ is a random uniform number from the $(0,1)$ interval.

In order to improve our algorithm, we considered the following types of assimilation:

- **Local assimilation**: Each colony moves toward its owner empire, equivalent to the solutions moving toward the current local minimum (Figure 4b).
- **Global assimilation**: Most countries move toward the best imperialist country, regardless of ownership. A smaller percentage maintains local assimilation to maintain the relevance of other imperialists. This form of assimilation is equivalent to most solutions moving toward the current global minimum. We find that a percentage of 75% of countries moving toward the best imperialist is suitable for our algorithm, whereas the remaining 25% move toward their owners in a local fashion (Figure 4c).
- **Free will assimilation:** Each country is free to choose which imperialist they move toward. The choice is made through a roulette wheel selection, where for each country, its destination empire is chosen using a distribution determined from the inverse costs of the empires. In this manner, each imperialist has a probability of being chosen, which is inversely proportional to its cost and equivalent to the colonies being more likely to choose better imperialists (Figure 4d).

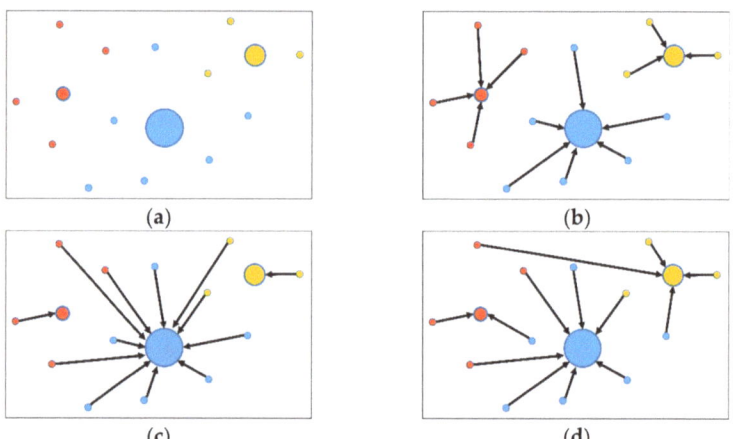

Figure 4. Illustration of the tested assimilation types: (**a**) The imperialist–colony configuration, where the imperialists are the larger points; the size of the imperialist points indicates their fitness; (**b**) local assimilation, where each country moves towards its imperialist owner; (**c**) global assimilation, where most countries move toward the best imperialist; (**d**) free will assimilation, where countries choose which imperialist to move toward.

Our analysis showed that global assimilation proved to be the most useful approach for our algorithm, primarily due to an improved convergence curve.

Revolution is a step where the countries typically change independently from each other. We implemented this step as a mutation of the values of each respective country. Specifically, we tested two types of revolution:

- **Uniform revolution**, where countries change via a uniform mutation operator. Considering that a country C is defined by variables c_i, $i \in \{1, \ldots, l_c\}$, where c_i are equivalent to the genes of a chromosome from genetic algorithms and l_c is the variable count (equivalent to the length of the chromosome), a uniform revolution involves applying a uniform mutation operator to C with probability p_r. This involves replacing variable c_i with a randomly generated value from a uniform distribution within its respective domain $[c_{i\_min}, c_{i\_max}]$, which for each c_i occurs with probability p_{rv} (the probability of per-variable revolution). Let $\alpha \sim U(0,1)$, $\beta_i \sim U(0,1)$ and $\gamma_i \sim U(c_{i\_min}, c_{i\_max})$. Then, the c_i values are updated as shown in Equation (2).

- **Normal revolution:** Countries change via a mutation operator that uses normal distribution. Considering the previously defined country C with variables c_i, a normal revolution occurs with probability p_r, where each variable c_i is modified via a normally generated value centered in c_i with a standard deviation of 1, scaled by step size s_r. Each variable is mutated with probability p_{rv}. The resulting value is then truncated within the respective domain $[c_{i\_min}, c_{i\_max}]$ of variable c_i. Let $\alpha \sim U(0,1)$, $\beta_i \sim U(0,1)$ and $\gamma_i \sim N(c_i, 1)$. Then, the mutated values c_i' are updated from the original ones, c_i, as shown in Equation (3).

$$c_i' = \begin{cases} \gamma_i & \text{if } p_r > \alpha \text{ and } p_{rv} > \beta_i \\ c_i & \text{otherwise} \end{cases} \quad (2)$$

$$c_i' = \begin{cases} s_r \cdot \gamma_i & \text{if } p_r > \alpha \text{ and } p_{rv} > \beta_i \\ c_i & \text{otherwise} \end{cases} \quad (3)$$

Competition is a step where imperialists attempt to gain additional colonies by taking them from other imperialists. The type of competition typically has a strong influence on convergence speed, as it is the main factor in controlling the rate at which imperialists are eliminated. As with the previously mentioned steps, we analyzed several types of competition, as follows:

- **Weakest competition:** At each iteration of the algorithm, an imperialist chosen by roulette-wheel selection conquers the weakest colony of the weakest imperialist. Eventually, the weakest empire is left without colonies and is removed. Statistically, stronger imperialists will accumulate the highest number of colonies. The total cost $tcost_I$ of an imperialist I with n_{cI} colonies is determined via a combination of the imperialist's own cost $cost_I$ and a fraction f_{cost} of the average cost of its colonies $cost_{C_i}, i \in \{1, \ldots, n_{cI}\}$ (Equation (4)).
- **Strongest competition:** At each iteration, the strongest imperialist conquers the weakest colony of an imperialist chosen by roulette-wheel selection. When choosing a source imperialist, the distribution used for selection is generated so that imperialists with a higher cost have a higher probability of being selected. Therefore, weaker imperialists have a higher chance of yielding their weakest colony to the strongest imperialist.
- **Multiple competition:** This version is a combination of the selection methods from the weakest and strongest competition types. A conquering imperialist is chosen by roulette-wheel selection, where the related distribution favors lower-cost imperialists, and the conquered imperialist is also chosen by roulette-wheel selection but using a distribution that favors weaker imperialists. Therefore, a statistically stronger imperialist takes the weakest colony of a statistically weaker one.
- **Aggressive competition:** This approach is similar to the weakest competition, the difference being that the weakest imperialist is conquered multiple times during the same iteration. Each time, the weakest colony of the weakest imperialist is yielded to a stronger imperialist chosen by roulette-wheel selection. This approach means that weaker imperialists are depleted of their colonies at a faster rate, resulting in an overall significantly faster convergence. The number of colonies n_{LC} lost by the weakest imperialist is decided by a hyperparameter of the algorithm, which we refer to as $comp_{Ag}$ (competition aggression). $comp_{Ag}$ is defined in the interval [0,1] and its value is used to determine the actual number of lost colonies n_{LC} according to the number of

initial countries n_{InitC}, the number of initial imperialists n_{InitI}, and the current iteration it (Equation (5)).

$$tcost_I = cost_I + \frac{f_{cost}}{n_{cI}} \sum_{i=1}^{n_c} cost_{Ci} \qquad (4)$$

$$n_{LC} = [\ln(comp_{Ag} \cdot \frac{n_{InitC}}{n_{InitI}} \cdot it + 1)] \qquad (5)$$

4.5. Backpropagation Boosting

Additionally, from the evolutionary approach described in previous sections, we employed a backpropagation step that was incorporated into the modified ICA pipeline, which served as a complementary boost for each country. At the beginning of each iteration, we applied an additional partial optimization of each solution via gradient-based backpropagation, where each neural network was trained in varying amounts to get closer to the optimum. This operation served as a supplementary boosting mechanism that slightly steered each solution in the "right" direction, i.e., toward the optimal solution. This approach worked in tandem with the evolutionary pipeline, making the overall algorithm a hybrid of two optimization strategies:

- **The evolutionary approach** contributed mainly to exploring the solution space and ensuring the diversity of the solution population. To this extent, assimilation, revolution, and competition operators were applied to the solutions in order to regroup and transform them accordingly. As described in previous sections, we analyzed multiple versions of the fundamental ICA steps in order to find the ones that best suited our needs in terms of convergence speed and efficiency, considering the complexity and dimensionality of our data.
- **Backpropagation boosting** further "pushes" the solutions toward the optimum. We found that, for our problem, this complementary approach had the most significant contribution to minimizing errors and eventually reaching a solution that was as close as possible to the optimum. As such, our approach leveraged the advantages of both an evolutionary algorithm and traditional gradient-based neural network training. Furthermore, the addition of backpropagation boosting added two hyperparameters to our algorithm: a parameter that controlled the number of epochs (backpropagation acceleration) and the learning rate used for backpropagation training.

4.6. Algorithm Parameters and Parameter Control Strategies

Considering the previously described steps and the versions of the said steps ultimately chosen for our approach (as seen in Figure 2), we defined several hyperparameters that impact the convergence of our hybrid evolutionary algorithm. For efficiency of discussion, we henceforth refer to these hyperparameters as "algorithm parameters" or simply "parameters" (Table 1). From the perspective of parameter control, we split the parameters into two categories: static parameters, which were globally set from the start of the algorithm, and variable parameters, whose values were steered during the iterations of the algorithm. The parameters in the second category were applied locally for each solution (they influenced countries at the individual level). These parameters were subjected to a mixed adaptive/self-adaptive parameter control strategy.

Table 1. The parameters of our algorithm, their values, and their role within the algorithm's iterations. The value "self-adaptive" refers to the fact that the values of the corresponding parameters were optimized by the algorithm itself via the self-adaptive control mechanism.

Parameter	Role	Default Value
n_{InitC}	Initial population count	100
n_{InitI}	The initial imperialist count	10
$comp_{Ag}$	Aggressiveness of the imperialist during the competition phase	0.4
f_{cost}	The fraction of the total imperialist cost contributed by its colonies	0.3
p_r	Probability of revolution occurring for a country	self-adaptive
p_{rv}	Probability of revolution occurring for each individual value of a country	self-adaptive
s_r	Step size used for normal revolution	self-adaptive
a_{dist}	Maximum distance to the destination imperialist during assimilation	self-adaptive
bp_a	Controls the number of epochs used for backpropagation boosting	self-adaptive
bp_{LR}	Learning rate used for backpropagation boosting	self-adaptive

In order to aid in finding optimal values for some of the parameters in Table 1, we used a mixed adaptive/self-adaptive parameter control strategy. When using the term "adaptive", we refer to the fact that during the iterations of the evolutionary algorithm, certain parameters were modified according to the state of the algorithm in each respective iteration in order to improve on the progress of the algorithm's convergence. The topic of adaptive parameters in the evolutionary algorithm has been widely discussed in the related literature [56–58]. Consequently, for our approach we employed a few simple adaptive parameter control strategies, as follows:

- During the aggressive competition phase, the number of colonies lost by the weakest imperialist was adjusted according to the current iteration (Equation (5)). As the evolutionary algorithm advanced and progressed toward the optimum solution, the aggressiveness of the imperialists increased to speed up convergence.
- During the normal revolution phase, the actual step size used for normal mutation was adjusted according to the current state of convergence. In order to achieve this, we multiplied the base step size s_r by the square of the lowest current cost. Consequently, the step size decreased as the algorithm converged and lower-cost countries are found. The justification for this modification is that, as the algorithm converged toward a minimum, the mutation step size should be reduced so that the algorithm searches for other solutions in narrower neighborhoods [58].
- The number of epochs used during the backpropagation boosting phase was influenced by the current iteration. Specifically, the number of epochs was defined as round ($bp_a \cdot iter$), i.e., we multiplied the backpropagation acceleration by the current iteration and rounded the result. This means that the solutions were boosted further as the algorithm converged in order to encourage finding the optimal one.
- The learning rate used during the backpropagation boosting phase was multiplied by the current lowest cost. As the algorithm converged and lower-cost solutions were found, the learning rate also decreased to permit more fine-grained backpropagation.

Aside from the adaptive measures, for the country local parameters we employed a self-adaptive control strategy. This refers to the fact that the parameter values were initialized and subjected to the same transformations as the solutions themselves (with the notable exception of backpropagation boosting). In essence, the evolutionary algorithm optimized its own parameters as it searched for the optimal solution. It is worth noting that self-adaptation in evolutionary algorithms is a well-known strategy that is frequently used for parameter control [57].

We implemented self-adaptive parameter control by extending the chromosome of each country with additional locations to represent the values of the self-adaptive parameters (Figure 5). Subsequently, we allowed the evolutionary algorithm to find both the optimal parameter values and the optimal solution (i.e., the optimal neural network). This means that, on the one hand, each country had its own set of self-adaptive parameters as opposed to using a global parameter set. On the other hand, as the algorithm converged, better countries with lower costs also contained better values of the self-adaptive parameters.

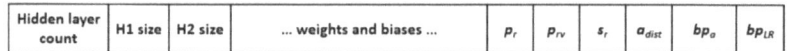

Figure 5. The extended variables of each country with added self-adaptive parameters.

5. Experimental Results

Our evaluation methodology first involved assessing the usefulness of the various alternative steps described in Section 4.4. To this extent, we tested several variations of some of the most important operators applied to the population during the main ICA loop. Secondly, we tested the contribution of the adaptive parameter control strategy as well as of the backpropagation boosting used in conjunction with the main algorithm. Our data set contained experimental data consisting of 177 instances with 7 input and 2 output values, as described in Section 2. For our test methodology, we aimed to select the strategies, steps, and parameter control mechanisms that produced a regression model that minimized the RMSE on our dataset. Although our main goal was to obtain the lowest possible error value, we also considered the convergence curve when evaluating the various employed strategies.

With regard to population initialization, we tested several initialization methods, as described in Section 4.3. The most commonly used sampling method used a uniform distribution to generate the values for the chromosomes. However, we explored a few other low-discrepancy alternatives. A low-discrepancy sampling method attempts to spread the generated values as evenly as possible throughout their domain. As such, lower-discrepancy sampling spaces out the initial population so that the density is relatively even throughout the problem space. To this extent, we compared uniform initialization with four other low-discrepancy initialization approaches. The resulting convergence curves are shown in Figure 6. Our tests showed that uniform initialization performed the worst, resulting in the highest RMSE, whereas the best initialization approach was Maximin Latin Hypercube sampling (MLHS), with Centered Latin Hypercube sampling (CLHS) coming close in terms of the results. Overall, using MLHS resulted in an improvement of about 15% compared to uniform initialization, which we consider to be a noticeable improvement, albeit not a dramatic one. The implementation overhead induced by one of the initialization strategies is worthy because (a) the initialization was performed only once at the beginning of the evolutionary algorithm, and (b) we consider a 15% improvement in RMSE to be satisfactory.

We used similar reasoning when trying the various alternative steps throughout the ICA loop. Of the three assimilation strategies tested, global assimilation demonstrated the best results and generated the fastest convergence with the steepest curve (Figure 7), whereas local assimilation performed the worst. Consequently, having most of the solutions migrate toward the strongest overall imperialist resulted in the lowest overall error value, whereas the classic approach where the solutions moved toward their owners provided the worst convergence. We observed a 15–20% improvement in RMSE by choosing an appropriate assimilation strategy.

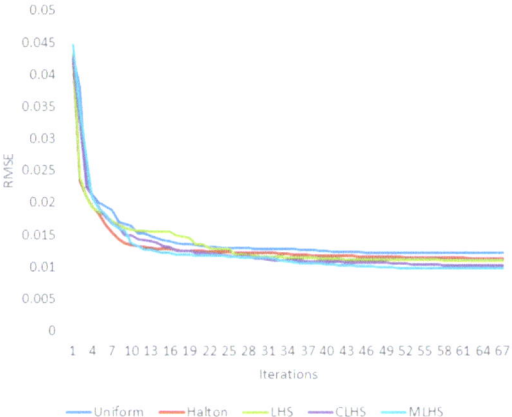

Figure 6. Comparison of convergence using multiple types of initialization methods: Uniform sampling, Halton sampling, classic Latin Hypercube sampling, (LHS), Centered Latin Hypercube sampling (CLHS), Maximin Latin Hypercube sampling (MLHS).

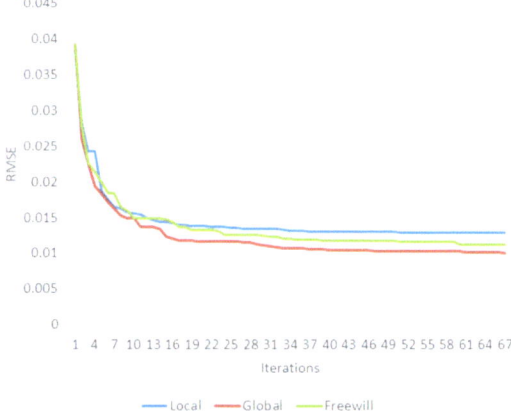

Figure 7. Comparison of convergence using different assimilation strategies: Local assimilation, where countries move toward their imperialist owner; Global assimilation, where a large percentage of the countries move toward the strongest imperialist; Freewill assimilation, where countries move toward an imperialist chosen via roulette-wheel selection.

In terms of competition strategies, surprisingly, the four tested approaches did not have substantial differences in terms of error minimization, resulting in an improvement of below 10%. One can see in Figure 8 that the aggressive competition strategy resulted in the fastest decreasing and overall lowest error value. These results were predictable since aggressive competition statistically leads to the fastest elimination of imperialists and therefore the imposed convergence criterion (one empire left) is reached the quickest. Consequently, the chosen competition strategy unintuitively had the least effect in terms of error minimization, though it ultimately proved to be an effective means of controlling the convergence speed and steepness.

Adopting an adaptive parameter control strategy and using backpropagation boosting to the population provided the biggest improvements to our method. Using a combination of adaptive and self-adaptive parameter controls, as described in Section 4.6, made a noticeable improvement to the resulting errors, compared to the non-adaptive approach.

Incorporating the algorithm parameters into the evolutionary optimization loop did not result in a noticeable penalty in terms of convergence speed, as the algorithm seemed to effectively optimize its own parameters. However, incorporating a backpropagation-based boosting led to the most significant improvement to our method. As presented in Section 4.5, for each iteration of the evolutionary algorithm, we steered the solutions toward the optimum via partial backpropagation-based training. We used the Adam optimizer during each backpropagation epoch [59], whereas the number of epochs and learning rate are part of the overall algorithm parameters. As such, the resulting algorithm was a hybrid that incorporated both an evolutionary and a gradient-based backpropagation approach. The convergence curves obtained using various improved and unimproved versions of the algorithm are shown in Figure 9, where it is clear that the hybrid-adaptive approach provided a significant improvement in terms of minimizing errors.

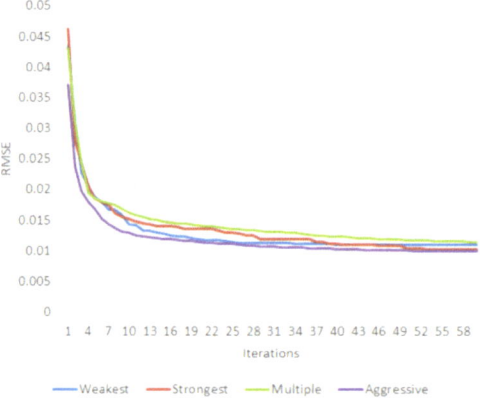

Figure 8. Comparison of convergence using various competition strategies: weakest—the highest-cost imperialist loses a colony to one of the other imperialists; strongest—the lowest-cost imperial gains a colony from one of the others; multiple—the conquering and conquered imperialists are both chosen based on their costs; aggressive—the highest-cost imperialist loses several colonies to the others.

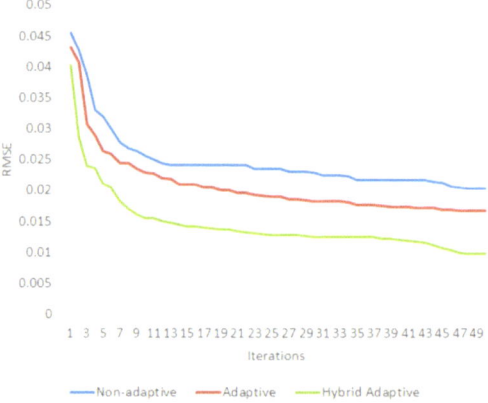

Figure 9. Comparison between the non-adaptive, adaptive, and hybrid adaptive versions of our algorithm. In the adaptive version, adaptive and self-adaptive parameter control strategies were employed. In the hybrid version, the solutions were subjected to backpropagation boosting.

We also evaluated our algorithm by testing it against several evolutionary metaheuristics from the related literature:

- Football Game Algorithm (FGA) [60];
- Imperialist Competitive Algorithm (the classic version of ICA [3];
- Simple Human Learning Optimization (SHLO) [61];
- Social Learning Optimization (SLO) [62];
- Teaching Learning-Based Optimization (TLBO) [63];
- Viral System (VS) [64];
- Virulence Optimization Algorithm (VOA) [65];
- Volleyball Premier League (VPL) [66].

These algorithms have also been compared in a previous work [67] for the optimization of another industrial chemical process.

Our test methodology was as follows: first, we minimized the RMSE using the entire dataset. Then, we minimized the RMSE on 70% of the data (the training subset) and tested the resulting models on the 30% remaining instances (the test subset). We performed these tests by optimizing both outputs simultaneously via multivariate regression, and each output individually, therefore generating a separate regression model for each output separately. The results obtained from optimizing both outputs are presented in Table 2, whereas the results for the individual outputs are shown in Tables 3 and 4, respectively. In each Table, we list the RMSE and the correlation coefficients r for the corresponding outputs presented in Section 2: η (yield in the crosslinked polymer) and α (swelling degree). The output values were obtained using all instances from the dataset (the columns titled "all"), as well as using the training subset ("train") and the test subset ("test").

Table 2. RMSE and r metrics for the two outputs (η, α) resulting from applying the tested algorithms for optimizing the neural network architecture and weights using the entire dataset ("all"), the training split ("train"), and subsequently testing on the test split ("test"). The optimization was carried out for both outputs simultaneously. ICAHY is our method.

Method	RMSE All	r η All	r α All	RMSE Train	r η Train	r α Train	RMSE Test	r η Test	r α Test
FGA	0.03223	0.26	0.036	0.03828	0.24	0.033	0.05966	0.139	0.009
ICA	0.02157	0.662	0.411	0.02533	0.443	0.407	0.04087	0.296	0.226
SHLO	0.02417	0.476	0.25	0.02834	0.414	0.227	0.04603	0.271	0.184
SLO	0.02524	0.434	0.216	0.02998	0.472	0.216	0.04672	0.261	0.217
TLBO	0.01964	0.841	0.481	0.02274	0.625	0.465	0.03838	0.387	0.433
VOA	0.03322	0.43	0.132	0.04013	0.321	0.087	0.06513	0.164	0.104
VPL	0.03366	0.404	0.085	0.0402	0.299	0.056	0.06153	0.191	0.13
VS	0.03556	0.313	0.019	0.0408	0.304	0.023	0.06596	0.132	0.092
ICAHY	0.0089	0.96	0.843	0.01061	0.934	0.732	0.01641	0.755	0.672

Table 3. RMSE and r metrics for the yield in the crosslinked polymer η, resulting from applying the tested algorithms for optimizing the neural network architecture and weights using the entire dataset ("all"), the training split ("train"), and subsequently testing on the test split ("test"). ICAHY is our method.

Method	RMSE η All	r η All	RMSE η Train	r η Train	RMSE η Test	r η Test
FGA	0.02096	0.472	0.02478	0.45	0.03904	0.242
ICA	0.01067	0.875	0.01243	0.802	0.0205	0.532
SHLO	0.01572	0.715	0.01866	0.695	0.0291	0.342

Table 3. Cont.

Method	RMSE η All	r η All	RMSE η Train	r η Train	RMSE η Test	r η Test
SLO	0.01288	0.81	0.01512	0.725	0.02441	0.356
TLBO	0.01497	0.729	0.01779	0.717	0.02757	0.338
VOA	0.02172	0.432	0.0237	0.433	0.04675	0.265
VPL	0.01964	0.686	0.02429	0.397	0.03277	0.308
VS	0.0215	0.425	0.02625	0.347	0.03719	0.266
ICAHY	0.00374	0.984	0.00474	0.963	0.0058	0.825

Table 4. RMSE and r metrics for the swelling degree α, resulting from applying the tested algorithms for optimizing the neural network architecture and weights using the entire dataset ("all"), the training split ("train"), and subsequently testing on the test split ("test"). ICAHY is our method.

Method	RMSE α All	r α All	RMSE α Train	r α Train	RMSE α Test	r α Test
FGA	0.02947	0.196	0.03466	0.187	0.05578	0.185
ICA	0.02221	0.587	0.02611	0.434	0.04205	0.343
SHLO	0.02579	0.437	0.03001	0.407	0.04983	0.338
SLO	0.02662	0.426	0.0309	0.409	0.05174	0.309
TLBO	0.02627	0.419	0.03077	0.411	0.05008	0.301
VOA	0.03172	0.214	0.0384	0.166	0.05614	0.103
VPL	0.02882	0.231	0.0339	0.329	0.05448	0.126
VS	0.03368	0.236	0.04058	0.106	0.06022	0.046
ICAHY	0.01142	0.828	0.01304	0.802	0.02012	0.659

These results cover all the above-mentioned algorithms, as well as our algorithm, which is labeled ICAHY (*ICA Hybrid*). The results show that our algorithm outperformed the others in terms of minimizing errors on all variations and splits of the data and the outputs, often by as much as an order of magnitude. Furthermore, our approach allowed for the optimization of the regression models, which provided the strongest correlations between their predictions and the target values from the dataset. We, therefore, surmise that our hybrid-evolutionary approach constitutes a dependable method for finding and optimizing neural networks capable of generating reliable regression models.

Although in the previous articles that addressed the same database the accuracy was satisfactory, from the point of view of the methodology, the present article has clear advantages. Thus, in [5], the neural networks were designed by the trial-and-error method—an expensive procedure that does not guarantee obtaining the best model. In [6], the successive trials method was also used, adding neural network stacks as a type of model. The present evaluation methodology automatically determined an optimal neural network model from both points of view, structure, and parameters. In addition, the method showed flexibility and generality and could be easily adapted and applied to other complex processes in chemical engineering.

The simulation study of the synthesis process of multicomponent hydrogels benefitted from the results obtained through the predictions for parameters difficult to determine experimentally (swelling degree), which means significant savings in time, materials, and energy.

Based on the data presented in Tables 2–4, we created some derived figures that can help the reader to better visualize the results. They mainly show some relative values of the error metrics employed. However, they have a qualitative character rather than a quantitative one, because, e.g., the correlation coefficient r has a nonlinear definition and a relative r cannot be defined by a direct ratio between two such values. Therefore, we use several quality indicators that can provide some insight into the results from a qualitative, possibly managerial, point of view. The greater the value of an indicator, the better.

Figure 10 displays, for each algorithm, the improvements using two separate networks to predict η and α (case 1) rather than using a single neural network with two outputs (case 2). The results are considered for the testing set only. Thus, we use four quality indicators:

- QI1, defined as the ratio between the RMSE obtained in case 2 and the average of the two RMSEs obtained in case 1.
- QI2, defined as the ratio between the correlation coefficient r obtained in case 1 for η and the r obtained in case 2.
- QI3, defined as the ratio between the correlation coefficient r obtained in case 1 for α and the r obtained in case 2.
- QI4, defined as the average of QI1, QI2, and QI3, as a global indicator.

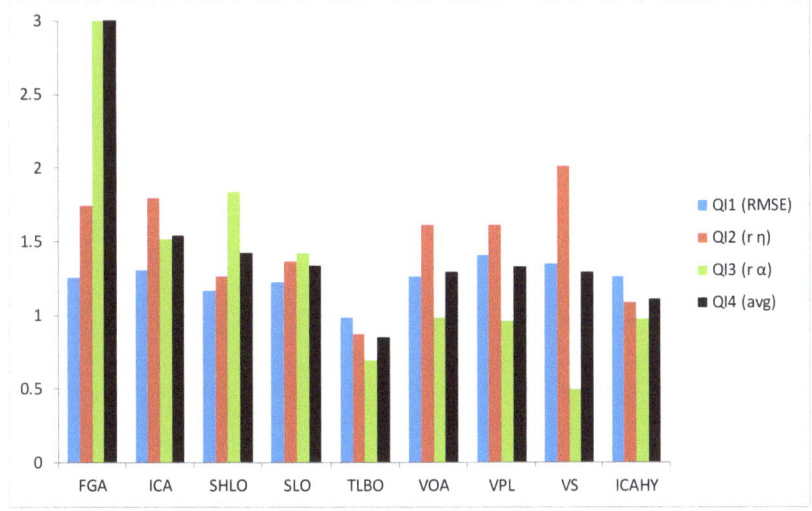

Figure 10. Improvements of two separate networks for each output over a single network with two outputs.

In the case of FGA, QI3 and consequently QI4 are outliers with very high values (about 20 and 7, respectively), therefore their values are cropped in order to provide a better level of detail for the rest of the values. It can be seen that most, but not all, algorithms benefitted from the separation of the models. In the case of the ICAHY, the values are close to 1, and therefore the single network succeeded in providing results of approximately the same quality as the two individual networks.

Figure 11 shows how much worse the results obtained for the testing set are compared with those obtained for the training set. The purpose of this analysis is to estimate the generalization capability of the models, and it is made for the separate models, i.e., one network for the η output and another network for the α output. If the training results are good and the testing results are bad, this is an indicator of overfitting. The closer the two results are, the better the generalization capability of the model. However, one can realistically expect the testing results to be (slightly) worse than the training results. Consequently, we use another five quality indicators:

- QI5, defined as the ratio between the RMSE for η obtained for the training set and the RMSE for η obtained for the testing set.
- QI6, defined as the ratio between the correlation coefficient r for η obtained for the testing set and the r for η obtained for the training set.

- QI7, defined as the ratio between the RMSE for α obtained for the training set and the RMSE for α obtained for the testing set.
- QI8, defined as the ratio between the correlation coefficient r for α obtained for the testing set and the r for α obtained for the training set.
- QI9, defined as the average of QI5, QI6, QI7, and QI8, as a global indicator.

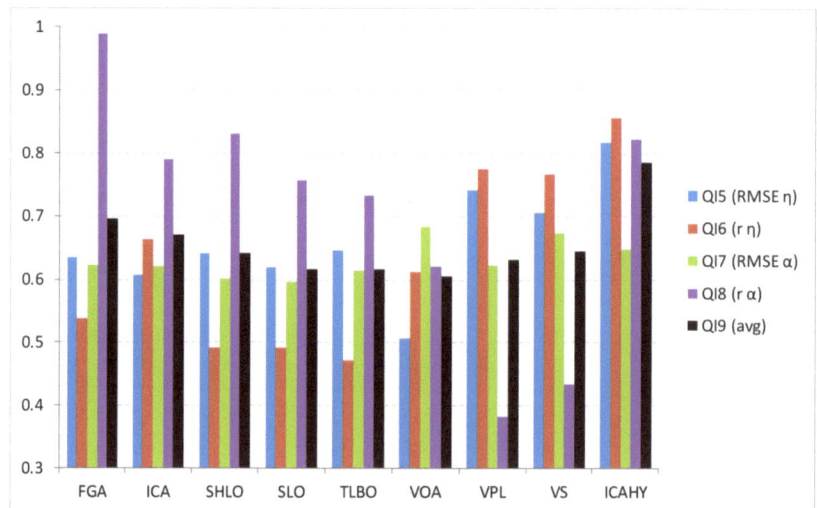

Figure 11. A comparison of the results obtained for the training and testing sets.

It can be seen that the proposed algorithm ICAHY has the highest value for QI9 among all the algorithms, which demonstrates that it can generalize very well.

Finally, in Figure 12, we compare the results of ICAHY obtained for the testing set with those of the other eight algorithms, and we use:

- QI10, defined as the ratio between the RMSE for η obtained with ICAHY and the RMSE for η obtained with each algorithm.
- QI11, defined as the ratio between the RMSE for α obtained with ICAHY and the RMSE for α obtained with each algorithm.
- QI12, defined as the ratio between the correlation coefficient r for η obtained with each algorithm and r for η obtained with ICAHY.
- QI13, defined as the ratio between the correlation coefficient r for α obtained with each algorithm and r for α obtained with ICAHY.
- QI14, defined as the average of QI10, QI11, QI12, and QI13, as a global indicator.

We can see that ICAHY clearly shows better performance than the other algorithms for every error metric. From the qualitative point of view defined by our conventions, its average indicator value is about twice as good as the algorithm in second place, i.e., the standard ICA.

This confirms that the proposed algorithm had very good potential for the optimization problem considered in the present paper and likely also for other optimization problems.

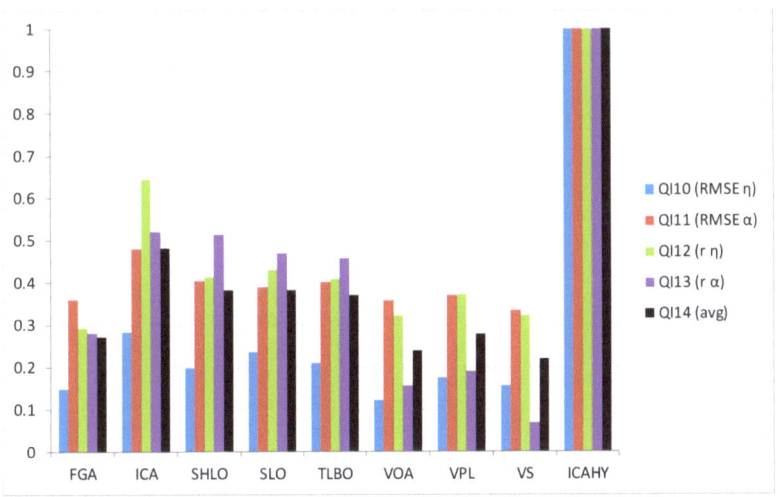

Figure 12. Relative quality of ICAHY results compared with the results of the other algorithms under study.

6. Conclusions

We developed a hybrid evolutionary algorithm that optimized a fully connected neural network, which successfully minimized the RMSE on a dataset from the field of chemical engineering. The data were collected from the synthesis of polyacrylamide-based multicomponent hydrogels; they consisted of 7 input parameters and 2 outputs and had as a goal the modeling of the yield and swelling degree as functions of the reaction conditions. In our experience, this dataset has proven difficult in terms of generating a regression model that properly characterizes the underlying phenomenon. Existing evolutionary metaheuristics have proven incapable of properly optimizing a neural network architecture, considering the high dimensionality and complexity of the corresponding neural network space. Consequently, we proposed a method that combined the advantages of two optimization approaches: an evolutionary optimization algorithm that was capable of thoroughly searching through the solution space and providing partial convergence and backpropagation-based optimization, which constituted a necessary boost toward minimizing errors further. For our evolutionary approach, we started with a loop inspired by the Imperialist Competitive Algorithm (ICA) and modified several key steps of the algorithm to better suit the requirements of our particular problem. To this end, we searched and tested various types of initializations, assimilations, and competition strategies. At the same time, we employed an adaptive/self-adaptive parameters control strategy so that the parameters of the algorithm were optimized by the algorithm itself, on the one hand, as well as altered during the algorithm's iterations, on the other hand. The result of this analysis was an ICA-based evolutionary algorithm that used global assimilation, during which most of the colonies moved toward the strongest imperialist nation as opposed to their owner imperialist; aggressive competition, where the imperialists repeatedly conquered the weaker countries from the weakest empire, thus depleting it of colonies much faster and contributing to the convergence speed; and Maximin Latin Hypercube initialization, which used a low-discrepancy sampling method to initialize the population so that it was relatively evenly dispersed throughout the solution space. All of the implemented steps contributed in varying degrees to improving the resulting evolutionary algorithm. Furthermore, the adaptive and self-adaptive strategies contributed in their own regard to improving the performance of the method, while at the same time alleviating the need for time-consuming parameter search and tuning. Ultimately, integrating a backpropagation boost proved to be the most significant enhancement in terms of optimizing a reliable neural network. Over each iteration of the evolutionary algorithm, the neural network population was slightly optimized with partial backpropagation-based training. This resulted in a much-improved convergence and more reliable neural network candidates.

We tested our method on the dataset in multiple scenarios: for instance, we used both the entire dataset for optimization, and a train/test split; we optimized the errors on the two outputs simultaneously as well as on each of them individually. Our results showed that the neural networks optimized using our approach minimized the RMSE further than alternative evolutionary algorithms and demonstrated better correlations among the predictions and the desired values of the outputs. We, therefore, conclude that our algorithm constitutes a suitable method for finding optimal neural network models that are capable of accurately characterizing the data and making reliable predictions.

Naturally, our work has limitations and there are still many ways to improve upon the method, both in terms of the algorithms themselves and with regard to performance. In terms of the actual approach, there are many versions and modifications of the ICA in the related literature that may provide suitable candidates for a reliable evolutionary algorithm. Currently, backpropagation-based optimization is integrated rather bluntly, and we intend to search for more elegant ways to exploit it for faster convergence. There are other optimizers that can be combined with the evolutionary algorithm to form even mode-capable hybrid methods. Although our method is currently limited to fully connected neural networks, in future work we plan to extend the use of evolutionary optimization to other, potentially more useful architectures, such as sparse neural networks and/or convolutional and recurrent networks. An additional direction for improvement is performance. Hybrid algorithms combine the advantages of multiple methods but require most of the computational resources of those methods. As such, the current implementation of our method could be improved in terms of performance, especially considering runtimes. We intend to expand this aspect of our work by searching for ways to reduce computational times and parallelizing as much of the implementation as the algorithms will allow. This may require possibly migrating the implementation to a GPGPU language to exploit the advantages of GPU-based computation. Finally, neural networks may not be the best and easiest to work with as candidates for regression models. Other functions/parametric models may prove more reliable. We, therefore, intend to explore the related state-of-the-art results for better alternatives that may converge easier or offer higher accuracies/fewer errors. Fortunately, the literature in the related field of this paper provides many resources for gathering information and which are reliable sources of inspiration and learning, for the continuous improvement of our methods.

Author Contributions: Conceptualization, F.L. and S.C.; Investigation, M.G. and S.-A.F.; Methodology, M.G. and F.L.; Software, M.G.; Validation, F.L. and S.C.; Writing—original draft, M.G., S.-A.F., F.L. and S.C.; Writing—review and editing, M.G., S.-A.F., F.L. and S.C.; funding acquisition, S.C. All authors have read and agreed to the published version of the manuscript.

Funding: This research was funded by UEFISCDI Romania, Exploratory Research Project PN-III-P4-ID-PCE-2020-0551, no. 91/2021.

Acknowledgments: This work was supported by Exploratory Research Project PN-III-P4-ID-PCE-2020-0551, no. 91/2021, financed by UEFISCDI Romania.

Conflicts of Interest: The authors declare no conflict of interest.

Nomenclature

Notation	Description
c_i	The values of a country i (equivalent to the genes of an individual in genetic algorithms)
l_c	The number of variables of a country (equivalent to the size of a chromosome in genetic algorithms)
I_{dest}	The destination imperial during the assimilation phase.

Notation	Description
$cost_{Ci}$	The cost of country c_i (countries with lower costs have higher "fitness", in genetic algorithm terms)
$cost_I$	The cost of imperialist I
$tcost_I$	The total cost of imperialist I (a combination of the imperialists' own cost and the costs of its colonies)
f_{cost}	The fraction of the total cost of an imperialist represented by the average cost of its colonies
n_{cI}	The number of colonies of imperialist I
n_{LC}	The number of colonies lost during the competition phase
it	Index of an iteration of the ICA loop
n_{InitC}	Initial ICA population count
n_{InitI}	Initial ICA imperialist count
$comp_{Ag}$	Aggressiveness of the imperialist during the competition phase
f_{cost}	The fraction of the total imperialist cost contributed by its colonies
p_r	Probability of revolution occurring for a country
p_{rv}	Probability of revolution occurring for each individual value of a country
s_r	Step size used for normal revolution (the ICA equivalent of mutation)
a_{dist}	Maximum distance to the destination imperialist during assimilation
bp_a	Scaling factor used to determine the number of epochs used for backpropagation boosting
bp_{LR}	Learning rate used for backpropagation boosting
α	The swelling degree of the semi- and interpenetrated multicomponent crosslinked structures
η	The yield in the crosslinked polymer

References

1. Antonio, L.M.; Coello Coello, C.A. Coevoluctionary Multiobjective Evolutionary Algorithms: Survey of the State-of-the-Art. *IEEE Trans. Evol. Comput.* **2022**, *22*, 851–865. [CrossRef]
2. Sebastian, R. An overview of gradient descent optimization algorithms. *arXiv* **2016**, arXiv:1609.04747.
3. Atashpaz-Gargari, E.; Lucas, C. Imperialist competitive algorithm: An algorithm for optimization inspired by imperialistic competition. In Proceedings of the 2007 IEEE Congress on Evolutionary Computation, Singapore, 25–28 September 2007; pp. 4661–4667. [CrossRef]
4. Curteanu, S.; Dumitrescu, A.; Mihailescu, C.; Simionescu, B. Neural Network Modeling Applied to Polyacrylamide based Hydrogels Synthetised by Single Step Process. *Polym. Plast. Technol. Eng.* **2008**, *47*, 1061. [CrossRef]
5. Curteanu, S.; Dumitrescu, A.; Mihailescu, C.; Simionescu, B.C. Stacked Neural Network Modeling Applied to the Synthesis of Polyacrylamide Based Multicomponent Hydrogels. *J. Macromol. Sci. Part A Pure Appl. Chem.* **2008**, *A46*, 368.
6. Leon, F.; Piuleac, C.G.; Curteanu, S. Stacked Neural Network Modeling Applied to the Synthesis of Polyacrylamide-Based Multicomponent Hydrogels. *Macromol. React. Eng.* **2010**, *4*, 591–598. [CrossRef]
7. Stanley, K.O.; Clune, J.; Lehman, J.; Miikkulainen, R. Designing neural networks through neuroevolution. *Nat. Mach. Intell.* **2019**, *1*, 24–35. [CrossRef]
8. Galvan, E.; Mooney, P. Neuroevolution in Deep Neural Networks: Current Trends and Future Challenges. *IEEE Trans. Artif. Intell.* **2021**, *2*, 476–493. [CrossRef]
9. Koppejan, R.; Whiteson, S. Neuroevolutionary reinforcement learning for generalized control of simulated helicopters. *Evol. Intell.* **2011**, *4*, 219–241. [CrossRef]
10. Aryan, H.; Khademi, M.; Pedram, M. Prediction of Photovoltaic Panels Output Power by using MLP, RNN and Neuroevolution Models. *Adv. Nat. Appl. Sci.* **2014**, *8*, 74–81.
11. Jalali, S.M.J.; Ahmadian, S.; Khosravi, A.; Mirjalili, S.; Mahmoudi, M.R.; Nahavandi, S. Neuroevolution-based autonomous robot navigation: A comparative study. *Cogn. Syst. Res.* **2020**, *62*, 35–43. [CrossRef]
12. Junior, F.E.F.; Yen, G.G. Particle swarm optimization of deep neural networks architectures for image classification. *Swarm Evol. Comput.* **2019**, *49*, 62–74. [CrossRef]
13. Wang, B.; Sun, Y.; Xue, B.; Zhang, M. A hybrid differential evolution approach to designing deep convolutional neural networks for image classification. In Proceedings of the Australasian Joint Conference on Artificial Intelligence, Wellington, New Zealand, 11–14 December 2018; pp. 237–250.
14. Kim, J.K.; Han, Y.S.; Lee, J.S. Particle swarm optimization–deep belief network–based rare class prediction model for highly class imbalance problem. *Concurr. Comput. Pract. Exp.* **2017**, *29*, e4128. [CrossRef]
15. Qiang, N.; Ge, B.; Dong, Q.; Ge, F.; Liu, T. Neural architecture search for optimizing deep belief network models of fmri data. In Proceedings of the International Workshop on Multiscale Multimodal Medical Imaging, Shenzhen, China, 13 October 2019; pp. 26–34.
16. Sun, Y.; Xue, B.; Zhang, M.; Yen, G.G. A particle swarm optimization-based flexible convolutional autoencoder for image classification. *IEEE Trans. Neural Netw. Learn. Syst.* **2018**, *30*, 2295–2309. [CrossRef]

17. Sun, Y.; Xue, B.; Zhang, M.; Yen, G.G. An experimental study on hyper-parameter optimization for stacked auto-encoders. In Proceedings of the 2018 IEEE Congress on Evolutionary Computation (CEC), Rio de Janeiro, Brazil, 8–13 July 2018; pp. 1–8.
18. Jalali, S.M.J.; Ahmadian, S.; Khosravi, A.; Shafie-khah, M.; Nahavandi, S.; Catalão, J.P.S. A Novel Evolutionary-Based Deep Convolutional Neural Network Model for Intelligent Load Forecasting. *IEEE Trans. Ind. Inform.* **2021**, *17*, 8243–8253. [CrossRef]
19. Rojas, M.G.; Olivera, A.C.; Vidal, P.J. Optimising Multilayer Perceptron weights and biases through a Cellular Genetic Algorithm for medical data classification. *Array* **2022**, *14*, 100173. [CrossRef]
20. Kaveh, M.; Khishe, M.; Mosavi, M.R. Design and implementation of a neighborhood search biogeography-based optimization trainer for classifying sonar dataset using multi-layer perceptron neural network. *Analog. Integr. Circuits Signal Process.* **2018**, *100*, 405–428. [CrossRef]
21. Yuan, C.; Moayedi, H. The performance of six neural-evolutionary classification techniques combined with multi-layer perception in two-layered cohesive slope stability analysis and failure recognition. *Eng. Comput.* **2019**, *36*, 1705–1714. [CrossRef]
22. Bahnsen, A.C.; Gonzalez, A.M. Evolutionary Algorithms for Selecting the Architecture of a MLP Neural Network: A Credit Scoring Case. In Proceedings of the 11th International Conference on Data Mining Workshops, Vancouver, BC, Canada, 11 December 2011. [CrossRef]
23. Ho, Y.-W.; Rawat, T.S.; Yang, Z.-K.; Pratik, S.; Lai, G.-W.; Tu, Y.-L.; Lin, A. Neuroevolution-based efficient field effect transistor compact device models. *IEEE Access* **2021**, *9*, 159048–159058. [CrossRef]
24. Sekaj, I.; Kenický, I.; Zúbek, F. Neuro-Evolution of Continuous-Time Dynamic Process Controllers. *MENDEL* **2021**, *27*, 7–11. [CrossRef]
25. Ororbia, A.; ElSaid, A.; Desell, T. Investigating Recurrent Neural Network Memory Structures using Neuro-Evolution. In Proceedings of the Genetic and Evolutionary Computation Conference 2019 (GECCO '19), Prague, Czech Republic, 13–17 July 2019. [CrossRef]
26. Lyu, Z.; Karns, J.; ElSaid, A.; Desell, T. Improving Neuroevolution Using Island Extinction and Repopulation. *arXiv* **2020**, arXiv:2005.07376v1.
27. Yilmaz, O.; Bas, E.; Egrioglu, E. The Training of Pi-Sigma Artificial Neural Networks with Differential Evolution Algorithm for Forecasting. *Comput. Econ.* **2022**, *59*, 1699–1711. [CrossRef]
28. Saporetti, C.M.; Goliatt, L.; Pereira, E. Neural network boosted with differential evolution for lithology identification based on well logs information. *Earth Sci. Inform.* **2021**, *14*, 133–140. [CrossRef]
29. Kaur, M.; Singh, D. Multi-modality medical image fusion technique using multi-objective differential evolution based deep neural networks. *J. Ambient. Intell. Humaniz. Comput.* **2021**, *12*, 2483–2493. [CrossRef]
30. Fernandes, F.E.; Yen, G.G. Pruning of generative adversarial neural networks for medical imaging diagnostics with evolution strategy. *Inf. Sci.* **2021**, *558*, 91–102. [CrossRef]
31. Zamani, H.; Nadimi-Shahraki, M.H.; Gandomi, A.H. Starling murmuration optimizer: A novel bio-inspired algorithm for global and engineering optimization. *Comput. Methods Appl. Mech. Eng.* **2022**, *392*, 114616. [CrossRef]
32. Nadimi-Shahraki, M.H.; Zamani, H.; Mirjalili, S. Enhanced whale optimization algorithm for medical feature selection: A COVID-19 case study. *Comput. Biol. Med.* **2022**, *148*, 105858. [CrossRef]
33. Nadimi-Shahraki, M.H.; Zamani, H. DMDE: Diversity-maintained multi-trial vector differential evolution algorithm for non-decomposition large-scale global optimization. *Expert Syst. Appl.* **2022**, *198*, 116895. [CrossRef]
34. Askari, R.; Sebt, M.V.; Amjadian, A. A Multi-product EPQ Model for Defective Production and Inspection with Single Machine, and Operational Constraints: Stochastic Programming Approach. In Proceedings of the International Conference on Logistics and Supply Chain Management LSCM 2020: Logistics and Supply Chain Management, Tehran, Iran, 23–24 December 2020; pp. 161–193. [CrossRef]
35. Gharaei, A.; Amjadian, A.; Amjadian, A.; Shavandi, A.; Hashemi, A.; Taher, M.; Mohamadi, N. An integrated lot-sizing policy for the inventory management of constrained multi-level supply chains: Null-space method. *Int. J. Syst. Sci. Oper. Logist.* **2022**, 1–14. [CrossRef]
36. Taleizadeh, A.A.; Safaei, A.Z.; Bhattacharya, A.; Amjadian, A. Online peer-to-peer lending platform and supply chain finance decisions and strategies. *Ann. Oper. Res.* **2022**, *315*, 397–427. [CrossRef]
37. Gharaei, A.; Amjadian, A.; Shavandi, A. An integrated reliable four-level supply chain with multi-stage products under shortage and stochastic constraints. *Int. J. Syst. Sci. Oper. Logist.* **2021**, 1–22. [CrossRef]
38. Amjadian, A.; Gharaei, A. An integrated reliable five-level closed-loop supply chain with multi-stage products under quality control and green policies: Generalised outer approximation with exact penalty. *Int. J. Syst. Sci. Oper. Logist.* **2022**, *9*, 429–449. [CrossRef]
39. Gharaei, A.; Shekarabi, S.A.H.; Karimi, M. Optimal lot-sizing of an integrated EPQ model with partial backorders and re-workable products: An outer approximation. *Int. J. Syst. Sci. Oper. Logist.* **2021**, 1–17. [CrossRef]
40. Hussein, S.; Chandra, R.; Sharma, A. Multi-step-ahead chaotic time series prediction using coevolutionary recurrent neural networks. In Proceedings of the Congress on Evolutionary Computation (CEC), Vancouver, BC, Canada, 24–29 July 2016. [CrossRef]
41. Chandra, R.; Zhang, M. Cooperative coevolution of Elman recurrent neural networks for chaotic time series prediction. *Neurocomputing* **2012**, *86*, 116–123. [CrossRef]
42. Si, T.; Bagchi, J.; Miranda, P.B.C. Artificial neural network training using metaheuristics for medical data classification: An experimental study. *Expert Syst. Appl.* **2022**, *193*, 116423. [CrossRef]
43. Salman, I.; Ucan, O.N.; Bayat, O.; Shaker, K. Impact of metaheuristic iteration on artificial neural network structure in medical data. *Processes* **2018**, *6*, 57. [CrossRef]

44. Kumar, N.; Kumar, D. An improved grey wolf optimization-based learning of artificial neural network for medical data classification. *J. Inf. Commun. Technol.* **2021**, *20*, 213–248. [CrossRef]
45. Das, S.; Mishra, S.; Senapati, M.R. New approaches in metaheuristic to classify medical data using artificial neural network. *Arab. J. Sci. Eng.* **2019**, *45*, 2459–2471. [CrossRef]
46. Cartwright, H.; Curteanu, S. Neural Networks Applied in Chemistry. II. Neuro-Evolutionary Techniques in Process Modeling and Optimization. *Ind. Eng. Chem. Res.* **2013**, *52*, 12673–12688. [CrossRef]
47. Cerecedo-Cordoba, J.A.; Barbosa, J.J.G.; Terán-Villanueva, J.D.; Frausto-Solís, J.; Martínez Flores, J.A. Use of Neuroevolution to Estimate the Melting Point of Ionic Liquids. *Int. J. Comb. Optim. Probl. Inform.* **2017**, *8*, 2–9.
48. Yin, W. Personalized Hybrid Education Framework Based on Neuroevolution Methodologies. *Comput. Intell. Neurosci.* **2022**, *2022*, 6925668. [CrossRef]
49. Risi, S.; Togelius, J. Neuroevolution in Games: State of the Art and Open Challenges. *IEEE Trans. Comput. Intell. AI Games* **2017**, *9*, 25–41. [CrossRef]
50. Waris, F.; Reynolds, R. Neuro-Evolution Using Game-Driven Cultural Algorithms. In Proceedings of the 2020 Genetic and Evolutionary Computation Conference Companion, Cancún, Mexico, 8–12 July 2020.
51. Tharwat, A.; Schenck, W. Population initialization techniques for evolutionary algorithms for single-objective constrained optimization problems: Deterministic vs. stochastic techniques. *Swarm Evol. Comput.* **2022**, *67*, 100952. [CrossRef]
52. Kazimipour, B.; Li, X.; Qin, A.K. A review of population initialization techniques for evolutionary algorithms. In Proceedings of the 2014 IEEE Congress on Evolutionary Computation (CEC), Beijing, China, 6–11 July 2014; pp. 2585–2592. [CrossRef]
53. Bangyal, W.H.; Nisar, K.; Ag Ibrahim, A.A.B.; Haque, M.R.; Rodrigues, J.J.P.C.; Rawat, D.B. Comparative Analysis of Low Discrepancy Sequence-Based Initialization Approaches Using Population-Based Algorithms for Solving the Global Optimization Problems. *Appl. Sci.* **2021**, *11*, 7591. [CrossRef]
54. Jassova, A.; Lertchoosakul, P.; Nair, R. On variants of the Halton sequence. *Mon. Math.* **2015**, *180*, 743–764. [CrossRef]
55. Gnewuch, M.; Hebbinghaus, N. Discrepancy bounds for a class of negatively dependent random points including Latin hypercube samples. *Ann. Appl. Probab.* **2021**, *31*, 1944–1965. [CrossRef]
56. Aleti, A.; Moser, I. A Systematic Literature Review of Adaptive Parameter Control Methods for Evolutionary Algorithms. *ACM Comput. Surv.* **2017**, *49*, 1–35. [CrossRef]
57. Sipper, M.; Fu, W.; Ahuja, K.; Moore, J.H. Investigating the parameter space of evolutionary algorithms. *BioData Mining* **2018**, *11*, 2. [CrossRef]
58. Meyer-Nieberg, S.; Beyer, H.G. Self-Adaptation in Evolutionary Algorithms. In *Parameter Setting in Evolutionary Algorithms. Studies in Computational Intelligence*; Lobo, F.G., Lima, C.F., Michalewicz, Z., Eds.; Springer: Berlin/Heidelberg, Germany, 2007; Volume 54. [CrossRef]
59. Kingma, D.P.; Ba, J. Adam: A method for stochastic optimization. *arXiv* **2014**, arXiv:1412.6980.
60. Djunaidi, A.V.; Juwono, C.P. Football game algorithm implementation on the capacitated vehicle routing problems. *Int. J. Comput. Algorithm* **2018**, *7*, 45–53.
61. Wang, L.; Ni, H.; Yang, R.; Fei, M.; Ye, W.A. Simple Human Learning Optimization Algorithm. In *Communications Computer and Information Science*; Book Series CCIS; Springer: Berlin/Heidelberg, Germany, 2014; Volume 462, pp. 56–65.
62. Liu, Z.-Z.; Chu, D.H.; Song, C.; Xue, X.; Lu, B.Y. Social learning optimization (SLO) algorithm paradigm and its application in QoS-aware cloud service composition. *Inf. Sci.* **2016**, *326*, 315–333. [CrossRef]
63. Rao, R.V.; Savsani, V.J.; Vakharia, D.P. Teaching–learning-based optimization: A novel method for constrained mechanical design optimization problems. *Comput. Aided Des.* **2011**, *43*, 303–315. [CrossRef]
64. Cortés, P.; García, J.M.; Muñuzuri, J.; Onieva, L. Viral systems: A new bio-inspired optimisation approach. *Comput. Oper. Res.* **2008**, *35*, 2840–2860. [CrossRef]
65. Jaderyan, M.; Khotanlou, H. Virulence optimization algorithm. *Appl. Soft Comput.* **2016**, *43*, 596–618. [CrossRef]
66. Moghdani, R.; Salimifard, K. Volleyball premier league algorithm. *Appl. Soft Comput.* **2018**, *64*, 161–185. [CrossRef]
67. Anton, C.; Leon, F.; Gavrilescu, M.; Drăgoi, E.-N.; Floria, S.-A.; Curteanu, S.; Lisa, C. Obtaining Bricks Using Silicon-Based Materials: Experiments, Modeling and Optimization with Artificial Intelligence Tools. *Mathematics* **2022**, *10*, 1891. [CrossRef]

Review

A Review of Intelligent Connected Vehicle Cooperative Driving Development

Biyao Wang [1], Yi Han [1,*], Siyu Wang [1], Di Tian [1], Mengjiao Cai [2], Ming Liu [3] and Lujia Wang [3]

[1] Department of Automobile, Chang'an University, Xi'an 710064, China
[2] Shaanxi Institute of Coal Science, Xi'an 710043, China
[3] Department of Electronic and Computer Engineering, The Hong Kong University of Science and Technology, Clear Water Bay, Kowloon, Hong Kong SAR, China
* Correspondence: hany@chd.edu.cn; Tel.: +86-132-2805-5890

Abstract: With the development and progress of information technology, especially V2X technology, the research focus of intelligent vehicles gradually shifted from single-vehicle control to multi-vehicle control, and the cooperative control system of intelligent connected vehicles became an important topic of development. In order to track the research progress of intelligent connected vehicle cooperative driving systems in recent years, this paper discusses the current research of intelligent connected vehicle cooperative driving systems with vehicles, infrastructure, and test sites, and analyzes the current development status, development trend, and development limitations of each object. Based on the analysis results of relevant references of the cooperative control algorithm, this paper expounds on vehicle collaborative queue control, vehicle collaborative decision making, and vehicle collaborative positioning. In the case of taking the infrastructure as the object, this paper expounds the communication security, communication delay, and communication optimization algorithm of the vehicle terminal and the road terminal of intelligent connected vehicles. In the case of taking the test site as the object, this paper expounds the development process and research status of the real vehicle road test platform, virtual test platform, test method, and evaluation mechanism, and analyzes the problems existing in the intelligent connected vehicle test environment. Finally, the future development trend and limitations of intelligent networked vehicle collaborative control system are discussed. This paper summarizes the intelligent connected car collaborative control system, and puts forward the next problems to be solved and the direction of further exploration. The research results can provide a reference for the cooperative driving of intelligent vehicles.

Keywords: intelligent connected vehicle; cooperative driving system; V2X; communication technology

JEL Classification: 68T01

Citation: Wang, B.; Han, Y.; Wang, S.; Tian, D.; Cai, M.; Liu, M.; Wang, L. A Review of Intelligent Connected Vehicle Cooperative Driving Development. *Mathematics* 2022, 10, 3635. https://doi.org/10.3390/math10193635

Academic Editor: Aydin Azizi

Received: 8 August 2022
Accepted: 29 September 2022
Published: 4 October 2022

Publisher's Note: MDPI stays neutral with regard to jurisdictional claims in published maps and institutional affiliations.

Copyright: © 2022 by the authors. Licensee MDPI, Basel, Switzerland. This article is an open access article distributed under the terms and conditions of the Creative Commons Attribution (CC BY) license (https://creativecommons.org/licenses/by/4.0/).

1. Introduction

Conducting research on intelligent connected vehicle systems will introduce a new stage of development in China's automotive industry and intelligent transportation industry [1]. In recent decades, single-vehicle-based intelligent driving technology made great progress. With sensors and processors loaded on the vehicles, some sample vehicles were implemented for demonstration operations on the road. However, there are still many problems to be solved [2], such as (1) inaccurate individual sensor readings; (2) the limited detection distance of on-board sensors; (3) the existence of blind areas for on-board sensor detection; (4) high costs of on-board computational processors; and (5) a lack of predictive mechanisms for other vehicle behaviors.

Specifically, the direction of automobile development is intelligent and networked. Intelligence includes the perception, decision making, and control of intelligent cars. Car intelligence is usually through the radar system (laser radar, millimeter wave radar, and ultrasonic radar) and visual system (camera) to collect the surrounding environment, and then through the vehicle computer and algorithm for data processing, it makes the optimal decision, the decision signal goes to the vehicle chassis control system, and the intelligent control is realized [3]. Networking refers to the function of communication and real-time information between the network environment and real-time information interaction, which can be divided into vehicle-to-vehicle (V2V), vehicle-to-infrastructure (V2I), vehicle-to-network (V2N), and vehicle-to-pedestrian (V2P). An intelligent connected vehicle generally refers to a single vehicle to achieve intelligence through sensor technology. At present, in order to improve the safety and comfort of intelligent vehicles, intelligent connected vehicles, in addition to directly perceiving the environment to make decisions, also need to have the ability to cooperate and act, and reflect the advantages of multi-vehicle intelligence through the cooperation and coordination of vehicle to vehicle [4].

In the development and advancement in vehicle-to-everything (V2X) technologies, including vehicle-to-vehicle communication technologies and vehicle and roadside infrastructure communication technologies, collaborative vehicle infrastructure systems (CVIS) and information factors play an increasingly important role in transportation systems [5–7]. Intelligent collaborative vehicle control based on vehicle–road cooperation will enable all-round information sensing and compensate for the lack of on-board computing power, which is a future direction in this field. Under the conditions of intelligent networks, vehicles on the road are no longer isolated individuals but multi-vehicle systems formed by wireless communication networks. In the vehicle network environment, intelligent vehicles can obtain information about other vehicles and roads within the communication range based on workshop communication and vehicle–road communication, and they use this information for distributed decision making and control in order to realize the collaborative control of the whole system. At present, the development of technologies, such as vehicle–road cooperation and vehicle–vehicle communication became a breakthrough in the development of single-vehicle agents in the intelligent network environment [8]. The European SAFESPOT project [9], the U.S. path project [10], and the Japanese Smartway project [11], etc., researched and explored the field of vehicle–road cooperation from various aspects by establishing an experimental platform to verify the technical problems in the process of vehicle–road cooperation in an effort to achieve intelligent information sharing between vehicles and road facilities, and ultimately ensure traffic safety and improve traffic efficiency. Among them, the intelligent connected vehicle formation, as a kind of both traffic efficiency and traffic safety mode, through the real-time communication and coordination between vehicles, makes full use of road infrastructure, simplifies the complexity of traffic control and management, improves road capacity, eases traffic congestion, reduces environmental pollution, has great potential, and is the new way of road vehicle traffic in the future. Intelligent connected vehicle formation is mainly for more intelligent snatched vehicles in a complex traffic environment. By adjusting their driving speed and steering, it makes itself and nearby intelligent connected vehicles keep relatively stable geometric posture and the same movement, and meets the task requirements and constraints (such as obstacle avoidance), so as to realize more intelligent connected vehicles between wireless communication collaborative driving behavior. The main technologies involved in the autonomous vehicle formation include: vehicle combination positioning and multi-sensor and multi-source information fusion technology, collaborative formation control technology, and cooperative perception and communication technology. In this context, this paper focuses on the intelligent vehicle cooperative control system in the vehicle networking environment.

In the 1980s, some scholars put forward the concept of formation system control. After the 1990s, the problem of multi-vehicle formation gradually attracted more and more researchers. At present, the formation control of multi-vehicle cooperative system mainly includes following the pilot method, virtual structure method, artificial potential energy field method, virtual pilot method, and behavior-based method. Benefits of a vehicle–road collaborative intelligent system are as follows: firstly, from the perspective of safety, many bicycle intelligent scenarios can be easily solved through intelligent roads and powerful cloud network facilities. Secondly, through the intensive construction of intelligent roads and the intelligent cloud network, intelligent capabilities can be shared by all the cars on the road to reduce the amount of cars, reduce the cost of the car, thus reducing the cost of the whole automatic system. From the perspective of the three parts of autonomous driving perception, decision making and control, the perception of bicycle intelligence is only based on its own sensors, with blind spots and dead corners. The vehicle-road collaborative "intelligent look" can be based on the sensor network on the road, namely based on the 5G "car-road-side-edge-cloud" level 4 fusion data processing system network, covering vehicle perception data, roadside perception data, edge, area, central cloud access of traffic/road data, environment/public service data, and other basic service platform data, no dead angle, and long distance, also called "god perspective". The intelligent decision of a bicycle vehicle can only be made based on its own incomplete information, which cannot be taken into account by other vehicles, so the decision result is locally optimal. Vehicle–road collaborative intelligence can comprehensively take into account the next movement trend of all cars, so as to make a comprehensive and optimal decision result. Based on such advantages, vehicle-to-road collaborative intelligence can achieve very good driving safety and economy.

In this context, the research of this paper focuses on intelligent connected vehicle cooperative driving development. The overall framework of the article is shown in Figure 1. The intelligent vehicle cooperative driving system is discussed, and the latest developments in vehicle network cooperative driving are introduced.

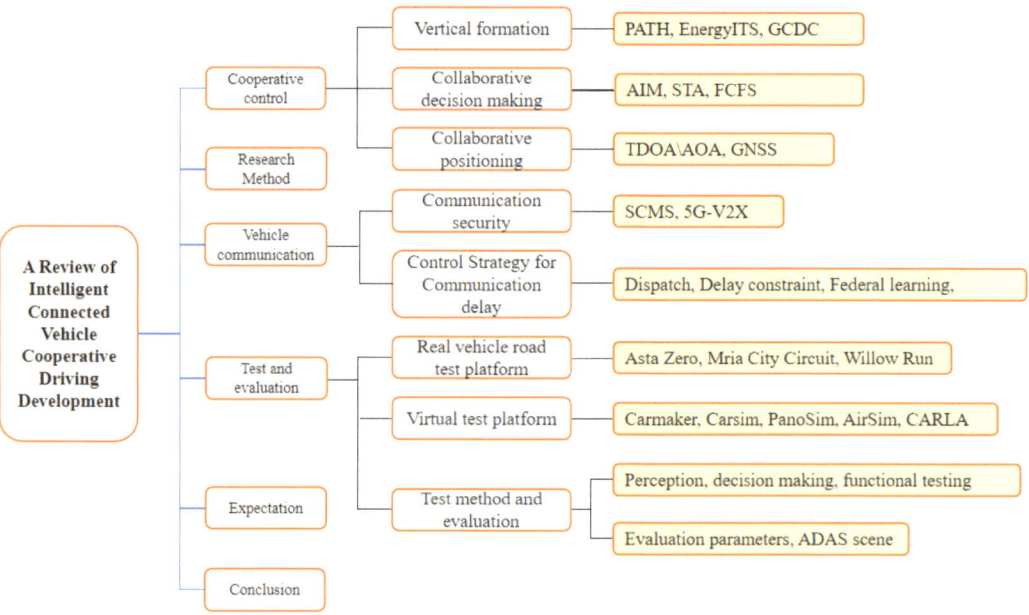

Figure 1. Structural framework.

The remainder of this paper is organized as follows: Section 2 presents the selection methods of the references and details the literature screening process for the systematic review and the preferred reporting guidelines for the meta-analysis. Section 3 describes the details and problems of the collaborative control algorithms for intelligent vehicles. Section 4 describes current situation and problems of the exit vehicle and internet communication. Section 5 explains the test platform and evaluation system of the intelligent vehicle collaborative control system. Section 6 summarizes the current status of the study and suggests directions for future research. Finally, the article is summarized in Section 7.

2. Research Method

In this paper, preferred reporting items for systematic reviews and meta-analysis (PRISMA) are used to analyze the literature to review the cooperative development of intelligent and connected vehicles [12,13].

2.1. Literature Search

Relevant Chinese and English literature of eight databases, including Google Academic, Web of Science Core Collection, Inspec, KCI-Korean Journal Database, SciELO Citation Index, IEEE Xplore, and China Knowledge Network of China and Baidu Academic, were searched. The following search keywords will include the following four categories:

(1) intelligent vehicle cooperative development, intelligent connected vehicles;
(2) vehicle queue, collaborative positioning, collaborative control and decision, multi-vehicle, CACC;
(3) communication security, communication delay, and internet of vehicles;
(4) intelligent connected vehicle test platform, test software, experimental method and evaluation system.

The selection of keywords can be divided into three levels: layer 1 is the Chinese and English keywords related to intelligent vehicle cooperative development; layer 2 is a general name, generic name or nickname, such as "vehicle collaborative control technology", "Intelligent connected vehicle communication", "Intelligent connected test platform, evaluation system" and its corresponding English name; layer 3 is the specific classification name, such as the vehicle queue, communication security, vehicle road collaborative positioning, and selects their respective names as the search keywords. The above three layers of keyword search and classification provide a complete summary of the collaborative control system from the aspects of concept, general classification and classification, so a comprehensive and detailed research literature can be obtained accordingly. Some of the search keywords were not listed because there was no relevant literature under the entry, or the retrieved literature was repeatedly recorded by other keywords.

2.2. Literature Screening

The literature screening process used in this paper and the literature screening situation at each stage are shown in Figure 2, and the n is the number of documents. First, the relevant literature of eight databases was searched according to the keywords mentioned above. Secondly, the repeated literature between databases was eliminated and the subject and content were screened. Finally, the evaluation indicators of these literature were scored for quality, and the literature finally included in the review was determined according to the scoring results.

In terms of literature quality scoring standards [14–16], this paper constructs the literature quality evaluation indicators required by the research of the intelligent connected vehicle cooperative control system, as shown in Table 1. Specifically, score 2 if the indicator answers "Yes", 1 if it answers "Not exactly Yes", and 0 if the indicator answers "No". Among them, the literature quality score of 17 or above is excellent, while 12–17 is classified as qualified, and that of 12 or below 12 points is unqualified. Only qualified and above documents are retained, and unqualified documents are excluded. The whole literature was scored by two authors, respectively, and the literature with a difference of less than three and the final score was decided by two people through discussion. If the scoring results of either literature are quite different (the score difference is greater than 3), the remaining two authors will make a decision on the scoring results.

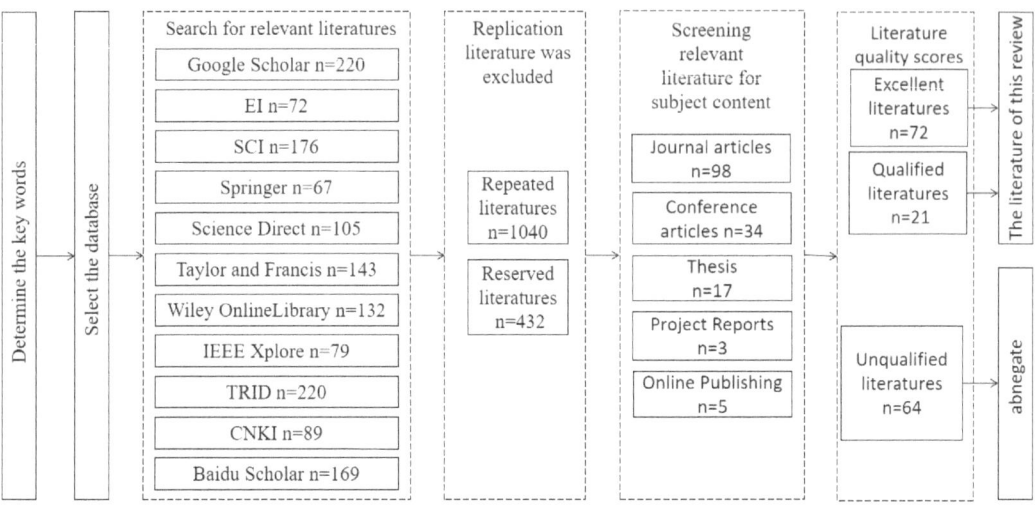

Figure 2. Literature screening process.

Table 1. Measurement Indexs of Literature Quality.

Number	Literature Quality Assessment Index	Marking
1	Is the motivation clear?	Yes is 2, Not exactly 1, No is 0
2	Are the hypotheses/questions under study clearly and adequately stated?	Yes is 2, Not exactly 1, No is 0
3	Is the study design suitable for the study purposes?	Yes is 2, Not exactly 1, No is 0
4	Does the study clearly describe the type or characteristics of collaborative control clearly?	Yes is 2, Not exactly 1, No is 0
5	Is the test environment clearly described?	Yes is 2, Not exactly 1, No is 0
6	Is the way of data collection is clear and reasonable?	Yes is 2, Not exactly 1, No is 0
7	Are all the influencing factors strictly restricted in the experimental studies?	Yes is 2, Not exactly 1, No is 0
8	Are the data fully analyzed?	Yes is 2, Not exactly 1, No is 0
9	Are the investigation or test results clearly stated?	Yes is 2, Not exactly 1, No is 0
10	Are the study conclusions fully discussed?	Yes is 2, Not exactly 1, No is 0
11	Is there any lack of research and prospects?	Yes is 2, Not exactly 1, No is 0

2.3. Information Extraction

After eliminating the unqualified literature of all the literature included in the review of standardized information extraction, the following data are extracted from the literature: ① author and publication year, ② country and region, ③ research object, ④ sample size, ⑤ research length, ⑥ research method, ⑦ research index, ⑧ influence factors, and ⑨ literature conclusion. In order to ensure the accuracy of literature information extraction, two authors were, respectively, responsible for the relevant literature information extraction, and two other authors randomly selected 10 documents from each part for information verification to ensure reliability.

2.4. Comprehensive Analysis of the Literature Results

Quantitative analysis cannot be performed directly due to the heterogeneity of the different studies. Therefore, the results of the screened literature were systematically summarized and reported by narrative comprehensive analysis. Specifically, the steps of this analysis include determining the review problem, sorting out and comparing the data, and drawing conclusions.

3. Cooperative Control
3.1. Vertical Formation

The development of intelligent transportation technology has advantages in solving the problems of low traffic efficiency, poor safety, and high energy consumption. V2X-based traffic environment information sensing and interaction technology enables vehicles in the road network to obtain real-time status information about other vehicles within communication range, identify vehicle driving intentions through model predictive reasoning, adjust driving strategies, and ensure vehicle driving safety [17]. V2X technology lays the foundation for the development of vehicle group operation. Vehicle group operation is an important means to improve road traffic efficiency; when vehicle group driving, on the one hand, with the increase in the number of vehicles in line, the driving resistance coefficient of each vehicle decreases, so the driving mode of the vehicle group can reduce the vehicle driving resistance and reduce energy consumption. On the other hand, vehicle group driving can reduce traffic stress by integrating vehicle driving states, reducing the vehicle following distance, and improving road occupancy [18]. Therefore, the team operation mode will be a future development trend in self-driving vehicles.

The vehicle platoon driving system is also called the cooperative adaptive cruise system, and its structure is shown in Figure 3. Through the introduction of inter-vehicle communication, the vehicle platoon driving system realizes the information transmission and sharing between connected vehicles, and can achieve continuous tracking control of multiple vehicles, ensure vehicle safety, and improve the performance of the entire vehicle plat. The research on vehicle platoons began in the early 1990s with the Partnership for Advanced Transportation Technology (PATH) project in the United States [19,20], as shown in Figure 4a. Japan and Europe also launched related projects on vehicle platoons, such as Japan's Energy ITS project [21], the Grand Cooperative Driving Challenge (GCDC) in Europe as shown in Figure 4b [22,23], etc. In recent years, there were many studies related to vehicle queues in China. For example, the vehicle platoon of Chang'an Automobile CS55 is shown in Figure 4c, and the Baidu 6-vehicle mixed fleet is shown in Figure 4d shown [24,25].

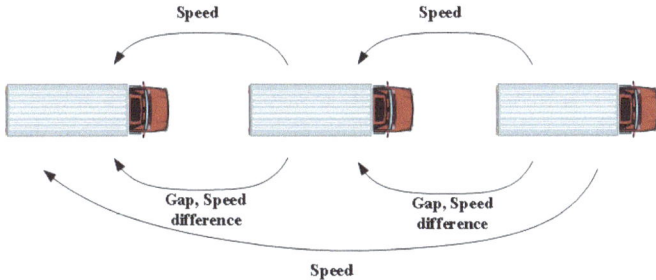

Figure 3. Vehicle platoon structure.

The ideal distance between vehicles is also referred to as the geometric configuration. It is used to describe the relative position or attitude between the controlled vehicle and the driver's vehicle in a steady state. Different spacing control strategies can affect the safety and stability of the vehicle queue. By maintaining a reasonable distance, aerodynamics can effectively use the traction effect to improve fuel economy. In the 1890s, scholars such as Loannou P.A. and Swaroop D. proposed a fixed forward constant time headway (CTH) strategy to maintain a distance between front and rear vehicles. In 1997, Yanakiev [26] also considered the vehicle speed and acceleration when developing a headway control strategy. In 2004, Fred Browand [27], a scholar at the University of Southern California, considered the situation of two trucks tailing each other. The model predictive control (MPC) approach has three typical features: model prediction, rolling optimization, and feedback correction. It allows for better advanced control and online roll optimization calculations. It is suitable for complex systems where it is difficult to build accurate numerical models. Memon [28] developed a continuous time-domain vehicle model based on MPC techniques that can capture the steady state and transient states of the vehicle in real time. It focuses on the critical state characteristics of the vehicle response of adaptive cruise control (ACC). Through simulation, it was verified that the ACC model controlled by MPC has high sensitivity and can truly reflect the behavior of the actual vehicle.

Figure 4. Vehicle queue display [25]: (**a**) US path truck queue; (**b**) European GCDC mixed queue driving competition; (**c**) driving demonstration of 55 Chang'an Cs55; and (**d**) Baidu 6-car mixed queue driving display.

In recent years, with the gradual maturity of the ACC system, its cost reduced, and ACC technology fell to the 100,000 range. For example, Nissan's Sylphy and Versa are equipped with an ACC system. Pan Chaofeng et al. [29] detailed the components, design methods, and research hotspots of the ACC, and reviewed future research directions and development trends. In addition, CACC can realize collaboration with traffic signals, and alvert Simeon C et al. [30] realized the interaction with intelligent traffic signals by queuing suburban trunk lines in real traffic. In addition, YuanHeng Zhu et al. [31] proposed a new control structure for the vehicle queue with multiple front vehicles, transforming the heterogeneous CACC problem into the adjustment problem of each error dynamic, and ensuring the stability of the minimum front time distance of the vehicle queue through the sum of square planning. Shuaidong Zhao et al. [32] proposed a model predictive control method based on distributed robust stochastic optimization for collaborative adaptive cruise control under uncertain traffic conditions, which then improves the stability, robustness, and safety of longitudinal collaborative autonomous driving with multiple CAVs. In the process of car following, CACC's coordination ability and adaptability of various goals are a very important part in the complex and changeable driving environment. Yang, Ld et al. [33] adjusts the weighted value according to the deceleration duration and the deceleration change, and increases the relative distance between the two cars under a deceleration condition. In addition, Chen JZ et al. [34] proposed an improved variable front time distance strategy for the collaborative cruise control system, which redesigned the second-layer controller on the basis of existing technologies, and verified the effectiveness of the strategy through the simulation of two traffic scenarios. Liang H et al. [35] proposed a new consensus-based input saturation and variable workshop time–distance control method, considering the communication delay in the algorithm. At present, some researchers carried out the study of applying the communication between the multiple front vehicles to the collaborative adaptive cruise system, so that the communication between the target vehicles and the multiple front vehicles is made. The current research on the CACC technology control method is mainly divided into classical control method, optimal control method, synovial control method, and machine learning-based method, which is the latest development trend.

3.2. Vehicle Collaborative Decision-Making and Control Strategy

Traffic congestion in signal road intersections became a central problem in both developed and developing countries. Collaborative decision making of vehicle control can solve this problem very well and reduce the traffic congestion problem at highway and road intersections [36]. Based on vehicle–road communication technology, vehicle–road cooperative decision making became a research hotspot within intelligent traffic organization systems. Vehicle–road collaborative decision making needs to realize active vehicle safety control and road collaborative management. Vehicle active safety control is divided into three directions, namely no signal intersection, road section between the adjacent intersection and road network. Seeking effective ways to maximize traffic at intersections, maximizing traffic flow, while considering various factors, the rapid development of truth–time strategy, signal timing limit, traffic system, speed, and other actual implementation are our goals [37]. First, for non-signalized crossing, autonomous intersection management (AIM) is more effective than signal timing assignment (STA) [38]. Research on the spatial dispersion of road intersections is mostly based on the first-come-first-served (FCFS) traffic principle [39–41], which is more prone to delays than STA. Based on the analysis of intersection conflict points, one can overcome the shortage of reserved space for an intelligent driving vehicle at the whole intersection [42–46]. Some researchers study methods that are different from FCFS by optimizing the departure sequences of intelligent vehicles at intersections, such as optimizing the departure sequence of conflict traffic flow [47–51], sharing control based on the real-time traffic state at intersections [52], adaptive traffic decision making based on insertion [53], distributed conflict resolution mechanisms [54], etc. Secondly, for the adjacent intersection link, the trajectory can be optimized by speed coordination. Hamilton and Euler–Lagrange equations are constructed to obtain the analytical expressions of vehicle motion parameters [55]. On this basis, the vehicle trajectories between two intersections are optimized [56], the trajectory solving process is extended [57], and the existence of feasible solutions is proven. Bichiou et al. [58] estimated the arrival time of vehicles at intersections and solved the convex programming problem of the vehicle movement process according to the minimum principle. Finally, for the road network, the road network traffic organization method for intelligent driving vehicles is still in the initial stage of research. Guo et al. [59] focused on the road network scenario with multiple intersections, and Huasknecht et al. [60] introduced the internet of vehicles to study the performance of aim. Huang et al. [61] studied the design and evaluation of vehicle trajectory planning methods in a multi-intersection traffic network using an integrated simulator, and Chu et al. [62] studied vehicle trajectory optimization in road networks based on dynamic variable lanes. Milanes et al. [63] used vehicle-to-vehicle (V2V) communication technology to determine the vehicle speed and location at a signalized intersection, estimated the intersection location through these data, designed a fuzzy logic decision algorithm according to vehicle speed, and predicted the optimal vehicle speed trajectory by using short-range radar and traffic signal information. Liu et al. [64] regarded drivers and signalized intersections as automatic agents in a multi-agent system, and elaborated new mechanisms to imitate traffic signals and stop signs in the system. Since the factors influencing the collaborative control of vehicles exhibit complex interactions, these factors must be identified to propose solutions that can address this complexity and still need to be implemented.

In terms of road collaborative management, the accurate and effective prediction of vehicle traffic flow plays an important role in the construction and planning of signal intersections. The application of the AI prediction model in traffic flow performance prediction achieves positive results. However, there is still great uncertainty in determining which AI approach can effectively solve traffic congestion problems. Isaac Oyeyemi Olayode [36] et al. compared an artificial neural network trained by a particle swarm optimization model (ANN-PSO) and a heuristic artificial neural network model (ANN) for vehicle traffic flow prediction, using the South Africa transportation system as a case study. Results show that the ANN-PSO model is more efficient than the neural network model in predicting vehicle traffic flow at four-way signal intersections, and is robust enough to predict traffic flow. This research idea provides traffic flow information and guidance for the collaborative control system to optimize its travel time decision.

In the multi-vehicle queue forming control system, the system needs to be specially designed when individual vehicles need to leave or join the fleet. Ying ZB et al. [65] added a dynamic AVP management protocol to the control system for how to effectively manage the addition of vehicles and the leaving of vehicles in the vehicle queue. Vehicles joining and leaving the queue will need to communicate with the queue leader, and all the messages will be related to the corresponding transactions specified by the smart contract. Cai MC et al., for the real-time collaborative lane change and queue switching problems, [66] proposed a dynamic staggered hierarchical queue generation method, which introduces the lane change function of all vehicles, establishes the optimal problem model, and develops the on-board local controller of vehicles to ensure a safe distance between vehicles. Gao W et al. [67] proposed a spectrum-aware scheduling scheme for queue communication resource management for the problems of communication between queues when vehicles join queues, and shown through simulation results that the scheme achieves a smaller queue error when vehicles join multi-vehicle queues. Won M [68] proposed the concept of L-Platooning for especially long heavy trucks, the first queuing protocol that can seamlessly, reliably, and quickly form a long platoon, introducing a new concept—the virtual leader, a vehicle that acts as a platoon leader, to support the addition and departure of the long platoon. Fina NA [69] proposes an improved multi-mobility management protocol (IMMP) for queue, join, leave, and disrupt scheduling operations, where IMMP manages multiple connections and leave operations through vehicle-to-vehicle infrastructure and vehicle-to-vehicle communication, simultaneously. By verifying the design features of various systems using PROMELA and SPIN validation tools, the logical flow of IMMP is proposed, and the simulation results and analysis verify the behavior of the connection and departure process without affecting the safety of the entire system, this study shows that IMMP works successfully within an acceptable duration of mobility. Santini S et al. [70] proposed a longitudinal controller based on distributed consensus, while maintaining the stability and performance of the formation topology and control gain, showing the dynamic characteristics of the system and the addition, leaving performance in the middle of a typical set of queue maneuvers, and finally the simulation confirmed the feasibility of the strategy. Liu B et al. [71], for multi-vehicle queue forming control problem, proposed a distributed reinforcement learning method based on the deep Q-network and consensus algorithm; the queue problem is decomposed into multiple bicycle tasks, each car by interacting with the front and rear car accumulated experience data samples, and then uses the consensus algorithm to make all the vehicles in the scattered queue close to each other, which only needs to directly connect the communication between vehicles. Li LH et al. [72] combined graph theory and safety potential field (G-SPF) theory and proposed a new model of networked automatic vehicle (cav) under different vehicle distribution, which compared with previous studies, innovatively introduced the concept of safety potential field, better described the actual driving risk, ensured the absolute safety of the vehicle, put forward the four-step team optimization strategy, realized the optimization control of team pre-formation and team drive, and finally verified the effectiveness of the vehicle queue forming method based on G-SPF theory through simulation results. Dai SL et al. [73] uses the prescribed performance control methods, neural network approximation, interference observer, dynamic surface control technology, and Lyapunov method to comprehensively propose an adaptive formation control strategy to ensure the internal stability of the closed-loop system while guaranteeing the specified performance. In the vehicle collaborative decision making and control, the researchers gradually study the indicators, such as ride comfort and fuel economy, on the premise of ensuring the vehicle safety. Multi-objective optimization is now the future development trend.

3.3. Collaborative Positioning

The vehicle–road collaboration technology in the automotive internet integrates modern communication technology and network platforms. Through information sharing among vehicles, roads, and people, it realizes complex environmental sensing, collaborative decision making, and intelligent control functions to build a safe, comfortable, and energy-efficient automotive internet platform. Vehicle GPS technology is usually used to achieve positioning. Due to signal blockage and the multiplex effect, GPS positioning technology often suffers from missing signals or insufficient accuracy to achieve lane-level positioning accuracy and cannot meet the requirements of vehicle–road collaboration applications [74]. Cooperative positioning (CP) technology is another method to improve the positioning accuracy of vehicle–road collaboration networks [75].

Currently, using various methods to obtain more and more meters or even centimeter-level high precision position information research, based on the global navigation satellite system positioning technology, based on computer vision sensor positioning technology, based on the laser radar sensor positioning technology, and based on super broadband signal positioning technology, the four methods are the mainstream of the high-precision positioning technology route.

The global navigation satellite system is the existing and widely used positioning technology in the field of road traffic, and the GPS, Beidou, and other systems are integrated to improve the positioning accuracy and reliability of the positioning system. Zeng Qinghua and others of Nanjing University of Aeronautics and Astronautics proposed that the positioning method of multi-constellation-combined navigation can improve the accuracy of users. [76]. Robert Odolinski and others of Otago University also did relevant research in order to reduce the cost of RTK and improve the positioning accuracy, and proposed that [77] uses the measurement antenna to improve the positioning accuracy of the receiver. However, the impact on the interference of streamers and tall buildings on satellite signals is [78], and satellite signals are vulnerable to road conditions and weather, which will cause signal drift and signal loss, affect normal driving, and even cause safety accidents, which cannot meet the conditions of the high reliability requirements of the positioning system.

Computer visual positioning can be divided into: monocular visual positioning navigation, binocular visual positioning navigation, and multiocular visual positioning navigation [79–82]. These positioning and navigation technologies achieved good results in the research of visual positioning. However, bad weather can lead to poor work normally, and existing technology can only well solve the identification of specific targets. The complex scene of the social road cannot well identify any problems, nor can it meet the requirements of real-time and the reliability of the positioning system.

Lidar positioning technology uses adjacent point cloud data to derive the rigid body transformation [83] between two adjacent frames through feature extraction and a registration algorithm. Compared with other sensors, lidar has incomparable advantages in the unmanned positioning system, and the positioning algorithm, based on lidar sensors, plays an important role in the intelligent driving positioning module of [84,85].

Ultra wiband technology is a new wireless communication technology. Its positioning technology has low system complexity, low power consumption, good anti-interference ability, high multi-path resolution, and high positioning accuracy [86,87]. Kegen et al. [88]

proposed that in order to locate and track the target, we applied the Kalman filtering algorithm in an ultra-wideband positioning system.

Car–car and car–road information collaborative interaction drives multiple collaborative positioning applications, for example, car–car collaborative positioning [89], based on roadside positioning enhancement [90], car–car collaborative integrity monitoring [91], and beyond visual distance detection perception [92]; at the same time, it also greatly expands the traditional bicycle autonomous positioning weight calculation based on the perceptual range in the weight distribution and actual satellite observation quality level to establish closer correlations. Liu [93] et al. established the overall framework of vehicle satellite positioning and collaborative positioning enhancement based on vehicle–road information interaction for the tracking and adaptation of navigation satellite positioning and weight allocation in a complex dynamic operating environment. Based on high-precision mapping and multi-sensor fusion positioning technology, Yao [94] and others complement the advantages of various sensing and positioning methods, such as the global navigation satellite system and roadside multi-sensor sensing, and realize the continuous tracking and high-precision positioning of vehicles in urban ground and underground garage scenes. In view of the problem of large positioning errors of unmanned vehicles in unstructured scenarios, combined with on-board lidar and a roadside binocular camera, the dual-layer fusion collaborative positioning algorithm is adopted to achieve high-precision positioning.

Figure 5 [95] shows a typical cooperative localization system in which the participating nodes include vehicles and roadside infrastructure. The location of the roadside infrastructure is known and can receive GPS signals. The vehicle with a brighter color knows its GPS location, while the vehicle with a darker color does not obtain sufficient GPS signals to obtain its location information. However, it can estimate its own position data from the position information of neighboring nodes, i.e., it calculates its own position information from the position information of neighboring nodes received from neighboring nodes and the estimated distance between neighboring nodes. Positioning observation data are limited, and the evaluation of a collaborative localization system based on GPS/RSS/CFO can effectively improve the localization accuracy.

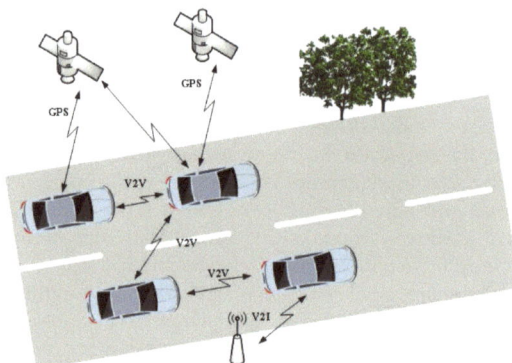

Figure 5. Collaborative positioning system in urban scene showing the block diagram of the system, consisting of four parts: RSS filter, GPS filter, decision center, and integrated Kalman filter.

In 2006, Europe achieved a breakthrough in the information exchange between vehicles and roadside units. In the preset platform, researchers initially achieved a mutual balance between the traffic infrastructure and vehicles, and freely used the information of various vehicles [96]. A weighted least squares algorithm based on the maximum likelihood estimation of the distance between the sensor and the target was proposed [97]. A simple filtering algorithm based on least squares was proposed, but the positioning accuracy was not high [98]. A total least squares target location algorithm based on the time difference of arrival (TDOA) and the angle of arrival (AOA) was proposed [99], but it had low accuracy and complex steps. The iterative constrained weighted least squares localization algorithm based on TDOA and frequency difference of arrival (FDOA) measurement was adopted in reference [100], which has high accuracy but complex implementation. Sensor-based location is a common method of vehicle location. However, the high cost, sensitivity to the environment, and the mapping and updating of maps also limit the rapid diffusion and spread of sensor-based positioning. No single technology, such as global navigation satellite systems (GNSS) or sensors, can guarantee high-accuracy positioning performance for vehicles in any environment, so a combination of inertial navigation, high-accuracy maps, and other complementary methods, such as cellular networks, is used to improve the positioning accuracy and stability. Among them, cellular networks are very important for improving positioning performance, such as real-time kinematic (RTK) data and sensor data transmission and high-precision map downloads. In addition, the positioning capability of 5G also provides strong support for the high-accuracy positioning of vehicles.

Due to the high technical difficulty and rich application scenarios of vehicle–road collaboration, the positioning research and application of vehicle–road collaboration in China is still in the stage of exploration and attempting, with more design schemes, less implementation, and no unified standard formed. Pilot application is in the Beijing–Hong Kong–Macao expressway Zhuozhou service section of the vehicle–road collaborative demonstration area construction. Four millimeter-wave radars will be installed in the pilot demonstration area, which are fixed to the surveillance lever or gantry by the back-to-back installation mode, and the installation position is close to the surveillance camera and millimeter-wave radar. China Mobile built 65G base stations in the vehicle–road collaborative demonstration area, realizing the full coverage of 5G signals. A total of 3 V2X roadside units were installed, with a single coverage radius of 800 m and a coverage range of 3 km. According to the application scenario of the expressway, the Zhuozhou service section of the G4 Beijing–Hong Kong–Macao expressway conducted the pilot application of the expressway collaborative positioning construction mode based on "5G + Beidou high-precision positioning", and the system functions of the typical application scenario are verified.

The development direction of the collaborative orientation for road cloud integration control, 5G + fusion high-precision positioning is based on AI multi-source heterogeneous data fusion, holographic simulation and consistency test public service platforms, and other key technologies, such as the formation of "car-road-road-edge-cloud" level 4 fusion of data processing, 5G + beidou dynamic cm/static millimeter-level high-precision positioning, real-time interaction, and all-round decision management of collaborative system.

4. Vehicle Communication

As one of the key technologies in this field, vehicle communication refers to the use of wireless communication, physical terminals, and intelligent sensors to realize V2V, vehicle–road communication (V2I), to enhance traffic efficiency, improve traffic safety and travel experiences, and construct the vehicle network (IOV) or vehicle self-organization network (VANET).

The frequency band of on-board communication is mainly divided into low frequency, intermediate frequency, and high frequency, and the name and scope are shown in Table 2. The application representative of low-frequency technology mainly includes automobile anti-theft and keyless systems. The product application of this technology mainly includes vehicle remote control keys; high-frequency communication mainly includes Bluetooth communication, mobile communication, dedicated short-range communication (DSRC), ultra-wideband (UWB) communication, etc.

Table 2. Name and range of frequency bands [101].

Classification/ Characteristics	Frequency Band	Band Range	Frequency Range
Ultra-long-wave	VLF	105~104 m	3~30 kHz
Long-wave	Low frequency	104~103 m	30~300 kHz
Medium-wave	Intermediate frequency	103~102 m	300~3000 kHz
Short-wave	High frequency	102~10 m	3~30 MHz
Ultra-short-wave	VHF	10~1 m	30~300 MHz
Microwave	Extra-high frequency UHF Very high frequency Ultra-high frequency	100~10 cm 10~1 cm 10~1 mm <1 mm	300~3000 MHz 3~30 GHz 30~300 GHz >300 GHz

The beginning of the development of vehicle communication systems can be traced back to a patent introduced in the United States in 1922 on the use of peer-to-peer (P2P) wireless communication vehicle alarm systems [102]. In recent years, with the development of wireless communication technology, on-board communication technology attracted increasing attention from a number of fields. The United States (CAMP/VSC-2) [103], Japan [104], and the European Union (SAFESPOT) successively carried out relevant research projects, taking place around 2010. As early as the 10th five-year plan, China began to strengthen its focus on and planning of intelligent transportation-related fields. Since 2010, a number of "863" projects and National Nature Science Foundation of China (NSFC) projects related to vehicle communication were launched. Collaborative data processing and security privacy are key issues in wireless sensor networks. We focus on network delays, external interference, impulsive behavior, and structural instability.

4.1. Communication Security

With the rapid development of wireless communication technology, intelligent vehicle communication is becoming more vulnerable to potential security attacks [105]. Due to the openness of wireless channels, the signal exposed in the open environment is likely to be stolen, interfered with, or even modified by the attacker [106]. If the attacker maliciously impersonates the vehicle to release false information and mislead other vehicles to form incorrect judgments, serious consequences may result. In 2018, the U.S. Department of transportation took the lead in proposing the security credential management system (SCMS), exploring the security process of V2X certificate management through a small-scale pilot. Vijayakumar et al. [107,108] proposed a dual group key management scheme, which distributes the group key to each vehicle and ensures the update of the group key when the vehicle joins or leaves the VANET. Combined with fingerprint authentication technology and hash codes, it improves the security of the vehicle terminal in the VANET environment and effectively prevents malicious vehicles from participating in communication. Ma et al. [109] proposed an energy-saving cooperative communication model for wireless sensor networks based on the genetic algorithm. In 2018, Kang et al. [110], drawing upon fog computing, constructed a privacy protection pseudonym scheme, which used the resources at the edge of the network for effective pseudonym management, in order to prevent the occurrence of overly centralized pseudonym management, resulting in large communication delays and high costs. Yang et al. designed a security architecture for the internet of vehicles based on digital signatures. Through in-depth study of the internal mechanism of the security framework, and the detailed design of the architecture, the whole life cycle's security mechanism is integrated into the design, and the identity authentication service in the whole life cycle of multiple scenarios is realized. Hubaux et al. [111] focused on the privacy protection and GPS positioning of vehicles, analyzed the main security problems in the internet of vehicles from different perspectives, and highlighted the relationship between the message accountability mechanism and the message anonymity mechanism.

Data privacy and scheme efficiency are the basic requirements for the application of the internet of vehicles system. In this section, various security and privacy threats are discussed from three aspects: the signature stage of the internet of vehicles, the data collection and transmission stage of the internet of vehicles users, and the data processing stage of the cloud platform. The characteristics and major security threats at the various stages of the internet of vehicles are shown in Table 3.

At present, the homomorphic aggregation scheme [112], elliptic curve encryption algorithm [113], and Chinese residual theorem [114] are often used to achieve data aggregation. The homomorphic encryption algorithm is the most commonly used technical method of data aggregation [115] because it satisfies the cipheric homomorphism operation properties. Homomorphic encryption (HE) refers to the specific calculation of the ciphertext after homomorphic encryption, and the ciphertext calculation results are equivalent to the same calculation [116] after the corresponding homomorphic data. Although the scheme in literature [117,118] can meet the basic privacy protection requirements and efficiency requirements in the internet of vehicles, it still has some deficiencies. The homomorphic encryption algorithm used in the scheme includes the elliptic curve-based encryption algorithm and the Paillier homomorphic encryption algorithm. The scheme based on the Paillier homomorphic encryption algorithm is not based on an elliptical curve.

Scheme [119] also adopts a homomorphic encryption algorithm and a data aggregation scheme based on heterogeneous fog layer nodes. The scheme uses resource-rich buses as dynamic fog nodes, and the roadside units are static fog nodes. At the same time, the scheme still does not support anti-collusion attack, and there is no reasonable and efficient method in the selection of dynamic fog nodes. In order to solve the above problems, Liu et al. [120] proposed the selection problem of dynamic fog nodes. The scheme adopted a heuristic algorithm to optimize the selection of core vehicles, and proposed a vehicle mobility measure based on relative average speed and a Convolutional Neural Networks (CNN)-based destination prediction method. Unfortunately, the programme also does not support anti-collusion attacks and has a high demand for resources. The current commonly used data aggregation schemes are limited by the computing performance of homomorphic encryption algorithms. Although the aggregation schemes basically meet the needs of data privacy protection, they still need to be optimized in terms of computational efficiency. At the same time, the related privacy and security issues caused by the highly centralized internet of vehicles also deserve the attention of researchers.

To protect the privacy of the internet of vehicles, there should be the following points: First, ensure that all the vehicles received by the nodes in the vehicle ad hoc network send and receive messages can be verified. The authentication is a method to determine whether the information received is true when the receiving vehicle successfully receives the information sent to it, as well as a method to determine whether the vehicle sending the message is a registered vehicle in the network. Second, ensure the integrity of the messages in the vehicle self-group network. Integrity refers to the message, from sending to receiving, not being tampered with by unauthorized vehicle nodes, add, delete, or packaging. However, a message integrity defect is not necessarily caused by an attacker, but also may be caused by the roadside units, relay vehicle node, routing, and other network line hardware or software equipment failure leading to timeout, packet loss, and other phenomena. Third, ensure that the communication of vehicles in the ad hoc network is confidential. Communication confidentiality means that only the parties sending and receiving the information can correctly interpret the information content, and other vehicle nodes or devices that relay the message cannot obtain the true content of the message. Fourth, ensure the traceability of messages in the vehicle ad hoc network. Traceability means that any message sent, received, relayed, or forwarded by the sender, relay, or receiver of the information will be recorded and retained. The vehicle cannot change or delete the sending, receiving, or relay records, nor can it deny the message sent, received, or relay by itself. Traceability plays an important role in investigating traffic crimes and confirming vehicle tracks. Fifth, it must be ensured that the spatiotemporal correlation of the vehicle's location is cut off for the attacker in the network. The spatial and temporal correlation of the location is cut off, which means that the attacker cannot know the name, position, and corresponding time of the vehicle at the same time. Once the attacker knows the three points, the location information of the owner or the vehicle can be judged according to the spatial and temporal correlation of the vehicle. There are two kinds of types of privacy protection for in-car ad hoc networks, namely the protection of information privacy and location privacy.

Table 3. Characteristics of each stage and major security threats [121].

Classification	Frequency Band	Data Security and Privacy Threats	Security Research Methods Addressed
The internet of vehicles signature phase	Calculation consumes large resources, dynamic changes of user attributes, diverse data types, etc.	Fake attack, witch attack, location attack, mission related attack	Homomorphism encryption, fuzzy generalization
Data collection and transmission stage of internet of vehicles users	Network topology changes frequently, data rights and user permissions are complex	Middle node attack, witch attack, position attack, background knowledge attack	Secure multi-party computing, homomorphic encryption
Cloud platform processing data stage	Easy to be vulnerable to malicious attacks, the security and benefit game between users, the vehicle parties to seek benefit maximization, highly centralized	Plot attack, time association attack	Game theory method, blockchain technology

With the development of 5G technology, information sharing among the complete internet of vehicles system is promoted. After the information is collected, it is processed and analyzed in a timely manner to recommend the best route for drivers to bypass congested roads. Boban et al. [122] analyzed the use cases and requirements of 5G-V2X, highlighted the gaps in existing communication technology, and provided guidance on how to overcome these gaps. Hameed et al. [123] used machine learning to enhance fog computing-related applications and services, effectively reduced the latency and energy consumption, improved the security, and provided more efficient resource management.

4.2. Control Strategy for Communication Delay

At present, the limited computing resources of vehicles are unable to meet the computing resource requirements of many delay-sensitive messages [124]. In order to cope with the expanding computing requirements of this vehicle terminal, the existing cloud computing technology can process a large amount of data information, which effectively reduces the local computing burden to a certain extent. However, when the security message is sent to the cloud server for processing through the core network, the processing delay of the message may be greatly affected. At the same time, the transmission of security messages often displays the phenomenon of redundant propagation, which causes a broadcast storm during message transmission and leads to the poor performance of message transmission. Generally, the transmission of emergency messages involves directional propagation, and the emergency messages are broadcast to the farthest receiving vehicles within the communication range [125].

The existence of communication delay will affect the following performance of the vehicle, and even threaten the driving safety. Therefore, it is necessary to design [126] for CACC control strategy for communication delay. On the one hand, the internal performance of the network can be studied from the perspective of communication, and the communication efficiency and quality can be improved by designing a reasonable network scheduling algorithm and communication protocol, so as to reduce its adverse impact on the control system. On the other hand, the optimization design of the control strategy under limited communication restriction gradually became a research hotspot, and a variety of solutions [127–130] were formed.

From the perspective of communication, Yin et al. designed a PID controller with a Smith estimation compensator to effectively control the [131] for the delay system. Xing et al. used the Smith estimator to effectively estimate the vehicle dynamics time delay and communication time delay, thus achieving the vehicle formation control [132] with a smaller following time distance. However, the delay estimation compensation control has some disadvantages, that is, it needs a more accurate prior cognition of the estimation system, and requires a high degree of accuracy and invariance.

Sun et al. [133] proposed a new multi-objective coverage optimization complex alliance strategy (CASMOC) algorithm, which can effectively improve the coverage of nodes. Wang et al. [134] proposed a dynamic clustering and cooperative scheduling algorithm based on SINR analysis of the signal-to-noise ratio in V2V communication for a two-way road data service. This algorithm can enable vehicles to dynamically join or leave a cluster according to the actual time and place. Yang et al. [135] proposed a system that can relax the communication attributes of the vehicle–road system by considering the time dependence. If the vehicle generates multiple signatures in the same time period, it indicates that the vehicle can be connected. Guo et al. [136] established delay constraints by introducing a delay index, and redistributed and controlled resources and power by using the method of distribution solution, so as to realize the high demand of the security mechanism of the vehicle network on the delay.

According to the relevant team of Intel [137], in the future, each intelligent vehicle will generate 4000 GB of data per day, which is equivalent to the amount of data consumed by around 3000 mobile users. Such prediction studies show that the future development of transportation systems will face severe challenges, and efficient sensor data processing needs reliable and efficient underlying technology to support the system. Therefore, in the face of this challenge, the vehicle edge information system (VEIS), which integrates vehicle communication technology and edge technology architecture, is proposed [138]. This vehicular edge information system is a new application that imposes strict requirements for communication and computing resources in the future intelligent transportation system by enhancing the communication, storage, and computing capabilities at the edge of the vehicular network and realizing the corresponding vehicular communication, edge cache, edge computing, and other technologies.

From the control point of view, due to the inevitable existence of wireless communication delay, the string stability of the cooperative adaptive cruise control queue system may not be guaranteed if the controller gain is not adjusted in time. Zhang Yuqin et al. [139] considered a dynamic gain regulation algorithm based on local traffic characteristics in collaborative adaptive cruise control considering wireless communication delay. The stability of CACC string is guaranteed by a dynamic C gain setting algorithm, which outperforms traditional methods and can significantly suppress interference along the upstream direction of the fleet. Vite Leopoldo et al. [140] proposed an adaptive cruise control based on dynamic predictors for input delay compensation, a filtered version of the standard finite spectrum allocation method, which overcomes the robustness problem, especially caused by the approximation of the distributed delay term, and finally, demonstrates the effectiveness of the study by performing simulations on five vehicles. Wang CJ et al. [141]

proposed ideas to dynamically optimize the IFT for CACC to optimize the string stability of the queue under environmental traffic conditions. When the CACC system is operating, the communication failure should be prepared at any time, because the CACC is too dependent on the communication quality, and is very sensitive to the communication failure. The safety impact of cooperative adaptive cruise control vehicle degradation under disruption of spatial continuous communication is described in paper [142] by Yu Weijie et al. Liu Yi et al. [143] proposed a safety-enhanced collaborative adaptive cruise control strategy for dynamic vehicle–vehicle communication failure, in which the safety-enhanced platoon control system is embedded with a dual-branch control strategy. When a fatal wireless communication failure is detected and confirmed, the SR-CACC system will automatically activate an alternative sensor-based adaptive cruise control strategy, which can significantly improve the safety performance of organized vehicle rows in extremely harsh communication environments. In order to reduce the impact of security vulnerabilities and network attacks possible when wireless communication networks work, Petrillo A et al. [144] handles and solves the network security tracking problem of a queue, embedding a distributed malicious information mitigation mechanism. Fiengo G et al. [145] investigated the leader tracking problem of connected autonomous vehicle queues in the presence of both uniform time variable parameter uncertainty and vehicle workshop time-varying communication delay.

Literature [146] proposes a strategy to mitigate communication delays between vehicle queues by using expected information from the lead and following vehicles. Literature [147] devised a strategy to mitigate communication latency in various traffic situations by providing flexible ad hoc links. Some researchers proposed a consensus strategy to alleviate the vehicle queue stability problem by designing more effective queue controllers or follower control strategies, such as the literature [148], as a dynamic network affected by time-varying heterogeneous communication delays. In addition, the distributed control protocol is derived based on graph theory. For example, literature [149] proposes a vehicle tracking control strategy based on considering the time-varying communication delay, and deduces and proves the sufficient conditions for local stability and serial stability in the frequency domain. Furthermore, the literature [150–152], to handle communication and parasitic delays, models the vehicle queue as multiple delay linear systems under various time-varying network topologies, investigating internal and serial stability, proposing an adaptive control method and a consensus method designed to mitigate the impact of communication delays.

Asadi and Muller [153] used an online machine learning algorithm to solve the problem of beam selection in vehicle millimeter-wave communication, which reduced the complexity of directional millimeter-wave communication and allowed a better application effect to be achieved in vehicle communication scenarios. Samarakoon and Bennis et al. [154] set up a distributed federated learning algorithm for the delay and reliability requirements of the edge side, especially in the vehicle dynamic scene, to ensure the stability of the queue by estimating the tail distribution of the length of the communication queue. Gyawali and Qian et al. [155] improved the reliability, safety, and stability of on-board communication by establishing an abnormal behavior detection mechanism based on machine learning. Hasselt et al. [156] evaluated the temporal and spatial patterns of traffic network flow using a multi-task learning architecture. Zhao et al. [157] combined a CNN with a deep Q-learning network (DQN) based on LSTM to identify surrounding vehicles by extracting features from input images to help vehicles identify the positions of adjacent vehicles and detect lane changes, and then to feed these features into the DQN based on LSTM, which can learn the optimal driving sequence of vehicles through input features after training. It can be seen that the application of artificial intelligence in vehicle edge information systems mainly focuses on distributed algorithms, online algorithms, and other intelligent learning algorithms, which require lower data training costs. At the same time, it also meets the requirements of data processing efficiency and response time in vehicle scenes. However, there are still many challenges in future research. Deep learning technology needs a large number of accurately labeled data for training, and the efficiency of processing largely depends on the training algorithm. On the other hand, due to the randomness of driver behavior and environmental impacts, the system may encounter many emergencies, which may lead to a system response delay. Therefore, the core deep learning method must ensure the robustness of the system through a large amount of learning so that the system can effectively deal with emergencies and be rapidly adjusted to account for them.

5. Test Method and Evaluation
5.1. Real Vehicle Road Test Platform

The real vehicle road test of an intelligent network includes three test scenarios: a closed scene test, a semi-open road test, and an open road test. Firstly, the representative closed test sites in foreign countries include the following: the Asta Zero test site in Sweden, which contains complete experimental facilities and has the capacity to test vehicle dynamics, driver behavior, and V2X technology; the Mria City Circuit test site in the UK, whose main features are simulated signal masking and various V2X communication facilities, with the flexible design of traffic lights and transmitting towers, and is oriented towards the testing of intelligent transportation systems and intelligent networked vehicles [158]; the Willow Run test site in Michigan, U.S., which is suitable for the extreme testing of V2X technology and autonomous driving technology, etc. [159]. The closed test sites also occupy a large proportion of the domestic real-world test sites. On July 30, 2021, the Ministry of Industry and Information Technology, the Ministry of Public Security, and the Ministry of Communications jointly issued the "Management Specification for Road Testing and Demonstration Application of Intelligent Connected Vehicles (Trial)" [160], adding the demonstration application of manned vehicles and special operating vehicles, and opening some expressway tests. At present, there are around 50 test sites in a state of completion or under construction, 30 of which are equipped with testing capability for intelligent networked vehicles. The intelligent driving test base of the Ministry of Transport in Beijing contains traffic scenes of various road shapes and surfaces, such as urban and rural roads, high-speed roads, and their ramps, and is equipped with street lights, traffic lights, weather simulation equipment, and other facilities, which can be used for intelligent driving, intelligent road networks, and other tests. Changsha, Wuhan, and other cities within intelligent network pilot demonstration areas can simulate a variety of road conditions, including wet roads, mountain roads, woodlands, high-speed roads, masonry, bridges, etc.; equipped with intelligent sensors and other monitoring equipment, they can be used for intelligent networked vehicle testing. Secondly, the domestic open test sites mainly include the following: the Shanxi (Yangquan) autonomous driving vehicle–road cooperation demonstration area, where roadside sensing, collection, and transmission systems are being built, and the deployment of the vehicle–road cooperation cloud control platform and autonomous driving vehicle supervision platform based on Baidu's public cloud was completed, so as to realize object detection technology based on environmental sensing and V2X communication technology to support L4-level autonomous driving vehicle over the horizon, etc. The Yongchuan Baidu Western Autonomous Driving Open Test Base is an open test and demonstration operation base for L4-level autonomous driving. The base deploys 5G communication in the road network environment in all aspects and includes more than 30 typical open road test scenarios in the mountain city, such as interchanges, tunnels, and bridges, with the unique traffic terrain of Chongqing, and it can accommodate 200 intelligent driving vehicles for testing at the same time. The efficient data transmission based on 5G technology and intelligent data processing based on artificial intelligence technology are of great significance for the application of intelligent connected vehicles. The Changsha test demonstration area has a wealth of intelligent connected vehicle test scenarios, and 5G widely covers the intelligent connected vehicle test area. It is the first [161] demonstration area to carry out high-speed tests and manned tests in China.

Domestic test areas are constructed in the following ways: 1. leading by application scenarios; 2. leading testing and demonstration application by standard formulation; 3. promoting the integrated development of intelligent connected vehicles and intelligent transportation with 5G commercialization; 4. policy exploration and demonstration operation promoting each other; and 4. national intelligent transportation comprehensive test base.

5.2. Virtual Test Platform

The simulation test experiments of intelligent network connected systems seek to establish a real static scene and carry out dynamic scene modeling according to the actual situation through computer simulation technology, so as to realize the model and algorithm of the network-connected vehicle. The system can carry out a variety of test verification experiments in the simulated traffic scene, reducing the dependence on real vehicle experiments to a certain extent, such as the current mainstream of intelligent driving vehicle sensor physical model simulation authenticity, intelligent transportation system V2X model construction, and the construction of dynamic traffic flow in the simulation scene. At present, a new generation of intelligent driving simulation systems integrating physical characteristic information is being gradually developed, which cannot only verify and iterate intelligent driving algorithms more effectively, but also meet the overall test requirements of intelligent driving simulation platforms for physical information systems more comprehensively. With the rapid development of advanced driver assistance systems (ADAS) and intelligent driving, the development of simulation software underwent the following stages: The early simulation test software mainly used dynamic simulation. The Simulink module of control design simulation software MATLAB was used to build the vehicle dynamics model and carry out real-time simulation, such as Carmaker [162], CarSim, Panosim [163], and other simulation software. With the further development of the ADAS function, simulation and test software to assist this function began to appear, such as Prescan [164]. In recent years, the ability of unreal engines to restore the virtual environment became stronger, and more researchers paid attention to the open-source simulators, such as AirSim [165], CARLA [166], and Unity. However, due to the diversity and functional complexity of the current mainstream intelligent driving simulation tools, most of them cannot support multi-agent co-simulation or simulation in large-scale scenarios, so the test verification of the off-vehicle networking system in large-scale complex traffic environments is not yet realized. At present, the optimization control of urban traffic in intelligent vehicle network systems is mainly concentrated within single-point traffic control, lacking real-time linkage control. However, the simulation of intelligent driving in large-scale open scenes shifted from macro-centralized control to meso-edge-side coordination control, and then to micro-single-car intelligent control. Therefore, it is necessary to develop simulation tools that can support this hierarchical control model. A microscopic traffic flow simulation model takes vehicles as the description unit, which can describe in detail the car-following and lane-changing behavior between vehicles. At present, the more common ones include SUMO [167] and PTV-Vissim [168], both of which have corresponding interfaces for secondary development. An intelligent driving simulation simulator based on SUMO and Unity3D [169] was proposed through the TraCI protocol. It can be seen that the use of intelligent driving simulation tools to provide single-vehicle intelligent decision making, traffic flow simulation models to provide specific traffic scene modeling and design, and the combination of the two through an interface, can support intelligent networked vehicle collaborative simulation in large-scale open scenes.

Elrofai et al. [170] believes that the scene is the dynamic interaction of various elements over a continuous period of time, and divides the scene into three main elements, namely, the tested vehicle, passive environment (such as road topology, traffic signs, etc.) and active environment (such as traffic lights, weather, etc.); De Gelder et al. [171] further defines the scene as a collection of internal movement, static environment, and actions related to the environment and autonomous vehicles. It can be seen that the above literature emphasizes that the test scenario is time-varying, and includes driving tasks, dynamic environment, and other elements of the environment. On this basis, this paper defines the test scenario as the dynamic description and abstraction of the behavior and operating environment of autonomous vehicles in certain times and airspace, with the characteristics of inexhaustible, extremely complex, infinite and rich, and difficult to predict [172]. The scale size of time and airspace needs to be formulated according to the specific test requirements. For example, the time domain of the lane change scene generally lasts from tens of seconds to several minutes; the space domain of the follow scene is a road network composed of several roads. Further decomposed from the elements, the scene generally includes the input flow of the road, weather, traffic rules and traffic popularity, as well as the output flow of the autonomous driving car to the environment.

In the construction of virtual scenes, the influence of the complexity of public transportation should be considered. Researchers will generally set up various traffic simulation scenarios, among which, rain and fog weather is an important environmental scenario in the traffic simulation scenarios. In the extreme environment test area of the project, there is an extreme environment warehouse and a signal-shielding warehouse, combined with augmented reality (AR) technology. The extreme environmental warehouse will simulate extreme weather conditions, such as "wind, rain, thunder and electricity", allowing vehicles to be tested under extreme weather conditions. When the intelligent car passes by from the warehouse, the warehouse can accurately adjust the rain and fog visibility that the vehicle can feel, observe the operation of the car when "being in it", so as to accelerate the research and development efficiency of intelligent vehicles, and provide effective support for improving the performance of intelligent vehicles. The signal-shielding warehouse will simulate the car communication environment after the tunnel, intelligent connected car into the tunnel, tunnel traffic internally and out of the tunnel, and the communication signal strength will present "strong-weak-no signal-weak-strong" change, thus the intelligent connected car in the case of weak signal control and operation status of the research and evaluation work.

In order to fully expose the design defects of autonomous vehicles, it is necessary to build a workflow, including a simulation test, closed site test, and open road test based on the scene, and solve the technical problems in scene definition, classification, data mining and analysis, scene generation, and other aspects. Table 4 shows the performance of virtual test, closed site test and real car road test under test specification.

Table 4. Virtual test, closed site test, real car road test comparison [173].

Test Specification	Virtual Test	Closed Site Test	Real Car Road Test
Test the truth	Depending on the authenticity of the model, the authenticity is relatively low in comparison.	More real, but not the real dynamic elements of other traffic participants.	Real, consistent with the actual driving environment of autonomous cars on the road.
Test cost	Low, the cost of the software systems is relatively low.	The construction cost of the test site is relatively high.	High, it requires too many people and over a long time to drive.
Testing efficiency	High, multi-core parallel testing can greatly improve the simulation speed.	High, can be targeted to strengthen the test for key scenarios.	Low, road mileage-based test methods require long driving times with multiple people and multiple cars.

Table 4. *Cont.*

Test Specification	Virtual Test	Closed Site Test	Real Car Road Test
Repeatability	Strong, you can build the same test scenario according to the defined data.	Strong, the scene elements can be reconstructed through the scene configuration requirements.	Poor, not a reproducible test on the public road.
Number of test scenarios	Many, any number of test scenarios can be generated given the logical scenario parameter space.	Less often, although as many scenarios can be built as possible according to scene element changes, the number of virtual test and open road test scenarios is still low.	Many, as many required test scenarios can be encountered long enough.
Test purpose	Embedded in each link of the system development, massive scene testing, to verify the boundaries of the autonomous driving function.	At the same time, the scene type that is not encountered or with low probability in reality can be built by configuring the field and the scene elements to verify the operation of the system under the boundary situations.	Clarify the statistical laws of related events, verify the system boundaries in practical situations, detect the interaction between autonomous vehicles and traditional vehicles, and find new scenarios that were not considered.

5.3. Test Method and Evaluation

The test and evaluation of intelligent connected vehicles is an important stage in the development of its vehicle functions. Similar to human drivers, the test method can be divided into three parts: the perception function test, the decision function test based on perception information, and the action function test. Vargas et al. [174] proposed a conceptual sensor testing framework for automatic driving vehicles, which is oriented towards different types of sensors and communication mechanisms, and provides a means of performing test scenarios similar to those occurring in the physical world. Wei et al. [175] implemented a parallel computing framework and system for intelligent driving tests and verification. It constructs a set of intelligent test models, which enables the system to develop a cognitive mechanism of automatic self-upgrading under the guidance of human experts, and further improves the ability of intelligent driving vehicles to adapt to complex environments. In order to speed up the scene testing, virtual environment simulation can be used. The mainstream virtual environment simulation software includes Prescan, Carmaker, dSpace, etc. At present, most of the tests only cover intelligent driving, and the test methods for intelligent driving vehicles in static, dynamic, and uncertain environments are not perfect. The vehicle decision-making ability test and V2X-based traffic integration test also need to be improved.

The evaluation mechanism design of intelligent driving vehicles is an important link in the research field. The evaluation of intelligent driving vehicles is affected by the interaction between the intelligent driving system, static traffic environment, and dynamic traffic environment, which is a more complex type of system engineering. At present, the main test and evaluation mechanisms are mostly for auxiliary intelligent driving. For example, the American Highway Safety Insurance Association issued the test procedures for automatic emergency braking systems in 2013, with the reduction in collision speed as the evaluation parameter. EU evaluation regulations for new cars cover most ADAS functions. In the process of continuously enriching the functional test scenarios, a rich and complete ADAS test and evaluation method system was gradually formed. In China, the 2021 evaluation regulations for new cars cover the ADAS test and evaluation system with automatic emergency braking, lane departure alarms, speed assist systems, and blind spot detection as the main content, and communication evaluation systems are rarely involved.

Domestic and foreign scholars and institutions carried out a lot of basic research work in simulation test methods, test scenarios, simulation modeling, tool chain reliability, and other aspects of [176–179]. For the different stages of the product, different types of simulation and simulation test methods are not only applied to the development process of intelligent and connected vehicles, but also gradually play an important role in the product verification, confirmation, and evaluation. The UN is in the automatic lane keeping system for L3 automated lane keeping systems (ALKS)-type approval regulations for test verification, and put forward the relevant requirements for the simulation tools and models [180,181]. Japan explicitly introduced the software in the rings in its software-in-the-loop (SIL) and hardware-in-the-loop (HIL) to test the [182]. The new test assessment method proposed by the United Nations Informal Working Group on Autonomous Driving Verification Methods requires the use of a proven simulation tool chain to conduct simulation tests to evaluate the safety of autonomous driving systems, and proposes SIL testing for driving safety and critical safety scenario assessment [183]. In the draft regulation on the type approval requirements of autonomous driving systems, the EU made it clear that simulation, closed sites, and practical law can be adopted, and roads introduced the United Nations study of [184] on the credibility of simulation tests. The vehicle dynamics simulation model and test methods developed by ISO provide the basic [185,186] for the vehicle dynamics simulation test and verification. The research of SCHONER et al. [187] proposed that SIL testing is an effective means to solve the verification of control algorithms, behavior, and rule compliance verification in complex and difficult scenarios. Domestic relevant institutions propose a set of intelligent connected vehicle safety tests and evaluation methods from the perspective of a third party, and clearly states that the simulation test is used to evaluate the function and performance verification of intelligent connected vehicles in diversified scenarios and complex conditions. Ahamed et al. [188] designed a framework for freely constructing vehicle models, and developed the SIL simulation platform in Gazebo using a robot operating system. Bachuwar et al. [189] proposed a software-in-loop simulation framework based on the open source autonomous driving software Autoware [190], which uses Simulink to communicate with the robot operating system (ROS). The above research shows that, with the maturity of technology and simulation tests for intelligent connected car safety test evaluation, among them, SIL test with its low cost, low risk, high advantages, high efficiency, and high coverage, become intelligent car safety, especially the lack of function and important means of algorithm defects. Hardware-in-loop simulation is a semi-physical test method where some components or systems of autonomous vehicles adopt real physical equipment, and the scene and charged objects are digital models. Hardware in loop simulation combines mathematical model and physical hardware equipment, and introduces the nonlinear physical characteristics, such as time delay, saturation, and friction, which significantly improves the confidence of the test results and overcomes the shortcomings of the model and data in MIL/SIL test to some extent.

At present, about 30 closed test sites for autonomous vehicles were built in China, basically covering typical traffic environments, such as rural areas and urban roads. Some of the closed sites also established a heterogeneous network of the internet of vehicles, [191]. However, the existing closed site has an inconsistent service level, high operating costs, mutual recognition, and other test results are very prominent. The main reason behind this is the lack of standard specifications. The specific performance, in two aspects, is as follows: The first is the lack of standard site construction. Construction levels are uneven, some site scenes have single scenes, are unable to support IoV testing, and fell behind the technological development level of self-driving cars. Secondly, the test passing standards are not uniform. For example, test preparation, vehicle technical status, scene setting, vehicle end, and roadside data collection and processing methods are inconsistent. This directly leads to the differences in the evaluation results among the closed sites. It restricts the development of test mutual recognition work.

Considering the complexity of the actual working conditions, the evaluation results of the simulation and the closed site may deviate from the real situation. Therefore, self-driving vehicles must be continuously tested on open roads before mass production. It is a necessary part for self-driving vehicles to accumulate test data, improve their technology, and ultimately commercialize it. However, there is still a lack of norms for testing autonomous driving vehicles on most open roads, especially highways.

Compared with simulation and site testing, the actual road test method is still in the preliminary exploration stage. The actual road test of autonomous driving can use the randomization characteristics of various targets and events on the actual road to verify the autonomous vehicles: (1) the safety impact of the vehicle and the surrounding traffic environment when running on the actual road; (2) whether the response to various typical goals and random dynamic events meets the expectations; and (3) the impact on the overall road traffic efficiency. Therefore, the actual road test is an indispensable link in the testing and evaluation process of autonomous vehicles. Since 2017, the major auto industry countries launched the exploration of the actual road testing of autonomous driving. In 2018–2019, 36 companies in California completed 5.635 million km of public road autonomous driving tests. Auto companies in Germany, Britain, Finland, Japan, and other countries also carried out a large number of practical road tests under the framework of their own autonomous driving-related laws and regulations. By October 2021, more than 3200 km of test roads were opened, more than 700 test licenses were issued, and the total length of road testing exceeded 5.3 million km. Shanghai and Beijing carried out demonstration applications of manned cargo loads. However, the current international actual, general road testing to improve the single model technology scheme for the purpose, due to the diversity of autonomous driving research and development technology, leads to strong research and development test scheme pertinence, test index, and research and development technology scheme correlation; such a test evaluation scheme does not have typical universality standardization characteristics.

6. Expectations

After decades of development, the vehicle collaborative driving system made great progress in all aspects. Facing the future intelligent vehicle collaboration technology under the network environment, it is suggested to carry out further work from the following three aspects:

(1) Multi-vehicle intelligence, instead of bicycle intelligence. became a current development trend, in addition to realizing comprehensive perception driving decision and control execution function, it is suggested to further enhance the intelligent road infrastructure, realize comprehensive intelligent cooperation between vehicles, namely vehicle–road collaborative perception, vehicle–road collaborative prediction decision and vehicle–road collaborative control system integration function, improve the commercial landing, thus forming the comprehensive development of car and road, and jointly promote the realization of automatic driving.

(2) Wireless communication delay inevitably exists in the internet of vehicles system. The collaborative system can consider the communication delay, the middle section, and other factors in the policy planning of the control system. The application of AI algorithms in vehicle communication became a new research hotspot. It is suggested that, to improve the quality of the data set, reduce the interference caused by emergencies, improve and optimize the control algorithm, and improve the ride comfort of the road.

(3) Scene-based test theories and methods became the mainstream technical route to deal with this challenge, but the research in this field is in its initial stage and is yet to receive enough attention from the academic community, which still needs to be further studied and explored. At present, the high-level automatic driving car test evaluation index,

evaluation model, and evaluation system of research is still in its infancy; in the future, there is a need to test scene classification, test task classification, improve the test system, and speed up the unified evaluation standards to further strengthen the comprehensive evaluation system of the integration of subjective and objective research.

7. Conclusions

This paper analyzes the collaborative control system of intelligent connected vehicles from three aspects of the collaborative control of intelligent vehicles, communication technology in vehicle networking environment, connected vehicle test platform, and evaluation system. At present, the future development of the collaborative control of intelligent connected vehicles has limitations, which are as follows: First, price restriction; the related hardware and software facilities, such as the internet of vehicles system and intelligent connected vehicles, are expensive, which poses great obstacles to the test of the intelligent networked collaborative control system. At present, most tests are still based on simulation. Second, laws and regulations limit it. At present, only a very small part of the intelligent connected vehicle testing sites are open in China, and the real vehicle testing sites and the testing process are greatly limited. Third, there is no uniform test standard. This paper puts forward the next urgent problems and the direction of in-depth exploration, and its related research can provide a reference for the intelligent vehicle–road collaboration technology.

Author Contributions: Conceptualization, B.W. and D.T.; methodology, B.W.; formal analysis, S.W.; investigation, M.L.; resources, B.W.; data curation, B.W. and L.W.; writing—original draft preparation, B.W. and M.C.; writing—review and editing, Y.H.; supervision, B.W.; project administration, Y.H.; funding acquisition, Y.H and B.W. All authors have read and agreed to the published version of the manuscript.

Funding: This research was funded by the National Key Research and Development Program of China under Grant 2021YFE0203600 and in part by the Fundamental Research Funds for the Central Universities-Research on the cultivation of Excellent Doctoral Dissertations in Chang'an University under Grant 300203211221.

Data Availability Statement: Not applicable.

Conflicts of Interest: The authors declare no conflict of interest.

References

1. Wang, W.; Xia, F.; Nie, H.; Chen, Z.; Gong, Z.; Kong, X.; Wei, W. Vehicle trajectory clustering based on dynamic representation learning of internet of vehicles. *IEEE Trans. Intell. Transp. Syst.* **2021**, *22*, 3567–3576. [CrossRef]
2. Wang, B.Y.; Han, Y.; Liu, F.; Hu, H.; Zhao, R.; Fang, H. Intelligent Distribution Framework and Algorithms for Connected Logistics Vehicles. *IEEE Access* **2020**, *8*, 204241–204255. [CrossRef]
3. Zhao, J.; Song, D.; Zhu, B.; Liu, B.; Chen, Z.; Zhang, P. Intelligent car following control strategy based on the hybrid drive of self-learning and supervised learning. *J. Highw. China* **2022**, *35*, 55–65.
4. Autonomous Driving Working Committee of China Highway Society. Development Trend and Suggestions of vehicle-road collaborative autonomous driving. *Intell. Connect. Car* **2019**, *4*, 50–60.
5. Daganzo, C.; Lehe, L. Traffic flow on signalized streets. *Transport. Res. B-Meth.* **2016**, *90*, 56–69. [CrossRef]
6. Evers, R.; Proost, S. Optimizing intersections. *Transport. Res. B-Meth.* **2015**, *71*, 100–119. [CrossRef]
7. Wong, S.; Sze, N.; Li, Y. Contributory factors to traffic crashes at signalized intersections in Hong Kong. *Accid. Anal. Prev.* **2007**, *39*, 1107–1113. [CrossRef] [PubMed]
8. Xu, Q.J.; Fu, R.; Wu, F.W.; Wang, B.Y. Roadside Estimation of a Vehicle's Center of Gravity Height Based on an Improved Single-Stage Detection Algorithm and Regression Prediction Technology. *IEEE Sens. J.* **2021**, *21*, 24520–24530. [CrossRef]
9. Samuel, W. D3.1. *Component Specification for the Overall Architecture*; European Commission: Brussels, Belgium, 2015.
10. Tan, H.; Huang, J. DGPS-based vehicle-to-vehicle cooperative collision warning: Engineering feasibility viewpoints. *IEEE Trans. Intell. Transp. Syst.* **2016**, *7*, 415–428. [CrossRef]
11. Yu, M. News: Japanese trucks are at 80 kilometers per hour. *Commer. Car News* **2013**, *10*, 20.
12. Shim, J.; Park, S.H.; Chung, S.; Jang, K. Enforcement avoidance behavior near automated speed enforcement areas in korean expressways. *Accid. Anal. Prev.* **2015**, *80*, 57–66. [CrossRef] [PubMed]
13. De, P.; Daniels, S.; Brijs, T.; Hermans, e.; Wets, E. Behavioural effects of fixed speed cameras on motorways: Overall improved speed compliance or kangaroo jumps? *Accid. Anal. Prev.* **2014**, *73*, 132–140.

14. Moher, D.; Liberati, A.; Tetzlaff, J.; Altman, D.G. Preferred Reporting Items for Systematic Reviews and Meta-analyses: The PRISMA Statement. *Ann. Intern. Med.* **2009**, *151*, 264–269. [CrossRef]
15. Liberati, A.; Altman, D.G.; Tetzlaff, J.; Mulrow, C.; Gøtzsche, P.C.; Ioannidis, J.P.A.; Clarke, M.; Devereaux, P.J.; Kleijnen, J.; Moher, D. The PRISMA Statement for Reporting Systematic Reviews and Meta-analyses of Studies that evaluation. *J. Clin. Epidemiol.* **2009**, *62*, e1–e34. [CrossRef]
16. Jiang, G.; Liu, H.; Zhou, Y.; Fu, C.Y. Research status and development trend of overspeed behavior interventions. *J. Highw. China* **2020**, *33*, 1–31.
17. Biswas, S.; Tatchikou, R.; Dion, F. Vehicle-to-vehicle wireless communication protocols for enhancing highway traffic safety. *IEEE Commun. Mag.* **2006**, *44*, 74–82. [CrossRef]
18. Rangesh, A.; Trivedl, M. No blind spots: Full-surround multi-object tracking for autonomous vehicles using cameras and lidars. *IEEE Trans. Intell. Veh.* **2019**, *4*, 588–599. [CrossRef]
19. Horowitz, R.; Varaiya, P. Control design of an automated highway system. *Proc. IEEE* **2000**, *88*, 913–925. [CrossRef]
20. Shladover, S. PATH at 20—History and major milestones. *IEEE Trans. Intell. Transp. Syst.* **2007**, *8*, 584–592. [CrossRef]
21. Tsugawa, S.; Jeschke, S.; Shladover, S. A Review of Truck Platooning Projects for Energy Savings. *IEEE Trans. Intell. Veh.* **2016**, *1*, 68–77. [CrossRef]
22. Hult, R.; Sancar, F.E.; Jalalmaab, M.; Vijayan, A.; Severinson, A.; Di Vaio, M.; Falcone, P.; Fidan, B.; Santini, S. Design and Experimental Validation of a Cooperative Driving Control Architecture for the Grand Cooperative Driving Challenge 2016. *IEEE Trans. Intell. Transp. Syst.* **2018**, *19*, 1290–1301. [CrossRef]
23. Ploeg, J.; Semsar-Kazerooni, E.; Medina, A.; de Jongh, J.F.C.M.; van de Sluis, J.; Voronov, A.; Englund, C.; Bril, R.J.; Salunkhe, H.; Arrue, A.; et al. Cooperative Automated Maneuvering at the 2016 Grand Cooperative Driving Challenge. *IEEE Trans. Intell. Transp. Syst.* **2018**, *19*, 1213–1226. [CrossRef]
24. Zheng, Y.; Li, S.; Wang, J.; Cao, D.P.; Li, K.Q. Stability and Scalability of Homogeneous Vehicular Platoon: Study on the Influence of Information Flow Topologies. *IEEE Trans. Intell. Transp. Syst.* **2016**, *17*, 14–26. [CrossRef]
25. Bian, Y.; Zheng, Y.; Ren, W.; Li, S.; Wang, J.Q.; Li, K.Q. Reducing time headway for platooning of connected vehicles via V2V communication. *Transport. Res. C-Emer.* **2019**, *102*, 87–105. [CrossRef]
26. Yanakiev, D.; Kanellakopoulos, I. Nonlinear spacing policies for automated heavy-duty vehicles. *IEEE Trans. Veh. Technol.* **1998**, *47*, 1365–1377. [CrossRef]
27. Browand, F.; Mcarthur, J.; Radovich, C. Fuel Saving Achieved in the Field of Two Tandems Trucks. In *California PATH Research Report UCB-ITS-PRR-2004-20*; eScholarship: Berkeley, CA, USA, 2004.
28. Memon, Z.A.; Unar, M.A.; Pathan, D.M. Parametric Study of Nonlinear Adaptive Cruise Control for a Road Vehicle Model by MPC. *Mehran Univ. Res. J. En.* **2016**, *31*, 301–314.
29. Pan, C.; Huang, A.; Chen, L. A review of the development trend of adaptive cruise control for ecological driving. *Proc. Inst. Mech. Eng. Part D J. Automob. Eng.* **2022**, *236*, 1931–1948. [CrossRef]
30. Calvert, S.C.; van Arem, B. Cooperative adaptive cruise control and intelligent traffic signal interaction: A field operational test with platooning on a suburban arterial in real traffic. *IET Intell. Transp. Syst.* **2020**, *14*, 1665–1672. [CrossRef]
31. Zhu, Y.H.; Zhao, D.B.; Zhong, C.G. Adaptive Optimal Control of Heterogeneous CACC System with Uncertain Dynamics. *IEEE Trans. Control. Syst. Technol.* **2019**, *27*, 1772–1779. [CrossRef]
32. Zhao, S.; Zhang, K. A distributionally robust stochastic optimization-based model predictive control with distributionally robust chance constraints for cooperative adaptive cruise control under uncertain traffic conditions. *Transp. Res. Part B* **2020**, *138*, 144–178. [CrossRef]
33. Yang, L.; Mao, J.; Liu, J. An Adaptive Cruise Control Method Based on Improved Variable Time Headway Strategy and Particle Swarm Optimization Algorithm. *IEEE Access* **2020**, *8*, 168333–168343. [CrossRef]
34. Chen, J.Z.; Zhou, Y.; Liang, H. Effects of ACC and CACC vehicles on traffic flow based on an improved variable time headway spacing strategy. *IET Intell. Transp. Syst.* **2019**, *13*, 1365–1373. [CrossRef]
35. Chen, J.Z.; Liang, H.; Lv, Z.K. Connected Automated Vehicle Platoon Control with Input Saturation and Variable Time Headway Strategy. *IEEE Trans. Intell. Transp. Syst.* **2021**, *22*, 4929–4940. [CrossRef]
36. Isaac, O.; Lagouge, K.; Modestus, O.; Alessandro, S. Comparative Traffic Flow Prediction of a Heuristic ANN Model and a Hybrid ANN-PSO Model in the Traffic Flow Modelling of Vehicles at a Four-Way Signalized Road Intersection. *Sustainability* **2021**, *13*, 10704.
37. Myungeun, E.; Byung-In, K. The traffic signal control problem for intersections: A review. *Eur. Transp. Res. Rev.* **2020**, *12*, 50.
38. Dresner, K.; Stone, P. A multiagent approach to autonomous intersection management. *J. Artif. Intell. Res.* **2018**, *31*, 591–656. [CrossRef]
39. Rosolia, U.; Bruyne, D.; Alleyne, A.G. Autonomous vehicle control: A nonconvex approach for obstacle avoidance. *IEEE Trans. Control. Syst. Technol.* **2016**, *25*, 469–484. [CrossRef]
40. Galceran, E.; Cunningham, A.G.; Eustice, R.M.; Olson, E. Multipolicy decision-making for autonomous driving via changepoint-based behavior prediction: Theory and experiment. *Auton. Robot.* **2017**, *41*, 1367–1382. [CrossRef]
41. Chen, L.; Englund, C. Cooperative intersection management: A survey. *IEEE Trans. Intell. Transp. Syst.* **2015**, *17*, 570–586. [CrossRef]

42. Levin, M.W.; Boyles, S.D.; Patel, R. Paradoxes of reservation-based intersection controls in traffic networks. *Transp. Res. Part A Policy Pract.* **2016**, *90*, 14–25. [CrossRef]
43. Jablonský, J. Benchmarks for current linear and mixed integer optimization solvers. *Acta Univ. Agric. Silvic. Mendel. Brun.* **2015**, *63*, 1923–1928. [CrossRef]
44. Zhou, Y.; Ahn, S.; Chitturi, M.; Noyce, D.A. Rolling horizon stochastic optimal control strategy for ACC and CACC under uncertainty. *Transp. Res. Part C Emerg. Technol.* **2017**, *83*, 61–76. [CrossRef]
45. Li, Z.; Pourmehrab, M.; Elefteriadou, L.; Ranka, S. Intersection control optimization for automated vehicles using genetic algorithm. *J. Transp. Eng. Part A Syst.* **2018**, *144*, 04018074. [CrossRef]
46. Wu, J.; Abbas-Turki, A.; Moudni, A.E. Cooperative driving: An ant colony system for autonomous intersection management. *Appl. Intell.* **2012**, *37*, 207–222. [CrossRef]
47. Guler, S.I.; Menendez, M.; Meier, L. Using connected vehicle technology to improve the efficiency of intersections. *Transp. Res. Part C Emerg. Technol.* **2014**, *46*, 121–131. [CrossRef]
48. Yang, H.; Jin, W.L. Instantaneous communication capacities of vehicular ad hoc networks. *Transp. Res. Part C Emerg. Technol.* **2016**, *72*, 325–341. [CrossRef]
49. Altché, F.; Fortelle, D.L. Analysis of optimal solutions to robot coordination problems to improve autonomous intersection management policies. In Proceedings of the 2016 IEEE Intelligent Vehicles Symposium (IV), Gothenburg, Sweden, 19–22 June 2016.
50. Meng, Y.; Li, L.; Wang, F.Y.; Li, K.Q.; Li, Z.H. Analysis of cooperative driving strategies for nonsignalized intersections. *IEEE Trans. Veh. Technol.* **2017**, *67*, 2900–2911. [CrossRef]
51. Levin, M.W.; Boyles, S.D. A multiclass cell transmission model for shared human and autonomous vehicle roads. *Transp. Res. Part C Emerg. Technol.* **2016**, *62*, 103–116. [CrossRef]
52. Tachet, R.; Santi, P.; Sobolevsky, S.; Reyes-Castro, L.I.; Frazzoli, E.; Helbing, D.; Ratti, C. Revisiting street intersections using slot-based systems. *PLoS ONE* **2016**, *11*, e0149607. [CrossRef]
53. Liu, C.; Lin, C.W.; Shiraishi, S.; Tomizuka, M. Distributed conflict resolution for connected autonomous vehicles. *IEEE Trans. Intell. Veh.* **2017**, *3*, 18–29. [CrossRef]
54. Mirheli, A.; Hajibabai, L.; Hajbabaie, A. Development of a signal-head-free intersection control logic in a fully connected and autonomous vehicle environment. *Transp. Res. Part C Emerg. Technol.* **2018**, *92*, 412–425. [CrossRef]
55. Rios-Torres, J.; Malikopoulos, A. Automated and cooperative vehicle merging at highway on ramps. *IEEE Trans. Intell. Transp. Syst.* **2016**, *18*, 780–789. [CrossRef]
56. Zhang, Y.J.; Malikopoulos, A.; Cassandras, C. Optimal control and coordination of connected and automated vehicles at urban traffic intersections. In Proceedings of the 2016 American Control Conference (ACC), Boston, MA, USA, 6–8 July 2016.
57. Malikopoulos, A.; Cassandras, C.; Zhang, Y.J. A decentralized energy-optimal control framework for connected automated vehicles at non-signalized crossing. *Automatica* **2018**, *93*, 244–256. [CrossRef]
58. Bichiou, Y.; Rakha, H.A. Real-time optimal intersection control system for automated/ cooperative vehicles. *Int. J. Transp. Sci. Technol.* **2019**, *8*, 1–12. [CrossRef]
59. Guo, Y.S.; Xu, Q.J.; Su, Y.Q.; Jiang, S.Y. Visibility detection based on the recognition of the preceding vehicle's taillight signals. *IEEE Access* **2020**, *8*, 206105–206117. [CrossRef]
60. Hausknecht, M.; Au, T.; Stone, P. Autonomous intersection management: Multi-intersection optimization. In Proceedings of the 2011 IEEE/RSJ International Conference on Intelligent Robots and Systems, San Francisco, CA, USA, 25–30 September 2011.
61. Huang, S.; Sadek, A.; Zhao, Y. Assessing the mobility and environmental benefits of reservation-based intelligent intersections using an integrated simulator. *IEEE Trans. Intell. Transp. Syst.* **2012**, *13*, 1201–1214. [CrossRef]
62. Chu, K.F.; Lam, A.; Li, V. Dynamic lane reversal routing and scheduling for connected autonomous vehicles. In Proceedings of the 2017 International Smart Cities Conference (ISC2), Wuxi, China, 14–17 September 2017.
63. Milanes, V.; Perez, J.; Onieva, E.; Gonzalez, C. Controller for urban intersections based on wireless communications and fuzzy logic. *IEEE Trans. Intell. Transp. Syst.* **2010**, *11*, 243–248. [CrossRef]
64. Liu, B.; Kamel, A.E. V2X-based decentralized cooperative adaptive cruise control in the vicinity of intersections. *IEEE Trans. Intell. Transp. Syst.* **2016**, *17*, 644–658. [CrossRef]
65. Ying, Z.B.; Ma, M.; Yi, L. Bavpm: Practical autonomous vehicle platoon management supported by blockchain technique. In Proceedings of the 2019 4th International Conference on Intelligent Transportation Engineering (ICITE), Singapore, 5–7 September 2019; pp. 256–260.
66. Cai, M.C.; Xu, Q.; Li, K.; Wang, J.Q. Multi-lane formation assignment and control for connected vehicles. In Proceedings of the 2019 IEEE Intelligent Vehicles Symposium (IV), Paris, France, 9–12 June 2019; pp. 1968–1973.
67. Gao, W.; Wu, C.; Zhong, L.; Yau, K.L.A. Communication Resources Management Based on Spectrum Sensing for Vehicle Platooning. *IEEE Trans. Intell. Transp. Syst.* **2022**. [CrossRef]
68. Won, M. L-Platooning: A protocol for managing a long platoon with DSRC. *IEEE Trans. Intell. Transp. Syst.* **2021**. [CrossRef]
69. Fida, N.A.; Ahmad, N.; Cao, Y.; Jan, M.A.; Ali, G. An improved multiple manoeuver management protocol for platoon mobility in vehicular ad hoc networks. *IET Intell. Transp. Syst.* **2021**, *15*, 886–901. [CrossRef]
70. Santini, S.; Salvi, A.; Valente, A.S.; Pescapè, A.; Segata, M.; Cigno, R.L. Platooning maneuvers in vehicular networks: A distributed and consensus-based approach. *IEEE Trans. Intell. Veh.* **2018**, *4*, 59–72. [CrossRef]

71. Liu, B.; Ding, Z.; Lv, C. Platoon control of connected autonomous vehicles: A distributed reinforcement learning method by consensus. *IFAC-Pap. OnLine* **2020**, *53*, 15241–15246. [CrossRef]
72. Li, L.H.; Gan, J.; Qu, X.; Mao, P.P.; Yi, Z.W.; Ran, B. A novel graph and safety potential field theory-based vehicle platoon formation and optimization method. *Appl. Sci.* **2021**, *11*, 958. [CrossRef]
73. Dai, S.L.; He, S.; Lin, H.; Wang, C. Platoon formation control with prescribed performance guarantees for USVs. *IEEE Trans. Ind. Electron.* **2017**, *65*, 4237–4246. [CrossRef]
74. Orujov, F.; Maskeliunas, R.; Damasevicius, R.; Wei, W.; Li, Y. Smartphone based intelligent indoor positioning using fuzzy logic. *Future Gener. Comput. Syst.* **2018**, *89*, 335–348. [CrossRef]
75. Liu, J.; Cai, B.; Wang, J. Cooperative Localization of Connected Vehicles: Integrating GNSS With DSRC Using a Robust Cubature Kalman Filter. *IEEE Trans. Intell. Transp. Syst.* **2017**, *18*, 111–2125. [CrossRef]
76. Zeng, Q.; Liu, J.; Hu, Q.; Yang, D. The Beidou system and GNSS multi-constellation combination navigation performance research. *Glob. Position.* **2011**, *36*, 53–57.
77. Odolinski, R.; Teunissen, P.J.G. Low-cost, high-precision, single-frequency GPS–BDS RTK positioning. *GPS Solut.* **2017**, *21*, 1315–1330. [CrossRef]
78. Yang, L.; Li, B.; Lou, L. Effect of different tropospheric models on the GPS localization results. *Surv. Mapp. Bull.* **2009**, *4*, 9–11.
79. Milford, M.J.; Wyeth, G.F. Single camera vision-only SLAM on a suburban road network. In Proceedings of the Robotics and Automation IEEE, Pasadena, CA, USA, 19–23 May 2008; pp. 3684–3689.
80. Mur-Artal, R.; Montiel, J.M.M.; Tardos, J.D. ORB-SLAM: A versatile and accurate monocular SLAM system. *IEEE Trans. Robot.* **2015**, *31*, 1147–1163. [CrossRef]
81. MPalzkill, T.; Ledermann, A. Verl. Anticipation-Preprocessing for Object Pose Detection. In Proceedings of the ISR 2010 and ROBOTIK 2010, Munich, Germany, 7–9 June 2010; pp. 1–6.
82. Brand, C.; Schuster, M.J.; Hirschmüller, H.; Suppa, M. Submap matching for stereo-vision based indoor/outdoor slam. In Proceedings of the IEEE/RSJ International Conference on Intelligent Robots and Systems (IROS), Hamburg, Germany, 28 September–2 October 2015; pp. 5670–5677.
83. Wang, L.; Zhang, Y.; Wang, J. Map-based localization method for autonomous vehicles using 3D-LIDAR. *IFAC-Pap.* **2017**, *50*, 276–281.
84. Javanmardi, E.; Gu, Y.; Javanmardi, M.; Kamijo, S. Autonomous vehicle self-localization based on abstract map and multi-channel Li DAR in urban area. *IATSS Res.* **2019**, *43*, 1–13. [CrossRef]
85. Magnusson, M.; Andreasson, H.; Nüchter, A.; Lilienthal, A.J. Automatic appearance-based loop detection from three-dimensional laser data using the normal distributions transform. *J. Field Robot.* **2009**, *26*, 892–914. [CrossRef]
86. Fontana, R.J. Recent system applications of short-pulse ultra-wideband (UWB) technology. *IEEE Trans. Microw. Theory Tech.* **2004**, *52*, 2087–2104. [CrossRef]
87. Parwari, N.; Joshua, N.A.; Kyperountas, S. Locating the Nodes-Cooperative localization in wireless sensor networks. *IEEE Signal Process. Mag.* **2005**, *22*, 54–59.
88. Oppermann, I.; Yu, K.; Montillet, J.P.; Rabbachin, A.; Cheong, P. UWB Location and Tracking for Wireless Embedded Networks. *Signal Process.* **2006**, *86*, 2153–2171.
89. Rohani, M.; Gingras, D.; Vigneron, V.; Gruyer, D. A new decentralized Bayesian approach for cooperative vehicle localization based on fusion of GPS and inter-vehicle distance measurements. In Proceedings of the 2013 International Conference on Connected Vehicles and Expo, Las Vegas, NV, USA, 2–6 December 2013.
90. Soatti, G.; Nicoli, M.; Garcia, N.; Denis, B.; Raulefs, R.; Wymeersch, H. Implicit cooperative positioning in vehicular networks. *IEEE Trans. Intell. Transp. Syst.* **2018**, *19*, 3964–3980. [CrossRef]
91. Ansari, K.; Feng, Y.; Tang, M. A runtime integrity monitoring framework for real-time relative positioning systems based on GPS and DSRC. *IEEE Trans. Intell. Transp. Syst.* **2015**, *16*, 980–992.
92. Xiong, J.; Cheong, J.W.; Xiong, Z.; Dempster, A.G.; Tian, S.; Wang, R. Integrity for multi-sensor cooperative positioning. *IEEE Trans. Intell. Transp. Syst.* **2021**, *22*, 792–807. [CrossRef]
93. Liu, J.; Tan, S.; Cai, B.; Wang, J. Based on Vehicle-Road information interaction. Transportation System Engineering and Information. 2022. Available online: https://kns.cnki.net/kcms/detail/11.4520.U.20220811.1444.008.html (accessed on 7 August 2022).
94. Yao, H.; Feng, F.; Chen, J. Practical Application of Vehicle-Road Cooperation Based on High Precision Map and Multi-sensor Fusion Positioning. *J. Geomat.* **2022**, *47*, 65–69.
95. Liu, S.Y.; He, D.Z.; Xu, Y.; Zhang, C.; Sun, S.B.; Ru, D.Y. Adaptive Vehicle Cooperative Positioning System with Uncertain GPS Visibility and Neural Network-based Improved Approach. In Proceedings of the IEEE/CIC International Conference on Communications in China (ICCC), Beijing, China, 16–18 August 2018.
96. Hu, L.; Ni, Q. IoT-Driven Automated Object Detection Algorithm for Urban Surveillance Systems in Smart Cities. *IEEE Internet Things* **2018**, *5*, 747–754. [CrossRef]
97. Xu, L.; He, J.; Wang, R.; Wang, X. Relative positioning coordinate estimation algorithm for Internet of vehicles independent of precise initial coordinates. *J. Comput. Sci.* **2017**, *40*, 1583–1599.
98. Han, Z.; Guo, K.; Xie, L.; Lin, Z.Y. Integrated Relative Localization & Leader-Follower Formation Control. *IEEE Trans. Autom. Control* **2019**, *64*, 20–34.

99. Jia, T.; Wang, H.; Shen, X.; Jiang, Z.; He, K. Target localization based on structured total least squares with hybrid TDOA-AOA measurements. *Signal Process.* **2018**, *143*, 211–221. [CrossRef]
100. Qu, X.; Xie, L.; Tan, W. Iterative Constrained Weighted Least Squares Source Localization Using TDOA and FDOA Measurements. *IEEE Trans. Signal Proces.* **2017**, *15*, 3990–4003. [CrossRef]
101. Jiang, X. *Research on Communication Performance Optimization and Control Method of Vehicle Belt C-V2X System*; Jiangsu University: Jiangsu, China, 2021.
102. Jelinek, J. Simulation and Analysis of Information Dissemination in Vehicular Ad-Hoc Networks. In Proceedings of the 10th International Conference on Advanced Computer Information Technologies (ACIT), Deggendorf, Germany, 16–18 September 2020.
103. Singh, J.; Singh, K. Advanced VANET Information Dissemination Scheme Using Fuzzy Logic. In Proceedings of the IEEE Annual Computing and Communication Workshop and Conference (CCWC), Las Vegas, NV, USA, 8–10 January 2018.
104. Zhao, H.T.; Zhang, M.K.; Gao, K.Q.; Mao, T.Q.; Zhu, H.B. A Multi-channel Cooperative Demand-Aware Media Access Control Scheme in Vehicular Ad-Hoc Network. *Wirel. Pers. Commun.* **2019**, *104*, 325–337. [CrossRef]
105. Wei, W.; Liu, S.; Li, W.; Du, D.Z. Fractal Intelligent Privacy Protection in Online Social Network Using Attribute-Based Encryption Schemes. *IEEE Trans. Comput. Soc. Syst.* **2018**, *6*, 189. [CrossRef]
106. Damaševičius, R.; Woźniak, M.; Alarcon-Aquino, V.; Ganchev, I.; Wei, W. Advances in security and privacy of multimodal interfaces. *J. Univers. Comput. Sci.* **2018**, *24*, 338–340.
107. Vijayakumar, P.; Azees, M.; Kannan, A.; Deborah, L.J. Dual authentication and key management techniques for secure data transmission in vehicular ad hoc networks. *IEEE Trans. Intell. Transp.* **2016**, *17*, 1015–1028. [CrossRef]
108. Vijayakumar, P.; Azees, M.; Chang, V.; Deborah, J.; Balusamy, B. Computationally efficient privacy preserving authentication and key distribution techniques for vehicular ad hoc networks. *Clust. Comput.* **2017**, *20*, 2439–2450. [CrossRef]
109. Ma, W.; Cao, Y.; Wei, W.; Hei, X.; Ma, J. Energy-efficient collaborative communication for optimization cluster heads selection based on genetic algorithms inwireless sensor networks. *Int. J. Distrib. Sens. N.* **2015**, *11*, 396121. [CrossRef]
110. Kang, J.; Yu, R.; Huang, X.; Zhang, Y. Privacy-preserved pseudonym scheme for fog computing supported Internet of Vehicles. *IEEE Trans. Intell. Transp.* **2018**, *19*, 2627–2637. [CrossRef]
111. Hubaux, J.P.; Capkun, S.; Luo, J. The security and privacy of smart vehicles. *IEEE Secur. Priv.* **2004**, *2*, 49–55. [CrossRef]
112. Sun, X.; Yu, F.; Zhang, P.; Xie, W.X.; Peng, X. A survey on secure computation based on homomorphic encryption in vehicular Ad Hoc networks. *Sensors* **2020**, *20*, 4253. [CrossRef]
113. Liu, Y.; Lang, X.; Pei, S. Encryption algorithm based on ECC and homomorphic encryption. *Comput. Eng. Des.* **2020**, *41*, 1243–1247.
114. Wei, X.; Lu, D. Forward secure aggregated signature scheme based on Chinese Remainder Theorem. *Comput. Technol. Dev.* **2021**, *31*, 137–141.
115. Abbasian Dehkordi, S.; Farajzadeh, K.; Rezazadeh, J.; Farahbakhsh, R.; Sandrasegaran, K.; Dehkordi, M.A. A survey on data aggregation techniques in IoT sensor networks. *Wirel. Netw.* **2020**, *26*, 1243–1263. [CrossRef]
116. Boudia, O.; Senouci, M. An efficient and secure multidimensional data aggregation for fog computing-based smart grid. *IEEE Internet Things J.* **2020**, *8*, 6143–6153. [CrossRef]
117. Chen, L.; Zhou, J.; Chen, Y.; Cao, Z.F.; Dong, X.; Choo, K.K.R. PADP: Efficient privacypreserving data aggregation and dynamic pricing for vehicle to grid networks. *IEEE Internet Things J.* **2020**, *8*, 7863–7873. [CrossRef]
118. Xie, Y.; Xu, F.; Li, D.; Nie, Y. Efficient message authentication scheme with conditional privacy-preserving and signature aggregation for vehicular cloud network. *Wirel. Commun. Mob. Comput.* **2018**, *2018*, 1875489. [CrossRef]
119. Lai, Y.; Zhang, L.; Yang, F.; Zheng, L.; Wang, T.; Li, K.C. CASQ: Adaptive and cloudassisted query processing in vehicular sensor networks. *Future Gener. Comput. Syst.* **2019**, *94*, 237–249. [CrossRef]
120. Liu, B.; Wang, Z.; Qin, J.; Jiang, Y.; Chen, X.H.; Wang, E.S.; Xiong, S.W. A novel framework for message dissemination with consideration of destination prediction in VFC. *Neural Comput. Appl.* **2021**, 1–11. [CrossRef]
121. Liu, H.; Zhang, L.; Li, J. Review of Privacy Protection Data Aggregation Research based on Internet of Vehicles. *Comput. Appl. Res.* **2022**, *39*, 1–12.
122. Boban, M.; Kousaridas, A.; Manolakis, K.; Eichinger, J. Connected roads of the future: Use cases, requirements, and design considerations for vehicle-to-everything communications. *IEEE Veh. Technol. Mag.* **2018**, *13*, 110–123. [CrossRef]
123. Abdulkareem, K.H.; Gunasekaran, S.; Al-Mhiqani, M.N.; Mutlag, A.A.; Mostafa, S.A.; Ali, N.S.; Ibrahim, D.A. A Review of Fog Computing and Machine Learning: Concepts, Applications, Challenges, and Open Issues. *IEEE Access* **2019**, *7*, 153123–153140. [CrossRef]
124. Otomo, M.; Sato, G.; Shibata, Y. In-vehicle Cloudlet Computing System for Disaster Information Based on Delay Tolerant Network Protocol. In Proceedings of the 31st IEEE International Conference on Advanced Information Networking and Applications (IEEE AINA), Taipei, Taiwan, 27–29 March 2017.
125. Zhao, H.; Zhu, Y.; Tang, J.; Han, Z.; Aujla, G.S. Message-Sensing Classified Processing and Transmission Scheme Based on Mobile Edge Computing in the Internet of Vehicles. *Softw. Pract. Exper.* **2020**, *51*, 2501–2518. [CrossRef]
126. Zeng, T.; Semiari, O.; Saad, W.; Bennis, M. Joint Communication and Control for Wireless Autonomous Vehicular Platoon Systems. *IEEE Trans. Commun.* **2019**, *67*, 7907–7922. [CrossRef]
127. Bahreini, M.; Zarei, J.; Razavi–Far, R.; Saif, M. Robust Finite-Time Stochastic Stabilization and Fault-Tolerant Control for Uncertain Networked Control Systems Considering Random Delays and Probabilistic Actuator Faults. *Trans. Inst. Meas. Control.* **2019**, *41*, 3550–3561. [CrossRef]

128. Tang, Y.; Peng, C.; Yin, S.; Qiu, J.B.; Gao, H.J.; Kaynak, O. Robust Model Predictive Control Under Saturations and Packet Dropouts With Application to Networked Flotation Processes. *IEEE Trans. Autom. Sci. Eng.* **2014**, *11*, 1056–1064. [CrossRef]
129. Zhang, L.; Xie, W.; Liu, J. Robust Control of Saturating Systems with Markovian Packet Dropouts under Distributed MPC. *ISA Trans.* **2019**, *85*, 49–59. [CrossRef]
130. Li, C.; Jing, H.; Wang, R.; Chen, N. Vehicle Lateral Motion Regulation under Unreliable Communication Links Based on Robust H∞ Output-Feedback Control Schema. *Mech. Syst. Signal Process.* **2018**, *104*, 171–187. [CrossRef]
131. Yin, C.; Gao, J.; Sun, Q. Enhanced PID Controllers Design Based on Modified Smith Predictor Control for Unstable Process with Time Delay. *Math. Probl. Eng.* **2014**, *2014*, 521460. [CrossRef]
132. Xing, H.; Ploeg, J.; Nijmeijer, H. Smith Predictor Compensating for Vehicle Actuator Delays in Cooperative ACC Systems. *IEEE Trans. Veh. Technol.* **2019**, *68*, 1106–1115. [CrossRef]
133. Sun, Z.; Zhang, Y.; Nie, Y.; Wei, W.; Lloret, J.; Song, H.B. CASMOC: A novel complex alliance strategy with multi-objective optimization of coverage in wireless sensor networks. *Wirel. Netw.* **2017**, *23*, 1201–1222. [CrossRef]
134. Wang, X.; Han, Y.; Wang, C.; Zhao, Q.; Chen, X.; Chen, M. In-Edge AI: Intelligentizing mobile edge computing, caching and communication by federated learning. *IEEE Netw.* **2019**, *33*, 156–165. [CrossRef]
135. Yang, H.; Liang, Y.; Yuan, J.; Yao, Q.; Zhang, J. Distributed blockchain-based trusted multi-domain collaboration for mobile edge computing in 5G and beyond. *IEEE Trans. Ind. Inform.* **2020**, *16*, 7094–7104. [CrossRef]
136. Guo, C.; Liang, L.; Li, G. Resource Allocation for Low-Latency Vehicular Communications: An Effective Capacity Perspective. *IEEE J. Sel. Area. Comm.* **2019**, *37*, 905–917. [CrossRef]
137. Oliveira, D.; Manera, L.T.; Luz, D. Development of a Smart Traffic Light Control System with Real-Time Monitoring. *IEEE Internet Things* **2021**, *8*, 3384–3393. [CrossRef]
138. Zhang, J.; Letaief, K.B. Mobile edge intelligence and computing for the internet of vehicles. *Proc. IEEE* **2019**, *108*, 246–261. [CrossRef]
139. Zhang, Y.; Tian, B.; Xu, Z. A local traffic characteristic based dynamic gains tuning algorithm for cooperative adaptive cruise control considering wireless communication delay. *Transp. Res. Part C* **2022**, *142*, 103766. [CrossRef]
140. Leopoldo, V.; Luis, J.; Marco, G.A. Dynamic predictor-based adaptive cruise control. *J. Frankl. Inst.* **2022**, *359*, 6123–6141.
141. Wang, C.J.; Gong, S.Y.; Peeta, S. Cooperative adaptive cruise control for connected autonomous vehicles by factoring communication-relatedconstraints. *Transp. Res. Part C-Emerg. Technol.* **2020**, *113*, 124–145. [CrossRef]
142. Yu, W.; Hua, X.; Zhao, D. Safety impact of cooperative adaptive cruise control vehicles' degradation under spatial continuous communication interruption. *IET Intell. Transp. Syst.* **2021**, *16*, 309–331. [CrossRef]
143. Liu, Y.; Wang, W. A Safety Reinforced Cooperative Adaptive Cruise Control Strategy Accounting for Dynamic Vehicle-to-Vehicle Communication Failure. *Sensors* **2021**, *21*, 6158. [CrossRef]
144. Petrillo, A.; Pescape, A.; Santini, S. A Secure Adaptive Control for Cooperative Driving of Autonomous Connected Vehicles in the Presence of Heterogeneous Communication Delays and Cyberattacks. *IEEE Trans. Cybern.* **2020**, *51*, 1134–1149. [CrossRef]
145. Fiengo, G.; Lui, D.G.; Tufo, M. Distributed Robust PID Control For Leader Tracking in Uncertain Connected Ground Vehicles With V2V Communication Delay. *IEEE-ASME Trans. Mechatron.* **2019**, *24*, 1153–1165. [CrossRef]
146. Fernandes, P.; Nunes, U. Platooning with IVC-Enabled autonomous vehicles:strategies to mitigate communication delays, improve safety and traffic flow. *Intell. Transp. Syst. IEEE Trans.* **2012**, *13*, 91–106. [CrossRef]
147. Ge, J.I.; Orosz, G. Dynamics of connected vehicle systems with delayed acceleration feedback. *Transp. Res.* **2014**, *46*, 46–64. [CrossRef]
148. Di Bernardo, M.; Salvi, A.; Santini, S. Distributed consensus strategy for platooning of vehicles in the presence of time- varying heterogeneous communication delays. *IEEE Trans. Intell. Transp. Syst.* **2015**, *16*, 102–112. [CrossRef]
149. Zhou, Y.; Ahn, S. Robust local and string stability for a decentralized car following control strategy for connected automated vehicles. *Transp. Res. Part B: Methodol.* **2019**, *125*, 175–196. [CrossRef]
150. Chehardoli, H.; Homaeinezhad, M.R. Third-order safe consensus of heterogeneous vehicular platoons with MPF network topology:Constant time headway strategy. *Proc. Inst. Mech. Eng. J. Automob. Eng.* **2018**, *232*, 1402–1413. [CrossRef]
151. Chehardoli, H.; Ghasemi, A. Adaptive centralized/ decentralized control and identification of 1- D heterogeneous vehicular platoons based on constant time headway policy. *Intell. Transp. Syst. IEEE Trans.* **2018**, *19*, 3376–3386. [CrossRef]
152. Hossein, C.; Ali, G. Formation control of longitudinal vehicular platoons under generic network topology with heterogeneous time delays. *J. Vib. Control.* **2018**, *25*, 655–665.
153. Asadi, A.; Müller, S.; Sim, G.; Klein, A.; Hollick, M. FML: Fast machine learning for 5G mmWave vehicular communications. In Proceedings of the IEEE International Conference on Computer Communications (INFOCOM), Honolulu, HI, USA, 16–19 April 2018.
154. Samarakoon, S.; Bennis, M.; Saad, W. Distributed federated learning for ultra-reliable low-latency vehicular communications. *IEEE Trans. Commun.* **2019**, *68*, 1146–1159. [CrossRef]
155. Gyawali, S.; Qian, Y. Misbehavior Detection using Machine Learning in Vehicular Communication Networks. In Proceedings of the IEEE International Conference on Communications (ICC), Shanghai, China, 20–24 May 2019.
156. Hasselt, H.; Guez, A.; Silver, D. Deep Reinforcement Learning with Double Q-learning. In Proceedings of the 30th Association-for-the-Advancement-of-Artificial-Intelligence (AAAI) Conference on Artificial Intelligence, Phoenix, AZ, USA, 12–17 February 2016.

157. Zhao, H.; Mao, T.; Duan, J.; Wang, Y.F.; Zhu, H.B. FMCNN: A Factorization Machine Combined Neural Network for Driving Safety Prediction in Vehicular Communication. *IEEE Access* **2019**, *7*, 11698–11706. [CrossRef]
158. Liu, T.Y.; Yu, Z.P.; Xiong, L.; Zhang, P. Development status and construction suggestions of intelligent Connected Vehicle Test ground. *Auto. Technol.* **2017**, *1*, 7–11.
159. Zhang, W.; Li, X.H.; Wu, X.Y.; Tang, F.M.; Guo, P.; He, J. Research status of autonomous driving simulation technology. *Auto Electric.* **2019**, *8*, 13–15.
160. Ministry of Industry and Information Technology; Ministry of Public Security; Ministry of Transport. Notice on the Issuance of the Management Code for Road Testing and Demonstration Application of Intelligent Connected Vehicles (Trial): The Ministry of Industry and Information Technology, No.97,2021. 21 July 2021. Available online: https://baike.baidu.com/item/Managementstandardforroadtestanddemonstrationapplicationofintelligentandconnectedvehicles/55766374?fr=aladdin (accessed on 1 January 2022).
161. Changsha Municipal Bureau of Industry and Information Technology. Notice on the issuance of the Implementation Rules of Road Test Management of Intelligent and Connected Vehicle in Changsha City (Trial) V3.0: Changgongxin Digital Issue No. 77,2020. 18 June 2020. Available online: https://baike.baidu.com/item/ImplementationRulesforRoadTestofIntelligentandConnectedVehiclesinChangshaCity(Trial)/23790739?fr=aladdin (accessed on 14 June 2022).
162. Varga, B.O.; Burnete, N.; Iclodean, C. Validation Procedure for Worldwide Harmonized Light Vehicles Test Cycle via Hardware in the Loop—Real Time Testing. In Proceedings of the 12th International Congress of Automotive and Transport Engineering (CONAT), Brasov, Romania, 26–29 October 2016.
163. Zhang, L.; Du, Z.; Zhao, S.; Zhai, Y.; Shen, Y. Development and Verification of Traffic Confrontation Simulation Test Platform Based on PanoSim. In Proceedings of the 4th IEEE Information Technology, Networking, Electronic and Automation Control Conference (ITNEC), Electr, Network, 12–14 June 2020.
164. Ortega, J.; Lengyel, H.; Szalay, Z. Overtaking maneuver scenario building for autonomous vehicles with PreScan software. *Transport. Engi.* **2020**, *2*, 100029. [CrossRef]
165. Ates, U. Long-Term Planning with Deep Reinforcement Learning on Autonomous Drones. In Proceedings of the 2020 Innovations in Intelligent Systems and Applications Conference (ASYU), Istanbul, Turkey, 15–17 October 2020.
166. Li, G.F.; Yang, Y.F.; Zhang, T.R.; Qu, X.D.; Cao, D.P.; Cheng, B.; Li, K.Q. Risk assessment based collision avoidance decision-making for autonomous vehicles in multi-scenarios. *Transport. Res. C-Emer.* **2021**, *122*, 102820. [CrossRef]
167. Akhter, S.; Ahsan, N.; Quaderi, S.; Sumit, S.; Rahman, M. A sumo based simulation framework for intelligent traffic management system. *Transport. Res. C-Emer.* **2020**, *8*, 1–5. [CrossRef]
168. Song, Z.; Wang, H.; Sun, J.; Tian, Y. Experimental findings with VISSIM and TransModeler for evaluating environmental and safety impacts using micro-simulations. *Transport. Res. Rec.* **2020**, *2674*, 566–580. [CrossRef]
169. Szalai, M.; Varga, B.; Tettamanti, T.; Tihanyi, V. Mixed reality test environment for autonomous cars using Unity 3D and SUMO. In Proceedings of the 18th IEEE World Symposium on Applied Machine Intelligence and Informatics (SAMI), Herlany, Slovakia, 23–25 January 2020.
170. Elrofai, H.; Paardekooper, J.; Gelder, E.; Kalisvaart, S.; Camp, O.; StreetWise: Scenario-Based Safety Validation of Connected and Automated Driving. *Neth. Organ. Appl. Sci. Res. TNO Tech. Rep.* 2018. Available online: https://repository.tno.nl/islandora/object/uuid:2b155e03-5c51-4c9f-8908-3fa4c34b3897 (accessed on 7 August 2022).
171. De Gelder, E.; Paardekooper, J.P.; Saberi, A.K.; Elrofai, H.; Camp, O.; Kraines, S.; Ploeg, J.; Schutter, B.D. Towards an Ontology for Scenario Definition for the Assessment of Automated Vehicles: An Object-Oriented Framework. *IEEE Trans. Intell. Veh.* **2022**, *7*, 300–314. [CrossRef]
172. China Automotive Technology and Research Center Co., Ltd. *Development and Application of Automated Driving Test Scenaro Technology*; Machine PressL: Beijing, China, 2020.
173. Xu, X.; Hu, W.; Dong, H.; Wang, Y.; Xiao, L.; Li, P. Summary of key technologies for the construction of autonomous vehicle test scenarios. *Automot. Eng.* **2021**, *43*, 610–619.
174. Vargas, J.; Alsweiss, S.; Jernigan, M.; Amin, A.; Brinkmann, M.; Santos, J.; Razdan, R. Development of Sensors Testbed for Autonomous Vehicles. In Proceedings of the IEEE SoutheastCon Conference, Huntsville, AL, USA, 11–14 April 2019.
175. Wei, B.; Xiao, L.; Wei, W.; Song, Y.; Yan, B.C.; Huo, Z.S. A high-bandwidth and low-cost data processing approach with heterogeneous storage architectures. *Pers. Ubiquit. Comput.* **2020**, 1–18. [CrossRef]
176. Zhu, B.; Zhang, P.; Zhao, J.; Chen, H.; Xu, Z.; Zhao, X.; Deng, W. Review of Scenario-Based Virtual Validation Methods for Automated Vehicles. *China J. Highw. Transp.* **2019**, *32*, 1–19.
177. Kirovskii, O. Determination of Validation Testing Scenarios for an ADAS Functionality: Case Study. *SAE Tech. Pap.* **2019**. [CrossRef]
178. Davision, A.J.; Reid, I.D.; Molton, N.D.; Stasse, O. MonoSLAM: Real-time Single Camera SLAM. *IEEE Trans. Pattern Anal. Mach. Intell.* **2007**, *29*, 1052–1067. [CrossRef] [PubMed]
179. Guo, J.; Deng, W.; Zhang, S.; Qi, S.Q.; Li, X. A Novel Method of Radar Modeling for Vehicle Intelligence. *SAE Tech. Pap.* **2017**, *10*, 50–57.
180. Economic Commission for Europe. *Uniform Provisions Concerning the Approval of Vehicles with Regard to Automated Lane Keeping Systems*; United Nations: New York, NY, USA; Economic Commission for Europe: Geneva, Switzerland, 2021.

181. Economic Commission for Europe. *Proposal for the 01 Series of Amendments to UN Regulation No. 157 (Automated Lane Keeping Systeme)*; United Nations: Geneva, Switzerland; Economic Commission for Europe: Geneva, Switzerland, 2022.
182. Ministry of Land and Communications. *TRIAS 48-R157-01 Automated Lane Keeping Systems Test (Agreement No.157)*; Ministry of Land and Communications: Tokyo, Japan, 2020.
183. Economic Commission for Europe. *New Assessment/Test Method for Automated Driving (NATMG) uidelines for Validating Automated Driving (ADS) Safety*; United Nations: Geneva, Switzerland; Economic Commission for Europe: Geneva, Switzerland, 2022.
184. European Commission. *Draft Commission Implementing Regulation: Laying Down Rules for the Application of Regulation (EU) 2019/2144 of the European Parliament and of the Council as Regards Uniform Procedures and Technical Specifications for the Type-Approval of Motor Vehicles with Regard to Their Automated Driving System (ADS) (G/TBT/N/EU/884)*; European Commission: Geneva, Switzerland, 2022.
185. ISO 11010-1: 2022. Passenger Cars—Simulation Model Classification—Part 1: Vehicle Dynamics. International Organization for Standardization: Geneva, Switzerland, 2021.
186. ISO 22140: 2021. Passenger Cars—Validation of Vehicle Dynamics Simulation—Lateral Transient Response Test Methods. International Organization for Standardization: Geneva, Switzerland, 2021.
187. Schöner, H.P. Simulation in Development and Testing of Autonomous Vehicles. In *18th Internationales Stuttgarter Symposium*; Springer: Wiesbaden, Germany, 2018.
188. Liu, F.; Xu, X.; Chen, Z.; Li, Y.; Li, J.; Pan, P.; Zhang, J.; Zhang, Z. Research on the safety testing and evaluation methods of intelligent connected vehicles equipped with autonomous driving function. *J. Automot. Eng.* **2022**, *12*, 221–227.
189. Ahamed MF, S.; Tewolde, G.; Kwon, J. Software-inthe-Loop Modeling and Simulation Framework for Autonomous Vehicles. In Proceedings of the 2018 IEEE International Conference on Electro/Information Technology (EIT), Rochester, MI, USA, 3–5 May 2018; pp. 305–310.
190. Bachuwar, S.; Bulsara, A.; Dossaji, H.; Gopinath, A.; Paredis, C.; Pilla, S.; Jia, Y. Integration of Autonomous Vehicle Frameworks for Software-in-the-Loop Testing. *SAE Tech. Pap.* **2020**, *2*, 2617–2622.
191. Kato, S.; Tokunaga, S.; Maruyama, Y.; Maeda, S.; Hirabayashi, M.; Kitsukawa, Y.; Monrroy, A.; Ando, T.; Fujii, Y.; Azumi, T. Autoware on Board: Enabling Autonomous Vehicles with Embedded Systems. In Proceedings of the 2018 ACM/IEEE 9th International Conference on Cyber-Physical Systems (ICCPS), Porto, Portugal, 11–13 April 2018; pp. 287–296.

Article

Optimization Methods for Redundancy Allocation in Hybrid Structure Large Binary Systems

Petru Cașcaval and Florin Leon *

Faculty of Automatic Control and Computer Engineering, "Gheorghe Asachi" Technical University of Iasi, Bd. Mangeron 27, 700050 Iasi, Romania
* Correspondence: florin.leon@academic.tuiasi.ro

Abstract: This paper addresses the issue of optimal redundancy allocation in hybrid structure large binary systems. Two aspects of optimization are considered: (1) maximizing the reliability of the system under the cost constraint, and (2) obtaining the necessary reliability at a minimum cost. The complex binary system considered in this work is composed of many subsystems with redundant structure. To cover most of the cases encountered in practice, the following kinds of redundancy are considered: active redundancy, passive redundancy, hybrid standby redundancy with a hot or warm reserve and possibly other cold ones, triple modular redundancy (TMR) structure with control facilities and cold spare components, static redundancy: triple modular redundancy or 5-modular redundancy (5MR), TMR/Simplex with cold standby redundancy, and TMR/Duplex with cold standby redundancy. A classic evolutionary algorithm highlights the complexity of this optimization problem. To master the complexity of this problem, two fundamentally different optimization methods are proposed: an improved evolutionary algorithm and a zero-one integer programming formulation. To speed up the search process, a lower bound is determined first. The paper highlights the difficulty of these optimization problems for large systems and, based on numerical results, shows the effectiveness of zero-one integer programming.

Keywords: redundancy allocation; hybrid structure binary systems; Markov chains; evolutionary algorithms; RELIVE algorithm; zero-one integer programming

MSC: 68M15; 68T20; 90C26

Citation: Cașcaval, P.; Leon, F. Optimization Methods for Redundancy Allocation in Hybrid Structure Large Binary Systems. *Mathematics* **2022**, *10*, 3698. https://doi.org/10.3390/math10193698

Academic Editor: Ioannis G. Tsoulos

Received: 7 September 2022
Accepted: 6 October 2022
Published: 9 October 2022

Publisher's Note: MDPI stays neutral with regard to jurisdictional claims in published maps and institutional affiliations.

Copyright: © 2022 by the authors. Licensee MDPI, Basel, Switzerland. This article is an open access article distributed under the terms and conditions of the Creative Commons Attribution (CC BY) license (https://creativecommons.org/licenses/by/4.0/).

1. Introduction

The problem of reliability optimization in large hybrid systems mainly refers to the type of the system (binary or multi-state), type of solution (reliability allocation and/or redundancy allocation), or the kind of redundancy, which can be static (TMR or 5MR, for example), dynamic (active redundancy or standby redundancy), or hybrid (TMR/Simplex or TMR/Duplex with spare components, etc.). Useful overviews covering models and methods for these reliability optimization problems (ROPs), including reliability allocation, redundancy allocation, and reliability-redundancy allocation can be found in many works, such as [1–3].

The mathematical formulation of a reliability optimization problem requires the specification of three elements: decision variables, imposed constraints, and objective function(s).

The decision variables describe those elements that can be changed or adjusted or the decisions that can be made to improve system performance, as expressed by the objective function(s). As examples of decision variables one can mention the types of components and their characteristics (reliability, cost, etc.), the type of redundancy for each subsystem, the number of spare components for each subsystem, etc.

The constraints reflect practical design limitations, e.g., a required level of reliability or the available budget, which occur in almost all cases. But in practice there may be other limitations, related to the volume or weight of the system, for example.

The objective function measures the performance of the system for a set of values of the decision variables. Thus, by optimizing the objective function(s) under the specified constraints it is possible to identify the combination of values of the decision variables that leads to the best possible design solution for the studied system.

Usually for ROPs, the goal of optimization is to maximize system reliability or minimize system cost. In reliability engineering the problem of system reliability maximization under two or more constraints often arises, e.g., under cost constraints, but also under weight and/or volume constraints. When an analytical approach is possible (e.g., in the case of active-redundancy-only subsystems), to ensure that two or more constraints are satisfied, Lagrangian multipliers are often introduced as part of the objective function [4–6].

In this paper we address a class of redundancy allocation problems (RAPs) where the decision variable is the number of redundant components for each subsystem in a series redundant reliability model. RAP is one of the most studied reliability optimization problems, because it has been proven to be quite difficult to solve, and many different optimization approaches have been used to determine optimal or near-optimal solutions. As [7] demonstrates, RAPs belong to the NP-hard class of optimization problems.

The RAPs we consider involves hybrid structures with no less than eight types of redundancy; these are conditions where the optimization problems are difficult to solve, even if we limit ourselves to single-constraint optimization problems. More specifically, our goal is to highlight the difficulty of these RAPs for large systems, when the number of subsystems grows to the order of tens or even hundreds.

In order to master the complexity of RAPs in case of large systems, for which the difficulty of the problem increases, special research efforts have been made in recent years. In addition, to cover a wide range of techniques used to increase the reliability encountered in practice, many hybrid reliability models have been considered for which the RAPs get even more complicated. For example, [8] investigates a complex reliability-redundancy allocation problem with a component mixing strategy, which changes the traditional RAP model to a heterogeneous one. Moreover, in the hybrid reliability models proposed in [9], the choice of redundancy strategy is considered as a decision variable. So, for each subsystem, an active or cold standby redundancy may be considered. In addition, components of different types can be used in each subsystem, i.e., a component mixing strategy. Consequently, this RAP involves determining a solution that maximizes system reliability in terms of the type of redundancy and the number of spare components of each type (for each subsystem). To solve this RAP, a genetic algorithm is developed. Also, a reliability model based on cold standby redundancy combined with component mixing is investigated by [10]. For this complex problem, the author proposes a simplified swarm optimization method in which a multi-role resource sharing strategy is adopted to provide the diverse system components. Another reliability model based on active or cold standby redundancy combined with component mixing is investigated in [11]. To solve this RAP, the authors propose a parallel stochastic fractal search algorithm. Other RAPs involving a heterogeneous structure and/or component allocation strategy of a different type can be found in [12–14].

Such a hybrid reliability model is also considered in this paper. In the previously cited works, RAPs are formulated by considering redundant systems with hybrid redundancy strategies and/or reliability models with heterogeneous components, which means that each component of a subsystem can have its own failure rate. In this paper we limit ourselves to the case where subsystems include homogeneous components, but we extend RAPs to cover more redundancy strategies (not just active redundancy or cold standby), including static redundancy or reconfigurable structures such as TMR/Simplex or TMR/Duplex with cold standby redundancy.

To solve redundancy allocation problems of this type, several techniques can be applied, such as heuristic methods [15–18], Lagrange multiplier analytical methods, and branch-and-bound techniques, especially for active redundancy [5,6,19,20], dynamic programming [21–23], evolutionary algorithms [9,10,24–27], linear programming methods [28–30] or a mix of integer and nonlinear programming [31]. As the RAPs we considered are complex, two evolutionary algorithms and a special model of zero-one integer programming are used.

As the highlights of our contribution we can mention:

- The formalization of two RAPs for binary systems with hybrid structure, which include no less than eight types of redundancy, where reliability modeling of redundant and reconfigurable structures is based on Markov chains;
- The design and implementation of two evolutionary algorithms and the formulation of a zero-one integer program for solving these complex optimization problems;
- Conducting an extensive performance evaluation study of the three proposed techniques on thousands of problems, which demonstrates the effectiveness of the zero-one integer programming approach for large systems with tens or even hundreds of subsystems.

This paper is organized as follows. Section 2 presents the issue addressed, whereas the types of redundancy considered here and the models or equations used for reliability evaluation are presented in detail in Section 3. Some related works are mentioned in Section 4. The algorithms used for these optimal allocation issues are described in Section 5. The objective functions adopted for the evolutionary algorithms and for the linear programming model are reported in Section 6, whereas in Section 7 a lower bound solution is proven. Experimental results are presented in Section 8. Further discussion is the subject of Section 9. The conclusions of the paper and several directions of future research are included in Section 10.

2. Problem Description

For systems with a large number of components without redundancy, reliability is often very low. To achieve the required reliability, a certain type of redundancy is applied to a certain element, depending on technical particularities, which can be static, dynamic, or hybrid redundancy. All of these types of redundancy are considered in this paper. The reliability model for this redundant system is a series-redundant one as presented in Figure 1.

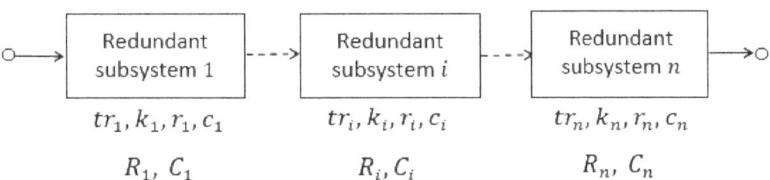

Figure 1. Series-redundant reliability model for a complex hybrid system.

The notations used to describe the redundant structures and their reliability evaluation models are presented at the end of the paper. Along with these notations we include a short nomenclature and some assumptions under which the reliability models are valid.

Typically, in this allocation process the criterion may be reliability, cost, weight, or volume. One or more criteria can be considered in an objective function, while the others may be considered constraints, as considered by [22] (pp. 331–338). In this paper, the criteria we consider are reliability and cost, and in this situation, two optimization problems are frequently encountered in practice:

1. Minimizing the cost of the redundant system for which a required reliability must be achieved;
2. Maximizing the reliability of the system within a maximum allowed cost.

In both cases, from the mathematical point of view, one must solve an optimization problem with an objective function and constrains. More exactly, for the first problem, one must minimize the cost function:

$$C_{rs} = f(C_1, C_2, \cdots, C_n) = \sum_{i=1}^{n} C_i \qquad (1)$$

with the constraint of reliability:

$$R_{rs} = \prod_{i=1}^{n} R_i \geq R^*. \qquad (2)$$

For the second problem, one must maximize the reliability function:

$$R_{rs} = f(R_1, R_2, \cdots, R_n) = \prod_{i=1}^{n} R_i \qquad (3)$$

with the cost constraint:

$$\sum_{i=1}^{n} C_i \leq C^*. \qquad (4)$$

For example, when for all the subsystems an active redundancy is considered, for the redundant system a series-parallel reliability model results. Thus, the cost and reliability functions can be expressed by the equations:

$$C_{rs} = \sum_{i=1}^{n} c_i k_i \qquad (5)$$

$$R_{rs} = 1 - \prod_{i=1}^{n} (1 - r_i)^{k_i} \qquad (6)$$

Thus, we have to determine the values $k_1, k_2, \ldots, k_n$ that minimize the cost function in Equation (5) with the reliability constraint in Equation (2), or maximize the reliability function in Equation (6) with the cost constraint in Equation (4), as the case may be.

3. Types of Redundancy

To cover most situations encountered in practice, the following types of redundancy are considered in this study, namely:

- active redundancy ($tr = A$);
- passive redundancy (or cold standby redundancy) ($tr = B$);
- hybrid standby redundancy with a hot reserve ($tr = C$) or a warm one ($tr = D$) and possibly other cold ones;
- hybrid redundancy consisting of a TMR structure with control facilities and possibly cold reserves ($tr = E$);
- static redundancy: TMR or 5MR ($tr = F$);
- reconfigurable TMR/Simplex type structure with possible other cold-maintained spare components ($tr = G$);
- reconfigurable TMR/Duplex type structure with possible other cold-maintained spare components ($tr = H$).

The reliability model and the equations used to evaluate the reliability for a subsystem, depending on the type of redundancy, are presented in this section. Since the time to failure for a component is assumed to have a negative exponential distribution, the following equations are valid:

$$r = e^{-\lambda T} \qquad (7)$$

and
$$\lambda T = -\ln r \tag{8}$$

Remember that for any redundant subsystem the spare components are considered identical to the basic ones.

3.1. Active Redundancy (tr = A)

For this parallel reliability model where all components operate simultaneously, the well-known equation is applied:
$$R = 1 - (1-r)^k, \ k = 2, 3, \ldots \tag{9}$$

3.2. Passive Redundancy (tr = B)

In this case, one component is in operation and all other identical $k-1$ spare components are maintained in a cold state, which means that a spare component is switched off until it is needed to replace the defective one (i.e., a redundant component does not fail in cold standby mode). The following equation can be applied to this model:
$$R = \sum_{j=0}^{k-1} \frac{(\lambda T)^j}{j!} e^{-\lambda T} = r \sum_{j=0}^{k-1} \frac{(-\ln r)^j}{j!}, \ k \geq 2 \tag{10}$$

Note that Equation (10) is the sum of the first k terms of the Poisson distribution of the parameter λT.

3.3. Hybrid Standby Redundancy with a Hot (tr = C) or a Warm (tr = D) Spare and Possibly Other Cold Ones

In this case of standby redundancy, a component is in operation, a spare component is active or kept in a warm state, and possibly other spare components are kept in cold conditions as illustrated in Figure 2.

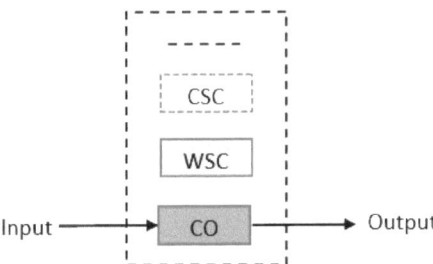

Figure 2. Standby redundancy with a hot/warm spare component and possibly other cold ones.

A warm component may fail before being put into operation and its failure rate is less than that of the same component in active mode. Therefore, let $\alpha\lambda$, $0 < \alpha \leq 1$, be the failure rate for this reserve. For this type of redundancy, the subsystem reliability function is obtained based on the Markov method, depending on the total number of components, as shown below.

3.3.1. Case 1: $k = 2$

Consider a subsystem consisting of a component in operation and a warm-maintained reserve. The evolution of this redundant subsystem until failure is illustrated by the Markov chain presented in Figure 3.

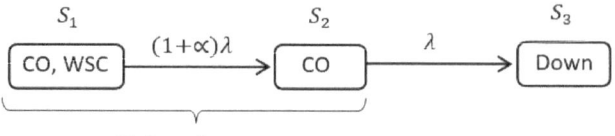

Figure 3. Markov chain for subsystem reliability evaluation ($k = 2$).

To begin with, let us refer to a general Markov model. Let $S_1, S_2, \ldots, S_N$ be the states of the Markov chain and $\mathbf{A} = [a_{x,y}]_{N \times N}$ be the matrix of state transition rates, where $a_{x,y}$, $x \neq y$, represents the rate of transition from state S_y to state S_x, while an element of the main diagonal (i.e., $x = y$) is the negative value of the sum of all the other elements in the column.

Let $s(t)$ be the state of the subsystem at the time t, and

$$p_x(t) = \text{prob}(s(t) = S_x), \quad x \in \{1, 2, \ldots, N\}. \tag{11}$$

To obtain the probability functions $p_x(t)$, $x = 1 : N$, the following system of differential equations must be solved:

$$\mathbf{P}' = \mathbf{A} \times \mathbf{P}, \tag{12}$$

where $\mathbf{P} = [p_1(t)\ p_2(t)\ \cdots\ p_N(t)]^T$, and $\mathbf{P}' = [p'_1(t)\ p'_2(t)\ \cdots\ p'_N(t)]^T$.

Note that the state probabilities for $t = 0$ are also known.

Let us resume the analysis of the subsystem under study. In the Markov chain presented in Figure 3, S_1 and S_2 are successful states, while S_3 is a failure state. Thus, the reliability function of this redundant subsystem can be defined as

$$R(t) = p_1(t) + p_2(t), \quad t \geq 0. \tag{13}$$

As the transition rate matrix is:

$$\mathbf{A} = \begin{bmatrix} -(1+\alpha)\lambda & 0 & 0 \\ (1+\alpha)\lambda & -\lambda & 0 \\ 0 & \lambda & 0 \end{bmatrix}, \tag{14}$$

to determine the probability functions $p_1(t)$ and $p_2(t)$, the following system of differential equations must be solved:

$$\begin{cases} p'_1(t) = -(1+\alpha)\lambda p_1(t) \\ p'_2(t) = (1+\alpha)\lambda p_1(t) - \lambda p_2(t) \end{cases} \tag{15}$$

With the initial values: $p_1(0) = 1$ and $p_2(0) = p_3(0) = 0$, by applying the Laplace transform ($\mathcal{L}$), the following system of algebraic equations results:

$$\begin{cases} sP_1(s) - 1 = -(1+\alpha)\lambda P_1(s) \\ sP_2(s) = (1+\alpha)\lambda P_1(s) - \lambda P_2(s) \end{cases} \tag{16}$$

where $P_i(s) = \mathcal{L}\{p_i(t)\}$, $i \in \{1, 2\}$, are functions in the frequency domain, and s is the Laplace operator. Based on (16), after some algebraic operations, the following functions are obtained:

$$P_1(s) = \frac{1}{s + (1+\alpha)\lambda}, \quad P_2(s) = \frac{(1+\alpha)\lambda}{s + (1+\alpha)\lambda} \cdot \frac{1}{s+\lambda} \tag{17}$$

After a partial-fraction-expansion, the function $P_2(s)$ can be expressed as follows:

$$P_2(s) = -\frac{1+\alpha}{\alpha}\frac{1}{s+(1+\alpha)\lambda} + \frac{1+\alpha}{\alpha}\frac{1}{s+\lambda} \tag{18}$$

As the function $\mathcal{R}(s) = \mathcal{L}\{R(t)\} = P_1(s) + P_2(s)$, the following expression results:

$$\mathcal{R}(s) = \frac{1+\alpha}{\alpha}\frac{1}{s+\lambda} - \frac{1}{\alpha}\frac{1}{s+(1+\alpha)\lambda} \tag{19}$$

The reliability function $R(t)$ can then be obtained by applying the inverse Laplace transform, $R(t) = \mathcal{L}^{-1}\{\mathcal{R}(s)\}$. Thus, the reliability function has the following form:

$$R(t) = \frac{1+\alpha}{\alpha}e^{-\lambda t} - \frac{1}{\alpha}e^{-(1+\alpha)\lambda t}, \quad t \geq 0, \quad 0 < \alpha \leq 1. \tag{20}$$

For a certain period of time T, the component reliability is $r = e^{-\lambda T}$, so that the subsystem reliability R as a function of r and α is given by the equation:

$$R(r, \alpha) = \frac{1+\alpha}{\alpha}r - \frac{1}{\alpha}r^{1+\alpha} = r + \frac{1}{\alpha}r(1-r^\alpha), \quad 0 < \alpha \leq 1. \tag{21}$$

For a redundancy subsystem with a larger number of components, the reliability function can be obtained based on the Markov method in the same way, but algebraic operations are more complicated. The results for the other two cases are presented below.

3.3.2. Case 2: $k = 3$

Take a redundant subsystem composed of an active component, a hot/warm spare component, and another one maintained in cold conditions. For this case, the following reliability function results:

$$R(r, \alpha) = \frac{(1+\alpha)^2}{\alpha^2}r - \left(\frac{1+2\alpha}{\alpha^2} - \frac{1+\alpha}{\alpha}\ln r\right)r^{1+\alpha}, \quad 0 < \alpha \leq 1. \tag{22}$$

3.3.3. Case 3: $k = 4$

For a redundant subsystem with an active component, a hot/warm spare component, and two other ones maintained in cold conditions, the reliability function is given by the following equation:

$$R(r, \alpha) = \frac{(1+\alpha)^3}{\alpha^3}r - \left(\frac{1+3\alpha+3\alpha^2}{\alpha^3} - \frac{1+3\alpha+2\alpha^2}{\alpha^2}\ln r + \frac{(1+\alpha)^2}{2\alpha}(\ln r)^2\right)r^{1+\alpha}, \quad 0 < \alpha \leq 1. \tag{23}$$

3.4. TMR Structure with Control Facilities and Cold Spare Components ($tr = E$)

In this case, another hybrid redundancy is considered. Thus, a redundant system is composed of a TMR structure with control facilities as a basic structure (i.e., static redundancy) and possibly one or more components maintained in cold conditions (i.e., standby redundancy). This type a hybrid redundancy is illustrated in Figure 4.

The decision logic works on the principle of majority logic, 2 out of 3, called voter and represented by the symbol V in Figure 4. When one of the three components in operation (CO_1, CO_2 or CO_3) fails, an error signal indicates the faulty component. Thus, the faulty component can be replaced with a cold-maintained standby one as soon as possible. In this way, this redundant hybrid subsystem can tolerate one or more defective components, as the case may be. For additional decision and control block the failure rate, denoted by λ_{dc}, is expressed based on the basic component rate, λ. In this study, the following expression is used:

$$\lambda_{dc} = \frac{\lambda}{\beta}, \quad \beta > 1. \tag{24}$$

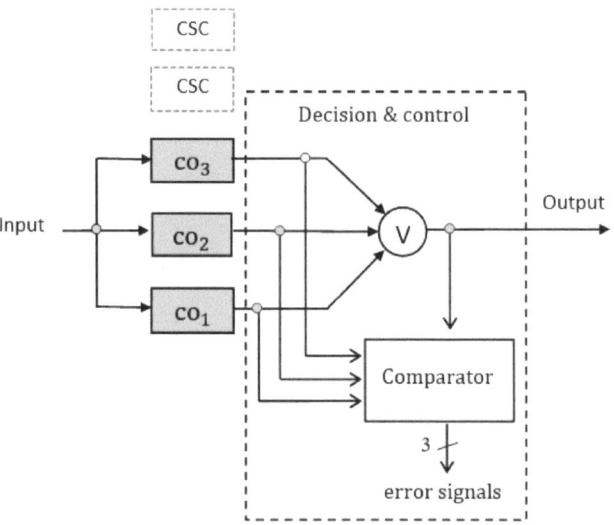

Figure 4. TMR structure with control facilities and cold spare components.

Consequently, the reliability function for logical decision and control block, denoted by r_{dc}, is expressed as:

$$r_{dc} = e^{-\lambda_{dc}T} = e^{-\frac{\lambda}{\beta}T} = \left(e^{-\lambda T}\right)^{\beta^{-1}} = r^{\beta^{-1}}, \quad \beta > 1. \tag{25}$$

3.4.1. Case 1: TMR Structure without Standby Redundancy

In case of a TMR structure without reserves (i.e., $k = 3$), the redundant subsystem can tolerate only one faulty component, so the subsystem reliability function is given by the well-known equation:

$$R(r, \beta) = (3r^2 - 2r^3)r_{dc} = (3r^2 - 2r^3)r^{\beta^{-1}}, \quad \beta > 1 \tag{26}$$

3.4.2. Case 2: TMR Structure and One Cold Spare Component

A redundant subsystem with hybrid redundancy composed of a TMR structure and one CSC (i.e., $k = 4$) may tolerate two faulty components. For a start, for the logical block of decision and control, the possibility of failure is neglected. The reliability evaluation is made based on the Markov graph given in Figure 5.

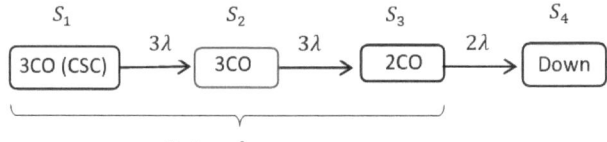

Figure 5. Markov chain for subsystem reliability evaluation ($k = 4$).

In this graph, S_1, S_2 and S_3 are successful states, while S_4 is a failure one. Given these aspects, the reliability function of this redundant subsystem is expressed as:

$$R(t) = p_1(t) + p_2(t) + p_3(t), \quad t \geq 0. \tag{27}$$

As the transition rate matrix is:

$$\mathbf{A} = \begin{bmatrix} -3\lambda & 0 & 0 & 0 \\ 3\lambda & -3\lambda & 0 & 0 \\ 0 & 3\lambda & -2\lambda & 0 \\ 0 & 0 & 2\lambda & 0 \end{bmatrix}, \qquad (28)$$

by applying Equation (12) in order to determine the probability functions $p_1(t)$, $p_2(t)$ and $p_3(t)$, the next system of differential equations results:

$$\begin{cases} p_1'(t) = -3\lambda p_1(t) \\ p_2'(t) = 3\lambda p_1(t) - 3\lambda p_2(t) \\ p_3'(t) = 3\lambda p_2(t) - 2\lambda p_3(t) \end{cases} \qquad (29)$$

With the initial values: $p_1(0) = 1$, and $p_2(0) = p_3(0) = 0$, by applying the Laplace transform, the following system of algebraic equations is obtained:

$$\begin{cases} sP_1(s) - 1 = -3\lambda P_1(s) \\ sP_2(s) = 3\lambda P_1(s) - 3\lambda P_2(s) \\ sP_3(s) = 3\lambda P_2(s) - 2\lambda P_3(s) \end{cases} \qquad (30)$$

By solving the system, the following functions in the frequency domain result:

$$\begin{cases} P_1(s) = \frac{1}{s+3\lambda} \\ P_2(s) = \frac{3\lambda}{(s+3\lambda)^2} \\ sP_3(s) = \frac{9\lambda^2}{(s+3\lambda)^2} \cdot \frac{1}{s+2\lambda} = \frac{9}{s+2\lambda} - \frac{9}{s+3\lambda} - \frac{9\lambda}{(s+3\lambda)^2}. \end{cases} \qquad (31)$$

As the function

$$\mathcal{R}(s) = \mathcal{L}\{R(t)\} = P_1(s) + P_2(s) + P_3(s), \qquad (32)$$

the following expression results:

$$\mathcal{R}(s) = \frac{9}{s+2\lambda} - \frac{8}{s+3\lambda} - \frac{6\lambda}{(s+3\lambda)^2} \qquad (33)$$

The reliability function $R(t)$, obtained by applying the inverse Laplace transform, is of the form:

$$R(t) = 9e^{-2\lambda t} - 8e^{-3\lambda t} - 6\lambda t e^{-3\lambda t}, \quad t \geq 0. \qquad (34)$$

Finally, taking also into account the reliability of the decision and control logic, the subsystem reliability R as a function of r and β is given by the equation:

$$R(r, \beta) = (9r^2 - r^3(8 - 6\ln r))r_{dc} = (9r^2 - r^3(8 - 6\ln r))r^{\beta^{-1}}, \quad \beta > 1 \qquad (35)$$

For a hybrid redundancy subsystem with a larger number of CSCs, the reliability function can be obtained by applying the Markov method in the same way, but algebraic operations are more complicated. A result obtained for another case is presented as follows.

3.4.3. Case 3: TMR Structure and Two Cold Spare Components

Take a redundant subsystem with hybrid redundancy composed of a TMR structure and two CSCs (i.e., $k = 5$). This redundant subsystem can tolerate three defective components. A Markov-based approach similar to the one presented above gives the following subsystem reliability as a function of r and β:

$$R(r, \beta) = \left(27r^2 - r^3(26 - 24\ln r + 9(\ln r)^2)\right)r^{\beta^{-1}}, \quad \beta > 1 \tag{36}$$

3.5. Static Redundancy: TMR or 5MR (tr = F)

This type of redundancy refers to those subsystems for which a static redundancy with majority logic (TMR or 5MR) can be adopted, depending on the desired level of reliability. Thus, in the process of finding an optimal solution, the valid values for variable k are 1, 3 and 5.

3.5.1. Case 1: TMR Structure

This case where $k = 3$ was also considered in Section 3.4, Case 1, so that the reliability function for this redundant subsystem is given by Equation (25).

3.5.2. Case 2: 5MR Structure

When a 5MR redundancy is adopted (i.e., $k = 5$), as [22] (pp. 165–176) appreciates, the additional logic of decision and control is more complex than that used for TMR redundancy. Consequently, the failure rate, denoted by λ'_{dc}, expressed on the basis of the failure rate of the basic components, is considered of the form:

$$\lambda'_{dc} = \frac{\lambda}{\gamma}, \quad \gamma > 1 \tag{37}$$

where the reduction factor γ is lower than the reduction factor β used for the TMR redundancy. Because the 5MR structure can tolerate two defective components, the reliability of the subsystem can be calculated as follows:

$$\begin{aligned} R(r, \gamma) &= (r^5 + 5r^4(1-r) + 10r^3(1-r)^2)\lambda'_{dc} \\ &= \left(10r^3 - 15r^4 + 6r^5\right)r^{\gamma^{-1}}, \quad \gamma > 1. \end{aligned} \tag{38}$$

3.6. TMR/Simplex and Cold Standby Redundancy (tr = G)

This is another case of hybrid redundancy in which the basic structure is reconfigurable. Specifically, the redundant subsystem consists of a TMR structure with control and reconfiguration facilities and other possible CSCs, as shown in Figure 6.

If one of the three components in operation fails, the subsystem continues to operate successfully based on redundancy, and the control logic generates an error signal indicating the faulty component. The status of the active component (good or failed) is reflected by three dedicated flip-flops. For example, Figure 6 illustrates the case where components CO_1 and CO_3 work successfully and component CO_2 is defective.

When an error signal is activated, the defective component must be replaced with a spare one as soon as possible to restore the initial fault tolerance state. Let us suppose this replacement is done quickly enough so reliability is not significantly affected. When only two components remain in good state, in order to increase the reliability, it is preferable for only one component to continue to work, not both. This reconfigurable structure is known as TMR/Simplex [32] (p. 233) or TMR 3-2-1 [22] (p. 152). Note that after a component has failed, the control logic can no longer correctly indicate another fault, so the values of the status flip-flops must be preserved until the fault tolerance is restored. This is the role of the 3-input NAND logic gate in Figure 6.

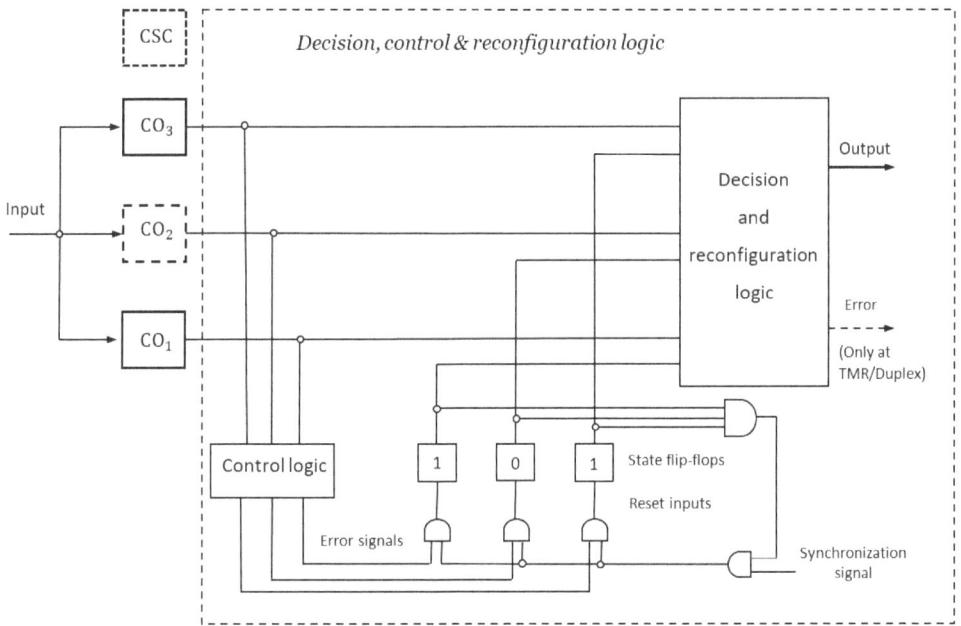

Figure 6. Reconfigurable TMR structure with cold redundancy.

For an additional decision, control and reconfiguration logic block, the faulty rate denoted by λ_{dcr} is expressed based on the basic component rate. In this study, the following equation is used:

$$\lambda_{dcr} = \frac{\lambda}{\delta}, \quad \delta > 1 \tag{39}$$

where the reduction factor δ is lower than the reduction factor β used for TMR redundancy. Consequently, the reliability function for the logic of decision, control and reconfiguration denoted by r_{dcr} is expressed as:

$$r_{dcr} = e^{-\lambda_{dcr}T} = e^{-\frac{\lambda}{\delta}T} = \left(e^{-\lambda T}\right)^{\delta^{-1}} = r^{\delta^{-1}}, \quad \delta > 1. \tag{40}$$

The reliability of the redundant subsystem depends on the number of CSCs, as shown below.

3.6.1. Case 1: TMR/Simplex without Standby Redundancy

In case of TMR/Simplex redundancy without spare components (i.e., $k = 3$), the subsystem reliability function is given by the well-known equation [32], (p. 233):

$$R(r,\delta) = (1.5r - 0.5r^3)r_{dcr} = (1.5r - 0.5r^3)r^{\delta^{-1}}, \quad \delta > 1. \tag{41}$$

3.6.2. Case 2: TMR/Simplex and One Cold Reserve

For this case of hybrid redundancy, the reliability evaluation is made by applying the Markov method. For starters, for the logical block of decision, control and configuration the possibility of failure is neglected. In this condition, the evolution of the redundant subsystem to failure is illustrated by the Markov chain shown in Figure 7.

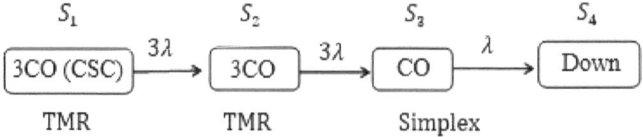

Figure 7. Markov chain for TMR/Simplex and one CSC ($k = 4$).

In this graph, S_1, S_2 and S_3 are states of success, while S_4 is a failure state. Consequently, the subsystem reliability is defined as:

$$R(t) = p_1(t) + p_2(t) + p_3(t), \quad t \geq 0. \tag{42}$$

Since the transition rate matrix is:

$$\mathbf{A} = \begin{bmatrix} -3\lambda & 0 & 0 & 0 \\ 3\lambda & -3\lambda & 0 & 0 \\ 0 & 3\lambda & -\lambda & 0 \\ 0 & 0 & \lambda & 0 \end{bmatrix}, \tag{43}$$

based on (12), the following system of differential equations results:

$$\begin{cases} p_1'(t) = -3\lambda p_1(t) \\ p_2'(t) = 3\lambda p_1(t) - 3\lambda p_2(t) \\ p_3'(t) = 3\lambda p_2(t) - \lambda p_3(t) \end{cases} \tag{44}$$

With the initial values: $p_1(0) = 1$, and $p_2(0) = p_3(0) = 0$, by applying the Laplace transform, the following system of algebraic equations is obtained:

$$\begin{cases} sP_1(s) - 1 = -3\lambda P_1(s) \\ sP_2(s) = 3\lambda P_1(s) - 3\lambda P_2(s) \\ sP_3(s) = 3\lambda P_2(s) - \lambda P_3(s) \end{cases} \tag{45}$$

By solving this equation system, the following functions in the field of Laplace transform are obtained:

$$\begin{cases} P_1(s) = \frac{1}{s+3\lambda} \\ P_2(s) = \frac{3\lambda}{(s+3\lambda)^2} \\ sP_3(s) = \frac{9\lambda^2}{(s+3\lambda)^2} \cdot \frac{1}{s+\lambda} = \frac{9}{4(s+\lambda)} - \frac{9}{4(s+3\lambda)} - \frac{9\lambda}{2(s+3\lambda)^2} \end{cases} \tag{46}$$

The reliability function in the field of Laplace transform is:

$$\mathcal{R}(s) = P_1(s) + P_2(s) + P_3(s) = \frac{9}{4(s+\lambda)} - \frac{5}{4(s+3\lambda)} - \frac{3\lambda}{2(s+3\lambda)^2} \tag{47}$$

The reliability function $R(t)$, obtained by applying the inverse Laplace transform, is of the form:

$$R(t) = \frac{9}{4}e^{-\lambda t} - \frac{5}{4}e^{-3\lambda t} - \frac{3}{2}\lambda t e^{-3\lambda t}, \quad t \geq 0. \tag{48}$$

Finally, taking also into account the reliability of the logical block of decision, control and configuration, the reliability of the subsystem R as a function of r and δ is given by the equation:

$$\begin{aligned} R(r, \delta) &= (2.25r - r^3(1.25 - 1.5 \ln r))r_{dcr} \\ &= (2.25r - r^3(1.25 - 1.5 \ln r))r^{\delta-1}, \quad \delta > 1 \end{aligned} \tag{49}$$

3.6.3. Case 3: TMR/Simplex and Two Cold Reserves

Take a reconfigurable subsystem with hybrid redundancy composed of a TMR/Simplex structure and two CSCs (i.e., $k = 5$). This redundant subsystem can tolerate three defective components. A Markov-based approach similar to the one presented above gives the following subsystem reliability as a function of r and δ:

$$R(r, \delta) = \left(\frac{27}{8}r - \frac{1}{8}\left(19 - 30\ln r + 18(\ln r)^2\right)r^3\right)r^{\delta-1}, \quad \delta > 1 \tag{50}$$

3.7. TMR/Duplex and Cold Standby Redundancy (tr = H)

As in the previous case, the redundant subsystem has a hybrid redundancy consisting of a reconfigurable TMR structure and possibly other CSCs, as shown in Figure 6. But this reconfigurable structure also aims at high operational safety. Thus, when one component of the TMR structure fails, the other two good components are put into operation in duplex mode. Specifically, the two components operate in parallel and their outputs are compared continuously. When the two components no longer generate the same response, an error signal is activated (as shown in Figure 6), so that the operation is stopped in safe mode. This reconfigurable structure is called by [32] TMR/Duplex.

Regarding the reliability assessment, note that this redundant subsystem can tolerate the same number of faulty components as the TMR structure presented in Section 3.4 for type E redundancy. Consequently, depending on the total number of components (k), Equations (26), (35) or (36) are valid in this case as well, with the only difference that the reduction factor β is replaced by δ.

4. Related Work

The problems of maximizing reliability with a cost constraint or minimizing cost with a reliability constraint can be solved using various methods. One is by solving an analytical model based on Lagrange multipliers with an alternative indicator for reliability [4]. The resulting system of algebraic equations can be solved but involve some approximate relations which may impact the accuracy of the solution. Also, this method gives real-valued results which must be converted into integers, and this may have a strong impact on solution quality. Therefore, heuristic methods can be appropriate. For example, one such technique described by [22] (p. 335) is a greedy approach that tries to make an optimal choice at each step: starting with the minimum system design, the system reliability is increased by adding one component to the subsystem with the lowest reliability. This process is repeated as long as the cost constraint is met.

Another method described by [33] (pp. 499–532) tries to accelerate the allocation process by noticing that the subsystem with the highest reliability should have the smallest number of components, and the least reliable subsystem should have the greatest number of components. Starting with the initial system, the reliability is increased by adding one component to each subsystem as long as the cost constraint is met. For the most reliable subsystem, this is the final allocation. The process continues with the other subsystems, until no allocation is possible any longer.

Pairwise Hill Climbing (PHC) [29] adapts the idea of classic hill climbing to the reliability-cost problem. Two candidate solutions are generated for each pair of subsystems. The first candidate is created by adding one component to the first subsystem, i.e., the direct hill climbing operation. The second is created by adding one component to the first subsystem and subtracting one from the second subsystem, i.e., a swapping operation. A hybrid approach starting from an approximate, but nearly-optimal solution given by the analytical approach, further improved by PHC was found to provide good results.

The problem can also be expressed as a quadratic unconstrained binary optimization (QUBO). This formulation has the potential of being solved by the D-Wave quantum computer as shown by [29] or [34].

The problem must be stated in the form of:

$$O(\mathbf{q};\mathbf{a},\mathbf{b}) = \sum_i a_i q_i + \sum_{(i,\ j)} b_{ij} q_i q_j. \tag{51}$$

The user needs to specify the parameters a_i (the weights associated with each qubit) and b_{ij} (the strengths of the couplers between qubits). The expression is minimized by quantum annealing when run on the quantum computer and the observed q_i values of either 0 or 1 represent the solution. A special procedure is required to transform the inequality constraint into additional terms to be optimized together with the main objective function in the same expression [29].

5. The Optimization Algorithms

The experimental studies presented in Section 9 are based on three approaches: a classical real-valued evolutionary algorithm, an improved evolutionary algorithm called RELIVE, that combines global search with local search, and a zero-one integer programming model, i.e., a special case of linear programming. While these techniques have been extensively used for various optimization problems, an original contribution of the current paper is the design of the objective functions corresponding to the problem under study, described in Section 6.

5.1. Classic Evolutionary Algorithm

Evolutionary algorithms (EAs) are inspired by biological natural selection [35,36]. They maintain a population of individuals (or chromosomes) which are potential solutions, i.e., different values of the **x** input of the objective function $f(\mathbf{x})$ that needs to be optimized. There are three main genetic operators which are repeatedly applied for a pre-specified number of generations or until a convergence criterion is satisfied: selection (which identifies "parents", such that individuals with better objective functions have a higher probability of being selected), crossover (which combines the genes of two parents and creates an offspring), and mutation (which may change some genes of a child before it is inserted into the new population). All these operators are stochastic, but the constant favoring of better individuals to reproduce drives the algorithm towards increasingly better solutions, while random changes in the chromosomes try to prevent it from convergence into local optima. For the experiments in Section 8, the standard evolutionary algorithm (SEA) uses the following types of operators and parameters:

- tournament selection with two individuals;
- elitism is used, i.e., the best individual is directly copied into the next generation;
- arithmetic crossover, where a child chromosome is a linear combination of the parent chromosomes, with a probability of 0.9;
- mutation by gene resetting, where the value of a randomly selected gene is set to a random number from a uniform distribution defined on its domain of definition, with a probability of 0.2;
- stopping criterion with a fixed number of generations; depending on the experiment 1000 or 10,000 generations are used.

5.2. RELIVE

The cross-generational evolutionary algorithm with local improvements (RELIVE) [4] is an original evolutionary algorithm which performs secondary local searches in addition to the main global search and includes the concept of personal improvement of individuals that survive for several generations, instead of just one. Since the lifespan of individuals is no longer fixed, the size of the population is variable. Personal improvement is based on a number of hill climbing steps in each generation. During a generation, the individuals undergo the classic evolution based on selection, crossover and mutation. Another typical feature of RELIVE is the way in which it encourages exploration. This has proved particularly useful for difficult optimization problems such as the one addressed in our work. First, a few newly created chromosomes are added in each generation. Secondly, to generate a neighbor state in the hill climbing stage, three types of mutation are used with different probabilities: Gaussian mutation, resetting mutation, and pairwise mutation, where two genes exchange a unit, i.e., one's value is incremented and the other's value is decremented. The latter type is again specifically designed for problems involving integer solutions, such as the present one. For the experiments in Section 8, RELIVE uses the following parameter values:

- the initial size of the population is 50;
- the fraction of newly generated chromosomes in a generation is 0.25;
- the life span of an individual is 4;
- the number of neighbors generated for hill climbing is 20;
- the number of hill climbing steps is 20;
- the probability of overall mutation is 0.2, divided into:
    - Gaussian mutation, with a probability of 0.05, where the value of a randomly selected gene is set to a normal random number with the mean equal to the original gene value and a standard deviation of 2;
    - resetting mutation, with a probability of 0.05, where the value of a randomly selected gene is set to a random number from a uniform distribution defined on its domain of definition is 0.25;
    - pairwise mutation, with a probability of 0.1, where two genes exchange a unit.

For the rest of the operators RELIVE uses, like SEA, tournament selection with two individuals, elitism, arithmetic crossover, with a probability 0.9, and a maximum number of 100 or 1000 generations.

5.3. Linear Programming

Linear programming (LP) is an optimization method aimed at problems with a linear objective function and linear constraints. There are several specific LP algorithms implemented in various libraries and programs. For our experiments, *lpsolve* [28] was used, which implements an optimized version of the simplex algorithm proposed by [37]. Depending on the nature of the optimization problem, it can select either the primal or the dual method, with factorization and scaling procedures to increase numerical stability. The problem we address in this paper is in fact cast as a zero-one integer programming (01IP) problem, a special case of LP.

6. Designing the Objective Functions

6.1. Evolutionary Algorithms

6.1.1. Problem Definition

For the two evolutionary algorithms, the objective (or fitness) function closely follows the definition of the two correlated problems stated in Section 3 and repeated here for convenience.

The maximization of the reliability with a maximum cost limit can be expressed as:

$$\begin{cases} \text{Maximize} : \prod_{i=1}^{n} R_i \\ \text{subject to} : \sum_{i=1}^{n} C_i \leq C^* \end{cases} \tag{52}$$

The minimization of the cost of the redundant system with a required reliability can be expressed as:

$$\begin{cases} \text{Minimize}: \sum_{i=1}^{n} C_i \\ \text{subject to}: \prod_{i=1}^{n} R_i \geq R^* \end{cases} \tag{53}$$

As C_i and R_i are computed by means of the equations detailed in Section 3, which depend on the number of components for each subsystem, the optimization problem reduces to finding $k_1, k_2, \ldots,$ and k_n.

For the two evolutionary algorithms, the fitness functions are the expressions in (52) and (53) that need to be optimized. Since an EA maximizes the fitness function by default, in case of (53), the negative of the sum of costs is actually used as the fitness function. The encoding of the problem uses real values, thus the chromosomes have n real genes, corresponding to k_i. The domain of the genes is $[1, k_{max}]$, i.e., $1 \leq k_i \leq k_{max}$. It depends on the problem and therefore k_{max} needs to be chosen by the user.

6.1.2. Genotype-Phenotype Mapping

The real values involved in the evolutionary search are interpreted as integer values for k_i before the computation of the fitness function. Therefore, the first step is to round the real values to the nearest integer:

$$k_i^p = \left\lfloor k_i^g + 0.5 \right\rfloor \tag{54}$$

where k_i^g reflects the genotype (the actual value of the gene), and k_i^p reflects the phenotype (its interpretation for further use).

Because in our case studies, for some types of redundancy we limited ourselves to a certain number of spare components as sufficient, another important issue is related to the unsuitability of some values of k_i for certain subsystems. Therefore, the adjustment rules in Table 1 are used to interpret the values of k_i as valid ones.

Table 1. Adjustment rules for phenotype interpretation.

Redundancy Type	Adjustment Rule
$tr = A$ or $tr = B$	No adjustment
$tr = C$	if $k_i^p > 5$ then $k_i^p \leftarrow 5$
$tr = D$	if $k_i^p > 4$ then $k_i^p \leftarrow 4$
$tr = E$	if $k_i^p < 3$ then $k_i^p \leftarrow 3$ if $k_i^p > 5$ then $k_i^p \leftarrow 5$
$tr = F$	if $k_i^p < 4$ then $k_i^p \leftarrow 3$ else $k_i^p \leftarrow 5$
$tr = G$	if $k_i^p < 3$ then $k_i^p \leftarrow 3$ if $k_i^p > 5$ then $k_i^p \leftarrow 5$
$tr = H$	if $k_i^p < 3$ then $k_i^p \leftarrow 3$ if $k_i^p > 5$ then $k_i^p \leftarrow 5$

It must be mentioned that trying to enforce a valid domain for each subsystem gene a priori would have caused discontinuities in the evolutionary search, would have decreased the genetic diversity, and thus would have led to inferior results.

6.1.3. Chromosom Repairing Procedure

Although expressed with a very simple equation, because of the possibly large size of a problem (e.g., $n = 50$ or $n = 100$, as considered in our case studies), the constraints are actually difficult to satisfy.

A naïve approach based on penalties for constraint violation decreases the genetic diversity to such an extent that the algorithms usually fail to find any solution at all, or find feasible solutions very far from the optimum.

Therefore, one can apply a repairing procedure for the chromosomes, such that even if a certain individual resulted from the application of the genetic operators is initially unfeasible, it can be slightly modified to become feasible. In this way, all the individuals in the population represent feasible solutions and the evolutionary algorithm focuses on optimizing the fitness function.

For the reliability maximization problem with cost constraints, a random repairing method is applied. Iteratively, a subsystem whose $k_i > 1$ is randomly selected and its k_i is decreased by 1, until the overall cost of the system becomes smaller than C^*.

Alternative methods were also attempted, but they were slower with no significant improvement of results:

- The selection of the subsystem with the highest cost. Because of the genotype-phenotype distinction, this could sometimes lead to infinite loops (e.g., the repairing procedure decrements a value, and the corresponding adjustment rule increments it);
- The selection of the subsystem with the highest reliability. This is even slower because it requires the recomputation of the system reliability after each k_i is decremented, with i from 1 to n.

The repairing procedure for the cost minimization with reliability constraints proved much more challenging. Eventually, a random repairing method was also applied in this case. Iteratively, a subsystem whose $k_i < k_{max}$ is randomly selected and its k_i is increased by 1, until the overall reliability of the system becomes greater than R^*. However, the way in which this increment affects the overall system reliability is nonlinear. Simple random selection may be very slow, because it may take several trials to choose the proper subsystem whose increased reliability may turn the overall reliability above the imposed threshold. That is why a specified number of repairing attempts trials is imposed (e.g., 10). If after these repeated trials the reliability does not exceed R^*, the individual is penalized with a very low value for its fitness function (e.g., -10^6) and thus becomes likely to be excluded from the evolutionary selection process.

Several other alternative methods were attempted as well, but they all had various drawbacks compared to the random method presented above:

- The selection of the subsystem with the lowest reliability. This method is slower and its results are not much better;
- A more elaborate method, where the number of components is increased on layers, with subsystems taken in a random order. When one layer of incrementation is completed, the next one begins. This method was the slowest, about an order of magnitude slower than random selection.

6.2. Linear Programming

The objective function is transformed in a different way in order to apply 01IP optimization. This is based on the idea proposed by [29]. The maximization of the product is equivalent to the maximization of the sum of logarithms. The desired solutions of the problem, i.e., k_i, $i = 1 : n$, are included as separate terms, one for each possible result, from 1 to k_{max}:

$$\text{Maximize}: \sum_{i=1}^{n} \sum_{j=1}^{k_{max}} x_{ij} \cdot \ln R_i(j) \tag{55}$$

where $x_{ij} \in \{0, 1\}$, $\forall i \in \{1, \ldots, n\}$, $\forall j \in \{1, \ldots, k_{max}\}$, is a binary variable that shows that for subsystem i, j components are needed to maximize reliability. The notation $R_i(j)$ signifies the reliability of subsystem i when it contains j redundant components.

For a subsystem i, only one solution is possible, i.e., its binary indicator must be 1, and the rest must be 0, and this can be written as an additional constraint:

$$\sum_{j=1}^{k_{max}} x_{ij} = 1, \forall i \in \{1, \ldots, n\} \tag{56}$$

The main constraint of the problem is also expressed by using a different term for each possible solution:

$$\sum_{i=1}^{n} \sum_{j=1}^{k_{max}} x_{ij} \cdot j \cdot c_i \leq C^* \tag{57}$$

For the cost minimization problem, the formulation becomes:

$$\begin{cases} \text{Maximize}: \\ \quad \sum_{i=1}^{n} \sum_{j=1}^{k_{max}} x_{ij} \cdot j \cdot c_i \\ \text{subject to}: \\ \quad \sum_{i=1}^{n} \sum_{j=1}^{k_{max}} x_{ij} \cdot \ln R_i(j) \geq R_* \\ \quad \sum_{j=1}^{k_{max}} x_{ij} = 1, \forall i \in \{1, \ldots, n\} \end{cases} \tag{58}$$

The genotype-phenotype mapping described above is also used here to compute the reliability of the subsystems by handling the k_i values that are not allowed for the corresponding subsystem type.

7. Lower Bound Solution

The minimum system design represents the first step toward achieving an optimized system design. Let us consider the optimization problem in which the required reliability R^* must be achieved at a minimum cost. To obtain a lower bound solution expressed by the values k'_i, $i = 1 : n$, as the first step for optimization, an improved version of Albert's method [22,38] is used. Albert's method assumes that as spare elements are added, the reliability of the subsystems tends to become more uniform. This method involves the following steps:

Step 1. The components are renumbered so that the reliabilities are in increasing order:

$$r_1 \leq r_2 \leq \cdots \leq r_n. \tag{59}$$

Step 2. Let m be the lower limit to which all subsystems certainly require an additional allocation. According to Albert's method, the limit m is adopted so that

$$r_m \leq R^* < r_{m+1}, \tag{60}$$

or $m = n$ in case of $r_n \leq R^*$.

As an improved version, we propose that the limit m be adopted as the highest value for which the following condition is met:

$$r_m r_{m+1} \cdots r_n < R^*. \tag{61}$$

Let R be the reliability level that the first m subsystems must reach. Based on the condition that:

$$R^m r_{m+1} r_{m+2} \cdots r_n \geq R^*, \tag{62}$$

for R the following condition results:

$$R \geq (R^*/(r_{m+1} r_{m+2} \cdots r_n))^{m-1}. \tag{63}$$

Step 3. With this intermediate result (reliability value R), for each subsystem i, $i = 1:m$, depending on the redundancy type, the lower bound k'_i is then determined. For example, for a subsystem i with active redundancy ($tr = A$), the following equations apply:

$$1 - (1 - r_i)^{k_i} \geq R = (1 - r_i)^{k_i} \leq 1 - R, \quad i = 1:m \tag{64}$$

After applying the logarithm we get:

$$k_i \ln(1 - r_i) \leq \ln(1 - R), \tag{65}$$

and then:

$$k_i \geq \frac{\ln(1-R)}{\ln(1-r_i)}, \quad i = 1:m \tag{66}$$

So, the lower bound as an integer value is:

$$k'_i = \left\lfloor \frac{\ln(1-R)}{\ln(1-r_i)} \right\rfloor + 1, \quad i = 1:m \tag{67}$$

where the equations are too complicated, the lower bound is determined iteratively, and not algebraically.

For other components with higher reliability, the lower bound corresponds to the non-redundant variant, so that:

$$k'_i = 1, \quad i = m+1:n \tag{68}$$

Based on this lower bound solution, the search for an optimal solution can decrease significantly.

8. Experimental Results

In order to evaluate the effectiveness of the proposed algorithms, a large number of optimization problems of the order of thousands were analyzed. For all these optimization problems, all eight types of redundancy presented in Section 3 are considered. For any of the n subsystems, the type of redundancy is randomly generated based on the predetermined weights, as shown in Table 2.

Table 2. Weights for types of redundancy considered in experimental studies.

Type of Redundancy	A, B, C, D	E, F, G, H
Weight	15%	10%

Component reliabilities and costs are also randomly generated. In terms of cost, the values are in the range of $[1, 50]$ units for all n subsystems. In terms of reliability, the value ranges depend on the type of redundancy, as shown in Table 3.

Table 3. Value ranges for component reliability by type of redundancy.

Type of Redundancy	A, B, C, D	E, F, G, H
Weight	[0.9, 1)	[0.95, 1)

Regarding the coefficient α and the reduction factors β and δ, the values are randomly generated in the ranges:

$$0 < \alpha < 1, \quad 50 \leq \beta \leq 100, \quad 40 \leq \delta \leq 80 \tag{69}$$

In the case of type F redundancy subsystems, the value of the reduction factor γ is taken as half of the value for β ($\gamma = \beta/2$).

For the optimization problems we address, two levels of complexity were taken into account, when $n = 50$ and $n = 100$. For each case, extensive experimental studies were performed, including thousands of optimization problems.

For each reliability model, the proposed algorithms were tested taking into account both optimization problems. Specifically, for any reliability model, the study on the optimal allocation of redundancy was conducted in this way. First, the issue of redundancy allocation is considered to maximize system reliability at a maximum allowable cost $C^* = 3 \times C_{ns}$. Let R_{max} be the maximum system reliability obtained in this way. Then, another redundancy allocation problem is solved to obtain the required reliability $R^* = R_{max}$ at a minimum cost. In this way, either the solution from the first optimization problem is validated, or an improved solution is obtained.

This is the final allocation that we consider, reflected by the vector **k** and for which the reliability and cost are R_{rs} and C_{rs}, respectively. For any allocation solution, the redundancy efficiency is then calculated as follows:

$$Ef = \frac{1 - R_{sn}}{1 - R_{rs}}. \tag{70}$$

Efficiency is a more intuitive indicator that shows how often the risk of a failure for the redundant system decreases compared to the basic, non-redundant one.

To illustrate this approach, the numerical results of four experimental studies (problems $P_1 - P_4$) are presented below. First, two reliability models for a system with 50 subsystems are considered (problems P_1 and P_2). All the details of these models are presented in Tables 4 and 5.

Each problem is defined by a set of n tuples corresponding to the parameters of its subsystems. In Table 4, we define a problem with 50 subsystems, therefore we have 50 tuples. The first number in the tuple, i, goes from 1 to 50. The second item of a tuple is the subsystem type. It is identified by a letter following the convention defined in Section 3. For example, the first tuple (1: D, 0.989, 39; α = 0.55) has tr_1 = D, which corresponds to hybrid standby redundancy with a warm reserve and possibly other cold ones. The following two numbers identify the reliability and the cost of a single component. Again, for the first tuple, the reliability is $r_1 = 0.989$ and the cost is $c_1 = 39$.

Table 4. Problem P_1 for $n = 50$ subsystems.

Structural Details: Tuples of (i: tr_i, r_i, c_i) Extended with Parameters α_i, β_i, or as Appropriate, $i = 1:n$.
(1: D, 0.989, 39; α = 0.55), (2: C, 0.958, 25), (3: C, 0.905, 41), (4: E, 0.952, 46; β = 50), (5: C, 0.975, 44), (6: A, 0.984, 14), (7: D, 0.939, 43; α = 0.86), (8: A, 0.944, 13), (9: G, 0.987, 48; δ = 74), (10: A, 0.914, 9), (11: H, 0.955, 32; δ = 65), (12: A, 0.986, 41), (13: D, 0.957, 16; α = 0.84), (14: D, 0.920, 1; α = 0.31), (15: C, 0.913, 27), (16: A, 0.985, 8), (17: A, 0.902, 9), (18: F, 0.956, 26; β = 80, γ = 40), (19: B, 0.910, 32), (20: F, 0.986, 42; β = 95, γ = 48), (21: F, 0.968, 47; β = 80, γ = 40), (22: D, 0.965, 47; α = 0.24), (23: H, 0.981, 31; δ = 72), (24: H, 0.982, 31; δ = 53), (25: F, 0.953, 45; β = 77, γ = 39), (26: B, 0.959, 18), (27: H, 0.962, 13; δ = 49), (28: E, 0.974, 46; β = 98), (29: C, 0.915, 26), (30: D, 0.983, 18; α = 0.74), (31: H, 0.975, 8; δ = 47), (32: A, 0.988, 12), (33: A, 0.971, 21), (34: C, 0.909, 17), (35: C, 0.953, 7), (36: C, 0.926, 7), (37: D, 0.989, 8; α = 0.74), (38: C, 0.906, 43), (39: H, 0.971, 11; δ = 66), (40: C, 0.944, 16), (41: E, 0.989, 21; β = 79), (42: A, 0.907, 36), (43: B, 0.942, 5), (44: C, 0.975, 18), (45: F, 0.961, 42; β = 95, γ = 48), (46: G, 0.979, 8; δ = 60), (47: E, 0.970, 38; β = 82), (48: H, 0.952, 23; δ = 48), (49: G, 0.958, 15; δ = 68), (50: C, 0.975, 7)
$C_{ns} = 1241$, $C^* = 3 \times C_{ns} = 3723$

Table 5. Problem P_2 for $n = 50$ subsystems.

Structural Details: Tuples of $(i: tr_i, r_i, c_i)$ Extended with Parameters α_i, β_i, or as Appropriate, $i = 1{:}n$.
(1: D, 0.925, 39; α = 0.42), (2: B, 0.985, 31), (3: E, 0.968, 29; β = 67), (4: A, 0.969, 35), (5: B, 0.904, 36), (6: A, 0.909, 18), (7: F, 0.973, 6; β = 92, γ = 46), (8: C, 0.976, 10), (9: C, 0.947, 19), (10: C, 0.940, 33), (11: A, 0.931, 22), (12: G, 0.970, 35; δ = 62), (13: H, 0.966, 14; δ = 69), (14: B, 0.989, 31), (15: A, 0.945, 41), (16: C, 0.974, 17), (17: B, 0.980, 47), (18: H, 0.972, 4; δ = 79), (19: C, 0.917, 44), (20: B, 0.902, 32), (21: B, 0.981, 1), (22: C, 0.983, 34), (23: F, 0.983, 12; β = 92, γ = 46), (24: G, 0.960, 12; δ = 54), (25: D, 0.936, 28; α = 0.41), (26: G, 0.965, 11; δ = 56), (27: F, 0.976, 7; β = 53, γ = 26), (28: B, 0.978, 10), (29: H, 0.972, 21; δ = 55), (30: C, 0.980, 2), (31: G, 0.975, 46; δ = 41), (32: B, 0.901, 46), (33: H, 0.972, 26; δ = 56), (34: C, 0.928, 7), (35: A, 0.909, 5), (36: A, 0.977, 49), (37: D, 0.973, 22; α = 0.72), (38: C, 0.918, 42), (39: A, 0.930, 29), (40: B, 0.986, 37), (41: G, 0.968, 37; δ = 60), (42: G, 0.977, 31; δ = 41), (43: F, 0.981, 41; β = 84, γ = 42), (44: G, 0.975, 33; δ = 40), (45: B, 0.975, 25), (46: E, 0.965, 37; β = 81), (47: B, 0.941, 20), (48: F, 0.979, 8; β = 86, γ = 43), (49: F, 0.964, 40; β = 58, γ = 29), (50: E, 0.967, 25; β = 64)
$C_{ns} = 1287$, $C^* = 3 \times C_{ns} = 3861$

The rest of the parameters depend on the subsystem type. They were defined in the mathematical description in Sections 3.1–3.7, but for convenience we include a summary here with the list of the parameters used for each type of subsystems:

- active redundancy ($tr = $ A), passive redundancy (or cold standby redundancy) ($tr = $ B), and hybrid standby redundancy with a hot reserve ($tr = $ C) and possibly other cold ones: no additional parameters;
- hybrid standby redundancy with a warm reserve ($tr = $ D) and possibly other cold ones: parameter α (the coefficient of reduction of the failure rate for a warm-maintained reserve compared to the failure rate of the component in operation);
- hybrid redundancy consisting of a TMR structure with control facilities and possibly cold reserves ($tr = $ E): parameter β (the reduction factor used to express the failure rate of the decision and control logic of a TMR structure based on the failure rate of the basic components);
- static redundancy: TMR or 5MR ($tr = $ F): parameters β (as above) and γ (the reduction factor used to express the failure rate of the decision and control logic of a 5MR structure based on the failure rate of the basic components);
- reconfigurable TMR/Simplex type structure with possible other cold-maintained spare components ($tr = $ G) and reconfigurable TMR/Duplex type structure with possible other cold-maintained spare components ($tr = $ H): parameter δ (the reduction factor used to express the failure rate of the decision, control and reconfiguration logic of a TMR/Simplex or a TMR/Duplex structure based on the failure rate of the basic components).

For example, in Table 4, since subsystem 1 is of type D, its parameter α_1 is 0.55. Since subsystem 4 is of type E, its parameter β_4 is 50. The subscripts were omitted to avoid cluttering the table, but the parameters have distinct values for each subsystem, i.e., they are α_i, β_i, γ_i or δ_i.

On the last line, one can see the cost of the non-redundant system C_{ns} and the maximum allowable cost of the system C^*, chosen to be three times greater than C_{ns}. C^* could have in fact any value, but greater values do not make the problem harder, because the main difficulty lies in finding the proper distribution of redundant components in the "upper" part of the allocation. Greater values for C^* would lead to a certain number of redundant components included for all subsystems, and then the main issue would also lie in this "upper" part of the allocation.

The redundancy allocation for these problems generated by the three proposed algorithms after the first optimization process, that tries to maximize system reliability at a maximum allowable cost C^*, is presented in Tables 6 and 7.

Table 6. Best solutions to problem P_1 after first optimization (maximizing reliability under cost constraint: $C^* = 3723$).

Algorithm	Optimal Allocation: $k_1, k_2, \ldots, k_n$	C_{rs}	R_{rs}	Ef
SEA	2, 2, 3, 4, 2, 2, 3, 4, 3, 5, 4, 2, 3, 3, 3, 3, 4, 3, 3, 3, 3, 2, 3, 3, 3, 2, 5, 4, 3, 2, 4, 3, 2, 3, 3, 4, 4, 3, 4, 3, 3, 3, 3, 3, 4, 3, 4, 4, 2	3719	0.973398	33.714
RELIVE	2, 3, 3, 4, 2, 2, 3, 3, 3, 4, 4, 2, 3, 4, 3, 2, 4, 3, 3, 3, 3, 2, 3, 3, 3, 3, 4, 4, 3, 2, 4, 2, 2, 3, 3, 4, 2, 3, 4, 3, 3, 3, 3, 2, 3, 4, 4, 4, 4, 3	3719	0.977724	40.260
LP	2, 3, 3, 4, 2, 2, 3, 3, 3, 4, 4, 2, 3, 4, 3, 2, 4, 3, 3, 3, 3, 2, 3, 3, 3, 3, 4, 4, 3, 2, 4, 2, 2, 3, 3, 4, 2, 3, 4, 3, 3, 3, 3, 2, 3, 4, 4, 4, 4, 3	3719	0.977724	40.260

Table 7. Best solutions to problem P_2 after first optimization (maximizing reliability under cost constraint: $C^* = 3861$).

Algorithm	Optimal Allocation: $k_1, k_2, \ldots, k_n$	C_{rs}	R_{rs}	Ef
SEA	3, 2, 4, 2, 3, 3, 3, 2, 3, 3, 4, 4, 5, 2, 3, 3, 2, 5, 3, 3, 8, 2, 3, 4, 3, 4, 3, 2, 4, 5, 3, 3, 4, 5, 4, 2, 4, 3, 3, 2, 3, 3, 3, 3, 2, 4, 3, 3, 3, 4	3856	0.978930	41.911
RELIVE	3, 2, 4, 3, 3, 4, 3, 3, 3, 3, 4, 4, 2, 3, 3, 2, 5, 3, 3, 4, 2, 3, 4, 3, 4, 3, 2, 4, 3, 3, 3, 4, 4, 4, 2, 2, 3, 3, 2, 4, 3, 3, 3, 2, 4, 3, 3, 3, 4	3861	0.981474	47.666
LP	3, 2, 4, 3, 3, 4, 3, 3, 3, 3, 4, 4, 2, 3, 3, 2, 5, 3, 3, 4, 2, 3, 4, 3, 4, 3, 2, 4, 3, 3, 3, 4, 4, 4, 2, 2, 3, 3, 2, 4, 3, 3, 3, 2, 4, 3, 3, 3, 4	3861	0.981474	47.666

The solutions after the second optimization process trying to minimize the cost under the reliability constraint $R_{rs} \geq R^* = R_{max}$ are presented in Tables 8 and 9.

Table 8. Best solutions to problem P_1 after second optimization (minimizing cost under reliability constraint R^*).

Algorithm	Optimal Allocation: $k_1, k_2, \ldots, k_n$	C_{rs}	R_{rs}	Ef
SEA $R^* = 0.973398$	2, 3, 3, 4, 2, 2, 3, 3, 3, 3, 4, 2, 3, 4, 3, 3, 4, 3, 3, 3, 3, 2, 3, 3, 3, 3, 5, 3, 3, 2, 4, 2, 2, 3, 3, 3, 2, 3, 4, 3, 3, 3, 3, 3, 3, 4, 3, 4, 4, 3	3658	0.973465	33.798
RELIVE $R^* = 0.977724$	2, 3, 3, 4, 2, 2, 3, 3, 3, 4, 4, 2, 3, 4, 3, 2, 4, 3, 3, 3, 3, 2, 3, 3, 3, 3, 4, 4, 3, 2, 4, 2, 2, 3, 3, 4, 2, 3, 4, 3, 3, 3, 3, 2, 3, 4, 4, 4, 4, 3	3719	0.977724	40.260
LP $R^* = 0.977724$	2, 3, 3, 4, 2, 2, 3, 3, 3, 4, 4, 2, 3, 4, 3, 2, 4, 3, 3, 3, 3, 2, 3, 3, 3, 3, 4, 4, 3, 2, 4, 2, 2, 3, 3, 4, 2, 3, 4, 3, 3, 3, 3, 2, 3, 4, 4, 4, 4, 3	3719	0.977724	40.260

Table 9. Best solutions to problem P_2 after second optimization (minimizing cost under reliability constraint R^*).

Algorithm	Optimal Allocation: $k_1, k_2, \ldots, k_n$	C_{rs}	R_{rs}	Ef
SEA $R^* = 0.978930$	3, 2, 4, 3, 3, 4, 3, 2, 3, 3, 3, 3, 4, 2, 3, 2, 2, 5, 3, 3, 2, 2, 3, 4, 3, 4, 3, 2, 4, 4, 3, 3, 4, 3, 5, 2, 3, 3, 3, 2, 4, 3, 3, 3, 2, 4, 3, 3, 3, 4	3819	0.979250	42.556
RELIVE $R^* = 0.981474$	3, 2, 4, 3, 3, 4, 3, 3, 3, 3, 4, 4, 2, 3, 3, 2, 5, 3, 3, 4, 2, 3, 4, 3, 4, 3, 2, 4, 3, 3, 3, 4, 4, 4, 2, 2, 3, 3, 2, 4, 3, 3, 3, 2, 4, 3, 3, 3, 4	3861	0.981474	47.666
LP $R^* = 0.981474$	3, 2, 4, 3, 3, 4, 3, 3, 3, 3, 4, 4, 2, 3, 3, 2, 5, 3, 3, 4, 2, 3, 4, 3, 4, 3, 2, 4, 3, 3, 3, 4, 4, 4, 2, 2, 3, 3, 2, 4, 3, 3, 3, 2, 4, 3, 3, 3, 4	3861	0.981474	47.666

For the second experiment, more complex reliability models corresponding to a system with 100 subsystems are considered (problems P_3 and P_4). These models are presented in Tables 10 and 11.

Table 10. Problem P_3 for $n = 100$ subsystems.

Structural Details: Tuples of $(i: tr_i, r_i, c_i)$ Extended with Parameters $\alpha_i, \beta_i, \gamma_i$ or as Appropriate, $i = 1{:}n$.
(1: F, 0.987, 9; β = 75, γ = 38), (2: H, 0.970, 16; δ = 40), (3: F, 0.959, 20; β = 82, γ = 41), (4: C, 0.984, 40), (5: B, 0.919, 23), (6: D, 0.953, 9; α = 0.34), (7: G, 0.985, 8; δ = 44), (8: A, 0.966, 23), (9: H, 0.978, 38; δ = 48), (10: B, 0.908, 5), (11: C, 0.919, 23), (12: A, 0.946, 18), (13: A, 0.969, 42), (14: F, 0.970, 15; β = 94, γ = 47), (15: B, 0.921, 17), (16: B, 0.913, 32), (17: D, 0.905, 15; α = 0.41), (18: H, 0.958, 14; δ = 58), (19: B, 0.963, 12), (20: B, 0.930, 29), (21: A, 0.954, 18), (22: C, 0.989, 27), (23: A, 0.990, 7), (24: C, 0.983, 23), (25: D, 0.928, 10; α = 0.22), (26: E, 0.958, 13; β = 93), (27: A, 0.962, 25), (28: F, 0.967, 20; β = 53, γ = 27), (29: G, 0.970, 36; δ = 67), (30: B, 0.972, 20), (31: C, 0.943, 23), (32: G, 0.982, 43; δ = 58), (33: H, 0.978, 45; δ = 64), (34: B, 0.952, 20), (35: A, 0.944, 7), (36: C, 0.969, 19), (37: F, 0.953, 43; β = 57, γ = 29), (38: G, 0.953, 18; δ = 47), (39: H, 0.987, 25; δ = 54), (40: A, 0.940, 25), (41: B, 0.962, 43), (42: H, 0.958, 31; δ = 77), (43: A, 0.947, 26), (44: E, 0.984, 48; β = 57), (45: E, 0.969, 6; β = 87), (46: A, 0.900, 46), (47: C, 0.945, 47), (48: G, 0.967, 8; δ = 52), (49: F, 0.961, 27; β = 64, γ = 32), (50: E, 0.971, 44; β = 82), (51: B, 0.912, 47), (52: F, 0.968, 34; β = 52, γ = 26), (53: G, 0.978, 19; δ = 51), (54: E, 0.966, 32; β = 69), (55: B, 0.946, 35), (56: C, 0.983, 32), (57: H, 0.970, 10; δ = 50), (58: D, 0.926, 46; α = 0.61), (59: H, 0.975, 30; δ = 77), (60: D, 0.902, 10; α = 0.99), (61: D, 0.982, 33; α = 0.30), (62: A, 0.940, 38), (63: C, 0.922, 37), (64: F, 0.986, 19; β = 78, γ = 39), (65: G, 0.975, 32; δ = 59), (66: D, 0.938, 30; α = 0.22), (67: B, 0.974, 22), (68: H, 0.958, 22; δ = 70), (69: E, 0.951, 9; β = 75), (70: G, 0.969, 48; δ = 77), (71: D, 0.905, 38; α = 0.21), (72: E, 0.989, 47; β = 64), (73: H, 0.962, 38; δ = 63), (74: B, 0.923, 37), (75: H, 0.976, 36; δ = 53), (76: A, 0.937, 36), (77: B, 0.942, 2), (78: C, 0.913, 8), (79: E, 0.968, 18; β = 69), (80: C, 0.928, 14), (81: B, 0.962, 16), (82: C, 0.924, 17), (83: A, 0.913, 42), (84: A, 0.987, 41), (85: A, 0.960, 22), (86: D, 0.902, 39; α = 0.72), (87: H, 0.953, 24; δ = 54), (88: B, 0.925, 13), (89: H, 0.953, 35; δ = 65), (90: E, 0.972, 24; β = 86), (91: D, 0.924, 9; α = 0.48), (92: B, 0.971, 46), (93: H, 0.969, 37; δ = 66), (94: D, 0.980, 15; α = 0.11), (95: E, 0.972, 41; β = 80), (96: B, 0.922, 6), (97: E, 0.988, 44; β = 54), (98: C, 0.955, 7), (99: F, 0.960, 16; β = 90, γ = 45), (100: A, 0.904, 25)
$C_{ns} = 2579$, $C^* = 3 \times C_{ns} = 7737$

Table 11. Problem P_4 for $n = 100$ subsystems.

Structural Details: Tuples of $(i: tr_i, r_i, c_i)$ Extended with Parameters $\alpha_i, \beta_i, \gamma_i$ or as Appropriate, $i = 1{:}n$.
(1: D, 0.974, 45; α = 0.98), (2: B, 0.902, 13), (3: C, 0.955, 24), (4: D, 0.958, 21; α = 0.91), (5: E, 0.954, 39; β = 82), (6: A, 0.923, 46), (7: D, 0.952, 8; α = 0.23), (8: B, 0.900, 33), (9: A, 0.926, 19), (10: D, 0.933, 3; α = 0.55), (11: D, 0.973, 4; α = 0.13), (12: E, 0.976, 2; β = 100), (13: D, 0.912, 12; α = 0.43), (14: G, 0.963, 19; δ = 45), (15: B, 0.975, 27), (16: D, 0.985, 11; α = 0.23), (17: C, 0.984, 34), (18: B, 0.940, 47), (19: F, 0.981, 35; β = 79, γ = 40), (20: F, 0.961, 20; β = 79, γ = 39), (21: D, 0.929, 17; α = 0.36), (22: H, 0.989, 7; δ = 63), (23: E, 0.977, 1; β = 57), (24: A, 0.943, 44), (25: F, 0.965, 40; β = 97, γ = 48), (26: E, 0.982, 34; β = 97), (27: F, 0.974, 49; β = 79, γ = 39), (28: H, 0.969, 12; δ = 42), (29: D, 0.949, 45; α = 0.44), (30: G, 0.977, 11; δ = 56), (31: D, 0.915, 2; α = 0.48), (32: C, 0.975, 10), (33: A, 0.904, 10), (34: A, 0.928, 16), (35: H, 0.976, 49; δ = 65), (36: E, 0.958, 25; β = 55), (37: D, 0.962, 47; α = 0.15), (38: B, 0.909, 1), (39: H, 0.960, 37; δ = 44), (40: B, 0.923, 49), (41: C, 0.907, 32), (42: E, 0.985, 49; β = 63), (43: B, 0.918, 4), (44: F, 0.964, 38; β = 90, γ = 45), (45: A, 0.952, 36), (46: B, 0.945, 41), (47: C, 0.906, 16), (48: D, 0.915, 24; α = 0.70), (49: B, 0.905, 21), (50: A, 0.902, 20), (51: C, 0.969, 15), (52: H, 0.964, 24; δ = 51), (53: D, 0.916, 44; α = 0.68), (54: E, 0.973, 37; β = 53), (55: C, 0.945, 13), (56: D, 0.976, 38; α = 0.23), (57: D, 0.931, 13; α = 0.09), (58: B, 0.912, 30), (59: F, 0.960, 31; β = 71, γ = 35), (60: A, 0.925, 5), (61: B, 0.958, 46), (62: E, 0.954, 46; β = 57), (63: F, 0.968, 38; β = 85, γ = 43), (64: B, 0.955, 8), (65: H, 0.958, 1; δ = 59), (66: B, 0.988, 44), (67: D, 0.954, 42; α = 0.19), (68: C, 0.974, 46), (69: G, 0.977, 19; δ = 47), (70: D, 0.958, 3; α = 0.04), (71: A, 0.922, 13), (72: A, 0.975, 33), (73: C, 0.918, 10), (74: D, 0.946, 36; α = 0.42), (75: C, 0.918, 38), (76: H, 0.968, 18; δ = 70), (77: F, 0.981, 3; β = 93, γ = 46), (78: H, 0.963, 12; δ = 78), (79: A, 0.981, 8), (80: D, 0.980, 48; α = 0.97), (81: B, 0.967, 19), (82: C, 0.939, 26), (83: F, 0.967, 40; β = 55, γ = 27), (84: C, 0.947, 25), (85: D, 0.982, 46; α = 0.07), (86: E, 0.982, 28; β = 84), (87: G, 0.976, 15; δ = 66), (88: D, 0.941, 22; α = 0.44), (89: F, 0.983, 3; β = 97, γ = 49), (90: C, 0.972, 12), (91: A, 0.976, 13), (92: B, 0.950, 18), (93: D, 0.976, 20; α = 0.07), (94: G, 0.989, 32; δ = 42), (95: H, 0.974, 3; δ = 66), (96: E, 0.989, 36; β = 93), (97: G, 0.967, 11; δ = 45), (98: H, 0.974, 46; δ = 68), (99: G, 0.956, 38; δ = 74), (100: G, 0.974, 42; δ = 73)
$C_{ns} = 2506$, $C^* = 3 \times C_{ns} = 7518$

The numerical results after the two optimization processes described above are presented in Tables 12–15.

Table 12. Best solutions to problem P_3 after first optimization (maximizing reliability under cost constraint: $C^* = 7737$).

Algorithm	Optimal Allocation: $k_1, k_2, \ldots, k_n$	C_{rs}	R_{rs}	Ef
SEA	5, 3, 3, 2, 4, 3, 5, 3, 3, 7, 4, 4, 2, 3, 3, 3, 4, 3, 3, 3, 2, 4, 7, 2, 3, 4, 3, 3, 3, 5, 2, 3, 4, 3, 2, 3, 3, 5, 3, 2, 2, 3, 2, 3, 3, 3, 2, 4, 3, 3, 3, 3, 3, 4, 2, 2, 4, 3, 4, 4, 3, 2, 4, 3, 3, 2, 2, 4, 5, 3, 3, 3, 3, 3, 3, 3, 5, 3, 3, 5, 2, 3, 3, 2, 2, 3, 4, 2, 3, 3, 4, 2, 3, 3, 3, 4, 3, 5, 3, 3	7722	0.894261	9.375
RELIVE	3, 4, 3, 2, 3, 3, 4, 2, 3, 4, 3, 3, 3, 3, 3, 3, 4, 3, 3, 3, 2, 2, 2, 3, 5, 2, 3, 3, 2, 2, 3, 3, 4, 3, 2, 3, 3, 3, 3, 3, 3, 2, 4, 3, 3, 5, 3, 2, 4, 3, 3, 3, 3, 4, 3, 3, 2, 4, 2, 3, 4, 2, 3, 2, 3, 3, 2, 2, 4, 5, 4, 3, 3, 4, 2, 4, 3, 8, 4, 4, 4, 2, 3, 3, 2, 3, 3, 4, 3, 4, 4, 3, 2, 4, 2, 4, 3, 3, 3, 4	7737	0.927214	13.619
LP	3, 4, 3, 2, 3, 4, 2, 3, 3, 3, 2, 3, 3, 3, 3, 4, 2, 3, 3, 2, 2, 2, 3, 4, 3, 3, 2, 3, 3, 3, 3, 2, 3, 4, 3, 3, 2, 4, 3, 3, 4, 3, 3, 4, 3, 4, 3, 3, 3, 4, 2, 2, 4, 3, 4, 4, 2, 3, 3, 3, 3, 2, 4, 4, 3, 3, 3, 4, 3, 3, 3, 3, 4, 4, 3, 2, 3, 3, 2, 3, 3, 4, 3, 4, 4, 3, 2, 4, 2, 4, 3, 3, 3, 3	7737	0.947769	18.979

Table 13. Best solutions to problem P_4 after first optimization (maximizing reliability under cost constraint: $C^* = 7518$).

Algorithm	Optimal Allocation: $k_1, k_2, \ldots, k_n$	C_{rs}	R_{rs}	Ef
SEA	2, 3, 3, 3, 4, 3, 4, 4, 3, 3, 4, 4, 4, 3, 3, 3, 2, 2, 3, 3, 4, 3, 4, 2, 3, 4, 3, 4, 2, 4, 4, 4, 4, 5, 3, 4, 2, 5, 4, 3, 3, 3, 8, 3, 3, 2, 3, 3, 4, 4, 3, 3, 3, 3, 3, 2, 4, 2, 3, 3, 2, 3, 3, 3, 2, 5, 2, 2, 2, 5, 3, 3, 4, 5, 2, 3, 5, 3, 5, 3, 2, 3, 5, 3, 3, 3, 3, 3, 2, 3, 2, 3, 3, 2, 4, 5, 3, 5, 4, 3, 3	7499	0.930610	14.281
RELIVE	3, 3, 2, 3, 4, 3, 3, 3, 4, 4, 2, 5, 4, 4, 2, 2, 2, 2, 3, 3, 3, 4, 3, 2, 3, 3, 3, 5, 3, 4, 4, 3, 5, 4, 3, 4, 2, 6, 4, 3, 4, 3, 4, 3, 3, 2, 4, 3, 3, 4, 3, 4, 3, 3, 2, 3, 3, 3, 4, 3, 4, 3, 2, 5, 2, 3, 2, 4, 4, 4, 2, 4, 3, 3, 4, 5, 5, 3, 2, 2, 3, 3, 3, 2, 4, 4, 3, 3, 3, 3, 3, 2, 3, 5, 3, 4, 3, 4, 3	7518	0.952116	20.695
LP	2, 3, 3, 3, 4, 3, 3, 3, 4, 3, 5, 3, 4, 2, 2, 2, 3, 3, 3, 3, 4, 5, 3, 3, 3, 3, 4, 3, 4, 4, 3, 4, 3, 4, 4, 2, 4, 4, 3, 3, 3, 3, 3, 3, 3, 4, 3, 3, 4, 3, 4, 3, 2, 3, 3, 3, 4, 2, 4, 3, 3, 5, 2, 2, 2, 4, 3, 4, 2, 3, 3, 3, 4, 3, 4, 3, 2, 2, 3, 3, 3, 2, 3, 4, 3, 3, 3, 3, 2, 3, 4, 3, 4, 4, 4, 3	7518	0.962884	26.699

Table 14. Best solutions to problem P_3 after second optimization (minimizing cost under the constraint of reliability R^*).

Algorithm	Optimal Allocation: $k_1, k_2, \ldots, k_n$	C_{rs}	R_{rs}	Ef
SEA $R^* = 0.894261$	3, 5, 3, 2, 2, 2, 3, 3, 4, 2, 2, 3, 2, 5, 3, 3, 4, 4, 2, 2, 3, 2, 3, 2, 4, 5, 4, 5, 3, 2, 2, 3, 3, 2, 7, 2, 3, 5, 3, 4, 2, 5, 3, 3, 4, 3, 2, 5, 3, 3, 3, 3, 3, 3, 2, 2, 3, 2, 3, 3, 4, 3, 3, 3, 3, 4, 2, 3, 5, 3, 3, 3, 4, 2, 3, 3, 2, 8, 3, 4, 5, 3, 3, 3, 2, 2, 3, 5, 4, 4, 3, 4, 2, 3, 3, 3, 6, 3, 5, 3, 3	7735	0.896609	9.588
RELIVE $R^* = 0.927214$	3, 4, 3, 2, 3, 4, 3, 2, 3, 3, 3, 3, 2, 3, 3, 3, 4, 4, 3, 3, 2, 2, 2, 3, 5, 3, 3, 3, 2, 3, 3, 3, 3, 2, 3, 4, 3, 3, 2, 4, 3, 3, 5, 3, 2, 5, 3, 5, 2, 3, 3, 4, 2, 2, 5, 3, 4, 4, 2, 2, 3, 3, 3, 2, 2, 4, 4, 3, 3, 4, 2, 3, 2, 3, 5, 5, 3, 3, 3, 3, 2, 3, 3, 4, 3, 4, 5, 4, 2, 3, 2, 3, 3, 5, 3, 3	7622	0.927251	13.626
LP $R^* = 0.947769$	3, 4, 3, 2, 3, 3, 4, 2, 3, 3, 3, 2, 3, 3, 3, 3, 4, 2, 3, 3, 2, 2, 2, 3, 4, 3, 3, 2, 3, 3, 3, 3, 2, 3, 4, 3, 3, 2, 4, 3, 3, 4, 3, 3, 4, 3, 4, 3, 3, 3, 4, 2, 2, 4, 3, 4, 4, 2, 3, 3, 3, 3, 2, 4, 4, 3, 3, 3, 4, 3, 3, 3, 3, 4, 4, 3, 2, 3, 3, 2, 3, 3, 4, 3, 4, 4, 3, 2, 4, 2, 4, 3, 3, 3, 3	7737	0.947769	18.979

Table 15. Best solutions to problem P_4 after second optimization (minimizing cost under the constraint of reliability R^*).

Algorithm	Optimal Allocation: $k_1, k_2, \ldots, k_n$	C_{rs}	R_{rs}	Ef
SEA $R^* = 0.930610$	2, 3, 5, 2, 4, 3, 4, 4, 2, 4, 2, 5, 3, 4, 4, 3, 3, 3, 5, 3, 3, 5, 4, 3, 3, 3, 3, 3, 3, 5, 4, 5, 6, 5, 5, 5, 2, 8, 3, 3, 3, 3, 8, 3, 3, 2, 5, 4, 4, 4, 5, 4, 3, 3, 4, 3, 2, 4, 3, 4, 2, 3, 3, 5, 5, 2, 2, 3, 5, 3, 4, 2, 4, 2, 3, 4, 5, 5, 3, 4, 2, 5, 3, 4, 2, 5, 3, 2, 5, 4, 2, 5, 2, 4, 3, 3, 5, 4, 3, 3	8213	0.932688	14.722
RELIVE $R^* = 0.952116$	2, 3, 3, 3, 4, 3, 4, 3, 3, 4, 4, 4, 3, 4, 2, 2, 2, 2, 3, 3, 3, 5, 5, 3, 3, 3, 3, 5, 3, 5, 4, 3, 4, 4, 3, 4, 2, 3, 4, 2, 3, 3, 3, 3, 3, 2, 3, 3, 4, 3, 3, 4, 3, 4, 3, 2, 3, 3, 3, 3, 2, 4, 3, 3, 4, 2, 2, 2, 4, 3, 4, 2, 3, 3, 3, 5, 5, 4, 3, 2, 3, 3, 3, 3, 2, 3, 5, 3, 5, 3, 3, 3, 2, 3, 4, 3, 4, 3, 4, 3	7384	0.952135	20.703
LP $R^* = 0.962884$	2, 3, 3, 3, 4, 3, 3, 3, 3, 4, 3, 5, 3, 4, 2, 2, 2, 3, 3, 3, 3, 4, 5, 3, 3, 3, 3, 4, 3, 4, 4, 3, 4, 3, 4, 4, 2, 4, 4, 3, 3, 3, 4, 3, 3, 3, 4, 3, 3, 4, 3, 4, 3, 4, 3, 2, 3, 3, 3, 4, 2, 4, 3, 3, 5, 2, 2, 2, 4, 3, 3, 2, 4, 3, 3, 4, 3, 4, 3, 2, 2, 3, 3, 3, 2, 3, 4, 3, 3, 3, 3, 3, 2, 3, 4, 3, 4, 4, 4, 3	7518	0.962884	26.699

For each algorithm, the reliability found by maximization was set as the threshold for the minimization problem. The goal is to find systems with a lower total cost for the same reliability. During maximization, if there are more candidates with the same reliability but different costs, the choice between them is indifferent from the point of view of the objective function. Therefore, a solution with a higher cost but still less or equal to the cost threshold can be selected. The second optimization can identify better solutions from both points of view. This is often the case for SEA, which usually gives suboptimal results for the first optimization. On the contrary, LP likely finds the optimal solution every time, and therefore, the results of the second optimization are the same as for the first.

The three optimization algorithms considered in our study generate different solutions. The following three examples illustrate how we can determine whether one is superior to the other:

- Consider problem P_1 for which the best solutions generated by the three optimization algorithms are shown in Table 6. All three solutions require 3719 cost units, but the solution given by SEA achieves lower reliability (0.973398) compared to that given by RELIVE and LP (0.977724);
- Consider problem P_3 for which the best solutions generated by the three optimization algorithms are shown in Table 12. The solutions given by RELIVE and LP both require 7737 cost units, but the solution generated by LP achieves higher reliability (0.947769) compared to that given by RELIVE (0.927214);
- Consider problem P_4 for which the best solutions generated by the three optimization algorithms are shown in Table 15. Please note that the solution given by SEA requires the highest cost and offers the lowest reliability compared to the solutions given by RELIVE and LP.

For a better comparison of the three proposed optimization algorithms, 1000 randomly generated problems were considered for both $n = 50$ and $n = 100$. The corresponding results are presented in Figures 8–11. Each graph presents the mean values as the height of the bars, with the standard deviations represented as two sigmas (one up from the mean, and one down from the mean).

First, the reliability maximization case for $n = 50$ was considered. Figure 8 shows some statistics of the final system reliability obtained by the algorithms. Since the performance of the evolutionary algorithm greatly depends on the number of generations, two versions were considered: 1000 and 10,000 generations for SEA, and 100 and 500 generations for RELIVE.

It must be mentioned that RELIVE performs additional function evaluations during the hill climbing procedure, therefore it is normal that its number of generations be less than for SEA. Figure 8a presents the actual efficiency values obtained by the algorithms.

Figure 8b includes a comparison relative to LP, where in each of the 1000 trials the efficiency found by LP was considered to correspond to 100% and the efficiency found by the other algorithms is represented as a percentage of that found by LP. It can be seen that the results of LP and RELIVE are very close, with LP being slightly better, while those of SEA are of a lower quality.

It can also be seen that there is no significant difference between the results of SEA and RELIVE with different numbers of generations: most likely, 1000 and 100 generations, respectively, are sufficient for such problems.

Similar statistics are displayed in Figure 9 for systems with $n = 100$. In this case, since the problems are more difficult, there are greater differences between algorithms. LP remains the best, while the relative average efficiency of RELIVE solutions is around 75%, and that of SEA is around 45%.

Figures 10 and 11 show the results obtained for the cost minimization problems. Since an increase in the number of generations does not seem to be a decisive factor, only 100 and 500 generations were considered for SEA and RELIVE, respectively. The relative performance of algorithms is similar: LP provides the best results, RELIVE results are comparable, slightly worse especially for $n = 100$, while SEA gives an average minimum cost around 120–130% higher than the optimal solution.

In addition, in order to better verify the effectiveness of the proposed algorithms, for the 2000 problems studied, the results obtained for the initial variant were compared with those for two other variants in which the order of the subsystems changed, being sorted by reliability. The LP algorithm provided the same results for all 2000 problems checked, which highlights its stability for this type of stress. This is not the case with the two evolutionary algorithms, RELIVE and SEA, but the differences that occurred were not statistically significant.

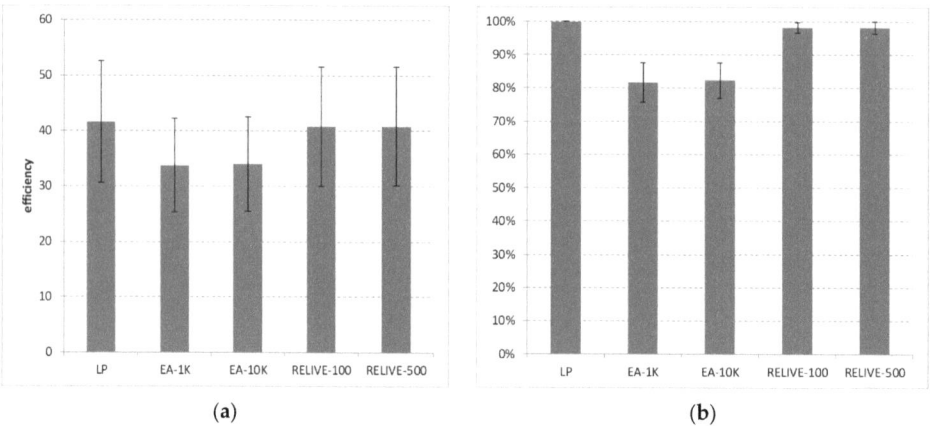

Figure 8. Comparison between algorithms performance for reliability maximization on systems with $n = 50$: (**a**) the average efficiency for 1000 random problem instances; (**b**) the results relative to the maximum efficiency found by LP considered as 100%.

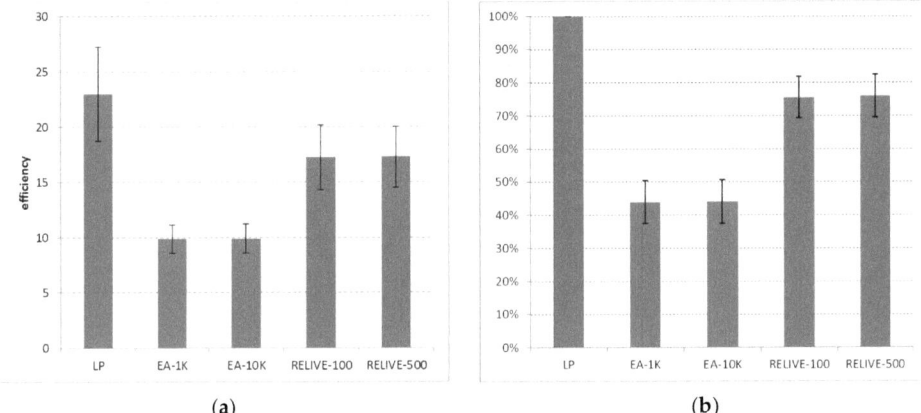

Figure 9. Comparison between algorithms performance for reliability maximization with systems with $n = 100$ subsystems: (**a**) average efficiency; (**b**) results relative to LP.

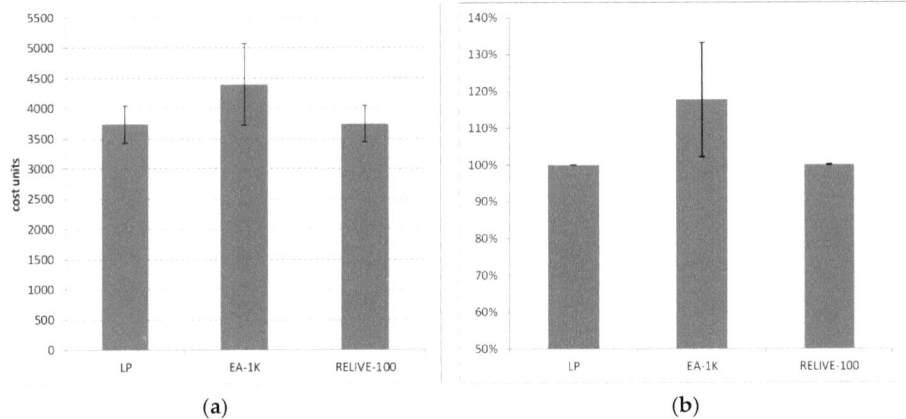

Figure 10. Comparison between the performance of the algorithms for cost minimization with systems of $n = 50$ subsystems: (**a**) average cost; (**b**) results relative to LP.

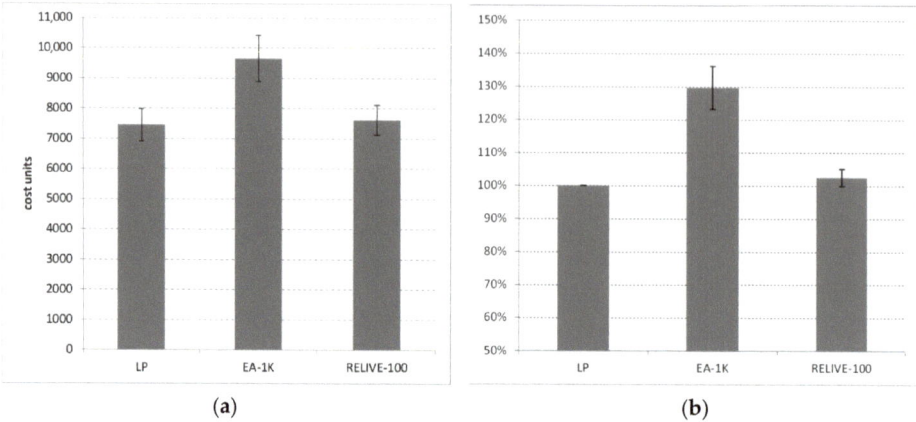

(a) (b)

Figure 11. Comparison between the performance of the algorithms for cost minimization with systems of $n = 100$ subsystems: (**a**) average cost; (**b**) results relative to LP.

9. Discussion

In the mathematical model, we assume that the time to failure of a component follows a negative-exponential distribution. For electronic components or electronic modules, especially for integrated circuits, the time to failure is usually considered to have such a distribution. This means that, for a given operating regime, the average failure rate is constant (and not a function of time). But for mechanical elements, for example, this assumption must be accepted with caution because of the physical wear and tear that can occur during system operation. In this case, a Weibull distribution may be more appropriate.

This assumption is important only for specifying the reliability of the redundant system. Only under this assumption the reliability function for most of the redundant structures we considered can be determined analytically, using Markov models, as presented in Section 3. For other distributions, the evaluation of subsystem reliability is more complicated and can be done in other ways, e.g., by using a Monte Carlo simulation.

The optimization methods used in this study are not fundamentally affected by this simplifying assumption. The only change concerns the calculation of the objective function, which otherwise should be done in a different way. Thus, we appreciate that the comparative performance results of the three optimization methods presented in this article are not significantly affected by this simplifying assumption.

The systems discussed in this paper are all series-aligned subsystems. Our study does not cover cases where a system component may have a redundant structure composed of elements other than the base component, as shown in Figure 12.

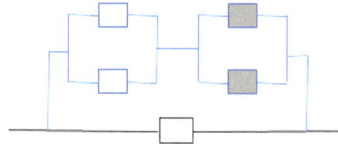

Figure 12. Alternative redundant subsystem structure.

In this situation, the optimization problem must be formulated differently, and it involves the inclusion of more types of components than those that form the non-redundant system.

Such cases are encountered in complex systems, e.g., with a network structure. Unfortunately, the conclusions regarding the performance of the three optimization algorithms compared in this paper cannot be extended to these more general cases. There is no evidence to support this.

Another point of discussion is needed about the number of generations used by the two evolutionary algorithms. The specific number of generations used in the study are powers of ten so that the reader can have an intuitive view about the results. A fairer comparison would need to assess their performance, e.g., with the same number of objective function evaluations, a common setting in the area of biologically-inspired optimization algorithms. The number of function evaluations is easy to determine in case of SEA. If the population consists of 50 chromosomes and 10,000 generations are used, then 500,000 evaluations are needed. However, RELIVE does not have a constant population size. Additional function evaluations are performed in the hill climbing step, although at most one of these solutions will be actually used subsequently in the next generation, i.e., the best local improvement. It was empirically estimated that RELIVE with 100 generations needs about 27 times more function evaluations than SEA with 1000 generations. Thus, a comparison could be made with SEA with about 27,000 generations. Still, from the statistical analysis presented above, we hypothesize that the poorer results of SEA are not caused by a smaller number of generations than required. The performance in both cases with 1000 and 10,000 generations is quite similar. Also, the main issue is not execution time, because this is not a real-time application, but the fact that SEA usually gets stuck into a local optimum because, e.g., at the "top" part of the allocation, one cannot include any more components without exceeding the cost limit. It would require one to add one component to a subsystem and remove one component from another subsystem in order to improve the optimization. SEA lacks any mechanisms to do so, and such improvements can come only from "lucky" mutations and removals of components during the chromosome repairing procedure. On the other hand, RELIVE has an especially designed mutation for this situation, based on exchanging a unit between a pair of genes. Because of this, we eventually chose to use the lower number of generations, i.e., 1000 for SEA and 100 for RELIVE, because in this case the optimization is faster and it seems to show the hierarchy of the used methods quite well.

Since evolutionary algorithms are stochastic, more runs may be necessary to obtain a good solution. In the case studies presented above, we used the following methodology:

- For the results presented in Figures 8–11, each algorithm was run a single time for a problem and 2000 problems were used, i.e., 1000 problems for $n = 50$ and another 1000 problems for $n = 100$. Due to the high number of problems, the results are statistically significant to assess the performance of the algorithms. These figures show this statistical analysis in terms of mean and standard deviation;
- For the results presented in Tables 6–9 and 12–15, the best out of ten runs was selected for SEA and RELIVE, because we were interested in the best solution. The LP algorithm was run only once.

10. Conclusions

Extensive experimental studies on the allocation of redundancy in large binary systems with a hybrid structure, which include a number of optimization problems of the order of thousands, highlight the difficulty of these optimization problems as the number of subsystems increases. Three algorithms were used for optimization: zero-one integer programming, a classic evolutionary algorithm and an original evolutionary algorithm, RELIVE, which combines global search with local fine tuning and includes a number of mutation strategies in order to escape from local optima.

The proposed algorithms are compared, but their effectiveness was also verified by solving two optimization problems, properly correlated. Specifically, a converse problem of minimizing cost for the reliability threshold found in the first case was also attempted as a means to verify the optimality of the solution and when the solution was not optimal, to attempt to improve it from either the cost or reliability perspectives, and possibly both. Experimental results demonstrate that for large instances of the reliability maximization problem, zero-one integer programming yields the best results, followed by RELIVE. The differences become apparent when the number of subsystems is large, e.g., when $n = 100$.

As future research, the authors intend to extend the study on the optimal allocation of reliability in hybrid structure binary systems in several directions, as shown below.

For the optimization issues considered in this paper, the type of redundancy is predetermined for all subsystems, as shown in Table 4, Table 5, Table 10 or Table 11. But for certain reliability models this condition may be relaxed. For example, if a redundancy technique based on majority logic is appropriate for a subsystem, then one of the following solutions can be adopted: TMR, TMR/Simplex or 5MR, with or without cold-maintained spare components. The same is true for dynamic redundancy, where active redundancy or hybrid standby redundancy with a hot component and other passive spare ones can be adopted. Therefore, the optimization process can be extended to find an optimal solution that refers to both the type of redundancy and the number of components for each of the n subsystems.

On the other hand, some redundant structures often adopt the technical solution in which the components are functionally compatible but different in design to avoid common errors. For example, this idea applies to majority logic structures (TMR, TMR/Simplex and 5MR) or duplex structure. A future direction of research also refers to these redundant subsystems with heterogeneous structure.

In reliability engineering the problem of system reliability maximization under two or more constraints often arises; for example, under cost constraints, but also under weight and/or volume constraints. We intend to extend the research to also cover this important problem of maximizing system reliability under two or more constraints.

We also plan to study the transformation of the problem into a multi-objective optimization problem, e.g., maximize the system's reliability while minimizing the associated cost. The solutions to be considered would be the solutions around the imposed threshold for cost or reliability. Previously we saw that an increase in the cost limit of only 5% can lead to a larger increase in system reliability. By using a multi-objective optimization approach, such analysis could be more principled.

Another direction of investigation would be to assess the effect of integer-based representation for the evolutionary algorithms instead of the real-valued representation used so far.

Author Contributions: Conceptualization, P.C. and F.L.; methodology, P.C. and F.L.; software, F.L.; validation, P.C.; formal analysis, P.C.; investigation, F.L.; writing—original draft preparation, P.C. and F.L.; writing—review and editing, P.C. and F.L. All authors have read and agreed to the published version of the manuscript.

Funding: This research received no external funding.

Institutional Review Board Statement: Not applicable.

Informed Consent Statement: Not applicable.

Data Availability Statement: All data used for the experimental studies are available on request.

Conflicts of Interest: The authors declare no conflict of interest.

Nomenclature

Reliability	The probability that a component or a system works successfully within a given period of time
Binary system	A system in which each component can be either operational or failed
Series-redundant model	A reliability model that reflects a redundant system composed of subsystems consisting of basic components or redundant structures, and possibly other spare components

Notations

n	The number of components in the non-redundant system or the number of subsystems in the redundant system, as appropriate
T	A certain period of time for which reliability is assessed
r_i	The reliability of a component of type i, $i \in \{1, \ldots, n\}$, for a given period of time T
c_i	The cost of a component of type i
λ_i	The failure rate for a component of type i
k_i	The number of components that make up the redundant subsystem i
R_i	The reliability of subsystem i (subsystem with redundant structure)
C_i	The cost of subsystem i
tr_i	The type of redundancy for subsystem i
α, $0 < \alpha < 1$	The coefficient of reduction of the failure rate for a warm-maintained reserve compared to the failure rate of the component in operation
β, $\beta > 1$	The reduction factor used to express the failure rate of the decision and control logic of a TMR structure based on the failure rate of the basic components
γ, $\gamma > 1$	The reduction factor used to express the failure rate of the decision and control logic of a 5MR structure based on the failure rate of the basic components
δ, $\delta > 1$	The reduction factor used to express the failure rate of the decision, control and reconfiguration logic of a TMR/Simplex or a TMR/Duplex structure based on the failure rate of the basic components
R_{ns}	The reliability of the non-redundant system (system with series reliability model)
C_{ns}	The cost of the non-redundant system
R_{rs}	The reliability of the redundant system (system with series-redundant reliability model)
R_{rs}	The reliability of the redundant system (system with series-redundant reliability model)
C_{rs}	The cost of the redundant system
R^*	The required level of reliability of the system
C^*	The maximum allowable cost of the system
CO	A component in operation (active component)
WSC	A warm-maintained spare component
CSC	A cold-maintained spare component

Note: For notations r_i to tr_i, when the subsystem is not indicated the index is not necessary, therefore the notations used are r, c, λ and so on.

Assumptions

- For any redundant subsystem, the spare components are considered identical to the basic one/ones.
- For the components in operating mode or for the spare components maintained in warm conditions, the time to failure has a negative-exponential distribution.
- The events of failure that may affect the components of the system are stochastically independent.

References

1. Coit, D.W.; Zio, E. The evolution of system reliability optimization. *Reliab. Eng. Syst. Saf.* **2019**, *192*, 106259. [CrossRef]
2. Soltani, R. Reliability optimization of binary state non-repairable systems: A state of the art survey. *Int. J. Ind. Eng. Comput.* **2014**, *5*, 339–364. [CrossRef]
3. Kuo, W.; Wan, R. *Recent Advances in Optimal Reliability Allocation, Computational Intelligence in Reliability Engineering*; Springer: Berlin/Heidelberg, Germany, 2007; pp. 1–36.
4. Leon, F.; Cașcaval, P.; Bădică, C. Optimization Methods for Redundancy Allocation in Large Systems. *Vietnam. J. Comput. Sci.* **2020**, *7*, 281–299. [CrossRef]
5. Kuo, W.; Lin, H.H.; Xu, Z.; Zhang, W. Reliability optimization with the Lagrange-multiplier and branch-and-bound technique. *IEEE Trans. Reliab.* **1987**, *36*, 624–630. [CrossRef]

6. Misra, K.B. Reliability Optimization of a Series-Parallel System, part I: Lagrangian Multipliers Approach, part II: Maximum Principle Approach. *IEEE Trans. Reliab.* **1972**, *21*, 230–238. [CrossRef]
7. Chern, M. On the Computational Complexity of Reliability Redundancy Allocation in Series System. *Oper. Res. Lett.* **1992**, *11*, 309–315. [CrossRef]
8. Dobani, E.R.; Ardakan, M.A.; Davari-Ardakani, H.; Juybari, M.N. RRAP-CM: A new reliability-redundancy allocation problem with heterogeneous components. *Reliab. Eng. Syst. Saf.* **2019**, *191*, 106–563. [CrossRef]
9. Gholinezhad, H.; Hamadani, A.Z. A new model for the redundancy allocation problem with component mixing and mixed redundancy strategy. *Reliab. Eng. Syst. Saf.* **2017**, *164*, 66–73. [CrossRef]
10. Hsieh, T.J. A simple hybrid redundancy strategy accompanied by simplified swarm optimization for the reliability–redundancy allocation problem. *Eng. Optim.* **2022**, *54*, 369–386. [CrossRef]
11. Ali Najmi, K.B.; Ardakan, M.A.; Javid, A.Y. Optimization of reliability redundancy allocation problem with component mixing and strategy selection for subsystems. *J. Stat. Comput. Simul.* **2021**, *91*, 1935–1959. [CrossRef]
12. Peiravi, A.; Karbasian, M.; Ardakan, M.A.; Coit, D.W. Reliability optimization of series-parallel systems with K-mixed redundancy strategy. *Reliab. Eng. Syst. Saf.* **2019**, *183*, 17–28. [CrossRef]
13. Feizabadi, M.; Jahromi, A.E. A new model for reliability optimization of series-parallel systems with non-homogeneous components. *Reliab. Eng. Syst. Saf.* **2017**, *157*, 101–112. [CrossRef]
14. Hsieh, T.-J.; Yeh, W.C. Penalty guided bees search for redundancy allocation problems with a mix of components in series–parallel systems. *Comput. Oper. Res.* **2012**, *39*, 2688–2704. [CrossRef]
15. Sadjadi, S.J.; Soltani, R. An efficient heuristic versus a robust hybrid meta-heuristic for general framework of serial–parallel redundancy problem. *Reliab. Eng. Syst. Saf.* **2009**, *94*, 1703–1710. [CrossRef]
16. Coit, D.W.; Konak, A. Multiple weighted objectives heuristic for the redundancy allocation problem. *IEEE Trans. Reliab.* **2006**, *55*, 551–558. [CrossRef]
17. Prasad, V.R.; Nair, K.P.K.; Aneja, Y.P. A Heuristic Approach to Optimal Assignment of Components to Parallel-Series Network. *IEEE Trans. Reliab.* **1992**, *40*, 555–558. [CrossRef]
18. Shi, D.H. A new heuristic algorithm for constrained redundancy optimization in complex system. *IEEE Trans. Reliab.* **1987**, *36*, 621–623.
19. Cașcaval, P.; Leon, F. Active Redundancy Allocation in Complex Systems by Using Different Optimization Methods. In Proceedings of the 11th International Conference on Computational Collective Intelligence (ICCCI 2019), Hendaye, France, 4–6 September 2019; Nguyen, N., Chbeir, R., Exposito, E., Aniorte, P., Trawinski, B., Eds.; Computational Collective Intelligence, Lecture Notes in Computer Science; Springer: Berlin/Heidelberg, Germany, 2019; Volume 11683, pp. 625–637.
20. Everett, H. Generalized Lagrange Multiplier Method of Solving Problems of Optimal Allocation of Resources. *Oper. Res.* **1963**, *11*, 399–417. [CrossRef]
21. Yalaoui, A.; Châtelet, E.; Chu, C. A new dynamic programming method for reliability & redundancy allocation in a parallel-series syste. *IEEE Trans. Reliab.* **2005**, *54*, 254–261.
22. Shooman, M. *Reliability of Computer Systems and Networks*; John Wiley & Sons: New York, NY, USA, 2002.
23. Misra, K.B. Dynamic programming formulation of the redundancy allocation problem. *Int. J. Math. Educ. Sci. Technol.* **1971**, *2*, 207–215. [CrossRef]
24. Sahoo, L.; Bhunia, A.K.; Roy, D. Reliability optimization with high and low level redundancies in interval environment via genetic algorithm. *Int. J. Syst. Assur. Eng. Manag.* **2014**, *5*, 513–523. [CrossRef]
25. Tavakkoli-Moghaddam, R.; Safari, J.; Khalili-Damghani, F.; Abtahi, K.; Tavana, A.-R. A new multi-objective particle swarm optimization method for solving reliability redundancy allocation problems. *Reliab. Eng. Syst. Saf.* **2013**, *111*, 58–75.
26. Coelho, L.D.S. Self-organizing migrating strategies applied to reliability-redundancy optimization of systems. *IEEE Trans. Reliab.* **2009**, *58*, 501–510. [CrossRef]
27. Agarwal, M.; Gupta, R. Genetic Search for Redundacy Optimization in Complex Systems. *J. Qual. Maint. Eng.* **2006**, *12*, 338–353. [CrossRef]
28. Berkelaar, M.; Eikland, K.; Notebaert, P. lpsolve, Mixed Integer Linear Programming (MILP) Solver. 2021. Available online: https://sourceforge.net/projects/lpsolve (accessed on 1 September 2022).
29. Leon, F.; Cașcaval, P. 01IP and QUBO: Optimization Methods for Redundancy Allocation in Complex Systems. In Proceedings of the 2019 23rd International Conference on System Theory, Control and Computing, Sinaia, Romania, 9–11 October 2019; pp. 877–882.
30. Misra, K.B.; Sharma, U. An efficient algorithm to solve integer-programming problems arising in system-reliability design. *IEEE Trans. Reliab.* **1991**, *40*, 81–91. [CrossRef]
31. Floudas, C.A. *Nonlinear and Mixed-Integer Optimization: Fundamentals and Applications*; Oxford University Press: New York, NY, USA, 1995.
32. Trivedi, K.S. *Probability and Statistics with Reliability, Queueing, and Computer Science Applications*; John Wiley & Sons: New York, NY, USA, 2002.
33. Misra, K.B. (Ed.) *Handbook of Performability Engineering*; Springer: London, UK, 2008.
34. McGeoch, C.C.; Harris, R.; Reinhardt, S.P.; Bunyk, P. Practical Annealing-Based Quantum Computing, Whitepaper, D-Wave Systems. 2019. Available online: https://www.dwavesys.com/media/vh5jmyka/ (accessed on 1 September 2022).

35. Holland, J.H. Genetic Algorithms. *Sci. Am.* **1992**, *267*, 66–73. Available online: http://www.jstor.org/stable/24939139 (accessed on 1 September 2022). [CrossRef]
36. De Jong, K.A. *Evolutionary Computation: A unified Approach*; MIT Press: Cambridge, MA, USA, 2006.
37. Dantzig, G.B.L. *Linear Programming and Extensions*; Princeton University Press: Princeton, NJ, USA, 1963.
38. Albert, A.A. *A Measure of the Effort Required to Increase Reliability*; Technical Report, No. 43; Stanfort University, Applied Mathematics and Statistics Laboratory: Stanford, CA, USA, 1958.

Article

Hateful Memes Detection Based on Multi-Task Learning

Zhiyu Ma [1,2], Shaowen Yao [1,2], Liwen Wu [1,2], Song Gao [1,2] and Yunqi Zhang [1,2,3,*]

1. Engineering Research Center of Cyberspace, Yunnan University, Kunming 650091, China
2. School of Software, Yunnan University, Kunming 650091, China
3. Yunnan Key Laboratory of Statistical Modeling and Data Analysis, School of Mathematics and Statistics, Yunnan University, Kunming 650091, China
* Correspondence: yunqizhang@ynu.edu.cn

Abstract: With the popularity of posting memes on social platforms, the severe negative impact of hateful memes is growing. As existing detection models have lower detection accuracy than humans, hateful memes detection is still a challenge to statistical learning and artificial intelligence. This paper proposed a multi-task learning method consisting of a primary multimodal task and two unimodal auxiliary tasks to address this issue. We introduced a self-supervised generation strategy in auxiliary tasks to generate unimodal auxiliary labels automatically. Meanwhile, we used BERT and RESNET as the backbone for text and image classification, respectively, and then fusion them with a late fusion method. In the training phase, the backward guidance technique and the adaptive weight adjustment strategy were used to capture the consistency and variability between different modalities, numerically improving the hateful memes detection accuracy and the generalization and robustness of the model. The experiment conducted on the Facebook AI multimodal hateful memes dataset shows that the prediction accuracy of our model outperformed the comparing models.

Keywords: hateful memes; deep learning; multimodal data; multi-task learning; self-supervised

MSC: 68T07

Citation: Ma, Z.; Yao, S.; Wu, L.; Gao, S.; Zhang, Y. Hateful Memes Detection Based on Multi-Task Learning. *Mathematics* **2022**, *10*, 4525. https://doi.org/10.3390/math10234525

Academic Editors: Florin Leon, Mircea Hulea and Marius Gavrilescu

Received: 29 October 2022
Accepted: 26 November 2022
Published: 30 November 2022

Publisher's Note: MDPI stays neutral with regard to jurisdictional claims in published maps and institutional affiliations.

Copyright: © 2022 by the authors. Licensee MDPI, Basel, Switzerland. This article is an open access article distributed under the terms and conditions of the Creative Commons Attribution (CC BY) license (https://creativecommons.org/licenses/by/4.0/).

1. Introduction

Memes are an element of a cultural or behavioral system transmitted from one person to another through imitation or other non-genetic behaviors. Memes come in various types and formats, including but not limited to images, videos, or posts, which are increasingly influential on social platforms. The vast amount of memes on the Internet constitutes an eye-catching problem. Memes not only express people's natural emotions but may also cause emotional damage to someone. The most popular form of memes is images containing text, which is the type we are interested in. Usually, an ordinary sentence or a picture does not have any special emotional meaning, but when combined, they become meaningful. Hateful memes thus emerge and are becoming an increasingly serious problem in modern society. People with malignant motives use such memes, with misleading content, hateful speech, and harmful images, to attack vulnerable people or target people.

Nowadays, social giants such as Facebook, Twitter, and Weibo, are engaged in identifying hateful memes and removing thousands of hateful memes to protect users. However, it is impossible to have humans detect every meme on a massive Internet scale manually. Researchers have explored statistical tools [1,2] and machine learning techniques [3,4] with optimization algorithms [5] to address this issue. The probability upper bounds of the generalization errors of simple models are well studied [6,7], but statisticians are still struggling to explain the generalization ability of large artificial neural networks [8]. Meanwhile, machines cannot understand contextual information like humans, and detecting hateful memes is still a challenging study for statistical learning and artificial intelligence. Owing to the development of sentiment analysis (hate is one emotion) and artificial intelligence, we can build our research on the work of previous researchers [9–12]. However, the available sentiment analysis methods have limited usefulness in practice because hate is not always as easy to identify as other emotions, and they do not explain generalization ability statistically. Most early studies for hateful memes focused on unimodal hateful text detection, classifying hateful, abusive, or offensive texts against individuals or groups according to gender, nationality, or sexual orientation [13,14]. These studies for hate detection are enlightening, but they cannot handle hateful memes detection, which combines visual and textual elements. In addition, some hateful attacks against specific groups are very subtle. To further improve the accuracy of detecting hateful memes, we have to extend them to multimodal learning.

Baltrušaitis et al. [15] figured that difficulties and challenges in multimodal learning are representation, translation, alignment, fusion, and co-learning, while representation learning may be the most critical impact on multimodal learning. According to the difference of guidance in representation learning, the existing methods are divided into forward guidance and backward guidance. The forward guidance projects unimodal representations together into a shared subspace [16] with the interaction module for obtaining information on different modalities [10,17–19]. However, the uniformity of multimodal labels makes it difficult to get information in a single modality. Backward guidance adds extra regularization terms to the optimization objectives [20] to guide feature learning by gradient descent and thus learn the variability across modalities [21,22], and we prefer this method.

Multi-task Learning is a learning paradigm in machine learning that learns multiple related tasks jointly and leverages useful information contained in multiple related tasks [23]. It can learn multiple related tasks together simultaneously and maximize the use of information from each modal in multimodal data. Therefore, it can be further used to enhance the accuracy of hateful meme detection. Usually, multi-task learning is designed with a primary classification task and some auxiliary tasks to enhance the feature learning capability. Nevertheless, this leads to a problem coming with a requirement of independent labels for auxiliary tasks, which is time-consuming and labor-intensive [22] by manual labeling. Yu et al. [24] designed a self-supervised unimodal label generation module to overcome this problem. This method can automatically get appropriate labels without requiring access to any further data.

Thus, we proposed a new idea to detect hateful memes using a multi-task learning method to balance the unilateral information exacting from different modalities separately and the fuzzy information from the multimodal without introducing further data or manual labels and reduce the generalization errors. We conducted a primary task to learn multimodal features and classify hateful memes. Meanwhile, two auxiliary tasks were used in the training phase to learn unimodal features and classify the hate of text and images. Moreover, we used two self-supervised label generation modules to generate unimodal labels in auxiliary tasks automatically. Finally, we applied our method to the Facebook AI hateful memes data sets [25] and achieved competitive results. In contrast with the previous works, the main contributions of this work are as follows:

- A new artificial intelligence model is proposed for hateful memes detection. It effectively improved the hateful memes detection accuracy in that our model outperformed the comparing models.
- The multi-task strategy and adaptive weight adjustment strategy used in our model captured the consistency and variability between different modalities and numerically improved the generalization and robustness of the model.
- Our auxiliary tasks using self-supervised unimodal auxiliary label generation module enhanced the feature learning capability without human-defined labels or additional data.

The remaining part of this paper is organized as follows. Section 2 introduces related works. Section 3 shows our hateful memes detection model's framework and algorithm.

Next, experiments with real data and their results are presented in Section 4. Section 5 summarizes this work.

2. Related Works

Hateful memes detection is a binary classification task from multimodal data containing text and images. As detection accuracy is still a big challenge for this task, we want to introduce a multi-task learning strategy into our model to address it. So we review some text, image, and multimodal classification models and bring ideas from them together with multi-task learning.

2.1. Datasets

As research on multimodal sentiment analysis constantly evolves, many multimodal sentiment analysis datasets have emerged. The CMU-MOSEI dataset [26] is one of the enormous trimodal sentiment analysis datasets and has both sentiment and emotion labels. It contains seven categories of sentiment, from negative to positive, and six categories of emotion, including anger, happiness, sadness, surprise, fear, and disgust. This CMU-MOSEI dataset has been extensively studied in the literature.

However, hate is a special emotion, and the expression of hateful emotion is subtle and not easy to detect, requiring more appropriate reasoning. A growing number of researchers are focusing on the study of hate analysis, especially for multimodal hateful memes detection. MMHS150K [27] is another multimodal hateful speech dataset collected and annotated from Twitter, consisting of images and text. Facebook announced the launch of a competition called the "Hateful Memes Challenge" with over 10,000 "hateful memes," which will be used as a data set [25]. It is also a multimodal dataset consisting of images and text, but it uses methods such as "benign confounders" to make its hateful samples challenging to distinguish by unimodal methods.

2.2. Textual Model

Much of the early research on hate detection was related to hateful text detection. Warner et al. [28] developed a support vector machine (SVM) classifier to detect offensive languages. The classifier can distinguish the features extracted from the text and classify whether a given text is malicious. At the same time, Djuric et al. [29] proposed using N-gram features to classify whether the text is offensive. As hateful text detection is a binary classification problem, many deep learning models are also available. TextCNN [30] has been proven to have good performance early, and a variety of more advanced models related to the task [31–36] have emerged in recent years. Among them, the best-performing model is BERT (Bidirectional Encoder Representation from Transformers) [37]. It is a pre-trained model proposed by Google AI Research to learn bidirectional representations with the help of Transformer [38]. By using an attention mechanism with Transformer, BERT can process entire sequences in parallel to collect information about the context of a word and encode it in a rich vector to represent it. The commonly used BERT has two versions, $BERT_{BASE}$ (L = 12, H = 768, A = 12, Total Parameters = 110 M) and $BERT_{LARGE}$ (L = 24, H = 1024, A = 16, Total Parameters = 340 M), where L is the number of layers (Transformer blocks), H is the hidden size, and A is the number of self-attention heads. The pre-trained BERT is a highly generalizable model that no longer needs to be trained with large datasets in a specific task, saving time and efficiency. Figure 1 shows the architecture of BERT.

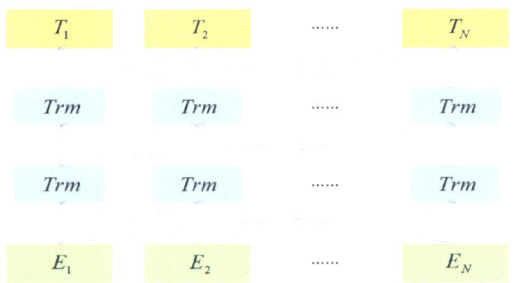

Figure 1. The structure of BERT using the structure of bidirectional transformer [37].

2.3. Visual Model

Another important part of memes is the image. Among many developed image classification models, they have their unique characteristics, and the research with the most significant progress is on neural networks for extracting image information. Early researchers focused on the analysis of convolutional neural networks, such as VGG (Visual Geometry Group) [39] and RESNET (Residual Neural Network) [40]. VGG is a large model with a few fully connected 3×3 convolution kernels, and it is famous for regularly designed, simple, and stackable convolution blocks. Compared with VGG and other neural networks, the most significant advantage of RESNET is that it introduces an identity mapping to construct a Residual Unit to calculate the residuals and solve the degradation problem generated by the high number of layers. RESNET has different versions depending on the number of convolution layer blocks, and five standard versions are RESNET18, RESNET34, RESNET50, RESNET101, and RESNET152. Figure 2 shows the architecture of RESNET18 as an example. Recently, many studies proved that the dependence on CNNs is unnecessary, and the Transformer model based on attention strategy can also perform well [41]. Currently, both of them are extensively applied to image classification tasks.

Figure 2. The structure of RESNET18 for ImagNet [40].

2.4. Multimodal Model

As hateful memes detection is a multimodal classification task, fusion techniques and attention strategies for multimodal models can be used. Many late fusion models have outstanding performance, such as the concatenation model [42] and the multiplicative combining model [43]. This concatenation fusion model [42] fused image features based on the VGG16 with text features based on BERT to train a multi-Layer perception network for hate detection. This multiplicative combining model [43] may automatically focus on information from more reliable modalities while reducing the emphasis on the less reliable modalities during the training process. Later more advanced multimodal models [44–50] were studied and designed. They extracted visual-textual relationships by introducing an attention strategy. These models can be divided into two main categories, single-stream models and dual-stream models. In the single-stream model, the language information and the visual information were fused at the beginning and fed directly into the encoder together. A typical single-stream model is VisualBERT [49], which inputs both text and images into the model, then aligns and fuses the text and image information through Transformer's self-attention. In the dual-stream model, the language and vision information first passed through two separate encoder modules, and then the different modal information was fused through the cross transformer, for example, the ViLBERT [50] model. It is a representative dual-stream model, which does not directly fuse linguistic and image information at the beginning. Instead, the image and text go through two different streams into the co-attention transformer layer first. Then the two streams pass through multiple layers of intersecting co-transformer and transformer layers. This allows the corresponding visual information to be embedded when generating text features by attention and vice versa.

2.5. Multi-Task Learning

Multi-task learning is prevalent in multimodal sentiment analysis [22,51–53], but few people have applied multi-task learning to hateful meme detection. As multi-task learning can improve performance on a primary task by using information from auxiliary tasks [23], we want to bring this idea to hateful memes detection. We can learn similarity information from multimodal tasks and differentiation information from unimodal tasks to improve classification accuracy. There are two main challenges to multi-task learning in the training phase compared to single-task learning. The first is how to share network parameters, and the leading solutions are soft parameter sharing and hard parameter sharing methods. Hard parameter sharing is achieved by sharing the hidden layer among all tasks while keeping a few task-specific output layers. For soft parameter sharing, each task has a separate model with its exclusive parameters. The distance between the model parameters is used as a regularization term to ensure that the parameters are as similar as possible. Another challenge is to solve the problem of inconsistent convergence speed and training importance of different tasks. We can refer to some optimization methods to solve this problem, such as Gradnorm [54]. So, we introduced two unimodal auxiliary tasks to help the primary task improve its accuracy in the hateful memes detection task. Meanwhile, we used the hard parameter sharing method and an adaptive weight adjustment strategy to solve the two challenges we faced.

3. Method

This paper aims to design a model that can balance the unilateral information exacting from different modalities separately and the fuzzy information from the multimodal without introducing further data or manual labels and reduce generalization errors. Nowadays, modern methods for predicting and understanding data are rooted in both statistical and computational thinking, and algorithmics are put on equal footing with intuition, properties, and the abstract arguments behind them [55]. So we proposed a new hateful memes detection method combing statistic theory with modern neural nets and optimization algorithms. And we will describe it detailly in this section.

First, we introduced the setup of our model to illustrate the inputs and outputs. Next, we constructed the multi-task learning model with a primary multimodal task and two unimodal auxiliary tasks to capture the consistency and variability between different modalities. As we only have manually labeled labels (y_m) in the dataset for the primary task, we adopt a self-supervised method [24] to generate the unimodal labels (y_u). And then, we designed an adaptive weight in our objective function to optimize this model and reduce the generalization errors. In the following, we call multimodal labels m-labels and unimodal labels u-labels, where $u = t, v$.

3.1. Setup

Hateful memes detection is a binary classification task that uses text and image signals to judge whether a meme is hateful. Our designed model takes I_t and I_v as inputs after data processing and the hateful intensity $\hat{y}_m \in R$ as outputs. In addition to the primary multimodal classification output $\hat{y}_m$, two unimodal auxiliary task outputs $\hat{y}_t$ and $\hat{y}_v$ are also set to improve the accuracy in the training phase. Obviously, $\hat{y}_m$ is the final result we are interested in.

3.2. Architecture

We designed a multi-task learning model that can generate auxiliary labels in a self-supervised way to detect multimodal hateful memes, as shown in Figure 3. The network consists of a primary multimodal task using BERT and RESNET to extract features and two unimodal auxiliary tasks that share the bottom feature learning network in a hard parameter sharing method.

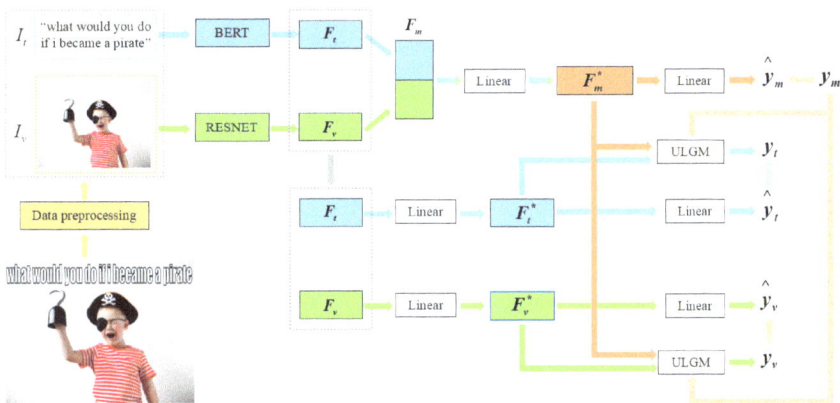

Figure 3. The architecture of our method. y_m is the labeled multimodal label in the dataset, and y_t, y_v are the auxiliary labels generated by the self-supervised label generation module for the unimodal text and image auxiliary tasks, respectively. $\hat{y}_m$ is the predicted output of the primary multimodal task, $\hat{y}_t$, $\hat{y}_v$ are the predicted outputs of the unimodal text and image auxiliary tasks, respectively.

The primary task part is a multimodal classification net, which consists of three steps, the extraction of features, the fusion of features, and the output of classification. Pre-trained models have performed very well in recent years, so we used two pre-trained models as the backbone for two unimodal tasks in the hateful memes detection task.

For text processing, we use the pre-trained twelve-layers BERT [37] to extract text feature F_t.

$$F_t = BERT\left(I_t; \theta_t^{bert}\right),$$

where I_t is the text input, θ_t^{bert} is all parameters of the BERT we used.

For image processing, we use the pre-trained RESNET101 [40] to extract image feature F_v.

$$F_v = RESNET\left(I_v; \theta_v^{resnet}\right),$$

where I_v is the image input, θ_v^{resnet} is all parameters of the RESNET we used.

Then, the text and image representations are concatenated as $F_m = [F_t; F_v]$ and projected onto a low-dimensional space.

$$F_m^* = \sigma(W_1^m F_m + b_1^m),$$

where W_1^m and b_1^m are the parameters of the first linear layer in the primary multimodal task, σ is the activation function.

After that, we use the representation of fusion obtained from the linear layer and activation function to detect whether the meme is hateful.

$$\hat{y}_m = W_2^m F_m^* + b_2^m,$$

where $W_2 \in R^{d_m \times 1}$, and W_2^m and b_2^m are the parameters of the second linear layer in the multimodal primary task.

The auxiliary tasks are two unimodal classification tasks that detect the presence of hateful sentiment in text and images, respectively. We project the unimodal features into a new feature space, which reduces the impact of the dimensional difference between different modalities. Moreover, the text and image auxiliary classification tasks share modal features with the primary multimodal classification task.

$$F_u^* = \sigma(W_1^u F_u + b_1^u),$$

where $u \in \{t, v\}$, W_1^u and b_1^u are parameters of the first linear layer in the unimodal auxiliary task.

Then, the results of unimodal auxiliary tasks are obtained by

$$\hat{y}_u = W_2^u F_u^* + b_2^u,$$

where $u \in \{t, v\}$, W_2^u and b_2^u are parameters of the second linear layer in the unimodal auxiliary task.

3.3. Unimodal Label Generation Module

While we need corresponding labels to guide the training in the two unimodal auxiliary tasks, and manual labeling is too costly, we adopt a strategy of self-supervised label generation to obtain u-labels. We call this module the "Unimodal Label Generation Module" (ULGM), that is

$$y_u = ULGM(y_m, F_m^*, F_u^*),$$

where $u \in \{t, v\}$.

The ULGM generates labels for unimodal auxiliary tasks based on multimodal labels and the feature of each modality. The unimodal label generation module does not have any parameters, which makes it a stand-alone module without any impact on the multitask network. Based on the fact that unimodal labels are closely related to multimodal labels, this module calculates the offset value based on the distance between each modal representation to the center of the hateful class and the non-hateful class.

Here, we calculate the relative distance rather than absolute distance values, which overcomes the error introduced by different modal features in different feature spaces. First, we keep the center of the hateful class (C_k^h) and the center of the not-hateful class (C_k^n) unchanged for different modal features in the training phase. And the hateful class center and the not-hateful class center can be defined as:

$$C_k^h = \frac{\sum_{j=1}^N I\left(y_{kj} > c\right) \cdot F_{kj}^g}{\sum_{j=1}^N I\left(y_{kj} > c\right)},$$

$$C_k^n = \frac{\sum_{j=1}^N I\left(y_{kj} < c\right) \cdot F_{kj}^g}{\sum_{j=1}^N I\left(y_{kj} < c\right)}, \quad (1)$$

where $k \in \{m, t, v\}$, N is the sample size of the training set. $I(\cdot)$ is an indicator function and F_{kj}^g is the global representation of the j-th sample in modality k, and c is a threshold value, which we chose it as 0.5 in our experiment.

Then we use the L2 norm to calculate the distance between features and the hateful/not-hateful class centers, that is

$$D_k^h = \frac{\left\|F_k^* - C_k^h\right\|_2^2}{\sqrt{d_k}},$$
$$D_k^n = \frac{\left\|F_k^* - C_k^n\right\|_2^2}{\sqrt{d_k}}, \quad (2)$$

where $k \in \{m, t, v\}$, d_k is a scaling factor used to represent the dimensions.

After doing the above calculations, we can calculate the relative distance α_k between the modality representation and the hateful/not-hateful center with

$$\alpha_k = \frac{D_k^n - D_k^h}{D_k^h + \epsilon}, \quad (3)$$

where $k \in \{m, t, v\}$, ϵ is a very small number to avoid zero exception.

Obviously, α_k is positively related to y_k, then the ratio relationship between y_u and y_m can be summarised as:

$$\frac{y_u}{y_m} \propto \frac{\hat{y}_u}{\hat{y}_m} \propto \frac{\alpha_u}{\alpha_m} \Rightarrow y_u = \frac{\alpha_u \cdot y_m}{\alpha_m}. \quad (4)$$

To avoid the "zero value problem", the difference relationship between y_s and y_m should also be considered, which means:

$$(y_u - y_m) \propto (\hat{y}_u - \hat{y}_m) \propto (\alpha_u - \alpha_m) \Rightarrow y_u = y_m + \alpha_u - \alpha_m. \quad (5)$$

By equal-weight summation Equations (4) and (5), we obtain the unimodal supervisions as follows.

$$\begin{aligned} y_u &= \frac{y_m \cdot \alpha_u}{2\alpha_m} + \frac{y_m + \alpha_u - \alpha_m}{2} \\ &= y_m + \frac{\alpha_u - \alpha_m}{2} \cdot \frac{y_m + \alpha_m}{\alpha_m} \\ &= y_m + \delta_{um}, \end{aligned} \quad (6)$$

where $u \in \{t, v\}$, δ_{um} is the offset value of the unimodal supervision values to the given multimodal labels.

3.4. Optimization Objectives

In the case of a binary classification task, since there are only positive and negative cases, and the probability sum of both is 1, it is not necessary to predict a vector, but only a probability. We choose the cross-entropy loss of binary classification as the base optimization objective, and the loss function is defined in a simplified way as follows.

$$loss_k = -[y_k \cdot \log(\hat{y}_k) + (1 - y_k) \cdot \log(1 - \hat{y}_k)], \quad (7)$$

where $k \in \{m, t, v\}$.

As the hateful memes data are complicated with two modalities, we designed multi-task learning to make the statistical inference. When we optimize the model, the extracted information may be fuzzy if we pay too much attention to the multimodal part. However, if we pay too much attention to the unimodal part, the extracted information may be much unilateral and weaken our primary task. In addition, the gradient magnitudes of the backpropagation of several tasks' losses may differ. When backpropagating to the shared bottom part, the task with a small gradient magnitude has less weight to update the model parameters, making the shared bottom not learn enough for that task. Of course, we can simply introduce static weights to balance the gradients for different tasks. However, this does not work well. If we assigned a fixed weight for a task with a large gradient magnitude at the beginning of training, this small weight would keep limiting this task by the end of the training, making this task not learned enough and enhancing the generalization errors [56,57]. Meanwhile, information may be with different intensities among different samples. Suppose the difference between the multimodal label $y_m^{(i)}$ and the generated unimodal label $\hat{y}_u^{(i)}$ is large. In that case, the results from different modalities are diverging, and we should impose a larger weight on this sample to learn more information. Therefore, a data-driving weight should be imposed on different samples so that the objective function can be adaptively adjusted to balance the learning process.

Thus, we use the absolute difference between the generated unimodal label and the existing multimodal label as a measure for weight adjustment, that is, $|y_u^{(i)} - y_m|$. As we want to make more significant adjustments for samples with large distances and slight adjustments for samples with small distances, an 'S'-type function $\in (0,1)$ may be preferred, such as $tanh(\cdot)$, $eliot(\cdot)$, $arctan(\cdot)$ and $logit(\cdot)$. We chose $tanh(\cdot)$ here to get more adjustment for the samples with large distances with rapid change, and the weight of i_{th} sample for auxiliary task u can be expressed as $\omega_u^i = tanh(|y_u^{(i)} - y_m|)$. Then the optimization objective is

$$L = \frac{1}{N} \sum_j^N \left(loss_m^j + \sum_u^{\{t,v\}} \omega_u^j * loss_u^j \right), \tag{8}$$

where N is the sample size, $loss_m^j$ is the binary cross-entropy loss between multimodal labels and multimodal predictions of the j-th sample, $loss_u^j$ is the binary cross-entropy loss between the self-supervised generated unimodal labels and the unimodal predictions of the j-th sample.

While the modal representations are changing dynamically, so the generated auxiliary labels are unstable. In order to mitigate the influence of this disadvantage, a momentum update strategy is introduced.

$$y_u^{(i)} = \begin{cases} y_m & i = 1 \\ \frac{i-1}{i+1} y_s^{(i-1)} + \frac{2}{i+1} y_s^i & i > 1 \end{cases}, \tag{9}$$

where $u \in \{t,v\}$, i means the i-th epoch [58].

Finally, supervised by the m-labels in the dataset and the u-labels generated by the self-supervised module, the final result $\hat{y}_m$ for detecting whether each meme is hateful or not can be obtained. Overall, the entire algorithm (Algorithm 1) of our model is defined as follows:

Algorithm 1: The algorithm of our model in training stage [24]

Input: m-labels y_m and unimodal inputs I_u, where $u \in \{t, v\}$
Output: predicted u-labels $\hat{y}_u$ and predicted m-labels $\hat{y}_m$
1 **Initialize** all the parameters θ of the model ;
2 **Initialize** $y_u^{(1)} = y_m^{(1)}$, where $u \in \{t, v\}$;
3 **Initialize** global representations $F_k^g = 0$, where $k \in \{m, t, v\}$;
4 **for** $n \in [1, end]$ **do**
5   **for** *batch in TrainDataLoader* **do**
6   Compute modality represenations of each batch F_k^*, where $k \in \{m, t, v\}$;
7   Compute loss L using Equation (8) ;
8   Compute parameters gradient $\frac{\partial L}{\partial \theta}$;
9   Update parameters of model $\theta = \theta - \eta \frac{\partial L}{\partial \theta}$, where η is the learning rate ;
10   Compute the predicted labels $\hat{y}_k^{(n)}$, where $k \in \{m, t, v\}$;
11   **if** $n \neq 1$ **then**
12   Compute α_k using Equations (1) $\sim$ (3), where $k \in \{m, t, v\}$;
13   Compute y_u using Equation (6), where $u \in \{t, v\}$;
14   Update $y_u^{(n)}$ using Equation (9), where $u \in \{t, v\}$;
15   **end**
16   Update F_k^g using F_k^*, where $k \in \{m, t, v\}$;
17   **end**
18 **end**
19 **return**
---

4. Experiments

4.1. Dataset

To validate the performance of our model, we choose the hateful memes dataset in the "Hateful Memes Challenge" [25] published by Facebook AI as our experimental dataset. It is a dataset of over 10,000 strictly labeled memes, where the memes are manually labeled as hate or not with a strict definition. The researchers carefully designed each meme and confounded the hateful memes with the benign memes by methods such as "benign confounders", as shown in Figure 4. These subtle designs make each meme challenging to detect accurately by unimodal detection methods and must be reasoned about both text and image to obtain accurate detection results.

Figure 4. Example pictures in the experimental dataset. The memes in the first column are all hateful memes, the second column replaces only their images to make them not hateful, and the third column replaces only their text to make them not hateful.

4.2. Compared Models

We compared our model with different advanced unimodal, multimodal models described in [59]. All models can be classified into two categories, unimodal models and multimodal models.

Unimodal models include the image and text classification models, while image classification models include Image-Grid and Image-Region regarding different features. Features of Image-Grid are ResNet-152 [40] convolutional features and are based on res-5c with average pooling. Features of Image-Region are from the fc6 layer of Faster-RCNN [60] and are based on ResNeXt-152. The text classification model is the Twelve-layer BERT.

Multimodal models include Late Fusion, Concat BERT, MMBT-Grid, MMBT-Region, ViLBERT, and VisualBERT. Late Fusion is a model that fused the mean of outputs of the unimodal text model BERT and the unimodal image model ResNet-152 through simple fusion methods. Concat BERT is a model that concatenates the unimodal image model ResNet-152 feature with the unimodal text model BERT. MMBT-Grid and MMBT-Region are both supervised multimodal transformers models, the former using Image-Grid features and the latter using Image-Region features. VisualBERT [49] is a single-stream model in which the text and image features are fused at the beginning of the model. ViLBERT and VisualBERT can be pretrained on unimodal and multimodal datasets. ViLBERT [50] model is a dual-stream model, where text and image features are first passed through two separate encoding modules. Then the different modal information is fused through a co-attention mechanism. We use VisualBERT and ViLBERT with unimodal pretraining, Visualbert COCO is VisualBERT trained on multimodal dataset COCO [61] and ViLBERT CC is ViLBERT trained on multimodal dataset Conceptual Captions [62].

4.3. Results

We compared the results of our model with all kinds of unimodal and multimodal models on the hateful memes dataset. The activation function in our model is selected as ReLU, and the threshold value to calculate the hateful/not-hatful class center is set as 0.5. The results of compared models on the dataset were from [59]. For the unimodal models, it can be found that their performance is generally less satisfactory. In addition, the unimodal text model outperformed the unimodal image model, reflecting the fact that the text features may contain more information. For the multimodal models, they outperformed the unimodal models. We also found that the fusion method affects their performance, while models using early fusion methods outperformed those using later fusion methods. For the multimodal pretrained process, there was little difference between the multimodal pretrained model and the unimodal pretrained model.

In contrast to the models mentioned above, our model used a late fusion method and two unimodal pre-training models. Although the late fusion method generally performed worse than the early fusion method, our model outperformed those early fusion models. Thanks to the additional auxiliary learning, which validated the idea that adding multi-task learning to hateful meme detection can improve the accuracy of the task. Moreover, it may help to fuse different unimodal pre-training models using our method in future studies for similar tasks. Prediction accuracy results of these models are presented in Table 1.

Table 1. The prediction accuracy of different models on the "Hateful Memes Challenge" data set.

Type	Model	Validation	Test
Unimodal	Image-Grid	52.73%	52.00%
	Image-Region	52.66%	52.13%
	Text BERT	58.26%	59.20%
Multimodal	Late Fusion	61.53%	59.66%
	Concat BERT	58.60%	59.13%
	MMBT-Grid	58.20%	60.06%
	MMBT-Region	58.73%	60.23%
	ViLBERT	62.20%	62.30%
	Visual BERT	62.10%	63.20%
	ViLBERT CC	61.40%	61.10%
	Visual BERT COCO	65.06%	64.73%
	Our model	65.92%	66.30%

The results of compared models on the dataset are from [59]. We show the best performance results of our model on Accuracy.

4.4. Ablation Study

We added a self-supervised multi-task learning of generating auxiliary labels to the task of hateful memes detection, which did greatly improve its accuracy. However, we wanted to further investigate the effect of each unimodal auxiliary learning on the overall model. Therefore, we set up this experiment to test the model by adding each unimodal auxiliary task separately and comparing the results in Table 2.

Table 2. The prediction accuracy of the multi-task learning models with the addition of different unimodal auxiliary tasks.

Model	Validation	Test
M	61.92%	63.40%
M,T_E	62.67%	63.10%
M,V_E	62.05%	62.24%
M,T	62.83%	63.45%
M,V	62.33%	62.60%
M,T_E,V_E	63.00%	64.65%
M,T,V	65.92%	66.30%

M is the model with the primary task of a multimodal classification only; M, T_E is the model with a primary task of multimodal classification and an auxiliary task of text classification using equal weights with $\omega_u^j = 1$; M, V_E is the model with a primary task of multimodal classification and an auxiliary task of image classification using equal weights with $\omega_u^j = 1$; M, T is the model with a primary task of multimodal classification and an auxiliary task of text classification; M, V is the model with a primary task of multimodal classification and an auxiliary task of image classification; M, T_E, V_E is the model with a primary task of multimodal classification and two auxiliary tasks including text and image classification using equal weights with $\omega_u^j = 1$; M, T, V is the model with a primary task of multimodal classification and two auxiliary tasks including text and image classification.

These results indicated that the accuracy of the multi-task model only with the unimodal textual auxiliary or only with the unimodal visual auxiliary task is very similar in hateful meme detection. Furthermore, both the results were also very close compared to the multimodal task, which showed that the accuracy of detecting hateful memes could hardly be improved by adding a single unimodal auxiliary task alone. In contrast, the multi-task learning model was greatly enhanced with the addition of a unimodal textual auxiliary task and a unimodal visual auxiliary task. Moreover, all the cases optimized using equal weights with $\omega_u^j = 1$ performed worse than the same model using the adaptive weight adjustment strategy. In conclusion, the multi-task learning and the adaptive weight adjustment strategy helped improve the testing accuracy and reduce the generation errors.

5. Conclusions

Our research aims to improve the accuracy and reduce generalization errors of detecting hateful memes, which are widely available on the Internet and have severe negative impacts. For this purpose, we selected a multimodal dataset of hateful memes published by Facebook AI as our experimental dataset. Moreover, we designed a multi-task learning model that can generate auxiliary labels self-supervised. A text classification model BERT and an image classification model RESNET were selected as the backbone, and a late fusion method was used. In the multi-task learning network, we added two unimodal auxiliary learning tasks, the textual and the visual auxiliary task, to the primary classification task. In order to solve the problem of lacking labels for the unimodal auxiliary tasks and the high cost of manual labeling, we chose a strategy of self-supervised label generation for the auxiliary tasks. In the phrase of optimization, we added a data-driving adaptive weight adjustment strategy to balance the learning process and reduce the generalization errors. By comparing our multi-task learning model with various advanced models for the detection of hateful memes, we can find that our multi-task learning model achieved more accurate results.

In the ablation experiments, we also found that it is difficult to improve the accuracy of the final classification results by simply adding a single unimodal auxiliary task to the multi-task learning network. Both the text and image auxiliary tasks should be introduced to the model to achieve better results. In addition to the good performance of the results, our method can easily be extended to fuse other unimodal models to solve similar problems. Although our experiments achieved good results, there is still much room for improvement. Our model and existing multimodal models are still far from reaching the accuracy of humans (84.7%) for the task. We are trying to improve the accuracy of hateful meme detection from other perspective. One is improving the adaptability of the backbone model and the multi-task learning network. Another is improving the feature fusion methods.

Author Contributions: Conceptualization, Y.Z. and S.Y.; software, Z.M. and S.G.; validation, Y.Z.; formal analysis, Z.M., L.W. and S.G.; investigation, Y.Z. and L.W.; resources, Y.Z., L.W. and S.Y.; writing—original draft preparation, Z.M. and Y.Z.; writing—review and editing, Y.Z. and S.G.; visualization, Z.M.; supervision, Y.Z. and S.Y.; project administration, Y.Z., L.W. and S.Y.; funding acquisition, Y.Z. and S.Y. All authors have read and agreed to the published version of the manuscript.

Funding: This research was funded by the National Natural Science Foundation of China (No. 61863036), the China Postdoctoral Science Foundation (No. 2021M702778), the Fundamental Research Funds for the Central Universities (No. 2042022KF0021), and the Fundamental Research Plan of "Release Management Service" in Yunnan Province: Research on Multi-source Data Platform and Situation Awareness Application for Cross-border Cyberspace Security (No. 202001BB050076).

Institutional Review Board Statement: Not applicable.

Informed Consent Statement: Not applicable.

Data Availability Statement: The datasets generated and analysed are available from the corresponding author on reasonable request.

Conflicts of Interest: The authors declare no conflict of interest.

References

1. Devroye, L.; Györfi, L.; Lugosi, G. *A Probabilistic Theory of Pattern Recognition*; Springer Science & Business Media: New York, NY, USA, 2013; Volume 31.
2. Fan, J.; Li, R.; Zhang, C.H.; Zou, H. *Statistical Foundations of Data Science*; Chapman and Hall/CRC: New York, NY, USA, 2020.
3. Hastie, T.; Tibshirani, R.; Friedman, J.H.; Friedman, J.H. *The Elements of Statistical Learning: Data Mining, Inference, and Prediction*; Springer: Berlin/Heidelberg, Germany, 2009; Volume 2.
4. Mohri, M.; Rostamizadeh, A.; Talwalkar, A. *Foundations of Machine Learning*; MIT Press: Cambridge, MA, USA, 2018.
5. Bertsekas, D.P. Nonlinear programming. *J. Oper. Res. Soc.* **1997**, *48*, 334. [CrossRef]
6. Tewari, A.; Bartlett, P.L. On the Consistency of Multiclass Classification Methods. *J. Mach. Learn. Res.* **2007**, *8*, 1007–1025.
7. Zhang, T. Statistical analysis of some multi-category large margin classification methods. *J. Mach. Learn. Res.* **2004**, *5*, 1225–1251.
8. Vapnik, V.N. An overview of statistical learning theory. *IEEE Trans. Neural Netw.* **1999**, *10*, 988–999. [CrossRef] [PubMed]

9. Zadeh, A.; Chen, M.; Poria, S.; Cambria, E.; Morency, L.P. Tensor fusion network for multimodal sentiment analysis. *arXiv* **2017**, arXiv:1707.07250.
10. Tsai, Y.H.H.; Bai, S.; Liang, P.P.; Kolter, J.Z.; Morency, L.P.; Salakhutdinov, R. Multimodal transformer for unaligned multimodal language sequences. In Proceedings of the 57th Annual Meeting of the Association for Computational Linguistics, Florence, Italy, 28 July–2 August 2019; NIH Public Access: Bethesda, MD, USA, 2019; Volume 2019, p. 6558.
11. Poria, S.; Hazarika, D.; Majumder, N.; Mihalcea, R. Beneath the tip of the iceberg: Current challenges and new directions in sentiment analysis research. *IEEE Trans. Affect. Comput.* **2020**, 1. [CrossRef]
12. Bartlett, P.L.; Jordan, M.I.; McAuliffe, J.D. Convexity, classification, and risk bounds. *J. Am. Stat. Assoc.* **2006**, *101*, 138–156. [CrossRef]
13. i Orts, Ò.G. Multilingual detection of hate speech against immigrants and women in Twitter at SemEval-2019 task 5: Frequency analysis interpolation for hate in speech detection. In Proceedings of the 13th International Workshop on Semantic Evaluation, Minneapolis, MN, USA, 6–7 June 2019; pp. 460–463.
14. Burnap, P.; Williams, M.L. Hate speech, machine classification and statistical modelling of information flows on Twitter: Interpretation and communication for policy decision making. In Proceedings of the Internet, Policy & Politics Conference, Oxford, UK, 26 September 2014.
15. Baltrušaitis, T.; Ahuja, C.; Morency, L.P. Multimodal machine learning: A survey and taxonomy. *IEEE Trans. Pattern Anal. Mach. Intell.* **2018**, *41*, 423–443. [CrossRef]
16. Guo, W.; Wang, J.; Wang, S. Deep multimodal representation learning: A survey. *IEEE Access* **2019**, *7*, 63373–63394. [CrossRef]
17. Zadeh, A.; Liang, P.P.; Mazumder, N.; Poria, S.; Cambria, E.; Morency, L.P. Memory fusion network for multi-view sequential learning. In Proceedings of the AAAI Conference on Artificial Intelligence, New Orleans, LA, USA, 2–7 February 2018; Volume 32.
18. Sun, Z.; Sarma, P.; Sethares, W.; Liang, Y. Learning relationships between text, audio, and video via deep canonical correlation for multimodal language analysis. In Proceedings of the AAAI Conference on Artificial Intelligence, New York, NY, USA, 7–12 February 2020; Volume 34, pp. 8992–8999.
19. Rahman, W.; Hasan, M.K.; Lee, S.; Zadeh, A.; Mao, C.; Morency, L.P.; Hoque, E. Integrating multimodal information in large pretrained transformers. In Proceedings of the 58th Annual Meeting of the Association for Computational Linguistics (ACL 2020), online, 5–10 July 2020; NIH Public Access: Bethesda, MD, USA, 2020; Volume 2020, p. 2359.
20. Wang, S.; Zhang, H.; Wang, H. Object co-segmentation via weakly supervised data fusion. *Comput. Vis. Image Underst.* **2017**, *155*, 43–54. [CrossRef]
21. Hazarika, D.; Zimmermann, R.; Poria, S. Misa: Modality-invariant and-specific representations for multimodal sentiment analysis. In Proceedings of the 28th ACM International Conference on Multimedia, Seattle, WA, USA, 12–16 October 2020; pp. 1122–1131.
22. Yu, W.; Xu, H.; Meng, F.; Zhu, Y.; Ma, Y.; Wu, J.; Zou, J.; Yang, K. Ch-sims: A chinese multimodal sentiment analysis dataset with fine-grained annotation of modality. In Proceedings of the 58th Annual Meeting of the Association for Computational Linguistics, Online, 5–10 July 2020; pp. 3718–3727.
23. Zhang, Y.; Yang, Q. A survey on multi-task learning. *IEEE Trans. Knowl. Data Eng.* **2021**, *34*, 5586–5609. [CrossRef]
24. Yu, W.; Xu, H.; Yuan, Z.; Wu, J. Learning modality-specific representations with self-supervised multi-task learning for multimodal sentiment analysis. In Proceedings of the AAAI Conference on Artificial Intelligence, Virtually, 2–9 February 2021; Volume 35, pp. 10790–10797.
25. Kiela, D.; Firooz, H.; Mohan, A.; Goswami, V.; Singh, A.; Ringshia, P.; Testuggine, D. The hateful memes challenge: Detecting hate speech in multimodal memes. *Adv. Neural Inf. Process. Syst.* **2020**, *33*, 2611–2624.
26. Zadeh, A.B.; Liang, P.P.; Poria, S.; Cambria, E.; Morency, L.P. Multimodal language analysis in the wild: Cmu-mosei dataset and interpretable dynamic fusion graph. In Proceedings of the 56th Annual Meeting of the Association for Computational Linguistics, Melbourne, Australia, 15–20 July 2018; Volume 1: Long Papers, pp. 2236–2246.
27. Gomez, R.; Gibert, J.; Gomez, L.; Karatzas, D. Exploring hate speech detection in multimodal publications. In Proceedings of the IEEE/CVF Winter Conference on Applications of Computer Vision, Snowmass Village, CO, USA, 1–5 March 2020; pp. 1470–1478.
28. Warner, W.; Hirschberg, J. Detecting hate speech on the world wide web. In Proceedings of the Second Workshop on Language in Social Media, Montréal, QC, Canada, 7 June 2012; pp. 19–26.
29. Djuric, N.; Zhou, J.; Morris, R.; Grbovic, M.; Radosavljevic, V.; Bhamidipati, N. Hate speech detection with comment embeddings. In Proceedings of the 24th International Conference on World Wide Web, Florence, Italy, 18–22 May 2015; pp. 29–30.
30. Chen, Y. Convolutional Neural Network for Sentence Classification. Master's Thesis, University of Waterloo, Waterloo, ON, Canada, 2015.
31. Waseem, Z.; Davidson, T.; Warmsley, D.; Weber, I. Understanding abuse: A typology of abusive language detection subtasks. *arXiv* **2017**, arXiv:1705.09899.
32. Benikova, D.; Wojatzki, M.; Zesch, T. What does this imply? Examining the impact of implicitness on the perception of hate speech. In Proceedings of the International Conference of the German Society for Computational Linguistics and Language Technology, Berlin, Germany, 13–14 September 2017; Springer: Berlin/Heidelberg, Germany, 2017; pp. 171–179.
33. Wiegand, M.; Siegel, M.; Ruppenhofer, J. Overview of the germeval 2018 shared task on the identification of offensive language. In Proceedings of the 14th Conference on Natural Language Processing (KONVENS 2018), Vienna, Austria, 21 September 2018.
34. Kumar, R.; Ojha, A.K.; Malmasi, S.; Zampieri, M. Benchmarking aggression identification in social media. In Proceedings of the First Workshop on Trolling, Aggression and Cyberbullying (TRAC-2018), Santa Fe, NM, USA, 25 August 2018; pp. 1–11.

35. Nobata, C.; Tetreault, J.; Thomas, A.; Mehdad, Y.; Chang, Y. Abusive language detection in online user content. In Proceedings of the 25th International Conference on World Wide Web, Montreal, QC, Canada, 11–15 May 2016; pp. 145–153.
36. Aggarwal, P.; Horsmann, T.; Wojatzki, M.; Zesch, T. LTL-UDE at SemEval-2019 Task 6: BERT and two-vote classification for categorizing offensiveness. In Proceedings of the 13th International Workshop on Semantic Evaluation, Minneapolis, MN, USA, 6–7 June 2019; pp. 678–682.
37. Devlin, J.; Chang, M.W.; Lee, K.; Toutanova, K. Bert: Pre-training of deep bidirectional transformers for language understanding. *arXiv* **2018**, arXiv:1810.04805.
38. Vaswani, A.; Shazeer, N.; Parmar, N.; Uszkoreit, J.; Jones, L.; Gomez, A.N.; Kaiser, Ł.; Polosukhin, I. Attention is all you need. In *Advances in Neural Information Processing Systems*; NIPS: La Jolla, CA, USA, 2017 ; Volume 30.
39. Simonyan, K.; Zisserman, A. Very deep convolutional networks for large-scale image recognition. *arXiv* **2014**, arXiv:1409.1556.
40. He, K.; Zhang, X.; Ren, S.; Sun, J. Deep residual learning for image recognition. In Proceedings of the IEEE Conference on Computer Vision and Pattern Recognition, Las Vegas, NV, USA, 27–30 June 2016; pp. 770–778.
41. Dosovitskiy, A.; Beyer, L.; Kolesnikov, A.; Weissenborn, D.; Zhai, X.; Unterthiner, T.; Dehghani, M.; Minderer, M.; Heigold, G.; Gelly, S.; et al. An image is worth 16 × 16 words: Transformers for image recognition at scale. *arXiv* **2020**, arXiv:2010.11929.
42. Sabat, B.O.; Ferrer, C.C.; Giro-i Nieto, X. Hate speech in pixels: Detection of offensive memes towards automatic moderation. *arXiv* **2019**, arXiv:1910.02334.
43. Liu, K.; Li, Y.; Xu, N.; Natarajan, P. Learn to combine modalities in multimodal deep learning. *arXiv* **2018**, arXiv:1805.11730.
44. Chen, Y.C.; Li, L.; Yu, L.; El Kholy, A.; Ahmed, F.; Gan, Z.; Cheng, Y.; Liu, J. Uniter: Universal image-text representation learning. In Proceedings of the European Conference on Computer Vision, Glasgow, UK, 23–28 August 2020; Springer: Berlin/Heidelberg, Germany, 2020; pp. 104–120.
45. Li, X.; Yin, X.; Li, C.; Zhang, P.; Hu, X.; Zhang, L.; Wang, L.; Hu, H.; Dong, L.; Wei, F.; et al. Oscar: Object-semantics aligned pre-training for vision-language tasks. In Proceedings of the European Conference on Computer Vision, Glasgow, UK, 23–28 August 2020; Springer: Berlin/Heidelberg, Germany, 2020; pp. 121–137.
46. Su, W.; Zhu, X.; Cao, Y.; Li, B.; Lu, L.; Wei, F.; Dai, J. Vl-bert: Pre-training of generic visual-linguistic representations. *arXiv* **2019**, arXiv:1908.08530.
47. Aken, B.v.; Winter, B.; Löser, A.; Gers, F.A. Visbert: Hidden-state visualizations for transformers. In Proceedings of the Companion Proceedings of the Web Conference 2020, Taipei, Taiwan, 20–24 April 2020; pp. 207–211.
48. Yu, F.; Tang, J.; Yin, W.; Sun, Y.; Tian, H.; Wu, H.; Wang, H. Ernie-vil: Knowledge enhanced vision-language representations through scene graphs. In Proceedings of the AAAI Conference on Artificial Intelligence, Virtually, 2–9 February 2021; Volume 35, pp. 3208–3216.
49. Li, L.H.; Yatskar, M.; Yin, D.; Hsieh, C.J.; Chang, K.W. Visualbert: A simple and performant baseline for vision and language. *arXiv* **2019**, arXiv:1908.03557.
50. Lu, J.; Batra, D.; Parikh, D.; Lee, S. Vilbert: Pretraining task-agnostic visiolinguistic representations for vision-and-language tasks. In *Advances in Neural Information Processing Systems*; NIPS: La Jolla, CA, USA, 2019 ; Volume 32.
51. Liu, W.; Mei, T.; Zhang, Y.; Che, C.; Luo, J. Multi-task deep visual-semantic embedding for video thumbnail selection. In Proceedings of the IEEE Conference on Computer Vision and Pattern Recognition, Boston, MA, USA, 7–12 June 2015; pp. 3707–3715.
52. Zhang, W.; Li, R.; Zeng, T.; Sun, Q.; Kumar, S.; Ye, J.; Ji, S. Deep model based transfer and multi-task learning for biological image analysis. In Proceedings of the 21th ACM SIGKDD International Conference on Knowledge Discovery and Data Mining, Sydney, NSW, Australia, 10–13 August 2015; pp. 1475–1484.
53. Akhtar, M.S.; Chauhan, D.S.; Ghosal, D.; Poria, S.; Ekbal, A.; Bhattacharyya, P. Multi-task learning for multi-modal emotion recognition and sentiment analysis. *arXiv* **2019**, arXiv:1905.05812.
54. Chen, Z.; Badrinarayanan, V.; Lee, C.Y.; Rabinovich, A. Gradnorm: Gradient normalization for adaptive loss balancing in deep multitask networks. In Proceedings of the International Conference on Machine Learning (PMLR 2018), Stockholm, Sweden, 10–15 July 2018; pp. 794–803.
55. Efron, B.; Hastie, T. *Computer Age Statistical Inference, Student Edition: Algorithms, Evidence, and Data Science*; Cambridge University Press: Cambridge, UK, 2021; Volume 6.
56. Zhang, T. Statistical behavior and consistency of classification methods based on convex risk minimization. *Ann. Stat.* **2004**, *32*, 56–85. [CrossRef]
57. Chen, D.R.; Sun, T. Consistency of multiclass empirical risk minimization methods based on convex loss. *J. Mach. Learn. Res.* **2006**, *7*, 2435–2447.
58. Su, W.; Boyd, S.; Candes, E. A differential equation for modeling Nesterov's accelerated gradient method: Theory and insights. In *Advances in Neural Information Processing Systems*; NIPS: La Jolla, California, USA, 2014; Volume 27.
59. Sandulescu, V. Detecting hateful memes using a multimodal deep ensemble. *arXiv* **2020**, arXiv:2012.13235.
60. Mao, H.; Yao, S.; Tang, T.; Li, B.; Yao, J.; Wang, Y. Towards real-time object detection on embedded systems. *IEEE Trans. Emerg. Top. Comput.* **2016**, *6*, 417–431. [CrossRef]

61. Lin, T.Y.; Maire, M.; Belongie, S.; Hays, J.; Perona, P.; Ramanan, D.; Dollár, P.; Zitnick, C.L. Microsoft coco: Common objects in context. In Proceedings of the European Conference on Computer Vision, Zurich, Switzerland, 6–12 September 2014; Springer: Berlin/Heidelberg, Germany, 2014; pp. 740–755.
62. Mokady, R.; Hertz, A.; Bermano, A.H. Clipcap: Clip prefix for image captioning. *arXiv* **2021**, arXiv:2111.09734.

Article

Manifold Regularized Principal Component Analysis Method Using L2,p-Norm

Minghua Wan [1,2,3], Xichen Wang [1], Hai Tan [1,*] and Guowei Yang [1,4]

1 School of Information Engineering, Nanjing Audit University, Nanjing 211815, China
2 Jiangsu Modern Intelligent Audit Integrated Application Technology Engineering Research Center, Nanjing Audit University, Nanjing 211815, China
3 Jiangsu Key Laboratory of Image and Video Understanding for Social Safety, Nanjing University of Science and Technology, Nanjing 210014, China
4 School of Electronic Information, Qingdao University, Qingdao 266071, China
* Correspondence: 270602@nau.edu.cn

Abstract: The main idea of principal component analysis (PCA) is to transform the problem of high-dimensional space into low-dimensional space, and obtain the output sample set after a series of operations on the samples. However, the accuracy of the traditional principal component analysis method in dimension reduction is not very high, and it is very sensitive to outliers. In order to improve the robustness of image recognition to noise and the importance of geometric information in a given data space, this paper proposes a new unsupervised feature extraction model based on $l_{2,p}$-norm PCA and manifold learning method. To improve robustness, the model method adopts $l_{2,p}$-norm to reconstruct the distance measure between the error and the original input data. When the image is occluded, the projection direction will not significantly deviate from the expected solution of the model, which can minimize the reconstruction error of the data and improve the recognition accuracy. To verify whether the algorithm proposed by the method is robust, the data sets used in this experiment include ORL database, Yale database, FERET database, and PolyU palmprint database. In the experiments of these four databases, the recognition rate of the proposed method is higher than that of other methods when $p = 0.5$. Finally, the experimental results show that the method proposed in this paper is robust and effective.

Keywords: principal component analysis; manifold learning; features extracting; $l_{2,p}$-norm; neighborhood preserving embedding

MSC: 68U10

1. Introduction

To solve the problem caused by high dimensions, researchers have summarized many dimensionality reduction methods [1–3], including principal component analysis (PCA) [4] that belongs to unsupervised learning and linear discriminant analysis (LDA) [5] that belongs to supervised learning, and these two methods generally project data from high-dimensional space to low dimensional space first. In order to solve the problem of ignoring the structure information embedded in the pixel when converting the two-dimensional image data into one-dimensional image vector [6], 2DPCA [7] was proposed. Inspired by 2DPCA, 2DLDA [8] and multi-directional principal component analysis (MPCA) [9] have also been proposed one after another. These algorithms can extract more effective features from the image itself.

In recent years, l_1-norm [10] has been greatly developed, and when the image is noisy, the recognition accuracy of the image is still high [11–15]. To further improve the robustness of subspace learning method, l_p-norm is proposed, and because of it, PCA [16] and LDA [17] are further developed. However, the above methods do not have the purpose of minimizing the reconstruction error. Therefore, Ding et al. [18] proposed a l_1-norm rotation invariant algorithm of PCA objective function, which is called rotation invariant l_1-norm PCA (R_1-PCA). To further improve the performance of PCA algorithm, $l_{2,p}$-norm [19] is proposed. Bi et al. [20] proposed locally invariant robust principal component analysis (LIRPCA), which uses $l_{2,p}$-norm to constrain PCA to solve the problem of underwater image recognition [21]. Although LIRPCA solves the problem of PCA in image reconstruction to a certain extent, it also reduces the influence of large distance as much as possible. However, LIRPCA is difficult to capture the nonlinear structure of manifolds, and there are also some limitations, for example, it is unable to generalize new samples, and its training time is too long.

The above methods can only deal with the dimensionality reduction of linear data. Therefore, in order to solve some nonlinear image data dimensionality reduction problems, scholars have proposed many dimensionality reduction methods that can solve nonlinear problems, and manifold learning [22] is one of them. Isometric mapping (Isomap) [23] and laplacian eigenmaps (LE) [24], which belongs to classical manifold learning methods, can learn some nonlinear manifold structures, but these methods lack the ability of generalization, in other words, it means that these algorithms have weak adaptability to new sample databases. Locally linear embedding (LLE) [25] and neighborhood preserving embedding (NPE) [26,27] based on manifold learning [28,29] solve this problem well. As a linear approximation of LLE, NPE has a very good effect on image dimensionality reduction and is easy to process new image samples. A manifold regularization is used to consider non-linearity, so kernel PCA (KPCA) [30], which is another popular extension of PCA that considers non-linearity, is proposed.

As we all know, images will be affected by various interferences in the process of recognition, such as occlusion, blurring, etc. First of all, in order to extract important features of an image, this paper improves the PCA algorithm, and proposes a new principal component analysis method called manifold regularized principal component analysis method using $l_{2,p}$-norm ($l_{2,p}$-MRPCA). This method uses $l_{2,p}$-norm to reconstruct the distance measurement between the error and the original input data. If the noise of the experimental data is relatively large, there is no obvious deviation between the expected projection direction and the desired solution of $l_{2,p}$-MRPCA, so as to minimize the reconstruction error of the data and improve the recognition accuracy. Secondly, in order to improve the modeling performance, manifold regularization terms are used. Manifold learning shows that observations are always collected from low dimensional manifolds embedded in high-dimensional environment space. $l_{2,p}$-MRPCA is a generalized robust metric learning method of PCA, and this method not only has strong robustness to outliers, but also maintains the good characteristics of PCA. Finally, the structure of $l_{2,p}$-MRPCA is relatively simple, belonging to unsupervised subspace learning algorithm, and the ability of model learning task is high. This paper mainly contains the following three contributions:

1. A new algorithm based on PCA is proposed. The model adopts $l_{2,p}$-norm as the function measure, which is a robust model.
2. This method combines the advantages of regularization and manifold learning, and has higher robustness and recognition effect.
3. In the non greedy iterative algorithm, the weighted covariance matrix is considered to further reduce the reconstruction error.

The following has four sections. Section 2 mainly presents the algorithms which are related to this paper, including PCA, R_1-PCA, NPE, and LIRPCA. Section 3 mainly presents the objective function, algorithm optimization, and algorithm flow of $l_{2,p}$-MRPCA. Section 4 analyses experimental comparisons on the ORL, Yale, FERET, and PolyU palmprint databases. Section 5 summarizes the full text.

2. Related Work

The related work includes the definition of the normal form mentioned in the paper and some related algorithms, such as PCA, R_1-PCA, NPE and LIRPCA.

2.1. Symbols and Definitions

Let the data set $X = (x_1, x_2, \ldots, x_n)$ to represent a standardized training sample matrix, which contains n samples, and each sample is an m dimensional column vector. In this paper, l_2-norm, R_1-norm and $l_{2,p}$-norm are adopted. The definition of l_2-norm is given as follows:

$$\|X\|_2 = \sqrt{\sum_{i=1}^{n} |x_i|^2} \tag{1}$$

R_1-norm is defined as:

$$\|X\|_{R_1} = \sum_{i=1}^{n} \sqrt{\sum_{j=1}^{m} |x_{ij}|^2} \tag{2}$$

$l_{2,p}$-norm is defined as:

$$\|X\|_{2,p} = \sqrt[p]{\sum_{i=1}^{n} \sqrt[p]{\sum_{j=1}^{m} |x_{ij}|^2}} \tag{3}$$

2.2. Principal Component Analysis (PCA)

PCA is a common feature extraction algorithm, which is mainly used in image recognition field. Assuming that $U \in R^{m \times q}$ is a projection matrix. This method uses l_2-norm as constraint, and we can obtain the optimal projection matrix U after finding the solution of the following optimization problem:

$$\min_{U} \sum_{i=1}^{n} \left\| x_i - UU^T x_i \right\|_2^2 \quad s.t.\ U^T U = I_q \tag{4}$$

where I_q is a $q \times q$ identity matrix. Through matrix tracing operation, we can convert Equation (4) into:

$$\max_{U} \sum_{i=1}^{n} \left\| UU^T x_i \right\|_2^2 = \max_{U} tr(U^T G_t U) \tag{5}$$

where $G_t = \sum_{i=1}^{n} x_i (x_i)^T$ is called the image covariance matrix, and the projection matrix U of Equation (4) is composed of G_t eigenvector corresponding to the maximum eigenvalue of q. However, because l_2-norm is sensitive to noise [31], and its robustness is low, and the iterative process is cumbersome, the traditional PCA method is relatively limited.

2.3. Rotation Invariant L1-PCA (R1-PCA)

In R_1-norm, we use l_2-norm to measure spatial dimension and l_1-norm to calculate the sum of different data points. R_1-PCA is not sensitive to noise [15], so it is easier to process some blurred images. Here is the specific definition of R_1-PCA:

$$\min_{U} \sum_{i=1}^{n} \left\| x_i - UU^T x_i \right\|_{R_1} \quad s.t.\ U^T U = I_q \tag{6}$$

After a series of optimization iterative algorithms, we can obtain the optimal projection matrix U. However, R_1-PCA uses l_2-norm to centralize the training samples, so it can not guarantee that the final calculated mean is optimal, so there is still room for improvement.

2.4. Neighborhood Preserving Embedding (NPE)

The idea of NPE is the same as LLE, which is to keep the local linear structure of manifold unchanged in the process of dimensionality reduction, so as to extract useful information from data. The local linear structure is represented by the reconstruction of the weight matrix, which is the coefficient matrix of the linear reconstruction of the neighbors to the nodes in the neighborhood.

Similar to other classical manifold learning algorithms, NPE has three steps:
1. Constructing Neighborhood Graph;
2. calculating Weight Matrix;
3. and computational mapping.

In conclusion, we can obtain the objective function of NPE in low dimensional space as follows:

$$\min_{U} \sum_{i=1}^{n} \left\| U^T x_i - \sum_{j=1}^{m} W_{ij} \cdot U^T x_j \right\|_2^2 \quad s.t. \ U^T X X^T U = I_q \tag{7}$$

where the weight matrix W_{ij} mentioned in Formula (7) can be defined as:

$$\sum_{j=1}^{m} W_{ij} = 1, i = 1, 2, \ldots, n \tag{8}$$

where W_{ij} represents the weight value of the edge from node i to node j. If there is no such edge, the value of W_{ij} is 0.

2.5. Locally Invariant Robust Principal Component Analysis (LIRPCA)

LIRPCA hopes to minimize the deviation between the reconstructed image and the original image of each projection data and further enhance the robustness of the model, so as to ensure that the extracted features can well reflect the main information of the original data space. Therefore, LIRPCA uses $l_{2,p}$-norm to constrain PCA. In order to recover low-dimensional information from high-dimensional environment space, we hope to find a U that ensures that $U x_k$ and $U x_j$ are adjacent. Based on the above objectives, LIRPCA is specifically defined as follows:

$$\min_{U} \sum_{i=1}^{n} \left(\frac{\|x_i - UU^T x_i\|_2^p}{\|x_i\|_2^p} + \frac{1}{2}\Psi \sum_{j=1}^{m} \left\| U^T(x_i - x_j) \right\|_2^2 W_{ij} \right) \tag{9}$$

where $\Psi > 0$, and W_{ij} is a weight matrix which can be defined as:

$$W_{ij} = \begin{cases} \exp\left(-\frac{\|x_i - x_j\|_2^2}{2\sigma^2}\right), & \text{if } x_i \in M_h(x_j), \\ \exp\left(-\frac{\|x_i - x_j\|_2^2}{2\sigma^2}\right), & \text{if } x_j \in M_h(x_i), \\ 0 & , \text{otherwise,} \end{cases} \tag{10}$$

where $\sigma > 0$, and $M_h(x_j)$ is the set of k nearest data of x_i, $M_h(x_i)$ is the set of k nearest data of x_j and W_{ij} represents the i-th, and the j-th column of the matrix W.

3. Manifold Regularized PCA Method Using $l_{2,p}$-norm($l_{2,p}$-MRPCA)

This chapter mainly includes the definition of $l_{2,p}$-MRPCA and its algorithm optimization process and convergence analysis.

3.1. Motivation and Objective Function

In order to reduce the influence of large distance as a measure and minimize the reconstruction error, combining with the LIRPCA mentioned above, we use $l_{2,p}$-norm instead of l_2-norm, and propose $l_{2,p}$-PCA as follows:

$$\min_U \sum_{i=1}^n \frac{\|x_i - UU^T x_i\|_2^p}{\|x_i\|_2^p} \quad s.t. \ U^T U = I_q \tag{11}$$

where p is $0 < p < 2$. By solving this constrained optimization problem, the optimal projection matrix U will be obtained.

However, considering the importance of considering the internal geometric information of data space to improve the performance of the algorithm and ensuring the rotation invariance of the data of the algorithm, popular learning, such as NPE, can be applied to this method. The specific formula of NPE is shown in Formula (7) mentioned above.

To sum up, combining Equations (4) and (11), we can obtain the following objective function:

$$\min_U \sum_{i=1}^n \frac{\|x_i - UU^T x_i\|_2^p}{\|x_i\|_2^p} + \phi \sum_{i=1}^n \left\| U^T x_i - \sum_{j=1}^m W_{ij} \cdot U^T x_j \right\|_2^2 \quad s.t. \ U^T U = I_q \tag{12}$$

where $\varphi > 0$.

3.2. Optimization

Formula (12) is divided into two parts: $\sum_{i=1}^n \frac{\|x_i - UU^T x_i\|_2^p}{\|x_i\|_2^p}$ and $\sum_{i=1}^n \left\| U^T x_i - \sum_{j=1}^m W_{ij} \cdot U^T x_j \right\|_2^2$.

First, we simplify the $\sum_{i=1}^n \frac{\|x_i - UU^T x_i\|_2^p}{\|x_i\|_2^p}$ part.

$$\begin{aligned}
&\sum_{i=1}^n \frac{\|x_i - UU^T x_i\|_2^p}{\|x_i\|_2^p} \\
&= \sum_{i=1}^n \frac{\|x_i - UU^T x_i\|_2^2 \|x_i - UU^T x_i\|_2^{p-2}}{\|x_i\|_2^p} \\
&= \sum_{i=1}^n tr\left[(x_i - UU^T x_i)^T (x_i - UU^T x_i) \right] q_i \\
&= \sum_{i=1}^n tr\left[\left((x_i)^T - (x_i)^T UU^T \right)(x_i - UU^T x_i) \right] q_i \\
&= \sum_{i=1}^n tr\left[(x_i)^T x_i - (x_i)^T UU^T x_i \right] q_i \\
&= tr(XDX^T) - tr(U^T XDX^T U)
\end{aligned} \tag{13}$$

where $q_i = \frac{\|x_i - UU^T x_i\|_2^{p-2}}{\|x_i\|_2^p}$ and D is a diagonal matrix whose elements on diagonal are q_i.

Then, we simplify the $\sum_{i=1}^n \left\| U^T x_i - \sum_{j=1}^m W_{ij} \cdot U^T x_j \right\|_2^2$ part.

$$\begin{aligned}
&\sum_{i=1}^n \left\| U^T x_i - \sum_{j=1}^m W_{ij} \cdot U^T x_j \right\|_2^2 \\
&= \sum_{i=1}^n \left(U^T x_i - \sum_{j=1}^m W_{ij} \cdot U^T x_j \right)^T \cdot \left(U^T x_i - \sum_{j=1}^m W_{ij} \cdot U^T x_j \right) \\
&= tr\left(U^T X (I - W)^T (I - W) X^T U \right) \\
&= tr(U^T X M X^T U)
\end{aligned} \tag{14}$$

where I is a $q \times q$ identity matrix.

Finally, Equations (13) and (14) are combined and we obtain the equation:

$$\min_U \sum_{i=1}^n tr\left(XDX^T\right) - tr\left(U^T XDX^T U\right) + \lambda tr\left(U^T XMX^T U\right) \quad (15)$$

where λ is a regularization parameter which should be set to a small real value.

3.3. Algorithm Optimization

Since the unknown variables U and D have a certain relationship with U, it is difficult to directly solve the optimal projection matrix U. However, in this case, we can use non greedy iterative algorithm to solve U and D. The Lagrangian function of Equation (15) is

$$L(U, \xi) = tr\left(XDX^T\right) - tr\left(U^T XDX^T U\right) + \lambda tr\left(U^T XMX^T U\right) + tr\left(\xi\left(U^T U - I\right)\right) \quad (16)$$

where $\xi \in R^{d \times d}$ is a symmetric matrix. Then we can apply the Karush–Kuhn–Tucker (KKT) condition to find the projection matrix. We set $\frac{\partial L(U,\xi)}{\partial U} = 0$, then,

$$\begin{aligned}
\frac{\partial L(U,\xi)}{\partial U} &= \frac{\partial tr\left(XDX^T\right)}{\partial U} - \frac{\partial tr\left(U^T XDX^T U\right)}{\partial U} + \lambda \frac{\partial tr\left(U^T XMX^T U\right)}{\partial U} \\
&\quad + \frac{\partial tr\left(\xi\left(U^T U - I\right)\right)}{\partial U} \\
&= 0 - \left(XDX^T U + \left(U^T XDX^T\right)^T\right) + \lambda\left(XMX^T U + \left(U^T XMX^T\right)^T\right) \\
&\quad + \xi(U + \left(U^T\right)^T) \\
&= -2XDX^T U + 2\lambda XMX^T U + 2U\xi \\
&= 0
\end{aligned} \quad (17)$$

and Equation (17) can be converted into

$$\left(XDX^T - \lambda XMX^T\right) U = U\xi \quad (18)$$

We set $\frac{\partial L(U,\xi)}{\partial \xi} = 0$, then,

$$U^T U = I_q \quad (19)$$

We can substitute Equations (18) and (19) into Equation (15), and the projection matrix U satisfies the objective function can be obtained. Algorithm 1 gives the whole flow of U and q_i calculation.

Algorithm 1. $l_{2,p}$-MRPCA

Input: Training set X, iterations T, parameters $\lambda, p, q, t = 1$
Output: $U^{(t+1)} \in R^{m \times q}$
Compute: $W \in R^{n \times n}$, $D \in R^{n \times n}$ and $M \in R^{n \times n}$ where $M = I - W$
Initialize: $U^{(t)}$ to a $m \times q$ orthogonal matrix
Repeat:

1. compute the diagonal matrix D by each diagonal element q_i.
2. Compute the weighted covariance matrix $XDX^T - \lambda XMX^T$
3. Update matrix $U^{(t+1)}$ which is called the optimal projection matrix by Equation (14).
4. If $J\left(U^{(t)}\right) - J\left(U^{(t+1)}\right) \leq \delta$ (δ is a small positive real number, such as 10^{-8}), where $J(U) = tr\left(XDX^T\right) - tr\left(U^T XDX^T U\right) + \lambda tr\left(U^T XMX^T U\right)$
5. $t \leftarrow t + 1$

Output the optimal projection matrix $U^{(t+1)}$, and the Algorithm 1 ends.

Theorem 1. Let any two vectors $e^t \in R^m$, $e^{t+1} \in R^m$, if $0 < p < 2$, we can obtain the following inequality:

$$\frac{\left\|e^{(t+1)}\right\|_2^p}{\left\|e^{(t)}\right\|_2^p} - \frac{p}{2}\frac{\left\|e^{(t+1)}\right\|_2^2}{\left\|e^{(t)}\right\|_2^2} - 1 + \frac{p}{2} \leq 0 \tag{20}$$

where e^t must be a non-zero vector, otherwise the denominator is zero, and the inequality is meaningless.

Proof of Theorem 1. Let $f(y) = y^p - \frac{p}{2}y^2 + \frac{p}{2} - 1$, through simple algebraic calculation, we can obtain:

$$\frac{\partial f}{\partial y} = py\left(y^{p-2} - 1\right) \tag{21}$$

It can be seen from Equation (21) that when $y > 0$ and $0 < p < 2$, $y = 1$ is the only extreme optimal solution of function f. In addition, we have $f'(y) > 0$ $(0 < y < 1)$ and $f'(y) < 0$ $(1 < y)$. So $y = 1$ is the maximum point of function f. Substitute $y = 1$ into the function y to obtain $f = 0$.

Combined with the previous analysis, we obtain that for any $y > 0$, $f(y) \leq 0$, Theorem 1 can be proved by setting $y = \frac{\|e^{t+1}\|_2}{\|e^t\|_2}$. □

Theorem 2. By using the iterative method which is described in Algorithm 1, we can obtain that the value of Equation (12) decreases monotonically in each iteration until it converges to the local optimum.

Proof of Theorem 2. As shown in Algorithm 1, in the $t+1$ iteration, we have:

$$\begin{aligned} &\sum_{i=1}^{n} tr\left((x_i)^T x_i q_i^{(t)}\right) - \sum_{i=1}^{n} tr\left(\left(U^{(t+1)}\right)^T x_i (x_i)^T U^{(t+1)} q_i^{(t)}\right) \\ &+ \lambda tr\left(\left(U^{(t+1)}\right)^T XMX^T U^{(t+1)}\right) \\ &\leq \sum_{i=1}^{n} tr\left((x_i)^T x_i q_i^{(t)}\right) - \sum_{i=1}^{n} tr\left(\left(U^{(t)}\right)^T x_i (x_i)^T U^{(t)} q_i^{(t)}\right) \\ &+ \lambda tr\left(\left(U^{(t)}\right)^T XMX^T U^{(t)}\right) \end{aligned} \tag{22}$$

Equation (22) can be transformed into:

$$\begin{aligned} &\sum_{i=1}^{n} \left\|x_i - U^{(t+1)}\left(U^{(t+1)}\right)^T x_i\right\|_2^2 q_i^{(t)} + \lambda tr\left(\left(U^{(t+1)}\right)^T XMX^T U^{(t+1)}\right) \\ &\leq \sum_{i=1}^{n} \left\|x_i - U^{(t)}\left(U^{(t)}\right)^T x_i\right\|_2^2 q_i^{(t)} + \lambda tr\left(\left(U^{((t))}\right)^T XMX^T U^{((t))}\right) \end{aligned} \tag{23}$$

Assuming that $e_i^{(t+1)} = x_i - U^{(t+1)}(U^{(t+1)T})x_i$, $e_i^{(t)} = x_i - U^{(t)}(U^{(t)T})x_i$ and $v^{(t)} = x_i$. As we already know that $q_i = \frac{\|x_i - UU^T\|_2^{p-2}}{\|x_i\|_2^p}$, so Equation (23) can be converted into

$$\begin{aligned} &\sum_{i=1}^{n} \frac{\left\|e_i^{(t+1)}\right\|_2^2}{\left\|v_i^{(t)}\right\|_2^p \left\|e_i^{(t)}\right\|_2^2} \left\|e_i^{(t)}\right\|_2^p + \lambda tr\left(\left(U^{(t+1)}\right)^T XMX^T U^{(t+1)}\right) \\ &\leq \sum_{i=1}^{n} \frac{\left\|e_i^{(t)}\right\|_2^p}{\left\|v_i^{(t)}\right\|_2^p} + \lambda tr\left(\left(U^{(t)}\right)^T XMX^T U^{(t+1)}\right) \end{aligned} \tag{24}$$

Equation (24) can be transposition into

$$\begin{aligned}&\sum_{i=1}^{n}\frac{\left\|e_i^{(t+1)}\right\|_2^2}{\left\|v_i^{(t)}\right\|_2^p\left\|e_i^{(t)}\right\|_2^2}\left\|e_i^{(t)}\right\|_2^p\\ &\leq \sum_{i=1}^{n}\frac{\left\|e_i^{(t)}\right\|_2^p}{\left\|v_i^{(t)}\right\|_2^p}+\lambda tr\left(\left(U^{(t)}\right)^T XMX^T U^{(t)}\right)-\lambda tr\left(\left(U^{(t+1)}\right)^T XMX^T U^{(t+1)}\right)\end{aligned} \quad (25)$$

According to the properties of Theorem 1, we multiply $\frac{1}{\left\|v_i^{(t)}\right\|_2^p} > 0$ on both sides of Equation (20) to obtain the inequality of each index i:

$$\sum_{i=1}^{n}\frac{p}{2}\frac{\left\|e_i^{(t+1)}\right\|_2^2}{\left\|v_i^{(t)}\right\|_2^p\left\|e_i^{(t)}\right\|_2^2}\left\|e_i^{(t)}\right\|_2^p \geq \sum_{i=1}^{n}\frac{\left\|e_i^{(t+1)}\right\|_2^p}{\left\|v_i^{(t)}\right\|_2^p}-\sum_{i=1}^{n}\frac{\left\|e_i^{(t)}\right\|_2^p}{\left\|v_i^{(t)}\right\|_2^p}+\sum_{i=1}^{n}\frac{p}{2}\frac{\left\|e_i^{(t)}\right\|_2^p}{\left\|v_i^{(t)}\right\|_2^p} \quad (26)$$

Then, we multiply the whole of Equation (25) by $\frac{p}{2}$ and substitute it into Equation (26), and we obtain

$$\begin{aligned}&\sum_{i=1}^{n}\frac{\left\|e_i^{(t+1)}\right\|_2^p}{\left\|v_i^{(t)}\right\|_2^p}-\frac{p}{2}\lambda tr\left(\left(U^{(t)}\right)^T XMX^T U^{(t)}\right)\\ &\leq \sum_{i=1}^{n}\frac{\left\|e_i^{(t)}\right\|_2^p}{\left\|v_i^{(t)}\right\|_2^p}-\frac{p}{2}\lambda tr\left(\left(U^{(t+1)}\right)^T XMX^T U^{(t+1)}\right)\end{aligned} \quad (27)$$

We substitute $e_i^{(t+1)} = x_i - U^{(t+1)}(U^{(t+1)T})x_i$, $e_i^{(t)} = x_i - U^{(t)}(U^{(t)T})x_i$ and $v^{(t)} = x_i$ into Equation (27), and we can obtain

$$\begin{aligned}&\sum_{i=1}^{n}\frac{\left\|x_i-U^{(t+1)}\left(U^{(t+1)}\right)^T x_i\right\|_2^p}{\|x_i\|_2^p}+\frac{p}{2}\lambda tr\left(\left(U^{(t+1)}\right)^T XMX^T U^{(t+1)}\right)\\ &\leq \sum_{i=1}^{n}\frac{\left\|x_i-U^{(t)}\left(U^{(t)}\right)^T x_i\right\|_2^p}{\|x_i\|_2^p}+\frac{p}{2}\lambda tr\left(\left(U^{(t)}\right)^T XMX^T U^{(t)}\right)\end{aligned} \quad (28)$$

Note that $0 < p < 2$, so $\frac{p}{2}\lambda > 0$ is true. Finally, ensuring that $\xi = \frac{p}{2}\lambda$ is established, and combine Equation (28) with Equation (15) to obtain Equation (28):

$$\begin{aligned}&\sum_{i=1}^{n}\frac{\left\|x_i-U^{(t+1)}\left(U^{(t+1)}\right)^T x_i\right\|_2^p}{\|x_i\|_2^p}+\xi tr\left(\left(U^{(t+1)}\right)^T XMX^T U^{(t+1)}\right)\\ &\leq \sum_{i=1}^{n}\frac{\left\|x_i-U^{(t)}\left(U^{(t)}\right)^T x_i\right\|_2^p}{\|x_i\|_2^p}+\xi tr\left(\left(U^{(t)}\right)^T XMX^T U^{(t)}\right)\end{aligned} \quad (29)$$

Equation (29) shows that the objective function of Equation (12) decreases monotonically in each iteration. Combining the convergence conditions given by Algorithm 1, it can be determined that the objective function (12) has a lower bound, and finally converges to the local optimal solution, so Theorem 2 is true. □

4. Experiments

The experiment part mainly includes the introduction of several databases, the presentation of the experimental results on each database, and the analysis of the experimental results. The whole experimental analysis is carried out under the windows system which is configured with i5-1035G1 processor, 8G memory, PCI-E 1T solid state disk, and MX250 2G single display. All codes are compiled by using matlab tools.

4.1. Data Sets and Experimental Parameters

In order to verify the effectiveness of $l_{2,p}$-MRPCA algorithm, this experiment compares $l_{2,p}$-MRPCA with PCA, R_1-PCA, KPCA, NPE, and LIRPCA. The databases used in this experiment include ORL face database, YALE face database and FERET face database, and PolyU palmprint database. In order to verify the robustness of the algorithm under different levels of occlusion, we add 5 × 5 occlusion block and 10 × 10 occlusion block to ORL face database and YALE face database respectively, and 5 × 5 occlusion block to the FERET face database. The original images and continuous occlusion images of the four libraries are shown in Figure 1. The ORL face database randomly selects training samples $n = 3, 4, 5, 6$, YALE face database randomly selects training samples $n = 4, 5$, and FERET face database randomly selects training samples $n = 2, 3, 4, 5$.

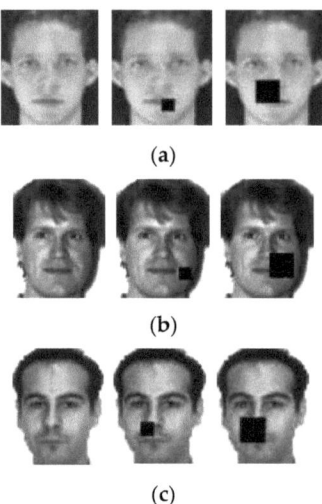

(a)

(b)

(c)

Figure 1. Partial original image and continuous occlusion image on ORL, YALE, and FERET database (**a**) ORL database (**b**) YALE database (**c**) FERET database.

For the parameters mentioned in $l_{2,p}$-MRPCA algorithm, λ, p, and q are briefly described. We select the optimal parameters of $l_{2,p}$-MRPCA by crossing validation strategy, and set parameters $\lambda = 0.1$ in the ORL face database, parameters $\lambda = 0.08$ in YALE face database, parameters $\lambda = 0.05$ in FERET face database. Parameter p is chosen as 0.5 and 1, and the two parameters values are substituted into the experiment to obtain the experimental results, so as to select better parameter values. The parameter q represents the number of extracted feature information, which can be determined empirically through Cumulative Percent Variance (CPV), and its formula is as follows:

$$CPV = \left[\sum_{i=1}^{q}\lambda_i \bigg/ \sum_{j=1}^{m}\lambda_j\right] \times 100\% \to 90\% \tag{30}$$

In order to ensure that CPV can reach 90% during the experiment, the corresponding q value is selected. In order to ensure the universality of the experimental results, the experiments in each database are repeated at least 100 times.

4.2. The ORL Face Database

The database has 400 images, including 40 people with 10 images, and each image is 56 × 46 pixels. The shooting background of these images is relatively dark, which is the front face collected in different time, light, facial expression, and facial detail environment (some images have slight deviation). We obtain the broken line diagram of the recognition rate of ORL database and its occlusion images in PCA, R_1-PCA, KPCA, NPE, LIRPCA ($p = 1$), LIRPCA ($p = 0.5$), $l_{2,p}$-MRPCA ($p = 1$), and $l_{2,p}$-MRPCA ($p = 0.5$), as shown in Figure 2.

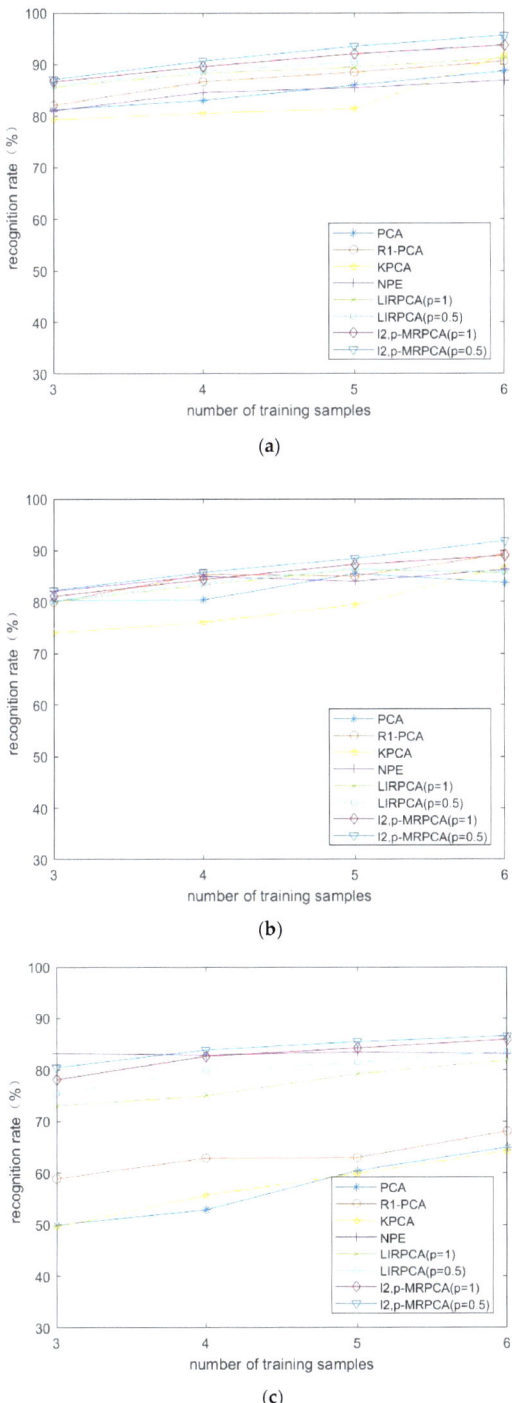

Figure 2. Recognition rate of PCA, R_1-PCA, KPCA, NPE, LIRPCA ($p = 0.5$), LIRPCA ($p = 1$), $l_{2,p}$-MRPCA ($p = 0.5$), $l_{2,p}$-MRPCA ($p = 1$) on ORL database (**a**) original image (**b**) occlusion block = 5 × 5 (**c**) occlusion block = 10 × 10.

First of all, it can be seen from Figure 2 that with the increase of the number of training samples, the recognition rates of PCA, R_1-PCA, KPCA, NPE, LIRPCA ($p = 1$), LIRPCA ($p = 0.5$), $l_{2,p}$-MRPCA ($p = 1$), and $l_{2,p}$-MRPCA ($p = 0.5$) also increase. Secondly, we compare the robustness of these algorithms. With the increase size of occlusion block, the recognition rate of NPE is improved, which shows that the robustness of NPE algorithm is relatively high, and it is suitable for recognizing occluded images. However, PCA, R_1-PCA, and KPCA reduce the recognition rate with the increase of occluded block size, which indicates that the two methods are not suitable for recognizing occluded images. Finally, the effect of parameter p on the experiment was observed. It can be seen from Figure 2 that the recognition rate of $l_{2,p}$-MRPCA is higher than that of LIRPCA when the number of training samples is the same, no matter whether the picture is occluded or not, no matter $p = 0.5$ or $p = 1$. Moreover, the recognition effect of $l_{2,p}$-MRPCA ($p = 0.5$) is higher than that of $l_{2,p}$-MRPCA ($p = 1$), which indicates that the value of p also has some influence on the recognition rate.

4.3. The Yale Face Database

The face dataset contains 15 volunteers with 11 images, and each image is 80×100 pixels. The shooting background of these images has more obvious changes in illumination, facial expression, posture, and occlusion than ORL face database. We obtain the histogram of the recognition rate of Yale database and its occlusion images in PCA, R_1-PCA, KPCA, NPE, LIRPCA ($p = 1$), LIRPCA ($p = 0.5$), $l_{2,p}$-MRPCA ($p = 1$), and $l_{2,p}$-MRPCA ($p = 0.5$), as shown in Figure 3.

First of all, the pixels of YALE is 80×100 where the pixels of ORL is 56×46, so YALE has a higher recognition rate than ORL. The reason may be that the shooting background of ORL database is dark, while that of YALE database is bright. It may also be because YALE database has high pixels. Secondly, in this experiment, the recognition rate of LIRPCA is only slightly higher than that of PCA, or even lower than that of NPE. This may be because LIRPCA is not able to capture the linear structure of manifolds. However, the recognition rate of $l_{2,p}$-MRPCA is still relatively high, which indicates that even if the methods are based on $l_{2,p}$-PCA, different regularization terms have a greater impact on the experimental results. Finally, in the YALE experiment, the recognition rate of $l_{2,p}$-MRPCA ($p = 1$) is higher than that of LIRPCA ($p = 0.5$) when the training samples are the same, regardless of whether the pictures are occluded or not. This shows that the robustness and stability of $l_{2,p}$-MRPCA are higher than that of LIRPCA. Therefore, the introduction of popular regularization in $l_{2,p}$-MRPCA has certain advantages.

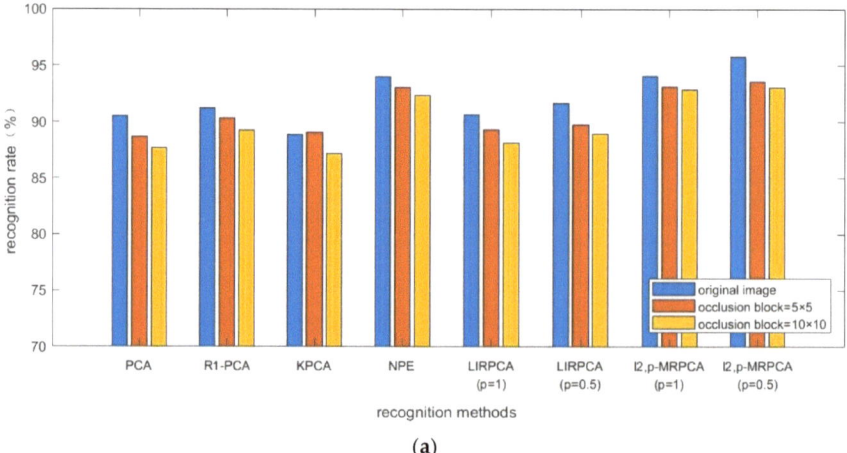

(a)

Figure 3. *Cont.*

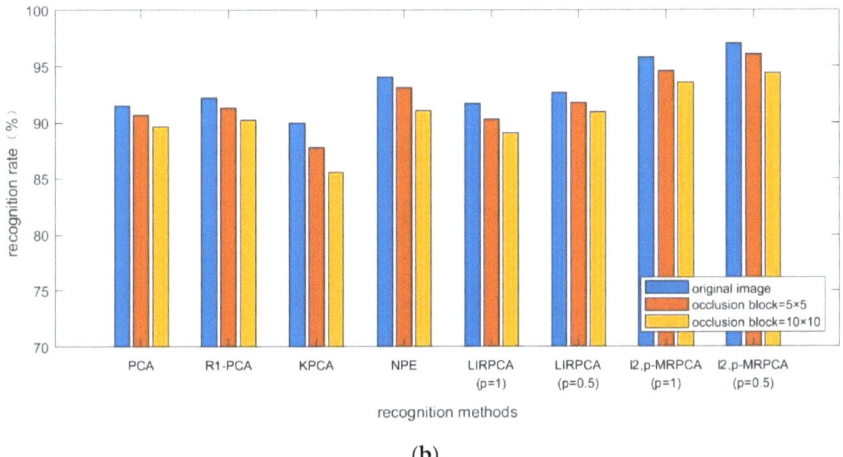

(b)

Figure 3. Recognition rate of PCA, R_1-PCA, KPCA, NPE, LIRPCA ($p = 0.5$), LIRPCA ($p = 1$), $l_{2,p}$-MRPCA ($p = 0.5$), $l_{2,p}$-MRPCA ($p = 1$) on YALE database (**a**) Number of training samples n = 4 (**b**) Number of training samples n = 5.

4.4. The FERET Face Database

There are 1400 images in this face dataset, including 200 people, and 7 images for each person, and each image is adjusted to 40×40 pixels. These images are collected under different illumination, facial expression, posture, and age. Most of the subjects are westerners, and the changes of face images contained by each person are relatively single. We obtain the original image of FERET database, and the database when block size is 5×5. The histogram of the recognition rate of the pictures of occlusion blocks in PCA, R_1-PCA, KPCA, NPE, LIRPCA ($p = 1$), LIRPCA ($p = 0.5$), $l_{2,p}$-MRPCA ($p = 1$), and $l_{2,p}$-MRPCA ($p = 0.5$) is shown in Figure 4.

First of all, from the results, the recognition rate of the database is relatively low, which may be because the database has more people but fewer images for each person, insufficient training samples, or the database image pixel is low. Since the recognition rate on the original data is low, the experiment is only carried out on the original database and 5×5 occlusion block. Secondly, on FERET database, the recognition rate of NPE is relatively low, but it is relatively high on ORL database and YALE database. This may be because the stability of NPE is not very strong, so the recognition rate varies greatly on different databases. The recognition rate of R_1-PCA decreases suddenly when the training sample is 3, and increases suddenly when the training sample is 4. Combined with previous experiments, it may be because of some errors in the experimental process, or because the stability of R_1-PCA is not very strong. Third, KPCA performs better on FERET database than on ORL database and YALE database, and it is greatly affected by the database and the number of training samples. Finally, the recognition rate of most methods in this experiment is lower when the training sample number is 5 than when the training sample number is 4, which is related to the number of each sample on FERET database. As the results of the previous two experiments, when the number of training samples is the same, the recognition rate of LIRPCA ($p = 0.5$) is higher than that of LIRPCA ($p = 1$), the recognition rate of $l_{2,p}$-MRPCA ($p = 0.5$) is higher than that of $l_{2,p}$-MRPCA ($p = 1$), which once again shows that the recognition rate effect of $p = 0.5$ is higher than that of $p = 1$.

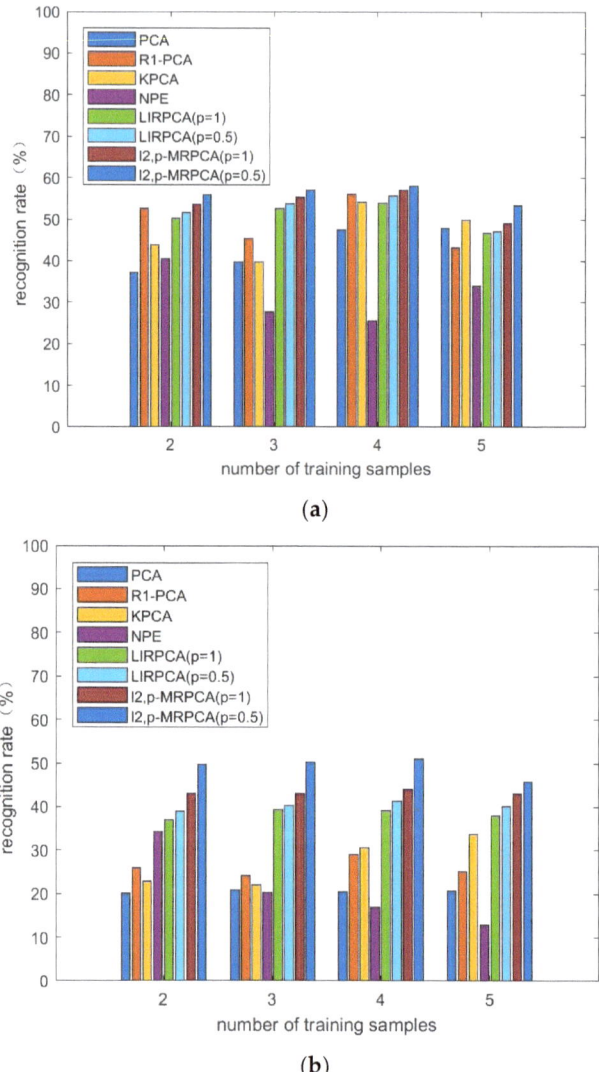

Figure 4. Recognition rate of PCA, R_1-PCA, KPCA, NPE, LIRPCA($p = 0.5$), LIRPCA($p = 1$), $l_{2,p}$-MRPCA ($p = 0.5$), $l_{2,p}$-MRPCA ($p = 1$) on FERET database (**a**) original image (**b**) block size = 5 × 5.

4.5. The PolyU Palmprint Verification Experiment

There are 600 images in this database, including the palmprint of 100 people. Each person has 6 images, and each image is cut into 50 × 40 pixels. To better verify the robustness of $l_{2,p}$-MRPCA, we add 5 × 5, 10 × 10 and 20 × 20 occlusion blocks to the database as shown in Figure 5, and three palmprint pictures of each person are selected as training samples. Finally, the average recognition accuracy of each algorithm when the number of training samples $n = 3$ can be obtained as shown in Table 1, the training time on PolyU palmprint database is shown in Figure 6, classification recognition rate on PolyU palmprint database is shown in Figure 7.

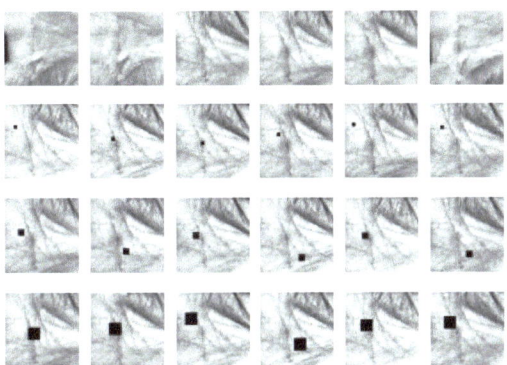

Figure 5. Partial original image and continuous occlusion image on the PolyU palmprint database.

Table 1. Experimental results of recognition rate (standard deviation)(%) on PolyU palmprint database.

TN		3		
Occlusion Block Size	None	5×5	10×10	20×20
PCA/%	76.32 (0.53)	67.32 (0.51)	61.98 (0.49)	43.12 (0.22)
R1-PCA/%	79.82 (0.42)	70.14 (0.44)	65.75 (0.53)	53.54 (0.35)
KPCA/%	77.23 (0.12)	73.04 (0.50)	58.33 (0.49)	40.98 (0.16)
NPE/%	83.06 (0.42)	71.17 (0.44)	67.38 (0.47)	54.17 (0.54)
LIRPCA ($p = 1$)/%	81.78 (0.27)	72.00 (0.33)	65.47 (0.35)	57.10 (0.41)
LIRPCA ($p = 0.5$)/%	86.53 (0.32)	73.15 (0.35)	66.56 (0.31)	57.64 (0.29)
$l_{2,p}$-MRPCA ($p = 1$)/%	86.91 (0.30)	73.03 (0.38)	68.96 (0.32)	61.82 (0.07)
$l_{2,p}$-MRPCA ($p = 0.5$)/%	89.01 (0.33)	74.54 (0.36)	69.34 (0.35)	63.01 (0.43)

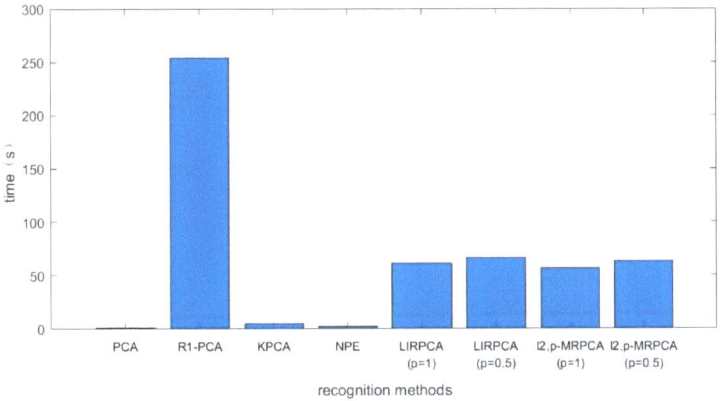

Figure 6. Training time on the PolyU palmprint database.

First, it can be seen from Table 1 that $l_{2,p}$-MRPCA ($p = 0.5$) has the best recognition effect. With the increase of the number of occluded blocks, the recognition rate of PCA, R_1-PCA, KPCA, NPE, LIRPCA ($p = 1$), LIRPCA ($p = 0.5$), $l_{2,p}$-MRPCA ($p = 1$), and $l_{2,p}$-MRPCA ($p = 0.5$) decreases gradually. Secondly, when the picture has no occlusion block, the recognition rate of $l_{2,p}$-MRPCA is only slightly higher than that of other algorithms. However, as the size of the occlusion block becomes higher, the advantages of $l_{2,p}$-MRPCA become larger, which shows that the method is robust and suitable for recognizing noisy images. Compared to PCA, R_1-PCA, and KPCA, LIRPCA has a certain recognition effect, but the recognition rate is always lower than that of $l_{2,p}$-MRPCA. Although LIRPCA, $l_{2,p}$-MRPCA all use $l_{2,p}$-PCA with good robustness, the regularization term of LIRPCA lacks a certain normalization ability, so the recognition effect is not as good as that of $l_{2,p}$-MRPCA. Finally, in general, $l_{2,p}$-MRPCA has good recognition effect and high robustness.

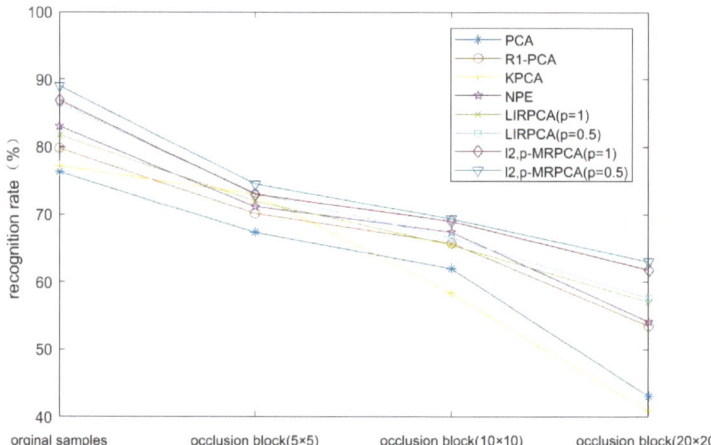

Figure 7. Classification recognition rate of PCA, R_1-PCA, KPCA, NPE, LIRPCA ($p = 0.5$), LIRPCA ($p = 1$), $l_{2,p}$-MRPCA ($p = 0.5$), $l_{2,p}$-MRPCA ($p = 1$) on the PolyU palmprint database.

4.6. Result Analysis

1. From the experimental results, R_1-PCA, as an improved algorithm of PCA algorithm, has a high recognition rate both in the original image database and in the occluded database.
2. When the experimental data is occluded, NPE, as a manifold learning method, most of the recognition rates are higher than PCA, indicating that the algorithm is less affected by occlusion. When the image is occluded, the recognition effect is better.
3. Compared to LIRPCA, $l_{2,p}$-MRPCA introduces manifold learning method, so the recognition rate is more significant. In addition, it takes into account the advantages of manifold regularization when the image is occluded, so the recognition effect is better. As the clarity of each database in the experiment is different, the recognition rate made by different databases is relatively different.
4. The training time on $l_{2,p}$-MRPCA is longer than PCA, KPCA and NPE, and is shorter than R_1-PCA and LIRPCA. Considering the recognition rate, robustness, and algorithm time of the algorithm, the training time on $l_{2,p}$-MRPCA is acceptable.
5. The parameter p also has a certain impact on the recognition effect. Whether it is LIRPCA or $l_{2,p}$-MRPCA, the recognition efficiency is slightly higher when $p = 0.5$ than when $p = 1$.

In order to further verify the stability of $l_{2,p}$-MRPCA, the algorithm is tested on PolyU palmprint dataset. The results show that even in the case of occlusion, $l_{2,p}$-MRPCA can still have a high recognition rate, so it shows that the algorithm has good robustness.

5. Conclusions

In this paper, we propose a manifold regularization principal component analysis method by using $l_{2,p}$-*norm* constraints. This method effectively combines $l_{2,p}$-PCA and manifold learning methods. It is not only robust to outliers, but also maintains the rotation invariance of the algorithm, and protects the true geometric information of the original data space. In the non greedy iterative algorithm of the model, the weight covariance matrix is considered to further reduce the reconstruction error. Therefore, the model has good expression ability, and it can effectively extract the algebraic features of images. This method is mainly divided into the following three steps:

1. Optimize the formula of $l_{2,p}$-MRPCA;
2. the equation of the optimal matrix is obtained by using KKT condition;
3. and according to the algorithm proposed in this paper, the convergence of the objective function is obtained, and the optimal projection matrix is obtained.

The experimental results show that the recognition rate of $l_{2,p}$-MRPCA algorithm is higher than some of the existing advanced algorithms, and it still has good robustness when there is occlusion. However, since this algorithm specifies many parameters in the implementation, which limits its application in practice, the following research will focus on parameter adjustment.

Author Contributions: Conceptualization, M.W. and X.W.; methodology, M.W.; software, X.W.; validation, M.W., X.W. and G.Y.; formal analysis, M.W.; investigation, X.W.; resources, G.Y. and H.T.; data curation, X.W.; writing—original draft preparation, X.W.; writing—review and editing, X.W.; visualization, G.Y.; supervision, M.W. and H.T.; project administration, M.W. and H.T.; funding acquisition, M.W and X.W. All authors have read and agreed to the published version of the manuscript.

Funding: This work is partially supported by the Postgraduate Research and Practice Innovation Program of Jiangsu Province Nos. SJCX21_0890; the National Science Foundation of China under Grant Nos. 61876213, 61861033, 61991401, 62172229, 61976117, 71972102, 61976118; the KeyR&D Program Science Foundation in Colleges and Universities of Jiangsu Province Grant Nos. 18KJA520005, 19KJA360001, 20KJA520002; the Natural Science Fund of Jiangsu Province under Grants Nos. BK20201397, BK20191409, BK20211295; and the Jiangsu Key Laboratory of Image and Video Understanding for Social Safety of Nanjing University of Science and Technology under Grants J2021-4. The Future Network Scientific Research Fund Project SRFP-2021-YB-25, and China's Jiangxi Province Natural Science Foundation (No. 20202ACBL202007). The Significant Project of Jiangsu College Philosophy and Social Sciences Research "Research on Knowledge Reasoning of Emergency Plan for Emergency Decision" (No: 2021SJZDA153). This work is funded in part by the "Qinglan Project" of Jiangsu Universities under Grant D202062032.

Institutional Review Board Statement: Not applicable.

Informed Consent Statement: Not applicable.

Data Availability Statement: Publicly available datasets were analyzed in this study. This data can be found here: [http://www.cl.cam.ac.uk/Research/DTG/attarchive:pub/data/att_faces.tar.Z; http://www.itl.nist.gov/iad/humanid/feret/; http://www.comp.polyu.edu.hk/~biometrics] (all accessed on 1 October 2022).

Conflicts of Interest: The authors declare no conflict of interest. The funders had no role in the design of the study; in the collection, analyses or interpretation of data; in the writing of the manuscript or in the decision to publish the results.

References

1. Wu, X.T.; Yan, Q.D. Analysis and Research on data dimensionality reduction method. *Comput. Appl. Res.* **2009**, *26*, 2832–2835.
2. Yu, X.X.; Zhou, N. Research on dimensionality reduction method of high-dimensional data. *Inf. Sci.* **2007**, *25*, 1248–1251.
3. Wan, M.H.; Lai, Z.H.; Yang, G.W. Local graph embedding based on maximum margin criterion via fuzzy set. *Fuzzy Sets Syst.* **2017**, *2017*, 120–131. [CrossRef]
4. Yang, J.; Zhang, D.D.; Yang, J.Y. Constructing PCA Baseline Algorithms to Reevaluate ICA-Based Face-Recognition Performance. *IEEE Trans Multimed.* **2007**, *37*, 1015–1021.
5. Zuo, W.; Zhang, D.; Yang, J.; Wang, K. BDPCA plus LDA:a novel fast feature extraction technique for face recognition. *IEEE Trans. Syst. Man Cybern. B Cybern.* **2006**, *36*, 946–953.
6. Kim, Y.G.; Song, Y.J.; Chang, U.D.; Kim, D.W.; Yun, T.S.; Ahn, J.H. Face recognition using a fusion method based on bidirectional 2DPCA. *Appl. Math. Comput.* **2008**, *205*, 601–607. [CrossRef]
7. Yang, J.; Zhang, D.; Frangi, A.F.; Yang, J.Y. Two dimensional PCA: A new approach to appearance-based face representation and recognition. *IEEE Trans. Pattern Anal. Mach. Intell.* **2004**, *26*, 131–137. [CrossRef]
8. Yang, J.; Zhang, D.; Yong, X.; Yang, J.Y. Two dimensional discriminant transform for face recognition. *Pattern Recognit.* **2005**, *38*, 1125–1129. [CrossRef]
9. Wang, J.; Barreto, A.; Wang, L.; Chen, Y.; Rishe, N.; Andrian, J.; Adjouadi, M. Multilinear principal component analysis for face recognition with fewer features. *Neurocomputing* **2010**, *73*, 1550–1555. [CrossRef]

10. Wan, M.; Yao, Y.; Zhan, T.; Yang, G. Supervised Low-Rank Embedded Regression (SLRER) for Robust Subspace Learning. *IEEE Trans. Circuits Syst. Video Technol.* **2022**, *32*, 1917–1927. [CrossRef]
11. Wright, J.; Ganesh, A.; Rao, S.; Peng, Y.; Ma, Y. Robust Principal Component Analysis: Exact Recovery of Corrupted Low-Rank Matrice. *Adv. Neural Inf. Process. Syst.* **2009**, *22*, 2080–2088.
12. Wan, M.; Chen, X.; Zhao, C.; Zhan, T.; Yang, G. A new weakly supervised discrete discriminant hashing for robust data representation. *Inf. Sci.* **2022**, *611*, 335–348. [CrossRef]
13. Ke, Q.F.; Kanade, T. Robust L1 norm factorization in the presence of outliers and missing data by alternative convex programming. In Proceedings of the IEEE Computer Society Conference on Computer Vision & Pattern Recognition, San Diego, CA, USA, 20–25 June 2005; Volume 1, pp. 739–746.
14. He, R.; Hu, B.G.; Zheng, W.S.; Kong, X.W. Robust Principal Component Analysis Based on Maximum Correntropy Criterion. *IEEE Trans. Image Process.* **2011**, *20*, 1485–1494.
15. Kwak, N. Principal Component Analysis Based on L1-Norm Maximization. *IEEE Trans. Pattern Anal. Mach. Intell.* **2008**, *30*, 1672–1680. [CrossRef] [PubMed]
16. Kwak, N. Principal Component Analysis by L-p-Norm Maximization. *IEEE Trans. Cybern.* **2014**, *44*, 594–609. [CrossRef] [PubMed]
17. Ye, Q.; Fu, L.; Zhang, Z.; Zhao, H.; Naiem, M. Lp- and Ls-Norm Distance Based Robust Linear Discriminant Analysis. *Neural Netw.* **2018**, *105*, 393–404. [CrossRef]
18. Ding, C.; Zhou, D.; He, X.; Zha, H. R1-PCA:Rotational invariant L1-norm principal component analysis for robust subspace factorization. In Proceedings of the 23rd International Conference on Machine Learning, ACM, New York, NY, USA, 25–29 June 2006; pp. 281–288.
19. Wang, Q.; Gao, Q.; Gao, X.; Nie, F. L2,p-norm based PCA for image recognition. *IEEE Trans. Image Process.* **2008**, *27*, 1336–1346. [CrossRef]
20. Bi, P.; Du, X. Application of Locally Invariant Robust PCA for Underwater Image Recognition. *IEEE Access* **2021**, *9*, 29470–29481. [CrossRef]
21. Xu, J.; Bi, P.; Du, X.; Li, J.; Chen, D. Generalized Robust PCA: A New Distance Metric Method for Underwater Target Recognition. *IEEE Access* **2019**, *7*, 51952–51964. [CrossRef]
22. Wan, M.; Chen, X.; Zhan, T.; Xu, C.; Yang, G.; Zhou, H. Sparse Fuzzy Two-Dimensional Discriminant Local Preserving Projection (SF2DDLPP) for Robust Image Feature Extraction. *Inf. Sci.* **2021**, *563*, 1–15. [CrossRef]
23. Tasoulis, S.; Pavlidis, N.G.; Roos, T. Nonlinear Dimensionality Reduction for Clustering. *Pattern Recognit.* **2020**, *107*, 107508. [CrossRef]
24. Luo, W.Q. Face recognition based on Laplacian Eigenmaps. In Proceedings of the International Conference on Computer Science and Service System, Nanjing, China, 27–29 June 2011; pp. 27–29.
25. Roweis, S.; Saul, L. Nonlinear Dimensionality Reduction by Locally Linear Embedding. *Science* **2000**, *290*, 2323–2326. [CrossRef] [PubMed]
26. Hu, K.L.; Yuan, J.Q. Statistical monitoring of fed-batch process using dynamic multiway neighborhood preserving embedding. *Chemom. Intell. Lab. Syst.* **2008**, *90*, 195–203. [CrossRef]
27. Song, B.; Ma, Y.; Shi, H. Multimode process monitoring using improved dynamic neighborhood preserving embedding. *Chemom. Intell. Lab. Syst.* **2014**, *135*, 17–30. [CrossRef]
28. Wan, M.; Chen, X.; Zhan, T.; Yang, G.; Tan, H.; Zheng, H. Low-rank 2D Local Discriminant Graph Embedding for Robust Image Feature Extraction. *Pattern Recognit.* **2023**, *133*, 109034. [CrossRef]
29. Chen, X.; Wan, M.; Zheng, H.; Xu, C.; Sun, C.; Fan, Z. A New Bilinear Supervised Neighborhood Discrete Discriminant Hashing. *Mathematics* **2022**, *10*, 2110. [CrossRef]
30. Li, W.H.; Gong, W.G.; Cheng, W.M. Method based on wavelet multiresolution analysis and KPCA for face recognition. *Comput. Appl.* **2005**, *25*, 2339–2341.
31. De, F.; Torre, L.; Black, M.J. A Framework for Robust Subspace Learning. *Int. J. Comput. Vis.* **2003**, *54*, 117–142.

Article

Multiagent Multimodal Trajectory Prediction in Urban Traffic Scenarios Using a Neural Network-Based Solution

Andreea-Iulia Patachi and Florin Leon *

Faculty of Automatic Control and Computer Engineering, "Gheorghe Asachi" Technical University of Iasi, Bd. Mangeron 27, 700050 Iasi, Romania
* Correspondence: florin.leon@academic.tuiasi.ro

Abstract: Trajectory prediction in urban scenarios is critical for high-level automated driving systems. However, this task is associated with many challenges. On the one hand, a scene typically includes different traffic participants, such as vehicles, buses, pedestrians, and cyclists, which may behave differently. On the other hand, an agent may have multiple plausible future trajectories based on complex interactions with the other agents. To address these challenges, we propose a multiagent, multimodal trajectory prediction method based on neural networks, which encodes past motion information, group context, and road context to estimate future trajectories by learning from the interactions of the agents. At inference time, multiple realistic future trajectories are predicted. Our solution is based on an encoder–decoder architecture that can handle a variable number of traffic participants. It uses vectors of agent features as inputs rather than images, and it is designed to run on a physical autonomous car, addressing the real-time operation requirements. We evaluate the method using the inD dataset for each type of traffic participant and provide information about its integration into an actual self-driving car.

Keywords: trajectory prediction; autonomous driving; neural network; multimodal prediction; group context; road context

MSC: 68T07

1. Introduction

Autonomous driving is an active research domain, pursued by both academia and private companies. Although fully automated driving, corresponding to the fifth level of automation [1], has not been achieved yet, progress has been made on the various subproblems underlying vehicle autonomous behavior, such as identifying and tracking objects, handling occlusions and varying light or weather conditions, predicting the trajectories and possible interactions of the agents in a traffic scene, route planning, and safety measures.

In this paper, we focus solely on the problem of trajectory prediction. This involves evaluating the possible future motion of traffic participants based on observed indicators in the recent past, such as positions, and sometimes heading angle, speed, or acceleration.

Trajectory prediction is a critical component of autonomous driving, allowing self-driving vehicles to anticipate the movement and behavior of other agents on the road, including other vehicles, pedestrians, bicycles, and more. It enables the vehicle to make informed decisions such as avoiding collisions, adjusting its speed and path, and anticipating traffic patterns.

To make accurate predictions, the vehicle must consider a wide range of inputs, including its own motion, the motion of other objects, road geometry, traffic signs, and environmental factors. By combining this information, the vehicle can build a predictive model of the environment, which it can use to make informed decisions about how to navigate the road safely and efficiently.

The main difficulties of the problem are related to the interactions of the agents, especially present in intersections, when a pedestrian approaches a crosswalk, or other situations where maneuvers are important, e.g., overtaking decisions, and also to the fact that trajectories may be multimodal, i.e., a common past set of observations may lead to different future trajectories.

Since the set of all possible maneuvers is virtually impossible to enumerate and evaluate exhaustively especially in situations with a large number of participants, the ego car needs to have an estimation about the most probable future states. Additionally, when the algorithms need to work in real time, i.e., on an actual autonomous car, computational efficiency becomes very important.

Accurate trajectory prediction is crucial for safe navigation. For example, safety can be increased if the ego car is able to predict whether another traffic participant will overtake another agent or if an agent in front will suddenly break. Furthermore, if autonomous vehicles are socially aware, their efficiency can be enhanced, and the overall traveling experience can become more comfortable.

The main contribution of this work is a neural network-based solution for predicting the future possible trajectories of traffic participants and their probabilities. By learning the effects of interactions between traffic participants, road features, and agent trajectories with different behavior patterns, the prediction quality can be improved.

This solution was developed as part of the PRORETA 5 project [2], which aimed to build an autonomous vehicle that incorporates artificial intelligence methods. The trajectory prediction presented in this paper is only a component of the full autonomy stack of an actual self-driving car, which was demonstrated in Darmstadt, Germany, in October 2022.

The first component of the general architecture involved image processing based on visual saliency models. It focused on traffic participant detection and also used driver attention information. Object tracking was performed using radar and lidar data. The following component was the trajectory prediction module that will be described in the current paper. Based on the previous information, trajectory planning was performed using a trajectory tree that was iteratively created using Monte Carlo tree search. Finally, there was a safety check module based on classic logical rules rather than artificial intelligence methods. Another aspect of the project addressed the hardware configuration of the vehicle, including various sensors and cameras, as well as the human–machine interface.

The project addressed all the General Data Protection Regulation (GDPR) requirements of the European Union for the data captured by cameras. The original images used for training were only accessible to the image processing team and were stored in a secure environment. Subsequent work, including trajectory prediction, was performed on vectors of object data that no longer contained any user-sensitive information.

The rest of the paper is organized as follows. In Section 2, we present an overview of the relevant literature. Section 3 details our methodology and the structure of the training data. In Section 4, we describe the developed model, while in Section 5 we present the experimental results. Finally, in Section 6 we include the conclusions and summarize the main findings.

2. Related Work

Many works address the problem of trajectory prediction. We would like to mention that the papers referenced for each category below are just examples and there are other authors that use those particular techniques as well.

Trajectory prediction methods can be broadly classified into two categories [3]: model-based and data-driven methods. Model-based methods use mathematical models to represent the motion of agents on the road and to predict their future trajectories based on physical or kinematic principles. Several authors use, e.g., Kalman filters [4], particle filters [5], and non-linear models [6]. On the other hand, data-driven methods rely on data to learn patterns and relationships in the motion of traffic participants and to make predictions based on these patterns. The most straightforward way of prediction is represented by rule-based methods, which use predefined rules to make predictions based on the behavior of road agents [7]. Although a positive aspect is that they rely on explicit knowledge, in general, identifying the proper rules may take time and they may not generalize very well in various traffic conditions. Probabilistic methods model the uncertainty and variability in the motion of road agents and make predictions based on probability distributions, e.g., employing Partially Observable Markov Decision Processes (POMDPs) or Gaussian mixture models (GMMs), especially for maneuver-based trajectory prediction [8–10].

The methods based on deep learning are arguably the most popular at this time and have contributed to a large extent to the state of the art. They use various kinds of deep neural networks to learn complex patterns from large amounts of training data and make predictions based on these patterns. A review of recent papers reporting such methods is [11].

Recurrent Neural Networks (RNNs) are well-suited for sequential data and have been applied to trajectory prediction by encoding the past motion of agents into a hidden state and using this state to make predictions about their future motion. Long-Short Term Memory (LSTM) models, in particular, have been successfully used [12–16]. The main advantage of recurrent networks is their ability to capture temporal dependencies, which is particularly relevant in the context of trajectory prediction, where the state of the traffic participants changes over time. Therefore, the models can incorporate complex patterns and trends in the data. Additionally, they can handle varying trajectory lengths. However, RNNs are complex models that usually require large amounts of data and may need long training times.

Convolutional Neural Networks (CNNs) are commonly used in trajectory prediction by utilizing image information from regular cameras, lidar sensors, or higher-level map projections [17–19]. This type of neural network is well-suited to handle spatial information efficiently. Due to their use of parameter sharing, they typically have shorter training times for larger datasets and faster predictions. Still, CNNs have limitations when it comes to temporal information and context because they typically consider only a fixed window of input data at a time. In many cases, CNNs are used to process video inputs while LSTMs contribute to the encoding and decoding of trajectories.

Other papers have reported the use of Conditional Variational Autoencoders (CVAEs) [20–23]. CVAEs can generate diverse trajectories by sampling from the learned latent space, which can be advantageous in dealing with complex and diverse traffic scenarios where multiple plausible trajectories exist. They can also estimate uncertainty in the predictions by providing a probability distribution over the possible trajectories and can reconstruct missing or corrupted inputs that may occur when sensor data are affected by noise. Nevertheless, CVAEs are complex models that can be challenging to train and may not be suitable for real-time applications due to the computational expense of generating a diverse set of trajectories. Additionally, the quality of the learned latent space representation is critical to the model's performance. If the latent space representation does not capture the underlying structure of the data, this can affect the output quality.

Generative Adversarial Networks (GANs) [24–26] can also be used for trajectory prediction. They can also generate diverse trajectories by training the model to create realistic trajectories that are expectantly indistinguishable from real ones. Many of the advantages and disadvantages of CVAEs apply to GANs as well. However, an additional issue related to both architectures is mode collapse, when the model generates only a small subset of possible trajectories while ignoring the rest, and this can lead to similar and unrealistic results.

Attention mechanisms [12,27] can also be used in conjunction with various models for trajectory prediction. They can capture global context by allowing the model to attend to different parts of the input sequence when generating the output sequence. This can be advantageous when dealing with complex and diverse traffic situations, where the context of the entire scene can be important for prediction. In many works, attention mechanisms refer to social attention, which can selectively aggregate information from nearby agents to predict the trajectory of the target agent. In this way, they capture the dependencies between the target agent and the scene context. This model has shown improved performance over other social pooling methods. Conversely, attention mechanisms can increase the complexity of the model and make it more difficult to train. They can also suffer from attention drift, where the model attends to irrelevant parts of the input sequence as the output sequence progresses, resulting in the model generating unrealistic trajectories.

Graph Neural Networks (GNNs) are suitable for modeling complex interactions between traffic participants by encoding the relationships between nodes (representing agents) and edges (representing interactions) in a graph structure [28–31]. GNNs can incorporate spatial information by using the relative positions of the nodes in the graph, which can be useful for trajectory prediction in complex scenarios. They can also scale to large graphs, which is important for modeling intricate traffic scenes. Yet GNNs require a large amount of data and are computationally expensive to train, especially for large graphs with many nodes and edges.

Transformer networks [32–34] represent a relatively recent architecture where operations can be highly parallelized, leading to faster training and inference times compared to sequential models such as LSTMs. Like the latter, they can capture both long-term dependencies and global context by attending to all positions in the input sequence. A disadvantage is that transformer networks may require large amounts of data to learn effective representations of the input sequence and may struggle to generalize to new and unseen scenarios, as they can be sensitive to the specific structure of the input sequence.

It must be emphasized that most approaches actually use hybrid methods, which combine the strengths of multiple techniques to make predictions.

Another direction related to reinforcement learning (RL)—in fact, inverse RL—is to use imitation learning to find out driving policies by estimating the cost function of human drivers [35].

Depending on the abstraction of level on which prediction is made, there are physics-based, maneuver-based, and interaction-aware motion models [36]. Physics-based models apply the laws of physics to estimate the trajectory, based, e.g., on speed, acceleration, steering, etc. They are useful as classic fail-safe techniques, but in general they are reliable only for short-term predictions. Maneuver-based models try to identify the maneuvers of the road agents but usually in isolation, while interaction-aware models take into account the influence of the neighbors on an agent but are more computationally complex.

Multiagent systems have also been used in the context of trajectory prediction to model the behavior of multiple agents in a scene, such as pedestrians or vehicles, and predict their future movements based on their past behavior and interactions with other agents. They are especially valuable for the latter, because interactions between agents play a crucial role in determining their future movements. Various methods have been proposed to model them, such as social force [37] or game theoretic [38] models.

Even if research on trajectory prediction constantly evolves, there are several key issues that still pose some challenges to the public use of autonomous vehicles. First, one can mention interpretability, i.e., the development of methods for making the predictions of autonomous vehicles explicit, so that the reasoning behind their decisions can be understood by humans. Secondly, one can think of interaction and cooperation between autonomous vehicles, i.e., how they can communicate and cooperate with one another to improve safety and efficiency on the road. Thirdly, there is the problem of unstructured and dynamic environments, which creates the need to develop prediction models that can handle complex, dynamically changing scenarios, such as urban environments with heavy traffic.

3. The Structure of the Training Data

The trajectory prediction problem can be formalized as follows. Let X_t^i be an observation vector with the position and possibly other motion indicators for agent i at time step t. If p designates the present time step, then for agent i the past trajectory (the input of the machine learning model) is a sequence of n_{in} vectors $\{X^i_{p-n_{in}+1}, \ldots, X^i_{p-1}, X^i_p\}$. The output of the model is the predicted trajectory, which is another sequence of n_{out} vectors $\{\widehat{Y}^i_{p+1}, \widehat{Y}^i_{p+2}, \ldots, \widehat{Y}^i_{p+n_{out}}\}$. In our case, the output consists of a set of such future trajectories, each with its corresponding probability.

The data that serves as an input to the model results after the segmentation and identification of the objects in the scene. The inputs refer to the representation of traffic participants (agents) and the representation of the road. In this approach, we considered the past information about an agent, the group context information, i.e., the surrounding agents, and the road context. An overview of the method is presented in Figure 1. The training phase uses information about the current agent's past trajectory and its desired trajectory, the group context that includes information about the past states of the surrounding agents, and road context that includes information about the road structure. The inference phase uses information about the past trajectory of the current agent, the group context, and the road context.

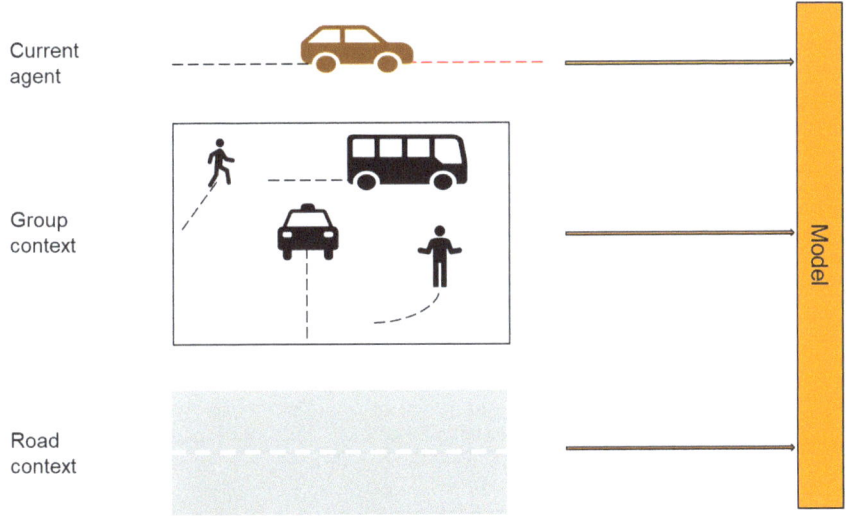

Figure 1. An overview of the multimodal method.

3.1. The Input Vectors

3.1.1. Agent Trajectory Representation

The presented approach aims to handle a variable number of agents of different types. Since the inputs to the neural model have a fixed size, we use a maximum number of agents n_{max} (Figure 2). When an observation is processed, the identified objects are considered "real" agents, and the rest, the unused placeholders, are considered "dummy" agents. The information corresponding to the dummy agents is ignored in the processing using a mechanism described in Section 4.1. In our case studies, n_{max} = 10.

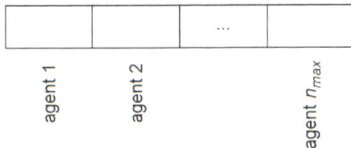

Figure 2. The structure of an input vector. The vector is divided into n_{max} blocks, each block corresponding to an agent.

The first components of an input block corresponding to an agent are displayed in Figure 3.

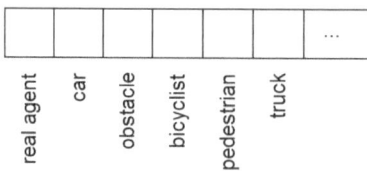

Figure 3. The identification of an agent. Each of the six attributes of the input instance has a binary value designating the presence or absence of a feature. The first attribute is 1 if the block identifies a real agent and 0 if it identifies a dummy agent. The following five attributes constitute a one-hot encoding of the agent type, e.g., the second attribute is 1 if the agent is a car and 0 if it not a car, and so on.

The rest of the input vector contains information about the past trajectory of the agent, including the present state. The trajectory is discretized into n_{in} samples (in our case, $n_{in} = 10$), as shown in Figure 4.

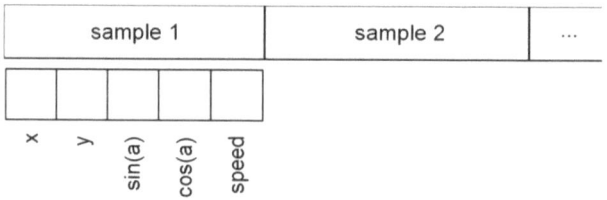

Figure 4. The representation of the past trajectory. Each trajectory sample is defined by the (x, y) position, a tuple $(\sin(a), \cos(a))$ representing the heading angle a, and the instantaneous speed.

For our problem, the x coordinate is normalized between −10 m and 10 m relative to the center line of the road. The y coordinate is normalized between −150 m and 150 m. Thus, the positions of the agents are in fact Frenet coordinates (described in the next paragraph) relative to the present position of the ego vehicle: x corresponds to the lateral displacement (the Frenet coordinate d) relative to the center line of the road, and y corresponds to the longitudinal displacement (the Frenet coordinate s) but relative to the ego agent position. The use of Frenet coordinates has the advantage that it avoids special cases caused by the change of perspective in curves and which may need more training data to cover various types of curves. Using the presented approach, curves are handled in the same way as straight road segments.

If the coordinates of the points representing the curve are in a Cartesian coordinate system, the Frenet transformation (Figure 5) interpolates linearly between the supporting points of the base curve. For the transformation of a 2D pose from Cartesian to Frenet coordinates, it is necessary at first to find the closest linear segment to the Cartesian coordinate. To find the point where the object is projected on this line, the perpendicular vector of the reference path is generated and it is intersected from the object position with the reference path. This results in the distance of the object to the reference path and the distance from the beginning of the path. The Cartesian points can fall onto areas where no perpendicular line can be drawn to a linear spline segment of the base curve, or where a perpendicular line can be drawn to two adjacent linear spline segments; a curve at that point is either convex or concave. In that case, the point is always projected on the first of the two segments. To transform a 2D pose from Frenet to Cartesian coordinates, a linear interpolation is used between the supporting points of the base curve even with the heading angle. A continuous distance function is employed, so that every point in the coordinate system is well defined.

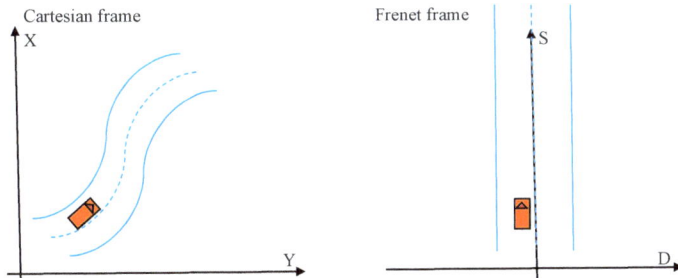

Figure 5. Cartesian frame to Frenet frame transformation.

For the heading angle, simply normalizing a value between [0, 2π) or [0°, 360°) introduces a discontinuity when the angle is around 0. This may happen very often since the "moving straight ahead" angle is considered 0. Therefore, a tuple (sin(a), cos(a)) is used to represent the angle. In this way, the variations are continuous for any value of the angle.

Finally, a trajectory sample contains the instantaneous speed measured in m/s.

An improvement of the representation of the y coordinate takes into account the fact that drivers usually pay more attention to the traffic participants nearby than to those situated at longer distances, especially in urban scenarios with lower speeds than highways and with more agents at lower distances.

Therefore, a technique that we name "focused normalization" can be used, which warps the longitudinal coordinate space in order to provide more details about the short-distance agents and fewer details about the long-distance ones (Figure 6).

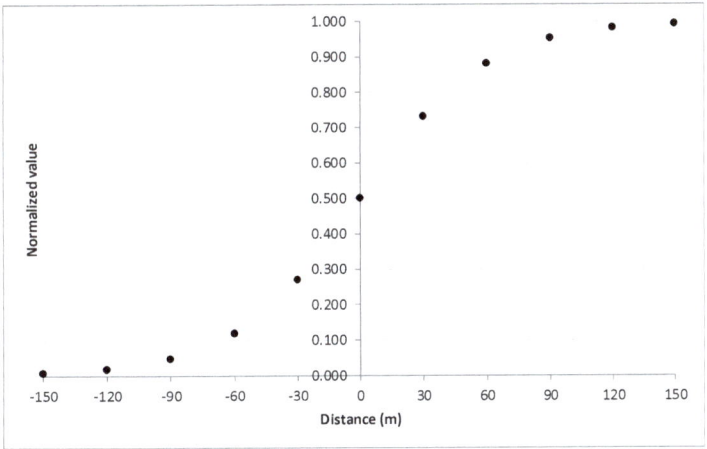

Figure 6. The effect of focused normalization.

This transformation uses a sigmoid function to change the y coordinate:

$$y' = \lambda \cdot (2y - 1)$$
$$y'' = \frac{1}{2} \cdot \left(\frac{1 - e^{-2y'}}{1 + e^{-2y'}} + 1 \right) \quad (1)$$

where λ is a coefficient that controls the width of the non-saturated region of the sigmoid function. In our case studies, $\lambda = 2.5$.

3.1.2. Group Context Representation

The group context is considered in a similar way as the agent trajectory representation. For each agent, the surrounding agents that can influence the behavior in traffic are considered, and we are including the ones that are around the current agent, e.g., 50 m around. As mentioned before, because the number of agents in the nearby area is variable and the inputs to the neural model have a fixed size, we use a maximum number of context agents n_n. For each agent included in the context, we have the agent type: (flags [0/1] [real/dummy agent] [is car] [is obstacle] [is bicycle] [is pedestrian] [is truck/bus]). For example, a truck can be defined as 100,001 and a bicycle as 100,100. For each past point, we consider the coordinates x, y, the pair $\sin(a)$, $\cos(a)$, where a is the heading angle, and the *speed*.

3.1.3. Road Context Representation

The road representation takes into account information about a general area (e.g., 40 m) around the ego agent (longitudinally) and complete information on the width of the road (transversally). Each traffic participant is considered ego in turn for trajectory prediction; therefore, road information may be slightly different for each traffic participant. Each road segment is encoded taking into account the following:

- The segment type: driving lane (100), parking (010), sidewalk (001). One-hot encoding is used, and more types can be included (e.g., crosswalks);
- The distinction between a real road segment or a dummy one (in the form of a binary flag), to account for a variable number of segments.

For each lane in the sight of view, five waypoints are encoded on the center of the lane, at −20 m, −10 m, 0 m, 10 m and 20 m relative to the y coordinate of the ego vehicle. Each waypoint is identified by $(x, y, \sin(a), \cos(a))$, where a is the angle of the road segment (e.g., 0 for "up"/the same direction as the ego, π or 180° for "down"/opposite direction). For a straight road, only 0° and 180° values are possible, therefore $(\sin(a), \cos(a))$ may be replaced by a binary 0/1 flag or a 01/10 encoding. For intersections, actual angle values are useful.

Each road segment, roughly defined by a quadrilateral, is also encoded by means of the four defining points (x_i, y_i) also relative to the ego agent. Their y coordinates are always clipped to the (−20 m, 20 m) range.

In addition, eight values are included for the corners of the rectangle. All in all, there are 32 values for a lane.

For the situation displayed in Figure 7, the following road information would be used:

- S1 (parking lane): [1] [0 1 0] [−5 −20 0 0] ... [−5 20 0 0] [−6 −20] ... [−6 20];
- S2 (driving lane): [1] [1 0 0] [−2 −20 0 −1] ... [−2 20 0 −1] [−4 −20] ... [−4 20];
- S3 (driving lane): [1] [1 0 0] [2 −20 0 1] ... [2 20 0 1] [0 −20] ... [0 20];
- S4 (parking lane): [1] [0 1 0] [5 −20 0 0] ... [5 20 0 0] [4 −20] ... [4 20].

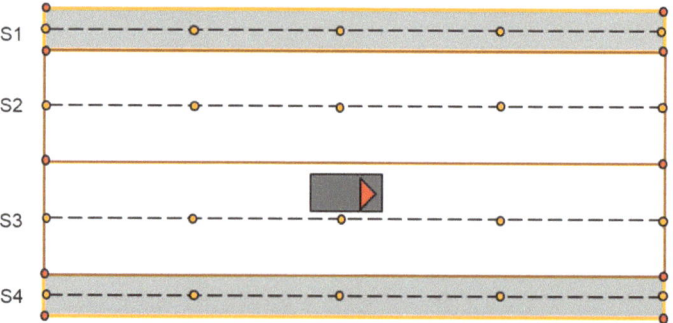

Figure 7. An example of road segment encoding.

In the model, each road segment is encoded into an embedding, as shown in Section 4.1. All the real (non-dummy) segment embeddings are encoded into segment embeddings using max pooling. The resulting road segment features are concatenated with the embeddings of the traffic participants, as part of the context.

3.2. The Output Vectors

Most of the information is contained in the input vectors. Comparatively, the structure of the output vectors is much simpler. It provides predictions for n_{out} steps into the future (in our case, n_{out} = 20). The predictions are made only for the ego agent; therefore, an output vector is a list of n_{out} tuples of (*x*, *y*, sin(*a*), cos(*a*), *speed*).

The ego car needs estimates about the future trajectories of all active traffic participants. Thus, for prediction, each non-dummy agent becomes the ego agent in turn and the model presented in Section 4.1 predicts its possible future trajectories. All these predicted trajectories are further used by the actual ego vehicle for trajectory planning.

4. The Proposed Model

As a distinct feature of the present approach, we use vectors of agent features as inputs into our model, rather than images, because we assume that a segmentation of the image has been performed in a previous step. This was conducted by a different team in the PRORETA 5 project mentioned in the Introduction. However, a large part of the existing work on trajectory prediction takes images as input. Although this may seem like an insignificant difference, working with vectors instead of images proved to have a big influence on the performance of the learning models, because several models proposed as recent state of the art performed worse than expected on this modified problem. Additionally, generative models such as CVAE need some time for sampling to assess the probabilities of different modes, and this may hinder their use for real-time applications. These are the reasons that lead us to develop the model described in this section.

4.1. Network Architecture

In order to correctly predict the movement of the surrounding agents, the system needs to account for their multimodal nature. Thus, we capture the idea that the same history may lead to multiple possible futures. For example, a car closing in behind the ego vehicle may follow it in the next predictable future or may overtake it. Both futures are possible, but the past trajectory of the approaching vehicle is the same in both cases. Based on such previous situations found in the training set, the model needs to compute multiple future trajectories (i.e., modes) and their probabilities.

The proposed model is therefore a neural network with n output heads, one for each mode. Its architecture is presented in Figure 8.

There is an encoding part for the ego vehicle and also for the rest of the agents (the closest n_n agents to the ego agent; in our case, n_n = 9). That consists in three fully connected layers with a leaky ReLU (leaky rectified linear unit) activation function for each case to encode the input information.

For the rest of the agents, a symmetric function must be used to represent the context, because such a function is insensitive to the order in which its operands are considered. In our case, a max pooling component is applied to the embeddings of the other traffic participants. When an agent is a dummy, its embedding is ignored: the embedding is multiplied by the 1/0 flag that shows whether the agent is real or a dummy; therefore, the embedding of a dummy agent becomes a vector of zeros. The context embedding is responsible for capturing the interactions between agents in an implicit form.

The road information is embedded using a similar approach like in the group context. That consists in three fully connected layers with a leaky ReLU activation function for each case to encode the input information, followed by the max pooling component.

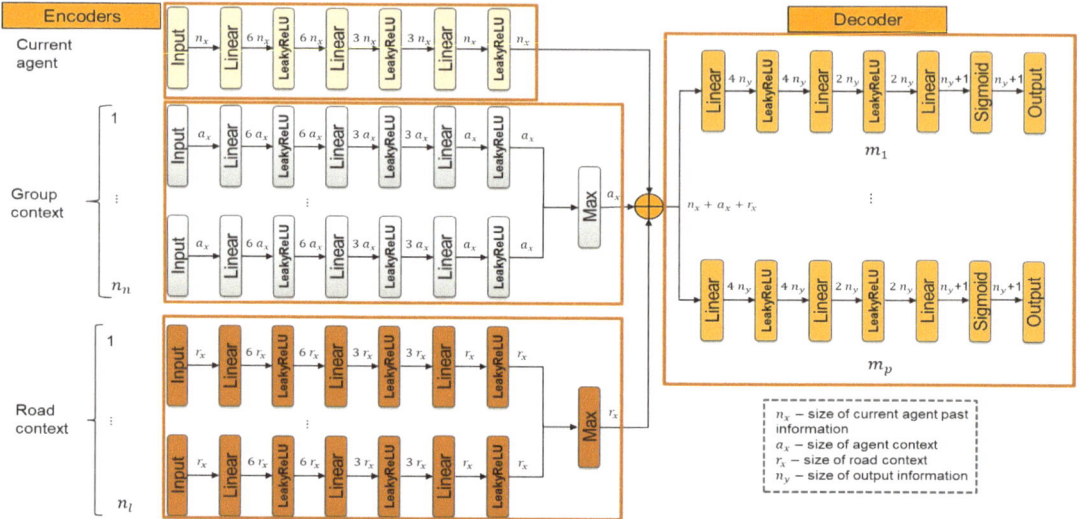

Figure 8. The architecture of the neural network.

The decoding part of the network extracts the information for future trajectories using three fully connected layers with a leaky ReLU activation function and a second fully connected layer with a sigmoid (logistic) activation function.

The outputs represent the future trajectories with a probability for each mode: m trajectories each with my steps into the future plus one value denoting its probability. In our case, $m = 3$ for the multimodal and of course $m = 1$ for the unimodal case.

4.2. The Conditional Loss Function

The training of the model is based on a conditional loss function (inspired by [39]) made up of two terms:

- L_1. A general loss, applied for all modes, which tries to decrease the mean square error (MSE) for the trajectories weighted by the mode probabilities:

$$L_1 = \sum_i p_i \cdot e_i \qquad (2)$$

where p_i is the probability of mode i and e_i is the MSE between the desired trajectory vector and the trajectory vector predicted by mode i. By minimizing L_1, when p_i is high (the mode matches the current instance well), e_i will further decrease, but when p_i is low, the influence on e_i will be small. Therefore, the effect of L_1 is especially strong for the modes with high probabilities. This is in fact a mixture-of-experts loss, where the computed value is an expected MSE given the probabilities of individual "experts", in our case, the individual modes.

- L_2. A special loss used only for the best mode (the best mode is the one with the smallest MSE):

$$L_2 = e_{best} - \log(p_{best}) \qquad (3)$$

On the one hand, L_2 tries to decrease the MSE, that is, to bring the predicted trajectory closer to the desired trajectory for that mode. On the other hand, it tries to increase the probability of the best mode. If the probability of one mode increases, the probabilities of the other modes automatically decrease. This second term of the L_2 loss function is actually a form of cross-entropy loss. Ideally, the best mode should match the current instance perfectly, and, therefore, its target value for the probability is 1, so the second term in Equation (3) is actually $-1 \cdot \log(p_i)$. The other modes should not predict the instance, and so their target values for the probability are 0, which cancel the terms $-0 \cdot \log(p_i)$. The term e_i imposes that the best mode becomes even closer to the desired trajectory of the current instance.

One implementation note may be useful. Since the neural network model was developed with PyTorch [40], the conditional loss involving the finding of the best mode is not straightforward, because a function involving "if" branches may not be continuous and thus not differentiable. Therefore, a matrix $\mathbf{A}$ is computed for each mode such that $A_{ji} = 1$ if mode i is the best mode for instance j and 0 otherwise. The implemented expression for L_2 is actually

$$L_2 = \sum_i (e_i - \log(p_i)) \cdot A_{ji} \quad (4)$$

The loss function is computed for one instance at the time; that is why j does not appear explicitly in Equation (4), but the losses corresponding to all instances in a training batch are eventually summed together.

The final composite loss is the sum of these two functions:

$$L_c = L_1 + L_2 \quad (5)$$

It causes the modes to specialize on distinct classes of agent behaviors, e.g., going straight or turning. Implicitly, this composite loss function encourages a clustering behavior of the modes over the predicted trajectories.

Computing the Mode Probabilities

The values computed by the neural networks for each mode must be converted into a valid probability distribution. This may seem simple at first sight, but it needs special attention because the training process is very sensitive to small probabilities given their use in the loss function, especially when it handles the situations when probabilities are very small, in fact close to 0, and this is often the case for unimodal trajectories. It was empirically found that different transformation formulas for avoiding the cases of 0/0 or log(0) lead to quite different results.

For example, a simple way of avoiding a zero division is to use a small non-zero number ε in the denominator when normalizing the probabilities:

$$p_i' = \frac{p_i}{\sum_i p_i + \varepsilon} \quad (6)$$

However, when the values provided by the neural networks are all very small, this equation may lead to invalid results. Let us assume a situation with two modes, with the computed values (0, 0). The probabilities according to Equation (6) are (0, 0). If the computed values are (0, ε), the probabilities according to Equation (6) are (0, 0.5). Since their sum is not 1, this is not a valid probability distribution.

The variant finally chosen for probability normalization is presented below:

$$p_i' = p_i \cdot (1 - 2\varepsilon) + \varepsilon$$
$$p_i'' = \frac{p_i'}{\sum_i p_i'} \quad (7)$$

First, the values from the neural network are scaled such that 0 becomes ε and 1 becomes $1 - \varepsilon$. The middle value of 0.5 remains unchanged. This is possible because the sigmoid activation function of the neural network provides values only in the [0, 1] interval. Secondly, the values are normalized to create a valid probability distribution, but without the risk of having a division by zero. In this case, (0, 0) becomes (0.5, 0.5) and

$(0, \varepsilon)$ becomes $(0.33, 0.67)$. Larger values provide normally expected results, e.g., $(0.4, 0.7)$ becomes $(0.36, 0.64)$.

4.3. The Fine-Tuning Loss Function

Since the training instances may be affected by noise and variability, a dilemma appears between fitting the training data as well as possible vs. ensuring a good generalization for new situations, especially because the model is meant to be used in a real-world urban scenario on an actual car. A similar problem is present, e.g., when assessing the value of the C parameter for support vector machine (SVM) models, where it controls the balance between trying to create a precise model and allowing training errors to increase the generalization capability.

In our case, if the trajectory points are not identical, overfitting causes mode collapse, where all instances are assigned to a single mode. However, a model with incomplete training may not be affected by this, and thus similar past histories may be assigned multiple modes, but also the training error is larger than desired.

Therefore, we decided to train the model for fewer training epochs, and finally added a fine-tuning phase to decrease the error of the predicted trajectories without changing their probabilities.

For this purpose, a mask **M** is calculated that identifies the dominant mode for each training instance. The outputs corresponding to the predicted trajectory points only for the mode with the lowest MSE are assigned a value of 1, and the rest remain 0. The outputs related to the probabilities also have their mask values equal to 0. Thus, the fine-tuning loss is defined as the mean square loss only for the elements identified by the mask:

$$L_{ft} = \frac{\sum_k \left(\left(y_k - y_k^d \right) \cdot M_{jk} \right)^2}{\sum_k M_{jk}} \qquad (8)$$

where k is the index of the elements of vectors y (the predicted network output), y_d (the desired output), and the columns of **M** (the mask), while j denotes a training instance. Basically, L_{ft} computes the MSE only for the elements included in the mask.

Although only two training cycles were adopted in the present case studies. i.e., one conditional training phase and then one fine tuning phase, it is possible to have more such alternating phases iteratively, in order to enhance both the multi-modal trajectory probabilities and the quality of the trajectories.

5. Case Studies

5.1. Simple Bimodal Trajectories

In this section, we include two very simple problems to demonstrate more clearly the type of problems addressed in our work and the obtained results. These trajectories have only two modes, and the network architecture is simpler, with a (3:24:3) configuration, i.e., 3 inputs, 24 neurons in a hidden layer, and 3 outputs.

First, let us consider a dataset of 1D trajectories with three points in the past and present and three points to be predicted in the future, as displayed in Table 1. These instances correspond to the multimodal trajectory problem displayed in Figure 9. One can see that the first five points are common between the two possible trajectories that diverge afterwards. Since only three points are considered in an instance, the model should identify the two possible trajectories for the inputs in instances 1–3, which are the same as in instances 6–8. Then, the inputs in instances 4–5 and 9–10 should uniquely identify a specific trajectory.

The obtained results are presented in Figure 10. The instances with the same inputs are not repeated, because the results would be the same. These results can be interpreted as follows. The unindented lines represent the three inputs' points. Then, the next two lines represent the computed outputs. In each such line, the three output values are presented.

In the brackets, p (the probability of a mode) and the MSE between the model output and the actual output are included. The content of lines 1–3 corresponds to instance 1 in Table 1; that is why the MSE in line 2 is much smaller than that in line 3, because the MSE is computed for the desired output of instance 1. If we had repeated the inputs for instances 6–8, the MSE corresponding to the second mode would have been close to 0.

Table 1. The dataset for a simple symmetric bimodal trajectory problem.

Instance	Input	Output
1	0.00 0.10 0.20	0.30 0.40 0.50
2	0.10 0.20 0.30	0.40 0.50 0.60
3	0.20 0.30 0.40	0.50 0.60 0.70
4	0.30 0.40 0.50	0.60 0.70 0.80
5	0.40 0.50 0.60	0.70 0.80 0.90
6	0.00 0.10 0.20	0.30 0.40 0.41
7	0.10 0.20 0.30	0.40 0.41 0.42
8	0.20 0.30 0.40	0.41 0.42 0.43
9	0.30 0.40 0.41	0.42 0.43 0.44
10	0.40 0.41 0.42	0.43 0.44 0.45

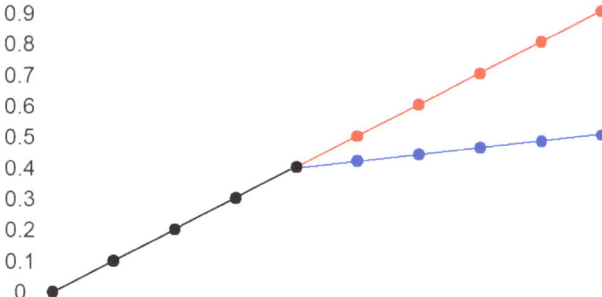

Figure 9. Simple bimodal trajectories.

```
0.0000 0.1000 0.2000
        0.3003 0.4001 0.5003 (p = 0.5044, MSE = 0.0004)
        0.3016 0.4001 0.4101 (p = 0.4956, MSE = 0.0899)
0.1000 0.2000 0.3000
        0.3998 0.5001 0.5998 (p = 0.4934, MSE = 0.0003)
        0.3969 0.4100 0.4200 (p = 0.5066, MSE = 0.2012)
0.2000 0.3000 0.4000
        0.5002 0.6001 0.7000 (p = 0.5050, MSE = 0.0002)
        0.4113 0.4201 0.4301 (p = 0.4950, MSE = 0.3362)
0.3000 0.4000 0.5000
        0.6002 0.7001 0.8006 (p = 0.9987, MSE = 0.0006)
        0.1181 0.4691 0.5013 (p = 0.0013, MSE = 0.6121)
0.3000 0.4000 0.4100
        0.4624 0.6002 0.7813 (p = 0.0001, MSE = 0.3837)
        0.4199 0.4301 0.4401 (p = 0.9999, MSE = 0.0002)
0.4000 0.5000 0.6000
        0.7001 0.8001 0.8997 (p = 1.0000, MSE = 0.0003)
        0.0042 0.5500 0.6196 (p = 0.0000, MSE = 0.7907)
0.4000 0.4100 0.4200
        0.4363 0.5960 0.8184 (p = 0.0000, MSE = 0.4001)
        0.4298 0.4401 0.4501 (p = 1.0000, MSE = 0.0003)
```

Figure 10. The prediction results for the symmetric bimodal problem.

Because the dataset is balanced between the two modes, the probabilities for the first three cases are close to 0.5. The last four cases are the situations where the future trajectory can be uniquely determined from the inputs, thus the result is unimodal. The probability of the dominant mode is close to 1, and the other mode, with a probability close to 0, is represented in gray. Still, it is interesting to see that the inactive modes continue the trends of their learned trajectories, either with a larger slope (the red one) or with a smaller slope (the blue one).

The dataset in Table 2 shows a similar situation, but the first five instances are repeated at the end in order to give them a higher weight in the computation of probabilities, because the network will encounter that case more frequently.

Table 2. The dataset for a simple asymmetric bimodal trajectory problem.

Instance	Input	Output
1	0.00 0.10 0.20	0.30 0.40 0.50
2	0.10 0.20 0.30	0.40 0.50 0.60
3	0.20 0.30 0.40	0.50 0.60 0.70
4	0.30 0.40 0.50	0.60 0.70 0.80
5	0.40 0.50 0.60	0.70 0.80 0.90
6	0.00 0.10 0.20	0.30 0.40 0.41
7	0.10 0.20 0.30	0.40 0.41 0.42
8	0.20 0.30 0.40	0.41 0.42 0.43
9	0.30 0.40 0.41	0.42 0.43 0.44
10	0.40 0.41 0.42	0.43 0.44 0.45
11	0.00 0.10 0.20	0.30 0.40 0.50
12	0.10 0.20 0.30	0.40 0.50 0.60
13	0.20 0.30 0.40	0.50 0.60 0.70
14	0.30 0.40 0.50	0.60 0.70 0.80
15	0.40 0.50 0.60	0.70 0.80 0.90

The results included in Figure 11 show that the probability of the corresponding mode increases to 0.67 as expected, while the unimodal trajectories are still identified by probabilities close to 1.

```
0.0000 0.1000 0.2000
        0.3000 0.4000 0.5000 (p = 0.6665, MSE = 0.0000)
        0.3000 0.4000 0.4100 (p = 0.3335, MSE = 0.0900)
0.1000 0.2000 0.3000
        0.4000 0.5000 0.6000 (p = 0.6658, MSE = 0.0000)
        0.4000 0.4100 0.4200 (p = 0.3342, MSE = 0.2012)
0.2000 0.3000 0.4000
        0.5000 0.6000 0.7000 (p = 0.6656, MSE = 0.0000)
        0.4100 0.4200 0.4300 (p = 0.3344, MSE = 0.3368)
0.3000 0.4000 0.5000
        0.6000 0.7000 0.8000 (p = 1.0000, MSE = 0.0000)
        0.2231 0.4320 0.4493 (p = 0.0000, MSE = 0.5804)
0.3000 0.4000 0.4100
        0.3072 0.4680 0.7430 (p = 0.0000, MSE = 0.3255)
        0.4200 0.4300 0.4400 (p = 1.0000, MSE = 0.0000)
0.4000 0.5000 0.6000
        0.7000 0.8000 0.9000 (p = 1.0000, MSE = 0.0000)
        0.0840 0.4470 0.4749 (p = 0.0000, MSE = 0.8275)
0.4000 0.4100 0.4200
        0.2181 0.4054 0.7808 (p = 0.0000, MSE = 0.3944)
        0.4300 0.4400 0.4500 (p = 1.0000, MSE = 0.0000)
```

Figure 11. The prediction results for the asymmetric bimodal problem.

Again, the non-selected modes still capture an approximation of the other "would-be" trajectory, e.g., going to 0.78 in the last case (according to the red trend), or to 0.47 in the penultimate one (according to the blue trend).

5.2. The inD Dataset

Our main case of study is based on the inD dataset (Intersection Drone Dataset) [41], a recently compiled collection of vehicle trajectories recorded at intersections in Germany using a drone. This method of data collection eliminates the limitations commonly encountered with conventional traffic data collection techniques, such as occlusions. Utilizing modern computer vision algorithms, the positional error is typically within 10 cm. Traffic was recorded at four different intersections and the trajectories of each road agent and its respective type have been extracted. The types of the traffic participants available are cars, buses or trucks, bicyclists, and pedestrians.

5.2.1. Implementation Details

For the InD dataset, for intersection A, information about each class of agent was extracted separately because a distinct model was trained for each type. The dataset contains 135,956 instances, of which 74,530 correspond to cars, 4518 correspond to buses or trucks, 51,121 correspond to pedestrians, and 5787 correspond to bicyclists. Of these instances, 25% were used for testing. Overall, 101,967 instances were used for training, and 33,989 instances were used for testing. The results presented in Section 5.2.2 were obtained only for the testing set.

The predicted trajectories correspond to a 5 s time horizon with 20 trajectory points, each at 0.25 s intervals. To train a model, 100,000 epochs are used, which are split into two parts: the conditional training phase and the fine-tuning phase, as described in Sections 4.2 and 4.3. For each model, the process takes approximately 4 h on a HP Z4 G4 station with a 3.6 GHz Intel 4 Core Xeon W-2123 processor, 32 GB of RAM, and an nVidia GeForce RTX 2080 graphics card.

During the experiments, different optimizers were used, including RMSProp (Root Mean Squared Propagation) and SGD (Stochastic Gradient Descent), as well as different types of activation functions for the hidden layers, such as sigmoid, hyperbolic tangent, ReLU (Rectified Linear Unit), and ELU (Exponential Linear Unit), together with different learning rates. Empirically, it was found that the configuration displayed in Figure 8 and the Adam optimization algorithm with a learning rate of 10^{-3} provided the best results.

5.2.2. Evaluation Metrics

The average displacement error (ADE) and the final displacement error (FDE) are the two most commonly applied metrics to measure the performance of trajectory prediction.

ADE is the average Euclidian distance between the desired data and the predicted data, summed over all time steps:

$$ADE = \frac{\sum_{t=1}^{T}\sqrt{\left(x_t^d - x_t\right)^2 + \left(y_t^d - y_t\right)^2}}{T} \qquad (9)$$

where T is the number of prediction steps, **x** and **y** are the predicted coordinates and $\mathbf{x}^d$ and $\mathbf{y}^d$ are the desired values, i.e., the ground truth.

FDE measures the Euclidian distance between the desired final position and the predicted final position:

$$FDE = \sqrt{\left(x_T^d - x_T\right)^2 + \left(y_T^d - y_T\right)^2} \qquad (10)$$

It measures the ability of a model to predict the destination and is more challenging as errors accumulate over time.

In our experiments, we evaluate the unimodal approach prediction and the best prediction for multimodal approach. We consider the best prediction the one that has the smallest ADE and FDE among the three predicted trajectories.

For each type of traffic participant such as car, truck, bicyclist, or pedestrian, a different model is trained in order to learn the specific behavior that depends on the class of the agent. In Tables 3 and 4, the results for each type of agent in unimodal and multimodal settings are presented.

Table 3. Unimodal results for different agent types.

Agent Type	Unimodal	
	ADE (m)	FDE (m)
Car	0.356	0.602
Truck and bus	0.355	0.571
Bicyclist	0.788	0.474
Pedestrian	0.274	0.473

Table 4. Multimodal results for different agent types.

Agent Type	Multimodal (3 Modes)	
	ADE (m)	FDE (m)
Car	4.532	23.912
Truck and bus	7.798	31.418
Bicyclist	7.571	32.632
Pedestrian	1.533	5.784

In Figure 12, some results are displayed using the unimodal approach when the current agent type is a car. Then, we show some predictions when the current agent type is a bus (Figure 13), a bicyclist (Figure 14), and a pedestrian (Figure 15). The past trajectory of the ego agent is drawn in red, the desired trajectory is drawn in blue, and the predicted trajectory is drawn with light blue. The surrounding agents are represented in blue and yellow. These color codes are the same for all unimodal scenarios.

Figure 12. Traffic scene prediction with the unimodal approach. In this scenario, the car is changing the lane.

Figure 13. Traffic scene prediction with the unimodal approach. In this scenario, the bus is stopping at the bus station.

Figure 14. Traffic scene prediction with the unimodal approach. In this scenario, the bicyclist is going to the sidewalk part of the road.

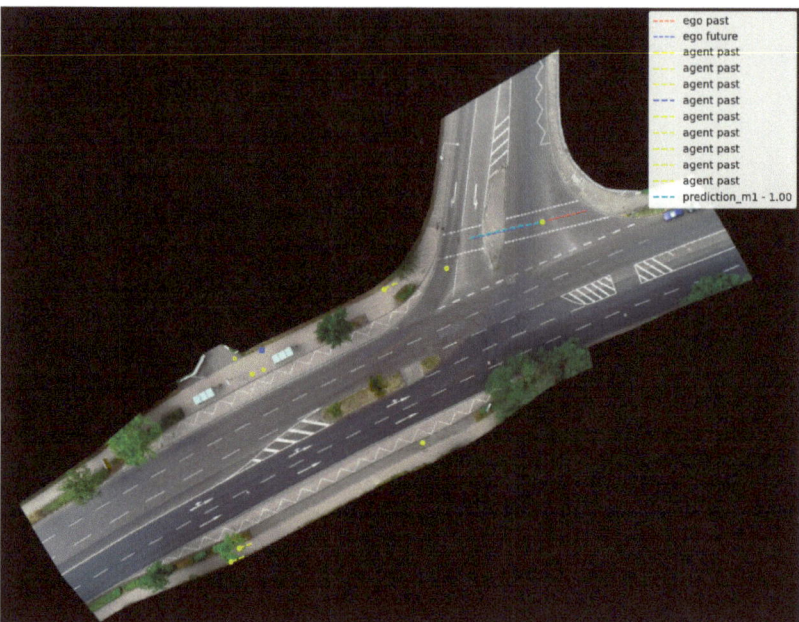

Figure 15. Traffic scene prediction with the unimodal approach. In this scenario, the pedestrian is crossing the street on the sidewalk.

Similar results are presented as follows, this time considering the multimodal prediction. In these scenarios, the predicted trajectory is drawn with light blue, magenta, and green. The current agent types are a car (Figure 16) and a bicyclist (Figure 17).

Figure 16. Traffic scene prediction with the multimodal approach. In this scenario, the car has the most probable maneuver with light blue (turning right) and the second one with magenta (turning left).

Figure 17. Traffic scene prediction with the multimodal approach. In this scenario, the bicyclist has the most probable maneuver drawn with magenta (going to the sidewalk), the second one drawn with green (going to the bus station), and the third one drawn with blue (following the lane).

5.2.3. Decreasing the Number of Predicted Points

An idea for a faster prediction of future trajectories for different traffic participants is to reduce the number of predicted points and to interpolate the values in order to obtain the entire trajectory. This can be observed in Figure 18.

Figure 18. Traffic scene prediction with the unimodal approach and a reduced number of prediction points.

Table 5 contains the results corresponding to fewer predicted points for cars with the unimodal approach.

Table 5. Unimodal results with fewer predicted points.

	Unimodal	
Agent Type	**ADE (m)**	**FDE (m)**
Car	0.355	0.601

5.2.4. Comparison with Other Models

In this section, we include some results obtained in recent years (2021–2023) by other researchers using various methods on the inD dataset. Tables 6–8 organize the results by paper, subset of the database used (e.g., certain intersections), and by model type. The same metrics (ADE and FDE) are considered. When a paper reports multiple results for a certain class of scenarios, only the best ones are included in Tables 6–8, i.e., the best results rather than the average results are selected. It is important to note that the data refer to the trajectory prediction for all vehicles, while our approach also takes into account the type of traffic participants for prediction.

It should be noted that these values should not be directly compared, as different authors use different parts of the inD dataset, different prediction horizons, or even certain predefined data splits to test the models' prediction capabilities. Therefore, a comparison with the results reported in the previous section should be considered from a qualitative point of view. Nevertheless, evaluating different methods for the same dataset can provide the reader with a general idea of the order of magnitude of the obtained errors.

There are other authors who focus only on trajectory prediction for pedestrians, e.g., [34], which uses the general inD dataset. The results are displayed in Table 9.

Upon analysis of the values presented by these authors, we observe that our results are comparable, and even better, in the unimodal case. However, it should be emphasized that our main goal was not solely to minimize some metric, but to create a model that can feasibly run in a real autonomous car. Due to real-time constraints, we were unable to explore more computationally expensive methods that may have resulted in lower errors. Nonetheless, we believe that the prediction quality obtained by our proposed model is on a par with other complex techniques that contribute to the current state of the art.

Table 6. Performance of vehicle trajectory prediction models on the inD dataset reported in [33].

Subset of inD	Model	ADE (m)	FDE (m)
General inD	S-LSTM	1.88	4.47
	S-GAN	2.38	4.66
	AMENet	0.73	1.59
	DCENet	0.69	1.52
	Vanilla-TF	1.07	2.65
	Oriented-TF	1.02	2.57
Intersections (mixed)	Vanilla-TF	2.09	5.85
	Oriented-TF	1.81	4.98
Roundabouts (mixed)	Vanilla-TF	2.75	7.78
	Oriented-TF	2.31	6.38

S-LSTM = Social Long Short-Term Memory; S-GAN = Social Generative Adversarial Network; AMENet = Attentive Maps Encoder Network; DCENet = Dynamic Context Encoder Network; TF = Transformer network.

Table 7. Performance of vehicle trajectory prediction models on the inD dataset reported in [23].

Subset of inD	Model	ADE (m)	FDE (m)
Intersection A	S-LSTM	2.04	4.61
	S-GAN	2.84	4.91
	AMENet	0.95	1.94
	DCENet	0.72	1.50
Intersection B	S-LSTM	1.21	2.99
	S-GAN	1.47	3.04
	AMENet	0.59	1.29
	DCENet	0.50	1.07
Intersection C	S-LSTM	1.66	3.89
	S-GAN	2.05	4.04
	AMENet	0.74	1.64
	DCENet	0.66	1.40
Intersection D	S-LSTM	2.04	4.80
	S-GAN	2.52	5.15
	AMENet	0.28	0.60
	DCENet	0.20	0.45

S-LSTM = Social Long Short-Term Memory; S-GAN = Social Generative Adversarial Network; AMENet = Attentive Maps Encoder Network; DCENet = Dynamic Context Encoder Network.

Table 8. Performance of vehicle trajectory prediction models on the inD dataset reported in [42].

Subset of inD	Model	ADE (m)	FDE (m)
Bendplatz intersection	VectorNet	3.80	7.52
	MTP (based on MLP)	1.10	2.13
Frankenburg intersection	VectorNet	2.19	4.44
	MTP (based on MLP)	1.85	3.62

MTP = Multi-vehicle Trajectory Prediction; MLP = Multi-Layer Perceptron.

Table 9. Performance of pedestrian trajectory prediction models on the inD dataset reported in [34].

Model	ADE (m)
Vanilla-LSTM	1.38
Vanilla-TF	1.07
Context-LSTM	1.03
Context-TF	0.80

LSTM = Long Short-Term Memory; TF = Transformer network.

5.3. Vehicle Integration within the PRORETA 5 Project

A separate dataset was created for vehicle integration, as no dataset was available that matched the specific scenarios required by the project. For this reason, the dataset was created based on real measurements from the vehicle and by using the CARLA simulator [43] with QGIS [44] with the same interfaces as in the real vehicle. The simulated scenarios were created to have more variation in the dataset.

The network models were developed using the PyTorch framework in Python. The trained networks were then exported in the ONNX (Open Neural Network Exchange) format and imported for use with the C language on the car computer.

By using the Frenet coordinate system, the reference path was considered to be the center of the road. This was extracted with a converter from a measurement as we can see in Figure 19. This is the test track that was used to develop the solution in the PRORETA 5 project.

Figure 19. Reference path used for the Frenet transformation.

Beside the difficulties arising from the fact that there were not enough data available for training, another challenge was to synchronize the module with the other modules running on the vehicle. In this case, the prediction approach was implemented to have two options, one to be input-triggered and the other one to be time-triggered (once every 100 ms). For the input-triggered concept, which was eventually used, the prediction module is triggered by the perception module which has a variable frequency of sending output data. Since the prediction must provide a predicted trajectory with a fixed timestamp, in our case 0.2 s, time synchronization is necessary. In order to accomplish this, an additional interpolation module was implemented.

Another important aspect is to check whether a predicted trajectory is valid or not, e.g., if some points are off road or if the distance between the current position and the first predicted point is too large. If it is not valid, it should be replaced by a backup trajectory that is computed based on the specific situation. This is important to ensure a valid output in a real vehicle and to improve the planned trajectory of the ego vehicle that takes into account the predicted trajectories of the other traffic participants.

In Figure 20, one can see some results from the real vehicle that include the planned trajectory of the ego vehicle and the predicted trajectory of the other agents.

 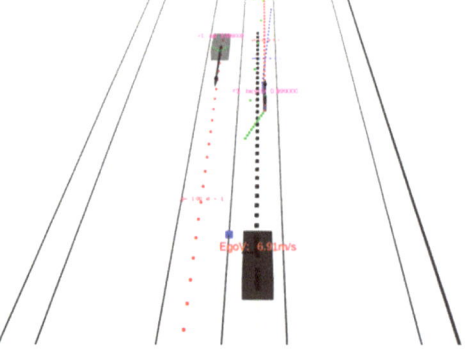

Figure 20. *Cont.*

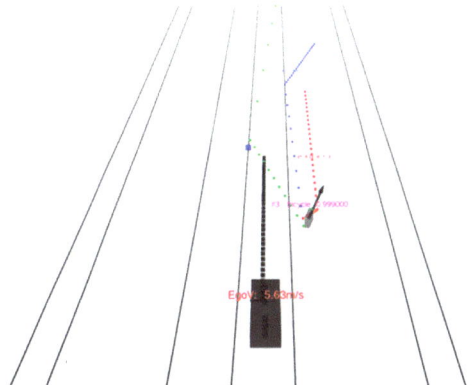

Figure 20. Two examples of traffic scene prediction from the vehicle.

6. Conclusions

In this paper, we propose a method for predicting the trajectories of various types of traffic participants using vectors and an original design of a neural network. This technique was developed using the inD dataset and a dataset created from real-world scenarios. One of the main advantages of this approach is that it is integrated and can be run on a real vehicle.

An important aspect of this research was the dataset used to develop and train the model. In this particular case, vectors were necessary, as opposed to images, because the information from the sensors was assumed to have already been created. Another challenge was that most of the available vector datasets did not match the scenarios required for the project. After studying and implementing various vector approaches, we discovered that some of them did not produce the desired results. This makes a fair comparison between the presented method and other methods difficult to achieve.

The paper shows that the unimodal implementation performs better than the multimodal implementation because most maneuvers follow the lane, and, therefore, many variations in the trajectories cannot be learned. In the case of bicyclists, there are more variations, resulting in better results.

We included many practical details about using prediction in a real-world case, providing a more hands-on approach to the topic. This level of detail is often omitted in other papers, but we have found that different approaches to handling these details can have a significant impact on the overall performance of prediction.

Our method takes into account the constraints related to real-time operation in an actual self-driving car, ensuring that the predictions made are feasible and relevant in a practical setting. Synchronization with other modules, such as the perception and trajectory planning module, is crucial for a successful implementation of this technique.

As future research directions, this method can be extended to newer vector-based datasets and can be applied to other time series, further increasing its scope and potential impact in the field. An additional parameter can be added to measure the level of noise and variation in the data for the multimodal case, in order to create a balance between trying to fit data to a conservative trajectory or allowing several different trajectories to be generated. This would provide a more comprehensive understanding of the data and its reliability, allowing for more informed predictions. An explicit analysis of the uncertainty of predictions is another valuable area for further investigation. This analysis can provide insight into the confidence level of the predictions made by the model and allow for a better understanding of its limitations. It can improve the reliability of the predictions and increase the confidence in the system.

Author Contributions: Conceptualization, F.L.; Investigation, A.-I.P.; Methodology, F.L. and A.-I.P.; Software, F.L. and A.-I.P.; Validation, F.L. and A.-I.P.; Writing—Original draft, F.L. and A.-I.P.; Writing—Review and editing, F.L. and A.-I.P.; funding acquisition, F.L. All authors have read and agreed to the published version of the manuscript.

Funding: This research was funded by Continental AG within the PRORETA 5 project (contracts no. 10118/16.05.2019, 1721/23.01.2020, 12371/21.05.2021, 15290/11.05.2022).

Data Availability Statement: Data sharing not applicable.

Acknowledgments: We kindly thank Continental AG for their great cooperation within PRORETA 5, which is a joint research project of the Technical University of Darmstadt, University of Bremen, "Gheorghe Asachi" Technical University of Iași and Continental AG.

Conflicts of Interest: The authors declare no conflict of interest.

References

1. SAE International. Taxonomy and Definitions for Terms Related to Driving Automation Systems for On-Road Motor Vehicles J3016_202104. 2021. Available online: https://www.sae.org/standards/content/j3016_202104 (accessed on 10 February 2023).
2. PRORETA 5—urbAn Driving. Available online: https://www.proreta.tu-darmstadt.de/proreta/index.en.jsp (accessed on 10 February 2023).
3. Singh, A. Prediction in Autonomous Vehicle–All You Need to Know. Available online: https://towardsdatascience.com/prediction-in-autonomous-vehicle-all-you-need-to-know-d8811795fcdc (accessed on 10 February 2023).
4. Ju, C.; Wang, Z.; Long, C.; Zhang, X.; Chang, D.E. Interaction-Aware Kalman Neural Networks for Trajectory Prediction. In Proceedings of the IEEE Intelligent Vehicles Symposium (IV), Las Vegas, NV, USA, 19 October–13 November 2020; pp. 1793–1800. [CrossRef]
5. Lin, M.; Yoon, J.; Kim, B. Self-Driving Car Location Estimation Based on a Particle-Aided Unscented Kalman Filter. *Sensors* **2020**, *20*, 2544. [CrossRef]
6. Nan, J.; Ye, X.; Cao, W. Nonlinear Model Predictive Control with Terminal Cost for Autonomous Vehicles Trajectory Follow. *Appl. Sci.* **2022**, *12*, 11359. [CrossRef]
7. Buehler, M.; Iagnemma, K.; Singh, S. (Eds.) *The DARPA Urban Challenge: Autonomous Vehicles in City Traffic*; Springer: Berlin/Heidelberg, Germany, 2009.
8. Zhou, B.; Schwarting, W.; Rus, D.; Alonso-Mora, J. Joint Multi-Policy Behavior Estimation and Receding-Horizon Trajectory Planning for Automated Urban Driving. In Proceedings of the 2018 IEEE International Conference on Robotics and Automation (ICRA), Brisbane, Australia, 21–25 May 2018; pp. 2388–2394.
9. Deo, N.; Rangesh, A.; Trivedi, M.M. How Would Surround Vehicles Move? A Unified Framework for Maneuver Classification and Motion Prediction. *IEEE Trans. Intell. Veh.* **2018**, *3*, 129–140. [CrossRef]
10. Schreier, M.; Willert, V.; Adamy, J. An Integrated Approach to Maneuver-Based Trajectory Prediction and Criticality Assessment in Arbitrary Road Environments. *IEEE Trans. Intell. Transp. Syst.* **2016**, *17*, 2751–2766. [CrossRef]
11. Leon, F.; Gavrilescu, M. A Review of Tracking and Trajectory Prediction Methods for Autonomous Driving. *Mathematics* **2021**, *9*, 660. [CrossRef]
12. Salzmann, T.; Ivanovic, B.; Chakravarty, P.; Pavone, M. Trajectron++: Dynamically-Feasible Trajectory Forecasting With Heterogeneous Data. In Proceedings of the European Conference on Computer Vision (ECCV), Glasgow, UK, 23–28 August 2020.
13. Messaoud, K.; Deo, N.; Trivedi, M.M.; Nashashibi, F. Trajectory Prediction for Autonomous Driving based on Multi-Head Attention with Joint Agent-Map Representation. *arXiv* **2020**, arXiv:2005.02545.
14. Chandra, R.; Bhattacharya, U.; Bera, A.; Manocha, D. TraPHic: Trajectory Prediction in Dense and Heterogeneous Traffic Using Weighted Interactions. In Proceedings of the 2019 IEEE/CVF Conference on Computer Vision and Pattern Recognition (CVPR), Long Beach, CA, USA, 15–20 June 2019; pp. 8475–8484.
15. Gao, H.; Su, H.; Cai, Y.; Wu, R.; Hao, Z.; Xu, Y.; Wu, W.; Wang, J.; Li, Z.; Kan, Z. Trajectory Prediction of Cyclist Based on Dynamic Bayesian Network and Long Short-Term Memory Model at Unsignalized Intersections. *Sci. China Inf. Sci.* **2021**, *64*, 172207. [CrossRef]
16. Yang, C.; Pei, Z. Long-Short Term Spatio-Temporal Aggregation for Trajectory Prediction. In *IEEE Transactions on Intelligent Transportation Systems*; IEEE Press: New York, NY, USA, 2023; Volume 24, pp. 4114–4126. [CrossRef]
17. Deo, N.; Trivedi, M.M. Trajectory Forecasts in Unknown Environments Conditioned on Grid-Based Plans. *arXiv* **2020**, arXiv:2001.00735.
18. Nikhil, N.; Morris, B.T. Convolutional Neural Network for Trajectory Prediction. In Proceedings of the Computer Vision—ECCV2018 Workshops, Munich, Germany, 8–14 September 2018; pp. 186–196.
19. Casas, S.; Luo, W.; Urtasun, R. IntentNet: Learning to Predict Intention from Raw Sensor Data. In Proceedings of the 2nd Annual Conference on Robot Learning, CoRL 2018, Zürich, Switzerland, 29–31 October 2018; pp. 947–956.
20. Monti, A.; Bertugli, A.; Calderara, S.; Cucchiara, R. DAG-Net: Double Attentive Graph Neural Network for Trajectory Forecasting. *arXiv* **2020**, arXiv:2005.12661.

21. Bhattacharyya, A.; Hanselmann, M.; Fritz, M.; Schiele, B.; Straehle, C.N. Conditional Flow Variational Autoencoders for Structured Sequence Prediction. *arXiv* **2020**, arXiv:1908.09008.
22. Lee, M.; Sohn, S.S.; Moon, S.; Yoon, S.; Kapadia, M.; Pavlovic, V. MUSE-VAE: Multi-Scale VAE for Environment-Aware Long Term Trajectory Prediction. In Proceedings of the 2022 IEEE/CVF Conference on Computer Vision and Pattern Recognition (CVPR), New Orleans, LA, USA, 18–24 June 2022; pp. 2211–2220. [CrossRef]
23. Cheng, H.; Liao, W.; Tang, X.; Yang, M.Y.; Sester, M.; Rosenhahn, B. Exploring Dynamic Context for Multi-Path Trajectory Prediction. *arXiv* **2020**, arXiv:2010.16267.
24. Lai, W.C.; Xia, Z.X.; Lin, H.S.; Hsu, L.F.; Shuai, H.H.; Jhuo, I.H.; Cheng, W.H. Trajectory Prediction in Heterogeneous Environmentvia Attended Ecology Embedding. In Proceedings of the 28th ACM International Conference on Multimedia, MM '20, Seattle, WA, USA, 12–16 October 2020; Association for Computing Machinery: New York, NY, USA, 2020; pp. 202–210.
25. Sadeghian, A.; Kosaraju, V.; Sadeghian, A.; Hirose, N.; Rezatofighi, H.; Savarese, S. SoPhie: An Attentive GAN for Predicting Paths Compliant to Social and Physical Constraints. In Proceedings of the IEEE Conference on Computer Vision and Pattern Recognition, CVPR 2019, Long Beach, CA, USA, 16–20 June 2019; pp. 1349–1358.
26. Wu, X.; Yang, H.; Chen, H.; Hu, Q.; Hu, H. Long-term 4D Trajectory Prediction Using Generative Adversarial Networks. Transportation Research. *Part C Emerg. Technol.* **2022**, *136*, 103554. [CrossRef]
27. Li, R.; Qin, Y.; Wang, J.; Wang, H. AMGB: Trajectory Prediction Using Attention-Based Mechanism GCN-BiLSTM in IOV. *Pattern Recognit. Lett.* **2023**, *169*, 17–27. [CrossRef]
28. Xu, Y.; Wang, L.; Wang, Y.; Fu, Y. Adaptive Trajectory Prediction via Transferable GNN. CVPR, 2022. *arXiv* **2022**, arXiv:2203.05046.
29. Singh, D.; Srivastava, R. Graph Neural Network with RNNs Based Trajectory Prediction of Dynamic Agents for Autonomous Vehicle. *Appl. Intell.* **2022**, *52*, 12801–12816. [CrossRef]
30. Li, G.; Luo, G.; Yuan, Q.; Li, J. Trajectory Prediction with Heterogeneous Graph Neural Network. In *Proceedings of PRICAI 2022: Trends in Artificial Intelligence*; Lecture Notes in Computer Science; Springer: Cham, Switzerland, 2022; Volume 13630, pp. 375–387. [CrossRef]
31. Deo, N.; Wolff, E.M.; Beijbom, O. Multimodal Trajectory Prediction Conditioned on Lane-Graph Traversals. In Proceedings of the 5th Conference on Robot Learning, London, UK, 8–11 November 2021; Proceedings of Machine Learning Research: Cambridge, MA, USA, 2022; Volume 164, pp. 203–212.
32. Wang, Z.; Guo, J.; Hu, Z.; Zhang, H.; Zhang, J.; Pu, J. Lane Transformer: A High-Efficiency Trajectory Prediction Model. *IEEE Open J. Intell. Transp. Syst.* **2023**, *4*, 2–13. [CrossRef]
33. Quintanar, A.; Fernández-Llorca, D.; Parra, I.; Izquierdo, R.; Sotelo, M.A. Predicting Vehicles Trajectories in Urban Scenarios with Transformer Networks and Augmented Information. *arXiv* **2021**, arXiv:2106.00559.
34. Saleh, K. Pedestrian Trajectory Prediction for Real-Time Autonomous Systems via Context-Augmented Transformer Networks. *Sensors* **2022**, *22*, 7495. [CrossRef] [PubMed]
35. He, C.; Chen, L.; Xu, L.; Yang, C.; Liu, X.; Yang, B. IRLSOT: Inverse Reinforcement Learning for Scene-Oriented Trajectory Prediction. *IET Intell. Transp. Syst.* **2022**, *16*, 769–781. [CrossRef]
36. Lefèvre, S.; Vasquez, D.; Laugier, C. A Survey on Motion Prediction and Risk Assessment for Intelligent Vehicles. *Robomech. J.* **2014**, *1*, 1–14. [CrossRef]
37. Chen, X.Z.; Liu, C.Y.; Yu, C.W.; Lee, K.F.; Chen, Y.L. A Trajectory Prediction Method Based on Social Forces, Scene Information and Motion Habit. In Proceedings of the 2020 IEEE International Conference on Consumer Electronics (ICCE), Las Vegas, NV, USA, 4–6 January 2020; pp. 1–3. [CrossRef]
38. Geiger, P.; Straehle, C.N. Learning Game-Theoretic Models of Multiagent Trajectories Using Implicit Layers. *arXiv* **2021**, arXiv:2008.07303. [CrossRef]
39. Cui, H.; Radosavljevic, V.; Chou, F.C.; Lin, T.H.; Nguyen, T.; Huang, T.K.; Schneider, J.; Djuric, N. Multimodal Trajectory Predictions for Autonomous Driving using Deep Convolutional Networks. In Proceedings of the 2019 International Conference on Robotics and Automation (ICRA), Montreal, QC, Canada, 20–24 May 2019; IEEE Press: New York, NY, USA; pp. 2090–2096. [CrossRef]
40. The Linux Foundation. PyTorch Library. Available online: https://pytorch.org (accessed on 10 February 2023).
41. Bock, J.; Krajewski, R.; Moers, T.; Runde, S.; Vater, L.; Eckstein, L. The inD Dataset: A Drone Dataset of Naturalistic Road User Trajectories at German Intersections. In Proceedings of the 2020 IEEE Intelligent Vehicles Symposium (IV), Las Vegas, NV, USA, 23–26 June 2020; pp. 1929–1934. [CrossRef]
42. Zhu, D.; Khan, Q.; Cremers, D. Multi-Vehicle Trajectory Prediction at Intersections Using State and Intention Information. *arXiv* **2023**, arXiv:2301.02561.
43. CARLA: Open-Source Simulator for Autonomous Driving Research. Available online: https://carla.org (accessed on 10 February 2023).
44. QGIS: A Free and Open-Source Geographic Information System. Available online: https://qgis.org (accessed on 10 February 2023).

Disclaimer/Publisher's Note: The statements, opinions and data contained in all publications are solely those of the individual author(s) and contributor(s) and not of MDPI and/or the editor(s). MDPI and/or the editor(s) disclaim responsibility for any injury to people or property resulting from any ideas, methods, instructions or products referred to in the content.

Article

Effects of Exploration Weight and Overtuned Kernel Parameters on Gaussian Process-Based Bayesian Optimization Search Performance

Yuto Omae

College of Industrial Technology, Nihon University, 1-2-1, Izumi, Narashino, Chiba 275-8575, Japan; oomae.yuuto@nihon-u.ac.jp

Abstract: Gaussian process-based Bayesian optimization (GPBO) is used to search parameters in machine learning, material design, etc. It is a method for finding optimal solutions in a search space through the following four procedures. (1) Develop a Gaussian process regression (GPR) model using observed data. (2) The GPR model is used to obtain the estimated mean and estimated variance for the search space. (3) The point where the sum of the estimated mean and the weighted estimated variance (upper confidence bound, UCB) is largest is the next search point (in the case of a maximum search). (4) Repeat the above procedures. Thus, the generalization performance of the GPR is directly related to the search performance of the GPBO. In procedure (1), the kernel parameters (KPs) of the GPR are tuned via gradient descent (GD) using the log-likelihood as the objective function. However, if the number of iterations of the GD is too high, there is a risk that the KPs will overfit the observed data. In this case, because the estimated mean and variance output by the GPR model are inappropriate, the next search point cannot be properly determined. Therefore, overtuned KPs degrade the GPBO search performance. However, this negative effect can be mitigated by changing the parameters of the GPBO. We focus on the weight of the estimated variances (exploration weight) of the UCB as one of these parameters. In a GPBO with a large exploration weight, the observed data appear in various regions in the search space. If the KP is tuned using such data, the GPR model can estimate the diverse regions somewhat correctly, even if the KP overfits the observed data, i.e., the negative effect of overtuned KPs on the GPR is mitigated by setting a larger exploration weight for the UCB. This suggests that the negative effect of overtuned KPs on the GPBO search performance may be related to the UCB exploration weight. In the present study, this hypothesis was tested using simple numerical simulations. Specifically, GPBO was applied to a simple black-box function with two optimal solutions. As parameters of GPBO, we set the number of KP iterations of GD in the range of 0–500 and the exploration weight as $\{1, 5\}$. The number of KP iterations expresses the degree of overtuning, and the exploration weight expresses the strength of the GPBO search. The results indicate that, in the overtuned KP situation, GPBO with a larger exploration weight has better search performance. This suggests that, when searching for solutions with a small GPBO exploration weight, one must be careful about overtuning KPs. The findings of this study are useful for successful exploration with GPBO in all situations where it is used, e.g., machine learning hyperparameter tuning.

Keywords: machine learning; Bayesian optimization; Gaussian process; overfitting

MSC: 68T01; 62J02

Citation: Omae, Y. Effects of Exploration Weight and Overtuned Kernel Parameters on Gaussian Process-Based Bayesian Optimization Search Performance. *Mathematics* 2023, 11, 3067. https://doi.org/10.3390/math11143067

Academic Editors: Florin Leon, Mircea Hulea and Marius Gavrilescu

Received: 7 June 2023
Revised: 4 July 2023
Accepted: 7 July 2023
Published: 11 July 2023

Copyright: © 2023 by the authors. Licensee MDPI, Basel, Switzerland. This article is an open access article distributed under the terms and conditions of the Creative Commons Attribution (CC BY) license (https://creativecommons.org/licenses/by/4.0/).

1. Introduction

Gaussian process-based Bayesian optimization (GPBO) optimizes black-box functions and is adopted to save time and/or reduce costs. For example, it is used for concrete design [1,2], material design [3–5], and tuning hyperparameters in machine learning (for support vector machines [6–8], random forest models [9,10] and neural networks [9,11,12], etc.). Appropriate parameters can be obtained more rapidly using GPBO compared with simple methods such as grid search. For example, Wu et al. [9] reported that the computation time of hyperparameter tuning in machine learning can be reduced significantly using GPBO. Snoek et al. [11] reported that when GPBO was used for tuning, the developed convolutional neural networks had higher generalization scores than networks with parameters tuned by an expert of machine learning.

To perform GPBO, a Gaussian process regression (GPR) model must be developed, which is computationally expensive. The computational cost of the kernel inverse matrix required in GPBO is $\mathcal{O}(n^3)$ for a data size of n [13]. Due to the fact that n increases with each successive GPBO iteration, the computational cost increases. Therefore, sparse matrix methods [13–16] and mini-batch methods [17] have been proposed for reducing the computational cost.

In the log-likelihood-based objective function, the kernel inverse matrix is used to tune the hyperparameters of the GPR model [18]. Gradient-based methods [17,19,20], evolutionary algorithms [21,22], and Markov chain Monte Carlo methods [23] have been adopted for hyperparameter tuning of the GPR model. Cross-validation [18] is adopted for tuning the kernel parameters (KPs) to avoid overfitting to the observed data. However, because the size of the observed data gradually increases, performing cross-validation at the beginning of GPBO is difficult. Therefore, we cannot perform cross-validation at the beginning of GPBO to tune the hyperparameters of the GPR model. Moreover, cross-validation increases the computational cost [18].

In the early stages of GPBO, the sample size is insufficient. Additionally, it is difficult to properly tune a GPR model by a small sample size [24,25]. Therefore, consider the situation wherein the KPs are tuned using all samples instead of using a method that reduces the number of data, such as cross-validation. In this case, because there are no data for validation, it is not known to what extent the KPs should be fitted to the observed data. Thus, there is a risk of overtuning the GPR model. Overtuned GPR models can correctly estimate observed regions but cannot properly estimate unobserved regions [26]. GPBO is an algorithm that searches for the optimal solution in unobserved regions. Therefore, if unobserved areas cannot be correctly estimated, a proper search cannot be performed. From this viewpoint, the search performance of Bayesian optimization using an overfitted GPR model is expected to be poor.

The negative effect of overtuned KPs on the search performance depends on other parameters of GPBO. We focus on the exploration weight of the upper confidence bound (UCB) [27,28], which is a GPBO parameter. Generally, when the exploration weight is set to a large value, the next search point tends to be selected from regions with insufficient observations; therefore, the observed samples appear in various areas. In this case, even if the KPs are overfitted to the observed samples, the GPR model can correctly estimate the various input domains. In contrast, with a small exploration weight, because the observed samples appear in only limited regions, the overfitted GPR model only estimates limited regions; therefore, its generalization score is worse.

This implies that the risk of overtuned KPs degrading the search performance depends on the exploration weight. We verified this hypothesis by analyzing the relationships among the overtuned KPs, exploration weight, and GPBO search performance. The results indicated that, for GPBO, more attention must be paid to the overtuning of the KPs in the case of smaller exploration weights. Additionally, it is necessary to pay attention to avoid overtuning KPs when searching for the solution via GPBO with a small exploration weight. These findings are useful for successful exploration with GPBO in all situations where it is used, e.g., hyperparameter tuning in machine learning.

As indicated by previous studies [21,24,25], the likelihood function in GPR may have multiple minimal solutions, making it difficult to find a globally optimal solution. Therefore, we focused on gradient descent (GD), which can rapidly obtain a local minimal solution, as a method for tuning the KPs. This method is widely used for tuning the KPs of GPR models [17,19,20].

2. Gaussian Process-Based Bayesian Optimization

2.1. Surrogate Model

In this study, we use the GPR model as a surrogate model for Bayesian optimization, which we call GPBO. This method outputs the estimated average and variance by assuming a Gaussian distribution from the dataset $\mathcal{D}$ consisting of pairs of observed input and output values.

Here, the output value y is obtained as

$$y = f(x) + \epsilon, \tag{1}$$

where $x = [x_1 \cdots x_D]^\top$ is the D-dimensional input vector, $f(x)$ is a black-box function, and ϵ denotes observation noise. In addition, we consider a situation in which a dataset

$$\mathcal{D} = \{(x_n, y_n) | n = 1, \cdots, N\} \tag{2}$$

is collected via N observations. In the case of GPR, assuming that the average of y is zero, the average and variance values of the output y' for the new input data x' are given as follows:

$$\mathbb{E}[y'|x', \mathcal{D}, \theta] = k'(\theta)^\top K(\theta)^{-1} y, \tag{3}$$

$$\mathbb{V}[y'|x', \mathcal{D}, \theta] = k''(\theta) - k'(\theta)^\top K(\theta)^{-1} k'(\theta) \tag{4}$$

where $y = [y_1 \cdots y_N]^\top$. $K(\theta)$ is a kernel matrix defined as follows:

$$K(\theta) = [k(x_i, x_j; \theta)] \in \mathbb{R}_{>0}^{N \times N} \tag{5}$$

where $k(x_i, x_j; \theta)$ denotes the kernel function. For Gaussian kernels, the kernel function is defined as

$$k(x_i, x_j; \theta) = \theta_1 \exp\left(-\frac{||x_i - x_j||_2^2}{\theta_2}\right) + \theta_3 \delta(i,j), \quad \delta(i,j) = \begin{cases} 0, & i \neq j \\ 1, & i = j \end{cases}, \quad \theta \in \mathbb{R}_{>0}^3 \tag{6}$$

where $\theta = (\theta_1, \theta_2, \theta_3)$ is a vector comprising three KPs. Due to the fact that the estimation accuracy depends on the KPs, appropriate tuning is important. $k''(\theta)$ and $k'(\theta)$ are the kernels related to the observed samples x_i and new sample x', respectively, and are defined as follows:

$$k''(\theta) = k(x', x'; \theta), \quad k'(\theta) = [k(x_i, x'; \theta)] \in \mathbb{R}_{>0}^N. \tag{7}$$

2.2. Tuning Kernel Parameters

As stated in the Introduction, the KP vector θ is tuned using GD. Due to the fact that the θ that maximizes the generation probability of the observed output y is desirable, using the log-likelihood, the objective function L is defined as

$$\begin{aligned} L(\theta) &= \log p(y|\theta) \\ &= \log \mathcal{N}(0, K(\theta)) \\ &= \log\left(\frac{1}{\sqrt{(2\pi)^N |K(\theta)|}} \exp\left(-\frac{1}{2} y^\top K(\theta)^{-1} y\right)\right) \\ &\propto -\log |K(\theta)| - y^\top K(\theta)^{-1} y. \end{aligned} \tag{8}$$

We assume that $p(y|\theta)$ is a Gaussian distribution consisting of the average 0 and the covariance matrix $K(\theta)$. When we adopt the gradient method for the objective function, θ

may be negative. Due to the fact that the Gaussian KP θ requires a plus (see Equation (6)), θ is redefined as follows:

$$\theta = g(\theta') \\ = \exp(\theta'), \quad \theta' = [\theta_1'\ \theta_2'\ \theta_3']^\top \quad (9)$$

where the map g is

$$g : \mathbb{R}^3 \mapsto \mathbb{R}^3_{>0}. \quad (10)$$

Therefore, when the gradient method is run as the search target θ' and the obtained parameter is transformed into θ using Equation (9), θ will certainly be positive. Therefore, we use the update equation for the KPs, as follows:

$$\theta'^{(t_g+1)} = \theta'^{(t_g)} + \gamma \nabla L\left(\exp(\theta'^{(t_g)})\right) \quad (11)$$

where t_g represents the iteration count, $\theta'^{(t_g)}$ is the t_g-th specific value of θ', and γ represents the learning rate. This partial differentiation is as follows:

$$\nabla L(\exp(\theta')) = -\operatorname{tr}\left(K(\exp(\theta'))^{-1}\nabla K(\exp(\theta'))\right) \\ + \left(K(\exp(\theta'))^{-1}y\right)^\top \nabla K(\exp(\theta')) \left(K(\exp(\theta'))^{-1}y\right). \quad (12)$$

Due to the fact that K is the matrix consisting of kernel functions, i.e., $\nabla K(\exp(\theta'))$, the partial derivative of $k(x_i, x_j; \exp(\theta'))$ with respect to $\theta_1', \theta_2', \theta_3'$ is required, i.e.,

$$\frac{\partial k(x_i, x_j; \exp(\theta'))}{\partial \theta_1'} = \exp(\theta_1') \exp\left(-\frac{||x_i - x_j||_2^2}{\exp(\theta_2')}\right), \quad (13)$$

$$\frac{\partial k(x_i, x_j; \exp(\theta'))}{\partial \theta_2'} = \frac{\exp(\theta_1')}{\exp(\theta_2')} ||x_i - x_j||_2^2 \exp\left(-\frac{||x_i - x_j||_2^2}{\exp(\theta_2')}\right), \quad (14)$$

$$\frac{\partial k(x_i, x_j; \exp(\theta'))}{\partial \theta_3'} = \exp(\theta_3')\delta(i,j). \quad (15)$$

This calculation technique was described by Mochihashi et al. [29].

After the parameter is updated T_g times, we obtain $\theta'^{(T_g)}$. Substituting this into Equation (9) yields the tuned KP $\theta^{(T_g)}$. According to Equation (10), the obtained parameter $\theta^{(T_g)}$ satisfies the condition of $\mathbb{R}^3_{>0}$.

2.3. Optimization Algorithm for Experiments

Using Equations (3) and (4), the acquisition function of GPBO is defined as

$$A(x'; \beta, \theta) = \mathbb{E}[y'|x', \mathcal{D}, \theta] + \beta\sqrt{\mathbb{V}[y'|x', \mathcal{D}, \theta]} \quad (16)$$

and it is called the UCB [27,28]. Here, with N observed samples, the $N+1$-th (next) observation sample is determined as follows:

$$x_{N+1} = \underset{x' \in \Psi}{\operatorname{argmax}}\ A(x'; \beta, \theta), \quad (17)$$

$$y_{N+1} = f(x_{N+1}) + \epsilon \quad (18)$$

where $\boldsymbol{\Psi}$ represents the domain of the input x'. The second term of the acquisition function, which is defined in Equation (16), controls the search weight. When β is set to a large value, exploration is emphasized. Subsequently, the observation dataset is updated as

$$\mathcal{D} = \mathcal{D} \cup \{(x_{N+1}, y_{N+1})\}. \tag{19}$$

By performing this process T_b times, we obtain the maximum value $y_{\max}$ and the approximate solution $x_{\max}$ as follows:

$$y_{\max} = \max \mathcal{D}_y, \quad x_{\max} = \operatorname*{argmax}_{x \in \mathcal{D}_x} \mathcal{D}_y \tag{20}$$

where $\mathcal{D}_y$ and $\mathcal{D}_x$ are the sets consisting of the output and input values, respectively, of the set $\mathcal{D}$. This procedure is presented in Algorithm 1.

Algorithm 1 Verification-targeted optimization algorithm

Input:
   Initial observation dataset $\mathcal{D}$, maximum number of BO iterations T_b,
   maximum number of GD iterations T_g, GD learning rate γ, exploration weight β,
   black-box function $f(x)$, observation noise ϵ,
   search space $\boldsymbol{\Psi}$, initial KP $\boldsymbol{\theta}^{(0)} = \exp(\boldsymbol{\theta}'^{(0)})$

Output:
   Solution $x_{\max}$ and its value $y_{\max}$

....

1: **for** $t_b = 1$ to T_b **do**
2:    **for** $t_g = 0$ to $T_g - 1$ **do**
3:      $\boldsymbol{\theta}'^{(t_g+1)} \leftarrow \boldsymbol{\theta}'^{(t_g)} + \gamma \nabla L\left(\exp(\boldsymbol{\theta}'^{(t_g)})\right)$
4:    **end for**
5:    $\boldsymbol{\theta}^{(T_g)} \leftarrow \exp\left(\boldsymbol{\theta}'^{(T_g)}\right)$
6:    $x_{N+1} \leftarrow \operatorname*{argmax}_{x' \in \boldsymbol{\Psi}} A(x'; \beta, \boldsymbol{\theta}^{(T_g)})$
7:    $y_{N+1} \leftarrow f(x_{N+1}) + \epsilon$
8:    $\mathcal{D} \leftarrow \mathcal{D} \cup \{(x_{N+1}, y_{N+1})\}$
9: **end for**
10: $y_{\max} \leftarrow \max \mathcal{D}_y, \ x_{\max} \leftarrow \operatorname*{argmax}_{x \in \mathcal{D}_x} \mathcal{D}_y$
11: **return** $x_{\max}, y_{\max}$

....

Notes:
· Lines 2–4: Tuning the KPs via GD;
· Lines 6–8: Decisions regarding the next search point and observation;
· Lines 10–11: Obtain an approximate solution.
"GD": gradient descent, "BO": Bayesian optimization

2.4. Indices

The GPBO search performance depends on the training and generalization errors of the surrogate model. Therefore, the training and generalization errors are, respectively, defined as

$$E_t(\boldsymbol{\theta}) = \frac{1}{N} \sum_{n=1}^{N} (y_n - \mathbb{E}[y_n | x_n, \mathcal{D}, \boldsymbol{\theta}])^2, \tag{21}$$

$$E_v(\boldsymbol{\theta}) = \frac{1}{|\boldsymbol{\Psi}|} \sum_{x \in \boldsymbol{\Psi}} (f(x) - \mathbb{E}[y | x, \mathcal{D}, \boldsymbol{\theta}])^2. \tag{22}$$

Moreover, the GPBO search performance depends on whether the next search point x_{N+1} and past observed points $x_1, \cdots, x_N$ are close, i.e., if the search is performed only near past observation points, the search performance is poor. Therefore, we determine whether they are close to each other as follows:

$$\min\{||x_{N+1} - x_n||_2 \mid n = 1, \cdots, N\} < \omega \tag{23}$$

where ω denotes the threshold value. When the minimum distance on the left side is less than ω, the next search point x_{N+1} is close to the previously observed points $x_1, \cdots, x_N$.

Furthermore, whether the KP vector $\theta'^{(T_g)}$ obtained as T_g times GD has converged is determined as follows:

$$\frac{||\theta'^{(T_g)} - \theta'^{(T_g-1)}||_2}{||\theta'^{(T_g-1)}||_2} < \tau \tag{24}$$

where τ is the threshold for the convergence criterion. The term on the left side is called the "relative change in parameters," and it is widely used as a convergence criterion [30–32].

Table 1. Input values for Algorithm 1. $\{\cdot\}$ is a set consisting of multiple elements, i.e., multiple patterns were adopted.

Parameters	Value(s)
Maximum number of GD iterations T_g	$\{0, 50, 100, \cdots, 500\}$
GD learning rate γ	0.01
Maximum number of BO iterations T_b	50
Exploration weight β	$\{1, 5\}$
Initial KP $\theta^{(0)}$	$[1\ 1\ 1]^\top$
Search space Ψ	Equation (25)
Black-box function $f(x)$	Equation (25)
Observation noise ϵ	0
Initial observation dataset $\mathcal{D}$	Four points randomly selected in Ψ

3. Experiments

3.1. Objective and Outline

From the definition of $A(x'; \beta, \theta)$, the search performance of GPBO depends on the KP θ. Due to the fact that the KP is obtained via GD, the maximum number of iterations for updating T_g significantly affects the GPBO search performance. When the number of iterations T_g is too high, the surrogate model is overfitted to the observation samples. In such cases, a relatively poor search performance is expected. When the exploration weight is set to a large value, because the observed samples occur in various regions in the input domain, the generalization error caused by overfitting may be mitigated. In contrast, when a small value is used for the exploration weight, because observation samples only occur in limited regions, the generalization error can be larger. Due to the fact that the generalization performance of the surrogate model affects the GPBO search performance, we consider that the negative effect of the overfitted KPs on the search performance depends on the exploration weight β. This hypothesis was verified through a simple numerical simulation.

We adopted the black-box function $f(x)$ and its search space Ψ as follows:

$$f(x) = \frac{1}{3} \sin \frac{x_1}{3} \sin \frac{x_2}{3} - \frac{(x_1)^2}{300} - \frac{(x_2)^2}{300} + \frac{5}{6}, \quad x \in \Psi := [-10, 10] \times [-10, 10]. \tag{25}$$

For simplicity, we set the observation noise to $\epsilon = 0$. The black-box function is shown in Figure 1. The adopted black-box function had two optimal solutions.

We used GPBO based on Algorithm 1, and the values of the input parameters are presented in Table 1. To verify the aforementioned hypothesis, the effects of the degree of kernel-parameter tuning and the exploration weight on the GPBO search performance were analyzed. Therefore, we adopted multiple values for the maximum number of GD iterations T_g and exploration weight β. Moreover, the initial observation dataset $\mathcal{D}$ comprised four randomly selected points $x_1, \cdots, x_4$ from the search space $\boldsymbol{\Psi}$. To enhance the reliability of the results, we performed 20 experiments in which the same parameter conditions were used but the random seed identification was changed.

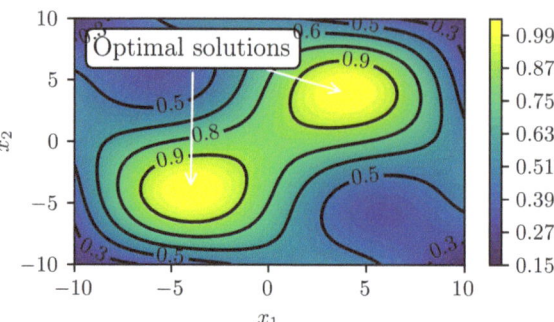

Figure 1. Adopted black-box function $f(x)$ defined by Equation (25).

3.2. Results and discussions

The relationship between the maximum number of GD iterations and the kernel-parameter tuning is presented in Figure 2A. The figure shows the rate at which the KPs $\theta^{(T_g)}$ obtained via the GD of each Bayesian optimization step of 50 iterations converged. We investigated whether the convergence was determined by Equation (24) for $\tau = 0.01$. The results represent the averages of 20 trials with different seeds. For $\beta = 1$ and 5, Figure 2A suggests that the log-likelihood converged when the maximum number of GD iterations T_g was set as more than approximately 300. Therefore, we regarded the KPs as overtuned at >300 GD iterations.

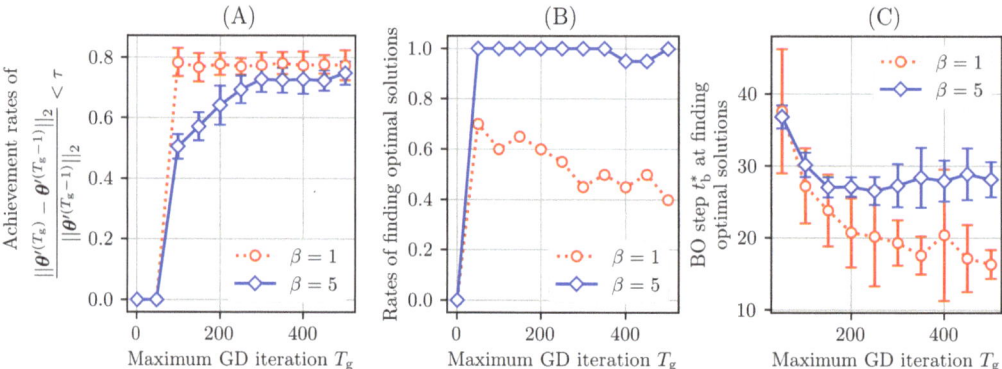

Figure 2. Relationships between the maximum number of GD iterations and other indices. Figure (**A**) presents the convergence achievement rates for Equation (24). (First, we averaged the results of all the Bayesian optimization steps ($T_b = 50$). Then, the averages and standard deviations of the results for 20 seeds were calculated.) Figure (**B**) presents the rates of finding two optimal solutions (total of 20 seeds). Figure (**C**) presents the average number of optimization steps needed for finding two optimal solutions calculated with only the results where two optimal solutions were successfully found (total of 20 seeds). The error bars indicate the standard deviations.

Figure 2B shows the rate of finding the two optimal solutions in 20 trials with different seeds. The maximum number of GD iterations was the degree of kernel-parameter tuning via GD. For $\beta = 1$, a larger maximum number of GD iterations corresponded to worse search performance. In contrast, for $\beta = 5$, even when the maximum number of GD iterations was large, the rates of finding solutions remained high. Therefore, we consider that even if KPs are overtuned to the observation dataset, in cases of a large exploration weight, GPBO can adequately search for solutions (of course, it is desirable to avoid overfitting). Figure 2C presents the average number of Bayesian optimization steps needed for finding two optimal solutions calculated using only the results where two optimal solutions were successfully found. As shown, for a smaller value of β and a larger number of KPs tuned, the optimal solutions were found faster. However, as shown in Figure 2B, the rate of correctly finding the optimal solutions was lower. Therefore, for a small β, the KPs should not be excessively tuned. In contrast, for a large β, the negative effect caused by the overtuned KPs was not observed.

Next, we verified the training error $E_t(\boldsymbol{\theta})$ and generalization error $E_v(\boldsymbol{\theta})$ defined by Equations (21) and (22) for analyzing the effect of the exploration weight β on the GPBO search performance. Figure 3A,B show the training errors. Figure 3C,D show the generalization errors. We transformed them into log errors, that is, using $\log E_t(\boldsymbol{\theta})$ instead of $E_t(\boldsymbol{\theta})$. As the maximum number of GD iterations T_g and number of Bayesian optimization steps t_b increased, the training errors decreased. In contrast, in the latter half of the Bayesian optimization process, a higher number of tuned KPs (i.e., larger T_g) corresponded to larger generalization errors. When the generalization error of the surrogate model was large, because the reliability of the first term of the acquisition function defined by Equation (16) was low, the GPBO search performance was poor. From these results, for $\beta = 1$, we attribute the degradation of the GPBO search performance to the overtuning of the KPs, which increased the generalization error. For $\beta = 5$, even when the KPs were overtuned, there were many regions with small generalization errors. Therefore, in this case, we consider that the GPBO search performance was not degraded.

When observation samples occur in a limited region, the generalization error is large, because the surrogate model based on these data cannot correctly estimate the output values of various regions in the search space. To verify this hypothesis, we used Equation (23) with $\omega = 0.5$ and calculated the rate at which the next search point determined by Equation (17) and the observed points were close. The results are presented in Figure 3E,F. Figure 3E suggests that, when the exploration weight was set as $\beta = 1$, the GPBO searched for areas close to previously observed samples. This was particularly true when large numbers of KPs were tuned. For example, in the case of $\beta = 1$ and $T_g = 500$, when the number of Bayesian optimization steps exceeded approximately 35 ($t_b > 35$), the search area of GPBO remained close to the previously observed samples. This trend was weaker for a smaller value of T_g. Thus, there was a stronger tendency to search close to the previously observed samples when the KPs were overtuned. Therefore, we considered the GPBO search performance to be poor. Figure 3F suggests that, for $\beta = 5$, the GPBO searched various areas even if the KPs were overtuned. In summary, from Figure 3E,F, the degree of kernel-parameter tuning affected whether GPBO searched areas close to previously observed samples. Moreover, a smaller exploration weight β corresponded to a higher risk. Thus, for a smaller value of β, there should be more focus on kernel-parameter tuning.

Next, we present the changes in the surrogate model for each Bayesian optimization step in Figures 4 and 5. These values were $\beta = 1, 5$, respectively. Due to the fact that we cannot show the results for all the seeds, the results for a specific seed are shown. In the case where no KPs were tuned, that is, $T_g = 0$, appropriate searches were not performed regardless of β. For $T_g = 0$, Figure 3A–D indicate that the training and generalization errors were large. We believe that, because the surrogate model was inappropriate, the GPBO search was inappropriate.

With a small number of KPs tuned, i.e., $T_g = 50$, the average $\mathbb{E}$ generated from the surrogate model nearly succeeded in reproducing the black-box function $f(x)$ regardless of β. Therefore, the rate of correctly finding the optimal solution was high (see Figure 2B).

Figures 4 and 5 suggest that, when the number of iterations of KP tuning was $T_g = 500$, the search results depended on the exploration weight β. For $\beta = 1$, because the GPBO searched only the neighborhood of the best point from the initial solutions, even if the search progressed, the output from the surrogate model $\mathbb{E}$ could not reproduce the black-box function $f(x)$. In contrast, for $\beta = 5$, because observation samples appeared in various areas, even if the KPs were overtuned, the output of the surrogate model $\mathbb{E}$ reproduced the black-box function $f(x)$. The results indicate that the negative effect of overtuning the KPs on the GPBO search performance can be mitigated by increasing the exploration weight β.

However, in both the $\beta = 1$ and 5 cases, when the number of iterations of KP tuning increased ($T_g = 500$), the surrogate model output was inappropriate when the number of BO steps t_b was approximately 30–35 (the cases of $T_g = 500$ are shown in Figures 4 and 5). In general, overfitting parameters to observed data increases the risk of reduced estimation performance in areas where there are no observed data. Therefore, overfitting can easily occur with high T_g values. Due to the fact that this occurs in both the cases of $\beta = 1$ and 5, it is important not to overtune the KPs, regardless of the exploration weight. Although the negative effects of overtuned KPs can be mitigated by increasing the exploration weight, they cannot be completely eliminated.

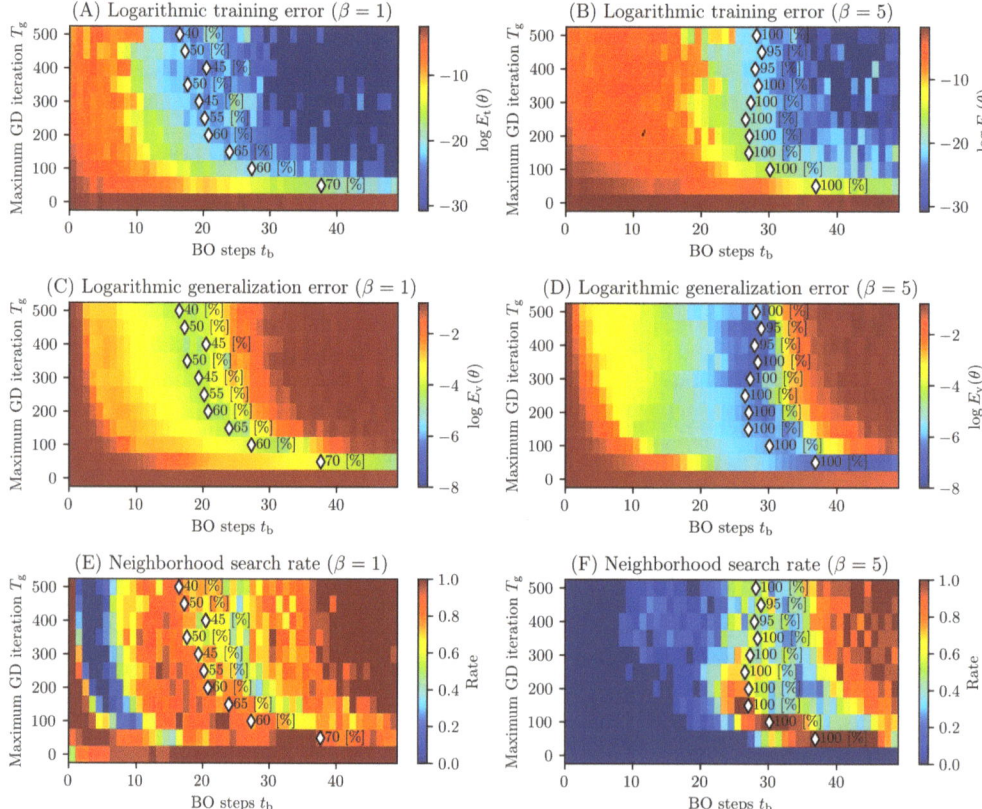

Figure 3. (**A**,**B**) Training errors of surrogate models calculated using Equation (21) for each maximum number of GD iterations; (**C**,**D**) generalization errors calculated using Equation (22); (**E**,**F**) rates of exploring the neighborhood of past observed samples. The values of (**A**–**D**) are the averages of 20 seeds, and those of (**E**,**F**) are the rates of 20 seeds. The white markers indicate the timings of finding two optimal solutions, and the percentages are the success rates of finding them in 20 trials with different seeds. These results are presented in Figure 2B,C. In the cases of $\beta = 1$, with a larger maximum number of GD iterations, although a solution was found faster, the success rate was worse. At $\beta = 5$, no such trend was observed.

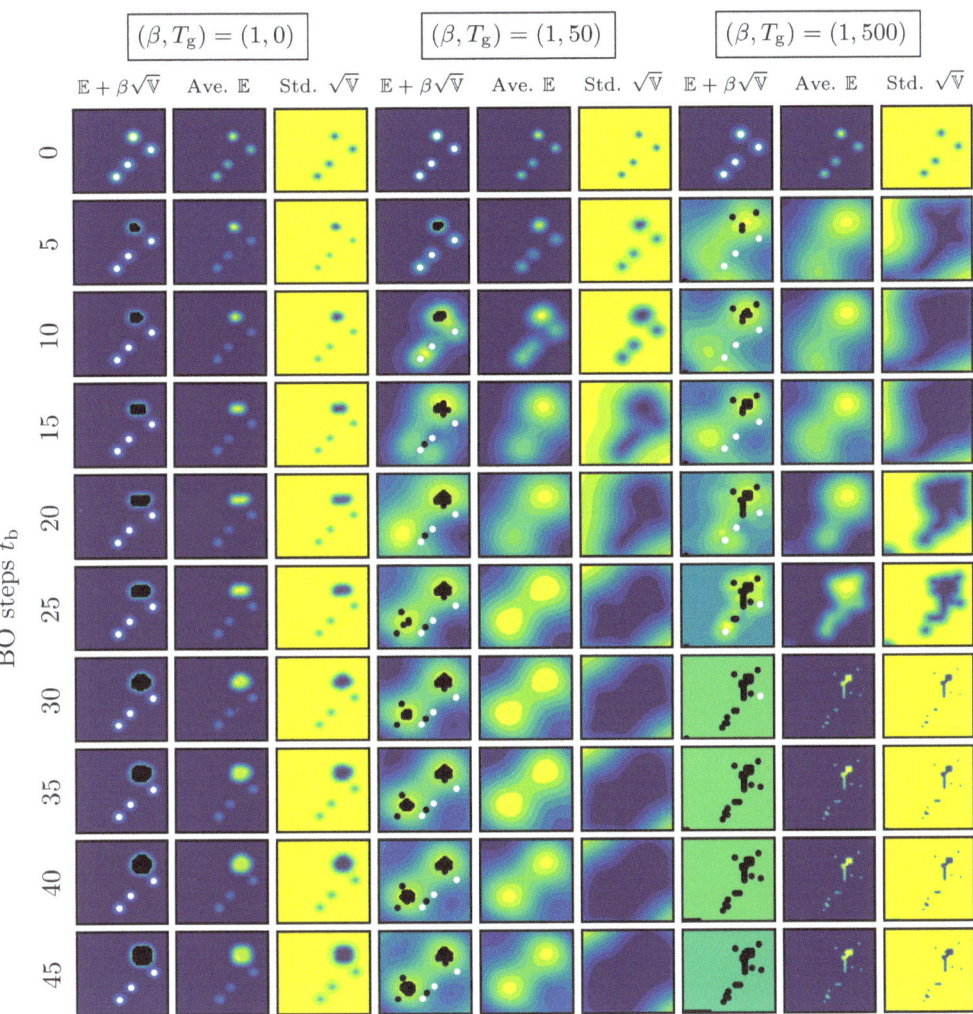

Figure 4. Average $\mathbb{E}$, standard deviation $\sqrt{\mathbb{V}}$ of the surrogate model, and the acquisition function $\mathbb{E} + \beta\sqrt{\mathbb{V}}$ for the maximum number of GD iterations T_g and exploration weight $\beta = 1$ calculated using Equations (3), (4) and (16). The white circles represent initial points, and the black circles represent observation points selected by the acquisition function.

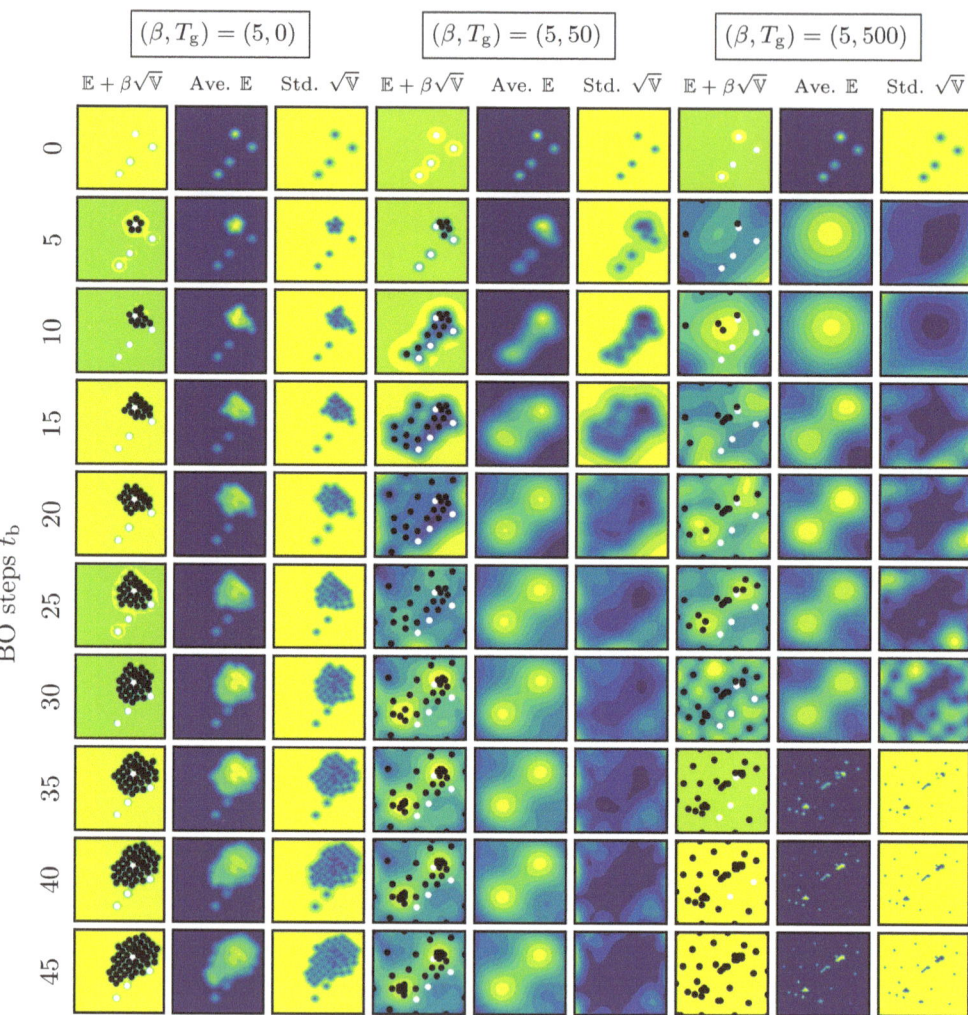

Figure 5. Average $\mathbb{E}$, standard deviation $\sqrt{\mathbb{V}}$ of the surrogate model, and the acquisition function $\mathbb{E} + \beta\sqrt{\mathbb{V}}$ for the maximum number of GD iterations T_g and exploration weight $\beta = 5$ calculated using Equations (3), (4) and (16). The white circles represent initial points, and the black circles represent observation points selected by the acquisition function.

4. Conclusions

The exploration weight affects the degree of exploration of GPBO. Therefore, the GPBO search performance depends on the exploration weight. In this study, we analyzed the mitigation of the negative effect of overtuning KPs as another effect of the exploration weight. The results indicate that we should pay attention to overtuning the KPs in the case of Bayesian optimization with a small exploration weight. It is preferable to use methods for avoiding the overtuning of KPs, e.g., early stopping of the GD. In contrast, for large exploration weights, the solution discovery rate is high even when overtuning the KPs. These findings are useful in all situations wherein GPBO is used, e.g., hyperparameter tuning in machine learning.

The results and discussions presented in this paper are entirely based on the blackbox function defined by Equation (25). The function has two optimal solutions clearly visible in the domain. However, it is not known whether the results of this study would be reproduced if flat functions such as the Beale function [33] or the Goldstein–Price function [34] (the minimum search) were adopted. As shown in Figure 6, the structure of these functions is apparent after log transformation. A similar result can be obtained with a flat function, or a logarithmic transformation may have to be performed. These points are unclear and will be discussed in a future work.

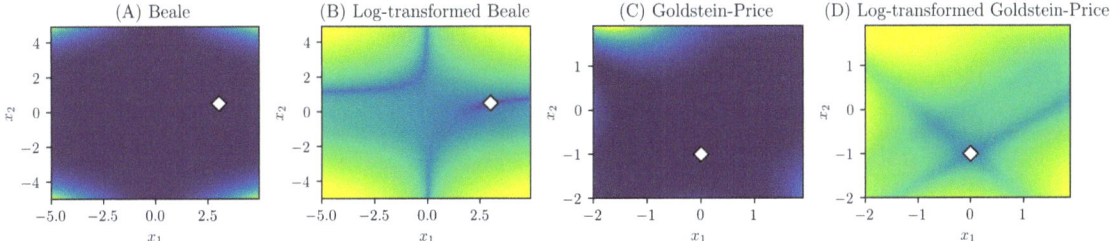

Figure 6. (**A**) Beale function [33], (**B**) log-transformed Beale function, (**C**) Goldstein–Price function [34], and (**D**) log-transformed Goldstein–Price function. The white diamond mark represents the global optimal solution.

Funding: This work was supported in part by JSPS Grants-in-Aid for Scientific Research (C) (Grant Nos. 21K04535 and 23K11310) and a JSPS Grant-in-Aid for Young Scientists (Grant No. 19K20062).

Institutional Review Board Statement: Not applicable.

Data Availability Statement: Not applicable.

Conflicts of Interest: The authors declare no conflict of interest.

References

1. Saleh, E.; Tarawneh, A.; Naser, M.Z.; Abedi, M.; Almasabha, G. You only design once (YODO): Gaussian Process-Batch Bayesian optimization framework for mixture design of ultra high performance concrete. *Constr. Build. Mater.* **2022**, *330*, 127270. [CrossRef]
2. Mathern, A.; Steinholtz, O.S.; Sjöberg, A.; Önnheim, M.; Ek, K.; Rempling, R.; Gustavsson, E.; Jirstrand, M. Multi-objective constrained Bayesian optimization for structural design. *Struct. Multidiscip. Optim.* **2021**, *63*, 689–701. [CrossRef]
3. Frazier, P.I.; Wang, J. Bayesian optimization for materials design. *Springer Ser. Mater. Sci.* **2015**, *225*, 45–75. [CrossRef]
4. Ohno, H. Empirical studies of Gaussian process based Bayesian optimization using evolutionary computation for materials informatics. *Expert Syst. Appl.* **2018**, *96*, 25–48. [CrossRef]
5. Ueno, T.; Rhone, T.D.; Hou, Z.; Mizoguchi, T.; Tsuda, K. COMBO: An efficient Bayesian optimization library for materials science. *Mater. Discov.* **2016**, *4*, 18–21. [CrossRef]
6. Elsayad, A.M.; Nassef, A.M.; Al-Dhaifallah, M. Bayesian optimization of multiclass SVM for efficient diagnosis of erythemato-squamous diseases. *Biomed. Signal Process. Control* **2022**, *71*, 103223. [CrossRef]
7. Agrawal, A.K.; Chakraborty, G. On the use of acquisition function-based Bayesian optimization method to efficiently tune SVM hyperparameters for structural damage detection. *Struct. Control. Health Monit.* **2021**, *28*, e2693. . [CrossRef]
8. Xie, W.; Nie, W.; Saffari, P.; Robledo, L.F.; Descote, P.Y.; Jian, W. Landslide hazard assessment based on Bayesian optimization–support vector machine in Nanping City, China. *Nat. Hazards* **2021**, *109*, 931–948. [CrossRef]
9. Wu, J.; Chen, X.Y.; Zhang, H.; Xiong, L.D.; Lei, H.; Deng, S.H. Hyperparameter Optimization for Machine Learning Models Based on Bayesian Optimization. *J. Electron. Sci. Technol.* **2019**, *17*, 26–40. [CrossRef]
10. Kumar, P.; Nair, G.G. An efficient classification framework for breast cancer using hyper parameter tuned Random Decision Forest Classifier and Bayesian Optimization. *Biomed. Signal Process. Control* **2021**, *68*, 102682. [CrossRef]
11. Snoek, J.; Larochelle, H.; Adams, R.P. Practical Bayesian Optimization of Machine Learning Algorithms. In Proceedings of the 25th International Conference on Neural Information Processing Systems, Lake Tahoe, NV, USA, 3–6 December 2012.
12. Kolar, D.; Lisjak, D.; Pajak, M.; Gudlin, M. Intelligent Fault Diagnosis of Rotary Machinery by Convolutional Neural Network with Automatic Hyper-Parameters Tuning Using Bayesian Optimization. *Sensors* **2021**, *21*, 2411. [CrossRef] [PubMed]
13. Snelson, E.; Ghahramani, Z. Local and global sparse Gaussian process approximations. In Proceedings of the Eleventh International Conference on Artificial Intelligence and Statistics, San Juan, Puerto Rico, 21–24 March 2007; pp. 524–531.
14. Snelson, E.; Ghahramani, Z. Sparse Gaussian Processes using Pseudo-inputs. In Proceedings of the 18th International Conference on Neural Information Processing Systems, Vancouver, BC, Canada 5–8 December 2005.
15. Csató, L.; Opper, M. Sparse On-Line Gaussian Processes. *Neural Comput.* **2002**, *14*, 641–668. [CrossRef] [PubMed]

16. Seeger, M.W.; Williams, C.K.I.; Lawrence, N.D. Fast Forward Selection to Speed Up Sparse Gaussian Process Regression. In Proceedings of the Ninth International Workshop on Artificial Intelligence and Statistics, Key West, FL, USA, 3–6 January 2003; pp. 254–261.
17. Chen, H.; Zheng, L.; Kontar, R.A.; Raskutti, G. Gaussian Process Parameter Estimation Using Mini-batch Stochastic Gradient Descent: Convergence Guarantees and Empirical Benefits. *J. Mach. Learn. Res.* **2022**, *23*, 1–59.
18. Martino, L.; Laparra, V.; Camps-Valls, G. Probabilistic cross-validation estimators for Gaussian Process regression. In Proceedings of the 25th European Signal Processing Conference, EUSIPCO 2017, Kos, Greece, 28 August–2 September 2017; pp. 823–827. [CrossRef]
19. Zhang, R.; Zhao, X. Inverse Method of Centrifugal Pump Blade Based on Gaussian Process Regression. *Math. Probl. Eng.* **2020**, *2020*, 4605625. [CrossRef]
20. Senanayake, R.; O'callaghan, S.; Ramos, F. Predicting Spatio-Temporal Propagation of Seasonal Influenza Using Variational Gaussian Process Regression. *Proc. AAAI Conf. Artif. Intell.* **2016**, *30*, 3901–3907. [CrossRef]
21. Petelin, D.; Filipic, B.; Kocijan, J. Optimization of Gaussian process models with evolutionary algorithms. In *Lecture Notes in Computer Science (Including Subseries Lecture Notes in Artificial Intelligence and Lecture Notes in Bioinformatics)*; Springer: Berlin/Heidelberg, Germany, 2011; Volume 6593, pp. 420–429. [CrossRef]
22. Ouyang, Z.L.; Zou, Z.J. Nonparametric modeling of ship maneuvering motion based on Gaussian process regression optimized by genetic algorithm. *Ocean Eng.* **2021**, *238*, 109699. [CrossRef]
23. Cheng, L.; Ramchandran, S.; Vatanen, T.; Lietzen, N.; Lahesmaa, R.; Vehtari, A.; Lähdesmäki, H. LonGP: An additive Gaussian process regression model for longitudinal study designs. *bioRxiv* **2018**, 259564. [CrossRef]
24. Israelsen, B.; Ahmed, N.; Center, K.; Green, R.; Bennett, W., Jr. Adaptive Simulation-Based Training of Artificial-Intelligence Decision Makers Using Bayesian Optimization. *J. Aerosp. Comput. Inf. Commun.* **2018**, *15*, 38–56. . [CrossRef]
25. Rasmussen, C.E.; Williams, C.K.I. *Gaussian Processes for Machine Learning*; MIT Press: Cambridge, MA, USA, 2006.
26. Deringer, V.L.; Bartók, A.P.; Bernstein, N.; Wilkins, D.M.; Ceriotti, M.; Csányi, G. Gaussian Process Regression for Materials and Molecules. *Chem. Rev.* **2021**, *121*, 10073–10141. . [CrossRef]
27. Oliveira, R.; Ott, L.; Ramos, F. Bayesian optimisation under uncertain inputs. In Proceedings of the Twenty-Second International Conference on Artificial Intelligence and Statistics, Naha, Japan, 16–18 April 2019; Volume 89, pp. 1177–1184.
28. Ath, G.D.; Everson, R.M.; Rahat, A.A.M.; Fieldsend, J.E. Greed is Good: Exploration and Exploitation Trade-offs in Bayesian Optimisation. *ACM Trans. Evol. Learn. Optim.* **2021**, *1*, 1–22. [CrossRef]
29. Mochihashi, D.; Oba, S. *Gaussian Process and Machine Learning*; Kodansha Scientific, Tokyo, Japan, 2019.
30. Blonigen, B.A.; Knittel, C.R.; Soderbery, A. Keeping it Fresh: Strategic Product Redesigns and Welfare. *Int. J. Ind. Organ.* **2017**, *53*, 170–214. [CrossRef]
31. Mareček, R.; Říha, P.; Bartoňová, M.; Kojan, M.; Lamoš, M.; Gajdoš, M.; Vojtíšek, L.; Mikl, M.; Bartoň, M.; Doležalová, I.; et al. Automated fusion of multimodal imaging data for identifying epileptogenic lesions in patients with inconclusive magnetic resonance imaging. *Hum. Brain Mapp.* **2021**, *42*, 2921–2930. [CrossRef] [PubMed]
32. Che, K.; Chen, X.; Guo, M.; Wang, C.; Liu, X. Genetic Variants Detection Based on Weighted Sparse Group Lasso. *Front. Genet.* **2020**, *11*, 155. [CrossRef] [PubMed]
33. Surjanovic, S.; Bingham, D. Beale Function. 2013. Available online: https://www.sfu.ca/~ssurjano/beale.html (accessed on 27 June 2023).
34. Surjanovic, S.; Bingham, D. Goldstein-Price Function. 2013. Available online: https://www.sfu.ca/~ssurjano/goldpr.html (accessed on 27 June 2023).

Disclaimer/Publisher's Note: The statements, opinions and data contained in all publications are solely those of the individual author(s) and contributor(s) and not of MDPI and/or the editor(s). MDPI and/or the editor(s) disclaim responsibility for any injury to people or property resulting from any ideas, methods, instructions or products referred to in the content.

Article

Breast Cancer Diagnosis Using a Novel Parallel Support Vector Machine with Harris Hawks Optimization

Sultan Almotairi [1,2,*], Elsayed Badr [3,4,*], Mustafa Abdul Salam [5,6] and Hagar Ahmed [3]

1. Department of Computer Science, College of Computer and Information Sciences, Majmaah University, Al-Majmaah 11952, Saudi Arabia
2. Department of Computer Science, Faculty of Computer and Information Systems, Islamic University of Madinah, Medinah 42351, Saudi Arabia
3. Scientific Computing Department, Faculty of Computers and Artificial Intelligence, Benha University, Benha 13511, Egypt; hagar.abdelhalim@fci.bu.edu.eg
4. Computer Science Department, Integrated Thebes Institutes, Cairo 11331, Egypt
5. Artificial Intelligence Department, Faculty of Computers and Artificial Intelligence, Benha University, Benha 13511, Egypt; mustafa.abdo@fci.bu.edu.eg
6. Faculty of Computer Studies, Arab Open University, Cairo 11211, Egypt
* Correspondence: almotairi@mu.edu.sa (S.A.); alsayed.badr@fci.bu.edu.eg (E.B.)

Abstract: Three contributions are proposed. Firstly, a novel hybrid classifier (HHO-SVM) is introduced, which is a combination between the Harris hawks optimization (HHO) and a support vector machine (SVM) is introduced. Second, the performance of the HHO-SVM is enhanced using the conventional normalization method. The final contribution is to improve the efficiency of the HHO-SVM by adopting a parallel approach that employs the data distribution. The proposed models are evaluated using the Wisconsin Diagnosis Breast Cancer (WDBC) dataset. The results show that the HHO-SVM achieves a 98.24% accuracy rate with the normalization scaling technique, outperforming other related works. On the other hand, the HHO-SVM achieves a 99.47% accuracy rate with the equilibration scaling technique, which is better than other previous works. Finally, to compare the three effective scaling strategies on four CPU cores, the parallel version of the proposed model provides an acceleration of 3.97.

Keywords: support vector machine; Harris hawks optimization; scaling techniques; parallel processing

MSC: 68T05; 68Q32

1. Introduction

Breast cancer is the most common disease in men and women of all ages, accounting for 11.7 percent of all cancer cases in 2020 [1]. It is the most common cancer in women worldwide, accounting for 24.5 percent of all new cases diagnosed in 2020. Breast cancer must be detected early in order to receive appropriate treatment and to reduce the number of fatalities caused by the disease.

Expert systems and artificial intelligence techniques can aid breast cancer detection professionals in avoiding costly mistakes. These expert systems can review medical data in less time and provide assistance to junior physicians. Breast cancer has been detected with excellent accuracy using a variety of artificial intelligence techniques. Marcano-Cedeo et al. [2] proposed the artificial metaplasticity MLP (AMMLP) method with a 99.26 percent accuracy. An RS-SVM classifier for breast cancer diagnosis was used by Chen et al. [3] and achieved 100% and 96.87% for the highest and average accuracy, respectively. Hui-Ling Chen et al. [4] obtained a 99.3% accuracy using a PSO-SVM. For the breast cancer dataset, Liu and Fu [5] presented the CS-PSO-SVM model, which merged a support vector machine (SVM), particle swarm optimization (PSO), and cuckoo search (CS) and obtained an accuracy of 91.3% versus 90% for both the PSO-SVM and GA-SVM models. Bashir, Qamar, and Khan [5] achieved a 97.4% accuracy with ensemble learning algorithms. Tuba et al. [6] proposed an adjusted bat algorithm to optimize the parameters of a support vector machine and showed that compared to the grid search, it led to a 96.49% better classifier versus 96.31% for the WDBC dataset. Shokoufeh Aalaei et al. [7] introduced a feature selection strategy based on GA, which achieved a 96.9% accuracy. In S. Mandal [8], different cancer classification models (naïve Bayes (NB), logistic regression (LR), decision tree (DT)) were compared to find the smallest subset of features that could warrant a high-accuracy classification of breast cancer. The author concluded that logistic regression classifier was the best classifier with the highest accuracy of 97.9%. The particle swarm optimization (PSO) algorithm was used as a feature option and to improve the C4.5 algorithm by Muslim et al. [9]. The accuracy of C4.5 was 95.61% versus 96.49% for the PSO C4.5 algorithm for the WBC dataset. Liu et al. [10] suggested an improved cost-sensitive support vector machine classifier (ICS-SVM), which took into consideration the unequal misclassification costs of breast cancer intelligent diagnosis and tested the approach on the (WBC) and (WDBC) breast cancer datasets. They scored 98.83% on the WDBC dataset. Agarap [11] performed a comparison of six ML techniques and obtained a 99.04% accuracy rate. The fruit fly optimization algorithm (FOA) enhanced by the Levy flight (LF) strategy (LFOA) was proposed by Huang et al. [12] to optimize the best parameters of an SVM and build an LFOA-based SVM for breast cancer diagnosis. Xie et al. [13] introduced a new technique based on an SVM, with a combined RBF and polynomial kernel functions, and the dragonfly algorithm (DA-CKSVM). Harikumar and Chakravarthy [14] proposed a model that applied two machine learning (ML) algorithms, a decision tree (DT) and the K-nearest neighbors (KNN) algorithm to the WDBC dataset after a feature selection using a principal component analysis (PCA), and the results of the comparative analysis indicated that the KNN classifier outperformed the DT classifier. Habib [15] used genetic programming and machine learning algorithms and achieved a 98.24% classification accuracy. Hemeida et al. [16] proposed four distinct optimization strategies for the classification of two datasets, the Iris dataset and the Breast Cancer dataset, using ANN. Telsang and Hegde [17] presented a prediction of breast cancer using various machine learning algorithms and compared the accuracy of their predictions using the WDBC dataset. After analysis, the SVM model had an accuracy of 96.25 percent. Umme and Doreswamy [18] proposed a hybrid diagnostic model that combined the bat method, gravitational search algorithm (GSA), and a feed-forward neural network (FNN). When training and testing, the accuracy on the WDBC dataset was found to be 94.28 percent and 92.10 percent, respectively. Singh et al. [19] proposed the grey wolf–whale optimization algorithm, a hybrid metaheuristic-swarm-intelligence-based SVM classifier (GWWOA-SVM). The hyperparameters of the SVM were tuned using the WOA and GWO. The WDBC dataset was used to test the effectiveness of the GWWOA-SVM. The model obtained a classification accuracy of 97.721 percent. Badr et al. [20] proposed three contributions. They used a recent grey wolf optimizer (GWO) to improve the performance of an SVM for diagnosing breast cancer utilizing efficient scaling strategies in contrast to the traditional normalization technique. They made use of a parallel technique that used task allocation to boost GWO's efficiency. The suggested model was tested on the WDBC dataset and obtained an accuracy rate of 98.60 percent with normalization scaling, and using scaling strategies also resulted in a fast convergence and a 99.30 percent accuracy rate. On four CPU cores, the parallel version of the proposed model provided a speedup of 3.9.

Scaling strategies can help classifiers become more accurate. For the SVM optimization, Elsayed Badr et al. [21] presented ten efficient scaling approaches. For linear programming approaches, these scaling techniques were effective [22–31]. On the WDBC dataset, they utilized the arithmetic mean and de Buchet scaling techniques for three cases ($p = 1, 2, \infty$), and the equilibration, geometric mean, IBM MPSX, and Lp-norm scaling techniques for three cases ($p = 1, 2, \infty$).

The parallel swarm technique was created by the authors of [32] for two-sided balancing problems. In [33], a parallel approach was applied to data testing in order to achieve massive passing. The authors of [34] introduced and discussed parallel dynamic programming methods. Reference [35] gives a survey of numerous strategies for parallelizing algorithms. Reference [36] introduces a parallel approach to constraint-solving methods. Polap et al. [37] proposed three strategies for improving traditional procedures that reduced the solution space by using a neighborhood search. The second was to reduce the calculation time by limiting the number of possible solutions. In addition, the two procedures indicated above were combined. Metaheuristic algorithms such as ABC, FPA, BA, PSO, and MFO have been used to optimize SVMs and extreme learning machines, allowing them to readily overcome local minima and overfitting difficulties. The reader can refer to [38,39], which present the advantages and disadvantages of traditional machine learning methods such as SVMs and deep learning methods.

Three achievements are presented in this work. The first is a new hybrid classifier (HHO-SVM) that combines the Harris hawks optimization (HHO) and support vector machine (SVM) techniques. In order to increase the HHO-SVM performance, the second contribution compares three efficient scaling algorithms with the usual normalizing methodology. The final contribution is to improve the efficiency of the HHO-SVM by adopting a parallel approach that employs the data distribution. The proposed models are tested on the Wisconsin Diagnosis Breast Cancer (WDBC) dataset. The results show that the HHO-SVM achieves a 98.24% accuracy rate with the normalization scaling technique outperforming the results in [6–8,15,17–19]. On the other hand, the HHO-SVM achieves a 99.47% accuracy rate with the equilibration scaling technique, better than the results in [6–8,10,11,15,17–20]. Finally, the parallel version of the suggested model achieves a speedup of 3.97 on four CPU cores.

The sections that follow are grouped as such: Section 2 delves into SVM and HHO. Section 3 contains an explanation of the suggested model. Section 4 provides a complete study of three unique scaling methods: the equilibration, arithmetic, and geometric means. Section 5 explains the parallel version of the HHO-SVM. Section 6 has an experimental design that includes data descriptions, experimental setup, performance evaluation measures, and a comparative analysis. The experimental results and discussion are found in Section 7. Finally, Section 8 provides a conclusion as well as future work.

2. Preliminaries

Support vector machines (SVM) and the Harris hawks optimization (HHO) are introduced and studied in this section.

2.1. Support Vector Machine (SVM)

The goal of an SVM is to find an N-dimensional hyperplane that classifies the available data vectors with the least amount of error. An SVM employs convex quadratic programming to avoid local minima [40]. If we assume a binary classification problem and have a training dataset with a class label: $(x_1, y_1) \ldots (x_n, y_n)$, $x_i \in R_d$ and $y_i \in (-1, +1)$ where x_i is the class label and y_i is the input or feature vector, the best hyperplane is as follows:

$$wx^T + b = 0 \qquad (1)$$

such that w, x, and b indicate the weight, input vector, and bias, respectively. The letters w and b fulfill the following requirements:

$$wx_i^T + b \geq +1 \quad if \ y_i = 1 \qquad (2)$$

$$wx_i^T + b \leq -1 \quad if \ y_i = -1 \qquad (3)$$

The goal of the SVM model training is to find the w and b that maximize the margin $\frac{1}{\|w\|^2}$.

Nonlinearly separable problems are common. To transform the nonlinear problem to a linear one, the input space is converted into a higher-dimensional space.

Kernel functions [41] could be used to extend the data's dimensions and turn the problem into a linear one. The linear and nonlinear SVMs are depicted in Figure 1. Furthermore, kernel functions may be useful in speeding up calculations in high-dimensional space. For example, in the extended feature space, the linear kernel can be used to compute the dot product of two features. The most frequent SVM kernels are RBF and polynomial. They can be expressed as:

$$K(x_i, x_j) = e^{-\gamma \|x_i - x_j\|^2} \tag{4}$$

$$K(x_i, x_j) = \left(1 + x_i^T x_j\right)^p \tag{5}$$

such that the parameters γ and p are the width of the Gaussian kernel and the polynomial order, respectively. Setting proper model parameters has been demonstrated to increase the accuracy of SVM classification [42]. The adjustment of SVM parameters is a very delicate process. These parameters are C, gamma, and the SVM kernel function which finds the mapping from the nonlinear to linear problem by increasing the dimension.

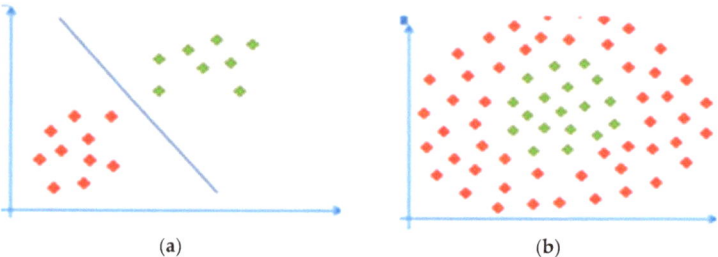

Figure 1. (**a**) Linear support vector machine and (**b**) nonlinear support vector machine.

2.2. Harris Hawks Optimization (HHO)

Heidari et al. [43] developed an algorithm called HHO (Harris hawks optimization). It derives from the hunting style and cooperation of Harris's hawks. Some hawks cooperate when attacking their prey from different directions to surprise and disable it. Furthermore, to aid in the selection of different hunting strategies, it is dependent on various sceneries and kinds of prey flying. Exploring a prey, transitioning from exploration to exploitation, and exploitation are the three primary phases of the HHO. In this diagram, all phases of the HHO are depicted (Figure 2). The following is a diagram of each phase:

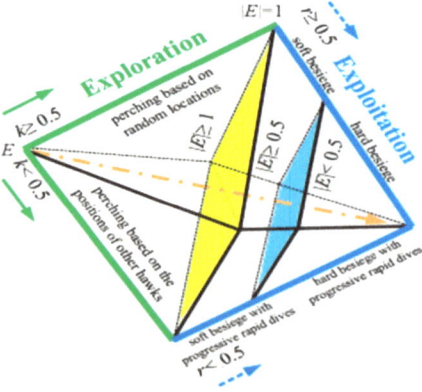

Figure 2. All phases of the HHO algorithm.

2.2.1. Exploration Phase

This phase is mathematically modeled primarily for waiting, searching, and prey detection. Harris's hawks are the alternative or best at every step. Harris's hawks' position $X(i+1)$ can be formulated according to Equation (6):

$$X(i+1) = \begin{cases} (X_{rand}(i)) - r_1|X_{rand}(i) - 2r_2X(i)| & \text{if } q \geq 0.5 \\ (X_{rabbit}(i) - X_m(i)) - badrr_3(LB + r_4(UB - LB)) & \text{if } q < 0.5 \end{cases} \quad (6)$$

where i is the current iteration, X_{rabbit} is the rabbit's position, X_{rand} is a randomly chosen hawk at the current population, r_j, $j = 1, 2, 3, 4$, q are random numbers between 0 and 1, and X_m is the average position of the hawks, which can be calculated by:

$$X_m(i) = \frac{1}{N}\sum_{j=1}^{N} X_j(i) \quad (7)$$

where the vector X_j denotes the position of each hawk j, and N is the number of hawks.

2.2.2. Transition from Exploration to Exploitation

The HHO alternates between exploration and exploitation depending on the rabbit's escaping energy. Moreover, the rabbit's energy can be calculated using the formula below:

$$E = 2E_0\left(1 - \frac{i}{T}\right) \quad (8)$$

where E indicates the rabbit's escaping energy, T denotes the maximum size of the iterations, and $E_0 \in (-1, 1)$ presents the initial energy at each step.

$$E_0 = 2\,rand(\,) - 1 \quad (9)$$

The HHO can determine the state of a rabbit based on the direction of E_0 (the HHO enters the exploration phase in order to locate the prey when $|E| \geq 1$, otherwise, during the exploitation steps, this strategy seeks to exploit the solutions' proximity).

2.2.3. Exploitation Phase

At this phase, hawks besiege the prey from all directions to hunt it, and this siege is hard or soft according to the remaining prey's energy. During this siege, the prey's escape depends on the chance r (it succeeds in escaping if r < 0.5). Moreover, if $|E| \geq 0.5$, the HHO is besieging softly, otherwise, it is besieging hard. According to the phenomenon of prey escape and hawks–hawks' strategies in pursuit, the HHO implements four attack strategies: a soft siege, a hard siege, a soft siege with progressive rapid dives, a hard siege with progressive rapid dives. In particular, the rabbit has enough energy to escape if $|E| \geq 0.5$; however, the prey's ability to escape or not depends on both values of $|E|$ and r.

Soft Siege (r ≥ 0.5 and |E| ≥ 0.5)

This procedure can be written as:

$$X(i+1) = \Delta X(i) - E|JX_{rabbit}(i) - X(i)| \quad (10)$$

$$\Delta X(i) = X_{rabbit}(i) - X(i) \quad (11)$$

where $\Delta X(i)$ indicates the difference between the rabbit's current location and the rabbit's location vector at the i iteration, $J = 2(1 - r_5)$ is the intensity of the rabbit's random jumping during the escape process, and $r_5 \in (0, 1)$ is a random number.

Hard Siege (r ≥ 0.5 and |E| < 0.5)

In this strategy, current positions can be updated with the following formula:

$$X(i+1) = X_{rabbit}(i) - E|\Delta X(i)| \tag{12}$$

Soft Siege with Progressive Rapid Dives (|E| ≥ 0.5 and r < 0.5)

As for the soft siege, hawks decide their next move with the following equation:

$$Y = X_{rabbit}(i) - E|JX_{rabbit}(i) - X(i)| \tag{13}$$

The hawks dive according to the following rules based on the LF-based patterns:

$$Z = Y + S \times LF(D) \tag{14}$$

in which D indicates the dimension of problem, and $S_{1 \times D}$ denotes a random vector. The levy flight (LF) can be calculated by Equation (15):

$$LF(D) = 0.01 \times \frac{\mu \times \sigma}{|v|^{\frac{1}{\beta}}}, \sigma = \left(\frac{\Gamma(1+\beta)\sin\left(\frac{\pi\beta}{2}\right)}{\Gamma\left(\frac{1+\beta}{2}\right) \times \beta \times 2^{\left(\frac{\beta-1}{2}\right)}} \right), \beta = 1.5 \tag{15}$$

where μ and v represent a range of random numbers between 0 and 1. As a result, Equation (16) can be used to describe the final strategy of this phase, which is to update the positions of the hawks:

$$X(i+1) = \begin{cases} Y & if \ F(Y) < F(X(i)) \\ Z & if \ F(Z) < F(X(i)) \end{cases} \tag{16}$$

Hard Siege with Progressive Rapid Dives (|E| < 0.5 and r < 0.5)

The hawk is always in close proximity to the prey during this step. The following is a model of the behavior:

$$X(i+1) = \begin{cases} Y & if \ F(Y) < F(X(i)) \\ Z & if \ F(Z) < F(X(i)) \end{cases} \tag{17}$$

The following formulas can be used to calculate Y and Z:

$$Y = X_{rabbit}(i) - E|JX_{rabbit}(i) - X_m(i)| \tag{18}$$

$$Z = Y + S \times LF(D) \tag{19}$$

$$\text{where } X_m(i) = \frac{1}{N} \sum_{i=1}^{N} X_i(i) \tag{20}$$

The main purpose of this study was to employ new scaling approaches to scale breast cancer data, compute the SVM parameter using the HHO algorithm to efficiently classify breast tumors, and use a parallel approach to reduce the proposed model's execution time.

3. The Proposed HHO-SVM Classification Model

The HHO-SVM system is implemented in two stages. The HHO algorithm determines the SVM parameters automatically for the first phase. The optimized SVM algorithm diagnoses a breast tumor as benign or malignant in the second phase. To obtain the best accurate result, a ten-fold cross-validation (CV) is used. To test the SVM parameters, the

HHO-SVM model applies the root-mean-square error (RMSE) as the fitness function. The following formula is used to calculate the RMSE:

$$RMSE = \sqrt{\frac{\sum_{i=1}^{N}(Predicted_i - Actual_i)}{N}} \qquad (21)$$

such that N is the number of entities in the test dataset.

In the HHO-SVM algorithm for breast cancer, the population size is set to N, and each hawk represents X_i ($i = 1, 2, \ldots, N$), the maximum number of iterations is set to T, the number of dimensions is set to dim, the upper bound is set to ub, the lower bound is set to lb, and the boundary of positions is set to X_{rabbit}. X_{rabbit} is the position of the rabbit, and all hawks update their positions. After that, random values are used to form the initial population ($N*dim$). After the data have been loaded, we use one of the scaling strategies to modify it. It uses a k-fold cross-validation and conducts several procedures for each fold to evaluate the model's efficiency. If the number of iterations does not equal T, the model repeats the steps below for each iteration.

To begin, it passes each bird through two specified functions and sets its output to the SVM (C and γ) parameters, then trains the SVM and classifies the test set. Then, it calculates the fitness function ($RMSE$) from Equation (21), updates X_{rabbit}, according to the smallest fitness value, and update the initial energy E_0, jump strength J, and the position of the current hawk according to the X_{rabbit}, E_0, J, E, and r values, where r is a random value and E is the energy. Then, the algorithm checks whether ($|E| \geq 1$); if it is, then it enters the exploration phase and updates the location vector using Equation (6); if ($|E| < 1$), then it enters the exploitation phase, which may be a soft siege, hard siege, soft siege with progressive rapid dives or a hard siege with progressive rapid dives.

Therefore, the algorithm checks whether ($|E| \geq 0.5$ and $r \geq 0.5$); if true, then it is a soft siege, and the location vector is updated using Equation (10). If ($|E| < 0.5$ and $r \geq 0.5$), then it is a hard siege, and the location vector is updated using Equation (12). If ($|E| \geq 0.5$ and $r < 0.5$), then it is a soft siege with progressive rapid dives and the location vector is updated using Equation (16), $F(Y)$ and $F(Z)$ are calculated by passing Y or Z to two particular functions, and the parameters of the SVM (C and γ) are equal to its output. Then, the algorithm trains the SVM and classifies the test set. It computes the $RMSE$ from Equation (21) as the value of $F(Y)$ or $F(Z)$. If ($|E| < 0.5$ and $r < 0.5$), then it is a hard siege with progressive rapid dives. The location vector is updated using Equation (17), $F(Y)$ and $F(Z)$ are calculated by passing Y or Z to two particular functions, and the parameters of the SVM (C and γ) are equal to its output; then, the algorithm trains the SVM and classifies the test set. It computes the $RMSE$ from Equation (21) as the value of $F(Y)$ or $F(Z)$. Then, if the number of iterations does not surpass T, it goes back to step 4 in the process (Algorithm 1). We move on to the next fold and return to step 3 if T is satisfied. If T and the fold number k are equal, we proceed to step 5. Finally, we compute the averages of the $RMSE$ and the accuracy of the k folds and return them.

Algorithm 1: HHO-SVM Algorithm

Input: *N*   *The population size*
         T   *Maximum number of Iterations*
         lb   *Lower_Bound*
         ub   *Upper_Bound*
         dim   *No. of dimensions*
         k   *No. of folds*
Output: *Average RMSE: Average classification accuracy rates*

1. Initialize the random population X_i (i = 1, 2, ..., N)
2. Apply one of the scaling techniques after loading the data.
3. **for** (each fold j) do
      Divide the data into train and test subsets randomly
4.   **while** (t < T) do
     for (each hawk (X_i)) do
       Pass X_i to particular functions
       Set function's output to parameter of SVM (C, γ)
       Train and test the SVM model
       Evaluate the fitness X_i with EQ (21)
       Update X_{rabbit} as the position of the rabbit (best position based on the fitness value)
     end (for)
     for (every hawk (X_i)) do
        Update E_0 and J (initial energy and jump strength)
        Update the E by EQ (8)
        if ($|E| \geq 1$) then   ▷ **Exploration phase**
        Update the position vector by EQ (6)
        if ($|E| < 1$) then   ▷ **Exploration phase**
        if ($r \geq 0.5$ and $|E| \geq 0.5$) then ▷ **Soft siege**
        Update the position vector by EQ (10)
        else if ($r \geq 0.5$ and $|E| < 0.5$) then ▷ **Hard siege**
          Update the position vector by EQ (12)
        else if ($r < 0.5$ and $|E| \geq 0.5$) then
        ▷ **Soft siege with PRD**
        Update the position vector by EQ (16)
        ▷$F(Y)$, $F(Z)$ *and* $F(X_i)$ calculated by using RMSE
        else if ($r < 0.5$ and $|E| < 0.5$) then ▷ **Hard siege with PRD**
          Update the position vector by EQ (17)
     end (for)
     t=t+1
   end (while)
   t=0
end (for)

5. **Return** averages of *RMSE* and classification accuracy for all folds

4. Scaling Techniques

Before introducing the scaling techniques, some of the necessary mathematical symbols should be presented. We treat the breast cancer data as a matrix and present some mathematical symbols as shown in Table 1. The final scaled matrix is denoted by RAS, where $R = diag(r_1, \ldots, r_m)$ and $S = diag(s_1, \ldots, s_n)$.

Table 1. Some mathematical terms for scaling techniques.

Term	Meaning
$A(a_{ij})$	$m \times n$ matrix (with m entities and n attributes)
r_i	The scaling factor of row i
s_j	The scaling factor of row j
R	$R = diag(r_1, \ldots, r_m)$ (diagonal matrix)
S	$S = diag(s_1, \ldots, s_n)$ (diagonal matrix)
N_i	$N_i = \{j \mid A_{ij} \neq 0\}$, such that $1 \leq i \leq m$
M_j	$M_j = \{i \mid A_{ij} \neq 0\}$, such that $1 \leq j \leq n$
n_i	The cardinality of the set N_i
m_j	The cardinality of the set M_j
$A^R(a_{ij}^R)$	The scaled matrix by row R scaling factor
$A^{RS}(a_{ij}^{RS})$	The scaled matrix in its final form.

All of the scaling approaches presented in this section scale the rows first, then the columns. Equations (22) and (23) show the steps for scaling the matrix.

$$A^R = RA \tag{22}$$

$$A^{RS} = A^R S \tag{23}$$

(1) *Arithmetic mean:*

The variance between nonzero entries in the coefficient matrix A is reduced using the arithmetic mean scaling technique. As shown in Equation (24), the rows are scaled by dividing each row by the mean of the absolute value of the nonzero values:

$$r_i = \frac{n_i}{\sum_{j \in N_i} a_{ij}} \tag{24}$$

Each column (attribute) is scaled by dividing the modulus value of the nonzero items in that column by the mean of the modulus of the nonzero entries in that column as shown in Equation (25):

$$s_j = \frac{m_j}{\sum_{i \in M_j} a_{ij}^R} \tag{25}$$

(2) *Equilibration scaling technique:*

This scaling method's cornerstone is the largest value in absolute value. The row scaling is done by dividing every row (instance) of matrix A by the absolute value of the row's largest value. Then, we divide every column of the matrix by the absolute value of the largest value in that column, which is scaled by the row factor. The final scaled matrix A has a range of $[-1, 1]$.

(3) *Geometric mean:*

To begin, Equation (26) depicts the scaling of the rows, in which every row is split by the geometric mean of the nonzero elements in that row.

$$r_i = \left(\max_{j \in N_i} a_{ij} \min_{j \in N_i} a_{ij} \right)^{-1/2} \tag{26}$$

Second, Equation (27) represents the column scaling where every column is divided by the geometric mean of the modulus of the nonzero elements in that column.

$$s_j = \left(\max_{j \in M_j} a_{ij}^R \min_{j \in M_j} a_{ij}^R \right)^{-1/2} \quad (27)$$

(4) Normalization $[-1, 1]$:

Equation (28) represents the normalization within the range $[-1, 1]$ where a, a', max_k, and min_k are the initial value, the scaled value, the maximum value, and the minimum value of feature k, respectively.

$$\dot{a} = \left(\frac{a - min_k}{max_k - min_k} \right) \times 2 - 1 \quad (28)$$

5. The Parallel Metaheuristic Algorithm

We implemented a parallel metaheuristic algorithm based on the population, where the population is divided into different parts that are easy to exchange, that evolve separately, and that are then later combined. In this paper, the parallel approach was implemented by dividing the population into several sets on different cores. The number of cores, Nc, was identified. The starting population consisted of n particles randomly initialized. The group size was calculated as follows:

$$n_g = \left\lceil \frac{n}{Nc} \right\rceil \quad (29)$$

The proposed model steps are shown in Algorithm 2.

Algorithm 2: Parallel Approach

1: Begin
    2: Identify Nc (no. of cores);
    3: Randomly initialize the population;
    4: Compute n_g particles with Equation (20);
    5: Make Nc sets;
    6: Distribute the particles on cores.
7: Run the HHO-SVM model on each core
    8: Choose the optimal particles from all cores;
        9: Update the model's parameters and particle positions;
            10: For all folds, return the average accuracy.
11: End

The ceil function was used to obtain an integer number of particles to be distributed on the cores. The basic algorithm steps were executed for all sets in a standalone thread. Nc best particles were chosen as a solution for the optimization problem when these phases were completed. Moreover, these particles were combined to obtain the best particles in general on all cores and update the position according to them.

6. Experimental Design

This part contains a description of the data, a performance evaluation measure, as well as a comparative study.

6.1. Data Description

The proposed model was tested on the Wisconsin diagnostic Breast Cancer (WDBC) dataset, which is available at the University of California, Irvine Machine Learning Repository [44]. There are 569 examples in the dataset, which are separated into two groups (malignant and benign). There are 357 cases of malignant tumors and 212 cases of benign tumors, respectively. Each database record has thirty-two attributes. Table 2 lists the thirty-two qualities.

Table 2. Description of dataset.

No	Attribute Name	Description
3	Radius	The range between the center and point on the perimeter
4	Texture	Gray-scale values' standard deviation
5	Perimeter	The total distance between the points that make up the nuclear perimeter
6	Area	The average of the cancer cell areas
7	Smoothness	The distance between a radial line's length and the mean length of the lines that surround it.
8	Compactness	Perimeter^2/area $-$ 1.0
9	Concavity	The severity of the contour's concave parts
10	Concave points	The number of concave contour parts
11	Fractal dimension	("coastline approximation"—1)
12	Symmetry	In both directions, the length difference between lines perpendicular to the major axis and the cell boundary.

6.2. Experimental Setup

MATLAB was used to create the suggested HHO-SVM detection method. Chang and Lin [45] created the SVM method, and their implementation was improved. The computing environment for the experiment is described in Table 3.

Table 3. Computational environment.

Center Processing Unit	Intel (R) Core (TM) i5—7200U CPU@ 2.70 GHz
RAM size	4 GB RAM
MATLAB ver.	R2015a

The *k-fold* CV was proposed by Salzberg [46], and it was used to ensure that the results were genuine. $k = 10$ in this study. The following are the HHO-SVM's detailed settings: 1000, 19, 25, and 10 were the values for the iterations, search agents, dimensions, and k-fold, respectively. The [*lb, ub*] lower and upper bounds were set to [$-5, 5$].

6.3. Performance Metrics

Six metrics, sensitivity, specificity, accuracy, precision, G-mean, and F-score, were used to assess the efficacy of the suggested HHO-SVM model. These metrics are defined as follows according to the confusion matrix:

$$Accuracy = \frac{TP + TN}{TP + TN + FP + FN} \times 100 \tag{30}$$

$$Sensitivity = \frac{TP}{TP + FN} \times 100 \tag{31}$$

$$Specificity = \frac{TN}{TN + FP} \times 100 \tag{32}$$

$$Precision = \frac{TP}{TP + FP} \times 100 \tag{33}$$

$$Gmean = \sqrt{Sensitivity \times Specificity} \tag{34}$$

$$Fmeasure = 2 \times \frac{Precision \times Sensitivity}{Precision + Sensitivity} \tag{35}$$

If the dataset has two classes ("M" for malignant and "B" for benign), then the true positives (TP) are the total number of cases with classification result "M" when they are actually "M" in the dataset; the true negatives (TN) are the total number of cases with classification result "B" when they are actually "B" in the dataset; the false positives (FP) are the total number of cases with classification result "M" when they are "B" in the dataset; and the false negatives (FN) are the total number of cases with classification result "B" when they are "M" in the dataset.

6.4. Comparative Study

In this study, the efficiency of the presented HHO-SVM algorithm was compared to the SVM algorithm with the grid search technique. Figure 3 shows how the SVM algorithm works with the grid search technique

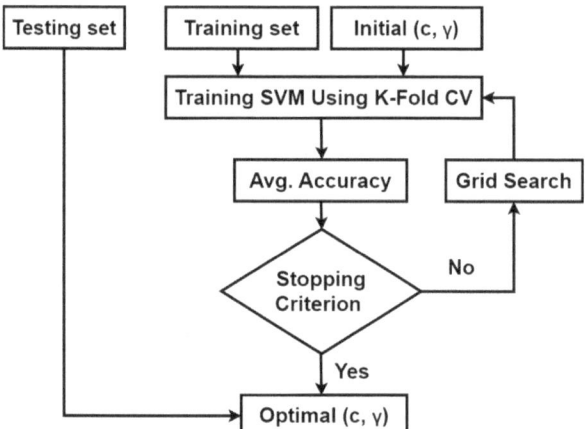

Figure 3. SVM algorithm with the grid search technique.

7. Empirical Results and Discussion

In this study, the abbreviations S0, S1, S2, S3, and S4 are used to denote no scaling, a normalization in $[-1, 1]$, the arithmetic mean, the geometric mean, and the equilibration scaling techniques, respectively. Experiments on the WBCD dataset were used to assess the efficacy of the proposed HHO-SVM model for breast cancer against the SVM algorithm with a grid search technique. First and foremost, our findings show the value of the grid search methodologies, the usefulness of the HHO-SVM model that was developed sequentially, and the superiority of the most recent scaling strategies over the previous normalizing methodology. Finally, the results show that the parallel version of the proposed model achieves a speedup of 3.97 for four cores.

Tables 4–6 demonstrate a comparison of the SVM classification accuracies using the grid search algorithm with S0, S1, S2, S3, and S4. Tables 4 and 5 show that the average accuracy rates obtained by the SVM using S3 (98.59%) are higher than those produced by the SVM using S1 (96.66%) (98.59%). On the other hand, the S4 technique outperforms all other scaling techniques with an accuracy of 98.95% compared to that obtained by the SVM.

Table 4. SVM using S0 and S1.

Fold	(S0)			(S1)		
	C	γ	Accuracy %	C	γ	Accuracy %
1	2^3	2^{-13}	94.76	2^{11}	2^1	94.64
2	2^7	2^{-15}	91.59	2^{15}	2^1	92.98
3	2^{15}	2^{-13}	100	2^{13}	2^1	100
4	2^5	2^{-13}	97.18	2^{13}	2^1	98.25
5	2^1	2^{-11}	96.23	2^{15}	2^1	96.49
6	2^{-1}	2^{-9}	91.29	2^{15}	2^{-1}	96.49
7	2^{11}	2^{-15}	97.59	2^{13}	2^1	100
8	2^9	2^{-15}	98.60	2^{15}	2^1	96.49
9	2^9	2^{-15}	97.59	2^{13}	2^1	94.74
10	2^{15}	2^{-9}	96.23	2^{13}	2^{-1}	96.49
Avg.	6877.9	0.00049	96.10	17408	1.7	96.66
Time		52.62167			19.208797	

Table 5. SVM using S2 and S3.

Fold	(S2)			(S3)		
	C	γ	Accuracy %	C	γ	Accuracy %
1	2^3	2^{-7}	100.00	2^1	2^{-5}	100
2	2^{15}	2^{-9}	98.25	2^9	2^{-5}	98.25
3	2^9	2^{-5}	96.49	2^9	2^{-5}	96.49
4	2^{-1}	2^{-5}	96.49	2^{-1}	2^{-5}	96.49
5	2^9	2^{-9}	100.00	2^9	2^{-9}	100
6	2^5	2^{-5}	98.25	2^7	2^{-5}	98.25
7	2^7	2^{-7}	98.25	2^3	2^{-3}	100.00
8	2^{-1}	2^{-3}	98.25	2^{15}	2^{-3}	98.25
9	2^9	2^{-9}	100.00	2^9	2^{-9}	100
10	2^{15}	2^{-9}	98.25	2^5	2^{-3}	98.25
Avg.	6724	0.024	98.42	3498.7	0.0535	98.59
Time		7.237509			6.822561	

Table 6. SVM using S4.

Fold	(S4)		
	C	γ	Accuracy %
1	2^5	2^{-1}	100.00
2	2^3	2^1	98.25
3	2^5	2^{-1}	100.00
4	2^{15}	2^1	98.25

Table 6. Cont.

Fold	(S4)		
	C	γ	Accuracy %
5	2^1	2^{-1}	100.00
6	2^9	2^{-1}	98.25
7	2^{15}	2^1	100.00
8	2^{15}	2^1	100.00
9	2^3	2^1	94.74
10	2^3	2^1	100.00
Avg.	9890.6	1.4	98.95
CPU Time		6.066946	

Tables 7–11 and Figure 4 show the importance of the data scaling techniques in improving classification accuracy, with the average classification accuracy rate without scaling the data (89.11%) being lower than the average classification accuracy rate when using any other scaling technique, and when comparing the normalization and other scaling techniques, we found that the novel scaling techniques outperformed the normalization in terms of both accuracy rates and CPU time. It is obvious that the HHO-SVM with the arithmetic mean scaling approach (98.25) achieved higher average accuracy rates than the HHO-SVM with normalization and the scaling strategy in the range $[-1, 1]$ (98.24%). With an accuracy of 99.47 percent, the equilibration scaling technique outperforms all the other scaling strategies, including the HHO-SVM.

Table 7. Grid-SVM accuracy with S0, S1, S2, S3, and S4.

No	Symbol	Accuracy	CPU Time
1	(S4)	98.95	6.066946
2	(S3)	98.59	6.822561
3	(S2)	98.42	7.237509
4	(S1)	96.66	19.208797
6	(S0)	96.10	52.62167

Table 8. Different metrics for the HHO-SVM model with S0.

Fold	HHO-SVM (S0)			
	Accuracy %	Sensitivity %	Specificity %	Precision %
1	91.07	90.48	91.43	91.07
2	98.98	81.82	100	98.98
3	100	100	100	100
4	96.49	95.24	97.22	96.49
5	63.16	0	100	63.16
6	92.98	80.95	100	92.98

Table 8. Cont.

Fold	HHO-SVM (S0)			
	Accuracy %	Sensitivity %	Specificity %	Precision %
7	96.49	95.24	97.22	96.49
8	63.16	0	100	63.16
9	96.49	95.24	97.22	96.49
10	98.25	100	97.22	98.25
Avg.	89.11	73.90	98.03	89.11
CPU Time	1.88×10^4			

Table 9. Different metrics for the HHO-SVM model with S0.

Fold	HHO-SVM (S0)			
	Recall %	F-Score %	G-Mean %	RMSE
1	90.48	90.95	0.2988	90.48
2	81.82	90.45	0.2649	81.82
3	100	100	0.00	100
4	95.24	96.23	0.1873	95.24
5	0.00	0.00	0.6070	0.00
6	80.95	89.97	0.2649	80.95
7	95.24	96.23	0.1873	95.24
8	0.00	0.00	0.6070	0.00
9	95.24	96.23	0.1873	95.24
10	100	98.60	0.1325	100
Avg.	73.90	75.87	0.2737	73.90
CPU Time	1.88×10^4			

Table 10. Different metrics for the HHO-SVM model with S1.

Fold	HHO-SVM (S1)			
	Accuracy %	Sensitivity %	Specificity %	Precision %
1	94.64	95.24	94.29	90.91
2	98.25	100	97.14	95.65
3	96.49	100	94.29	91.67
4	100	100	100	100
5	98.25	95.24	100	100
6	100	100	100	100
7	100	100	100	100

Table 10. Cont.

Fold	HHO-SVM (S1)			
	Accuracy %	Sensitivity %	Specificity %	Precision %
8	94.74	85.71	100	100
9	100	100	100	100
10	100	100	100	100
Avg.	98.24	97.62	98.57	97.82
CPU Time	1.13×10^5			

Table 11. Different metrics for the HHO-SVM model with S1.

Fold	HHO-SVM (S1)			
	Recall %	F-Score %	G-Mean %	RMSE
1	95.24	93.02	94.76	0.2315
2	100	97.78	98.56	0.1325
3	100	95.65	97.1	0.1873
4	100	100	100	0
5	95.24	97.56	97.59	0.1325
6	100	100	100	0
7	100	100	100	0
8	85.71	92.31	92.58	0.2294
9	100	100	100	0
10	100	100	100	0
Avg.	97.62	97.63	98.06	0.0913
CPU Time	1.13×10^5			

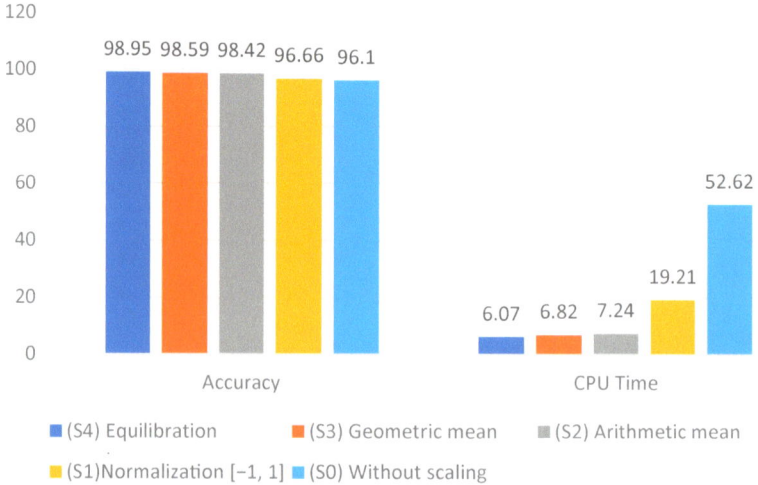

Figure 4. The accuracy and CPU time of Grid-SVM with S0, S1, S2, S3, and S4.

Tables 8–17 show the importance of the data scaling techniques in improving the classification accuracy, with the average classification accuracy rate without scaling the data (89.11 percent) being lower than the average classification accuracy rate when using any other scaling technique, and when comparing the normalization and other scaling techniques, we found that the novel scaling techniques outperformed the normalization in terms of both accuracy rates and CPU time. The HHO-SVM with the arithmetic mean scaling approach (98.25) clearly outperformed the HHO-SVM with the normalization scaling strategy in the range $[-1, 1]$ (98.24%). With an accuracy of 99.47%, S4 outperformed all other scaling procedures.

Table 12. Different metrics for the HHO-SVM model with S2.

Fold	HHO-SVM (S2)			
	Accuracy %	Sensitivity %	Specificity %	Precision %
1	100	100	100	100
2	100	100	100	100
3	94.74	90.91	97.14	95.24
4	98.25	95.24	100	100
5	100	100	100	100
6	100	100	100	100
7	100	100	100	100
8	94.74	90.48	97.22	95
9	98.25	95.24	100	100
10	96.49	90.48	100	100
Avg.	98.25	96.23	99.44	99.02
CPU Time	2.20×10^4			

Table 13. Different metrics for the HHO-SVM model with S2.

Fold	HHO-SVM (S2)			
	Recall %	F-Score %	G-Mean %	RSME
1	100	100	100	0
2	100	100	100	0
3	90.91	93.02	93.97	0.2294
4	95.24	97.56	97.59	0.1325
5	100	100	100	0
6	100	100	100	0
7	100	100	100	0
8	90.48	92.68	93.79	0.2294
9	95.24	97.56	97.59	0.1325
10	90.48	95	95.12	0.1873
Avg.	96.23	97.58	97.81	0.0911
CPU Time	2.20×10^4			

Table 14. Different metrics for the HHO-SVM model with S3.

Fold	HHO-SVM (S3)			
	Accuracy %	Sensitivity %	Specificity %	Precision %
1	96.43	90.48	100	100
2	100	100	100	100
3	96.49	90.91	100	100
4	100	100	100	100
5	96.49	90.48	100	100
6	100	100	100	100
7	96.49	95.24	97.22	95.24
8	98.25	100	97.22	95.45
9	98.25	95.24	100	100
10	100	100	100	100
Avg.	98.24	96.23	99.44	99.07
Time	2.71×10^4			

Table 15. Different metrics for the HHO-SVM model with S3.

Fold	HHO-SVM (S3)			
	Recall %	F-Score %	G-Mean %	RSME
1	90.48	95	95.12	0.1890
2	100	100	100	0
3	90.91	95.24	95.35	0.1873
4	100	100	100	0
5	90.48	95	95.12	0.1873
6	100	100	100	0
7	95.24	95.24	96.23	0.1873
8	100	97.67	98.60	0.1325
9	95.24	97.56	97.59	0.1325
10	100	100	100	0
Avg.	96.23	97.57	97.80	0.1016
CPU Time	2.71×10^4			

Table 16. Different metrics for the HHO-SVM model with S4.

Fold	HHO-SVM (S4)			
	Accuracy %	Sensitivity %	Specificity %	Precision %
1	100	100	100	100
2	96.49	90.91	100	100
3	100	100	100	100
4	100	100	100	100
5	100	100	100	100

Table 16. Cont.

Fold	HHO-SVM (S4)			
	Accuracy %	Sensitivity %	Specificity %	Precision %
6	100	100	100	100
7	100	100	100	100
8	100	100	100	100
9	100	100	100	100
10	98.25	95.24	100	100
Avg.	99.47	98.61	100	100
CPU Time	8.14×10^3			

Table 17. Different metrics for the HHO-SVM model with S4.

Fold	HHO-SVM (S4)			
	Recall %	F-Score %	G-Mean %	RMSE
1	100	100	100	0
2	90.91	95.24	95.35	0.1873
3	100	100	100	0
4	100	100	100	0
5	100	100	100	0
6	100	100	100	0
7	100	100	100	0
8	100	100	100	0
9	100	100	100	0
10	95.24	97.56	97.59	0.1325
Avg.	98.61	99.28	99.29	0.0320
CPU Time	8.14×10^3			

The results of all scaling strategies obtained by the HHO-SVM in terms of accuracies and CPU times are summarized in Table 18 and Figures 5 and 6. In terms of accuracy and CPU time, the equilibration scaling technique clearly outperformed all other scaling techniques. In terms of precision, however, the equilibration scaling technique was the least accurate. According to CPU time, the normalization scaling in the range $[-1, 1]$ was the greatest.

Table 18. The accuracy of the HHO-SVM model with S1, S2, S3, and S4.

No	Symbol	Accuracy	CPU Time
1	(S0)	89.11	18,800
1	(S1)	98.24	113,000
2	(S2)	98.25	22,000
3	(S3)	98.24	27,100
4	(S4)	99.47	8140

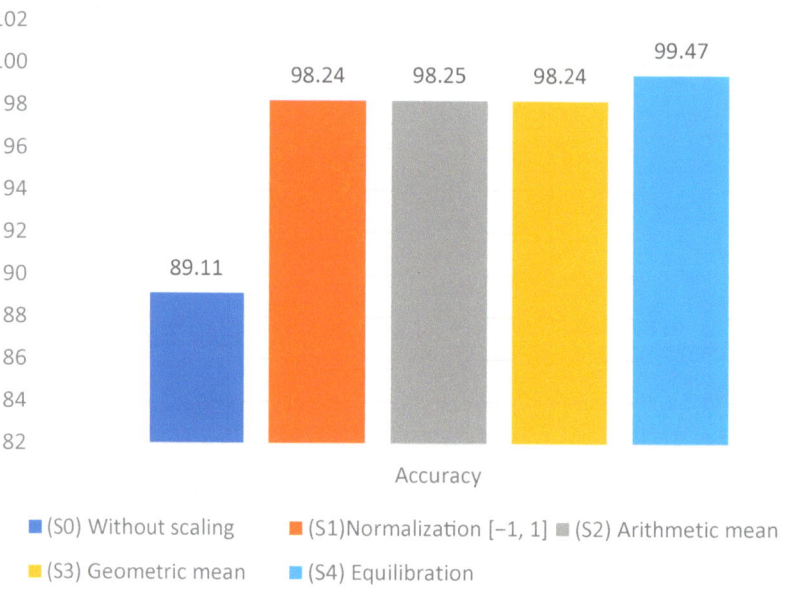

Figure 5. Accuracy of the HHO-SVM model with S0, S1, S2, S3, and S4.

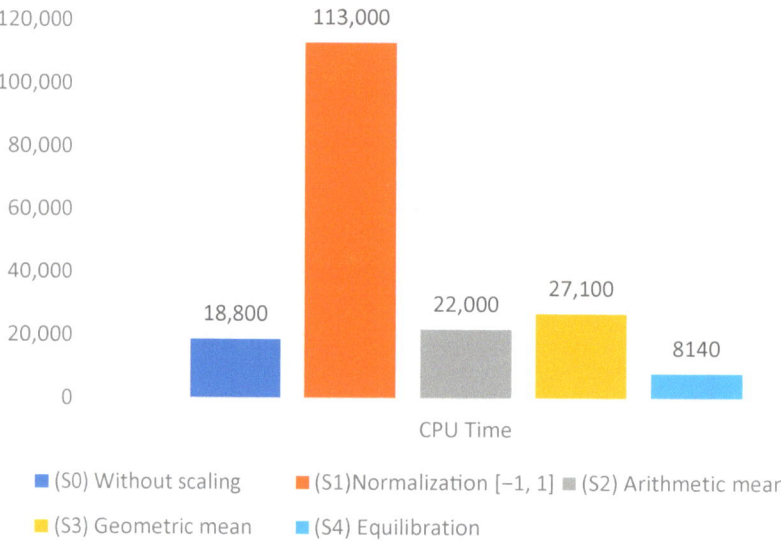

Figure 6. CPU time of the HHO-SVM model with S0, S1, S2, S3, and S4.

The accuracy rate of the proposed HHO-SVM model was compared to that of the conventional SVM employing a grid search technique in Table 19. For the scaling procedures S4, S2, S3, and S1, the accuracy rates of the proposed HHO-SVM model were 99.47, 98.25, 98.24, and 98.24, respectively. For the scaling approaches S4 and S1, the accuracy rates of the classic SVM with a grid search algorithm were 98.95 and 96.49, respectively.

Table 19. Accuracy comparison between HHO-SVM and Grid-SVM.

Symbol	Scaling Techniques	HHO-SVM Accuracy	Grid-SVM Accuracy
(S1)	Normalization $[-1, 1]$	98.24	96.49
(S2)	Arithmetic mean	98.25	98.42
(S3)	Geometric mean	98.24	98.59
(S4)	Equilibration	99.47	98.95

The parallel version of the HHO-SVM algorithm was provided to reduce its running time. CPU timings for all scaling strategies produced by the HHO-SVM on different cores are shown in Table 20 and Figure 7.

Table 20. CPU time comparison between HHO-SVM and Grid-SVM.

Symbol	Scaling Techniques	HHO-SVM		
		Core1	Core2	Core4
(S1)	Normalization $[-1, 1]$	91,600	47,461.14	23,073.04
(S2)	Arithmetic mean	8560	4703.30	2338.80
(S3)	Geometric mean	11,000	5820.11	2941.18
(S4)	Equilibration	3500	2023.12	980.39

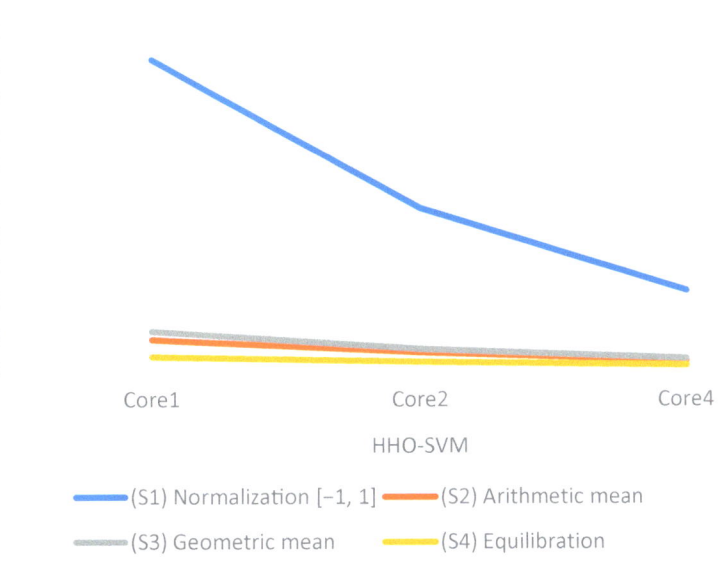

Figure 7. CPU time of the parallel HHO-SVM model for different cores.

In addition, Table 21 and Figure 8 show the speedup obtained by the HHO-SVM for all scaling strategies.

Table 21. Speedup on the WBCD database using the HHO-SVM with S1, S2, S3, and S4.

Symbol	HHO-SVM		
	Core1	Core2	Core4
(S1)	1	1.93	3.97
(S2)	1	1.82	3.66
(S3)	1	1.89	3.74
(S4)	1	1.73	3.57

For the scaling techniques S4, S3, S2, and S1, the speedups for four cores were 3.57, 3.74, 3.66, and 3.97, respectively.

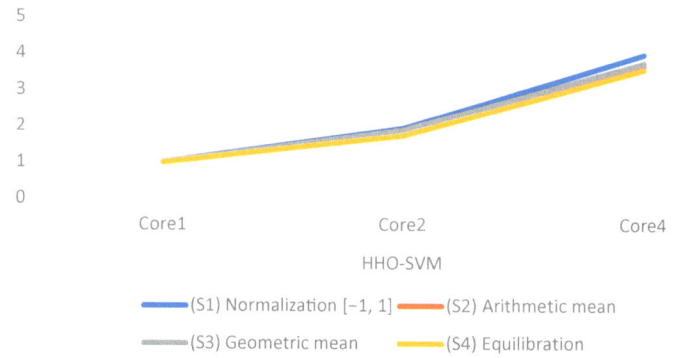

Figure 8. CPU time of the parallel HHO-SVM on different cores for all scaling techniques.

Table 22 shows that the performance of the presented HHO-SVM model against other related models developed in the literature, demonstrating the usefulness of our method. Table 22 shows that the classification accuracy of our created HHO-SVM diagnostic system is equivalent to or better than that of existing classifiers on the WBCD database.

Table 22. A comparison between related works against to our model.

Study	Year	Method	Accuracy (%)
Tuba et al. [6]	(2016)	ABA-SVM	96.49 %
Aalaei et al. [7]	(2016)	GA-ANN	97.30%
S. Mandal [8]	(2017)	Logistic regression	97.90%
Liu et al. [10]	(2018)	ICS-SVM	98.83%
Agarap [11]	(2018)	GRU-SVM	93.80%
Dhahri et al. [15]	(2019)	GA-AB	98.23%
Telsang et al. [17]	(2020)	SVM	96.25%
Umme et al. [18]	(2020)	BATGSA-FNN	92.10%
Singh et al. [19]	(2020)	GWWOA-SVM	97.72%
Badr et al. [20]	(2021)	GWO-SVM	99.3%
Our study	**(2023)**	**HHO-SVM**	**99.47%**

8. Conclusions

Three achievements were proposed. The first achievement was a novel hybrid classifier (HHO-SVM), which was a combination of the Harris hawks optimization (HHO) and a support vector machine (SVM). In order to increase the HHO-SVM performance, the second goal was to compare three efficient scaling algorithms to the old normalizing methodology.

The final contribution was to improve the efficiency of the HHO-SVM by adopting a parallel approach that employed the data distribution. On the Wisconsin Diagnosis Breast Cancer (WDBC) dataset, the proposed models were tested. The results showed that the HHO-SVM achieved a 98.24% accuracy rate with the normalization scaling technique, thus outperforming the results in [6–8,11,15,17–19]. On the other hand, the HHO-SVM achieved a 99.47% accuracy rate with the equilibration scaling technique, outperforming the results in [6–8,10,11,15,17–20]. Finally, on four CPU cores, the parallel HHO-SVM model delivered a speedup of 3.97. The proposed approach will be evaluated in various medical datasets in future research. In addition, we are attempting to incorporate various measuring techniques that will reduce the running time and improve the proposed diagnostic system's efficiency.

Author Contributions: Conceptualization, S.A.; Methodology, S.A.; Software, E.B.; Validation, E.B.; Formal analysis, M.A.S.; Investigation, M.A.S.; Resources, H.A.; Data curation, H.A. All authors have read and agreed to the published version of the manuscript.

Funding: The author would like to thank Deanship of Scientific Research at Majmaah University for supporting this work under Project Number No. R-2023-519.

Data Availability Statement: The data used to support the findings of this study are available from the corresponding author upon request.

Acknowledgments: The help from Benha University and Thebes Academy, Cornish El Nile, El-Maadi, Egypt for publishing is sincerely and greatly appreciated. We also thank the referees for suggestions to improve the presentation of this paper.

Conflicts of Interest: The authors declare no conflict of interest.

References

1. Sung, H.; Ferlay, J.; Siegel, R.L.; Laversanne, M.; Soerjomataram, I.; Jemal, A.; Bray, F. Global Cancer Statistics 2020: GLOBOCAN Estimates of Incidence and Mortality Worldwide for 36 Cancers in 185 Countries. *CA Cancer J. Clin.* **2021**, *71*, 209–249. [CrossRef] [PubMed]
2. Marcano-Cedeño, A.; Quintanilla-Domínguez, J.; Andina, D. WBCD breast cancer database classification applying artificial metaplasticity neural network. *Expert Syst. Appl.* **2011**, *38*, 9573–9579. [CrossRef]
3. Chen, H.-L.; Yang, B.; Liu, J.; Liu, D.-Y. A support vector machine classifier with rough set-based feature selection for breast cancer diagnosis. *Expert Syst. Appl.* **2011**, *38*, 9014–9022. [CrossRef]
4. Chen, H.L.; Yang, B.; Wang, G.; Wang, S.J.; Liu, J.; Liu, D.Y. Support vector machine based diagnostic system for breast cancer using swarm intelligence. *J. Med. Syst.* **2012**, *36*, 2505–2519. [CrossRef] [PubMed]
5. Bashir, S.; Qamar, U.; Khan, F.H. Heterogeneous classifiers fusion for dynamic breast cancer diagnosis using weighted vote based ensemble. *Qual. Quant.* **2015**, *49*, 2061–2076. [CrossRef]
6. Tuba, E.; Tuba, M.; Simian, D. Adjusted bat algorithm for tuning of support vector machine parameters. In Proceedings of the 2016 IEEE Congress on Evolutionary Computation (CEC), Vancouver, BC, Canada, 24–29 July 2016; pp. 2225–2232. [CrossRef]
7. Aalaei, S.; Shahraki, H.; Rowhanimanesh, A.; Eslami, S. Feature selection using genetic algorithm for breast cancer diagnosis: Experiment on three different datasets. *Iran. J. Basic. Med. Sci.* **2016**, *19*, 476–482.
8. Mandal, S.K. Performance Analysis of Data Mining Algorithms for Breast Cancer Cell Detection Using Naïve Bayes, Logistic Regression and Decision Tree. *Int. J. Eng. Comput. Sci.* **2017**, *6*, 20388–20391.
9. Muslim, M.A.; Rukmana, S.H.; Sugiharti, E.; Prasetiyo, B.; Alimah, S. Optimization of C4.5 algorithm-based particle swarm optimization for breast cancer diagnosis. *J. Phys. Conf. Ser.* **2018**, *983*, 012063. [CrossRef]
10. Liu, N.; Shen, J.; Xu, M.; Gan, D.; Qi, E.-S.; Gao, B. Improved Cost-Sensitive Support Vector Machine Classifier for Breast Cancer Diagnosis. *Math. Probl. Eng.* **2018**, *2018*, 3875082. [CrossRef]
11. Agarap, A.F.M. On breast cancer detection: An application of machine learning algorithms on the wisconsin diagnostic dataset. In Proceedings of the 2nd International Conference on Machine Learning and Soft Computing, Phuoc Island, Vietnam, 2–4 February 2018; pp. 5–9. [CrossRef]
12. Huang, H.; Feng, X.; Zhou, S.; Jiang, J.; Chen, H.; Li, Y.; Li, C. A new fruit fly optimization algorithm enhanced support vector machine for diagnosis of breast cancer based on high-level features. *BMC Bioinform.* **2019**, *20*, 290. [CrossRef]
13. Xie, T.; Yao, J.; Zhou, Z. DA-Based Parameter Optimization of Combined Kernel Support Vector Machine for Cancer Diagnosis. *Processes* **2019**, *7*, 263. [CrossRef]
14. Rajaguru, H.; SR, C.S. Analysis of Decision Tree and K-Nearest Neighbor Algorithm in the Classification of Breast Cancer. *Asian Pac. J. Cancer Prev.* **2019**, *20*, 3777–3781. [CrossRef] [PubMed]
15. Dhahri, H.; Al Maghayreh, E.; Mahmood, A.; Elkilani, W.; Nagi, M.F. Automated Breast Cancer Diagnosis Based on Machine Learning Algorithms. *J. Health Eng.* **2019**, *2019*, 4253641. [CrossRef] [PubMed]

16. Hemeida, A.; Alkhalaf, S.; Mady, A.; Mahmoud, E.; Hussein, M.; Eldin, A.M.B. Implementation of nature-inspired optimization algorithms in some data mining tasks. *Ain Shams Eng. J.* **2020**, *11*, 309–318. [CrossRef]
17. Telsang, V.A.; Hegde, K. Breast Cancer Prediction Analysis using Machine Learning Algorithms. In Proceedings of the 2020 International Conference on Communication, Computing and Industry 4.0 (C2I4), Bangalore, India, 17–18 December 2020; pp. 1–5. [CrossRef]
18. Salma, M.U.; Doreswamy, N. Hybrid BATGSA: A metaheuristic model for classification of breast cancer data. *Int. J. Adv. Intell. Paradig.* **2020**, *15*, 207. [CrossRef]
19. Singh, I.; Bansal, R.; Gupta, A.; Singh, A. A Hybrid Grey Wolf-Whale Optimization Algorithm for Optimizing SVM in Breast Cancer Diagnosis. In Proceedings of the 2020 Sixth International Conference on Parallel, Distributed and Grid Computing (PDGC), Waknaghat, India, 6–8 November 2020; pp. 286–290. [CrossRef]
20. Badr, E.; Almotairi, S.; Salam, M.A.; Ahmed, H. New Sequential and Parallel Support Vector Machine with Grey Wolf Optimizer for Breast Cancer Diagnosis. *Alex. Eng. J.* **2021**, *61*, 2520–2534. [CrossRef]
21. Badr, E.; Salam, M.A.; Almotairi, S.; Ahmed, H. From Linear Programming Approach to Metaheuristic Approach: Scaling Techniques. *Complexity* **2021**, *2021*, 9384318. [CrossRef]
22. Badr, E.S.; Paparrizos, K.; Samaras, N.; Sifaleras, A. On the Basis Inverse of the Exterior Point Simplex Algorithm. In Proceedings of the 17th National Conference of Hellenic Operational Research Society (HELORS), Rio, Greece, 16–18 June 2005; pp. 677–687.
23. Badr, E.S.; Paparrizos, K.; Thanasis, B.; Varkas, G. Some computational results on the efficiency of an exterior point algorithm. In Proceedings of the 18th National conference of Hellenic Operational Research Society (HELORS), Kozani, Greece, 15–17 June 2006; pp. 1103–1115.
24. Badr, E.M.; Moussa, M.I. An upper bound of radio k-coloring problem and its integer linear programming model. *Wirel. Netw.* **2020**, *26*, 4955–4964. [CrossRef]
25. Badr, E.; AlMotairi, S. On a Dual Direct Cosine Simplex Type Algorithm and Its Computational Behavior. *Math. Probl. Eng.* **2020**, *2020*, 7361092. [CrossRef]
26. Badr, E.S.; Moussa, M.; Paparrizos, K.; Samaras, N.; Sifaleras, A. Some computational results on MPI parallel implementation of dense simplex method. *Trans. Eng. Comput. Technol.* **2006**, *17*, 228–231.
27. Elble, J.M.; Sahinidis, N.V. Scaling linear optimization problems prior to application of the simplex method. *Comput. Optim. Appl.* **2012**, *52*, 345–371. [CrossRef]
28. Ploskas, N.; Samaras, N. The impact of scaling on simplex type algorithms. In Proceedings of the 6th Balkan Conference in Informatics, Thessaloniki Greece, 19–21 September 2013; pp. 17–22. [CrossRef]
29. Triantafyllidis, C.; Samaras, N. Three nearly scaling-invariant versions of an exterior point algorithm for linear programming. *Optimization* **2015**, *64*, 2163–2181. [CrossRef]
30. Ploskas, N.; Samaras, N. A computational comparison of scaling techniques for linear optimization problems on a graphical processing unit. *Int. J. Comput. Math.* **2015**, *92*, 319–336. [CrossRef]
31. Badr, E.M.; Elgendy, H. A hybrid water cycle-particle swarm optimization for solving the fuzzy underground water confined steady flow. *Indones. J. Electr. Eng. Comput. Sci.* **2020**, *19*, 492–504. [CrossRef]
32. Tapkan, P.; Özbakır, L.; Baykasoglu, A. Bee algorithms for parallel two-sided assembly line balancing problem with walking times. *Appl. Soft Comput.* **2016**, *39*, 275–291. [CrossRef]
33. Tian, T.; Gong, D. Test data generation for path coverage of message-passing parallel programs based on co-evolutionary genetic algorithms. *Autom. Softw. Eng.* **2016**, *23*, 469–500. [CrossRef]
34. Maleki, S.; Musuvathi, M.; Mytkowicz, T. Efficient parallelization using rank convergence in dynamic programming algorithms. *Commun. ACM* **2016**, *59*, 85–92. [CrossRef]
35. Sandes, E.F.D.O.; Boukerche, A.; De Melo, A.C.M.A. Parallel Optimal Pairwise Biological Sequence Comparison. *ACM Comput. Surv.* **2016**, *48*, 1–36. [CrossRef]
36. Truchet, C.; Arbelaez, A.; Richoux, F.; Codognet, P. Estimating parallel runtimes for randomized algorithms in constraint solving. *J. Heuristics* **2016**, *22*, 613–648. [CrossRef]
37. Połap, D.; Kęsik, K.; Woźniak, M.; Damaševičius, R. Parallel Technique for the Metaheuristic Algorithms Using Devoted Local Search and Manipulating the Solutions Space. *Appl. Sci.* **2018**, *8*, 293. [CrossRef]
38. Jiao, S.; Gao, Y.; Feng, J.; Lei, T.; Yuan, X. Does deep learning always outperform simple linear regression in optical imag-ing? *Opt. Express* **2020**, *28*, 3717–3731. [CrossRef] [PubMed]
39. Chauhan, D.; Anyanwu, E.; Goes, J.; Besser, S.A.; Anand, S.; Madduri, R.; Getty, N.; Kelle, S.; Kawaji, K.; Mor-Avi, V.; et al. Comparison of machine learning and deep learning for view identification from cardiac magnetic resonance images. *Clin. Imaging* **2022**, *82*, 121–126. [CrossRef]
40. Sain, S.R.; Vapnik, V.N. *The Nature of Statistical Learning Theory*; Springer Science & Business Media: Berlin/Heidelberg, Germany, 1996; Volume 38.
41. Cristianini, N.; Shawe-Taylor, J. *An Introduction to Support Vector Machines and Other Kernel-Based Learning Meth-Ods*; Cambridge University Press: Cambridge, UK, 2000.
42. Boser, B.E.; Guyon, I.M.; Vapnik, V.N. A training algorithm for optimal margin classifiers. In Proceedings of the Fifth Annual Workshop on Computational Learning Theory, Pittsburgh, PA, USA, 27–29 July 1992; pp. 144–152. [CrossRef]

43. Heidari, A.A.; Mirjalili, S.; Faris, H.; Aljarah, I.; Mafarja, M.; Chen, H. Harris hawks optimization: Algorithm and applications. *Futur. Gener. Comput. Syst.* **2019**, *97*, 849–872. [CrossRef]
44. UCI Machine Learning Repository. Breast Cancer Wisconsin (Diagnostic) Data Set 1995. Available online: https://archive.ics.uci.edu/dataset/17/breast+cancer+wisconsin+diagnostic (accessed on 1 January 2015).
45. Chang, C.; Lin, C. LIBSVM: A Library for Support Vector Machines. *ACM Trans. Intell. Syst. Technol.* **2013**, *2*, 1–27. [CrossRef]
46. Salzberg, S.L. On Comparing Classifiers: Pitfalls to Avoid and a Recommended Approach. *Data Min. Knowl. Discov.* **1997**, *1*, 317–328. [CrossRef]

Disclaimer/Publisher's Note: The statements, opinions and data contained in all publications are solely those of the individual author(s) and contributor(s) and not of MDPI and/or the editor(s). MDPI and/or the editor(s) disclaim responsibility for any injury to people or property resulting from any ideas, methods, instructions or products referred to in the content.

Article

Structure-Aware Low-Rank Adaptation for Parameter-Efficient Fine-Tuning

Yahao Hu, Yifei Xie, Tianfeng Wang, Man Chen and Zhisong Pan *

Command and Control Engineering College, Army Engineering University of PLA, Nanjing 210007, China; yahao_hu@163.com (Y.H.); xieyifei10@163.com (Y.X.); tianfengw97@163.com (T.W.); 19205060770@stu.csust.edu.cn (M.C.)
* Correspondence: panzhisong@aeu.edu.cn

Abstract: With the growing scale of pre-trained language models (PLMs), full parameter fine-tuning becomes prohibitively expensive and practically infeasible. Therefore, parameter-efficient adaptation techniques for PLMs have been proposed to learn through incremental updates of pre-trained weights, such as in low-rank adaptation (LoRA). However, LoRA relies on heuristics to select the modules and layers to which it is applied, and assigns them the same rank. As a consequence, any fine-tuning that ignores the structural information between modules and layers is suboptimal. In this work, we propose structure-aware low-rank adaptation (SaLoRA), which adaptively learns the intrinsic rank of each incremental matrix by removing rank-0 components during training. We conduct comprehensive experiments using pre-trained models of different scales in both task-oriented (GLUE) and task-agnostic (Yelp and GYAFC) settings. The experimental results show that SaLoRA effectively captures the structure-aware intrinsic rank. Moreover, our method consistently outperforms LoRA without significantly compromising training efficiency.

Keywords: pre-trained language models; parameter-efficient fine-tuning; low-rank adaptation; intrinsic rank; training efficiency

MSC: 68T50

Citation: Hu, Y.; Xie, Y.; Wang, T.; Chen, M.; Pan, Z. Structure-Aware Low-Rank Adaptation for Parameter-Efficient Fine-Tuning. *Mathematics* **2023**, *11*, 4317. https://doi.org/10.3390/math11204317

Academic Editors: Florin Leon, Mircea Hulea and Marius Gavrilescu

Received: 3 September 2023
Revised: 8 October 2023
Accepted: 10 October 2023
Published: 17 October 2023

Copyright: © 2023 by the authors. Licensee MDPI, Basel, Switzerland. This article is an open access article distributed under the terms and conditions of the Creative Commons Attribution (CC BY) license (https://creativecommons.org/licenses/by/4.0/).

1. Introduction

With the scaling of model and corpus size [1–5], large language models (LLMs) have demonstrated an ability for in-context learning [1,6,7] in various natural language processing (NLP) tasks, that is, learning from a few examples within context. Although in-context learning is now the prevalent paradigm for using LLMs, fine-tuning still outperforms it in task-specific settings. In such scenarios, a task-specific model is exclusively trained on a dataset comprising input–output examples specific to the target task. However, full parameter fine-tuning, which updates and stores all the parameters for different tasks, becomes impractical when dealing with large-scale models.

In fact, LLMs with billions of parameters can be effectively fine-tuned by optimizing only a few parameters [8–10]. This has given rise to a branch of parameter-efficient fine-tuning (PEFT) techniques [11–16] for model tuning. These techniques optimize a small fraction of the model parameters while keeping the rest fixed, thereby significantly reducing computational and storage costs. For example, LoRA [15] introduces trainable low-rank decomposition matrices into LLMs, enabling the model to adapt to a new task while preserving the integrity of the original LLMs and retaining the acquired knowledge. Fundamentally, this approach is built upon the assumption that updates to the weights of the pre-trained language model have a lower rank during adaptation to specific downstream tasks [8,9]. Thus, by reducing the rank of the incremental matrices, LoRA optimizes less than 0.5% of the additional trainable parameters. Remarkably, this optimization achieves comparable or even superior performance to that of full parameter fine-tuning.

However, despite its advantages, LoRA also comes with certain limitations that warrant consideration. One limitation lies in LoRA's reliance on heuristics to select the modules and layers to which it is applied. Though heuristics can be effective under specific circumstances, their lack of generalizability is a concern. This lack of generalizability can result in suboptimal performance, or even complete failure, when applied to new data. Another limitation is the assignment of the same rank to incremental matrices across different modules and layers. This tends to oversimplify the complex structural relationships and important disparities that exist within neural networks. This phenomenon is illustrated in Figure 1.

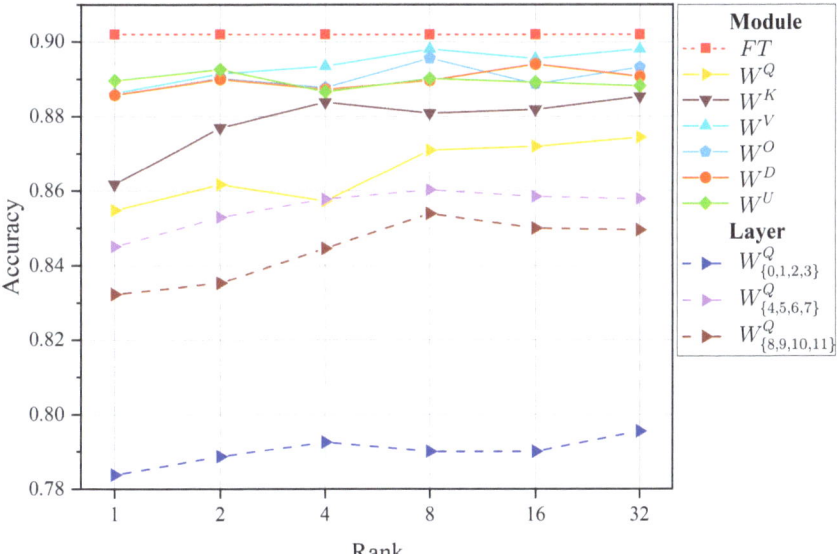

Figure 1. Fine-tuning performance of LoRA across different modules and layers with varying ranks on MRPC.

In this paper, we propose a novel approach called structure-aware low-rank adaptation (SaLoRA), which adaptively learns the intrinsic rank of each incremental matrix by removing rank-0 components. As shown in Figure 2, we introduce a diagonal gate matrix $G = \text{diag}(g_1, \ldots, g_r)$ for each incremental matrix. The modified incremental matrix can be represented as $\Delta W = BGA$. The incremental matrix is divided into triplets, where each triplet $\mathcal{T}_i$ contains the i-th column of B, the i-th gate mask of G and the i-th row of A. Here, g_i represents the binary "gate" that indicates the presence or absence of the i-th triplet. Although incorporating the active triplet count as a penalty term in the learning objective is unfeasible, we employ a differentiable relaxation method to selectively remove non-critical triplets by considering the L_0 norm [17,18]. The L_0 norm is equal to the number of non-zero triplets and encourages the model to deactivate less essential triplets. This strategy assigns a higher rank to crucial incremental matrices to capture task-specific information. Conversely, less significant matrices are pruned to possess a lower ranks preventing overfitting. However, A and B are not orthogonal, implying potential dependence among the triplets. Removing these triplets can result in a more significant deviation from the original matrix. To enhance training stability and generalization, we introduce orthogonality regularization for B and A. Furthermore, we integrate a density constraint and leverage Lagrangian relaxation [19] to control the number of valid parameters.

We conduct extensive experiments on a wide range of tasks and models to evaluate the effectiveness of SaLoRA. Specifically, we conduct experiments on the General Language Understanding Evaluation [20] benchmark in a task-oriented setting to assess the model's performance. In addition, we evaluate the model's performance in a task-agnostic setting by fine-tuning LLaMA-7B with a 50K cleaned instruction-following dataset [21], and then perform zero-shot task inference on two text style transfer tasks: sentiment transfer [22] and formality transfer [23]. The experimental results demonstrate that SaLoRA consistently outperforms LoRA without significantly compromising training efficiency.

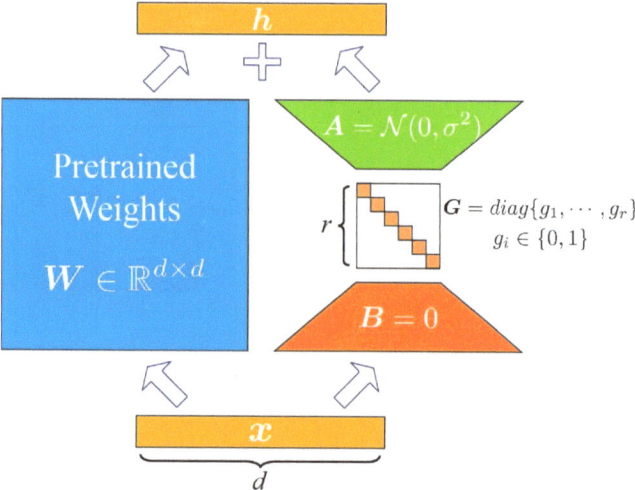

Figure 2. Structure-aware low-rank adaptation.

2. Backgound

Transformer Architecture. The Transformer [24] is primarily constructed using two key submodules: a multi-head self-attention (MHA) layer and a fully connected feed-forward (FFN) layer. The MHA is defined as follows:

$$
\begin{aligned}
MHA(Q, K, V) &= Concat(head_1, \ldots, head_h)W^O, \\
head_i &= Atention(QW_i^Q, KW_i^K, VW_i^V)
\end{aligned}
\quad (1)
$$

where $Q, K, V \in \mathbb{R}^{n \times d}$ are input-embedding matrices; $W^O \in \mathbb{R}^{d \times d}$ is an output projection; $W_i^Q, W_i^K, W_i^V \in \mathbb{R}^{d \times d_k}$ are query, key and value projections of head i, respectively; n is sequence length; d is the embedding dimension; h is the number of heads and $d_k = d/h$ is the hidden dimension of the projection subspaces. The FFN consists of two linear transformations separated by a ReLU activation:

$$FFN(x) = ReLU(xW^U + b^U)W^D + b^D \quad (2)$$

where $W^U \in \mathbb{R}^{d \times d_m}$ and $W^D \in \mathbb{R}^{d_m \times d}$.

Parameter-Efficient Fine-Tuning. With the growing size of models, recent works have developed three main categories of parameter-efficient fine-tuning (PEFT) techniques. These techniques optimize a small fraction of model parameters while keeping the rest fixed, thereby significantly reducing computational and storage costs [10]. For example, addition-based methods [11–13,25,26] introduce additional trainable modules or parameters that are not part of the original model or process. Specifcation-based methods [14,27,28] specify certain parameters within the original model or process as trainable, whereas the others remain frozen. Reparameterization-based methods [15,16,29], including LoRA, reparameterize existing parameters into a parameter-efficient form by transformation. In this study, we focus on reparameterization-based methods, with particular emphasis on LoRA.

Low-Rank Adaptation. LoRA, as introduced in the work of Hu et al. [15], represents a typical example of a reparameterization-based method. In LoRA, some pre-trained weights of LLMs' dense layers are reparameterized by injecting trainable low-rank incremental matrices. This reparameterization only allows low-rank matrices to be updated, while keeping the original pre-trained weights frozen. By reducing the rank of these matrices, LoRA effectively reduces the number of parameters during the fine-tuning process of LLMs. Consider a pre-trained weight matrix $W \in \mathbb{R}^{d \times k}$, accompanied by a low-rank incremental matrix $\Delta W = BA$. For $h = Wx$, the modified forward pass is as follows:

$$h = Wx + \frac{\alpha}{r} \Delta W x = Wx + \frac{\alpha}{r} BAx \tag{3}$$

where $B \in \mathbb{R}^{d \times r}$, $A \in \mathbb{R}^{r \times k}$, with the rank $r \ll \min(d,k)$, and α is a constant scale hyperparameter. The matrix A adopts a random zero-mean Gaussian initialization, while the matrix B is initialized as a zero matrix. Consequently, the product $\Delta W = BA$ is initially set to zero at the beginning of training. Let B_{*j} and A_{j*} denote the j-th column of B and the j-th row of A, respectively. Using this notation, ΔW can be expressed as $\Delta W = \sum_{j=1}^{r} B_{*j} A_{j*}$.

3. Method

In this section, we will first give a brief introduction to parameter-efficient fine-tuning, and then discuss our proposed model based on the problem definition.

3.1. Problem Formalization

We consider the general problem of efficiently fine-tuning LLMs for specific downstream tasks. Firstly, let us introduce some notations. Consider a training corpus $\mathcal{D} = (x_i, y_i)_{i=1}^{N}$, where N represents the number of samples. Each sample consists an input, x_i, and its corresponding output, y_i. We use the index i to refer to the incremental matrix, i.e., $\Delta W_i = B_i A_i$ for $i = 1, \ldots, K$, where K is the number of incremental matrices. However, LoRA's assumption of identical ranks for each incremental matrix overlooks structural relationships and the varying importance of weight matrices across different modules and layers during fine-tuning. This oversight can potentially impact overall model performance. Our objective is to determine the optimal $\{rank^*(\Delta W_i)\}_{i=1}^{K}$ on the fly. The optimization objective can be formulated as follows:

$$\min_{\mathcal{W}} \mathcal{R}(\mathcal{W}) \triangleq \frac{1}{N} (\sum_{i=1}^{N} \mathcal{L}(f(x_i; \mathcal{W}), y_i)) \tag{4}$$
$$s.t. \quad rank(\Delta W_i) \leq r, k = 1, \ldots, K.$$

where $\mathcal{W} = \{\Delta W_i, \ldots, \Delta W_K\}$ represents the sets of trainable parameters and $\mathcal{L}$ corresponds to a loss function, such as cross-entropy for classification. Note that $rank(\Delta W_i) \in \{0, 1, \ldots, r\}$ is an unknown parameter that needs to be optimized.

3.2. Structure-Aware Intrinsic Rank Using L_0 Norm

To find the optimal $\{rank^*(\Delta W_i)\}_{i=1}^{K}$ on the fly, with minimal computational overhead during training, we introduce a gate matrix G to define the structure-aware intrinsic rank:

$$\Delta W = BGA = \sum_{j=1}^{r} g_j B_{*j} A_{j*} \tag{5}$$

where the $g_j \in \{0, 1\}$ serves as a binary "gate", indicating the presence or absence of the j-th rank. The gate matrix $G = \text{diag}(g_1, \ldots, g_r)$ is a diagonal matrix consisting of the pruning variables. By learning the variable g_j, we can control the rank of each incremental matrix individually, rather than applying the same rank to all matrices. To deactivate non-critical rank-0 components, the ideal approach would be to apply L_0 norm regularization to the gate matrix G:

$$\|G\|_0 = \sum_{j=1}^{r} g_j \tag{6}$$

where r is the rank of incremental matrices. The L_0 norm measures the number of non-zero triplets; thus, optimizing L_0 would encourage the model to deactivate less important incremental matrices.

Unfortunately, the optimization objective involving $\|G\|_0$ is computationally intractable due to its non-differentiability, making it impossible to directly incorporate it as a regularization term in the objective function. Instead, we use a stochastic relaxation approach, where the gate variables g are treated as continuous variables distributed within the interval $[0,1]$. We leverage the reparameterization trick [30,31] to ensure that g remains differentiable. Following prior studies [17,19], we adopt the Hard-Concrete (HC) distribution as a continuous surrogate for random variables g, illustrated in Figure 3. The HC distribution applies a hard-sigmoid rectification to s, which can easily be sampled by first sampling $u \in U(0,1)$ and then computing as follows:

$$s = Sigmod\left(\frac{\log \frac{u}{1-u} + \log \theta}{\tau}\right) \times (\zeta - \gamma) + \gamma \tag{7}$$
$$g = \min(1, \max(0, s))$$

where θ is the trainable parameter of the distribution and τ is the temperature. The interval (γ, ζ), with $\gamma < 0$ and $\zeta > 1$, enables the distribution to concentrate probability mass at the edge of the support. The final outputs g are rectified into $[0,1]$. By summing up the probabilities of the gates being non-zero, the L_0 norm regularization can be computed via a closed form, as follows:

$$\mathbb{E}[\|G\|_0] = \sum_{j=1}^{r} \mathbb{E}[g_j > 0] = \sum_{j=1}^{r} Sigmod\left(\log \theta_j - \tau \log \frac{-\gamma}{\zeta}\right) \tag{8}$$

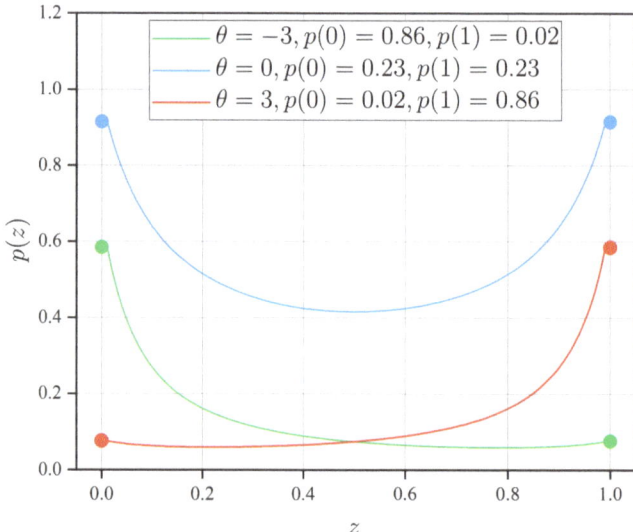

Figure 3. Hard-Concrete distribution with different parameters.

As g now represents the output of the parameterized HC distribution function and serves as an intermediate representation for the neural network, gradient-based optimization methods can perform gradient updates for $\theta = \{\theta_1, \ldots, \theta_r\}$. For each training batch, we sample the gate mask and then share it across the training examples within the batch to enhance sampling efficiency.

3.3. Enhanced Stability Using Orthogonal Regularization

In deep networks, orthogonality plays a crucial role in preserving the norm of the original matrix during multiplication, preventing signal vanishing or exploding [32]. However, in LoRA, where B and A are not orthogonal, the dependence can lead to larger variations when removing certain columns or rows through L_0 regularization. This, in turn, leads to training instability and the potential for negative effects on generalization [16]. For this, we turn to orthogonal regularization, which enforces the orthogonality condition:

$$\mathcal{R}_{orth}(B, A) = ||B^T B - I||_F^2 + ||AA^T - I||_F^2 \qquad (9)$$

where I is the identity matrix.

Now, let us substitute Equations (8) and (9) into Equation (4) to derive the new training objective:

$$\min_{\mathcal{W}, \Theta} \mathcal{R}(\mathcal{W}, \Theta) \triangleq \frac{1}{N}(\sum_{i=1}^{N} \mathcal{L}(f(x_i; \mathcal{W}), y_i)) + \lambda \sum_{i=1}^{K} \mathbb{E}[||G_i||_0] + \beta \sum_{i=1}^{K} \mathcal{R}_{orth}(B_i, A_i) \qquad (10)$$

where $\Theta = \{\theta_i, \ldots, \theta_K\}$ represents the sets of trainable parameters, and λ and β are two constant hyperparameters.

3.4. Controlled Budget Using Lagrangian Relaxation

If we only rely on Equation (10) to learn the intrinsic rank for each incremental matrix, the resulting parameter budget cannot be directly controlled. This limitation becomes problematic in many real-world applications that require a specific model size or parameter budget. To address this issue, we further introduce an additional density constraint on $\mathcal{R}(\mathcal{W}, \Theta)$ to guide the network towards achieving a specific desired budget.

$$\min_{\mathcal{W}} \mathcal{R}(\mathcal{W}) \triangleq \frac{1}{N}(\sum_{i=1}^{N} \mathcal{L}(f(x_i; \mathcal{W}), y_i)) + \beta \sum_{i=1}^{K} \mathcal{R}_{orth}(B_i, A_i)$$
$$s.t. \quad C(\Theta) \triangleq \sum_{i=1}^{K} \frac{\mathbb{E}[||G_i||_0] \times (d_i + k_i)}{\#(B_i) + \#(A_i)} = b \qquad (11)$$

where b represents the target density and $\#(x)$ counts the total number of parameters in matrix x. $\Delta W_i = B_i A_i$, where B_i is of $d_i \times r_i$, and A_i is of $r_i \times k_i$. However, lowering the density constraint poses a challenging and (not necessarily strictly) constrained optimization problem. To tackle this challenge, we leverage Lagrangian relaxation as an alternative approach, along with the corresponding min-max game:

$$\max_{\lambda} \min_{\mathcal{W}, \Theta} \mathcal{L}(\mathcal{W}, \Theta, \lambda) \triangleq \mathcal{R}(\mathcal{W}, \Theta) + \lambda(C(\Theta) - b)^2 \qquad (12)$$

where $\lambda \in \mathbb{R}$ is the Lagrangian multiplier, which is jointly updated during training. The updates to λ would increase the training loss unless the equality constraint is satisfied, resulting in the desired parameter budget. We optimize the Lagrangian relaxation by simultaneously performing gradient descent on $(\mathcal{W}, \Theta)$ and projected gradient ascent (to $\mathbb{R}^+$) on λ, as demonstrated in previous works [19,33]. During the experiments, we observed that the term $\lambda(C(\Theta) - b)^2$ converged quickly. To enhance training efficiency, we only optimize (Θ, λ) between T_{start} and T_{end} time steps. We provide a summarized algorithm in Algorithm 1.

Algorithm 1 SaLoRA

Input: Dataset $\mathcal{D}$; total iterations T; target density b; hyperparameters $\tau, \gamma, \zeta, \beta, \eta_p, \eta_c$.
Output: The fine-tuned parameters $\{\mathcal{W}, \Theta\}$.
   for $t = 1, \ldots, T$ **do**
      Sample a mini-batch from $\mathcal{D}$
      if $T_{start} \leq t < T_{end}$ **then**
         Sample a gate mask set $\mathcal{G}$ from HC distribution and share it across the mini-batch
         Compute the gradient $\mathcal{L}(\mathcal{W}, \Theta, \lambda)$
         Update $\mathcal{W}^{(t+1)} = \mathcal{W}^{(t)} - \eta_p \nabla_{\mathcal{W}} \mathcal{L}(\mathcal{W}^{(t)}, \Theta^{(t)}, \lambda^{(t)})$
         Update $\Theta^{(t+1)} = \Theta^{(t)} - \eta_c \nabla_{\Theta} \mathcal{L}(\mathcal{W}^{(t)}, \Theta^{(t)}, \lambda^{(t)})$
         Update $\lambda^{(t+1)} = \lambda^{(t)} + \eta_c \nabla_{\lambda^{(t)}} \mathcal{L}(\mathcal{W}^{(t)}, \Theta^{(t)}, \lambda^{(t)})$
      else
         Compute the gradient $\mathcal{L}(\mathcal{W})$
         Update $\mathcal{W}^{(t+1)} = \mathcal{W}^{(t)} - \eta_p \nabla_{\mathcal{W}} \mathcal{L}(\mathcal{W}^{(t)})$
      end if
   end for
   return The fine-tuned parameters $\{\mathcal{W}^{(T)}, \Theta^{(T)}, \lambda^{(T)}\}$.

3.5. Inference

During training, the gate mask g_i is a random variable drawn from the HC distribution. At inference time, we first calculate the expected value of each g_i in $\mathbf{G}$. If the value of g_i is greater than 0, we retain the corresponding i-th low-rank triplet. This procedure enables us to obtain the deterministic matrices $\mathbf{B}$ and $\mathbf{A}$.

4. Experiments

We evaluated the effectiveness of the proposed SaLoRA on RoBERTa [34] and LLaMA-7B in both task-oriented and task-agnostic settings.

Baselines. We compared SaLoRA with the following methods:

- **Fine-tuning (FT)** is the most common approach for adaptation. To establish an upper bound for the performance of our proposed method, we fine-tuned all parameters within the model.
- **Adapting tuning**, as proposed by Houlsby et al. [25], incorporates adapter layers between the self-attention module (and the MLP module) and the subsequent residual connection. Each adapter module consists of two fully connected layers with biases and a nonlinearity in between. This original design is referred to as **Adapter^H**. Recently, Pfeiffer et al. [11] introduced a more efficient approach, applying the adapter layer only after the MLP module and following a LayerNorm. We call it **Adapter^P**.
- **Prefix-tuning (Prefix)** [12] prepends a sequence of continuous task-specific activations to the input. During tuning, prefix-tuning freezes the model parameters and only backpropagates the gradient to the prefix activations.
- **Prompt-tuning (Prompt)** [13] is a simplified version of prefix-tuning, allowing the additional k tunable tokens per downstream task to be prepended to the input text.
- **LoRA**, introduced by Hu et al. [15], is a state-of-the-art method for parameter-efficient fine-tuning. The original implementation of LoRA applied the method solely to query and value projections. However, empirical studies [16,35] have shown that extending LoRA to all matrices, including W^Q, W^K, W^V, W^O, W^U and W^D, can further improve its performance. Therefore, we compare our approach with this generalized LoRA configuration to maximize its effectiveness.
- **AdaLoRA**, proposed by Zhang et al. [16], utilizes singular value decomposition (SVD) to adaptively allocate the parameter budget among weight matrices based on their respective importance scores. However, this baseline involves computationally intensive operations, especially for large matrices. The training cost can be significant, making it less efficient for resource-constrained scenarios.

4.1. Task-Oriented Performance

Models and Datasets. We evaluated the performance of different adaptive methods on the GLUE benchmark [20] using pre-trained RoBERTa-base (125M) and RoBERTa-large (355 M) [34] models from the HuggingFace Transformers library [36]. See Appendix A for additional details on the datasets we used.

Implementation Details. For running all the baselines, we utilized a publicly available implementation [37]. We evaluated the performance of LoRA, AdaLoRA and SaLoRA at $r = 8$. To maintain a controlled parameter budget, we set the desired budget ratio (b) to 0.50 for both SaLoRA and AdaLoRA. During training, we used the AdamW optimizer [38], along with the linear learning rate scheduler. During our experiments, we observed that using a larger learning rate (η_c) significantly improved the learning process for both the gate matrices and Lagrange multiplier. Therefore, we set η_c to 0.01 for all conducted experiments. We fine-tuned all models using an NVIDIA A100 (40 GB) GPU. Additional details can be found in Appendix B.

Main Results. We compared SaLoRA with the baseline methods under different model scale settings, and the experimental results on the GLUE development set are presented in Table 1. We can see that SaLoRA consistently achieved better or comparable performance compared with existing approaches for all datasets. Moreover, it even outperformed the FT method. SaLoRA's superiority was particularly striking when compared with LoRA, despite both models having a similar parameter count of 1.33 M/3.54 M for base/large model scales. After training, SaLoRA effectively utilized only 0.5×1.33 M/0.5×3.54 parameters, yet still attained superior performance. This observation emphasizes the effectiveness of our method in learning the intrinsic rank for incremental matrices.

Table 1. Results with RoBERTa-base and RoBERTa-large on GLUE development set. We report the Pearson correlation for STS-B, Matthew's correlation for CoLA, and accuracy for other tasks. We report the mean and maximum deviation of 5 runs using different random seeds. The best results are shown in bold. † indicates numbers published in prior works.

Model and Method	# Trainable Parameters	MNLI ACC	SST-2 ACC	CoLA Mathew	QQP ACC	QNLI ACC	RTE ACC	MRPC ACC	STS-B Pearson	ALL Avg
RoB$_{base}$(FT) †	125.00 M	87.6	94.8	63.6	**91.9**	92.8	78.7	90.2	91.2	86.4
RoB$_{base}$(Prefix)	1.33 M	82.58$_{\pm0.24}$	91.65$_{\pm0.44}$	47.45$_{\pm4.47}$	85.98$_{\pm0.11}$	85.91$_{\pm0.44}$	60.47$_{\pm0.54}$	88.09$_{\pm1.37}$	87.49$_{\pm0.63}$	78.70
RoB$_{base}$(Prompt)	0.62 M	79.14$_{\pm0.99}$	88.33$_{\pm1.44}$	42.35$_{\pm5.12}$	73.30$_{\pm5.84}$	80.51$_{\pm1.64}$	55.81$_{\pm2.67}$	69.75$_{\pm0.59}$	76.94$_{\pm3.59}$	70.77
RoB$_{base}$(LoRA)	1.33 M	87.49$_{\pm0.44}$	94.77$_{\pm0.53}$	61.22$_{\pm2.09}$	91.39$_{\pm0.18}$	92.85$_{\pm0.28}$	79.24$_{\pm.21}$	89.46$_{\pm1.23}$	90.89$_{\pm0.18}$	85.91
RoB$_{base}$(AdaLoRA)	1.33 M	**87.93**$_{\pm0.20}$	94.59$_{\pm0.21}$	59.29$_{\pm1.06}$	90.94$_{\pm0.13}$	92.61$_{\pm0.10}$	76.39$_{\pm1.30}$	87.35$_{\pm0.39}$	90.87$_{\pm0.15}$	85.00
RoB$_{base}$(SaLoRA)	1.33 M	87.83$_{\pm0.04}$	**95.14**$_{\pm0.73}$	**63.39**$_{\pm1.79}$	91.46$_{\pm0.09}$	**92.99**$_{\pm0.21}$	**81.01**$_{\pm0.87}$	**90.20**$_{\pm0.74}$	**91.13**$_{\pm0.17}$	**86.64**
RoB$_{large}$(FT) †	356.05 M	90.2	96.4	68.0	**92.2**	94.7	86.6	90.9	92.4	88.9
RoB$_{large}$(Adapt^P) †	4.05 M	90.2$_{\pm0.3}$	96.1$_{\pm0.3}$	68.3$_{\pm1.0}$	91.9$_{\pm0.1}$	94.8$_{\pm0.2}$	83.8$_{\pm2.9}$	90.2$_{\pm0.7}$	92.1$_{\pm0.7}$	88.4
RoB$_{large}$(Adapt^H) †	7.05 M	89.5$_{\pm0.5}$	96.2$_{\pm0.3}$	66.5$_{\pm4.4}$	92.1$_{\pm0.1}$	94.7$_{\pm.2}$	83.4$_{\pm1.1}$	88.7$_{\pm2.9}$	91.0$_{\pm1.7}$	87.8
RoB$_{large}$(Prefix)	3.02 M	88.61$_{\pm0.12}$	94.70$_{\pm0.44}$	60.06$_{\pm1.44}$	87.57$_{\pm0.25}$	89.60$_{\pm0.37}$	77.33$_{\pm1.37}$	89.85$_{\pm.88}$	89.97$_{\pm3.37}$	84.71
RoB$_{large}$(Prompt)	1.09 M	85.65$_{\pm2.54}$	93.95$_{\pm0.83}$	58.34$_{\pm2.63}$	83.98$_{\pm1.45}$	84.92$_{\pm3.28}$	58.70$_{\pm4.83}$	74.22$_{\pm2.65}$	80.47$_{\pm0.71}$	77.53
RoB$_{large}$(LoRA)	3.41 M	89.96$_{\pm0.12}$	96.10$_{\pm0.11}$	**68.76**$_{\pm1.75}$	88.67$_{\pm0.88}$	94.86$_{\pm0.07}$	85.49$_{\pm1.51}$	90.93$_{\pm0.74}$	92.25$_{\pm0.17}$	88.38
RoB$_{large}$(AdaLoRA)	3.54 M	**90.84**$_{\pm0.03}$	96.29$_{\pm0.19}$	67.61$_{\pm0.12}$	91.12$_{\pm0.26}$	94.82$_{\pm0.11}$	86.28$_{\pm0.36}$	89.89$_{\pm0.31}$	92.27$_{\pm0.16}$	88.64
RoB$_{large}$(SaLoRA)	3.54 M	90.67$_{\pm0.07}$	**96.63**$_{\pm0.28}$	68.37$_{\pm0.34}$	91.95$_{\pm0.08}$	**94.98**$_{\pm0.09}$	**87.80**$_{\pm1.29}$	**91.81**$_{\pm1.57}$	**92.43**$_{\pm0.18}$	**89.33**

4.2. Task-Agnostic Performance

Models and Datasets. We present the experiments conducted to evaluate the performance of the self-instruct tuned LLaMA-7B models on instruction-following data [21]. Our objective was to assess their capability in comprehending and executing instructions for arbitrary tasks. We evaluated model performance on two text style transfer datasets: Yelp [22] and GYAFC [23]). Text style transfer refers to the task of changing the style of a sentence to the desired style while preserving the style-independent content. The prompts used in these experiments can be found in Appendix C.

Implementation Details. We tuned the learning rate η_p from $\{8 \times 10^{-5}, 3 \times 10^{-5}, 1 \times 10^{-4}, 3 \times 10^{-4}, 8 \times 10^{-4}, 1 \times 10^{-3}\}$ and kept the following hyperparameters fixed: $r = 8, b = 0.5$,

$\eta_c = 0.01$, $\beta = 0.1$, $\tau = 1.0$, $\gamma = -0.1$ and $\zeta = 1.1$. All models were fine-tuned on an NVIDIA A800 (80 G) GPU.

Furthermore, we compared the performance of SaLoRA with dataset-specific style transfer models, including StyTrans [15], StyIns [16] and TSST [17]. In contrast to SaLoRA, these models were trained on a specific dataset. To evaluate the performance of style transfer models, we used the following metrics: (1) Transfer accuracy (ACC) using a fine-tuned BERT-base [39] classifier with each dataset. (2) Semantic similarity to human references via BLEU [40] score. (3) Sentence fluency (PPL) via perplexity, as measured by KenLM [41].

Main Results. Table 2 presents our experimental results on the Yelp and GYAFC datasets. Compared with LoRA, our method SaloRA achieved better or comparable performance across all directions on both datasets. This demonstrates the effectiveness of our method. In the negative-to-positive transfer direction, though SaloRA's transfer accuracy was lower than the dataset-specific models (e.g., StyIns achieved 92.40 compared with SaLoRA's 71), it still aligned with the human reference accuracy of 64.60. Furthermore, SaloRA exhibited a lower perplexity (PPL) compared with dataset-specific models. These results show that SaloRA (including LoRA) aligns more closely with human writing tendencies. In the formal-to-informal transfer direction, we also observed that our transfer accuracy was lower than dataset-specific models. This disparity may be attributed to the inherent bias of a large model for generating more formal outputs. This can be verified from the fact that SaLoRA exhibited a significant improvement in the transfer accuracy compared with dataset-specific models.

Table 2. Automatic evaluation results on Yelp and GYAFC datasets. ↑ indicates that higher values mean better performance, and vice versa.

Model and Method	Yelp						GYAFC					
	Negative to Positive			Positive to Negative			Informal to Formal			Formal to Informal		
	ACC↑	BLEU↑	PPL↓	ACC↑	BLEU↑	PPL↓	ACC↑	BLEU↑	PPL↓	ACC↑	BLEU↑	PPL↓
Reference	64.60	100	102.62	93.80	100	77.53	88.44	100	66.86	87.63	100	105.28
StyTrans	88.40	25.85	173.35	94.20	24.90	141.88	32.81	54.91	144.15	80.86	27.69	201.78
StyIns	**92.40**	25.98	116.01	89.60	26.08	105.79	54.73	60.87	96.53	80.57	30.25	132.54
TSST	91.20	28.95	112.86	94.40	28.83	101.92	65.62	**61.83**	87.04	**85.87**	33.54	128.78
LaA$_{7B}$	2.20	**33.58**	208.69	0.80	31.12	156.14	12.01	60.18	189.78	7.75	34.61	145.43
LaA$_{7B}$(LoRA)	71.00	25.96	82.20	92.80	31.83	**83.03**	89.34	61.06	68.52	34.45	**41.59**	82.96
LaA$_{7B}$(SaLoRA)	73.20	24.76	**76.49**	**94.60**	**31.96**	87.41	**89.63**	61.76	**67.53**	39.04	40.91	**79.54**

4.3. Analysis

The Effect of Rank r. Figure 4 illustrates the experimental results of fine-tuning RoBERTa-large across different ranks. We see that the rank r significantly influenced the model's performance. Both large and small values of r led to suboptimal results. This observation emphasizes that selecting the optimal value for r through heuristic approaches is not always feasible. Notably, SaLoRA consistently improved performance across all ranks when compared with the baseline LoRA. This suggests that SaLoRA effectively captured the "intrinsic rank" of the incremental matrix.

The Effect of Sparsity b. Figure 5 shows the experimental results of fine-tuning RoBERTa-large across various levels of sparsity. Remarkably, SaLoRA consistently exhibited enhanced performance across all sparsity levels compared with the baseline. This result suggests that SaLoRA's modifications facilitated the acquisition of the "intrinsic rank" of the incremental matrix under different sparsities. It is noteworthy that SaLoRA's performance even surpassed the results of LoRA under low sparsity conditions (0.125). The fact that SaLoRA can outperform LoRA even under low sparsity conditions highlights its capacity to capture and leverage parameters with a constrained budget. Consequently, SaLoRA's efficacy could be expanded on a limited budget, making it a versatile method with a broader range of applications.

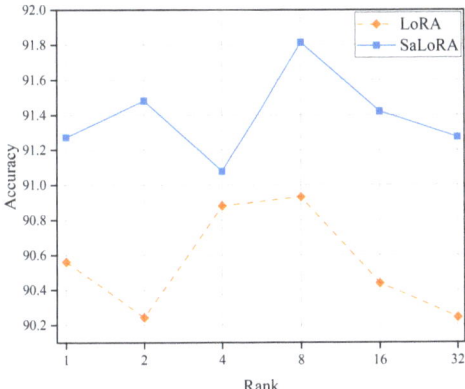

Figure 4. Fine-tuning performance under different ranks.

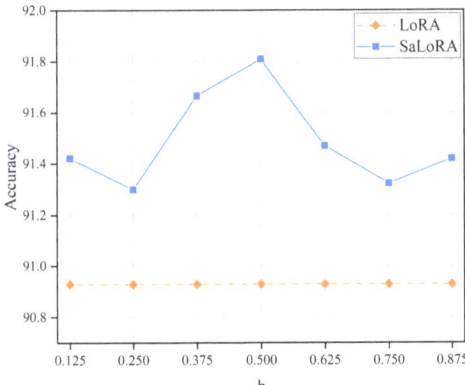

Figure 5. Fine-tuning performance under different sparsity levels.

Ablation Study. We investigated the impact of Lagrangian relaxation and orthogonal regularization in SaLoRA. Specifically, we compared SaLoRA with the following variants: (i) SaLoRA$_{\lambda=0}$: SaLoRA without Lagrangian relaxation; (ii) SaLoRA$_{\beta=0}$: SaLoRA without orthogonal regularization. These variations involved the fine-tuning of the RoBERTa-base model on the CoLA, STS-B, and MRPC datasets. The target sparsity was set to 0.5 by default. SPS represented the expected sparsity of the incremental matrix. From Table 3, we see that:

1. Without Lagrangian relaxation, the parameter budget was uncontrollable, being 0.37, 0.42 and 0.43 on the three datasets, respectively. Such results highlight the pivotal role that Lagrangian relaxation plays in controlling the allocation of the parameter budget. Nonetheless, it is worth noting that omitting Lagrange relaxation may lead to slight enhancements in performance. However, given the emphasis on control over the parameter budget, this incremental enhancement should be disregarded.
2. Without orthogonal regularization, the performance of SaLoRA degenerated. These results validate that incorporating orthogonal regularization into SaLoRA ensures the independence of doublets from one another, leading to a significant enhancement in its performance.

Table 3. Ablation studies on Lagrangian relaxation and orthogonal regularization.

Method	MRPC		STS-B		CoLA	
	ACC	SPS	ACC	SPS	ACC	SPS
SaLoRA	**90.20**$_{\pm 0.74}$	0.51$_{\pm 0.00}$	91.13$_{\pm 0.17}$	0.52$_{\pm 0.00}$	63.39$_{\pm 1.79}$	0.52$_{\pm 0.00}$
SaLoRA$_{\lambda=0}$	89.95$_{\pm 0.49}$	0.37$_{\pm 0.02}$	**91.20**$_{\pm 0.12}$	0.42$_{\pm 0.03}$	**63.65**$_{\pm 3.39}$	0.43$_{\pm 0.02}$
SaLoRA$_{\beta=0}$	90.00$_{\pm 0.94}$	0.51$_{\pm 0.00}$	90.78$_{\pm 0.27}$	0.52$_{\pm 0.00}$	62.89$_{\pm 2.16}$	0.52$_{\pm 0.00}$

Visualization of Four Components. We plotted the visualization of expected sparsity $\hat{b}$, the Lagrangian multiplier λ and $||A^T A - I||_F^2$ and $||B^T B - I||_F^2$ to show whether these four components were regularized by Lagrangian relaxation and orthogonal regularization, respectively. Specifically, we fine-tuned the RoBERTa-base using SaLoRA on the CoLA, STS-B and MRPC datasets. The initial Lagrangian multiplier λ was 0 and the target sparsity b was 0.5. From Figure 6, we see that:

1. The expected sparsity $\hat{b}$ decreased from 0.92 to about 0.50, and the Lagrangian multiplier λ kept increasing during training. The results indicate that the SaLoRA algorithm placed more emphasis on satisfying the constraints, eventually reaching a trade-off between satisfying the constraints and optimizing the objective function.
2. The values of $||A^T A - I||_F^2$ and $||B^T B - I||_F^2$ could be optimized to a highly negligible level (e.g., 0.001). Therefore, this optimization process enforced orthogonality upon both matrices A and B, guaranteeing the independence of doublets from one another.

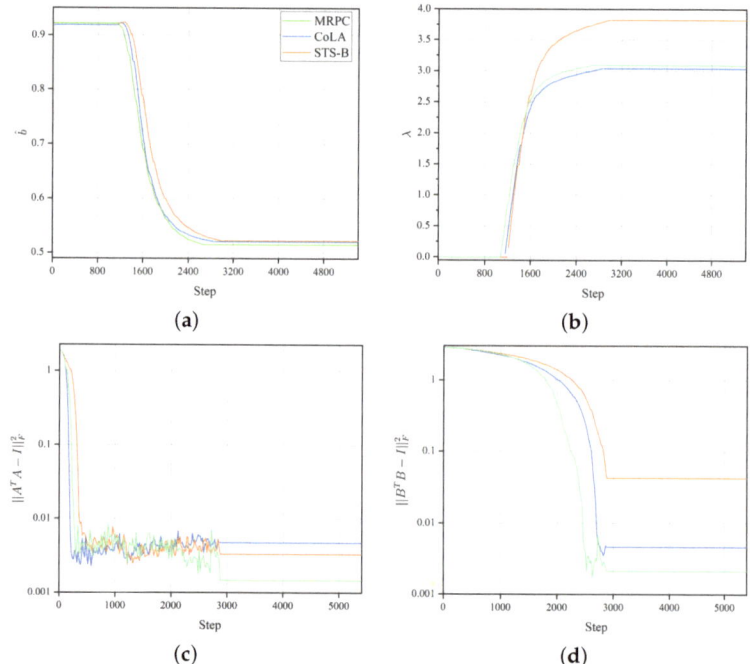

Figure 6. Visualization of expected sparsity $\hat{b}$ and the Lagrangian multiplier λ under Lagrangian relaxation, and $||A^T A - I||_F^2$ and $||B^T B - I||_F^2$ under orthogonal regularization: (**a**) expected sparsity $\hat{b}$; (**b**) Lagrangian multiplier λ; (**c**) A of W^O at the first layer; and (**d**) B of W^O at the first layer.

Comparison of Training Efficiency. We analyzed the efficiency of SaLoRA in terms of memory and computational efficiency, as shown in Table 4. Specifically, we selected two scales of the RoBERTa model, that is, RoB_{base} and RoB_{large}, and measured the peak GPU memory and training time under different batch sizes on an NVIDIA A100 (40 GB) GPU. From Table 4, we see that:

1. The GPU memory usages of both methods were remarkably similar. Such results demonstrate that SaLoRA does not impose significant memory overhead. The reason behind this is that SaLoRA only introduces gate matrices in contrast to LoRA. The total number of parameters was $r \times L \times M$. In this experiment, r denotes the rank of the incremental matrix (set at 8), L corresponds to the number of layers within the model (12 for RoB_{base} and 24 for RoB_{large}) and M stands for the number of modules in each layer (set at 6).

2. The training time of SaLoRA increased by 11% when using a batch size of 32 compared with LoRA. This suggests that the additional computational requirements introduced by SaLoRA are justified by its notable gains in performance. This is because SaLoRA is only utilized during a specific training phase (T_{start} to T_{end}) comprising 30% of the overall training time. With the remaining 70% being equivalent to LoRA, the overall impact on training time remains manageable.

Table 4. Comparison of training efficiency between LoRA and SaLoRA on the MRPC dataset.

Model	BS	Method	GPU Mem	Time
RoB$_{base}$	16	LoRA	3.54 GB	15 min
		SaLoRA	3.54 GB	20 min
	32	LoRA	5.34 GB	14 min
		SaLoRA	5.35 GB	15 min
	64	LoRA	9.00 GB	13 min
		SaLoRA	9.00 GB	14 min
RoB$_{large}$	16	LoRA	7.44 GB	44 min
		SaLoRA	7.46 GB	53 min
	32	LoRA	12.16 GB	40 min
		SaLoRA	12.18 GB	44 min
	64	LoRA	21.80 GB	38 min
		SaLoRA	21.82 GB	41 min

The Resulting Rank Distribution. Figure 7 shows the resulting rank of each incremental matrix obtained from fine-tuning RoBERTa-base with SaLoRA. We observed that SaLoRA always assigned higher ranks to modules (W^U, W^O and W^V) and layers (4, 5, 6 and 7). This aligns with the empirical results shown in Figure 1, indicating that modules (W^U, W^O and W^V) and layers (4, 5, 6 and 7) play a more important role in model performance. Hence, these findings not only validate SaLoRA's effective prioritization of critical modules and layers, but also emphasizes its capacity to learn the structure-aware intrinsic rank of the incremental matrix.

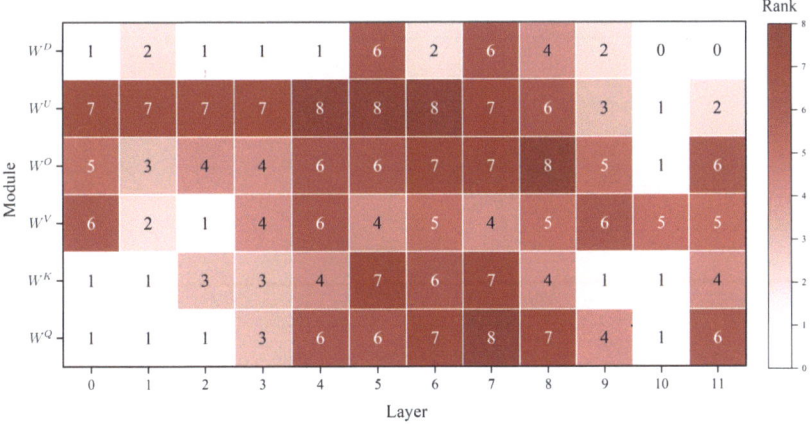

Figure 7. The resulting rank of each incremental matrix obtained from fine-tuning RoBERTa-base on MRPC with SaLoRA. The initial rank is set at 8, and the target sparsity is 0.5. The x-axis is the layer index and the y-axis represents different types of modules.

5. Conclusions

In this paper, we present SaLoRA, a structure-aware low-rank adaptation method that adaptively learns the intrinsic rank of each incremental matrix. In SaLoRA, we introduced a diagonal gate matrix to adjust the rank of the incremental matrix by penalizing the L_0 norm based on the count of activated gates. To enhance training stability and model generalization, we orthogonally regularized B and A. Furthermore, we integrated a density constraint and employed Lagrangian relaxation to control the number of valid ranks. In our experiments, we demonstrated that SaLoRA effectively captures the structure-aware intrinsic rank and consistently outperforms LoRA without significantly compromising training efficiency.

Author Contributions: Conceptualization, Y.H. and Z.P.; methodology, Y.H. and M.C.; validation, Y.H. and M.C.; formal analysis, Y.H. and Y.X.; investigation, Y.X.; resources, Y.X.; data curation, Y.H.; writing—original draft preparation, Y.H.; visualization, Y.H. and T.W.; supervision, Z.P.; project administration, Z.P.; funding acquisition, Z.P. All authors have read and agreed to the published version of the manuscript.

Funding: This research was funded by the National Natural Science Foundation of China (No. 62076251).

Data Availability Statement: Data sharing is not applicable.

Conflicts of Interest: The authors declare no conflict of interest.

Abbreviations

The following abbreviations are used in this manuscript:

PLMs	Pre-trained language models
LLMs	Large language models
NLP	Natural language process
LoRA	Low-rank adaptation
MHA	Multi-head self-attention
FFN	Feed-forward network
FT	Fine-tuning
PEFT	Parameter-efficient fine-tuning
HC	Hard-concrete distribution

Appendix A. Description of Datasets

Table A1. Description of datasets.

Dataset	Description	Train	Valid	Test	Metrics
GLUE Benchmark					
MNLI	Inference	393.0k	20.0k	20.0k	Accuracy
SST-2	Sentiment analysis	7.0k	1.5k	1.4k	Accuracy
MRPC	Paraphrase detection	3.7k	408	1.7k	Accuracy
CoLA	Linguistic acceptability	8.5k	1.0k	1.0k	Matthews correlation
QNLI	Inference	108.0k	5.7k	5.7k	Accuracy
QQP	Question answering	364.0k	40.0k	391k	Accuracy
RTE	Inference	2.5k	276	3.0k	Accuracy
STS-B	Textual similarity	7.0k	1.5k	1.4k	Pearson correlation
Text Style Transfer					
Yelp-Negative	Negative reviews of restaurants and businesses	17.7k	2.0k	500	Accuracy Similarity Fluency
Yelp-Positive	Positive reviews of restaurants and businesses	26.6k	2.0k	500	Accuracy Similarity Fluency
GYAFC-Informal	Informal sentences from the Family and Relationships domain	5.2k	2.2k	1.3k	Accuracy Similarity Fluency
GYAFC-Formal	Formal sentences from the Family and Relationships domain	5.2k	2.8k	1.0k	Accuracy Similarity Fluency

Appendix B. Training Details

We tuned the learning rate η_p from $\{5 \times 10^{-5}, 7 \times 10^{-5}, 9 \times 10^{-5}, 2 \times 10^{-4}, 3 \times 10^{-4}, 4 \times 10^{-4}, 5 \times 10^{-4}, 7 \times 10^{-4}\}$ and selected the best learning rate.

Table A2. The hyperparameters we used for RoBERTa on the GLUE benchmark.

	Model	MNLI	SST-2	CoLA	QQP	QNLI	RTE	MRPC	STS-B
# Epoch	RoB$_{base}$	15	20	20	20	15	40	40	30
	RoB$_{large}$	15	20	20	20	15	40	40	30
η_p	RoB$_{base}$	9×10^{-5}	4×10^{-4}	5×10^{-4}	4×10^{-4}	5×10^{-4}	4×10^{-4}	4×10^{-4}	7×10^{-4}
	RoB$_{large}$	9×10^{-5}	5×10^{-4}	4×10^{-4}	4×10^{-4}	4×10^{-4}	5×10^{-4}	2×10^{-4}	4×10^{-4}

$T_{start} = 0.2 \times$ # Epochs, $T_{end} = 0.5 \times$ # Epochs. $r = 8$, $b = 0.5$, $\alpha = 16$, $\eta_c = 0.01$, $\beta = 0.1$, $\tau = 1.0$, $\gamma = -0.1$, $\zeta = 1.1$.

Appendix C. Prompts

Table A3. The prompts used in text style transfer.

Yelp: Negative $\rightarrow$ Positive
"Below is an instruction that describes a task. Write a response that appropriately completes the request. ### Instruction: {Please change the sentiment of the following sentence to be more positive.} ### Input: {$Sentence} ### Response:"

Yelp: Positive $\rightarrow$ Negative
"Below is an instruction that describes a task. Write a response that appropriately completes the request. ### Instruction: {Please change the sentiment of the following sentence to be more negative.} ### Input: {$Sentence} ### Response:"

GYAFC: Informal $\rightarrow$ Formal
"Below is an instruction that describes a task. Write a response that appropriately completes the request. ### Instruction: {Please rewrite the following sentence to be more formal.} ### Input: {$Sentence} ### Response:"

GYAFC: Formal $\rightarrow$ Informal
"Below is an instruction that describes a task. Write a response that appropriately completes the request. ### Instruction: {Please rewrite the following sentence to be more informal.} ### Input: {$Sentence} ### Response:"

References

1. Brown, T.; Mann, B.; Ryder, N.; Subbiah, M.; Kaplan, J.D.; Dhariwal, P.; Neelakantan, A.; Shyam, P.; Sastry, G.; Askell, A.; et al. Language Models are Few-Shot Learners. In *Proceedings of the Advances in Neural Information Processing Systems, Virtual, 6–12 December 2020*; Larochelle, H., Ranzato, M., Hadsell, R., Balcan, M., Lin, H., Eds.; Curran Associates, Inc.: Red Hook, NY, USA, 2020; Volume 33, pp. 1877–1901.
2. Zeng, A.; Liu, X.; Du, Z.; Wang, Z.; Lai, H.; Ding, M.; Yang, Z.; Xu, Y.; Zheng, W.; Xia, X.; et al. Glm-130b: An open bilingual pre-trained model. *arXiv* **2022**, arXiv:2210.02414.
3. Touvron, H.; Lavril, T.; Izacard, G.; Martinet, X.; Lachaux, M.; Lacroix, T.; Rozière, B.; Goyal, N.; Hambro, E.; Azhar, F.; et al. LLaMA: Open and Efficient Foundation Language Models. *arXiv* **2023**, arXiv:2302.13971. [CrossRef]
4. OpenAI. GPT-4 Technical Report. *arXiv* **2023**, arXiv:2303.08774. [CrossRef]
5. Pavlyshenko, B.M. Financial News Analytics Using Fine-Tuned Llama 2 GPT Model. *arXiv* **2023**, arXiv:2308.13032. [CrossRef]
6. Kossen, J.; Rainforth, T.; Gal, Y. In-Context Learning in Large Language Models Learns Label Relationships but Is Not Conventional Learning. *arXiv* **2023**, arXiv:2307.12375. [CrossRef]
7. Dong, Q.; Li, L.; Dai, D.; Zheng, C.; Wu, Z.; Chang, B.; Sun, X.; Xu, J.; Li, L.; Sui, Z. A Survey on In-context Learning. *arXiv* **2022**, arXiv:2301.00234. [CrossRef]
8. Li, C.; Farkhoor, H.; Liu, R.; Yosinski, J. Measuring the Intrinsic Dimension of Objective Landscapes. In Proceedings of the International Conference on Learning Representations, Vancouver, BC, Canada, 30 April–3 May 2018.
9. Aghajanyan, A.; Gupta, S.; Zettlemoyer, L. Intrinsic Dimensionality Explains the Effectiveness of Language Model Fine-Tuning. In Proceedings of the 59th Annual Meeting of the Association for Computational Linguistics and the 11th International Joint Conference on Natural Language Processing (Volume 1: Long Papers), Online, 1–6 August 2021; pp. 7319–7328. [CrossRef]
10. Ding, N.; Qin, Y.; Yang, G.; Wei, F.; Yang, Z.; Su, Y.; Hu, S.; Chen, Y.; Chan, C.; Chen, W.; et al. Parameter-efficient fine-tuning of large-scale pre-trained language models. *Nat. Mac. Intell.* **2023**, *5*, 220–235. [CrossRef]
11. Pfeiffer, J.; Kamath, A.; Rücklé, A.; Cho, K.; Gurevych, I. AdapterFusion: Non-Destructive Task Composition for Transfer Learning. In Proceedings of the 16th Conference of the European Chapter of the Association for Computational Linguistics: Main Volume, Online, 19–23 April 2021; pp. 487–503. [CrossRef]
12. Li, X.L.; Liang, P. Prefix-Tuning: Optimizing Continuous Prompts for Generation. In Proceedings of the 59th Annual Meeting of the Association for Computational Linguistics and the 11th International Joint Conference on Natural Language Processing (Volume 1: Long Papers), Online, 1–6 August 2021; pp. 4582–4597. [CrossRef]
13. Lester, B.; Al-Rfou, R.; Constant, N. The Power of Scale for Parameter-Efficient Prompt Tuning. In Proceedings of the 2021 Conference on Empirical Methods in Natural Language Processing, Online and Punta Cana, Dominican Republic, 7–11 November 2021; pp. 3045–3059. [CrossRef]
14. Ben Zaken, E.; Goldberg, Y.; Ravfogel, S. BitFit: Simple Parameter-efficient Fine-tuning for Transformer-based Masked Language-models. In Proceedings of the 60th Annual Meeting of the Association for Computational Linguistics (Volume 2: Short Papers), Dublin, Ireland, 22–27 May 2022; pp. 1–9. [CrossRef]
15. Hu, E.J.; Shen, Y.; Wallis, P.; Allen-Zhu, Z.; Li, Y.; Wang, S.; Wang, L.; Chen, W. LoRA: Low-Rank Adaptation of Large Language Models. In Proceedings of the International Conference on Learning Representations, Virtual Event, 25–29 April 2022.
16. Zhang, Q.; Chen, M.; Bukharin, A.; He, P.; Cheng, Y.; Chen, W.; Zhao, T. Adaptive Budget Allocation for Parameter-Efficient Fine-Tuning. In Proceedings of the the Eleventh International Conference on Learning Representations, Kigali, Rwanda, 1–5 May 2023.
17. Louizos, C.; Welling, M.; Kingma, D.P. Learning Sparse Neural Networks through L_0 Regularization. In Proceedings of the International Conference on Learning Representations, Vancouver, BC, Canada, 30 April–3 May 2018.
18. Wang, Z.; Wohlwend, J.; Lei, T. Structured Pruning of Large Language Models. In Proceedings of the 2020 Conference on Empirical Methods in Natural Language Processing (EMNLP), Online, 8–12 November 2020; pp. 6151–6162. [CrossRef]
19. Gallego-Posada, J.; Ramirez, J.; Erraqabi, A.; Bengio, Y.; Lacoste-Julien, S. Controlled Sparsity via Constrained Optimization or: How I Learned to Stop Tuning Penalties and Love Constraints. In *Proceedings of the Advances in Neural Information Processing Systems, New Orleans, LA, USA, 29 November–1 December 2022*; Koyejo, S., Mohamed, S., Agarwal, A., Belgrave, D., Cho, K., Oh, A., Eds.; Curran Associates, Inc.: Red Hook, NY, USA, 2022; Volume 35, pp. 1253–1266.
20. Wang, A.; Singh, A.; Michael, J.; Hill, F.; Levy, O.; Bowman, S.R. GLUE: A Multi-Task Benchmark and Analysis Platform for Natural Language Understanding. In Proceedings of the International Conference on Learning Representations, New Orleans, LA, USA, 6–9 May 2019.
21. Taori, R.; Gulrajani, I.; Zhang, T.; Dubois, Y.; Li, X.; Guestrin, C.; Liang, P.; Hashimoto, T.B. Stanford Alpaca: An Instruction-Following LLaMA Model. 2023. Available online: https://github.com/tatsu-lab/stanford_alpaca (accessed on 14 March 2023).
22. Li, J.; Jia, R.; He, H.; Liang, P. Delete, Retrieve, Generate: A Simple Approach to Sentiment and Style Transfer. In Proceedings of the 2018 Conference of the North American Chapter of the Association for Computational Linguistics: Human Language Technologies, Volume 1 (Long Papers), New Orleans, LA, USA, 1–6 June 2018; pp. 1865–1874. [CrossRef]

23. Rao, S.; Tetreault, J. Dear Sir or Madam, May I Introduce the GYAFC Dataset: Corpus, Benchmarks and Metrics for Formality Style Transfer. In Proceedings of the 2018 Conference of the North American Chapter of the Association for Computational Linguistics: Human Language Technologies, Volume 1 (Long Papers), New Orleans, LA, USA, 1–6 June 2018; pp. 129–140. [CrossRef]
24. Vaswani, A.; Shazeer, N.; Parmar, N.; Uszkoreit, J.; Jones, L.; Gomez, A.N.; Kaiser, L.u.; Polosukhin, I. Attention is All you Need. In *Proceedings of the Advances in Neural Information Processing Systems, Long Beach, CA, USA, 4–9 December 2017*; Guyon, I., Luxburg, U.V., Bengio, S., Wallach, H., Fergus, R., Vishwanathan, S., Garnett, R., Eds.; Curran Associates, Inc.: Red Hook, NY, USA, 2017; Volume 30.
25. Houlsby, N.; Giurgiu, A.; Jastrzebski, S.; Morrone, B.; De Laroussilhe, Q.; Gesmundo, A.; Attariyan, M.; Gelly, S. Parameter-Efficient Transfer Learning for NLP. In Proceedings of the 36th International Conference on Machine Learning, Long Beach, CA, USA, 9–15 June 2019; Volume 97, pp. 2790–2799.
26. Mo, Y.; Yoo, J.; Kang, S. Parameter-Efficient Fine-Tuning Method for Task-Oriented Dialogue Systems. *Mathematics* **2023**, *11*, 3048. [CrossRef]
27. Lee, J.; Tang, R.; Lin, J. What Would Elsa Do? Freezing Layers during Transformer Fine-Tuning. *arXiv* **2019**, arXiv:1911.03090. [CrossRef]
28. Guo, D.; Rush, A.; Kim, Y. Parameter-Efficient Transfer Learning with Diff Pruning. In Proceedings of the 59th Annual Meeting of the Association for Computational Linguistics and the 11th International Joint Conference on Natural Language Processing (Volume 1: Long Papers), Online, 1–6 August 2021; pp. 4884–4896. [CrossRef]
29. Valipour, M.; Rezagholizadeh, M.; Kobyzev, I.; Ghodsi, A. DyLoRA: Parameter-Efficient Tuning of Pre-trained Models using Dynamic Search-Free Low-Rank Adaptation. In Proceedings of the 17th Conference of the European Chapter of the Association for Computational Linguistics, Dubrovnik, Croatia, 2–6 May 2023; pp. 3274–3287.
30. Kingma, D.P.; Welling, M. Auto-encoding variational bayes. *arXiv* **2013**, arXiv:1312.6114.
31. Rezende, D.J.; Mohamed, S.; Wierstra, D. Stochastic Backpropagation and Approximate Inference in Deep Generative Models. In Proceedings of the 1st International Conference on Machine Learning, Bejing, China, 22–24 June 2014; Xing, E.P., Jebara, T., Eds.; PMLR: Bejing, China, 2014; Volume 32, pp. 1278–1286.
32. Brock, A.; Lim, T.; Ritchie, J.; Weston, N. Neural Photo Editing with Introspective Adversarial Networks. In Proceedings of the International Conference on Learning Representations, Toulon, France, 24–26 April 2017.
33. Lin, T.; Jin, C.; Jordan, M. On Gradient Descent Ascent for Nonconvex-Concave Minimax Problems. In Proceedings of the 37th International Conference on Machine Learning, Vienna, Austria, 13–18 July 2020; Daumé, H., III, Singh, A., Eds.; PMLR: Vienna, Austria, 2020; Volume 119, pp. 6083–6093.
34. Liu, Y.; Ott, M.; Goyal, N.; Du, J.; Joshi, M.; Chen, D.; Levy, O.; Lewis, M.; Zettlemoyer, L.; Stoyanov, V. RoBERTa: A Robustly Optimized BERT Pretraining Approach. *arXiv* **2019**, arXiv:1907.11692.
35. He, J.; Zhou, C.; Ma, X.; Berg-Kirkpatrick, T.; Neubig, G. Towards a Unified View of Parameter-Efficient Transfer Learning. In Proceedings of the International Conference on Learning Representations, Virtual Event, 25–29 April 2022.
36. Wolf, T.; Debut, L.; Sanh, V.; Chaumond, J.; Delangue, C.; Moi, A.; Cistac, P.; Rault, T.; Louf, R.; Funtowicz, M.; et al. Transformers: State-of-the-Art Natural Language Processing. In Proceedings of the 2020 Conference on Empirical Methods in Natural Language Processing: System Demonstrations, Online, 16–20 November 2020; pp. 38–45. [CrossRef]
37. Mangrulkar, S.; Gugger, S.; Debut, L.; Belkada, Y.; Paul, S. PEFT: State-of-the-Art Parameter-Efficient Fine-Tuning Methods. 2022. Available online: https://github.com/huggingface/peft (accessed on 6 July 2023).
38. Loshchilov, I.; Hutter, F. Decoupled Weight Decay Regularization. In Proceedings of the International Conference on Learning Representations, New Orleans, LA, USA, 6–9 May 2019.
39. Devlin, J.; Chang, M.W.; Lee, K.; Toutanova, K. BERT: Pre-training of Deep Bidirectional Transformers for Language Understanding. In Proceedings of the 2019 Conference of the North American Chapter of the Association for Computational Linguistics: Human Language Technologies, Volume 1 (Long and Short Papers), Minneapolis, MN, USA, 3–5 June 2019; pp. 4171–4186. [CrossRef]
40. Papineni, K.; Roukos, S.; Ward, T.; Zhu, W.J. Bleu: A Method for Automatic Evaluation of Machine Translation. In Proceedings of the 40th Annual Meeting of the Association for Computational Linguistics, Philadelphia, PA, USA, 6–12 July 2002; pp. 311–318. [CrossRef]
41. Heafield, K. KenLM: Faster and Smaller Language Model Queries. In Proceedings of the Sixth Workshop on Statistical Machine Translation, Edinburgh, UK, 30–31 July 2011; pp. 187–197.

Disclaimer/Publisher's Note: The statements, opinions and data contained in all publications are solely those of the individual author(s) and contributor(s) and not of MDPI and/or the editor(s). MDPI and/or the editor(s) disclaim responsibility for any injury to people or property resulting from any ideas, methods, instructions or products referred to in the content.

Article

Efficient Federated Learning with Pre-Trained Large Language Model Using Several Adapter Mechanisms

Gyunyeop Kim , Joon Yoo * and Sangwoo Kang *

School of Computing, Gachon University, 1342, Seongnam-daero, Sujeong-gu, Seongnam-si 13120, Republic of Korea; gyop0817@gachon.ac.kr
* Correspondence: joon.yoo@gachon.ac.kr (J.Y.); swkang@gachon.ac.kr (S.K.)

Abstract: Recent advancements in deep learning have led to various challenges, one of which is the issue of data privacy in training data. To address this issue, federated learning, a technique that merges models trained by clients on servers, has emerged as an attractive solution. However, federated learning faces challenges related to data heterogeneity and system heterogeneity. Recent observations suggest that incorporating pre-trained models into federated learning can mitigate some of these challenges. Nonetheless, the main drawback of pre-trained models lies in their typically large model size, leading to excessive data transmission when clients send these models to the server. Additionally, federated learning involves multiple global steps, which means transmitting a large language model to multiple clients results in too much data exchange. In this paper, we propose a novel approach to address this challenge using adapters. Adapters demonstrate training efficiency by training a small capacity adapter layer alongside a large language model. This unique characteristic reduces the volume of data transmission, offering a practical solution to the problem. The evaluation results demonstrate that the proposed method achieves a reduction in training time of approximately 20–40% and a transmission speed improvement of over 98% compared to previous approaches.

Keywords: federated learning; deep learning; transfer learning; adapter transformer

MSC: 68T50

Citation: Kim, G.; Yoo, J.; Kang, S. Efficient Federated Learning with Pre-Trained Large Language Model Using Several Adapter Mechanisms. *Mathematics* **2023**, *11*, 4479. https://doi.org/10.3390/math11214479

Academic Editors: Florin Leon, Mircea Hulea and Marius Gavrilescu

Received: 27 September 2023
Revised: 22 October 2023
Accepted: 26 October 2023
Published: 29 October 2023

Copyright: © 2023 by the authors. Licensee MDPI, Basel, Switzerland. This article is an open access article distributed under the terms and conditions of the Creative Commons Attribution (CC BY) license (https://creativecommons.org/licenses/by/4.0/).

1. Introduction

Deep learning has emerged as a powerful and evolutionary technology, improving the quality of life across various fields. The demand for a proficient understanding of deep learning models has surged, driven by the availability of vast datasets. However, this pursuit has raised concerns about data privacy during the training process. One attractive method to mitigate these costs is federated learning [1]. In federated learning, each client trains its own model and shares only the trained model's parameters with the server, without actually sending raw data. Since the server only receives the model parameters, it cannot access the clients' data directly. Therefore, federated learning enables training that ensures the privacy of client data. While federated learning mitigates privacy risks, it is not without its drawbacks. In comparison to conventional learning methods, it often experiences performance degradation due to client heterogeneity. And data transfer costs are required for model aggregation. In this paper, we propose a novel methodology aimed at ameliorating the transmission challenges, with a specific focus on mitigating large data transmission needs. Our approach involves the use of adapters, which serve to enhance the efficiency of data transmission, thus addressing a key limitation of federated learning.

In general, federated learning, which combines the results from multiple clients, often exhibits a lower performance compared to the traditional centralized learning methods. This performance degradation can be attributed to the heterogeneity of the systems and data in federated learning. Since clients train models using their own devices (systems) and individual data, variations in device performance can lead to differences in learning speed. In extreme cases, due to some clients' performance limitations, they cannot even participate in the learning process. Furthermore, in federated learning each client trains models using its own diverse data, where the quantity and quality of data held by each client may differ. For example, in tasks that require various labels, certain clients may lack data for some labels, causing problems.

Many methodologies have been proposed to solve the heterogeneity of federated learning. Many methodologies have improved the aggregation method and training method of federated learning. There were methods for resolving heterogeneity based on model weight, such as FedProx [2] and FedDyn [3]. Feature-based heterogeneity solutions, such as FedUFO [4] and MOON [5], have been proposed. Some tried to solve the heterogeneity problem by improving the global model performance, and the APFL algorithm [6] was proposed through this. Also, incorporating pre-trained models into federated learning has proven to mitigate the performance degradation caused by data heterogeneity [7].

In [7], it was experimentally confirmed that the pre-trained model solves various problems of federated learning without using any special aggregation method. Pre-trained models are models trained on general and large-scale datasets. In the field of natural language processing, the methodology of fine-tuning these pre-trained language models for downstream tasks through transfer learning has shown state-of-the-art performance in most areas. Moreover, in federated learning pre-trained models consistently outperform non-pre-trained deep learning models [7].

In the field of natural language processing, pre-training generally utilizes large-scale language models. The recent rapid development of deep learning is closely related to the increase in model capacity. Each year, the size of the model is increasing, which leads to an increase in performance. For example, the BERT-base [8] model proposed in 2018, a large-scale language model commonly used in natural language processing, has a parameter number of about 340 M. The T5 model [9] proposed in 2019 has a size of 11 B. In addition, the GPT-3-base [10] and Megatron-Tuning [11] models proposed in 2020 have parameter numbers of up to 175 B and 530 B, respectively. In federated learning, however, sending large-scale language models can be burdensome, since the trained parameters need to be transmitted over the network. In federated learning, during each global epoch, the trained models need to be downloaded from all clients, and then the models are aggregated and uploaded. However, uploading/downloading large-scale language models during each global epoch poses challenges in terms of time and network resources.

In this paper, we propose a novel methodology to address these issues and save network transmission time in federated learning. The proposed method applies Adapters [12], which were introduced for efficient transfer learning, to federated learning. This allows federated learning to proceed with less model transmission. We conduct experiments in the areas of natural language processing and computer vision to demonstrate how the proposed methodology can significantly reduce the network transmission time compared to existing approaches.

The main contributions of our paper are three-fold: First, we identify that pre-trained models can mitigate the data heterogeneity problem in federated learning but render a new challenge of large data transmission requirements. Second, we introduce the adapter mechanism, which involves training large language models using smaller-sized adapters. This approach effectively addresses the problem of excessive data transmission issues in federated learning that uses transformer-based pre-trained models. Finally, we conduct extensive experiments on diverse federated learning datasets in both natural language processing and computer vision domains, to demonstrate the efficiency and performance of our proposal. The evaluation results highlight a significant reduction in training time of approximately 20–40% and a remarkable improvement in transmission speed, surpassing 98% compared to previous approaches.

The structure of the remainder of this paper is outlined as follows. Section 2 provides an overview of the related work in the field. Section 3 elaborates on the details and design of the proposed approach. Section 4 presents the results of the evaluation conducted. Finally, Section 6 concludes the paper.

2. Related Work

2.1. Federated Learning

Deep learning has emerged as a powerful and evolutionary technology, revolutionizing various research fields across the spectrum. By leveraging large-scale neural networks and vast amounts of data, deep learning has made significant contributions to diverse domains, ranging from healthcare and finance to computer vision and natural language processing. While it is easy to collect massive amounts of data for some tasks to effectively train deep learning models, there are often difficulties in collecting data for certain tasks due to security concerns. In the case of medical or conversational data, data privacy is crucial, requiring extensive security measures and de-identification processes for data collection.

Solving security and privacy issues incurs significant costs, thus increasing the cost of collecting privacy-preserving data. One attractive method to mitigate these costs is federated learning [1]. The process of federated training is divided into clients with private data and servers for model aggregation. The client trains the local model through private learning data. Then, the trained model parameter is transmitted to the server. The server aggregates the received model parameters and overwrites them on the global model. This method can protect privacy by not sending raw data directly to the server. Federated learning, which gained significant attention after its initial introduction in [1], was officially introduced in a 2017 Google AI Blog [13] and has been successfully applied in technologies such as the Mobile G Keyboard. Federated learning is a methodology in deep learning that enables data decentralization by utilizing multiple local clients and a central server to train a global model. In this approach, each local client possesses its own data and trains each local model, which is then transmitted to the central server and aggregated by the central server to form the global model.

However, in federated learning some problems occurred instead of protecting data privacy. One of them is performance degradation due to model aggregation. In the process of aggregating the model, the performance was degraded by various factors, such as the data heterogeneity and system heterogeneity of each client. Until recently, various aggregation methodologies and training methodologies have been proposed as a way to solve this problem. In general, the most basic aggregation method is FedAvg [1], which averages and aggregates the value of each local model. Since then, FedProx [2] and FedNova [14], which are aggregation methodologies, have been proposed to solve data heterogeneity. FedProx adds near-field terms to the local objective function to limit local updates to be closer to the global model. FedNova uses momentum to accurately weight local models when updating global models. FedDyn [3] modifies the local goal with a dynamic normalizer consisting of linear terms based on primary conditions and Euclidean distance terms so that the local minimum matches the global minimum. FedUFO [4] shares client models with each other to sort features and log outputs. In addition, some tried to solve the heterogeneity problem by improving the global model performance, and, through this, the APFL algorithm [6] was proposed. There have been attempts to solve heterogeneity in various ways. Since then, [7] has tried to solve the problem using a pre-trained model. According to [7], it was experimentally confirmed that various heterogeneity problems were solved despite the use of FedAvg when using the pre-trained model in federated learning.

2.2. Adapter

Recently, transfer learning-based methodologies have shown state-of-the-art performances in natural language processing. Transfer learning approaches pre-train large-scale language models on readily available and commonly collected massive datasets, such as the wiki dataset. In turn, these pre-trained language models are fine-tuned for downstream tasks.

Most pre-trained language models require large model capacity. BERT, a representative pre-trained language model with transfer learning, has a significantly higher capacity than LSTM; newer models, like GPT3 [10] and T5 [9], require even larger capacities than BERT. While these large-scale language models exhibit high performances, they demand considerable resources and time for training.

To address these challenges, Dosovitskiy et al. [12] proposed the fine-tuning methodology using adapters. Instead of training all the parameters of a pre-trained language model, they demonstrated that training only the proposed adapter layers for downstream tasks can achieve a comparable performance. Many pre-trained language models form stacked transformer blocks, where self-attention and feed-forward networks are interconnected. In AdapterFusion [15], adapter layers with lower capacities were inserted between each transformer block of the pre-trained model. Furthermore, it was shown that training only these adapter layers can yield a similar performance to previous methods. Subsequently, structurally enhanced adapters, such as the Houlsby adapter [12] and LoRA [16], were proposed to achieve a high performance with a smaller adapter capacity.

3. Methodology

This paper proposes to use adapters in federated learning, to improve transmission efficiency during the process of federated learning with large transformer-based pre-trained language models. Ref. [7] has shown that using a large language model can solve various problems with federated learning. Various problems caused by heterogeneity were alleviated and the performance of the global model was improved. However, federated learning is trained using model transmission of servers and clients. At this time, using a large model causes network overload from transmission. The proposed method of this paper uses adapters to solve the transmission problem. The reason is that the adapter can train the large language model with fewer parameters. Experiments on NLP and CV are conducted to confirm the efficiency and performance of the methodology. They also measure the amount of reduction in transmission.

One of the biggest issues of federated learning is performance degradation due to data heterogeneity and system heterogeneity. The study [7] showed that the pre-trained large language model could improve the problem. However, pre-trained large language models require a high model capacity. When a large-capacity deep learning model is used in federated learning, a very large amount of transmission is required. Federated learning requires the parameters of clients to be uploaded/downloaded at each global step, so using a large capacity model increases the amount of transmission exponentially.

For example, popular transformer models in natural language processing and computer vision, such as BERT-base [8] and ViT-base [17], have sizes of 440 MB and 330 MB, respectively. In federated learning, it is necessary to transmit and receive the trained model parameters to and from each client at every global epoch. Therefore, transmitting and downloading large model parameters multiple times becomes problematic in federated learning. For instance, if 10 clients perform federated learning for 30 global epochs using BERT-base, it would result in a total transmission of approximately 264,000 MB, or 263 GB.

$$T = 2E_g N_c C \qquad (1)$$

The amount of transmission in federated learning is calculated as shown in Equation (1). Federated learning should upload/download to all clients at every global step. Therefore, the total transmission amount T of federated learning is calculated by multiplying the global epoch E_g, the number of clients N_c, and the capacity C of the model transmission size and then doubling the result (upload and download).

Hence, we propose using adapters to reduce the size of the model parameters that need to be transmitted.

The overall structure of the proposed methodology is illustrated in Figure 1, which consists of three main steps. The first step is the preparation and downloading of the pre-trained model. In the first step, the pre-trained model is downloaded so that each client has the same model structure and parameter value before starting the first global step of federated learning. The second step is the client model training and upload. In the second step, clients train the local model. After that, each client uploads the trained adapter and classification head to the server.The final step is the aggregation and download of the models. In the final step, the learned models are merged. The learned model parameter value transmitted in the second step is aggregated to the global model. Each client then downloads the aggregated global model to start the next global step. Each step is described in Sections 3.2–3.4.

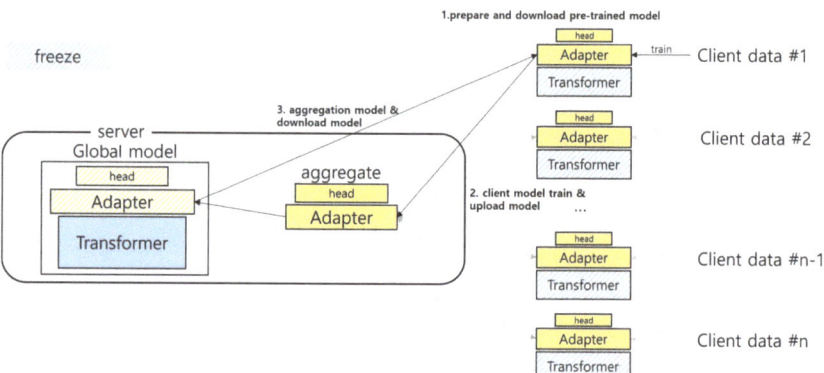

Figure 1. Overall architecture of federated learning with adapter.

3.1. Pre-Trained Model with Adapter

In this section, we discuss the deep learning model used in this paper. Firstly, the paper employs a pre-trained large language model. A pre-trained language model refers to a model that has been trained on a large-scale dataset and is typically divided into pre-trained transformer layers and embedding layers. The pre-trained large language model is fine-tuned to fit the downstream task. The classification head is added to classify the label for the purpose of each downstream task. The classification head is typically implemented as a one-layer feed-forward network. The classification head derives the probability for each label in the downstream task. For example, next word prediction predicts the probability that each word in every word will be used as the next word. Image classification predicts probabilities for all candidate categories.

Ref. [12] confirms that learning with adapter layers can achieve a similar performance. In this paper, we reduce the amount of training parameters by using adapter layers. The adapter mechanism trains only the adapter layer and classification head while freezing the pre-trained language model. As a result, the adapter mechanism can achieve a similar performance even with a small amount of training resources. The adapter layer, trained using adapter models, such as LoRA [16], Houslby [12], and Preffier [15], is an additional layer used to train the language model. In other words, the model to be used for federated learning in this paper consists of an embedding layer, transformer layer, adapter layer, and classification head. And according to [12], the model training process freezes the embedding and transformer layers.

3.2. Prepare Pre-Trained Language Model

In this section, we provide detailed explanations on the first steps shown in Figure 1. The first step is the preparation of the model for client training. In our proposed federated learning approach, each client performs downstream task training using a pre-trained large language model with adapters. Federated learning use the global model and the local model. The global model is a deep learning model owned by the server, and the local model is a deep learning model owned by each client. Federated learning is when each client trains the local model through their dataset and aggregates it to the global model at the server. Therefore, each local model and global model have the same model structure. You must also have the same parameter value at the beginning of the training of the local model.

In summary, in the proposed methodology all clients receive the full model (pre-trained large language model) from the server before starting federated learning. Note that this is a one-time download. This ensures that all clients begin with the same pre-trained parameters for federated learning.

3.3. Train Local Model

The next step involves clients training the local model and uploading it to the server. Each client fine-tunes the local model for the downstream task. After the local learning epoch, each client uploads the model parameter value to the server. However, using the pre-trained large language model in conventional federated learning requires a large amount of transmission capacity to be uploaded to the server, because federated learning involves servers and clients transmitting the full model. Typically, pre-trained large language models have hundreds of MB or several GB of capacity, which requires too much transmission. In addition, the server is required to receive trained model parameter values from all clients, which creates a network bottleneck.

In this paper, learning is conducted using adapters to reduce transmission. For learning with adapters, such as that explained in Section 3.1, the pre-trained model is frozen. There is no change in the model parameter values of the transformer layer and embedding layer because only the adapter layer and classification head are learned. Only the adapter layer and the model parameter value of the classification head change. In this step, clients train the local model as much as the local epoch through each of their datasets. As a result of clients learning their respective datasets from the local model, only the adapter layer and classification head are learned. Therefore, clients send only the adapter layer and classification head to the server. Compared to the transformer layer and embedding layer, the capacities of the adapter layer and the classification layer are very small, which can increase transmission efficiency.

3.4. Aggregation into Global Model

Lastly, the server aggregates the trained parameters, and the clients download them. The final step aggregates the adapter layer uploaded by clients in the second step and the model parameter value of the classification head layer. The aggregated model parameter value is overwritten on the global model. The above process completes the global model learning in one global step. In this process, the federated learning aggregation method uses FedAvg [1]. FedAvg is the most basic method of averaging model parameter values for each local model. At this point, the server aggregates only adapter layers and classification heads, because the transformer layer and embedding layer did not change the values at client's training step.

After one global step is completed, all clients must synchronize their model parameter value before starting learning for the next global step. Therefore, all clients download the global model learned on the server. The downloaded parts are the adapter layer and classification head, because the transformer layer and embedding layer did not change the values at aggregation step. Therefore, each client downloads only the model parameter values of the adapter layer and the classification head layer, which can increase transmission efficiency.

The proposed methodology solves the increased network transmission problem when using pre-trained large language models in federated learning. Instead of training the transformer layers and embedding layers, which takes most of the model capacity in the pre-trained language model, the proposed approach trains and transmits only the smaller-sized classification head and adapter layers. In result, the proposed method reduces the network transmission and the number of parameters to be trained and potentially decreases the overall training time.

4. Experiments

In this section, we conduct experiments on two types of datasets, namely, natural language processing and computer vision, to demonstrate the efficiency and performance of the proposed methodology.

4.1. Datasets and Downstream Task

For the experiments in natural language processing, the federated Stack Overflow dataset [18] and federated Shakespeare dataset [18], which are federated learning datasets for natural language processing, are used for training. The federated Stack Overflow dataset consists of question posts and their corresponding answers uploaded on Stack Overflow. The Shakespeare dataset contains various phrases from Shakespeare's literary works. We use the titles and contents of the posts in these datasets as input and then measure the performance of the next word prediction task [7]. Next, word prediction predicts the $n + 1$th word when up to n words are entered. The accuracy of the predicted word is measured for performance evaluation of the next word prediction task.

For the experiments in computer vision, the EMNIST dataset [19] and CIFAR100 dataset [20], which are computer vision federated learning datasets, are used for training. EMNIST is a dataset of handwritten characters and digits, while CIFAR100 is an image classification dataset with 100 classes. The performance of image classification is measured using these datasets. All datasets were downloaded using the TensorFlow Federated API [18].

4.2. Experiment Setup

We detail the experiment setup in this section. We conduct federated learning using large language models. For natural language processing, we use a pre-trained language model in the form of a transformer decoder for the next word prediction task. We utilize the gpt2-base [21] pre-trained language model, which has a parameter size of approximately 490 MB.

For computer vision image classification, we use a large encoder-based language model called ViT [17]. We use ViT-base [17] for training, which has a parameter size of approximately 330 MB. Additionally, we perform the experiment using three different types of adapters. For the experiment, we use the Pfeiffer adapter [15], Houlsby adapter [12], and LoRA [16].

The baseline uses the methodology proposed by [7]. Ref. [7] confirmed that using the pre-trained language model to conduct federated learning showed a high performance. The baseline uses a large language model as a global model and a local model for federated learning. Before starting federated learning, all clients download the model parameter value of the pre-trained large language model. After that, in each global step, clients pull-train the large language model and upload/download the large language model.

We also employ the experiments from [1] for comparison with traditional federated learning. The deep learning model for CV performance measurement is a 3-layer CNN (5×5 kernelsize) with ReLu activation and max pooling (2×2 kernelsize). And the classification layer is a 2-layer feed-forward network. The first layer has 1000 dimensions. In addition, the embedded layer and the 2-layer LSTM or RNN in 768 dimensions are used as models for measuring the performance of NLP, and the 1-layer feed-forward network for the classification head is used at the end.

The federated learning setup for this experiment is as follows. We conduct federated learning on both IID and non-IID datasets. For non-IID training, we use a total of 9 clients datasets for 9 clients. For IID training, we convert a total of 27 client datasets into 9 clients by grouping them in sets of 3. The experiments in this paper were conducted in a local environment; thus, the real transmission rate was not measured. The experiments were performed on a total of 4 RTX3090 GPUs, with 3 GPUs used for parallel training on 3 clients. The server independently uses 1 GPU for aggregating client model parameters and conducting tests for performance evaluation.

The hyperparameters used in the experiment are shown in Table 1. Since each experiment was conducted with different models and environments, we experimented with various learning rates and considered the highest performance achieved by each model as its performance. The learning rates used in the experiment are 0.005, 0.001, 0.0005, and 0.0001, and the differences between each learning rate are mentioned in Section 4.3.2.

Table 1. Hyperparameters used in the experiments.

Hyperparameter	Value
Global epoch (NLP)	30
Global epoch (CV)	50
Local step	5
Number of clients	9
Optimizer	Adam
Epsilon	0.0005
Batch size (NLP)	16
Batch size (CV)	12
Pre-trained model (NLP)	gpt2-base
Pre-trained model (CV)	ViT-base
GPU	RTX 3090 × 4

4.3. Experimental Results

4.3.1. Accuracy

We examine the accuracy of the next word prediction to verify the performance of the pre-trained model. The results of the Stack Overflow dataset are shown in Table 2. We conduct next word prediction using the gpt2 model, employ federated learning for training, and compare the performance with and without adapters. Traditional federated learning methods using an RNN and LSTM without using the pre-trained large language model showed performance of about 13.26 and 14.66. In contrast, when the pre-trained large language model was used the performance improvement was more than 10 compared to traditional combined learning. When adapters were not used, an accuracy of 26.97 was observed. When adapters were used, the performances with the Pfeiffer, LoRA, and Houlsby adapters were 26.69, 25.87, and 26.58, respectively. In summary, not using adapters results in a slight accuracy improvement compared to using adapters, but the performance is comparable.

Table 2. Next word prediction accuracy of Stack Overflow non-IID dataset.

Method	Language Model	lr	Pre-Trained	Adapter	Accuracy
McMahan et al. [1]	RNN	0.005	X	X	13.26
	LSTM	0.005	X	X	14.66
Nguyen et al. [7]	gpt2-base	0.0005	O	X	26.97
Proposed	gpt2-base	0.0001	O	Pfeiffer adapter	26.69
	gpt2-base	0.0001	O	LoRA adapter	25.87
	gpt2-base	0.0001	O	Houlsby adapter	26.58

We next examine the performance of image classification in computer vision (CV), and the results on CIFAR100 are presented in Table 3. In this experiment, ViT and adapters were used. Traditional federated learning methods using a CNN without using the pre-trained large language model showed performance of about 19.5. The Cifar-100 dataset is difficult to solve with a small model, and when using the baseline ViT without adapters an accuracy of 61.51 was achieved. When federated learning was performed with adapters, the performances were 64.09, 60.91, and 64.19, respectively. The Pfeiffer and Houlsby adapters showed better performances than the baseline, while the LoRA adapter had a similar performance to the baseline. The accuracy graphs from using the pre-trained large language model for each epoch are shown in Figures 2 and 3.

Table 3. Image classification accuracy of CIFAR100 non-IID dataset.

Method	Language Model	lr	Pre-Trained	Adapter	Accuracy
McMahan et al. [1]	CNN	0.001	X	X	19.5
Nguyen et al. [7]	ViT-base	0.0005	O	X	61.51
Proposed	ViT-base	0.005	O	Pfeiffer adapter	64.09
	ViT-base	0.005	O	LoRA adapter	60.91
	ViT-base	0.005	O	Houlsby adapter	64.19

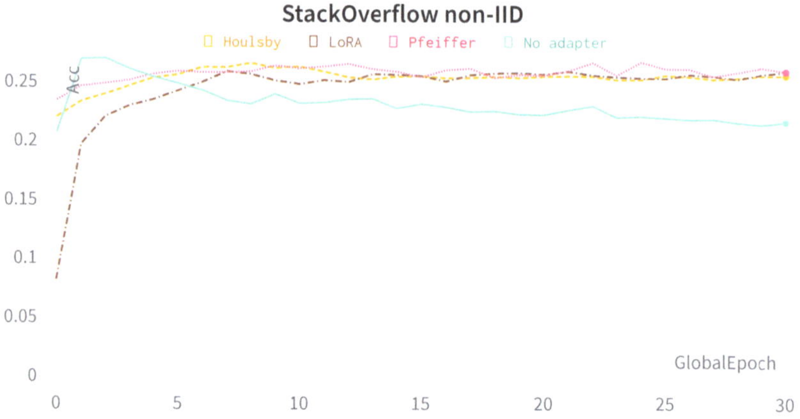

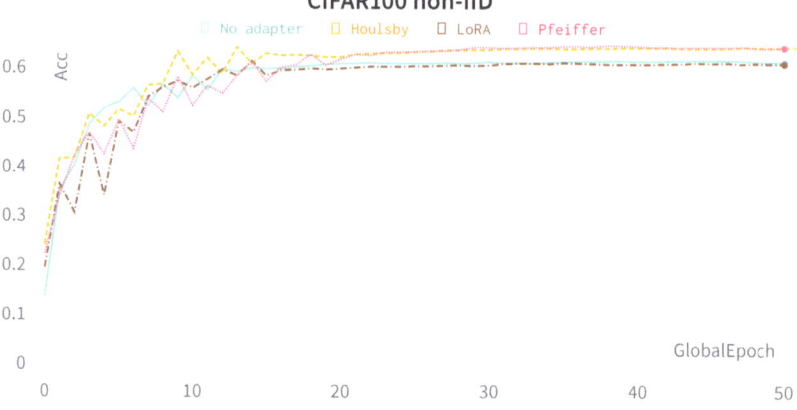

Figure 2. Test accuracy graph of Stack Overflow IID dataset using GPT2-base.

Figure 3. Test accuracy graph of CIFAR100 IID dataset using ViT-base.

To ensure the reliability of the experimental results, additional experiments were conducted on the Shakespeare dataset in NLP and the EMNIST dataset in CV. The results and accuracy graphs for these experiments are presented in Tables 4 and 5 and Figures 4 and 5. Overall, these experiments showed similar trends to the results in Tables 2 and 3 and Figures 2 and 3.

Table 4. Next word prediction accuracy of Shakespeare non-IID dataset.

Method	Language Model	lr	Pre-Trained	Adapter	Accuracy
McMahan et al. [1]	RNN	0.005	X	X	16.49
	LSTM	0.001	X	X	17.48
Nguyen et al. [7]	gpt2-base	0.0001	O	X	28.46
Proposed	gpt2-base	0.0005	O	Pfeiffer adapter	29.18
	gpt2-base	0.0005	O	LoRA adapter	27.75
	gpt2-base	0.0005	O	Houlsby adapter	28.29

Table 5. Image classification accuracy of EMNSIT non-IID dataset.

Method	Language Model	lr	Pre-Trained	Adapter	Accuracy
McMahan et al. [1]	CNN	0.005	X	X	94.64
Nguyen et al. [7]	ViT-base	0.0005	O	X	99.17
Proposed	ViT-base	0.005	O	Pfeiffer adapter	100
	ViT-base	0.001	O	LoRA adapter	95.83
	ViT-base	0.005	O	Houlsby adapter	100

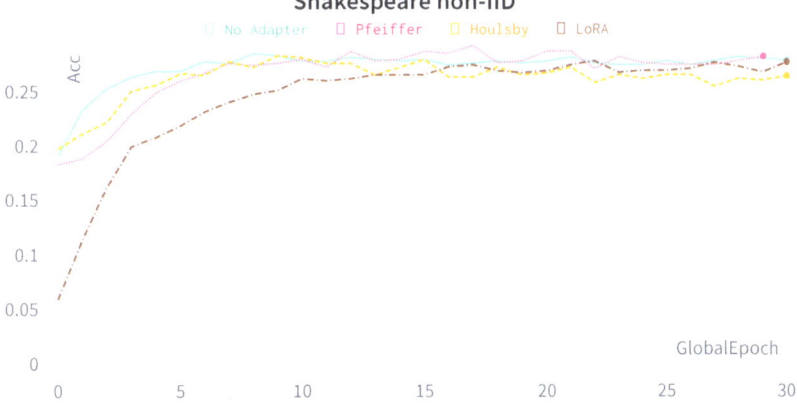

Figure 4. Test accuracy graph of Shakespeare non-IID dataset.

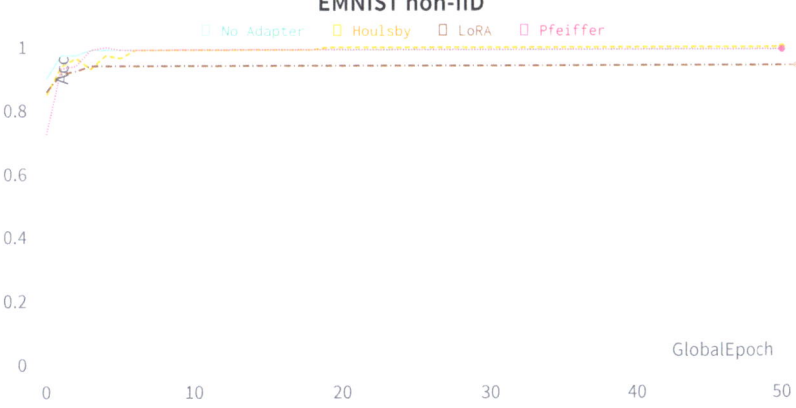

Figure 5. Test accuracy graph of EMNIST non-IID dataset.

The results of experiments on IID datasets are shown in Tables 6 and 7, which present the results assuming that each client has datasets from three individuals. Overall, the IID datasets showed better performances compared to the non-IID datasets in Tables 2 and 3. In the Stack Overflow dataset, when using the pre-trained large language model the performance improvement was more than 10 compared to traditional federated learning using an RNN and LSTM. And the highest performance was achieved with the Pfeiffer adapter, with an accuracy of 28.71. Similarly, in the CIFAR100 dataset the highest performance was achieved with the Pfeiffer adapter, with an accuracy of 79.0. Also, when the model was not pre-trained it showed a low performance. In summary, we observe that using adapters generally improves the performance in IID datasets. Even in cases where the performance degraded, it still showed a comparable performance to the baseline. The accuracy graphs from using a pre-trained large language model for each epoch are shown in Figures 6 and 7.

Table 6. Next word prediction accuracy of Stack Overflow IID dataset.

Method	Language Model	lr	Pre-Trained	Adapter	Accuracy
McMahan et al. [1]	RNN	0.001	X	X	14.94
	LSTM	0.005	X	X	16.96
Nguyen et al. [7]	gpt2-base	0.001	O	X	28.57
Proposed	gpt2-base	0.0001	O	Pfeiffer adapter	28.71
	gpt2-base	0.0005	O	LoRA adapter	28.16
	gpt2-base	0.0001	O	Houlsby adapter	28.04

Table 7. Image classification accuracy of CIFAR100 IID dataset.

Method	Language Model	lr	Pre-Trained	Adapter	Accuracy
McMahan et al. [1]	CNN	0.0001	X	X	249
Nguyen et al. [7]	ViT-base	0.0005	O	X	74.8
Proposed	ViT-base	0.001	O	Pfeiffer adapter	79.0
	ViT-base	0.001	O	LoRA adapter	76.3
	ViT-base	0.005	O	Houlsby adapter	76.9

We conduct additional experiments on the Shakespeare dataset and EMNIST dataset, to further investigate non-IID datasets. The results of these experiments are presented in Tables 8 and 9 and Figures 8 and 9. Overall, these experiments showed similar trends to the results in Tables 6 and 7 and Figures 6 and 7.

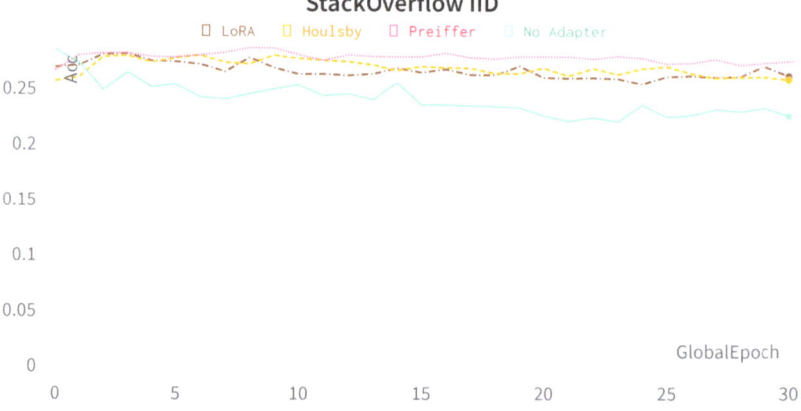

Figure 6. Test accuracy graph of Stack Overflow IID dataset.

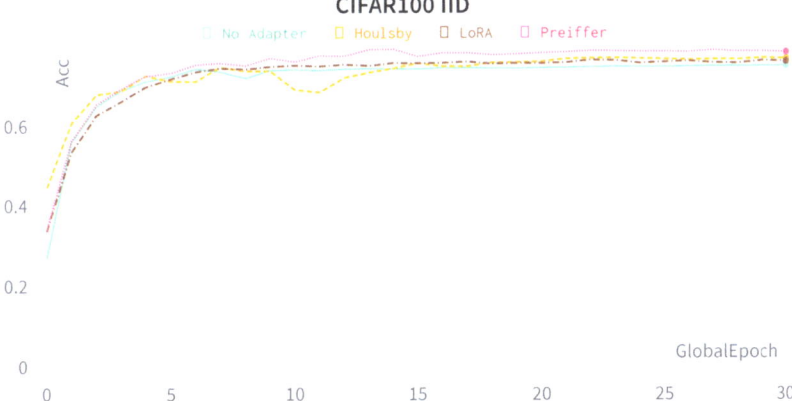

Figure 7. Test accuracy graph of CIFAR100 IID dataset.

Table 8. Next word prediction accuracy of Shakespeare IID dataset.

Method	Language Model	lr	Pre-Trained	Adapter	Accuracy
McMahan et al. [1]	RNN	0.005	X	X	19.83
	LSTM	0.005	X	X	19.79
Nguyen et al. [7]	gpt2-base	0.0001	O	X	31.10
Proposed	gpt2-base	0.0005	O	Pfeiffer adapter	30.6
	gpt2-base	0.001	O	LoRA adapter	30.73
	gpt2-base	0.0005	O	Houlsby adapter	31.01

Table 9. Image classification accuracy of EMNIST IID dataset.

Method	Language Model	lr	Pre-Trained	Adapter	Accuracy
McMahan et al. [1]	CNN	0.0005	X	X	98.21
Nguyen et al. [7]	ViT-base	0.0001	O	X	99.10
Proposed	ViT-base	0.005	O	Pfeiffer adapter	100
	ViT-base	0.005	O	LoRA adapter	99.10
	ViT-base	0.005	O	Houlsby adapter	100

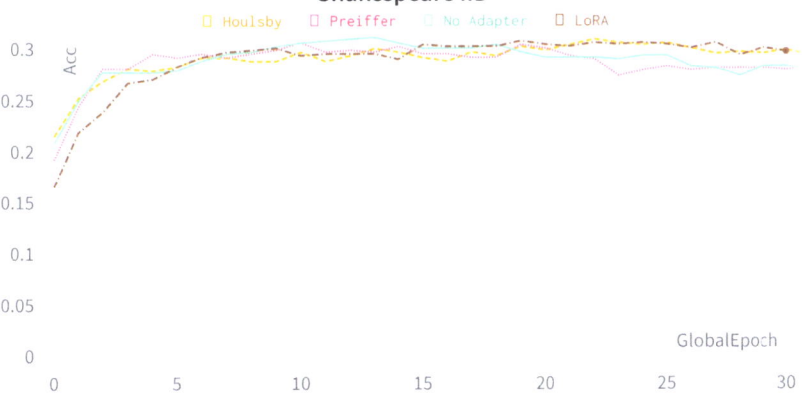

Figure 8. Test accuracy graph of Shakespeare IID dataset.

Figure 9. Test accuracy graph of EMNIST IID dataset.

4.3.2. Learning Rate

In this section, we conduct experiments with various learning rates. Figures 10 and 11 present the performance tables of the Stack Overflow dataset and CIFAR100 non-IID experiments, respectively, based on different learning rates. In Stack Overflow, which is an NLP dataset, there was not a significant change in performance according to the learning rate. However, in the CV dataset, CIFAR100, using adapters generally showed better performance at higher learning rates, while in smaller datasets, it showed a better performance at lower learning rates. This trend was observed to some extent in the Shakespeare dataset, but in EMNIST, where most adapters achieved an accuracy of 100, no significant differences were observed based on the learning rate. The corresponding performance and accuracy graphs of these experiments are provided in Figures 12 and 13.

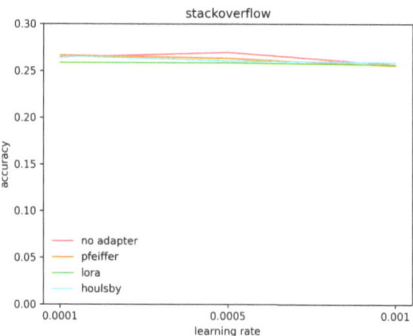

Figure 10. Test accuracy graph of each learning rate in Stack Overflow non-IID dataset.

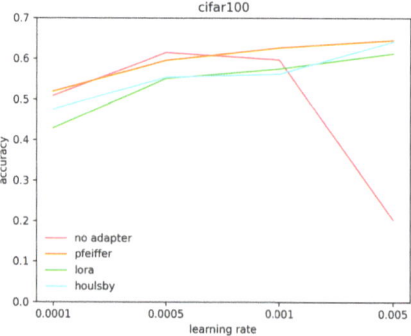

Figure 11. Test accuracy graph of each learning rate in CIFAR100 non-IID dataset.

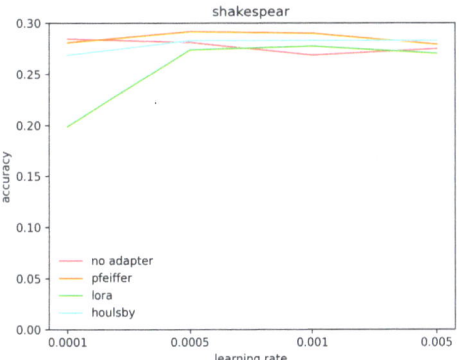

Figure 12. Test accuracy graph of each learning rate in Shakespeare non-IID dataset.

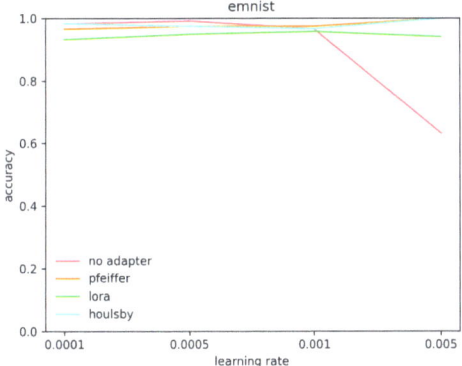

Figure 13. Test accuracy graph of each learning rate in EMNIST non-IID dataset.

4.4. Time Efficiency

4.4.1. Training Time

When using adapters in training a large language model, optimization is achieved with fewer parameters. This means there are fewer weights to compute gradients and to update. Therefore, fine-tuning only the adapters consumes less time compared to fine-tuning the entire model. This experiment measures the training time in federated learning, excluding the transmission time. This experiment shows the reduced local model training time due to the use of adapters. Note that in our experiments we measure the training time without considering the transmission time, since the experiments were conducted on a local machine. This allowed us to measure the efficiency in terms of pure training time.

The results are presented in Tables 10 and 11. In this experiment, only the case of using the same language model was compared because the structure and size of the model greatly affect the training speed. Table 10 measures the time taken for federated learning on the Stack Overflow dataset, for 30 epochs at the server. The results showed that using adapters allowed for a faster training time. For the Stack Overflow dataset, using the adapter methodology resulted in an approximately 20% reduction in training time compared to the baseline. The training speed results for the Shakespeare dataset are shown in Table 11. In this dataset, it was found that using adapters could save up to 40% of the training time.

Table 10. Training time in local environment with Stack Overflow non-IID dataset.

Method	Language Model	Pre-Trained	Adapter	Training Time	Time Compared to Baseline
Nguyen et al. [7]	gpt2-base	O	X	2 h 10 m 59 s	1
Proposed	gpt2-base	O	Pfeiffer adapter	1 h 38 m 43 s	0.75
	gpt2-base	O	LoRA adapter	1 h 45 m 28 s	0.80
	gpt2-base	O	Houlsby adapter	1 h 43 m 54 s	0.79

Table 11. Training time in local environment with Shakespeare non-IID dataset.

Method	Language Model	Pre-Trained	Adapter	Training Time	Time Compared to Baseline
Nguyen et al. [7]	gpt2-base	O	X	12 m 20 s	1
Proposed	gpt2-base	O	Pfeiffer adapter	7 m 11 s	0.58
	gpt2-base	O	LoRA adapter	7 m 43 s	0.65
	gpt2-base	O	Houlsby adapter	7 m 42 s	0.65

4.4.2. Transmission Time

Although we did not conduct experiments to measure the actual transmission time, the transmission efficiency can be computed based on the model's size. Table 12 presents the transmission sizes of the pre-trained models and adapters used in this paper.

Table 12. Transmission size for each model.

Model Name	Size
RNN	219.34 MB
LSTM	241.87 MB
Nguyen et al. [7] (gpt2-base)	487.82 MB
gpt2+Pfeiffer adapter	3.41 MB
gpt2+LoRA adapter	1.12 MB
gpt2+Houlsby adapter	6.82 MB
CNN	18.36 MB
Nguyen et al. [7] (ViT-base)	330.96 MB
ViT+Pfeiffer adapter	3.41 MB
ViT+LoRA adapter	1.12 MB
ViT+Houlsby adapter	6.82 MB

Firstly, gpt2-base, which is the NLP pre-trained model, had a large size of 487 MB, while each of the three adapters had sizes of 3.41 MB, 1.12 MB, and 6.82MB, respectively, which are significantly smaller. In the federated learning methodology used in this paper, after the initial download of the pre-trained large language model, only the adapters need to be transmitted at each global epoch, resulting in an efficient transmission time. In addition, the model sizes of the RNN and LSTM are 219 MB and 241 MB, respectively. Because the embedding layer of the NLP shows a very large model size, the proposed methodology in NLP shows better time efficiency than traditional federated learning that uses RNNs and LSTM. A similar trend is shown in the CV model ViT-base. Compared to the full model size of the large language model, the model size of the adapter is very small. Since the CNN model does not include an embedding layer, the model size is significantly small at 18 MB.

Based on the above Table 12, we measure the efficiency of transmission. Equation (1) shows the calculation of the amount of transmission in the federated learning methodology. In an experiment using gpt2-base, about 262,980 MB of transmission is required if federated learning is conducted using the Table 1 environment. However, when using an adapter, the transmission size decreases, as shown in Table 12. However, the transmission size is reduced when the proposed methodology is used. The transmission amount of the proposed methodology is calculated using the following Equation (2).

$$T = C_p N_c + (2E_g - 1) N_c C \qquad (2)$$

C_p is the model capacity of the large pre-trained loan model. E_g is the global peer, and N_c is the number of clients. C is the size of the model transmission. As in Section 3.2, C_p and N_c are multiplied to calculate the amount of transmission that clients initially use to download the pre-trained model. Then, it is multiplied by the number of up/downloads for the global epoch, excluding the initial download by the transfer model capacity C. If the LoRA adapter is used, only about 4977 MB of transmission is required. If the server could perform 10 MBps of upload/download speed, it would take approximately 7 h and 18 min for gpt2-base transmission but only approximately 8 min and 17 s for LoRA adapter transmission. In addition, the amount of transmission in traditional federated learning using LSTM calculated through (1) is 130,610 MB, or 128 GB. If the server could perform 10 MBps of upload/download speed, it would take approximately 3 h and 37 min. Using the proposed method in NLP can show better time efficiency than traditional federated learning using LSTM.

We can expect the same time efficiency for the CV pre-trained model. In the conventional federated learning methodology, if ViT-base is used for federated learning, then a total of 297,000 MB of transmission would be required. However, when conducting federated learning using the LoRA adapter, only approximately 3967 MB of transmission would be needed. This means that with a capability of 10 MBps of upload/download speed the conventional federated learning methodology would require 8 h and 15 min of transmission time, while using adapters would only require approximately 6 min and 36 s, enabling efficient federated learning. In addition, transmission in traditional federated learning using CNN is 16,524 MB, or 16 GB, which takes approximately 27 min and 32 s. Therefore, the proposed methodology can save time than traditional federated learning.

5. Discussion and Limitations

The evaluation of the proposed method in this paper revolves around two primary issues. Firstly, it addresses the question of whether the use of the adapter mechanism can effectively decrease both the data transmission and learning time. Secondly, it investigates whether the reduction in training time and data transmission does not lead to performance degradation. These aspects are rigorously examined through experiments conducted using the federated learning datasets of both computer vision and natural language processing.

This paper validates the reduction in training time and data transmission detailed in Section 4.4.2. Adapters significantly reduce the size of the model to be transferred by up to 98%. We mathematically calculated the decrease in transmission when the model size is reduced, which causes the reduction in transmission time during the training time. As a result, the reduction in transmission time shows is about 98%. Furthermore, the use of adapters reduces the training time of the local model by minimizing the number of layers that need training. In this paper, we experimentally check the reduction in training time when the transmission time is excluded in the local environment through Section 4.4.1. This shows that the reduction in training time, excluding the transmission time, can be about 20%. This confirms that the proposed methodology may show a reduction in training time and transmission time. In addition, Section 4.3.1 shows that performance degradation does not occur despite the reduced training time. Experimental results of NLP generally show a slight performance degradation. Experiments with CV generally show performance improvements. We confirm from the experimental results that the proposed method represents a reduction in training time, and this does not lead to significant performance degradation.

In this paper, experiments on CV tasks were not described, which prevented us from confirming the reduction in training time for these applications. Despite our efforts in conducting the experiments, we were unable to observe a decrease in the training time, regardless of whether the adapter was used or not. This limitation arose due to the speed discrepancy on the CPU-based image pre-processing and training speed using the GPU. Unfortunately, our computational resources did not permit us to bridge the gap effectively. In addition, we note that the experiments were conducted solely in a local environment. We did not perform transmission speed experiments on an actual network due to these limitations. Instead, we calculated the reduction in transmission speed based on our experiments in the local settings. Addressing these constraints in future studies will provide a more comprehensive understanding of the proposed methodology's applicability and effectiveness across diverse scenarios.

Furthermore, note that our methodology operates exclusively during the fine-tuning process and is not applicable in the pre-training phase. This limitation arises from the need to individually train the pre-trained large language model. Consequently, even though pre-training demands the most extensive dataset, the proposed method cannot be employed during this crucial phase. Additionally, while this paper successfully reduces the training time, there is a slight performance degradation observed in the NLP tasks. For future work, there is a need for research focused on reducing both the training time and data transmission during the full training of large language models in federated learning. Simultaneously, efforts should be directed towards eliminating performance degradation in NLP tasks through advancements in the adapter mechanism research.

6. Conclusions

In this paper, we addressed the problem of the increased transmission time caused by the pre-trained large language model in federated learning. To overcome this issue, we proposed and experimented with a federated learning approach using adapters, which previously have been suggested as an efficient fine-tuning method. As a result, the transmission time was reduced by about 98% compared to the methodology using the pre-trained large language model without adapters. In addition, the training time was also reduced by 20–40% as the number of parameters to be learned decreased. Nevertheless, the predictive performance was similar. Through this, it was confirmed that time-efficient federated learning is possible without performance degradation when an adapter is used in federated learning using a large language model, such as [7]. Also, the proposed methodology showed lower transmission sizes than traditional federated learning without a large language model. In addition, because the proposed methodology uses a large language model, it showed a higher predictive performance than traditional federated learning. Through this, it was confirmed that the proposed methodology can induce performance improvements with the same or lower transmission amount as traditional federated learning.

The significance of our proposed method lies in its ability to improve the transmission efficiency of federated learning. Therefore, it enables the use of a large language model, such as ChatGPT, powered by the GPT-3 model, in real-world federated learning environments. While large language models, such as ChatGPT, have shown impressive performances, it is practically challenging to use GPT-3 in an actual federated learning environment. This is mainly due to the substantial time and transmission costs incurred by clients with limited computational resources when learning and transmitting the large GPT-3 model. In contrast, the proposed methodology offers an attractive solution to significantly reduce the transmission costs. Furthermore, our experiments showed that the training time was partially mitigated. In summary, our proposal stands as a key enabler, facilitating the use of large models in a real-world federated learning environment.

Author Contributions: Conceptualization, G.K. and S.K.; methodology, G.K.; software, G.K.; validation, G.K.; investigation, G.K. and S.K.; resources, G.K. and S.K.; data curation, G.K.; writing—original draft preparation, G.K. and J.Y.; writing—review and editing, J.Y.; visualization, J.Y.; supervision, S.K. and J.Y.; project administration, S.K.; funding acquisition, S.K. All authors have read and agreed to the published version of the manuscript.

Funding: This work was supported in part by the National Research Foundation of Korea (NRF) grant funded by the Korean government (MSIT) (2022R1A2C1005316 and 2021R1F1A1063640) and in part by the Gachon University research fund of 2023 (GCU-202300660001).

Data Availability Statement: Publicly available datasets were analyzed in this study. This data can be found here: Tensorflow Federated api [18] (https://www.tensorflow.org/federated).

Conflicts of Interest: The authors declare no conflict of interest.

Abbreviations

The following abbreviations are used in this manuscript:

LSTM	Long Short-Term Memory
NLP	Natural Language Processing
CV	Computer Vision
IID	Independent Identically Distributed
Non-IID	Non-Independent Identically Distributed

References

1. McMahan, B.; Moore, E.; Ramage, D.; Hampson, S.; Arcas, B.A.y. Communication-Efficient Learning of Deep Networks from Decentralized Data. In Proceedings of the 20th International Conference on Artificial Intelligence and Statistics, Fort Lauderdale, FL, USA, 20–22 April 2017; Volume 54, pp. 1273–1282.
2. Li, T.; Sahu, A.K.; Zaheer, M.; Sanjabi, M.; Talwalkar, A.; Smith, V. Federated Optimization in Heterogeneous Networks. *Proc. Mach. Learn. Syst.* **2020**, *2*, 429–450.
3. Acar, D.A.E.; Zhao, Y.; Matas, R.; Mattina, M.; Whatmough, P.; Saligrama, V. Federated Learning Based on Dynamic Regularization. In Proceedings of the International Conference on Learning Representations, Vienna, Austria, 4 May 2021.
4. Zhang, L.; Luo, Y.; Bai, Y.; Du, B.; Duan, L.Y. Federated Learning for Non-IID Data via Unified Feature Learning and Optimization Objective Alignment. In Proceedings of the 2021 IEEE/CVF International Conference on Computer Vision (ICCV), Montreal, BC, Canada, 11 October 2021; pp. 4400–4408. [CrossRef]
5. Li, Q.; He, B.; Song, D. Model-Contrastive Federated Learning. In Proceedings of the IEEE/CVF Conference on Computer Vision and Pattern Recognition (CVPR), Nashville, TN, USA, 20–25 June 2021; pp. 10713–10722.
6. Deng, Y.; Kamani, M.M.; Mahdavi, M. Adaptive Personalized Federated Learning. *arXiv* **2020**, arXiv:2003.13461.
7. Nguyen, J.; Wang, J.; Malik, K.; Sanjabi, M.; Rabbat, M.G. Where to Begin? On the Impact of Pre-Training and Initialization in Federated Learning. *arXiv* **2022**, arXiv:2210.08090.
8. Devlin, J.; Chang, M.W.; Lee, K.; Toutanova, K. BERT: Pre-training of Deep Bidirectional Transformers for Language Understanding. In Proceedings of the 2019 Conference of the North American Chapter of the Association for Computational Linguistics: Human Language Technologies, Volume 1 (Long and Short Papers), Minneapolis, MN, USA, 2–7 June 2019; pp. 4171–4186. [CrossRef]
9. Raffel, C.; Shazeer, N.; Roberts, A.; Lee, K.; Narang, S.; Matena, M.; Zhou, Y.; Li, W.; Liu, P.J. Exploring the Limits of Transfer Learning with a Unified Text-to-Text Transformer. *J. Mach. Learn. Res.* **2020**, *21*, 1–67.
10. Brown, T.; Mann, B.; Ryder, N.; Subbiah, M.; Kaplan, J.D.; Dhariwal, P.; Neelakantan, A.; Shyam, P.; Sastry, G.; Askell, A.; et al. Language Models are Few-Shot Learners. In *Proceedings of the Advances in Neural Information Processing Systems*; Larochelle, H., Ranzato, M., Hadsell, R., Balcan, M., Lin, H., Eds.; Curran Associates, Inc.: Red Hook, NY, USA, 2020; Volume 33, pp. 1877–1901.
11. Shoeybi, M.; Patwary, M.; Puri, R.; LeGresley, P.; Casper, J.; Catanzaro, B. Megatron-LM: Training Multi-Billion Parameter Language Models Using Model Parallelism. *arXiv* **2019**, arXiv:1909.08053.
12. Houlsby, N.; Giurgiu, A.; Jastrzebski, S.; Morrone, B.; De Laroussilhe, Q.; Gesmundo, A.; Attariyan, M.; Gelly, S. Parameter-Efficient Transfer Learning for NLP. In Proceedings of the 36th International Conference on Machine Learning, Long Beach, CA, USA, 9–15 June 2019; Volume 97, pp. 2790–2799.
13. Federated Learning: Collaborative Machine Learning without Centralized Training Data. Available online: https://ai.googleblog.com/2017/04/federated-learning-collaborative.html (accessed on 4 May 2023).
14. Wang, J.; Liu, Q.; Liang, H.; Joshi, G.; Poor, H.V. Tackling the Objective Inconsistency Problem in Heterogeneous Federated Optimization. In *Proceedings of the Advances in Neural Information Processing Systems*; Larochelle, H., Ranzato, M., Hadsell, R., Balcan, M., Lin, H., Eds.; Curran Associates, Inc.: Red Hook, NY, USA, 2020; Volume 33, pp. 7611–7623.

15. Pfeiffer, J.; Kamath, A.; Rücklé, A.; Cho, K.; Gurevych, I. AdapterFusion: Non-destructive task composition for transfer learning. In Proceedings of the EACL 2021–16th Conference of the European Chapter of the Association for Computational Linguistics, Proceedings of the Conference, Association for Computational Linguistics (ACL), Virtual Event, 19–23 April 2021; pp. 487–503.
16. Hu, E.; Shen, Y.; Wallis, P.; Allen-Zhu, Z.; Li, Y.; Wang, L.; Chen, W. LoRA: Low-Rank Adaptation of Large Language Models. *arXiv* **2021**, arXiv:2106.09685.
17. Dosovitskiy, A.; Beyer, L.; Kolesnikov, A.; Weissenborn, D.; Zhai, X.; Unterthiner, T.; Dehghani, M.; Minderer, M.; Heigold, G.; Gelly, S.; et al. An Image is Worth 16 × 16 Words: Transformers for Image Recognition at Scale. In Proceedings of the International Conference on Learning Representations, Virtual Event, Austria, 3–7 May 2021.
18. Abadi, M.; Agarwal, A.; Barham, P.; Brevdo, E.; Chen, Z.; Citro, C.; Corrado, G.S.; Davis, A.; Dean, J.; Devin, M.; et al. TensorFlow: Large-Scale Machine Learning on Heterogeneous Systems. 2015. Available online: http://tensorflow.org/ (accessed on 13 December 2022).
19. Cohen, G.; Afshar, S.; Tapson, J.; van Schaik, A. EMNIST: Extending MNIST to handwritten letters. In Proceedings of the 2017 International Joint Conference on Neural Networks (IJCNN), Anchorage, AK, USA, 14–19 May 2017; pp. 2921–2926. [CrossRef]
20. Krizhevsky, A. Learning Multiple Layers of Features from Tiny Images. Master's Thesis, University of Toronto, Toronto, ON, Canada, 2009; pp. 32–33.
21. Radford, A.; Wu, J.; Child, R.; Luan, D.; Amodei, D.; Sutskever, I. Language Models are Unsupervised Multitask Learners. *OpenAI Blog* **2019**, *1*, 9.

Disclaimer/Publisher's Note: The statements, opinions and data contained in all publications are solely those of the individual author(s) and contributor(s) and not of MDPI and/or the editor(s). MDPI and/or the editor(s) disclaim responsibility for any injury to people or property resulting from any ideas, methods, instructions or products referred to in the content.

Review

Analysis of Colorectal and Gastric Cancer Classification: A Mathematical Insight Utilizing Traditional Machine Learning Classifiers

Hari Mohan Rai * and **Joon Yoo ***

School of Computing, Gachon University, Seongnam-si 13120, Republic of Korea
* Correspondence: drhmrai@gachon.ac.kr (H.M.R.); joon.yoo@gachon.ac.kr (J.Y.)

Abstract: Cancer remains a formidable global health challenge, claiming millions of lives annually. Timely and accurate cancer diagnosis is imperative. While numerous reviews have explored cancer classification using machine learning and deep learning techniques, scant literature focuses on traditional ML methods. In this manuscript, we undertake a comprehensive review of colorectal and gastric cancer detection specifically employing traditional ML classifiers. This review emphasizes the mathematical underpinnings of cancer detection, encompassing preprocessing techniques, feature extraction, machine learning classifiers, and performance assessment metrics. We provide mathematical formulations for these key components. Our analysis is limited to peer-reviewed articles published between 2017 and 2023, exclusively considering medical imaging datasets. Benchmark and publicly available imaging datasets for colorectal and gastric cancers are presented. This review synthesizes findings from 20 articles on colorectal cancer and 16 on gastric cancer, culminating in a total of 36 research articles. A significant focus is placed on mathematical formulations for commonly used preprocessing techniques, features, ML classifiers, and assessment metrics. Crucially, we introduce our optimized methodology for the detection of both colorectal and gastric cancers. Our performance metrics analysis reveals remarkable results: 100% accuracy in both cancer types, but with the lowest sensitivity recorded at 43.1% for gastric cancer.

Keywords: traditional machine learning; cancer detection; colorectal cancer; gastric cancer; mathematical formulation; preprocessing; feature extraction

MSC: 68T07

Citation: Rai, H.M.; Yoo, J. Analysis of Colorectal and Gastric Cancer Classification: A Mathematical Insight Utilizing Traditional Machine Learning Classifiers. *Mathematics* **2023**, *11*, 4937. https://doi.org/10.3390/math11244937

Academic Editors: Florin Leon, Mircea Hulea and Marius Gavrilescu

Received: 19 November 2023
Revised: 9 December 2023
Accepted: 11 December 2023
Published: 12 December 2023

Copyright: © 2023 by the authors. Licensee MDPI, Basel, Switzerland. This article is an open access article distributed under the terms and conditions of the Creative Commons Attribution (CC BY) license (https://creativecommons.org/licenses/by/4.0/).

1. Introduction

Cancer, a longstanding enigma in human history, has experienced a notable upsurge in its prevalence in recent decades due to several contributing causes. These reasons encompass the inexorable aging of populations, the embracing of detrimental lifestyles, and heightened exposure to carcinogens in the environment, food, and beverages [1,2]. The term "cancer" has its origins in the Greek word "kapkivoc", which carries a dual meaning, referring to both a neoplasm and a crustacean of the crab genus. This nomenclature was first introduced in the medical lexicon in the 17th century and signifies a condition characterized by the invasive spread of cells to different anatomical sites, potentially causing harm [3–5]. In the human anatomy, composed of countless innumerable cells, cancer can emerge in diverse locations, from the extremities to the brain. While cells typically divide and multiply to meet the body's needs and undergo programmed cell death, when necessary, deviations can lead to the uncontrolled replication of damaged or abnormal cells, resulting in the formation of a neoplasm or tumor. These tumors can be categorized as benign (non-malignant) or malignant (cancerous), with the latter having the potential to travel to distant body parts from the original location, often affecting nearby tissues along the way. Notably, blood cancers, like leukemia, do not follow the typical pattern of solid tumor formation but rather tend to involve the proliferation of abnormal blood cells that circulate within the body and may not form solid masses as seen in other types of cancer. Cancer arises from genetic anomalies that disrupt the regulation of cellular proliferation. These genetic anomalies compromise the natural control mechanisms that prevent excessive cell proliferation. The body has inherent mechanisms designed to remove cells that possess damaged DNA, but, in certain cases, these fail, allowing abnormal cells to thrive and potentially develop into tumors, disrupting regular bodily functions; these defenses can diminish with age or due to various factors [6].

Each instance of cancer exhibits a distinct genetic modification that evolves as the tumor grows. Tumors often showcase a diversity of genetic mutations across various cells existing within the same cluster. Genetic abnormalities primarily affect three types of genes: DNA repair genes, proto-oncogenes, and tumor suppressor genes. Proto-oncogenes are typically immersed in healthy cell division and proliferation. The transformation of these genes into oncogenes, brought on by specific alterations or increased activity, fuels uncontrolled cell growth and plays a role in cancer development. Meanwhile, tumor suppressor genes meticulously manage cellular division while imposing restraints on unbridled and unregulated cellular proliferation, and mutations in these genes disable their inhibitory function, increasing the risk of cancer. Mutations in DNA repair genes are significant in rectifying DNA damage, and these genes can lead to the accumulation of further genetic abnormalities, making cells more prone to developing cancer. Metastasis is the movement of cancer cells from the initial site to new parts. It includes cell detachment, local tissue invasion, blood or lymph system entry, and growth in distant tissues [7,8]. Understanding the genetic and cellular mechanisms underlying cancer development and metastasis is crucial for improving diagnostics, developing effective treatments, and advancing cancer research. Researchers can work toward better strategies for prevention, early detection, and targeted therapies by unraveling the intricacies of cancer at the molecular level. The early diagnosis of cancer developments across different body areas requires accurate and automated computerized techniques. While numerous researchers have made significant strides in cancer detection, there remains substantial scope for improvement in this field. In this manuscript, we have scrutinized colorectal and gastric cancers employing conventional ML techniques solely based on medical imaging datasets. Medical images offer finer and more specific details compared to other medical data sources.

Literature Review

This section provides an evaluative comparison of the most recent review articles available, analyzing current review articles dedicated to the utilization of machine learning and deep learning classifiers for cancer detection across diverse types. The objective is to summarize the positive aspects and limitations of these review articles, as per the review presented, on various cancer types. The papers selected for analysis include those that cover more than two cancer types, are peer-reviewed, and were published between 2019 and 2023. This present study extends our prior works [9,10] by providing an extensive review that now encompasses seven distinct cancer types. Levine et al. (2019) [9] focused on cutaneous, mammary, pulmonary, and various other malignant conditions, emphasizing radiological practices and diagnostic workflows. The study detailed the construction and deployment of a convolutional neural network for medical image analysis. However, limitations included a relative underemphasis on malignancy detection, sparse literature sources, and examination of a limited set of performance parameters. Huang et al. (2020) [10] explored prostatic, mammary, gastric, colorectal, solid, and non-solid malignancies. The study presented a comparative analysis of artificial intelligence algorithms and human pathologists in terms of prognostic and diagnostic performance across various cancer classifications. However, limitations included a lack of literature for each malignancy category, the absence of consideration for machine learning and deep learning classifiers, and a lack of an in-depth literature review. Saba (2020) [11] examined mammary, encephalic, pulmonary, hepatic, cutaneous, and leukemic cancers, offering concise explanations of benchmark datasets and a comprehensive evaluation of diverse performance metrics. However, limitations included a combined treatment of machine learning and deep learning without a separate analysis and the absence of a comparative exploration between the two methodologies. Shah et al. (2021) [12] proposed predictive systems for various cancer types but had limitations. It used a data, prediction technique, and view (DPV) framework to assess cancer detection. The focus was on data type, modality, and acquisition. However, the study included a limited number of articles for each cancer type, lacked a performance evaluation, and only considered deep learning-based methods.

Majumder and Sen (2021) [13] centered its focus on the domains of mammary, pulmonary, solid, and encephalic malignancies. The findings embraced the demonstration of artificial intelligence's application in the domains of oncopathology and translational oncology. However, limitations included a limited consideration of cancer types and literature sources, along with variations in performance metrics across different sources. Tufail et al. (2021) [14] evaluated astrocytic, mammary, colorectal, ovarian, gastric, hepatic, thyroid, and various other cancer types, emphasizing publicly accessible datasets, cancer detection, and segmentation. However, the exclusive focus on deep learning-based cancer detection limited a comprehensive examination of each cancer type. Kumar and Alqahtani (2022) [15] examined mammary, encephalic, pulmonary, cutaneous, prostatic, and various other malignancies, detailing diverse deep learning models and architectures based on image types. However, limitations included the exclusive focus on deep learning methods and variations in performance metrics across different literature sources. Kumar et al. (2022) [3] evaluated various malignancies, offering comprehensive coverage across diverse cancer categories. The study drew from numerous literature sources, presenting a wide array of performance metrics and acknowledging challenges. However, limitations included the amalgamation of all cancer types in a single analysis and the absence of a separate assessment of machine learning and deep learning approaches. Painuli et al. (2022) [16] concentrated on mammary, pulmonary, hepatic, cutaneous, encephalic, and pancreatic malignancies. The study examined benchmark datasets for these cancer types and provided an overview of the utilization of machine learning and deep learning methodologies. The research identified the most proficient classifiers based on accuracy but unified the examination of deep learning and machine learning techniques instead of offering individual assessments.

Rai (2023) [17] conducted a comprehensive analysis of cancer detection and segmentation, utilizing both deep neural network (DNN) and conventional machine learning (CML) methods, covering seven cancer types. The review separately scrutinized the strengths and challenges of DNN and CML classifiers. Despite limitations, such as a limited number of research articles and the absence of a database and feature extraction analysis, the study provided valuable insights into cancer detection, laying the foundation for future research directions. Maurya et al. (2023) [18] assessed encephalic, cervical, mammary, cutaneous, and pulmonary cancers, providing a comprehensive analysis of the performance parameters and inherent challenges. However, it lacked an independent assessment of machine learning and deep learning techniques and a dataset description. Mokoatle et al. (2023) [19] focused on pulmonary, mammary, prostatic, and colorectal cancers, proposing novel detection methodologies utilizing SBERT and the SimCSE approach. However, limitations included the study's focus on four cancer types, the lack of a dataset analysis, and reliance on a single assessment metric. Rai and Yoo (2023) [20] enhanced cancer diagnostics by classifying four cancer types with computational machine learning (CML) and deep neural network (DNN) methods. The study reviewed 130 pieces of literature, outlined benchmark datasets and features, and presented a comparative analysis of CML and DNN models. Limitations included a focus on four cancer types and reliance on a single metric (accuracy) for classifier validation.

This study offers an expansive and in-depth examination of the current landscape and potential prospects for diagnosing colorectal and gastric cancers through the application of traditional machine learning methodologies. The key contributions and highlights of this review can be distilled into the following key points.

- **Mathematical Formulations to Augment Cognizance:** Inaugurating the realm of mathematical formulations, meticulously addressing the most frequently utilized preprocessing techniques, features, machine learning classifiers, and the intricate domain of assessment metrics.
- **Mathematical Deconstruction of ML Classifiers:** Engaging in a profound exploration of the mathematical intricacies underpinning machine learning classifiers commonly harnessed in the arena of cancer detection.
- **Colorectal and Gastric Cancer Detection:** Dedicating an analytical focus to the nuanced landscape of colorectal and gastric cancer detection. Our scrutiny unfurled a detailed examination of the methodologies and techniques germane to the diagnosis and localization of these particular cancer types.
- **Preprocessing Techniques and Their Formulation:** Penetrating the intricate realm of preprocessing techniques and probing their pivotal role in elevating the quality and accuracy of models employed in cancer detection.
- **Feature Extraction Strategies and Informative Features:** Embarking on a comprehensive journey, scrutinizing the multifaceted domain of feature extraction techniques, meticulously counting and discerning the number of features wielded in research articles.
- **A Multidimensional Metrics Analysis:** Conducting an holistic examination encompassing a spectrum of performance evaluation metrics, encapsulating accuracy, sensitivity, specificity, precision, negative predictive value, F-measure (F1), area under the curve, and the Matthews correlation coefficient (MCC).
- **Evaluation Parameters for Research Articles:** Systematically analyzing diverse parameters, including publication year, preprocessing techniques, features, techniques, image count, modality nuances, dataset details, and integral metrics (%).
- **Prominent Techniques and Their Effectiveness:** Expertly identifying the techniques most prevalently harnessed by researchers in the realm of cancer detection and meticulously pinpointing the most effective among the gamut of options.
- **Key Insights and Ongoing Challenges:** Highlighting key insights from the scrutinized research papers, encompassing advances, groundbreaking revelations, and challenges in cancer detection using traditional machine learning techniques.
- **Architectural Design of Proposed Methodology:** Laying out in meticulous detail an architectural blueprint derived from the reviewed literature. These architectural formulations present invaluable guides for the enhancement of cancer detection models.
- **Recognizing Opportunities for Improvement:** Executing a methodical comparative analysis of an array of metrics, meticulously scrutinizing their zenith and nadir values, as well as the interstitial chasm. This granular evaluation aids in the strategic pinpointing of areas harboring untapped potential for enhancement in cancer detection practices.

2. Materials and Methods

2.1. Literature Selection Process

In this section, we will provide a broad overview of the procedures involved in selecting and employing research articles for the purpose of cancer classification through traditional ML approaches. These selection criteria encompass both inclusion and exclusion standards, which we will delineate in depth. The PRISMA flow diagram delineates the systematic review process employed for the detection of colorectal and stomach (gastric) cancer utilizing conventional machine learning (CML) methodologies, as illustrated in Figure 1. Commencing with an initial identification of 571 records through meticulous database searching, the subsequent removal of 188 duplicates yielded 383 distinct records. Through a rigorous screening process, 197 records were deemed ineligible, prompting a detailed assessment of eligibility for 186 full-text articles. Within this subset, the exclusion of 150 articles on various grounds culminated in the inclusion of 36 studies. This select group of 36 studies served as the foundational basis for the scoping review, offering a comprehensive exploration of cancer detection methods employing CML approaches for both colorectal and stomach cancers.

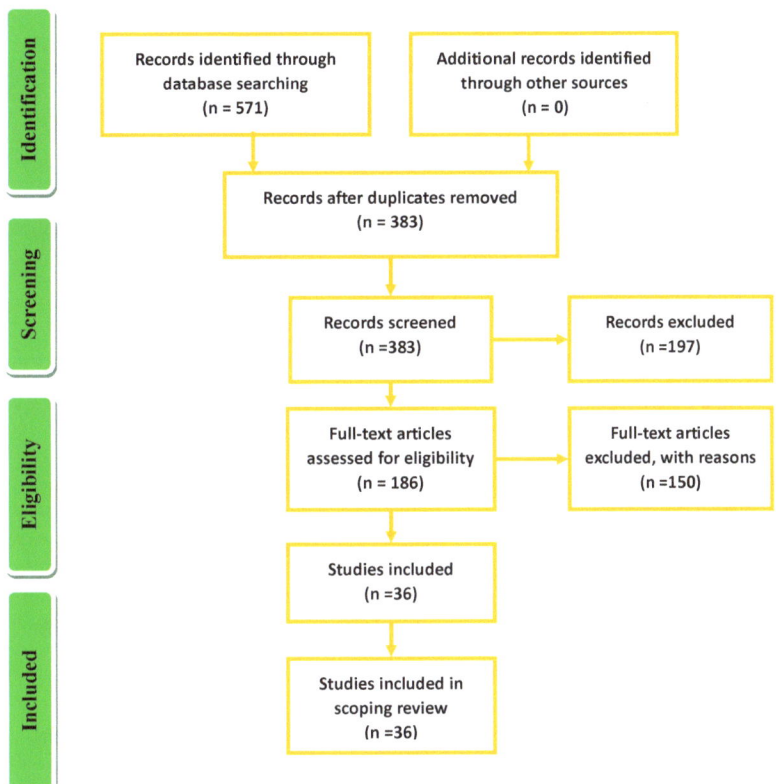

Figure 1. PRISMA flow diagram for the literature selection process.

2.1.1. Inclusion Criteria

The inclusion criteria for the review of research articles focused on cancer detection were defined across several specific parameters. Firstly, the articles had to pertain exclusively to the classification of cancer using conventional machine learning classifiers. These articles were specifically chosen if they were peer-reviewed and published between 2017 and 2023. The selection was limited to journal articles, omitting conference papers, book chapters, and similar sources to maintain the analytical scope. The studies selected for review utilized medical image datasets related to colorectal and gastric cancers. Additionally, a key criterion was the inclusion of accuracy as a performance metric in the chosen articles. Accuracy stands as a fundamental measure in evaluating the effectiveness of cancer detection models. The selected studies also strictly employed traditional machine learning classifiers for their classification tasks. The review was narrowed down to studies covering two specific high-mortality cancer types: colorectal and gastric cancer. Furthermore, articles were required to be in the English language, a criterion implemented to ensure the enhanced accessibility and comprehension of the research, thereby contributing to clarity and accuracy in the assessment process. Figure 2 illustrates the parameters governing the inclusion and exclusion of research articles in the selection process employed in this manuscript.

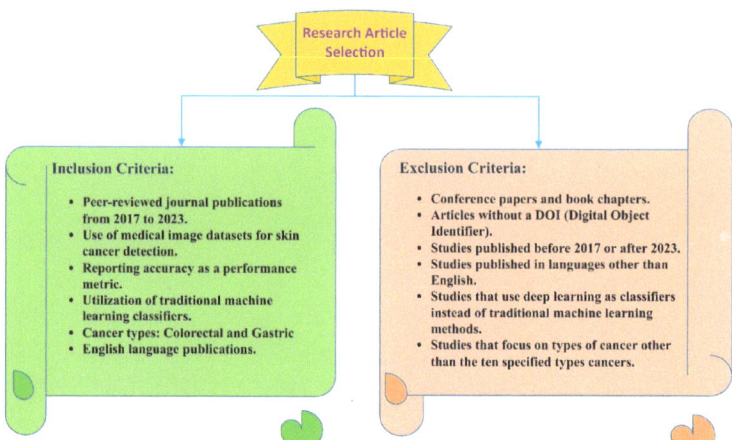

Figure 2. Parameters governing the inclusion and exclusion of research articles in the selection process.

2.1.2. Exclusion Criteria

The exclusion criteria, a pivotal aspect of the research review process for cancer detection, served as a strategic filter to ensure the selection of high-quality, pertinent articles. Omitting conference papers and book chapters was a deliberate choice to uphold a superior standard, guided by the in-depth scrutiny and comprehensive nature typically associated with peer-reviewed journal articles. Additionally, the requirement for digital object identifiers (DOIs) within the selected studies aimed to guarantee the reliability and accessibility of the articles, facilitating easy citation, retrieval, and verification processes. The temporal boundary set the scope within a specific timeframe, excluding research published before 2017 or after 2023, with the intention of focusing on the most recent advancements within the field of cancer detection. Language limitations were incorporated, allowing only English publications to ensure a consistent understanding and analysis. Moreover, the exclusion of deep learning classifiers in favor of traditional machine learning methods aligned with the specific objective of assessing the performance and effectiveness of the latter in cancer detection. By narrowing the focus exclusively to colorectal and gastric cancers, the exclusion criteria aimed to ensure a concentrated and comprehensive analysis across these specific high-mortality cancer types. This approach facilitated a deeper understanding of the efficacy of traditional machine learning methods in the context of different cancer types.

To illuminate the research hotspots, we have detailed the quantity of literature references pertaining annually to each cancer category (colorectal and gastric), along with the cumulative total, visually represented in Figure 3. This visual aid is designed to aid readers in identifying pertinent literature related to these specific cancer categories, fostering a more nuanced analysis within the specified years.

2.2. Medical Imaging Datasets

Data collection is the essential first step in any machine learning endeavor, and the performance of classifiers and detection tasks depends on the characteristics of the datasets used. The approach for identifying or classifying diseases, particularly cancers, is closely linked to the nature of the dataset. Various data types, such as images, text, and signal data, may require distinct processing methods. In the context of cancer detection, medical image datasets are of paramount importance. These datasets contain images that provide valuable information about the presence and characteristics of cancerous tissues. Specialized techniques, including image segmentation and feature extraction, are applied to extract relevant information for classification or detection. Analyzing image datasets differs significantly from text or signal datasets due to differences in data structures and feature extraction techniques. Dataset availability can be categorized as offline or real-time. In the domain of cancer detection, most research relies on offline datasets sourced from healthcare institutions, research centers, and platforms like Kaggle and Mendeley. Researchers often use local datasets from these sources to conduct studies and develop innovative cancer detection methods. In Table 1, we have described some benchmarked imaging datasets of lung and colorectal cancers.

Table 1. Benchmark and public medical imaging datasets for colorectal and gastric cancer with download links.

Dataset	Cancer Category	Modality	Downloadable Link	No. of Data Samples	Pixel Size
NCT-CRC-HE-100K	Colorectal	H&E	https://zenodo.org/record/1214456 (accessed on 15 September 2023)	100,000	224 × 224
Lung and colon histopathological images (LC25000)		H&E	https://academictorrents.com/details/7a638ed187a6180fd6e464b3666a6ea0499af4af (accessed on 15 September 2023)	10,000	768 × 768
CRC-VAL-HE-7K		H&E	https://zenodo.org/record/1214456 (accessed on 15 September 2023)	7180	224 × 224
Kather-CRC-2016 (KCRC-16)		H&E	https://zenodo.org/record/53169#.W6HwwP4zbOQ (accessed on 15 September 2023)	5000 10	150 × 150 5000 × 5000
Kvasir V-2 dataset (KV2D)	Stomach (Gastric)	Endoscopy	https://dl.acm.org/do/10.1145/3193289/full/ (accessed on 15 September 2023)	4000	720 × 576 to 1920 × 1072
HyperKvasir dataset (HKD)		Endoscopy	https://osf.io/mh9sj/ (accessed on 15 September 2023)	110,079 images and 374 videos	----
Gastric histopathology sub-size image database (GasHisSDB)		H&E	https://gitee.com/neuhwm/GasHisSDB	245,196	160 × 160, 120 × 120, 80 × 80

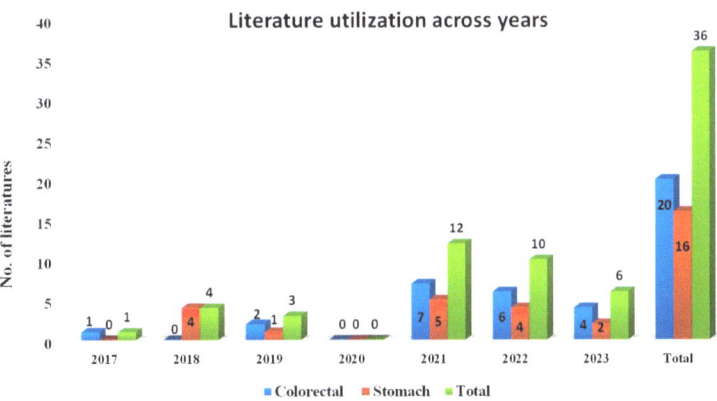

Figure 3. Temporal Analysis of Literature Utilization Across Cancer Categories (2017–2023).

2.3. Preprocessing

In cancer detection, preprocessing is essential to prepare data for analysis and classification. It refines diverse data types, like medical images and genetic and clinical data, addressing noise and inconsistencies. Medical image preprocessing includes noise reduction, enhancement, normalization, and format standardization. Augmentation enhances data diversity. Quality preprocessed data improves cancer detection model performance. Common tasks include noise reduction, data cleaning, transformation, normalization, and standardization. Preprocessing optimizes data for analysis, contributing to effective cancer diagnosis. Key preprocessing techniques are summarized in Table 2.

Table 2. Fundamental preprocessing techniques, associated formulas, and detailed descriptions.

Preprocessing Technique	Formula	Description
Image Filtering	$I_{\text{filtered}}(A, B) = \sum_{x=-N}^{N} \sum_{y=-N}^{N} I(A - x, B - y) \cdot K(x, y)$	$I_{\text{filtered}}(A, B)$ epitomizes the clean image pixel at location (A, B). $I(A - x, B - y)$ is the pixel significance at location $(A - x, B - y)$ in the original image. $K(x, y)$ is the value of the convolution kernel at location (x, y). The summation is performed over a window of size $(2N + 1) \times (2N + 1)$ centered at (A, B).
Image Denoising	$I_{\text{denoised}} = \text{argmin}(E(I_{\text{denoised}}) + R(I_{\text{denoised}}))$	I_{denoised} represents the denoised image. $E(I_{\text{denoised}})$ is the data fidelity term, which measures how well the denoised image matches the noisy input image. $R(I_{\text{denoised}})$ is the regularization term, which imposes a prior on the structure of the denoised image [21].
Gaussian Filtering	$Filtered_{value} = \frac{1}{(2\pi\sigma^2)} * e^{\frac{-(x^2+y^2)}{2\sigma^2}}$	$Filtered_{value}$ represents the resulting value after applying Gaussian filtering. x and y are the spatial coordinates. σ is the standard deviation, controlling the amount of smoothing or blurring.
Contrast Enhancement of Images (CEI)	$Pixel_{OP} = \frac{Pixel_{IP} - Min_{IP}}{(Max_{IP} - Min_{IP})} * (Max_{OP} - Min_{OP}) + Min_{OP}$	$Pixel_{OP}$ is the enhanced pixel value, derived from $Pixel_{IP}$ in the input image. Min_{IP} and Max_{IP} are the minimum and maximum pixel values in the input image. Min_{OP} and Max_{OP} represent the desired minimum and maximum pixel values in the output image [22].
Linear Transformation	$T(v) = Av$	where T is the transformation operator, v is the input vector, and A is a matrix defining the transformation.
Contrast Limited Adaptive Histogram Equalization (CLAHE)	$O(A, B) = T(I(A, B))$	$O(A, B)$ is the enhanced output pixel at (A, B) using contrast-enhancing transformation function $T(\cdot)$ based on pixel intensity using cumulative distribution function (CDF).
Discrete Cosine Transform (DCT)	$X[m] = \sum_{k=0}^{N-1} x[k] \cdot \cos\left(\frac{\pi(2k+1)m}{2N}\right)$	$X[m]$ represents the DCT coefficient at frequency index m. $x[k]$ is the input signal. N is the number of samples in the signal. The summation is performed over all samples in the signal
Wavelet Transform (WT)	$W(x, y) = \sum_{a=0}^{N-1} \sum_{b=0}^{M-1} I(a, b) \cdot \psi_{x,y}(a, b)$	$W(x, y)$ is the DWT coefficient, $(I(a, b))$ is the pixel value at (a, b), and $\psi_{x,y}(a, b)$ is the 2D wavelet function.

Table 2. Cont.

Preprocessing Technique	Formula	Description
RGB to Gray Conversion (RGBG)	$Gray\_value = (0.2989 * Red_{value}) + (0.5870 * Green_{value}) + (0.1140 * Blue_{value})$	$Gray_{value}$ is the converted gray value from RGB channels (Red_{value}, $Green_{value}$, $Blue_{value}$). Coefficients 0.2989, 0.5870, and 0.1140 are weights assigned to the R, G, and B channels, respectively [23].
Cropping (ROI)	$I_{cropped} = I[y : y + h, x : x + w]$	The cropped image $I_{cropped}$ is obtained by cropping the input image I at coordinates (x, y) with width w and height h.

2.4. Feature Engineering

Feature engineering is a critical component in solving classification problems, particularly with traditional machine learning methods. Features represent dataset attributes used by the model to classify or predict. Instead of using the entire dataset, relevant features are extracted and serve as classifier inputs, delivering the desired outcomes. Proper preprocessing is essential before feature engineering to ensure data quality. Feature engineering involves selecting which features to extract, choosing methods, defining the domain, and specifying the number of features. Categories of feature engineering include extraction, selection, reduction, fusion, and enhancement. Commonly used features for predicting lung and colorectal cancers in medical images are outlined below.

2.4.1. Histogram-Based First-Order Features (FOFs)

These are statistical features extracted from an image's histogram, providing valuable information about the distribution and characteristics of pixel intensities [24]. Here are some significant FOFs, along with their mathematical formulae presented in Equations (1)–(4).

Skewness (s): Skewness quantifies the asymmetry of the histogram and is calculated as:

$$s = \frac{1}{\sigma^3} \sum_{i=1}^{G_{max}} \left\{ (i - \mu)^3 * h_i \right\} \quad (1)$$

Here, i is the gray level, h_i is its frequency, G_{max} is the highest grayscale intensity, and μ and σ^2 are the mean and variance, respectively.

Excess Kurtosis (k): Excess kurtosis measures the peakedness of the histogram and is calculated as:

$$k = \frac{1}{\sigma^4} \sum_{i=1}^{G_{max}} \left\{ (i - \mu)^4 * h_i \right\} - 3 \quad (2)$$

Energy: Energy reflects the overall intensity in the image and is computed as:

$$Energy = \sum_{i=1}^{G_{max}} \left\{ [h_i]^2 \right\} \quad (3)$$

Entropy (HIST): Entropy quantifies the information or randomness in the histogram and is calculated as:

$$Entropy = \sum_{i=1}^{G_{max}} \{ h_i * \ln(h_i) \} \quad (4)$$

2.4.2. Gray-Level Co-Occurrence Matrix (GLCM) Features

GLCM is a technique used for texture analysis in image processing. It assesses the association between pixel values in an image, relying on the likelihood of specific pixel pairs with particular gray levels occurring within a defined spatial proximity [25–27]. Here are some important GLCM features, along with their mathematical formulas as provided in Equations (5)–(10).

Here, (x, y) pairs typically refer to the intensity values of adjacent or neighboring pixels.

Sum of Squares Variance (SSV): SSV quantifies the variance in gray levels within the texture.

$$SSV = \sum_{x,y}(x-\mu)^2 * GLCM(x,y) \quad (5)$$

Inverse Different Moment (IDM): IDM measures the local homogeneity and is higher for textures with similar gray levels.

$$IDM = \sum_{x,y} \frac{1}{1+(x-y)^2} * GLCM(x,y) \quad (6)$$

Correlation (Corr): Correlation quantifies the linear dependency between pixel values in the texture. It spans from −1 to 1, with 1 signifying flawless positive correlation.

$$Corr = \frac{\sum_{x,y}(x*y*GLCM(x,y))(\mu_a * \mu_b)}{\sigma_a * \sigma_b} \quad (7)$$

Dissimilarity: Dissimilarity quantifies how different neighboring pixel values are.

$$Dissimilarity = \sum_{x,y}|(x-y)| * GLCM(x,y) \quad (8)$$

Autocorrelation (AuCorr): Autocorrelation measures the similarity between pixel values at different locations in the texture.

$$AuCorr = \sum_{x,y} x * y * GLCM(x,y) \quad (9)$$

Inverse Difference (ID): ID measures the local homogeneity and is higher for textures with similar gray levels at different positions.

$$ID = \sum_{x,y} \frac{GLCM(x,y)}{1+|(x-y)|} \quad (10)$$

2.4.3. Gray-Level Run Length Matrix (GLRLM)

This is a statistical procedure employed in image processing and texture assessment to quantify the distribution of run lengths of specific gray levels within an image. Here are some significant GLRLM features along with their corresponding mathematical formulas, as presented in Equations (11)–(22).

Short Run Emphasis (SRE): SRE evaluates the dispersion of shorter runs characterized by lower gray-level values.

$$SRE = \sum_{x,y} \frac{C(x,y)}{x^2} \quad (11)$$

Here, (x,y) are gray levels, and $C(x,y)$ is the co-occurrence matrix value reflecting the frequency of each gray-level combination.

Long Run Emphasis (LRE): LRE assesses the presence of extended runs marked by higher gray-level values [28].

$$LRE = \sum_{x,y} C(x,y) * x^2 \quad (12)$$

Gray Level Nonuniformity (GLN): GLN Quantifies the nonuniformity of gray-level values in runs.

$$GLN = \sum_{x,y} C(x,y)^2 \qquad (13)$$

Run Length Nonuniformity (RLN): RLN evaluates the irregularity in the lengths of runs.

$$RLN = \sum_{x,y} \frac{C(x,y)}{y^2} \qquad (14)$$

Run Percentage (RP): RP represents the percentage of runs in the matrix.

$$RP = \sum_{x,y} \frac{C(x,y)}{N^2} \qquad (15)$$

Run Entropy (RE): RE calculates the entropy of run lengths and gray levels.

$$RE = -\sum_{x,y} (C(x,y) * \log C(x,y) + \in) \qquad (16)$$

Low Gray-Level Run Emphasis (LGRE): LGRE accentuates shorter runs with lower gray-level values.

$$LRGE = \sum_{x,y} \frac{C(x,y)}{y^2}, \text{ for } y \leq \frac{N+1}{2} \qquad (17)$$

High Gray-Level Run Emphasis (HGRE): HGRE highlights longer runs with higher gray-level values.

$$HRGE = \sum_{x,y} C(x,y) * y^2, \text{ for } y > \frac{N+1}{2} \qquad (18)$$

Short Run Low Gray-Level Emphasis (SRLGLE): SRLGLE highlights shorter runs that contain lower gray-level values.

$$SRLGLE = \sum_{x,y} \frac{C(x,y)}{(x^2 * y^2)}, \text{ for } x, y \leq \frac{N+1}{2} \qquad (19)$$

Short Run High Gray-Level Emphasis (SRHGLE): SRHGLE highlights shorter runs that contain higher gray-level values.

$$SRHGLE = \sum_{x,y} \frac{C(x,y) * x^2}{y^2}, \text{ for } x, y \leq \frac{N+1}{2}, y > \frac{N+1}{2} \qquad (20)$$

Long Run Low Gray-Level Emphasis (LRLGLE): LRLGLE emphasizes longer runs featuring lower gray-level values.

$$LRLGLE = \sum_{x,y} \frac{\frac{C(x,y)}{x^2}}{y^2}, \text{ for } x > \frac{N+1}{2}, y \leq \frac{N+1}{2} \qquad (21)$$

Long Run High Gray-Level Emphasis (LRHGLE): LRHGLE highlights extended sequences with higher gray-level values.

$$LRHRGLE = \sum_{x,y} C(x,y) * x^2 * y^2, \text{ for } x, y > \frac{N+1}{2} \qquad (22)$$

2.4.4. Neighborhood Gray-Tone Difference Matrix (NGTDM)

This is another texture analysis method used in image processing to characterize the spatial arrangement of gray tones in an image. Here are some key NGTDM features along with their respective mathematical formulas, as outlined in Equations (23)–(27).

Coarseness: Measures the coarseness of the texture based on differences in gray tones.

$$Coars = \sum_{x=1}^{N_g} \frac{C(x,y)}{(\Delta x)^2} \qquad (23)$$

Ng refers to the highest achievable discrete intensity level within the image.

Contrast (NGTD): Quantifies the contrast or sharpness in the texture.

$$Contrast_{NGTD} = \sum_{x=1}^{N_g} \sum_{y=1}^{N_g} C(x,y) * |x - y| \qquad (24)$$

Busyness: Represents the level of activity or complexity in the texture.

$$Busyness = \sum_{x=1}^{N_g} \sum_{y=1}^{N_g} C(x,y) * y \qquad (25)$$

Complexity: Measures the complexity or intricacy of the texture.

$$Complexity = \sum_{x=1}^{N_g} \sum_{y=1}^{N_g} \frac{P(x,y)}{1 + |x-y|^2} \qquad (26)$$

Texture Strength (TS): Quantifies the strength or intensity of the texture.

$$TS = \sqrt{\sum_{x=1}^{N_g} \sum_{y=1}^{N_g} P(x,y) * \left(\frac{x}{N_g} - \frac{y}{N_g}\right)^2} \qquad (27)$$

These features provide a detailed analysis of texture patterns in images, making them valuable for various applications, including image classification, quality control, and texture discrimination in fields such as geology, material science, and medical imaging.

2.5. Traditional Machine Learning Classifiers

Machine learning-based classifiers, renowned for their advanced capabilities in detecting cancer, notably stand out in their effectiveness when harmonized with non-invasive diagnostic techniques, providing a significant edge in the domain of cancer detection. Researchers have employed a range of ML classifiers to identify different malignancies and disorders. Some commonly used classifiers include:

2.5.1. K-Nearest Neighbors (KNN)

K-Nearest Neighbors (KNN) is a widely used and simple machine learning algorithm, suitable for classification and regression tasks. It relies on the assumption that similar inputs lead to similar outputs, assigning a class label to a test input based on the prevalent class among its k closest neighbors. The formal definition involves representing a test point 'x' and determining its set of 'k' nearest neighbors, denoted as 'Nx', where 'k' is a user-defined parameter.

The Minkowski distance is a flexible distance metric that can be tailored by adjusting the value of the parameter 'p.' The Minkowski distance between two data points 'x' and 'z' in a 'd'-dimensional space is defined by Equation (28):

$$dist(x,z) = \left(\sum_{r=1}^{d} |x_r - z_r|^p\right)^{1/p} \qquad (28)$$

The "1-NN Convergence Proof" states that, as your dataset grows infinitely large, the 1-Nearest Neighbor (1-NN) classifier's error will not be more than twice the error of the Bayes optimal classifier, which represents the best possible classification performance. This also holds for k-NN with larger values of k. It highlights the ability of the K-Nearest Neighbors algorithm to approach optimal performance with increasing data [29]. As n approaches infinity, Z_{NN} converges to Z_t, and the probability of different labels for Z_t when returning (Z_{NN})'s label is described in Equation (29) [30].

$$\in_{NN} = P(y*|Z_t)(1 - P(y*|Z_{NN})) + P(y*|Z_{NN})(1 - P(y*|Z_t)) \leq (1 - P(y*|Z_{NN})) + (1 - P(y*|Z_t)) \\ = 2(1 - P(y*|Z_t)) = 2 \in_{BO} \quad (29)$$

Here, BO is the Bayes optimal classifier. If the test point and its nearest neighbor are indistinguishable, misclassification occurs if they have different labels. This probability is outlined in Equation (30) and Figure 4 [29,31].

$$(1 - p(s|x))p(s|x) + p(s|x)(1 - p(s|x)) = 2p(s|x)(1 - p(s|x)) \quad (30)$$

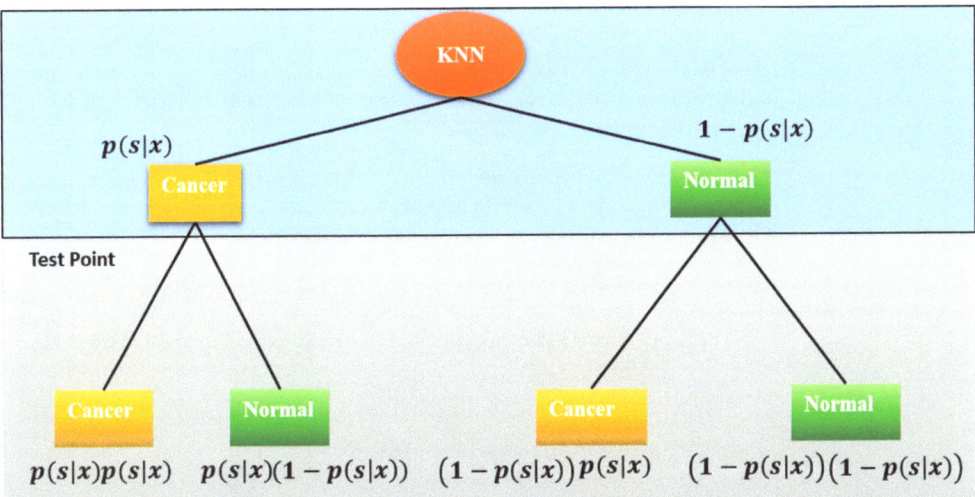

Figure 4. Probabilistic analysis of misclassification for identical test point and nearest neighbor scenario.

Equation (30) represents the misclassification probability when the test point and its nearest neighbor have differing labels.

2.5.2. Multilayered Perceptron (MLP)

In contrast to static kernels, neural network units have adaptable internal parameters for an adjustable structure. A perceptron, inspired by biological neurons, comprises three components: (i) weighted edges for individual multiplications, (ii) a summation unit for calculating the sum, and (iii) an activation unit applying a non-linear function [32–34]. The single-layer unit function involves a linear combination passed through a non-linear activation, represented by Equation (31) and Figure 5 [33,34].

$$y^{(1)}f = \left(w_0^{(1)} + \sum_{j=1}^{N} w_j^{(1)} x_j \right) \quad (31)$$

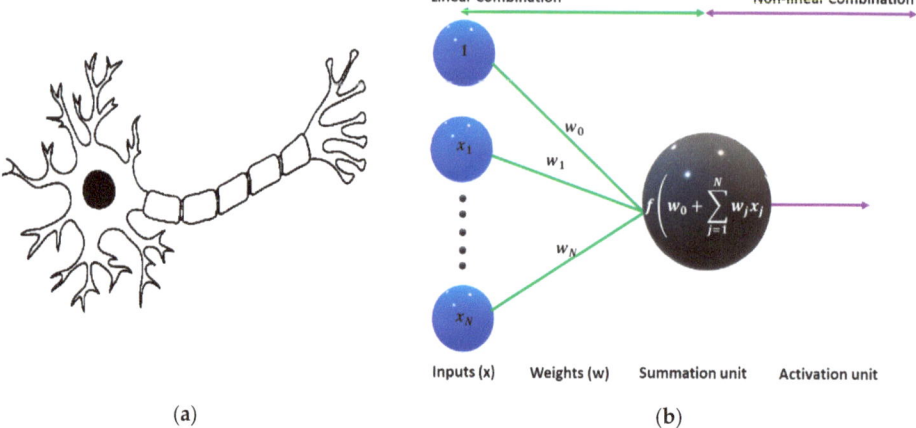

Figure 5. Contrasts (**a**) biological neurons, showcasing intricate neural architecture, with (**b**) artificial perceptrons in neural networks, depicting simplified representations and emphasizing structural differences.

In a single-layer neural network unit, $y^{(1)}f$ is the output, $w_0^{(1)}$ is the bias, and $\sum_{j=1}^{N} w_j^{(1)} x_j$ is the weighted sum of inputs. In general, we compute U_1 units as feature transformations in learning models, described in an Equation (32) [33,34].

$$\text{model}(x, w) = w_0 + y_1^{(1)}(x)w_1 + \cdots + y_{U_1}^{(1)}(x)w_{U_1} \tag{32}$$

The input vector x can be denoted as represented in Equation (33) [33,34].

$$x = \begin{bmatrix} 1 \\ x_1 \\ \cdot \\ \cdot \\ \cdot \\ x_N \end{bmatrix} \tag{33}$$

The vector representation comprises input values x_1 to x_N, and an additional element of 1. Internal parameters of single-layer units include bias $w_{0,j}^{(1)}$ and weights $w_{1,j}^{(1)}$ through $w_{N,j}^{(1)}$. These parameters form the *j*th column of a matrix $W^{(1)}$ with dimensions $(N+1) \times U_1$, as demonstrated in Equation (34) below [34]:

$$W_1 = \begin{bmatrix} w_{0,1}^{(1)} & w_{0,2}^{(1)} & \cdots & w_{0,U_1}^{(1)} \\ w_{1,1}^{(1)} & w_{1,2}^{(1)} & \cdots & w_{1,U_1}^{(1)} \\ \vdots & \vdots & \vdots & \vdots \\ w_{N,1}^{(1)} & w_{N,2}^{(1)} & \cdots & w_{N,U_1}^{(1)} \end{bmatrix} \tag{34}$$

Notably, the matrix–vector product $W_1^T x$ encompasses all linear combinations within our U_1 units as given in Equation (35) [33].

$$\left(W_1^T x\right)_j = w_{0,j}^{(1)} + \sum_{n=1}^{N} w_{n,j}^{(1)} x_n, \; j = 1, \ldots, U_1 \tag{35}$$

We extend the activation function f to handle a general $d \times 1$ vector v in Equation (36) [34]:

$$f(v) = \begin{bmatrix} f(v_1) \\ \vdots \\ f(v_d) \end{bmatrix} \quad (36)$$

In Equation (37), $f\left(W_1^T x\right)$ is a $U_1 \times 1$ vector containing all U_1 single-layer units [33,34]:

$$f\left(W_1^T x\right)_j = f\left(w_{0,j}^{(1)} + \sum_{n=1}^{N} w_{n,j}^{(1)} x_n\right), \, j = 1, \ldots, U_1 \quad (37)$$

The mathematical expression for an L-layer unit in a general multilayer perceptron, built recursively from single-layer units, is given by Equation (38) [33,34].

$$y^{(L)}(x) = f\left(w_0^{(L)} + \sum_{i=1}^{U^{(L-1)}} w_i^{(L)} f_i^{(L-1)}(x)\right) \quad (38)$$

2.5.3. Support Vector Machine (SVM)

SVMs, employed for regression and classification tasks, stand out in supervised machine learning for their precision with complex datasets. Particularly effective in binary classification, SVMs aim to discover an optimal hyperplane, maximizing the boundary between classes. Serving as a linear classifier, SVMs build on the perceptron introduced by Rosenblatt in 1958 [35–37]. Unlike perceptrons, SVMs identify the hyperplane (H) with the maximum separation margin, defined in Equation (39).

$$h(x) = \text{sign}\left(w^{Tx} + b\right) \quad (39)$$

The SVM classifies in $\{+1, -1\}$, emphasizing the key concept of finding a hyperplane with maximum margin σ. Figure 6 illustrates this importance, with the margin expressed in Equation (40) [35]

$$\sigma = \min_{(x_j, y_j) \in D} \left| w \cdot x_j \right| \quad (40)$$

where input vectors x_j are within the unit sphere, σ is the closest data point from the hyperplane, and the vector w resides on the unit sphere.

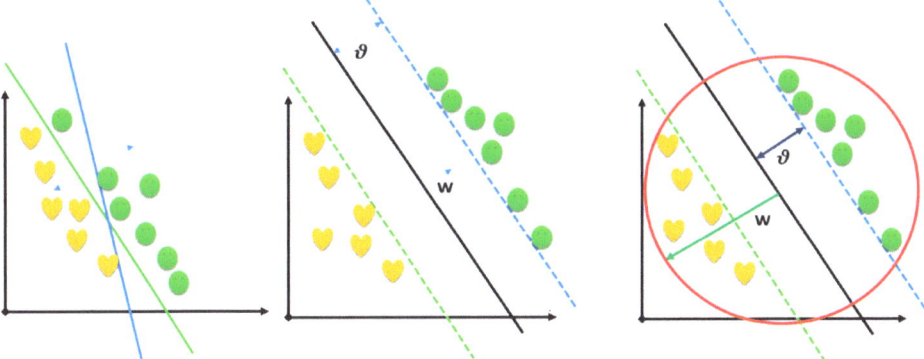

Figure 6. Separating Hyperplanes and Maximum Margin Hyperplane in Support Vector Machines.

Max Margin Classifier: We formulate our pursuit of the maximizing-margin hyperplane as a constrained optimization task, aiming to enhance the margin while ensuring correct classification of all data points. This is expressed in Equation (41) [35,37]:

$$[\underbrace{\max_{u,\delta} \sigma(u,\delta)}_{\text{maximize margin}} \text{ such that } \underbrace{\forall i \, y_i \left(u^T x_i + \delta\right) \geq 0}_{\text{separating hyperplane}}] \tag{41}$$

Upon substituting the definition of σ, Equation (42) is derived, as given below.

$$[\max_{u,\delta} \underbrace{\frac{1}{\|u\|_2} \min_{x_i \in D} \left|u^T x_i + \delta\right|}_{\sigma(u,\delta)} \text{ s.t. } \underbrace{\forall i \, y_i \left(u^T x_i + \delta\right) \geq 0}_{\text{separating hyperplane}}] \tag{42}$$

Scaling invariance enables flexible adjustment of u and δ. Smart value selection ensures $\left(\min_{x \in D}\left|u^T x + \delta\right| = 1\right)$, introduced as an equality constraint in the objective per Equation (43) [37]:

$$\left[\max_{u,\delta} 1 \cdot |u|_2 = \min_{u,\delta}|u|_2 = \min_{u,\delta} u^\top u\right] \tag{43}$$

Utilizing the fact that $f(z) = z^2$ is monotonically increasing for $z \geq 0$ and $|u| \geq 0$, where u maximizing $|u|_2$ also maximizes $u^\top u$. This reformulates the optimization problem in Equation (44), and a structural diagram of a multi-SVM has been visualized in Figure 7.

$$\min_{u,\delta} u^\top u \text{ subject to } \forall i, y_i \left(u^T x_i + \delta\right) \geq 0, \min_i \left|u^T x_i + \delta\right| = 1 \tag{44}$$

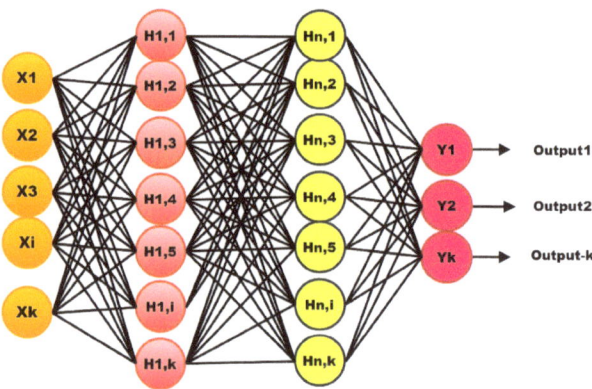

Figure 7. Structural diagram of the multi-class support vector machine (SVM).

2.5.4. Bayes and Naive Bayes (NB) Classifier

The Bayes classifier, an ideal algorithm, assigns class labels based on class probabilities given observed features and prior knowledge. It predicts the class with the highest estimated probability, often used as a benchmark but requiring complete knowledge of underlying probability distributions. To estimate $P(y|\overline{x})$ for the Bayes classifier, the common approach is maximum likelihood estimation (MLE), especially for the discrete variable y, as outlined in Equation (45) [37]:

$$P(y|\overline{x}) = \frac{\sum_{k=1}^{m} I(\overline{x_k} = \overline{x} \wedge \overline{y_i} = y)}{\sum_{i=1}^{n} I(\overline{x_i} = \overline{x})} \tag{45}$$

Naive Bayes addresses MLE's limitations with sparse data by assuming feature independence. It estimates $P(y)$ and $P(\bar{x}|y)$ instead of $P(y|\bar{x})$ using Bayes' rule (Equation (46)) [37]:

$$P(y|\bar{x}) = \frac{P(\bar{x}|y)P(y)}{P(\bar{x})} \qquad (46)$$

Generative learning estimates $P(y)$ and $P(\bar{x}|y)$, with $P(y)$ resembling tallying occurrences for discrete binary values (Equation (47)).

$$P(y = c) = \frac{\sum_{i=1}^{n} I(y_i = c)}{n} = \pi^c \qquad (47)$$

To simplify estimation, the Naive Bayes (NB) assumption is introduced, a key element of the NB classifier. It assumes feature independence given the class label, formalized in Equation (48) for $P(\bar{x}|y)$.

$$P(\bar{x}|y) = \prod_{\alpha=1}^{d} P(x_\alpha|y) \qquad (48)$$

Here, x_α is the value of feature α, assuming feature values, given class label y, are entirely independent. Despite potential complex relationships, NB classifiers are effective. The Bayes classifier, defined in Equation (49), further simplifies to (50) due to $P(\bar{x})$ independence from y, and using logarithmic property, it can be expressed as (51).

$$h(\bar{x}) = \mathrm{argmax}_y P(y|\bar{x}) = \mathrm{argmax}_y P(\bar{x}|y)P(y) \qquad (49)$$

$$h(\bar{x}) = \mathrm{argmax}_y \prod_{\alpha=1}^{n} P(x_\alpha|y)P(y) \qquad (50)$$

$$h(\bar{x}) = \mathrm{argmax}_y \sum_{\alpha=1}^{n} \log(P(x_\alpha|y)) + \log(P(y)) \qquad (51)$$

Estimating $\log(P(x_\alpha|y))$ is straightforward for one dimension. $P(y)$ remains unaffected and is calculated independently. In Gaussian NB, where features are continuous ($x_\alpha \in R$), $P(x_\alpha|y)$ follows a Gaussian distribution (Equation (52)). This assumes each feature (x_α) follows a class-conditional Gaussian distribution with mean $\mu_{\alpha c}$ and variance $\sigma_{\alpha c}^2$ (Equations (53) and (54)), using parameter estimates in the Gaussian NB classifier for each class [37].

$$P(x_\alpha|y = d) = \frac{1}{\sqrt{2\pi\sigma_{\alpha c}^2}} \exp\left(-\frac{(x_\alpha - \mu_{\alpha c})^2}{2\sigma_{\alpha c}^2}\right) \qquad (52)$$

$$\mu_{\alpha c} = \frac{1}{n_d} \sum_{k=1}^{n} I(y_k = d) x_{i\alpha} \qquad (53)$$

$$\sigma_{\alpha c}^2 = \frac{1}{n_d} \sum_{k=1}^{n} I(y_k = d)(x_{i\alpha} - \mu_{\alpha c})^2 \qquad (54)$$

2.5.5. Logistic Regression (LR)

Logistic regression, commonly used in classification, calculates the probability of a binary label based on input features. In logistic regression (LR), the logistic (sigmoid) function transforms a linear combination of input features x, weights w, and a bias term b into a likelihood estimate between 0 and 1. Mathematically, logistic regression is defined in Equation (55) [38]:

$$P(y = 1|x) = \frac{1}{1 + e^{-(w^T x + b)}} \qquad (55)$$

Equation (71): $P(y = 1|x)$ is the likelihood of class 1 given features x. w and b are estimated using statistical methods, minimizing assumptions about $P(x_i|y)$, allowing flexibility in underlying distributions [38].

The Maximum Likelihood Estimate (MLE): MLE maximizes $P(y \mid x, w)$, the probability of observing $y \in R^n$ given feature values x_i. It aims to find parameters maximizing this function, assuming independence among y_i given x_i and w. Equation (56) captures the mathematical expression for the conditional data likelihood.

$$P(y|x,w) = \prod_{k=1}^{m} P(y_k|x_k, w) \tag{56}$$

Now, by taking the logarithm of the product of Equation (57), we obtain Equation (73):

$$\log\left(\prod_{k=1}^{m} P(y_k|x_k, w)\right) = -\sum_{k=1}^{m} \log\left(1 + e^{-y_k w^T x_k}\right) \tag{57}$$

To find the MLE for w, we aim to minimize the function provided in Equation (58):

$$w^{MLE} = \mathrm{argmax}(w) - \sum_{k=1}^{m} \log\left(1 + e^{-y_k w^T x_k}\right) = \mathrm{argmin}(w) \sum_{k=1}^{m} \log\left(1 + e^{-y_k w^T x_k}\right) \tag{58}$$

Minimizing the function in Equation (58) is our goal, achieved through gradient descent on the negative log likelihood in Equation (59).

$$\mathcal{L}(w) = \sum_{k=1}^{m} \log\left(1 + e^{-y_k w^T x_k}\right) \tag{59}$$

Maximum a Posteriori (MAP): In maximum a posteriori (MAP), assuming a Gaussian prior, the objective is to find w^{MAP} that maximizes the posterior probability, represented mathematically in Equation (60). Reformulating, this becomes an optimization problem, as shown in Equation (61), where $\lambda = \frac{1}{2\sigma^2}$, and gradient descent is employed on the negative log posterior $l(w)$ for parameter optimization [32,37].

$$w^{MAP} = \mathrm{argmax}_{w} \log(P(y|x,w)P(w)) \propto P(y|x,w)P(w) \tag{60}$$

$$w^{MAP} = \mathrm{argmin}_{w} \sum_{k=1}^{m} \log\left(1 + e^{-y_k w^T x_k}\right) + \lambda w^T w \tag{61}$$

2.5.6. Decision Tree (DT)

Decision trees, used for regression and classification, form a hierarchical structure with nodes for decisions, branches for outcomes, and leaves for predictions. The goal is a compact tree with pure leaves, ensuring each contains instances from a single class. Achieving consistency is computationally challenging due to the NP-hard complexity of finding a minimum-size tree [37]. Impurity functions in decision trees, evaluated on a dataset D with pairs $(a_1, b_1), \ldots, (a_n, b_n)$, where b_i takes values in $\{1, \ldots, m\}$ representing m classes, are crucial for assessing tree quality.

Gini Impurity: Gini impurity in a decision tree is calculated for a leaf using Equation (62), and the Gini impurity for the entire tree is given by Equation (63).

$$I(D) = \sum_{m=1}^{k} q_m(1 - q_m) \tag{62}$$

$$G_T(D) = \frac{|D_L|}{|D|} G_T(D_L) + \frac{|D_R|}{|D|} G_T(D_R) \tag{63}$$

where: $D = D_L \cup D_R$, $D_L \cap D_R = \emptyset$, $\frac{|D_L|}{|D|}$ represents the fraction of inputs in the left subtree, and $\frac{|D_R|}{|D|}$ represents the fraction of inputs in the right subtree. The binary decision tree with class levels has been visualized in Figure 8.

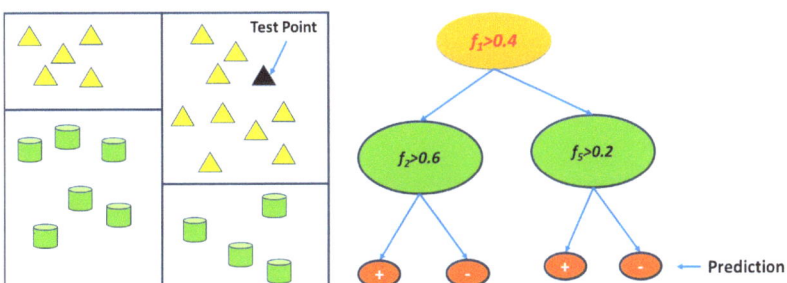

Figure 8. Binary Decision Tree with Sole Storage of Class Labels.

Entropy in Decision Trees: Entropy in decision trees measures disorder using class fractions. Minimizing entropy aligns with a uniform distribution, promoting randomness. KL-Divergence $KL(p||q)$ gauges the closeness of p to a uniform distribution q, as in Equation (64).

$$\begin{aligned} KL(p||q) &= \sum_{n=1}^{c} p_n \log \frac{p_n}{q_n} > 0 \leftarrow KL - Divergence \\ &= \sum_n p_n \log(p_n) - p_n \log(q_n), where\ q_n = \frac{1}{c} \\ &= \sum_n p_n \log(p_n) + p_n \log(c) \\ &= \sum_n p_n \log(p_n) + \log(c) \sum_n p_n, where\ \log(c) \leftarrow constant, \sum_n p_n = 1 \\ \max_p KL(p||q) &= \max_p \sum_n p_n \log(p_n) = \min_p -\sum_n p_n \log(p_n) = \min_p H(s) \leftarrow Entropy \end{aligned} \quad (64)$$

ID3 Algorithm: The ID3 algorithm stops tree-building when all labels are the same or no more attributes can split further. If all share the same label, a leaf with that label is created. If no more splitting attributes exist, a leaf with the most frequent label is generated (Equation (65)) [39].

$$ID3(S): \begin{cases} if\ \exists\ \vec{y}\ s.t.\ \forall (x,y) \in S,\ y = \vec{y}, return\ leaf\ with\ label\ \vec{y} \\ if\ \exists\ \vec{x}\ s.t.\ \forall (x,y) \in S,\ x = \vec{x}\ return\ leaf\ without\ mode\ (y: (x,y) \in S) \end{cases} \quad (65)$$

CART (Classification and Regression Trees): CART (classification and regression trees) is suitable for continuous labels ($y_i \in R$), using the squared loss function (Equation (66)). It efficiently finds the best split (attribute and threshold) by minimizing the average squared difference from the average label y_s [37].

$$L(S) = \frac{1}{|S|} \sum_{(i,j) \in S} \left(y - \vec{y_s}\right)^2 \leftarrow Average\ squared\ difference\ from\ average\ label \quad (66)$$

where $\vec{y_s} = \frac{1}{|S|} \sum_{(i,j) \in S} y \leftarrow average\ label$

2.5.7. Ensemble Classifier (EC)

Ensemble classifiers represent a sophisticated class of machine learning techniques aimed at enhancing the precision and resilience of predictive models. Their fundamental premise revolves around the amalgamation of predictions from multiple foundational models. Below, we delve into several prominent types of ensemble classifiers, each with its distinct modus operandi.

Bagging (Bootstrap Aggregating): Bagging orchestrates the training of multiple foundational models in parallel. Each model operates independently on distinct, resampled subsets of the training data. This decomposition helps us understand the sources of error in our models. Bias/variance decomposition is described by Equation (67) [37,40]:

$$\underbrace{E\left[(f_k(x) - b)^2\right]}_{Error} = \underbrace{E\left[(f_k(x) - \vec{f}(x))^2\right]}_{Variance} + \underbrace{E\left[(\vec{f}(x) - \vec{c}())^2\right]}_{Bias} + \underbrace{E\left[(\vec{c}(x) - d(x))^2\right]}_{Noise} \quad (67)$$

In Equation (67), we decompose the error into four components: "Error", "Variance", "Bias", and "Noise". Our primary objective is to minimize the "Variance" term, which is expressed as Equation (68):

$$\underbrace{E[(f_k(x) - \vec{f}(x))^2]}_{Variance} \quad (68)$$

Ensemble learning minimizes variance by averaging individual predictions $f_k(x)$. Bagging enhances ML classifiers by creating multiple datasets, training individual classifiers $h_i()$, and aggregating predictions in the final ensemble classifier $h(z)$, through averaging (Equation (69)) [40]:

$$h(z) = \frac{1}{n}\sum_{i=1}^{n} h_i(z) \quad (69)$$

In practice, a larger value of n often leads to a better-performing ensemble, as it leverages diverse base models for more robust predictions.

Random Forest (RF): RF stands as one of the most renowned and beneficial bagging algorithms. The RF algorithm entails creating multiple datasets, building decision trees with random feature subsets for each dataset, and averaging their predictions for the final classifier [37,40] $\left(\left(h(x) = \frac{1}{m}\Sigma h_j(x)\right)\right)$.

Boosting: Boosting addresses high bias in machine learning models, specifically when dealing with the hypothesis class H. Boosting reduces bias by iteratively constructing an ensemble of weak learners $\left(H_T(\vec{x}) = \sum_{t=1}^{T} \alpha_t h_t(\vec{x})\right)$ with each iteration introducing a new classifier, guided by gradient descent in function space [37,41].

Gradient descent: Gradient descent in functional space optimizes the loss function ℓ within hypothesis class H by finding the appropriate step size α and weak learner h that minimizes $l(H + \alpha h)$. The technique uses Taylor approximation to approximate the optimal weak learner h with a fixed α around 0.1 (Equation (70)) [34].

$$argmin_{h \in Hl}(H + \alpha h) \approx argmin_{h \in H} < \nabla l(H), h \geq argmin_{h \in H} \sum_{i=1}^{n} \frac{\partial l}{\partial [H(x_i)]} h(x_i) \quad (70)$$

Here, each prediction serves as an input to the loss function. The function $\ell(H)$ can be expressed by Equation (71).

$$l(H) = \sum_{i=1}^{nl}(H(x_i)) = l(H(x_1), \ldots, H(x_n)) \quad (71)$$

This approximation enables the utilization of boosting as long as there exists a method, denoted as A, capable of solving Equation (72).

$$h_{t+1} = argmin_{h \in H} \sum_{i=1}^{n} \underbrace{\frac{\partial l}{\partial [H(x_i)]}}_{r_i} h(x) \quad (72)$$

where $A(\{(x_1, r_1), \ldots, (x_n, r_n)\}) = argmin_{h \in H} \sum_{i=1}^{n} r_i h(x_i)$; progress is made as long as $\sum_{i=1}^{n} r_i h(x_i) < 0$, even if h is not an excellent learner.

AnyBoost (Generic Boosting): AnyBoost, a versatile boosting technique, iteratively combines weak learners, prioritizing challenging data points for enhanced accuracy. It creates a strong learner from weak ones, effectively reducing bias and improving predictions. See Algorithm 1 for the pseudo-code [41].

Algorithm 1: Pseudo-code for the AnyBoost.

Input: $l, a, \{(x_i, y_i)\}, A$
$H_0 = 0$
for $t = 0$: $T - 1$ **do**
    $\forall I : r_i = \frac{\partial l((H_t(x_1), y_1), \ldots, (H_t(x_n), y_n))}{\partial H(x_i)}$
    $h_{t+1} = A(\{(x_1, r_1), \ldots, (x_n, r_n)\}) = argmin_{h \in H} \sum_{i=1}^{n} r_i h(x_i)$
    if $\sum_{i=1}^{n} r_i h_{t+1}(x_i) < 0$ **then**
        $H_{t+1} = H_t + \alpha_{t+1} h_{t+1}$
    else
        return H_t (Negative gradient orthogonal to descent direction.)
    end
end
return H_T

Gradient Boosted Regression Trees (GBRT): GBRT, a sequential regression algorithm, combines decision trees to correct errors iteratively for precise predictions. Applicable to both classification and regression, it uses weak learners, often shallow regression trees, with a fixed depth. The step size (α) is a small constant, and the loss function (l) must be differentiable, convex, and decomposable over individual samples. The ensemble's overall loss is defined in Equation (73) [41].

$$\mathcal{L}(H) = \sum_{i=1}^{n} l(H(x_i)) \tag{73}$$

GBRT minimizes the loss by iteratively adding weak learners to the ensemble. Pseudo-code is in Algorithm 2 [41].

Algorithm 2: Pseudo-code for GBRT

Input: $l, \alpha, \{(x_i, y_i)\}, A$
$H = 0$
for $t = 1$: T **do**
    $\forall i : t_i = y_i - H(x_i)$
    $h = argmin_{h \in H}(h(x_i) - t_i)^2$
    $H \leftarrow H + \alpha h$
end
return H

AdaBoost: AdaBoost is a binary classification algorithm utilizing weak learners h producing binary predictions. Key components include step-size α and exponential loss $\ell(H)$, given by Equation (74):

$$l(H) = \sum_{i=1}^{n} e^{-y_i H(x_i)} \tag{74}$$

The gradient function r_i needed to find the optimal weak learner is computed using Equation (75).

$$r_i = \frac{\partial \mathcal{L}}{\partial H(x_i)} = -y_i e^{-y_i H(x_i)} \tag{75}$$

Introducing $w_i = \frac{1}{Z}e^{-y_i H(x_i)}$, for clarity and convenience, where $Z = \sum_{i=1}^{n} e^{-y_i H(x_i)}$, normalizing the weights. Each w_i signifies the role of (x_i, y_i) in the global loss. To find the next weak learner, we solve the optimization problem in Equation (76) with $h(x_i) \in \{+1, -1\}$ [42].

$$\begin{aligned} h(x_i) &= \text{argmin}_{h \in H} \sum_{i=1}^{n} r_i h(x_i) \left(\text{substitute in}: r_i = e^{-H(x_i)y_i}\right) \\ &= \text{argmin}_{h \in H} - \sum_{i=1}^{n} y_i e^{-H(x_i)y_i} h(x_i) \left(\text{substitute in}: w_i = \frac{1}{Z}e^{-H(x_i)y_i}\right) \\ &= \text{argmin}_{h \in H} - \sum_{i=1}^{n} w_i y_i h(x_i) \ (y_i h(x_i) \in \{+1, -1\} \text{with } h(x_i)y_i = 1 \iff h(x_i) = y_i) \\ &= \text{argmin}_{h \in H} \sum_{i:h(x_i) \neq y_i} w_i - \sum_{i:h(x_i) = y_i} w_i \left(\sum_{i:h(x_i) = y_i} w_i = 1 - \sum_{i:h(x_i) \neq y_i} w_i\right) \\ &= \text{argmin}_{h \in H} \sum_{i:h(x_i) \neq y_i} w_i \ (\text{This is the weighted classification error.}) \end{aligned} \qquad (76)$$

In (76), $\epsilon = \sum_{i:h(x_i) \neq y_i} w_i$, representing the weighted classification error. AdaBoost seeks a classifier minimizing this error without requiring high accuracy. The optimal step size, denoted as α, minimizes the loss l most effectively in the closed-form optimization problem (77) [41].

$$\begin{aligned} \alpha &= \text{argmin}_\alpha l(H + \alpha h) \\ &= \text{argmin}_\alpha \sum_{i=1}^{n} e^{-y_i[H(x_i) + \alpha h(x_i)]} \end{aligned} \qquad (77)$$

Taking the derivative with respect to α and setting it to zero, as shown by Equations (78)–(80):

$$\sum_{i=1}^{n} y_i h(x_i) e^{-y_i[H(x_i) + \alpha y_i h(x_i)]} = 0 \ (y_i h(x_i) \in \{+1 \text{ or } -1\}) \qquad (78)$$

$$-\sum_{i:h(x_i)y_i=1} e^{-(y_i H(x_i) + \alpha \underbrace{y_i h(x_i)}_{1})} + \sum_{i:h(x_i)y_i \neq 1} e^{-(y_i H(x_i) + \alpha \underbrace{y_i h(x_i)}_{-1})} = 0 \ \left(w_i = \frac{1}{Z}e^{-y_i H(x_i)}\right) \qquad (79)$$

$$-\sum_{i:h(x_i)y_i=1} w_i e^{-\alpha} + \sum_{i:h(x_i)y_i \neq 1} w_i e^{\alpha} = 0 \ \left(\epsilon = \sum_{i:h(x_i)y_i=-1} w_i\right) \qquad (80)$$

For further simplification, with ϵ representing the sum over misclassified examples, as given in Equation (81):

$$-(1-\epsilon)e^{-\alpha} + \epsilon e^{\alpha} = 0 \qquad (81)$$

Solving for α, as shown in Equation (82):

$$e^{2\alpha} = \frac{1-\epsilon}{\epsilon} \qquad (82)$$

$$\alpha = \frac{1}{2}\ln\frac{1-\epsilon}{\epsilon} \qquad (83)$$

The optimal step size α, derived from the closed-form solution in (83), facilitates rapid convergence in AdaBoost. After each step $H_{t+1} = H_t + \alpha h$, recalculating and renormalizing all weights is crucial for the algorithm's progression. The pseudo-code for AdaBoost Ensemble classifier is presented in Algorithm 3 [37,41].

Algorithm 3: Pseudo-code for AdaBoost

Input: l, α, $\{(x_i, y_i)\}$, A
H = 0
$\forall i \ : \ w_i = \frac{1}{n}$
for $t = 1: T$ **do**
$\quad h = A\,(w_1,\,x_1,\,y_1),\ldots\ldots\ldots,(w_n,\,x_n,\,y_n)$
$\quad \epsilon = \sum\limits_{i:h(x_i)\neq y_i} w_i$
$\quad$ **if** $\epsilon < \frac{1}{2}$ **then**
$\quad\quad \alpha = \frac{1}{2}\ln\frac{1-\epsilon}{\epsilon}$
$\quad\quad H_{t+1} = H_t + \alpha h$
$\quad\quad \forall i \ : \ w_i \leftarrow \frac{w_i e^{-\alpha h(x_i)y_i}}{2\epsilon(1-\epsilon)^{\frac{1}{2}}}$
$\quad$ **else**
$\quad\quad$ return (H_t)
$\quad$ **end**
$\quad$ return H
end

2.6. Assessment Metrics

The crucial next step in evaluating machine learning classifiers is the use of a separate test dataset that has not been part of the training process. Evaluation involves various parameters, with the confusion matrix being a widely adopted tool. This matrix forms the basis for determining assessment metrics, essential for validating model performance, whether it is a traditional or deep neural network classifier. In cancer prediction tasks, numerous metrics are employed to assess effectiveness, including error rate, accuracy, sensitivity, specificity, recall, precision, predictivity, F1 score, area under the curve (AUC), negative predictive value (NPR), false positive rate (FPR), and false negative rate (FNR), and Matthews correlation coefficient (MCC) [43]. These metrics quantify predictive capabilities and are vital for diverse prediction tasks. Multiple performance evaluation metrics rely on the confusion matrix, as visualized in Figure 9, for multiclass classification.

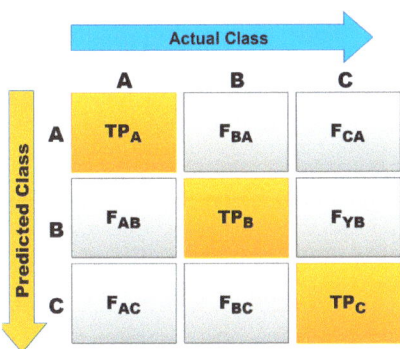

Figure 9. Confusion Matrix for Multiclass Classification Evaluation.

Accuracy (Acc): This metric is a fundamental indicator of a model's overall performance. It measures the ratio of accurately categorized cases (both cancer and non-cancer) to the overall cases in the test dataset. It may not be suitable when the dataset is imbalanced.

$$Accuracy\,(\%ACC) = \frac{(TP + TN)}{Total\ Samples} \times 100$$

Error Rate (ER): The reciprocal of accuracy equates to the error rate. It quantifies the proportion of instances that the model incorrectly classifies. A lower error rate suggests a more accurate model, and it is especially useful when you want to know how often the model makes incorrect predictions.

$$Error\ rate\ (ER) = 1 - Acc$$

$$\%ER = \frac{FP + FN}{Total\ Samples} \times 100 = 100 - (\%ACC)$$

Specificity (% Spe): True negative rate, commonly known as specificity, is a metric that evaluates a model's accuracy in correctly identifying true negative cases. This is crucial in minimizing false alarms.

$$Specificity(\%Sp) = True\ Negative\ Rate\ (\%TNR) = \frac{TN}{Total\ Negative} \times 100$$

Sensitivity (% Sen): This metric, also termed recall or the true positive rate (TPR), gauges the model's capability to accurately identify true positive values, which correspond to cases of cancer, among the total positive cases within a dataset [42].

$$Sensitivity(\%Sen) = Recall(\%Re) = True\ Positive\ Rate\ (\%TPR) = \frac{TP}{Total\ Positive} \times 100$$

Precision (% Pr): Precision, also recognized as positive predictive value (PP), denotes the ability to accurately predict positive values among the true positive predictions. A high precision score signifies that the model effectively reduces false positive errors.

$$Precision(\%Pr) = Positive\ Predictivity(\%PP) = \frac{TP}{True\ Prediction} \times 100$$

F1 Score (% F1): An equitable metric that amalgamates positive predictive value and recall forms the F1 score [44]. It is particularly valuable when you require a singular metric that contemplates both incorrect positive predictions and missed positive predictions.

$$F1\text{-}score\ (\%F1) = \frac{2 \times TP}{(2 \times TP + FP + FN)} \times 100 = \frac{2PP \times TPR}{(PP + TPR)} \times 100$$

Area Under the Curve (AUC): The AUC assesses the classifier's capacity to differentiate between affirmative and negative occurrences. It gauges the general efficacy of the model concerning receiver operating characteristic (ROC) graphs. A superior AUC score signifies enhanced differentiation capability.

Negative Predictive Value (% NPV): It measures the classifier's capability to accurately predict negative instances among all instances classified as negative. A high NPV suggests that the classifier is effective at identifying non-cancer cases when it predicts them as such, reducing the likelihood of unnecessary treatments.

$$Negative\ Predictive\ Value\ (\%NPV) = \frac{TN}{Total\ Negative} \times 100$$

False Positive Rate (%FPR): This quantifies how often the classifier falsely identifies a negative instance as positive. It provides insights into the model's propensity for false positive errors. In cancer detection, a high FPR can lead to unnecessary distress and treatments for individuals who do not have cancer.

$$False\ Positive\ Rate\ (\%FPR) = \frac{FP}{Total\ Negative} \times 100$$

False Negative Rate (%FNR): It determines the classifier's tendency to falsely identify a positive instance as negative. It reveals the model's performance regarding false negative errors, which is critical in cancer detection to avoid missing real cases. High FNR can lead to undiagnosed cancer cases and potentially delayed treatments.

$$False\ Negative\ Rate\ (\%FNR) = \frac{FN}{Total\ Positive} \times 100$$

Matthews Correlation Coefficient (MCC): The Matthews correlation coefficient (MCC) represents a pivotal metric utilized for evaluating the effectiveness of binary (two class) predictions, prominently beneficial when dealing with scenarios where classes are asymmetrically distributed in their volume and representation within the dataset. The formula to calculate MCC is:

$$\frac{[(TN*TP)-(FN*FP)]}{\sqrt{((True\ Prediction)*(False\ Predication)*(Total\ Positive)*(Total\ Negative))}}$$

where TN (True Negative) is accurately recognized negatives, TP (True Positive) is accurately recognized positives, FP (False Positive) is negatives incorrectly identified as positives, FN (False Negative) is positives incorrectly recognized as negatives, Total Positive is the Sum of TP and FN (all actual positives), Total Negative is the Sum of TN and FP (all actual negatives), True Prediction: Sum of TP and FP (correctly identified positives), False Predication: Sum of FN and TN (incorrectly identified negatives), Total Samples: Sum of TP, TN, FP, and FN (entire dataset).

3. Review Analysis

In this section, we present a thorough and extensive analysis of cancer detection utilizing conventional machine learning models applied to medical imaging datasets. Our study is focused exclusively on the detection of two specific types of cancer: colorectal and stomach cancer. For each of these cancer types, we have meticulously compiled a comprehensive review table that encompasses the relevant literature published during the period spanning 2017 to 2023. This table encompasses a range of crucial review parameters, including the year of publication, the datasets utilized, preprocessing methods, feature extraction techniques, machine learning classifiers employed, the number of images involved, the imaging modality, and various performance metrics. In total, our review encompasses 36 research articles that have harnessed medical imaging datasets to detect these specific types of cancer. Our primary emphasis lies in scrutinizing the utilization of traditional machine learning methodologies in the context of cancer detection using image datasets. We have conducted this analysis based on the meticulously assembled review tables. Subsequent subsections provide in-depth and comprehensive reviews for both colorectal and stomach cancer. Within our analysis, we delve into the intricate application of machine learning approaches for the intent of cancer prediction. Our overarching goal is to furnish valuable insights into the efficacy and constraints of conventional machine learning models when applied to the realm of cancer detection using medical imaging datasets. Through a meticulous examination and comparative analysis of results derived from various studies, our objective is to make a meaningful contribution to the evolution of cancer detection methodologies and to offer guidance for future research endeavors in this critical domain.

3.1. Analysis of Colorectal Cancer Prediction

Table 3 showcases 20 studies conducted from 2017 to 2023, focusing on machine learning-based colorectal cancer detection. These studies underscore the vital role of preprocessing methods in enhancing detection accuracy. The highest accuracy achieved is 100%, with the lowest at 76.00%. Various techniques, including cropping, stain normalization, contrast enhancement, smoothing, and filtering, were employed in conjunction with segmentation, feature extraction, and machine learning algorithms like SVM, MLP,

RF, and KNN. These approaches successfully detect colorectal cancer using modalities such as endocytoscopy, histopathological images, and clinical data. The studies employed varying quantities of images, patients, or slices, ranging from 54 to 100,000. The "KCRC-16" datasets are prominently featured in these analyses.

In a comparative analysis of colorectal cancer detection studies, (Talukder et al., 2022) [15] stood out with an impressive accuracy of 100%. Their approach included preprocessing steps like resizing, BGR2RGB conversion, and normalization. Deep learning models such as DenseNet169, MobileNet, VGG19, VGG16, and DenseNet201 were employed. Performance assessment was conducted using a combination of voting, XGB, EC, MLP, LGB, RF, SVM, LR, and hybrid techniques on a dataset comprising 2800 H&E images from the LC25000 dataset. Their best model achieved a flawless 100% accuracy. In contrast, (Ying et al., 2022) [46] achieved the lowest accuracy of 76.0% in colorectal cancer detection. Their approach involved manual region of interest (ROI) selection and various preprocessing techniques. They leveraged multiple features, including FOS, shape, GLCM, GLSZM, GLRLM, NGTDM, GLDM, LoG, and WT. Classification was carried out using the MLR technique on a dataset consisting of 276 CECT images from a private dataset. Their least-performing model achieved an accuracy of 76.00%. Moreover, their study exhibited a sensitivity of 65.00%, specificity of 80.00%, and precision of 54.00%, indicating relatively suboptimal performance in accurately identifying colorectal cancer cases.

(Khazaee Fadafen and Rezaee 2023) [47] conducted a remarkable colorectal cancer detection study by utilizing a substantial dataset (the highest number of images among all) comprising a total of 100,000 medical images sourced from the H&E NCT-CRC-HE-100K dataset. Their preprocessing methodology encompassed the conversion of RGB images to the HSV color space and the utilization of the lightness space. For classification, they harnessed the dResNet architecture in conjunction with DSVM, which resulted in an outstanding accuracy rate of 99.76%. (Jansen-winkeln et al., 2021) [48] conducted a study with a notably smallest dataset, comprising only 54 medical images. Their preprocessing approach included smoothing and normalization. For classification purposes, they employed a combination of MLP, SVM, and RF techniques. This approach yielded commendable results with an accuracy of 94.00%, sensitivity at 86.00%, and specificity reaching 95.00%. Notably, their analysis identified MLP as the most effective model in their study.

Within the corpus of 20 studies dedicated to the realm of colorectal cancer detection, researchers have deployed an array of diverse preprocessing strategies encompassing endocytoscopy, cropping, IPP, stain normalization, CEI, smoothing, normalization, filtering, THN, DRR, augmentation, UM-SN, resizing, BGR2RGB, normalization, scaling, labeling, RGBG, VTI, HOG, RGB to HSV, lightness space, edge preserving, and linear transformation. These sophisticated methodologies collectively served as the linchpin for optimizing machine learning-based colorectal cancer detection, ushering in a new era of precision and accuracy. However, it is captivating to note that, within the comprehensive assessment of 23 studies, a select quartet of research endeavors chose to forgo the utilization of any specific preprocessing techniques. This exceptional cluster includes the works of (Bora et al., 2021) [49], (Fan et al., 2021) [50], and (Lo et al., 2023) [51]. Astonishingly, these studies defied conventional wisdom by attaining commendable accuracies that spanned the spectrum from 94.00% to an impressive 99.44%. Such outcomes suggest that, in cases where the dataset is inherently pristine and impeccably aligned with the demands of the classification task, the impact of preprocessing techniques on the classifier's performance might indeed exhibit a marginal influence.

In the comprehensive analysis of the research studies under scrutiny, it is noteworthy that only the works of (Grosu et al., 2021) [52] and (Ying et al., 2022) [46] registered accuracy figures falling below the 90% threshold, specifically at 84.7% and 76%, respectively. This observation underscores the intriguing possibility that traditional machine learning models can indeed yield highly accurate cancer detection performance, provided they are meticulously optimized.

Table 3. Performance comparison of traditional ML-based colorectal cancer prediction methods.

Year	References	Pre-Processing	Features	Techniques	Dataset	Data Samples	Train Data	Test Data	Modality	Metrics (%)
2017	[53]	Endocytoscopy	Texture, nuclei	SVM	Private	5843	5643	200	ENI	Acc 94.1 Sen 89.4 Spe 98.9 Pre 98.8 NPV 90.1
2019	[54]	IPP	CSQ, Color histogram	WSVMCS	Private	180	108	72	H&E	Acc 96.0
2019	[55]	Cropping	Biophysical characteristic, WLD,	NB, **MLP**,	OMIS data	316	237	79	OMIS	Acc 92.6 Sen 96.3 Spe 88.9
2021	[56]	Filtering	HOS, FOS, GLCM, Gabor, WPT, LBP	**ANN**, RSVM,	KCRC-16	5000	4550	450	H&E	Acc 95.3
2021	[57]	IPP, Augmentation	VGG-16	**MLP**	KCRC-16	5000	4825	175	H&E	Acc 99.0 Sen 96.0 Spe 99.0 Pre 96.0 NPV 99.0 F1 96.0
2021	[50]	---	AlexNet	EC, SVM, AlexNet,	LC25000	10,000	4-fold cross validation		H&E	Acc 99.4
2021	[58]	THN, DRR	BmzP	NN	MALDI MSI	559	Leave-One-Out cross-validation		H&E	Acc 98.0 Sen 98.2 Spe 98.6
2021	[52]	Filtering	Filters, Texture, GLHS, Shape	RF	Private	287	169	77	CT	Acc 84.7 * Sen 82.0 Spe 85.0 AUC 91.0
2021	[49]	---	GFD, NSCT, Shape	**MLP** LSSVM,	Private	734	five-fold cross-validation		NBI, WLI	Acc 95.7 Sen 95.3 Spe 95.0 Pre 93.2 F1 90.5
2021	[48]	Normalization, smoothing	Spatial Information	**MLP**, SVM, RF	Private	54	Leave-One-Out cross-validation		HSI	Acc 94.0 Sen 86.0 Spe 95.0
2022	[59]	VTI	Haralick, VTF	RF	Private	63	cross-validation method		CT	Acc 92.2 Sen 88.4 Spe 96.0 AUC 96.2
2022	[60]	RGBG	GLCM	**ANN**, RF, KNN	KCRC-16	5000	4500	500	H&E	Acc 98.7 Sen 98.6 Spe 99.0 Pre 98.9
2022	[45]	Resize, BGR2RGB, Normalization,	Deep Features	EC, **Hybrid**, LR, LGB, MLP, RF, SVM, XGB, Voting	LC25000	2800	10-fold cross-validation		H&E	Acc 100.0
2022	[46]	ROI	FOS, GLCM, GLDM, GLRLM, GLSZM, LoG, NGTDM, Shape, WT	MLR	Private	276	194	82	CECT	Acc 76.0 Sen 65.0 Spe 80.0 Pre 54.0 NPV 86.0

Table 3. Cont.

Year	References	Pre-Processing	Features	Techniques	Dataset	Data Samples	Train Data	Test Data	Modality	Metrics (%)
2022	[61]	UM-SN	HIM, GLCM, Statistical	LDA, MLP, RF, SVM, **XGB**, LGB	LC25000	1000	900	100	H&E	Acc 99.3 Sen 99.5 Pre 99.5 F1 99.5
2022	[26]	---	Color Spaces, Haralick	ANN, DT, KNN, **QDA**, SVM	KCRC-16	5000	3504	1496	H&E	Acc 97.3 Sen 97.3 Spe 99.6 Pre 97.4
2023	[62]	Filtering, linear Transformation, normalization	Color characteristic, DBCM, SMOTE	CatBoost, DT, **GNB**, KNN, RF	NCT-CRCHE-7K	12,042	8429	3613	H&E	Acc 90.7 Sen 97.6 Spe 97.4 Pre 90.6 Rec 90.5 F1 90.5
2023	[51]	---	Clinical, FEViT	SEKNN	Private	1729	tenfold cross-validation		ENI	Acc 94.0 Sen 74.0 Spe 98.0 AUC 93.0
2023	[47]	Lightness space, RGB to HSV	dResNet	DSVM	KCRC-16	5000	4000	1000	H&E	Acc 98.8
					NCT-CRC-HE-100K	100,000	80,003	19,997	H&E	Acc 99.8
2023	[63]	HOG, RGBG, Resizing	Morphological	SVM	Private	540	420	120	ENI	Acc 97.5

* Not given in the paper, calculated from the result table, bold font signifies the best model in the 'Techniques' column. **Abbreviations:** BGR2RGB, Blue-Green-Red to Red-Green-Blue; BmzP, Binning of m/z Points; catBoost, Categorical Boosting; CECT, Contrast-Enhanced CT; CSQ, Color Space Quantization; DBCM, Differential Box Count Method; DSVM, Deep Support Vector Machine; dResNet, Dilated ResNet; DRR, Dynamic Range Reduction; DSVM, Deep Support Vector Machine; ENI, Endomicroscopy Images; FEViT, Feature Ensemble Vision Transformer; FOS, First-Order Statistics; GFD, Generic Fourier Descriptor; GNB, Gaussian Naive Bayes; GLDM, Gray-Level Dependence Matrix; GLHS, Gray Level Histogram Statistics; GLSZM, Gray Level Size Zone Matrix; GNB, Gaussian Naive Bayes; HOG, Histogram of Oriented Gradients; HOS, Higher-Order Statistic; HIM, Hu Invariants Moments; HSI, Hyperspectral Imaging; HSV, Hue-Saturation-Value; LBP, Local Binary Pattern; LDA, Linear Discriminant Analysis; LGB, Light Gradient Boosting; LoG, Laplacian of Gaussian; LSSVM, Least Square Support Vector Machine; MLR, Multivariate Logistic Regression; NGTDM, Neighboring Gray Tone Difference Matrix; NSCT, Non-Subsampled Contourlet Transform; OMIS, Optomagnetic Imaging Spectroscopy; QDA, Quadratic Discriminant Analysis; SEKNN, Subspace Ensemble K-Nearest Neighbor; THN, TopHat and Normalization; UMSN, Unsharp Masking and Stain Normalization; VTF, Vector Texture Features; VTI, Vector Texture Images; WLD, Wavelength Difference; WLI, White Light Imaging; WPT, Wavelet Packet Transform; WSVMCS, Wavelet Kernel SVM with Color Histogram; XGB, Extreme Gradient Boosting.

The analysis of colorectal cancer detection using traditional machine learning techniques reveals a notable disparity in model performance across various crucial metrics, showcasing substantial discrepancies between the models with the highest and lowest values as shown in Figure 10. The most proficient model achieved an extraordinary accuracy of 100.0%, whereas the least effective model achieved an accuracy of 76.0%, resulting in a substantial difference of 24.0%. When considering sensitivity, the top-performing model reached an impressive 99.5%, whereas the lowest-performing model registered a mere 65.0%, leading to a remarkable disparity of 34.5%. Similarly, concerning specificity, the superior model attained 99.6%, while the inferior model managed only 80.0%, resulting in a significant difference of 19.6%. In terms of precision, the best model demonstrated 99.5%, while the worst model exhibited a precision of only 54.0%, resulting in a substantial difference of 45.5%. When examining the F1-score, the model with the highest performance achieved 99.5%, whereas the least proficient model attained a score of 63.2%, yielding a notable difference of 36.3%. Lastly, in the case of the area under the curve (AUC), the top model achieved a score of 96.2%, while the bottom model scored 76.0%, marking a significant difference of 20.2%. These conspicuous differences underscore the pivotal role of choosing appropriate machine learning techniques and feature sets in the effectiveness of colorectal cancer detection. Effective cancer detection has far-reaching implications, influencing not only patient outcomes but also the operational efficiency of healthcare systems and the allocation of valuable medical resources.

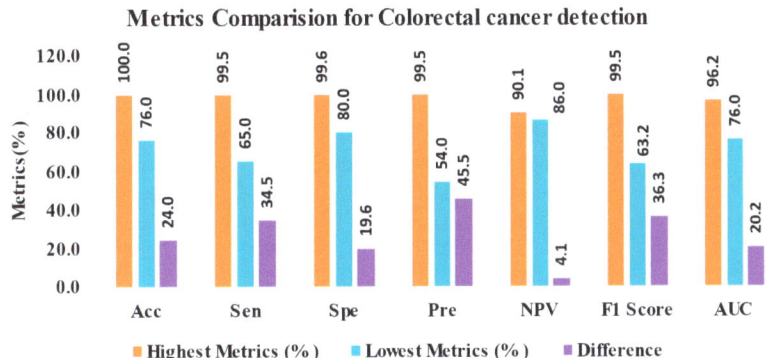

Figure 10. Metrics comparison for the prediction of colorectal cancer.

3.2. Analysis of Gastric Cancer Prediction

Table 4 meticulously encapsulates 16 distinct studies conducted within the temporal frame of 2018 to 2023, each ardently devoted to machine learning-based gastric cancer detection. These investigations collectively underscore the pivotal role of preprocessing in elevating the accuracy of stomach cancer detection models. Notably, the pinnacle of achievement in this realm reached a remarkable 100.0% accuracy, whereas the lowest point stood at 71.2%. This diverse spectrum of performance underscores the profound influence of preprocessing techniques, spanning resizing, filtering, cropping, and color enhancement. These preprocessing strategies, in harmony with segmentation, feature extraction, and the adept utilization of machine learning algorithms encompassing SVM, MLP, RF, and KNN, have collectively converged to engender a triumphant era of stomach cancer detection. This progress extends across diverse modalities such as endoscopy, CT, MRI, and histopathology images. The quantity of images, patients, or slices underpinning these studies spanned a substantial range, from 30 to a staggering 245,196. It is intriguing to note that the enigmatic "Private" dataset emerged as the most recurrently harnessed resource in this insightful analysis.

The research conducted by (Ayyaz et al., 2022) [64] achieved outstanding results in stomach cancer detection, with a remarkable accuracy of 99.80%. They employed various preprocessing techniques, including resizing, contrast enhancement, binarization, and filtering. However, the segmentation method used was not specified in the study. Feature extraction was carried out with deep learning models like VGG19 and AlexNet. For classification, they used multiple techniques such as DT, NB, KNN, SVM, and more. Among these, the cubic SVM model performed the best, achieving an accuracy of 99.80%. This model also had a high sensitivity, precision, F1-score, and an AUC of 100.0%. On the other hand, the study conducted by (Mirniaharikandehei et al., 2021) [65] achieved comparatively lower performance in stomach cancer detection, with an accuracy of 71.20%. Their preprocessing techniques involved filtering and ROI selection, and they utilized the HTS segmentation method. Feature extraction was done using radiomics features such as GLRLM, GLDM, and WT LoG. The classification was carried out using various machine learning models, including SVM, LR, RF, DT, and GBM. The worst-performing model in their analysis was GBM, with an accuracy of 71.20%. This model had lower sensitivity but a higher specificity, precision, and F1-score. (Hu et al., 2022) [66] conducted a stomach cancer detection study with a large dataset of 245,196 medical images. They used various preprocessing techniques, including ROI selection, cropping, filtering, rotation, and disruption. The study extracted features such as color histograms, LBP, and GLCM. For classification, they applied RF and LSVM classifiers, achieving an accuracy of 85.99%. RF was the best-performing model in their analysis. On the other hand, (Naser and Zeki 2021) [67] conducted a stomach cancer detection study with a smaller dataset of only 30 medical images. They applied DIFQ-based preprocessing techniques, and their study used FCM for classification and achieved an accuracy of 85.00%. Table 4 provides an overview of different machine learning-based techniques for stomach (gastric) cancer detection, encompassing 16 reviewed studies. Notably, three of these studies specifically, namely, (Korkmaz and Esmeray 2018) [68], (Nayyar et al., 2021) [69], and (Hu et al., 2022a) [70], opted not to employ any preprocessing techniques. Surprisingly, they achieved noteworthy accuracies of 87.77%, 99.8%, and 85.24%, respectively. This demonstrates the potential for effective stomach cancer detection even in the absence of preprocessing methods. However, it is essential to highlight that a significant portion of the studies examined in the table chose to implement various preprocessing techniques, including CEI, filtering, resizing, Fourier transform, cropping, ROI selection, rotation, disruption, binarization, augmentation, and RSA. These preprocessing steps underscore their pivotal role in enhancing the performance of machine learning models for stomach cancer detection.

Out of the 16 studies focused on gastric cancer detection, 50% of them (8 studies) achieved an accuracy rate of over 90%, indicating highly accurate results. However, the other 50% of the studies received less than 90% accuracy. This discrepancy in performance might be attributed to the utilization of private datasets in these studies. Private datasets may not undergo the same level of processing or standardization as publicly available datasets, potentially leading to variations in data quality and affecting the performance of the machine learning models.

Table 4. Performance comparison of traditional ML-based gastric cancer prediction methods.

Year	References	Preprocessing	Features	Techniques	Dataset	Data Samples	Train Data	Test Data	Modality	Metrics (%)
2018	[71]	Fourier transform	BRISK, SURF, MSER	**DT**, DA	Private	180	90	90	H&E	Acc 86.7
2018	[72]	Resizing	LBP, HOG	**ANN**, RF	Private	180	90	90	H&E	Acc 100.0
2018	[68]	---	SURF, DFT	**NB**	Private	180	90	90	H&E	Acc 87.8
					Private	720	360	360	H&E	Acc 90.3
2018	[73]	CEI, filtering, resizing	GLCM	**SVM**	Private	207	126	81	NBI	Acc 96.3 Sen 96.7 Spe 95.0 Pre 98.3
2019	[74]	Resizing, cropping	GLCM, Shape, FOF, GLSZM	**SVM**	Private	490	326	164	CT	Acc 71.3 Sen 72.6 Spe 68.1 Pre 82.0 NPV 50.0
2021	[67]	DIFQ	SMI	**FCM**, KMC	Private	30	---	---	MRI	Acc 85.0
2021	[75]	Resizing	Extract HOG	RF, **MLP**	Private	180	90	90	H&E	Acc 98.1
2021	[76]	Resizing	TSS	BP, **BPSVM**, SVM	Private	78	---	---	MRI	Acc 94.6
2021	[69]	---	Deep Features	**CSVM**, Bagged Trees, KNNs, SVMs	Private	4000	2800	1200	WCE	Acc 99.8 Sen 99.0 Pre 99.3 F1 99.1 AUC 100

Table 4. Cont.

Year	References	Preprocessing	Features	Techniques	Dataset	Data Samples	Train Data	Test Data	Modality	Metrics(%)
2021	[65]	Filtering, ROI	LoG, WT, GLDM, GLRLM	**GBM**, DT, RF, LR, SVM.	Private	159	Leave-One-Out cross-validation		CT	Acc 71.2 Sen 43.1 Spe 87.1 Pre 65.8
2022	[77]	Augmentation, resizing, filtering	InceptionNet, VGGNet	**SVM**, RF, KNN.	HKD	10,662 (47,398 Augmneted)	37,788	9610	Endoscopy	Acc 98.0 Sen 100 Pre 100 F1 100 MCC 97.8
2022	[70]	---	GLCM, LBP, HOG, histogram, luminance, Color histogram	NSVM, LSVM, LR, NB, RF, ANN, **KNN**	GasHisSDB	245196	196,157	49,039	H&E	Acc 85.2 Sen 84.9 # Pre 84.6 # Spe 84.9 # F1 84.8 #
2022	[64]	Binarization, CEI, filtering, resizing	VGG19 Alexnet	Bagged Tree, Coarse Tree, **CSVM**, CKNN, DT, Fine Tree, KNN, NB	Private	2590	10-fold cross-validation		EUS	Acc 99.8 Sen 99.8 Pre 99.8 F1 99.8 AUC 100
2022	[66]	Cropping, disruption, filtering, ROI, Rotation	Color histogram, GLCM, LBP	LSVM, **RF**	GasHisSDB	245,196	196,157	49,039	H&E	Acc 85.9 Sen 86.2 # Spe 86.2 # Pre 85.7 # F1 85.9 #
2023	[78]	Augmentation, CEI	MobileNet-V2	Bayesian, CSVM, LSVM, QSVM, **Softmax**	KV2D	4854	10-fold cross-validation		Endoscopy	Acc 96.4 Pre 97.6 Sen 93.0 F1 95.2
2023	[79]	RSA	RSF	PLS-DA, LOO, **SVM**	Private	450	Leave-One-Out cross validation		H&E	Acc 94.8 Sen 91.0 Spe 100 AUC 95.8

Calculated by averaging the normal and abnormal class, Bold Font techniques represent the best model.
Abbreviations: BPSVM, Binary Robust Invariant Scalable Keypoints; BRISK, Binary Robust Invariant Scalable Keypoints; CKNN, Cosine K-Nearest Neighbor; CSVM, Cubic SVM; DA, Discriminant Analysis; DIFQ, Dividing an image into four quarters; FCM, Fuzzy C-Means; GGF, Global Graph Features; HOG, Histogram of Oriented Gradients; HTSS, Hybrid Tumor Segmentation; KMC, K-Means Clustering; LOO, Leave-One-Out; LSVM, Linear Support Vector Machine; MSER, Maximally Stable Extremal Regions; NSVM, Non-Linear Support Vector Machine; OAT, Otsu Adaptive Thresholding; PLS-DA, Partial Least-Squares Discriminant Analysis; QSVM, Quadratic SVM; RSA, Raman Spectral Analysis; RSF, Raman Spectral Feature; SM, Seven Moments Invariants; SMI, Seven Moments Invariants; SURF, Speeded Up Robust Features; TSS, Tumor Scattered Signal.

The analysis of gastric cancer detection reveals substantial variations in model performance across key metrics, with significant differences observed between the highest and lowest values as shown in Figure 11. Accuracy (Acc) showcased a noteworthy contrast, with the best-performing model achieving a flawless 100.00% and the least effective model scoring 71.20%. This substantial 28.80% difference underscores the pivotal role of model selection in achieving accurate gastric cancer detection. Sensitivity (Sen) displayed a considerable gap, with the top model achieving a perfect 100.00%, while the lowest model only reached 43.10%. This marked difference of 56.90% emphasizes the necessity of sensitive detection techniques in identifying gastric cancer. Similarly, specificity (Spe) followed suit, with the highest model reaching 100.00% and the lowest model achieving 68.10%. The substantial 31.90% difference highlights the importance of correctly identifying non-cancer cases in diagnostic accuracy. Precision (Pre) also exhibited a significant disparity, with the best model achieving 100.00%, and the least effective model achieving 65.80%. The difference of 34.20% underscores the significance of precise identification of gastric cancer cases. It is noteworthy that the negative predictive value (NPV) remained constant at 50.00% for both the highest and lowest models, signifying that neither model excelled in ruling out non-cancer cases. However, since NPV is only used in a single article, its impact on the overall analysis may be limited.

Additionally, the F1-score showed a substantial difference, with the top model achieving a perfect 100.00%, while the lowest model reached 84.80%. The 15.20% difference emphasizes the balance between precision and sensitivity in gastric cancer detection. Lastly, in terms of the area under the curve (AUC), the best model achieved a near-perfect 100.00%, while the lowest model attained a still impressive 95.80%. The modest 4.20% difference indicates that both models performed well in distinguishing between gastric cancer and non-cancer cases. It is also worth noting that the area under the curve (AUC) metric was utilized in only three articles, and the differences in AUC were relatively modest. Therefore, the impact of AUC on the overall analysis may be less generalized. These findings underscore the critical role of model choice and feature selection in the effective detection of gastric cancer. Accurate and sensitive diagnostic tools are crucial for improving patient outcomes and optimizing healthcare resources. While NPV and AUC may have a limited impact in this context due to their restricted usage, the other metrics highlight the significance of selecting appropriate models for reliable gastric cancer detection.

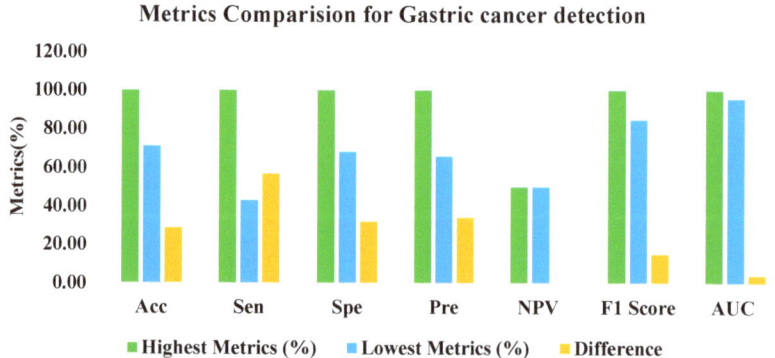

Figure 11. Metrics comparison for the prediction of gastric cancer.

4. Proposed Methodology

In this section, we delineate our proposed methodology for the detection of colorectal and gastric cancer through the application of traditional machine learning techniques. These approaches have been meticulously crafted based on the discerning insights and observations gleaned from the comprehensive review tables. Our primary goal is to introduce a Proposed (optimized) approach, accompanied by the most suitable parameters, in order to attain the most superior results. Our endeavor is to provide an efficient, effective, automated, and highly precise technique for the detection of colorectal and gastric cancer.

4.1. Detection of Colorectal Cancer

Figure 12 is a comprehensive visualization of the architectural framework that underpins our proposed model for the detection of colorectal cancer. This blueprint draws its inspiration from the wealth of insights extracted from Table 3, which provides a foundational understanding of the methodologies that have proven effective in this domain. While we have opted to use the H&E modality as an illustrative example, it is imperative to recognize that our model can seamlessly accommodate other modalities. This flexibility is a testament to the adaptability and robustness of our approach, as it allows for the incorporation of diverse data sources to enrich the depth and scope of our analysis. At the crux of our methodology lies the preprocessing phase, an instrumental step that sets the stage for the rigorous examination of input images. Within this phase, we meticulously execute four pivotal steps: Image Enhancement, Pixel Enhancement, RGB-to-Gray Conversion, and Image Segmentation. These sequential operations are not arbitrary but have been thoughtfully selected and implemented to systematically prepare the input images. Their collective objective is to optimize the images, ensuring they are in a suitable form for efficient feature extraction and subsequent in-depth analysis. The realm of feature engineering is where our approach truly shines. Here, we introduce an innovative and nuanced strategy. Instead of relying solely on one type of feature, we merge two distinct categories: deep learning-based features, which are often referred to as "deep features", and a varied assortment of other features. This assortment includes Discrete Wavelet Transform (DWT), Gray Level Co-occurrence Matrix (GLCM), Local Binary Pattern (LBP), Texture, and Gray Level Size Zone Matrix (GLSZM). The fusion of these diverse feature sets is not a random choice but a deliberate effort to enhance the robustness and comprehensiveness of our analysis. This fusion is designed to ensure that our model captures both the intricate, high-level representations obtained through deep learning and handcrafted features meticulously tailored to highlight specific aspects of tumor characteristics. By incorporating these different types of features, our model becomes versatile, capable of effectively identifying patterns and characteristics in the data that may not be discernible when using only one type of feature. By executing this innovative approach, we aim to enhance the model's ability to interpret and understand the complex information contained within medical images. This, in turn, contributes to the accuracy and efficiency of colorectal cancer detection. Furthermore, it enables our model to adapt and excel in different scenarios and datasets, making it a powerful tool for healthcare professionals and researchers working in the field of cancer detection.

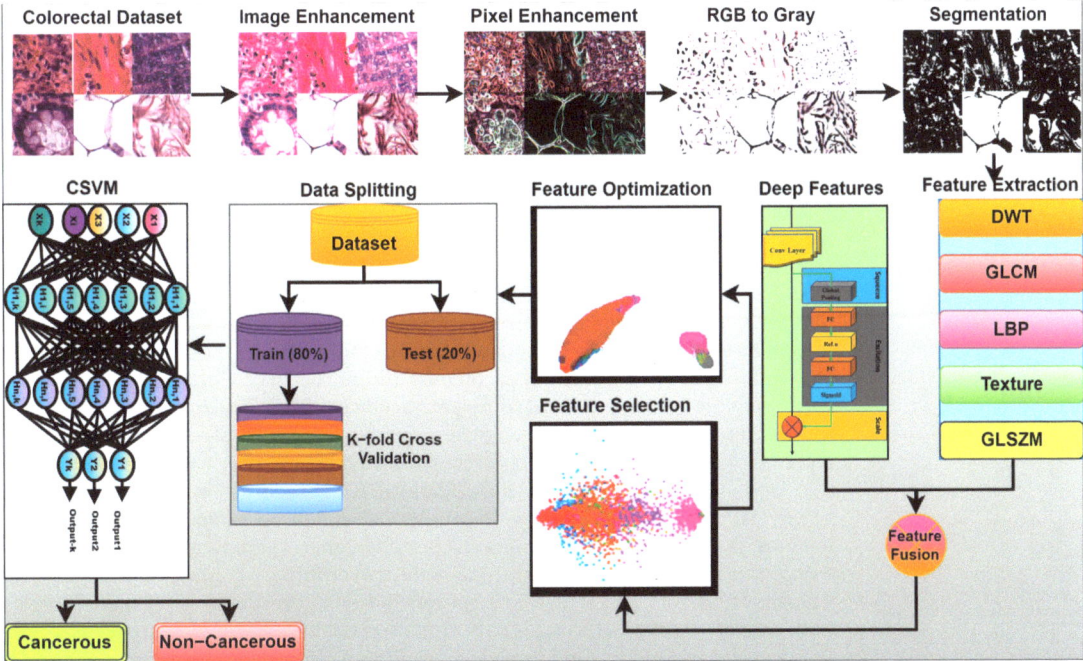

Figure 12. Proposed architectural flow diagram for the detection of colorectal cancer using traditional machine learning models from imaging database.

The combination of these diverse features enhances the model's capability to encompass both intricate, high-level representations acquired through deep learning and meticulously tailored handcrafted features that accentuate distinct tumor characteristics. Moving forward in the workflow, we encounter the crucial stages of feature selection and optimization. This pivotal process serves a dual role: it reduces feature redundancy while enhancing the overall model performance by focusing on the most distinctive attributes. Our model evaluation process is underpinned by a rigorous data-partitioning strategy, effectively splitting the dataset into training and testing subsets. The training dataset undergoes additional scrutiny through a k-fold cross-validation approach, fortifying the model's training and facilitating a robust performance assessment. This approach not only guards against overfitting but also assesses the model's adaptability to various data scenarios. The test dataset becomes the arena for predicting colorectal cancer, with the cubic support vector machine (SVM) taking the lead in this classification task. The SVM is a formidable presence among traditional machine learning classifiers, known for its prowess in handling high-dimensional data and executing binary classification tasks, making it ideally suited for the intricacies of cancer detection. In summary, our proposed model architecture harmoniously integrates advanced image preprocessing techniques, innovative feature-engineering methodologies, and the proven machinery of a traditional machine learning classifier. This synthesis yields an efficient and accurate framework for colorectal cancer detection. Pending further validation and testing on diverse datasets, this approach has the potential to revolutionize early cancer detection and diagnosis, potentially leading to improved patient outcomes and a transformation in healthcare effectiveness.

4.2. Detection of Gastric Cancer

The system architecture flow diagram, as depicted in Figure 13, outlines our comprehensive and adaptable approach to stomach cancer (Gastric) detection employing traditional machine learning classifiers. Informed by the top-performing models scrutinized in Table 4, our proposed architecture is intentionally crafted to accommodate both endoscopy video datasets, which have gained prominence in recent years, and static image datasets. Initiating with endoscopy video datasets as the primary data source, our architecture seamlessly extends its capabilities to image datasets by extracting individual frames from the video sequences. Subsequently, these extracted frames undergo preprocessing, which encompasses various techniques such as noise reduction, RGB-to-grayscale conversion, or other pertinent methods contingent on the specific application and dataset attributes. Acknowledging the potential constraint of limited video datasets, we introduce data augmentation techniques as part of our solution. This augmentation process generates an ample supply of augmented image datasets, enabling the model to undergo training on a more diverse and representative set of samples. This augmentation strategy empowers the model to generalize better, ultimately leading to enhanced performance outcomes. Moving into the feature extraction phase, we advocate the simultaneous use of deep features and texture-based features. Deep features are sourced from state-of-the-art deep learning models, while texture-based features encompass attributes like GLCM, GLRLM, and GLSZM, harnessed through conventional feature extraction methods. This fusion of diverse feature types ensures that the model possesses the capability to encapsulate both abstract high-level representations and the specific characteristics embedded in the stomach cancer data.

Upon the amalgamation of these features, the subsequent step in our approach involves feature optimization. Here, we employ well-suited algorithms to meticulously select the most pertinent attributes among the fused features. This optimization process serves a dual function: firstly, it mitigates the peril of overfitting, a common pitfall in machine learning endeavors, and secondly, it bolsters the overall efficiency of the model. The carefully curated selection of features enhances the model's capacity to discriminate between different classes, resulting in improved classification accuracy. Following the optimization phase, the dataset undergoes a deliberate partitioning into two distinct subsets: the training set and the testing set. This partitioning is a strategic maneuver that ensures the robust training and rigorous evaluation of traditional machine learning classifiers. The distribution of the dataset is thoughtfully orchestrated to prevent any data leakage and to create a reliable foundation for our model's assessment. Depending on the specific nature of the classification task and the unique requirements of the application, we employ a range of classifiers known for their effectiveness in various scenarios. These classifiers include but are not limited to support vector machines (SVM), Random Forest (RF), logistic regression (LR), backpropagation neural networks (BPNN), and artificial neural networks (ANN). Each of these classifiers is chosen judiciously to cater to the specific characteristics of the dataset and the intricacies of the task at hand. These classifiers excel in categorizing stomach cancer into distinct types, thereby providing valuable insights essential for accurate diagnosis and tailored treatment. A standout feature of our proposed system architecture is its inherent adaptability. This architectural flexibility empowers the system to seamlessly accommodate both image and video datasets, thereby rendering it versatile and suitable for a wide spectrum of applications. By harnessing the capabilities of traditional machine learning methods and integrating the novel approaches of feature fusion and optimization, our system architecture exhibits substantial potential for delivering heightened efficiency and heightened accuracy in the realm of stomach cancer detection. Nonetheless, it is imperative to emphasize the essentiality of conducting further validation and in-depth evaluation of our system's performance.

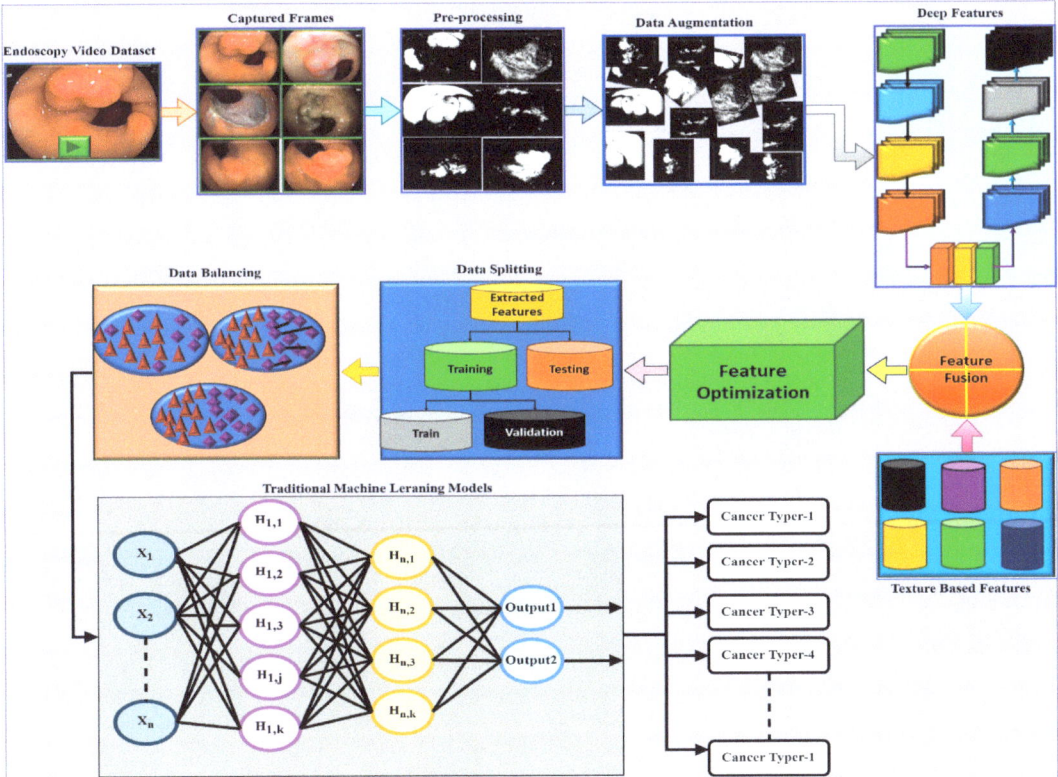

Figure 13. Proposed architectural flow diagram for the detection of stomach cancer using traditional machine learning models from imaging dataset.

4.3. Key Observations

The comprehensive assessment of colorectal and gastric cancer detection techniques using traditional machine learning methods and medical image datasets has revealed several key insights:

Dataset Diversity: Evaluation includes colorectal and gastric cancer datasets, ranging from 30 to 100,000 images. The varied dataset sizes showcase machine learning classifier effectiveness with appropriate tuning.

Exceptional Model Performances: Models achieve 100% accuracy for both colorectal and gastric cancer, with perfect scores in key metrics like sensitivity, specificity, precision, and F1-score, showcasing the potential of traditional ML classifiers with optimal parameters.

Preprocessing Techniques: Researchers employ various preprocessing techniques, including image filtering, denoising, wavelet transforms, RGB-to-gray conversion, normalization, cropping (ROI), sampling, and binarization, to optimize model performance and minimize biases during data manipulation.

Literature Review Significance: This analysis spans 36 literature sources related to colorectal and gastric cancer, underscoring the significant interest in cancer detection through traditional ML classifiers. Researchers have explored an extensive range of cancer types, diverse evaluation metrics, and datasets, collectively advancing the field.

Dominant Traditional ML Techniques: SVM is a commonly used traditional ML classifier in cancer detection tasks, emphasizing the need to understand each classifier's strengths and limitations for optimal selection.

Insightful Dataset and Feature Analysis: Reviewed studies predominantly utilized benchmark medical image datasets, with researchers employing feature extraction techniques like GLCM for informative feature extraction in cancer detection.

Prudent Model Architecture Design: Optimal results in cancer detection require thoughtful and optimized model architectures, which can enhance accuracy, generalizability, and interpretability, addressing challenges in medical image analysis.

4.4. Key Challenges and Future Scope

Traditional ML classifiers have shown remarkable potential in cancer detection. However, several challenges and the future scope in their application have been identified:

Variability in Accuracy: Traditional ML classifiers exhibit variable accuracy rates across cancer types, ranging from 76% to 100%. Overcoming these variations poses a challenge, underscoring the need for enhanced models. Future research should prioritize refining models for consistent and accurate performance across diverse cancer types.

Metric Disparities: Metric variations, especially in sensitivity (43.1% to 100%) for gastric cancer, suggest potential data imbalance challenges. Addressing these issues is crucial for accurate model assessments. Future research should focus on developing strategies to handle imbalanced data and improve model robustness.

Preprocessing Challenges: Balancing raw and preprocessed data is crucial to ensure input data quality and reliability, contributing to robust cancer detection model performance. Future research should explore advanced preprocessing techniques and optimization methods to further enhance model robustness.

Limited use of evaluation metrics: Limited use of metrics like NPV, AUC, and MCC in the reviewed literature highlights the challenge of comprehensive model assessment. Addressing this limitation and exploring a broader range of metrics is crucial for future research to enhance understanding and effectiveness in cancer detection tasks.

Generalizing to novel cancer types: The literature primarily focuses on colorectal and gastric cancers, posing a challenge for extending traditional ML classifiers to less-explored cancer types. Future research should aim to develop versatile ML models with robust feature extraction techniques to adapt to diverse cancer types and domains.

Addressing overfitting and model selection: The diversity in ML classifiers poses challenges in model selection for specific cancers, emphasizing the need for careful evaluation

5. Conclusions

In this manuscript, a thorough review and analysis of colorectal and gastric cancer detection using traditional machine learning techniques are presented. We have meticulously scrutinized 36 research papers published between 2017 and 2023, specifically focusing on the domain of medical imaging datasets for detecting these types of cancers. Mathematical formulations elucidating frequently employed preprocessing techniques, feature extraction methods, traditional machine learning classifiers, and assessment metrics are provided. These formulations offer valuable guidance to researchers when selecting the most suitable techniques for their cancer detection studies. To conduct this analysis, a range of criteria such as publication year, preprocessing methods, dataset particulars, image quantities, modality, techniques, best models, and metrics (%) were considered. An extensive array of metrics was employed to evaluate model performance comprehensively. Notably, the study delves into the highest and lowest metric values and their disparities, highlighting opportunities for enhancement. Remarkably, we found that the highest achievable value for all metrics reached an astonishing 100%, with gastric cancer detection registering the lowest sensitivity at 43.10%. This underscores the potential of traditional ML classifiers, while indicating areas for further refinement. Drawing from these insights, we present a proposed (optimized) methodology for both colorectal and gastric cancer detection, aiding in the selection of an optimized approach for future cancer detection research. The manuscript concludes by delineating key findings and challenges that offer valuable directions for future research endeavors.

In our future research endeavors, we plan to implement the proposed optimized methodology for the detection of colorectal and gastric cancer within the specified experimental framework. This proactive approach aligns with our commitment to enhancing the effectiveness of cancer detection methodologies. Furthermore, we will conscientiously incorporate and address the challenges and limitations identified in this study, ensuring a comprehensive and iterative improvement in our investigative efforts.

Author Contributions: Original Draft Preparation: H.M.R.; Review and Editing: H.M.R.; Visualization: H.M.R.; Supervision: J.Y.; Project Administration: J.Y.; Funding Acquisition: J.Y. All authors have read and agreed to the published version of the manuscript.

Funding: This work was supported by the National Research Foundation of Korea (NRF) Grant funded by the Korea government (MSIT) (NRF-2021R1F1A1063640).

Data Availability Statement: Data sharing is not applicable to this article as no datasets were generated or analyzed during the current study.

Conflicts of Interest: The authors declare no conflict of interest.

References

1. Faguet, G.B. A brief history of cancer: Age-old milestones underlying our current knowledge database. *Int. J. Cancer* **2014**, *136*, 2022–2036. [CrossRef] [PubMed]
2. Afrash, M.R.; Shafiee, M.; Kazemi-Arpanahi, H. Establishing machine learning models to predict the early risk of gastric cancer based on lifestyle factors. *BMC Gastroenterol.* **2023**, *23*, 6. [CrossRef] [PubMed]
3. Kumar, Y.; Gupta, S.; Singla, R.; Hu, Y.-C. A systematic review of artificial intelligence techniques in cancer prediction and diagnosis. *Arch. Comput. Methods Eng.* **2021**, *29*, 2043–2070. [CrossRef] [PubMed]
4. Nguon, L.S.; Seo, K.; Lim, J.-H.; Song, T.-J.; Cho, S.-H.; Park, J.-S.; Park, S. Deep learning-based differentiation between mucinous cystic neoplasm and serous cystic neoplasm in the pancreas using endoscopic ultrasonography. *Diagnostics* **2021**, *11*, 1052. [CrossRef] [PubMed]
5. Kim, S.H.; Hong, S.J. Current status of image-enhanced endoscopy for early identification of esophageal neoplasms. *Clin. Endosc.* **2021**, *54*, 464–476. [CrossRef] [PubMed]
6. NCI. What Is Cancer?—NCI. National Cancer Institute. Available online: https://www.cancer.gov/about-cancer/understanding/what-is-cancer (accessed on 9 June 2023).

7. Zhi, J.; Sun, J.; Wang, Z.; Ding, W. Support vector machine classifier for prediction of the metastasis of colorectal cancer. *Int. J. Mol. Med.* **2018**, *41*, 1419–1426. [CrossRef] [PubMed]
8. Zhou, H.; Dong, D.; Chen, B.; Fang, M.; Cheng, Y.; Gan, Y.; Zhang, R.; Zhang, L.; Zang, Y.; Liu, Z.; et al. Diagnosis of Distant Metastasis of Lung Cancer: Based on Clinical and Radiomic Features. *Transl. Oncol.* **2017**, *11*, 31–36. [CrossRef] [PubMed]
9. Levine, A.B.; Schlosser, C.; Grewal, J.; Coope, R.; Jones, S.J.; Yip, S. Rise of the Machines: Advances in Deep Learning for Cancer Diagnosis. *Trends Cancer* **2019**, *5*, 157–169. [CrossRef] [PubMed]
10. Huang, S.; Yang, J.; Fong, S.; Zhao, Q. Artificial intelligence in cancer diagnosis and prognosis: Opportunities and challenges. *Cancer Lett.* **2019**, *471*, 61–71. [CrossRef]
11. Saba, T. Recent advancement in cancer detection using machine learning: Systematic survey of decades, comparisons and challenges. *J. Infect. Public Health* **2020**, *13*, 1274–1289. [CrossRef]
12. Shah, B.; Alsadoon, A.; Prasad, P.; Al-Naymat, G.; Beg, A. DPV: A taxonomy for utilizing deep learning as a prediction technique for various types of cancers detection. *Multimed. Tools Appl.* **2021**, *80*, 21339–21361. [CrossRef]
13. Majumder, A.; Sen, D. Artificial intelligence in cancer diagnostics and therapy: Current perspectives. *Indian J. Cancer* **2021**, *58*, 481–492. [CrossRef] [PubMed]
14. Bin Tufail, A.; Ma, Y.-K.; Kaabar, M.K.A.; Martínez, F.; Junejo, A.R.; Ullah, I.; Khan, R. Deep Learning in Cancer Diagnosis and Prognosis Prediction: A Minireview on Challenges, Recent Trends, and Future Directions. *Comput. Math. Methods Med.* **2021**, *2021*, 9025470. [CrossRef] [PubMed]
15. Kumar, G.; Alqahtani, H. Deep Learning-Based Cancer Detection-Recent Developments, Trend and Challenges. *Comput. Model. Eng. Sci.* **2022**, *130*, 1271–1307. [CrossRef]
16. Painuli, D.; Bhardwaj, S.; Köse, U. Recent advancement in cancer diagnosis using machine learning and deep learning techniques: A comprehensive review. *Comput. Biol. Med.* **2022**, *146*, 105580. [CrossRef] [PubMed]
17. Rai, H.M. Cancer detection and segmentation using machine learning and deep learning techniques: A review. *Multimed. Tools Appl.* **2023**, 1–35. [CrossRef]
18. Maurya, S.; Tiwari, S.; Mothukuri, M.C.; Tangeda, C.M.; Nandigam, R.N.S.; Addagiri, D.C. A review on recent developments in cancer detection using Machine Learning and Deep Learning models. *Biomed. Signal Process. Control.* **2023**, *80*, 104398. [CrossRef]
19. Mokoatle, M.; Marivate, V.; Mapiye, D.; Bornman, R.; Hayes, V.M. A review and comparative study of cancer detection using machine learning: SBERT and SimCSE application. *BMC Bioinform.* **2023**, *24*, 112. [CrossRef]
20. Rai, H.M.; Yoo, J. A comprehensive analysis of recent advancements in cancer detection using machine learning and deep learning models for improved diagnostics. *J. Cancer Res. Clin. Oncol.* **2023**, *149*, 14365–14408. [CrossRef]
21. Ullah, A.; Chen, W.; Khan, M.A. A new variational approach for restoring images with multiplicative noise. *Comput. Math. Appl.* **2016**, *71*, 2034–2050. [CrossRef]
22. Azmi, K.Z.M.; Ghani, A.S.A.; Yusof, Z.M.; Ibrahim, Z. Natural-based underwater image color enhancement through fusion of swarm-intelligence algorithm. *Appl. Soft Comput.* **2019**, *85*, 105810. [CrossRef]
23. Alruwaili, M.; Gupta, L. A statistical adaptive algorithm for dust image enhancement and restoration. In Proceedings of the 2015 IEEE International Conference on Electro/Information Technology (EIT), Dekalb, IL, USA, 21–23 May 2015; IEEE: Piscataway, NJ, USA, 2015; pp. 286–289.
24. Cai, J.-H.; He, Y.; Zhong, X.-L.; Lei, H.; Wang, F.; Luo, G.-H.; Zhao, H.; Liu, J.-C. Magnetic Resonance Texture Analysis in Alzheimer's disease. *Acad. Radiol.* **2020**, *27*, 1774–1783. [CrossRef]
25. Chandrasekhara, S.P.R.; Kabadi, M.G.; Srivinay, S. Wearable IoT based diagnosis of prostate cancer using GLCM-multiclass SVM and SIFT-multiclass SVM feature extraction strategies. *Int. J. Pervasive Comput. Commun.* **2021**, *ahead-of-print*. [CrossRef]
26. Alqudah, A.M.; Alqudah, A. Improving machine learning recognition of colorectal cancer using 3D GLCM applied to different color spaces. *Multimed. Tools Appl.* **2022**, *81*, 10839–10860. [CrossRef]
27. Vallabhaneni, R.B.; Rajesh, V. Brain tumour detection using mean shift clustering and GLCM features with edge adaptive total variation denoising technique. *Alex. Eng. J.* **2018**, *57*, 2387–2392. [CrossRef]
28. Rego, C.H.Q.; França-Silva, F.; Gomes-Junior, F.G.; de Moraes, M.H.D.; de Medeiros, A.D.; da Silva, C.B. Using Multispectral Imaging for Detecting Seed-Borne Fungi in Cowpea. *Agriculture* **2020**, *10*, 361. [CrossRef]
29. Cover, T.; Hart, P. Nearest neighbor pattern classification. *IEEE Trans. Inf. Theory* **1967**, *13*, 21–27. [CrossRef]
30. Callen, J.L.; Segal, D. An Analytical and Empirical Measure of the Degree of Conditional Conservatism. *J. Account. Audit. Financ.* **2013**, *28*, 215–242. [CrossRef]
31. Weinberger, K. Lecture 2: K-Nearest Neighbors. Available online: https://www.cs.cornell.edu/courses/cs4780/2017sp/lectures/lecturenote02_kNN.html (accessed on 12 November 2023).
32. Weinberger, K. Lecture 3: The Perceptron. Available online: https://www.cs.cornell.edu/courses/cs4780/2017sp/lectures/lecturenote03.html (accessed on 12 November 2023).
33. Watt, J.; Borhani, R.; Katsaggelos, A.K. *Machine Learning Refined*; Cambridge University Press (CUP): Cambridge, UK, 2020; ISBN 9781107123526.
34. Watt, R.B.J. 13.1 Multi-Layer Perceptrons (MLPs). Available online: https://kenndanielso.github.io/mlrefined/blog_posts/13_Multilayer_perceptrons/13_1_Multi_layer_perceptrons.html (accessed on 12 November 2023).
35. Weinberger, K. Lecture 9: SVM. Available online: https://www.cs.cornell.edu/courses/cs4780/2017sp/lectures/lecturenote09.html (accessed on 13 November 2023).

36. Balas, V.E.; Mastorakis, N.E.; Popescu, M.-C.; Balas, V.E. Multilayer Perceptron and Neural Networks. 2009. Available online: https://www.researchgate.net/publication/228340819 (accessed on 18 September 2023).
37. Murphy, K.P. *Machine Learning: A Probabilistic Perspective*; MIT Press: Cambridge, MA, USA, 2012.
38. Islam, U.; Al-Atawi, A.; Alwageed, H.S.; Ahsan, M.; Awwad, F.A.; Abonazel, M.R. Real-Time Detection Schemes for Memory DoS (M-DoS) Attacks on Cloud Computing Applications. *IEEE Access* **2023**, *11*, 74641–74656. [CrossRef]
39. Houshmand, M.; Hosseini-Khayat, S.; Wilde, M.M. Minimal-Memory, Noncatastrophic, Polynomial-Depth Quantum Convolutional Encoders. *IEEE Trans. Inf. Theory* **2012**, *59*, 1198–1210. [CrossRef]
40. Bagging. Available online: https://www.cs.cornell.edu/courses/cs4780/2017sp/lectures/lecturenote18.html (accessed on 13 November 2023).
41. Boosting. Available online: https://www.cs.cornell.edu/courses/cs4780/2017sp/lectures/lecturenote19.html (accessed on 13 November 2023).
42. Dewangan, S.; Rao, R.S.; Mishra, A.; Gupta, M. Code Smell Detection Using Ensemble Machine Learning Algorithms. *Appl. Sci.* **2022**, *12*, 10321. [CrossRef]
43. Tharwat, A. Classification assessment methods. *Appl. Comput. Inform.* **2018**, *17*, 168–192. [CrossRef]
44. Leem, S.; Oh, J.; So, D.; Moon, J. Towards Data-Driven Decision-Making in the Korean Film Industry: An XAI Model for Box Office Analysis Using Dimension Reduction, Clustering, and Classification. *Entropy* **2023**, *25*, 571. [CrossRef] [PubMed]
45. Talukder, A.; Islam, M.; Uddin, A.; Akhter, A.; Hasan, K.F.; Moni, M.A. Machine learning-based lung and colon cancer detection using deep feature extraction and ensemble learning. *Expert Syst. Appl.* **2022**, *205*, 117695. [CrossRef]
46. Ying, M.; Pan, J.; Lu, G.; Zhou, S.; Fu, J.; Wang, Q.; Wang, L.; Hu, B.; Wei, Y.; Shen, J. Development and validation of a radiomics-based nomogram for the preoperative prediction of microsatellite instability in colorectal cancer. *BMC Cancer* **2022**, *22*, 524. [CrossRef]
47. Fadafen, M.K.; Rezaee, K. Ensemble-based multi-tissue classification approach of colorectal cancer histology images using a novel hybrid deep learning framework. *Sci. Rep.* **2023**, *13*, 8823. [CrossRef]
48. Jansen-Winkeln, B.; Barberio, M.; Chalopin, C.; Schierle, K.; Diana, M.; Köhler, H.; Gockel, I.; Maktabi, M. Feedforward artificial neural network-based colorectal cancer detection using hyperspectral imaging: A step towards automatic optical biopsy. *Cancers* **2021**, *13*, 967. [CrossRef]
49. Bora, K.; Bhuyan, M.K.; Kasugai, K.; Mallik, S.; Zhao, Z. Computational learning of features for automated colonic polyp classification. *Sci. Rep.* **2021**, *11*, 4347. [CrossRef]
50. Fan, J.; Lee, J.; Lee, Y. A Transfer learning architecture based on a support vector machine for histopathology image classification. *Appl. Sci.* **2021**, *11*, 6380. [CrossRef]
51. Lo, C.-M.; Yang, Y.-W.; Lin, J.-K.; Lin, T.-C.; Chen, W.-S.; Yang, S.-H.; Chang, S.-C.; Wang, H.-S.; Lan, Y.-T.; Lin, H.-H.; et al. Modeling the survival of colorectal cancer patients based on colonoscopic features in a feature ensemble vision transformer. *Comput. Med. Imaging Graph.* **2023**, *107*, 102242. [CrossRef] [PubMed]
52. Grosu, S.; Wesp, P.; Graser, A.; Maurus, S.; Schulz, C.; Knösel, T.; Cyran, C.C.; Ricke, J.; Ingrisch, M.; Kazmierczak, P.M. Machine learning–based differentiation of benign and premalignant colorectal polyps detected with CT colonography in an asymptomatic screening population: A proof-of-concept study. *Radiology* **2021**, *299*, 326–335. [CrossRef]
53. Takeda, K.; Kudo, S.-E.; Mori, Y.; Misawa, M.; Kudo, T.; Wakamura, K.; Katagiri, A.; Baba, T.; Hidaka, E.; Ishida, F.; et al. Accuracy of diagnosing invasive colorectal cancer using computer-aided endocytoscopy. *Endoscopy* **2017**, *49*, 798–802. [CrossRef] [PubMed]
54. Yang, K.; Zhou, B.; Yi, F.; Chen, Y.; Chen, Y. Colorectal Cancer Diagnostic Algorithm Based on Sub-Patch Weight Color Histogram in Combination of Improved Least Squares Support Vector Machine for Pathological Image. *J. Med. Syst.* **2019**, *43*, 306. [CrossRef] [PubMed]
55. Dragicevic, A.; Matija, L.; Krivokapic, Z.; Dimitrijevic, I.; Baros, M.; Koruga, D. Classification of Healthy and Cancer States of Colon Epithelial Tissues Using Opto-magnetic Imaging Spectroscopy. *J. Med. Biol. Eng.* **2018**, *39*, 367–380. [CrossRef]
56. Trivizakis, E.; Ioannidis, G.S.; Souglakos, I.; Karantanas, A.H.; Tzardi, M.; Marias, K. A neural pathomics framework for classifying colorectal cancer histopathology images based on wavelet multi-scale texture analysis. *Sci. Rep.* **2021**, *11*, 15546. [CrossRef]
57. Damkliang, K.; Wongsirichot, T.; Thongsuksai, P. Tissue classification for colorectal cancer utilizing techniques of deep learning and machine learning. *Biomed. Eng. Appl. Basis Commun.* **2021**, *33*, 2150022. [CrossRef]
58. Mittal, P.; Condina, M.R.; Klingler-Hoffmann, M.; Kaur, G.; Oehler, M.K.; Sieber, O.M.; Palmieri, M.; Kommoss, S.; Brucker, S.; McDonnell, M.D.; et al. Cancer tissue classification using supervised machine learning applied to MALDI mass spectrometry imaging. *Cancers* **2021**, *13*, 5388. [CrossRef]
59. Cao, W.; Pomeroy, M.J.; Liang, Z.; Abbasi, A.F.; Pickhardt, P.J.; Lu, H. Vector textures derived from higher order derivative domains for classification of colorectal polyps. *Vis. Comput. Ind. Biomed. Art* **2022**, *5*, 16. [CrossRef]
60. Deif, M.A.; Attar, H.; Amer, A.; Issa, H.; Khosravi, M.R.; Solyman, A.A.A. A New Feature Selection Method Based on Hybrid Approach for Colorectal Cancer Histology Classification. *Wirel. Commun. Mob. Comput.* **2022**, *2022*, 7614264. [CrossRef]
61. Chehade, A.H.; Abdallah, N.; Marion, J.-M.; Oueidat, M.; Chauvet, P. Lung and colon cancer classification using medical imaging: A feature engineering approach. *Phys. Eng. Sci. Med.* **2022**, *45*, 729–746. [CrossRef]
62. Tripathi, A.; Misra, A.; Kumar, K.; Chaurasia, B.K. Optimized Machine Learning for Classifying Colorectal Tissues. *SN Comput. Sci.* **2023**, *4*, 461. [CrossRef]

63. Kara, O.C.; Venkatayogi, N.; Ikoma, N.; Alambeigi, F. A Reliable and Sensitive Framework for Simultaneous Type and Stage Detection of Colorectal Cancer Polyps. *Ann. Biomed. Eng.* **2023**, *51*, 1499–1512. [CrossRef] [PubMed]
64. Ayyaz, M.S.; Lali, M.I.U.; Hussain, M.; Rauf, H.T.; Alouffi, B.; Alyami, H.; Wasti, S. Hybrid deep learning model for endoscopic lesion detection and classification using endoscopy videos. *Diagnostics* **2021**, *12*, 43. [CrossRef] [PubMed]
65. Mirniaharikandehei, S.; Heidari, M.; Danala, G.; Lakshmivarahan, S.; Zheng, B. Applying a random projection algorithm to optimize machine learning model for predicting peritoneal metastasis in gastric cancer patients using CT images. *Comput. Methods Programs Biomed.* **2021**, *200*, 105937. [CrossRef]
66. Hu, W.; Li, C.; Li, X.; Rahaman, M.; Ma, J.; Zhang, Y.; Chen, H.; Liu, W.; Sun, C.; Yao, Y.; et al. GasHisSDB: A new gastric histopathology image dataset for computer aided diagnosis of gastric cancer. *Comput. Biol. Med.* **2022**, *142*, 105207. [CrossRef] [PubMed]
67. Naser, E.F.; Zeki, S.M. Using Fuzzy Clustering to Detect the Tumor Area in Stomach Medical Images. *Baghdad Sci. J.* **2021**, *18*, 1294. [CrossRef]
68. Korkmaz, S.A.; Esmeray, F. A New Application Based on GPLVM, LMNN, and NCA for Early Detection of the Stomach Cancer. *Appl. Artif. Intell.* **2018**, *32*, 541–557. [CrossRef]
69. Nayyar, Z.; Khan, M.A.; Alhussein, M.; Nazir, M.; Aurangzeb, K.; Nam, Y.; Kadry, S.; Haider, S.I. Gastric tract disease recognition using optimized deep learning features. *Comput. Mater. Contin.* **2021**, *68*, 2041–2056. [CrossRef]
70. Hu, W.; Chen, H.; Liu, W.; Li, X.; Sun, H.; Huang, X.; Grzegorzek, M.; Li, C. A comparative study of gastric histopathology sub-size image classification: From linear regression to visual transformer. *Front. Med.* **2022**, *9*, 1072109. [CrossRef]
71. Korkmaz, S.A. Recognition of the Gastric Molecular Image Based on Decision Tree and Discriminant Analysis Classifiers by using Discrete Fourier Transform and Features. *Appl. Artif. Intell.* **2018**, *32*, 629–643. [CrossRef]
72. Korkmaz, S.A.; Binol, H. Classification of molecular structure images by using ANN, RF, LBP, HOG, and size reduction methods for early stomach cancer detection. *J. Mol. Struct.* **2018**, *1156*, 255–263. [CrossRef]
73. Kanesaka, T.; Lee, T.-C.; Uedo, N.; Lin, K.-P.; Chen, H.-Z.; Lee, J.-Y.; Wang, H.-P.; Chang, H.-T. Computer-aided diagnosis for identifying and delineating early gastric cancers in magnifying narrow-band imaging. *Gastrointest. Endosc.* **2018**, *87*, 1339–1344. [CrossRef] [PubMed]
74. Feng, Q.-X.; Liu, C.; Qi, L.; Sun, S.-W.; Song, Y.; Yang, G.; Zhang, Y.-D.; Liu, X.-S. An Intelligent Clinical Decision Support System for Preoperative Prediction of Lymph Node Metastasis in Gastric Cancer. *J. Am. Coll. Radiol.* **2019**, *16*, 952–960. [CrossRef]
75. Korkmaz, S.A. Classification of histopathological gastric images using a new method. *Neural Comput. Appl.* **2021**, *33*, 12007–12022. [CrossRef]
76. Dai, H.; Bian, Y.; Wang, L.; Yang, J. Support Vector Machine-Based Backprojection Algorithm for Detection of Gastric Cancer Lesions with Abdominal Endoscope Using Magnetic Resonance Imaging Images. *Sci. Program.* **2021**, *2021*, 9964203. [CrossRef]
77. Haile, M.B.; Salau, A.; Enyew, B.; Belay, A.J. Detection and classification of gastrointestinal disease using convolutional neural network and SVM. *Cogent Eng.* **2022**, *9*, 2084878. [CrossRef]
78. Noor, M.N.; Nazir, M.; Khan, S.A.; Song, O.-Y.; Ashraf, I. Efficient Gastrointestinal Disease Classification Using Pretrained Deep Convolutional Neural Network. *Electronics* **2023**, *12*, 1557. [CrossRef]
79. Yin, F.; Zhang, X.; Fan, A.; Liu, X.; Xu, J.; Ma, X.; Yang, L.; Su, H.; Xie, H.; Wang, X.; et al. A novel detection technology for early gastric cancer based on Raman spectroscopy. *Spectrochim. Acta Part A Mol. Biomol. Spectrosc.* **2023**, *292*, 122422. [CrossRef]

Disclaimer/Publisher's Note: The statements, opinions and data contained in all publications are solely those of the individual author(s) and contributor(s) and not of MDPI and/or the editor(s). MDPI and/or the editor(s) disclaim responsibility for any injury to people or property resulting from any ideas, methods, instructions or products referred to in the content.

Article
Multi-Target Feature Selection with Adaptive Graph Learning and Target Correlations

Yujing Zhou [†] and Dubo He *,[†]

Department of Management Engineering and Equipment Economics, Naval University of Engineering, Wuhan 430033, China; 1920191045@nue.edu.cn
* Correspondence: 21000801@nue.edu.cn
[†] These authors contributed equally to this work.

Abstract: In this paper, we present a novel multi-target feature selection algorithm that incorporates adaptive graph learning and target correlations. Specifically, our proposed approach introduces the low-rank constraint on the regression matrix, allowing us to model both inter-target and input–output relationships within a unified framework. To preserve the similarity structure of the samples and mitigate the influence of noise and outliers, we learn a graph matrix that captures the induced sample similarity. Furthermore, we introduce a manifold regularizer to maintain the global target correlations, ensuring the preservation of the overall target relationship during subsequent learning processes. To solve the final objective function, we also propose an optimization algorithm. Through extensive experiments on eight real-world datasets, we demonstrate that our proposed method outperforms state-of-the-art multi-target feature selection techniques.

Keywords: feature selection; multi-target regression; graph learning

MSC: 68T09

1. Introduction

Multi-target regression (MTR) aims to predict multiple target (response) variables by a common set of features. Unlike the Multi-Label Classification (MLC), where the multivariate outputs are all binary variables, the multi-outputs in MTR are all real-valued variables. Recently, MTR is enjoying increasing popularity in machine-learning community because of its ability to predict multiple outputs simultaneously and better generalization performance. Moreover, due to its superior ability, MTR has been widely employed in solving challenging problems in numerous applications such as data mining [1–4], computer vision [5], medical diagnosis [6], stock price prediction [7], load forecasting [8]. MTR takes into account the relationship between features and targets and the underlying correlation among targets, ensuring a better representation and interpretability of real-world problems. Another advantage of MTR is that it can generate cleaner models with better computational efficiency.

In order to obtain desirable and reliable predictions for multiple target variables, many potentially relevant variables are typically involved in the formulation of high-dimensional data which would represent and explain the target variables. However, high dimensional input features not only induce a complex correlation structure between features and targets but also result in the problem of the "curse of dimensionality". In addition, unrelated and redundant features adversely affect the effectiveness of the modeling and reduce the generalization performance. As an efficient dimensionality reduction technique to choose a subset of features from the primitive high-dimensional data, feature selection contributes to prevent the "curse of dimensionality" and enables the selection of an optimal subset from the primitive feature space with specific criterion. As feature selection does not modify the primitive semantics of the original variables, it makes the model more interpretable with reduced training time and space requirements [9].

The Multi-Target Feature Selection (MTFS) methods generally fall into one of three categories [10]: filter [11,12], wrapper [13,14] and embedded approaches [15,16]. The filter approaches use specific evaluation metrics such as mutual information [11] and Laplacian score [12] to measure the importance of features and select the most relevant features to form a subset. The family of filter methods is independent of the algorithm, which makes them computationally efficient. They can effectively remove irrelevant features from a dataset. However, one limitation of filter methods is that they may include redundant features in the selected subset since they ignore the correlation between features. On the other hand, wrapper methods select a subset of features by inputting them into a specific model for training. This process continues until satisfactory performance is achieved. Wrapper methods take into account the correlation between features and consider their impact on the model performance. Wrapper methods can be computationally expensive since the performance of the selected subset needs to be verified after each feature selection. To balance the trade-off between filter and wrapper methods, embedded methods treat feature selection as an optimization problem. Embedded methods can select the most informative features with a relatively low computational cost compared to wrapper methods. By embedding feature selection within the model building process, embedded methods are able to take into account the correlation between features while also minimizing computational costs. These methods weigh the importance of each feature and select the most relevant ones by optimizing the model performance. As a result, embedded methods often lead to better model performance compared to filter methods, while still being more computationally efficient than wrapper methods. Therefore, embedded methods are increasingly drawing attention due to their superior performance.

Closely related to MTR, multi-label learning is generally viewed as a particular case of MTR in statistics analysis [17]. Inspired by the intimate relationship between multi-label classification (MLC) and MTR, Various MTR models have been proposed based on the thought of handling label relevance in the context of MLC, such as the ensemble of regressor chains (ERC), stacked single-target (SST), Random Linear Target Combinations (RLC) [18,19]. Spyromitros-Xioufis et al. discrete the output space by product quantization and thus convert the MTR problem into a MLC problem [11]. It is evident that there are favorable similarities between MLC and MTR, and various methods of MLC have been transferred to handle MTR problems with excellent performance. However, there are a few approaches to solving the feature selection problem in MTR by exploiting various feature selection strategies in MLC. Indeed, various supervised, semi-supervised and unsupervised feature selection methods in MLC can also be transferred to feature selection tasks in MTR scenarios, such as incorporating local and global correlation structures of labels, features or samples into the learning process to improve the feature selection performance, which is inspiring for MTFS [20–22].

The significant challenges of MTR arise from jointly addressing input–output and inter-target correlations [23]. By exploring the correlation information between the targets accurately and effectively, the MTR model can obtain improved performance compared to the single-target model. Therefore, most existing MTR models focus on exploring target correlations. The general technique imposes various sparse regularizer or low-rank constraints on the regression matrix [6,23,24]. However, the above methods do not consider the structure information of features or samples. Both the global and local structures of features and samples have been previously demonstrated in the literature to provide complementary information for reinforcing the performance of feature selection [20,22,25]. Specifically, preserving the geometric structure of samples can strengthen the feature selection performance since the effects of noises and outliers could be mitigated [21,22]. Moreover, in MTR scenarios, the intrinsic inter-target relationships can also provide discriminate information to feature selection and discover the essential features that are highly correlated to the relationships between targets. Incorrect inter-target relationships could also deteriorate the generalization capability of feature selection model.

To address the above-mentioned issues, we design a novel MTFS method by integrating an adaptive graph structure learning and manifold learning of global target correlations into a general multi-target sparse regression model. The key contributions of this paper are highlighted below:

- A novel MTFS method with low-rank constraint is designed to generate low redundancy yet informative feature subset for MTR by imposing a low-rank constraint on the regression matrix, to conduct subspace learning and thus decouple the inter-input as well as the inter-target relationships, which can reduce the influence of redundant or irrelevant features.
- Based on the nearest neighbors of the samples, the similarity-induced graph matrix is learned adaptively, and the local geometric structure of the data can be preserved during the feature selection process, thus mitigating the effects of noise and outliers.
- A manifold regularizer based on target correlation is designed by considering the statistical correlation information between multiple targets over the training set, which is beneficial to discover informative features that are associated with inter-target relationships.
- The alternative optimization algorithm is proposed to solve the proposed objective function, and the convergence of the algorithm is proved theoretically. Extensive experiments are conducted on a benchmark data sets to validate the feasibility and effectiveness of the proposed method.

The rest of this paper is organized as follows. In Section 2, some related works on multi-objective feature selection and multi-label classification feature selection methods are briefly reviewed. The proposed multi-objective feature selection method is described in detail in Section 3, followed by the proposed optimization algorithm in Section 4. Section 5 proves the convergence of the proposed algorithm and analyzes the corresponding time complexity. In Section 6, experimental results are reported and analyzed to demonstrate the effectiveness of the proposed method. Finally, a brief conclusion is summarized in Section 7.

2. Related Work

To date, different MTFS methods have been proposed. Hashemi et al. [26] proposed a feature selection method incorporating the VIKOR algorithm to rank the features in the MTR problem. Sechidis et al. [11] proposed a feature selection method for both MLC and MTR. The method considers correlation, redundancy and complementarity between features by calculating the interaction among targets, thus ensuring that the acquired subset of features can have less redundancy and higher correlation. Petkovic et al. [27] proposed a feature-ranking method based on predictive clustering tree integration and RReliefF method extensions, and the optimal feature ranking is determined by integrating the feature scores of these two groups of methods. Masmoudi et al. [28] presented a multi-target feature ranking method based on regression chain ensemble and random forest; the final feature ranking is obtained by combining the feature importance information from both methods.

Recently, different embedded approaches have also been proposed. Yuan et al. [29] proposed an embedded Sparse Structural Feature Selection (SSFS) model based on a multi-layer multi-output framework. This model achieves improved feature selection performance by simultaneously applying sparsity constraints on the objective function, regression coefficients, and structure matrix. Similarly, Zhu et al. [30] utilized low-rank constraint to identify correlations between output variables and impose $\ell_{2,1}$-norm regularization on regression matrix to achieve feature selection. The above-mentioned methods impose sparsity or low rank on the loss function or parameter matrix to achieve the feature selection. However, these embedded methods either consider the similarity structure of samples or the statistical correlations between different targets, which may constrain the performance of feature selection.

In fact, the feature selection method in MLC tasks can also be deployed in MTR tasks when the model can handle continuous output variables. Fan et al. [31] proposed a feature selection method based on both label correlations and feature redundancies; the label correlations are explored through low-dimensional embedding, which maintains the global and local structure of the original label space. Xu et al. [32] proposed to perform feature extraction by maximizing feature variance and feature–label dependence to achieve better performance in MLC problems. Zhu et al. [21] proposed a robust unsupervised spectral feature selection method that maintains the local structure of features by exploiting the self-representation of features and maintains the global structure of samples as features via imposing low-rank constraints on the weight matrix. Mahsa et al. [33] proposed a low-redundant unsupervised feature selection method based on data structure learning and feature orthogonalization. Obviously, the above method introduces other information such as the local and global structure of the labels, the structure of the data and the relationship between the features by considering not only the relationship between the features and the labels in the feature selection process.

Recently, graph-based methods, such as spectral clustering, graph learning and hypergraph learning, have played an important role in machine learning due to their ability to encode similarity relationships among data. Ma et al. [34] proposed a feature selection method named discriminative multi-label feature selection with adaptive graph diffusion, and the graph embedding learning framework is constructed with adaptive graph diffusion to uncover a latent subspace that preserves the higher-order structure information. Zhang et al. [35] proposed a novel unsupervised feature selection via adaptive graph learning and constraint. Zhu et al. [36] proposed an unsupervised spectral feature selection method with dynamic hypergraph Learning. You et al. [37] proposed an unsupervised feature selection method via Neural Networks (NN) and self-expression with adaptive graph constraint. Deepak et al. [38] extended the feature selection algorithm presented in via Gumbel softmax to Graph Neural Networks (GNN). It can be seen that graph learning can effectively mine the similarity or structural relationship between data, and thus improve the performance of feature selection.

From the above research, it is evident that maintaining the various structural information contained in the original data, such as the geometric or similar structure of the samples, the structural information among the features and different outputs, can provide supplementary information for feature selection in different perspectives, thereby improve the feature selection performance. However, existing MTFS methods rarely consider the above information simultaneously.

3. The Proposed Approaches

3.1. Notations

For a $n \times m$ matrix $\mathbf{A} = [a_{i,j}] \in \mathbb{R}^{n \times m}$, and $a_{i,j}$ denotes the (i,j)-th entry of $\mathbf{A}$. $\mathbf{A}^T$ denotes its transpose. $tr(\mathbf{A})$ is $\mathbf{A}$'s trace. The Frobenius norm of $\mathbf{A}$ is defined as $\|\mathbf{A}\|_F = \sqrt{\sum_{i=1}^{n} \sum_{j=1}^{m} a_{i,j}^2}$, and the $\ell_{p,q}$-norm of matrix $\mathbf{A}$ is defined as

$$\|\mathbf{A}\|_{p,q} = \left[\sum_{i=1}^{n} \left(\sum_{j=1}^{m} |a_{i,j}|^p \right)^{\frac{q}{p}} \right]^{\frac{1}{q}} \tag{1}$$

and hence the $\ell_{2,1}$-norm of $\mathbf{A}$ is defined as

$$\|\mathbf{A}\|_{2,1} = \sum_{i=1}^{n} \sqrt{\sum_{j=1}^{m} a_{i,j}^2} \tag{2}$$

For a n-dimensional vector $\mathbf{c} \in \mathbb{R}^n$, $\|\mathbf{c}\|_2 = \sqrt{\sum_{i=1}^{n} c_i^2}$ is its ℓ_2-norm, $\mathbf{I}$ denotes an identity matrix, and let $\mathbf{H} = \mathbf{I} - \frac{1}{n}\mathbf{1}_n\mathbf{1}_n^T$ denote the center matrix, where $\mathbf{1}_n \in \mathbb{R}^n$ and the value of each element is 1.

3.2. MTR Based on Low-Rank Constraint

Given a training set consisting of n instances $\{(\mathbf{x}_i, \mathbf{y}_i)\}_{i=1}^n$, and $\mathbf{X} = [\mathbf{x}_1, \ldots, \mathbf{x}_n]^T \in \mathbb{R}^{n \times d}$ represents feature or input matrix, where $\mathbf{x}_i = [x_{i,1}, \ldots, x_{i,q}]^T \in \mathbb{R}^d$, and $\mathbf{Y} = [\mathbf{y}_1, \ldots, \mathbf{y}_n]^T \in \mathbb{R}^{n \times q}$ represents target or output matrix, where $\mathbf{y}_i = [y_{i,1}, \ldots, y_{i,q}]^T \in \mathbb{R}^q$ is the multi-target output corresponding to $\mathbf{x}_i$. The traditional ridge regression can be extended to multi-dimension, and we reach the following objective function:

$$\min_{\mathbf{W},\mathbf{b}} \|\mathbf{XW} + \mathbf{1}_n \mathbf{b}^T - \mathbf{Y}\|_F^2 + \alpha \|\mathbf{W}\|_F^2 \tag{3}$$

where $\mathbf{W} \in \mathbb{R}^{d \times q}$ is the regression coefficients, $\mathbf{b} \in \mathbb{R}^q$ is the bias, and $\alpha > 0$ is the regularization parameter. d and q are dimensions of features and targets. To select the features, the $\ell_{2,1}$-norm regularizer is imposed on regression matrix $\mathbf{W}$, and we have

$$\min_{\mathbf{W},\mathbf{b}} \|\mathbf{XW} + \mathbf{1}_n \mathbf{b}^T - \mathbf{Y}\|_F^2 + \alpha \|\mathbf{W}\|_{2,1} \tag{4}$$

where the sparse learning of $\mathbf{W}$ based on $\ell_{2,1}$-norm encourages the row sparsity to unselect the irrelevant features in the original feature matrix $\mathbf{X}$. Evidently, Equation (4) does not take into account the correlation among targets, which leads to poor performance in MTFS. Therefore, we impose a low-rank constraint on $\mathbf{W}$, i.e., $\mathbf{W} = \mathbf{AB}$, where $\mathbf{A} \in \mathbb{R}^{d \times r}$, $\mathbf{B} \in \mathbb{R}^{r \times q}$, $r \leq \min(d, q)$. Hence, Equation (4) is modified to

$$\min_{\mathbf{A},\mathbf{B},\mathbf{b}} \|\mathbf{XAB} + \mathbf{1}_n \mathbf{b}^T - \mathbf{Y}\|_F^2 + \alpha \|\mathbf{AB}\|_{2,1} \tag{5}$$

In Equation (5), the parameter matrix $\mathbf{A}$ can be viewed as transforming the original feature space $\mathbb{R}^d$ into an latent variable space $\mathbb{R}^r$ geometrically, and then parameter matrix $\mathbf{B}$ transforms $\mathbf{XA}$ to the target space $\mathbb{R}^q$. Considering the correlation among q targets, $\mathbf{B}$ can be served to encode inter-target correlations explicitly. Thus, the low-rank constraint takes into account global target correlations to leverage subspace learning and enables the simultaneous modeling of input–output correlations as well as inter-target relationships. In addition, the effects of redundant features and anomalous variables can be mitigated by low-rank learning, resulting in the output of robust feature selection models [39,40].

3.3. Adaptive Graph-Learning Based on Local Sample Structure

So far, the majority of studies have shown that, in addition to characterizing the significance of features in the regression model through sparse learning, the local structural information of the sample can also contribute additional information to feature selection [20–22,25]. By preserving the nearest neighbour structure of instances, the distribution of samples in the learned low-dimensional space can maintain consistency with the original sample space [21,22]. Even for a MTR problem with a complex correlation structure, The output $\mathbf{Y}$ can be reasonably hypothesized to be a continuous and smooth function of the input $\mathbf{X}$. It is natural to expect close samples $\mathbf{x}_i$ and $\mathbf{x}_j$ to have close output values $\mathbf{y}_i$ and $\mathbf{y}_j$; thereby, the corresponding prediction outputs $\hat{\mathbf{y}}_i$ and $\hat{\mathbf{y}}_j$ should also be adjacent to each other [41]. Based on the hypothesis, the geometric structure information of different instances in the feature space is leveraged to ensure that the predicted output of the model also maintains a similar geometric structure.

The existing literature obtains the local distribution structure and information of samples by learning the graph matrix $\mathbf{S}$ between samples, and given the input matrix $\mathbf{X}$ and the corresponding weight coefficients $\mathbf{W}$, according to the literature [42], we have:

$$\min_{\mathbf{W}} \sum_{i,j=1}^n \|\mathbf{x}_i^T \mathbf{W} - \mathbf{x}_j^T \mathbf{W}\|_2^2 s_{i,j} \tag{6}$$

where $\mathbf{W} \in \mathbb{R}^{d \times q}$ and $\mathbf{S} = [s_{i,j}] \in \mathbb{R}^{n \times n}$, and $s_{i,j}$ represents the similarity between $\mathbf{x}_i$ and $\mathbf{x}_j$. Traditional methods are often based on heat kernel functions to calculate the similarity between nearest neighbors samples, the similarity between nearest neighbor samples x_i and x_j is defined as

$$s_{i,j} = \exp\left(-\frac{\|x_i - x_j\|_2^2}{2\sigma^2}\right) \tag{7}$$

otherwise $s_{i,j} = 0$. Although Equation (7) has been widely applied, the similarity matrix is highly sensitive to the existence of noise and outliers in the original data [21,22]. To deal with this, we learn the similarity matrix of the target space adaptively to mitigate the effect of noise and outliers. The hypothesis in manifold learning is that if two samples are close in the dimension reduction space, then their corresponding multivariate prediction outputs should also be closed in target space, which gives rise to

$$\min_{S,A,B} \sum_{i,j=1}^{n} \left(\|x_i^T W - x_j^T W\|_2^2 s_{i,j} + \gamma \|s_i\|_2^2\right)$$
$$s.t. \; \forall i, \mathbf{1}^T s_i = 1, s_{i,i} = 0, \tag{8}$$
$$s_{i,j} \geq 0 \text{ if } j \in \mathcal{N}(i), \text{otherwise } 0.$$

where γ is a tuning parameter, The second item in (8) deals with avoiding trivial solutions. $\mathcal{N}(i)$ represents the nearest neighbours set of the ith sample, and $\mathbf{1}^T s_i = 1$ has been proved to reinforce the robustness for noises and outliers in [43], where s_i is the ith column of matrix S. Combining the low-rank constraint and Equation (8), which leads to

$$\min_{S,A,B} \sum_{i,j=1}^{n} \left(\|x_i^T AB - x_j^T AB\|_2^2 s_{i,j} + \gamma \|s_i\|_2^2\right)$$
$$s.t. \; \forall i, \mathbf{1}^T s_i = 1, s_{i,i} = 0, \tag{9}$$
$$s_{i,j} \geq 0 \text{ if } j \in \mathcal{N}(i), \text{otherwise } 0.$$

Based on Equation (9), we can ensure that the nearest neighbour relationship in the predicted output is consistent with the original data, which benefits the subsequent learning of different output correlation structures. Moreover, preserving the nearest neighbour relationship between samples is beneficial to lessen the impact of redundant or irrelevant features to improve the performance of feature selection.

3.4. Manifold Regularization of Global Target Correlations

Since different target correlation structures can also affect the performance of MTFS, we propose a manifold regularization term for global target correlations, which automatically exacts the correlations from the target matrix. By incorporating the target manifold regularization via exploiting the correlation of the target variables to filter out the noises of target variables indirectly. First, we use the commonly used cosine similarity to measure the similarity between target variables, which is calculated as follows,

$$\tilde{s}_{i,j} = \frac{\langle y_{:,i}, y_{:,j} \rangle}{\|y_{:,i}\| \|y_{:,j}\|}, i,j = 1,\ldots,q \tag{10}$$

where $y_{:,i}$ and $y_{:,j}$ are the ith and jth column of Y, respectively. We assume that for the coefficient matrix $B \in \mathbb{R}^{r \times q}$, if the target output vectors $y_{:,i}$ and $y_{:,j}$ are similar to each other, their corresponding weight vectors b_i and b_j should also be close. Based on the assumptions, we have:

$$\min_{B} \sum_{i,j=1}^{q} \|b_i - b_j\|_2^2 \tilde{s}_{i,j} \tag{11}$$

where b_i and b_j are the ith and jth column of B. Equation (11) encourages the similarity of the weight vectors corresponding to similar target outputs. The advantage of Equation (11) is that it can use the similarity information among different target outputs, thus improving the feature selection performance in MTR problems.

3.5. Objective Function

By incorporating the model (9) and (11) into the generalized low-rank MTR model (5), we can obtain the final feature selection model based on adaptive graph learning and global target correlations for MTR, which is described as follows:

$$\min_{\mathbf{A},\mathbf{B},\mathbf{S},\mathbf{b}} \|\mathbf{XAB} + \mathbf{1}_n\mathbf{b}^T - \mathbf{Y}\|_F^2 + \alpha\|\mathbf{AB}\|_{2,1}$$
$$+ \beta \sum_{i,j=1}^{n} \left(\|\mathbf{x}_i^T\mathbf{AB} - \mathbf{x}_j^T\mathbf{AB}\|_2^2 s_{i,j} + \gamma \sum_{i=1}^{n} \|\mathbf{s}_i\|_2^2 \right)$$
$$+ \lambda \sum_{i,j=1}^{q} \|\mathbf{b}_i - \mathbf{b}_j\|_2^2 \tilde{s}_{i,j}$$
$$s.t. \begin{cases} \forall i, \mathbf{1}^T\mathbf{s}_i = 1, s_{i,i} = 0, \\ s_{i,j} \geq 0 \text{ if } j \in \mathcal{N}(i), \text{otherwise } 0. \end{cases} \quad (12)$$

where α, β, γ and λ are tuning parameter. The proposed objective function (12) has the following important characteristics. On the one hand, the low-rank constraint on the regression matrix can decouple the input–target and inter-target correlations and enables robust learning of the correlation. On the other hand, by integrating the adaptive graph learning based on local sample structure and manifold regularization of global target correlations, we can consider both local sample structure and global target correlations. Moreover, the graph structure and regression parameter matrices learning could be iteratively updated by each other, and the global target correlations can be extracted from data automatically.

Consequently, given the optimal parameter matrix **A** and **B**, we evaluate the importance of each feature based on the ℓ_2-norm of $(\mathbf{AB})_i$, and rank them in descending order, then the top-ranked subset of features can be obtained.

4. Optimization Algorithm

This section presents an alternating optimization algorithm to solve the problem (12), i.e., iteratively optimizing each variable while fixing the others until convergence.

First, by setting the derivative of Equation (12) w.r.t. **b** to zero, we have

$$\mathbf{b}^T = \frac{1}{n}\left(\mathbf{1}_n^T\mathbf{Y} - \mathbf{1}_n^T\mathbf{XAB}\right) \quad (13)$$

Substituting the result of Equation (13) into (12), and the objective function can be rewritten as

$$\min_{\mathbf{A},\mathbf{B},\mathbf{S}} \|\mathbf{H}(\mathbf{XAB} - \mathbf{Y})\|_F^2 + \alpha\|\mathbf{AB}\|_{2,1}$$
$$+ \beta \sum_{i,j=1}^{n} \left(\|\mathbf{x}_i^T\mathbf{AB} - \mathbf{x}_j^T\mathbf{AB}\|_2^2 s_{i,j} + \gamma \sum_{i=1}^{n} \|\mathbf{s}_i\|_2^2 \right)$$
$$+ \lambda \sum_{i,j=1}^{q} \|\mathbf{b}_i - \mathbf{b}_j\|_2^2 \tilde{s}_{i,j}$$
$$s.t. \begin{cases} \forall i, \mathbf{1}^T\mathbf{s}_i = 1, s_{i,i} = 0, \\ s_{i,j} \geq 0 \text{ if } j \in \mathcal{N}(i), \text{otherwise } 0. \end{cases} \quad (14)$$

where **H** is a symmetric center matrix. Since Equation (14) is convex for each parameter matrix while fixing others. Hence, the alternating optimization algorithm is introduced.

4.1. Fix **S** *Update* **A** *and* **B**

With **S** is fixed, problem (14) can be rewritten as follows:

$$\min_{\mathbf{A},\mathbf{B}} \|\mathbf{H}(\mathbf{XAB} - \mathbf{Y})\|_F^2 + \alpha\|\mathbf{AB}\|_{2,1}$$
$$+ \beta \sum_{i,j=1}^{n} \|\mathbf{x}_i^T\mathbf{AB} - \mathbf{x}_j^T\mathbf{AB}\|_2^2 s_{i,j} + \lambda \sum_{i,j=1}^{q} \|\mathbf{b}_i - \mathbf{b}_j\|_2^2 \tilde{s}_{i,j} \quad (15)$$

To prevent the non-differentiable problem in (15), we transform problem (15) as follows,

$$\min_{\mathbf{A},\mathbf{B}} \|\mathbf{H}(\mathbf{XAB} - \mathbf{Y})\|_F^2 + \alpha tr\left(\mathbf{B}^T\mathbf{A}^T\mathbf{DAB}\right) \\ + \beta tr\left(\mathbf{B}^T\mathbf{A}^T\mathbf{X}^T\mathbf{LXAB}\right) + \lambda tr(\mathbf{B}\widetilde{\mathbf{L}}\mathbf{B}^T) \tag{16}$$

where $\mathbf{L}$ and $\widetilde{\mathbf{L}}$ are the Laplacian matrices corresponding to $s_{i,j}$ and $\tilde{s}_{i,j}$, respectively. $\mathbf{D} \in \mathbb{R}^{d \times d}$ is the diagonal matrix and

$$D_{i,i} = \frac{1}{2\|(\mathbf{AB})_i\|_2^2}, i = 1, 2, \ldots, d \tag{17}$$

where $(\mathbf{AB})_i$ is the ith row of matrix $\mathbf{AB}$. Similarly, by fixing $\mathbf{B}$, we set the derivative of Equation (16) with respect to $\mathbf{A}$ to zero and further to obtain

$$\mathbf{A}^* = \mathbf{P}^{-1}\mathbf{X}^T\mathbf{HYB}^T\left(\mathbf{BB}^T\right)^{-1} \tag{18}$$

where $\mathbf{P} = \mathbf{X}^T\mathbf{HX} + \alpha\mathbf{D} + \beta\mathbf{X}^T\mathbf{LX}$. In the same way, by fixing $\mathbf{A}$ we can obtain the following expression,

$$\min_{\mathbf{B}} \; tr\left(\mathbf{B}^T\mathbf{A}^T\mathbf{PAB} - 2\mathbf{B}^T\mathbf{A}^T\mathbf{X}^T\mathbf{HY}\right) + \lambda tr\left(\mathbf{B}\widetilde{\mathbf{L}}\mathbf{B}^T\right) \tag{19}$$

We set the derivative of Equation (19) $w.r.t.$ $\mathbf{B}$ to zero and obtain

$$\mathbf{A}^T\mathbf{PAB} + \lambda\mathbf{B}\widetilde{\mathbf{L}} = \mathbf{A}^T\mathbf{X}^T\mathbf{HY} \tag{20}$$

Obviously, Equation (20) is a standard Sylvester equation $\mathcal{A}\Theta + \Theta\mathcal{B} = \mathcal{C}$, where Θ is the unknown corresponding to $\mathbf{B}$, $\mathcal{A} = \mathbf{A}^T\mathbf{PA}$, $\mathcal{B} = \lambda\widetilde{\mathbf{L}}$, and $\mathcal{C} = \mathbf{A}^T\mathbf{X}^T\mathbf{HY}$. Therefore, Equation (20) has a closed-form solution and can be solved analytically. The optimization of $\mathbf{A}$ and $\mathbf{B}$ is shown in Algorithm 1.

Algorithm 1 The procedure of optimizing $\mathbf{A}$ and $\mathbf{B}$

Input: $\mathbf{X} \in \mathbb{R}^{n \times d}$, $\mathbf{Y} \in \mathbb{R}^{n \times q}$, $\mathbf{L} \in \mathbb{R}^{n \times n}$, $\widetilde{\mathbf{L}} \in \mathbb{R}^{q \times q}$, $\alpha, \beta, \lambda, k$ and r;
Output: $\mathbf{A} \in \mathbb{R}^{d \times r}$, $\mathbf{B} \in \mathbb{R}^{r \times q}$;
1. Initialize $\mathbf{D} = \mathbf{I} \in \mathbb{R}^{d \times d}$;
2. Update the matrix $\mathbf{P}$;
3. **repeat**:
    3.1. Calculate $\mathbf{B}$ by Equation (18);
    3.2. Update $\mathbf{A}$ by Equation (20);
    3.3. Update $\mathbf{D}$ and $\mathbf{P}$ by Equation (17);
until *converge*;

4.2. Fix A and B Update S

With fixed $\mathbf{A}$ and $\mathbf{B}$ we have:

$$\min_{\mathbf{S}} \sum_{i,j=1}^{n} \left(\|\mathbf{x}_i^T\mathbf{AB} - \mathbf{x}_j^T\mathbf{AB}\|_2^2 s_{i,j} + \gamma\|\mathbf{s}_i\|_2^2 \right) \\ s.t. \; \forall i, \mathbf{1}^T\mathbf{s}_i = 1, s_{i,i} = 0, \\ s_{i,j} \geq 0 \; \text{if} \; j \in \mathcal{N}(i), \text{otherwise } 0. \tag{21}$$

Initially, we set the value of $s_{i,j} = 0$ if $j \notin \mathcal{N}(i)$, where $\mathcal{N}(i)$ is the k nearest neighbors of sample i. Otherwise, the $s_{i,j}$ value can be calculated by the following Equation (22). Since different $\mathbf{s}_i$ ($i = 1, ..., n$) are independent of each other, the solutions of $\mathbf{s}_i$ can be solved separately by parallel optimization. Therefore, rewrite Equation (21) as

$$\min_{\mathbf{1}^T\mathbf{s}_i=1, s_{i,i}=0, s_{i,j}\geq 0} \sum_{j=1}^n \left(\|\mathbf{x}_i^T \mathbf{AB} - \mathbf{x}_j^T \mathbf{AB}\|_2^2 s_{i,j} + \gamma s_{i,j}^2 \right) \tag{22}$$

By denoting $\mathbf{G} = [\mathbf{g}_1, \ldots, \mathbf{g}_n] \in \mathbb{R}^{n \times n}$ where $g_{i,j} = \|\mathbf{x}_i \mathbf{AB} - \mathbf{x}_j \mathbf{AB}\|_2^2$, and rewrite Equation (23) as follows:

$$\min_{\mathbf{1}^T\mathbf{s}_i=1, s_{i,i}=0, s_{i,j}\geq 0} \frac{1}{2}\|\mathbf{s}_i + \frac{1}{2\gamma}\mathbf{g}_i\|_2^2 \tag{23}$$

Then we further derive the Lagrangian function of Equation (23) as

$$\begin{aligned}\mathcal{L}(\mathbf{s}_i, \zeta, \boldsymbol{\eta}) &= \frac{1}{2}\|\mathbf{s}_i + \frac{\mathbf{g}_i}{2\gamma}\|_2^2 - \zeta\left(\mathbf{1}^T\mathbf{s}_i - 1\right) - \boldsymbol{\eta}^T\mathbf{s}_i. \\ &= \frac{1}{2}\sum_{j=1}^n \left(s_{i,j} + \frac{g_{i,j}}{2\gamma}\right)^2 - \zeta\left(\sum_{j=1}^n s_{i,j} - 1\right) - \sum_{j=1}^n \eta_j s_{i,j}\end{aligned} \tag{24}$$

where ζ and η be the Lagrangian multipliers. By using the Karush–Kuhn–Tucker (KKT) conditions, we further achieve

$$\begin{cases} \forall j, s_{i,j} + \frac{g_{i,j}}{2\gamma} - \zeta - \eta_j = 0 \\ \forall j, s_{i,j} \geq 0 \\ \forall j, s_{i,j}\eta_j = 0 \\ \forall j, \eta_j \geq 0 \end{cases} \tag{25}$$

According to the KKT conditions, we can summarize the following three scenarios based on Equation (25):

$$\begin{cases} \text{scenario 1: } s_{i,j} > 0, \eta_j = 0 \Leftrightarrow s_{i,j} = -\frac{g_{i,j}}{2\gamma} + \zeta > 0 \\ \text{scenario 2: } s_{i,j} = 0, \eta_j > 0 \Leftrightarrow -\eta_j = -\frac{g_{i,j}}{2\gamma} + \zeta < 0 \\ \text{scenario 3: } s_{i,j} = \eta_j = 0 \Leftrightarrow -\frac{g_{i,j}}{2\gamma} + \zeta = 0 \end{cases} \tag{26}$$

Finally we have $s_{i,j} = \left(-\frac{g_{i,j}}{2\gamma} + \zeta\right)_+$. To ensure the sparsity of the similarity matrix and thus improve the model robustness, we only consider the k-nearest neighbours of each training sample. Without loss of generality, we suppose that $g_{i,1} \leq g_{i,2} \leq \ldots \leq g_{i,n}, \forall i$. For the vector $\mathbf{s}_i$ we have

$$\begin{cases} s_{i,k} > 0 \Rightarrow -\frac{g_{i,k}}{2\gamma} + \zeta > 0 \\ s_{i,k+1} \leq 0 \Rightarrow -\frac{g_{i,k+1}}{2\gamma} + \zeta \leq 0 \end{cases} \tag{27}$$

according to the constraint $\mathbf{1}^T\mathbf{s}_i = 1$, we have

$$\sum_{j=1}^k \left(-\frac{g_{i,j}}{2\gamma} + \zeta\right) = 1 \Rightarrow \zeta = \frac{1}{k} + \frac{1}{2k\gamma}\sum_{j=1}^k g_{i,j} \tag{28}$$

based on Equation (27) and (28), we can induce that

$$\frac{kg_{i,k} - \sum_{j=1}^k g_{i,j}}{2} < \gamma \leq \frac{kg_{i,k+1} - \sum_{j=1}^k g_{i,j}}{2} \tag{29}$$

let $\gamma = \frac{kg_{i,k+1} - \sum_j^k g_{i,j}}{2}$, the closed-form solution of $s_{i,j}$ can be yielded as

$$s_{i,j} = \begin{cases} \frac{g_{i,k+1} - g_{i,j}}{kg_{i,k+1} - \sum_{j=1}^k g_{i,j}}, & j \leq k, \\ 0, & j > k. \end{cases} \tag{30}$$

In summary, the overall pseudo-code of the proposed algorithm to solve the problem (14) is concluded in Algorithm 2.

Algorithm 2 MTFS Method based on Alternating Optimization Algorithm

Input: $\mathbf{X} \in \mathbb{R}^{n \times d}$, $\mathbf{Y} \in \mathbb{R}^{n \times q}$, α, β and λ, k and r;
Output: $\mathbf{A} \in \mathbb{R}^{d \times r}$, $\mathbf{B} \in \mathbb{R}^{r \times q}$, $\mathbf{S} \in \mathbb{R}^{n \times n}$
1. Calculate k nearest neighbors of all training samples;
2. Initialize $\mathbf{S}$ by Equation (8) where $\mathbf{W}$ is an identity matrix;
3. Update the Laplacian matrix $\tilde{\mathbf{L}}$;
4. **repeat**:
      4.1. Update $\mathbf{A}$ and $\mathbf{B}$ via Algorithm 1;
      4.2. Calculate $\mathbf{S}$ via Equation (27);
      4.3. Calculate the Laplacian matrix $\mathbf{L}$ corresponding to $\mathbf{S}$;
until *converge*;

---

5. Convergence and Complexity Analysis

To demonstrate the convergence of the proposed algorithm, a Lemma is first listed as follows [44]:

Lemma 1. *For any two non-zero vectors $\mathbf{u}, \mathbf{v} \in \mathbb{R}^m$, the following equation is always holds.*

$$\|\mathbf{u}\|_2 - \frac{\|\mathbf{u}\|_2^2}{2\|\mathbf{v}\|_2} \leq \|\mathbf{v}\|_2 - \frac{\|\mathbf{v}\|_2^2}{2\|\mathbf{v}\|_2} \tag{31}$$

5.1. Convergence Analysis of Algorithm 2

The convergence of Algorithm 2 is guaranteed by the following Theorem.

Theorem 1. *The value of objective function (15) is monotonically decreases until Algorithm 2 converges.*

Proof. Denote $\mathcal{J}\left(\mathbf{A}_{(t)}, \mathbf{B}_{(t)}\right)$ as the objective function of (15) in tth iteration. $\mathbf{W}_{(t)} = \mathbf{A}_{(t)}\mathbf{B}_{(t)}$, where $\mathbf{A}_{(t)}$ and $\mathbf{B}_{(t)}$ are the $\mathbf{A}$ and $\mathbf{B}$ in the tth iteration, respectively. After fixing $\mathbf{S}$, according to Algorithm 1, we can obtain

$$\left\langle \mathbf{A}_{(t)}, \mathbf{B}_{(t)} \right\rangle = \arg\min_{\mathbf{A},\mathbf{B}} \|\mathbf{H}\left(\mathbf{X}\mathbf{W}_{(t)} - \mathbf{Y}\right)\|_F^2 + \alpha tr\left(\mathbf{W}^T \mathbf{D} \mathbf{W}\right) \\ + \beta tr\left(\mathbf{W}_{(t)}^T \mathbf{X}^T \mathbf{L} \mathbf{X} \mathbf{W}_{(t)}\right) + \lambda tr\left(\mathbf{B}_{(t)} \tilde{\mathbf{L}} \mathbf{B}_{(t)}^T\right) \tag{32}$$

Since $\|\mathbf{W}\|_{2,1} = \sum_{i=1}^d \|\mathbf{w}_i\|_2$, hence

$$\|\mathbf{H}\left(\mathbf{X}\mathbf{W}_{(t+1)} - \mathbf{Y}\right)\|_F^2 + \beta tr\left(\mathbf{W}_{(t+1)}^T \mathbf{X}^T \mathbf{L} \mathbf{X} \mathbf{W}_{(t+1)}\right) + \lambda tr\left(\mathbf{B}_{(t+1)} \tilde{\mathbf{L}} \mathbf{B}_{(t+1)}^T\right) \\ + \alpha \|\mathbf{W}_{(t+1)}\|_{2,1} + \alpha \sum_{i=1}^d \left(\frac{\|\mathbf{w}_{i(t+1)}\|_2^2}{2\|\mathbf{w}_{i(t)}\|_2} - \|\mathbf{w}_{i(t+1)}\|_2^2\right) \\ \leq \|\mathbf{H}\left(\mathbf{X}\mathbf{W}_{(t)} - \mathbf{Y}\right)\|_F^2 + \beta tr\left(\mathbf{W}_{(t)}^T \mathbf{X}^T \mathbf{L} \mathbf{X} \mathbf{W}_{(t)}\right) + \lambda tr\left(\mathbf{B}_{(t)} \tilde{\mathbf{L}} \mathbf{B}_{(t)}^T\right) \\ + \alpha \|\mathbf{W}_{(t)}\|_{2,1} + \alpha \sum_{i=1}^d \left(\frac{\|\mathbf{w}_{i(t)}\|_2^2}{2\|\mathbf{w}_{i(t)}\|_2} - \|\mathbf{w}_{i(t)}\|_2^2\right) \tag{33}$$

where $\mathbf{w}_{i(t)}$ and $\mathbf{w}_{i(t+1)}$ denote the ith row of $\mathbf{W}_{(t)}$ and $\mathbf{W}_{(t+1)}$, respectively. According to Lemma 1, we have

$$\|\mathbf{w}_{i(t+1)}\|_2 - \frac{\|\mathbf{w}_{i(t+1)}\|_2^2}{2\|\mathbf{w}_{i(t)}\|_2} \leq \|\mathbf{w}_{i(t)}\|_2 - \frac{\|\mathbf{w}_{i(t)}\|_2^2}{2\|\mathbf{w}_{i(t)}\|_2} \tag{34}$$

By plugging Equation (34) into Equation (33), we have

$$\begin{aligned}
&\|\mathbf{H}\left(\mathbf{X}\mathbf{W}_{(t+1)} - \mathbf{Y}\right)\|_F^2 + \beta tr\left(\mathbf{W}_{(t+1)}^T \mathbf{X}^T \mathbf{L} \mathbf{X} \mathbf{W}_{(t+1)}\right) \\
&+ \alpha \sum_{i=1}^d \|\mathbf{w}_{i(t+1)}\|_2^2 + \lambda tr\left(\mathbf{B}_{(t+1)} \widetilde{\mathbf{L}} \mathbf{B}_{(t+1)}^T\right) \\
&\leq \|\mathbf{H}\left(\mathbf{X}\mathbf{W}_{(t)} - \mathbf{Y}\right)\|_F^2 + \beta tr\left(\mathbf{W}_{(t)}^T \mathbf{X}^T \mathbf{L} \mathbf{X} \mathbf{W}_{(t)}\right) \\
&+ \alpha \sum_{i=1}^d \|\mathbf{w}_{i(t)}\|_2^2 + \beta tr\left(\mathbf{B}_{(t)} \widetilde{\mathbf{L}} \mathbf{B}_{(t)}^T\right)
\end{aligned} \tag{35}$$

and further we have

$$\begin{aligned}
&\|\mathbf{H}\left(\mathbf{X}\mathbf{W}_{(t+1)} - \mathbf{Y}\right)\|_F^2 + \beta tr\left(\mathbf{W}_{(t+1)}^T \mathbf{X}^T \mathbf{L} \mathbf{X} \mathbf{W}_{(t+1)}\right) \\
&+ \alpha \|\mathbf{W}_{i(t+1)}\|_{2,1} + \lambda tr\left(\mathbf{B}_{(t+1)} \widetilde{\mathbf{L}} \mathbf{B}_{(t+1)}^T\right) \\
&\leq \|\mathbf{H}\left(\mathbf{X}\mathbf{W}_{(t)} - \mathbf{Y}\right)\|_F^2 + \beta tr\left(\mathbf{W}_{(t)}^T \mathbf{X}^T \mathbf{L} \mathbf{X} \mathbf{W}_{(t)}\right) \\
&+ \alpha \|\mathbf{W}_{i(t)}\|_{2,1} + \lambda tr\left(\mathbf{B}_{(t)} \widetilde{\mathbf{L}} \mathbf{B}_{(t)}^T\right)
\end{aligned} \tag{36}$$

Hence, we have the following inequality:

$$\mathcal{J}\left(\mathbf{A}_{(t+1)}, \mathbf{B}_{(t+1)}\right) \leq \mathcal{J}\left(\mathbf{A}_{(t)}, \mathbf{B}_{(t)}\right).$$

Therefore, $\mathcal{J}\left(\mathbf{A}_{(t)}, \mathbf{B}_{(t)}\right)$ is monotonically decreasing until convergence, and Theorem 1 proved. □

5.2. Convergence Analysis of Algorithm 1

Likewise, we also prove the convergence of Algorithm 1 according to the following Theorem 2.

Theorem 2. *The objective function (21) monotonically decreases with each optimization step until Algorithm 1 converges.*

Proof. According to Theorem 1, after the tth iteration, the optimal $\mathbf{A}_{(t)}$, $\mathbf{B}_{(t)}$ and $\mathbf{S}_{(t)}$ have obtained, we need to calculate $\mathbf{S}_{(t+1)}$ by fixing $\mathbf{A}_{(t)}$ and $\mathbf{B}_{(t)}$ in the $(t+1)$th iteration. Furthermore, the $\mathbf{S}_{(t+1)}$ can converge to the globally optimal solution according to Equation (30) since $s_{i,j}^{(t+1)}$ has the closed-form solution. Therefore, we have

$$\|\mathbf{H}(\mathbf{XW}_{(t)} - \mathbf{Y})\|_F^2 + \alpha\|\mathbf{W}_{(t)}\|_{2,1}$$
$$+ \beta\left(\sum_{i,j=1}^n \|\mathbf{x}_i^T\mathbf{W}_{(t)} - \mathbf{x}_j^T\mathbf{W}_{(t)}\|_2^2 s_{i,j}^{(t+1)} + \gamma\sum_{i=1}^n \|\mathbf{s}_i^{(t+1)}\|_2^2\right)$$
$$+ \lambda\sum_{i,j=1}^d \|\mathbf{b}_i^{(t)} - \mathbf{b}_j^{(t)}\|_2^2 \tilde{s}_{i,j}$$
$$\leq \|\mathbf{H}(\mathbf{XW}_{(t)} - \mathbf{Y})\|_F^2 + \alpha\|\mathbf{W}_{(t)}\|_{2,1}$$
$$+ \beta\left(\sum_{i,j=1}^n \|\mathbf{x}_i^T\mathbf{W}_{(t)} - \mathbf{x}_j^T\mathbf{W}_{(t)}\|_2^2 s_{i,j}^{(t)} + \gamma\sum_{i=1}^n \|\mathbf{s}_i^{(t)}\|_2^2\right)$$
$$+ \lambda\sum_{i,j=1}^d \|\mathbf{b}_i^{(t)} - \mathbf{b}_j^{(t)}\|_2^2 \tilde{s}_{i,j} \tag{37}$$

where $\mathbf{s}_i^{(t)}$ and $\mathbf{s}_i^{(t+1)}$ are the ith row of $\mathbf{S}_{(t)}$ and $\mathbf{S}_{(t+1)}$, respectively. When fixing $\mathbf{S}_{(t+1)}$ to update $\mathbf{A}_{(t+1)}$ and $\mathbf{B}_{(t+1)}$, we have the following inequality,

$$\|\mathbf{H}(\mathbf{XW}_{(t+1)} - \mathbf{Y})\|_F^2 + \alpha\|\mathbf{W}_{(t+1)}\|_{2,1} + \lambda\sum_{i,j=1}^d \|\mathbf{b}_i^{(t+1)} - \mathbf{b}_j^{(t+1)}\|_2^2 \tilde{s}_{i,j}$$
$$+ \beta\left(\sum_{i,j=1}^n \|\mathbf{x}_i^T\mathbf{W}_{(t+1)} - \mathbf{x}_j^T\mathbf{W}_{(t+1)}\|_2^2 s_{i,j}^{(t+1)} + \gamma\sum_{i=1}^n \|\mathbf{s}_i^{(t+1)}\|_2^2\right)$$
$$\leq \|\mathbf{H}(\mathbf{XW}_{(t)} - \mathbf{Y})\|_F^2 + \alpha\|\mathbf{W}_{(t)}\|_{2,1} + \lambda\sum_{i,j=1}^d \|\mathbf{b}_i^{(t)} - \mathbf{b}_j^{(t)}\|_2^2 \tilde{s}_{i,j}$$
$$+ \beta\left(\sum_{i,j=1}^n \|\mathbf{x}_i^T\mathbf{W}_{(t)} - \mathbf{x}_j^T\mathbf{W}_{(t)}\|_2^2 s_{i,j}^{(t+1)} + \gamma\sum_{i=1}^n \|\mathbf{s}_i^{(t+1)}\|_2^2\right) \tag{38}$$

By combining Equation (37) and (38), we obtain

$$\|\mathbf{H}(\mathbf{XW}_{(t+1)} - \mathbf{Y})\|_F^2 + \alpha\|\mathbf{W}_{(t+1)}\|_{2,1}$$
$$+ \beta\left(\sum_{i,j=1}^n \|\mathbf{x}_i^T\mathbf{W}_{(t+1)} - \mathbf{x}_j^T\mathbf{W}_{(t+1)}\|_2^2 s_{i,j}^{(t+1)} + \gamma\sum_{i=1}^n \|\mathbf{s}_i^{(t+1)}\|_2^2\right)$$
$$+ \lambda\sum_{i,j=1}^d \|\mathbf{b}_i^{(t+1)} - \mathbf{b}_j^{(t+1)}\|_2^2 \tilde{s}_{i,j}$$
$$\leq \|\mathbf{H}(\mathbf{XW}_{(t)} - \mathbf{Y})\|_F^2 + \alpha\|\mathbf{W}_{(t)}\|_{2,1}$$
$$+ \beta\left(\sum_{i,j=1}^n \|\mathbf{x}_i^T\mathbf{W}_{(t)} - \mathbf{x}_j^T\mathbf{W}_{(t)}\|_2^2 s_{i,j}^{(t)} + \gamma\sum_{i=1}^n \|\mathbf{s}_i^{(t)}\|_2^2\right)$$
$$+ \lambda\sum_{i,j=1}^d \|\mathbf{b}_i^{(t)} - \mathbf{b}_j^{(t)}\|_2^2 \tilde{s}_{i,j} \tag{39}$$

According to Equation (38), the value of objective function monotonically decreases after each iteration of Algorithm 1, Theorem 2 is proved. □

5.3. Complexity Analysis

We further analyze the computational complexity of the proposed algorithm. In each iteration, the computation cost of Algorithm 1 focuses on calculating $\mathbf{P}^{-1}\mathbf{X}^T\mathbf{H}\mathbf{Y}\mathbf{B}^T\left(\mathbf{B}\mathbf{B}^T\right)^{-1}$ and solving the Sylvester function, the corresponding complexity are $\max\{\mathcal{O}(r^3), \mathcal{O}(d^3), \mathcal{O}(ndq), \mathcal{O}(dqr)\}$ and $\mathcal{O}(q^3)$, respectively. The complexity of Algorithm 2 stems from calculating the matrix **G**, the computation cost is $\max\{\mathcal{O}(n^2d),\mathcal{O}(n^2q)\}$. Since $r \leq \min(d,q)$, $n,d \gg r,q$, and it is experimentally observed that Algorithm 1 can converge within 30 iterations on different data sets. Hence, the computational complexity of the proposed method is approximate $\mathcal{O}(td^3 + tnd^2)$, where t ($n,d \gg t$) is the iteration of the whole alternating optimization.

6. Experiments

6.1. Datasets

We test the proposed approach on eight high-dimensional datasets (http://mulan.sourceforge.net/datasets-mtr.html, accessed on 18 January 2024), which are all from the public website Mulan [45]. All selected datasets are commonly used benchmark datasets for measuring MTR modeling performance. The detailed statistics of these datasets are shown in Table 1. We follow the strategies in [18] to impute the datasets with missing values, i.e., RF1 and RF2, which are replaced with sample means in the datasets.

Table 1. Characters of the datasets.

Datasets	Instances	Features	Targets	#-Fold	Domains
ATP1d	337	411	6	10	Price prediction
ATP7d	296	411	6	10	Price prediction
OES10	403	298	16	10	Artificial
OES97	334	263	16	10	Artificial
RF1	9125	64	8	2	Environment
RF2	9125	576	8	2	Environment
SCM1d	9803	280	16	2	Environment
SCM20d	8966	61	16	2	Environment

6.2. Compared Methods

In this paper, different MTFS methods are selected to compare the performance with the proposed approach.

- **MTFS** [44]: The row sparsity constraint is imposed on the weight matrix by $\ell_{2,1}$-norm regularization,

$$\min_{\mathbf{W}}\|\mathbf{X}\mathbf{W} - \mathbf{Y}\|_F^2 + \lambda\|\mathbf{W}\|_{2,1} \tag{40}$$

where λ is the tuning parameter, we set the parameters to range as $\{10^{-3}, 10^{-2}, \ldots, 10^3\}$ empirically.

- **RFS** [46]: By jointly imposing $\ell_{2,1}$-norm regularization on the loss function and the weight matrix, the objective function of RFS is:

$$\min_{\mathbf{W}}\|\mathbf{X}\mathbf{W} - \mathbf{Y}\|_{2,1} + \lambda\|\mathbf{W}\|_{2,1} \tag{41}$$

where the parameter λ range as $\{10^{-3}, 10^{-2}, \ldots, 10^3\}$.

- **SSFS** [29]: The multi-layer regression structure is constructed by low-dimensional embedding, and the loss function, weight matrix and structure matrix are joint $\ell_{2,1}$-norm regularized, and the objective function is:

$$\min_{\mathbf{W},\mathbf{U}}\|\mathbf{Z}\mathbf{U} - \mathbf{Y}\|_{2,1} + \lambda\|\mathbf{W}\|_{2,1} + \beta\|\mathbf{U}\|_{2,1} \tag{42}$$

where $\mathbf{Z} = \mathbf{X}\mathbf{W}$, λ and β are tuning parameters. All tuning parameters' range as $10^{[-3:1:3]}$.

- **HLMR-FS** [47]: The method introduces a hyper-graph Laplacian regularization to maintain the correlation structure between samples and find the hidden correlation structure among different target variables via the low-rank constraint.

$$\min_{A,B} \|Y - XAB\|_F^2 + \alpha \|AB\|_{2,p} + \beta tr\left(B^T A^T X^T L_H XAB\right)$$
$$s.t.\ A^T A = I \tag{43}$$

where L_H is the graph Laplacian matrix between the predicted output vectors of different training samples. α and β searched in the grid $10^{[-3:1:3]}$, and p searched in the grid $\{0.1, \ldots, 1.9\}$.

- **LFR-FS** [30]: The method captures the correlation between different objectives through low-rank constraint, and by designing $\ell_{2,p}$-norm regularization on the loss function and the regression matrix, the learning of the orthogonal subspace enables multiple outputs to share the same low-rank data structure to obtain the corresponding feature selection results.

$$\min_{A,B} \|Y - XAB\|_{2,p} + \alpha \|A\|_{2,p}$$
$$s.t.\ A^T A = I \tag{44}$$

where α searched in the grid $10^{[-3:1:3]}$, and p varied in $\{0.1, \ldots, 1.9\}$.

- **VMFS** [26]: VMFS ranks each feature in MTR via the famous Multi-Criteria Decision-Making (MCDM) method called VIKOR.
- **RSSFS** [48]: RSSFS uses the mixed convex and non-convex $\ell_{2,p}$-norm minimization on both regularization and loss function for joint sparse feature selection, and the objective function is:

$$\min_{W,H,Q} \left\|X^T W - Y\right\|_{2,p}^p + \alpha \|W\|_{2,p}^p + \beta \|W - QH\|_F^2$$
$$s.t.\ Q^T Q = I \tag{45}$$

In the experiments, the regularization parameter α and β were set in $10^{[-3:1:3]}$, and p varied in $\{0.1, \ldots, 0.9\}$.

In addition to choosing the above-compared methods, we also perform regressions by using the original data without feature selection as a **Baseline** to test and validate the effectiveness of the proposed method. We adopt the Multi-output Kernel Ridge Regression (mKRR) [49] to obtain the regression result corresponding to feature subsets obtained by different MTFS methods. In mKKR, Radial Basis Function (RBF) is utilized as the kernel function, and the kernel parameter and the regularization parameter range as $10^{[-3:1:3]}$ on the training data [29]. For different data sets, 70% of the samples are selected as the training set and the rest as the test set. As is shown in Table 1, we use two-fold cross-validation for RF1/RF2 and SCM1d/SCM20d and five-fold cross-validation on the training data for the rest of the datasets to conduct model selection.

6.3. Evaluation Metrics

Two evaluation metrics are employed in experiment, including average Correlation Coefficient (aCC) and average Relative Root Mean Squared Error (aRRMSE) [47]. The definition of aCC is as follows,

$$aCC = \frac{1}{q} \sum_{i=1}^{q} \frac{\sum_{j=1}^{N_{test}} \left(y_i^{(j)} - \bar{y}_i\right)\left(\hat{y}_i^{(j)} - \bar{\hat{y}}_i\right)}{\sqrt{\sum_{j=1}^{N_{test}} \left(y_i^{(j)} - \bar{y}_i\right)^2 \sum_{j=1}^{N_{test}} \left(\hat{y}_i^{(j)} - \bar{\hat{y}}_i\right)^2}} \tag{46}$$

where $y_i^{(j)}$ and $\hat{y}_i^{(j)}$ are the real and predicted values of the jth sample on the target i, $\bar{y}_i$ and $\tilde{y}_i$ are the mean of true value and the predicted value on target i over the test set, respectively. Likewise, the formula for aRRMSE is given:

$$aRRMSE = \frac{1}{q}\sum_{i=1}^{q}\sqrt{\frac{\sum_{j=1}^{N_{test}}\left(y_i^{(j)} - \hat{y}_i^{(j)}\right)^2}{\sum_{j=1}^{N_{test}}\left(y_i^{(j)} - \mathbf{y}_i\right)^2}} \qquad (47)$$

where $\mathbf{y}_i$ is the average value of the training samples on the ith target.

6.4. Results on the Data Sets

Figures 1 and 2 show the aRRMSE and aCC values for different MTFS methods on different data sets, respectively. For ATP1d and ATP7d, we choose 60, 70, 80, 90, 100, 110 features. For OES10, RF2 and SCM1d, we choose 60, 70, 80, 90, 100 and 110 features. For OES97, we choose 40, 60, 80, 100, 120 and 140 features. For RF1, we choose 10, 15, 20, 25, 30 and 35 features. For SCM20d, we choose 20, 25, 30, 35, 40 and 45 features.

Meanwhile, the best aCC and aRRMSE values of compared MTFS methods on various datasets are ranked, and the average rank of different methods on all datasets is calculated. The *Friedman* test [50] with the significant level $\alpha = 0.05$ is employed, and we utilize *Bonferroni-Dunn* test [50] as the post hoc test to further analysis of the comparison. The critical difference (CD) is calculated to measure the difference between the proposed method and other algorithms. The calculation of CD is as follows:

$$CD = q_\alpha \sqrt{\frac{n(n+1)}{6T}}. \qquad (48)$$

where n is the number of algorithms compared, and T is the number of datasets. At significance level $\alpha = 0.05$, the corresponding $q_\alpha = 3.73$, thus we have CD = 2.41 ($n = 9, T = 8$). Figures 3 and 4 show the average ranks of different feature selection methods based on aRRMSE and aCC metrics.

Obviously, from Figures 1 and 2, we can observe that for different data sets, selecting the correct number of feature subsets can achieve better results than the baseline, which indicates that for MTR problems, a practical feature selection method can not only improve the computational efficiency of the model but also improve the comprehensive performance of the model on different targets. Furthermore, the regression performance does not necessarily improve as the size of the selected features increases. On the contrary, in most cases, such as OES97, RF1, SCM20d, etc., the performance decreases as the number of selected features increases, indicating the presence of redundant or irrelevant features in the original feature set may significantly reduce the performance of regression.

For most cases, SSFS, HLMR-FS and the proposed method can obtain a lower aRRMSE and higher aCC than MTFS, RFS and VMFS. It shows that the performance of MTFS can be improved via a low-rank constraint. The proposed method not only considers the structural information of different samples in feature space but also uses the intrinsic correlation information between targets to improve the performance of MTFS. Furthermore, the proposed method can outperform the baseline in most cases, regardless of the number of features. It indicates that the proposed method can effectively alleviate the influence of redundant features, thereby maintaining outstanding performance on the selected subset even if some redundant features are included.

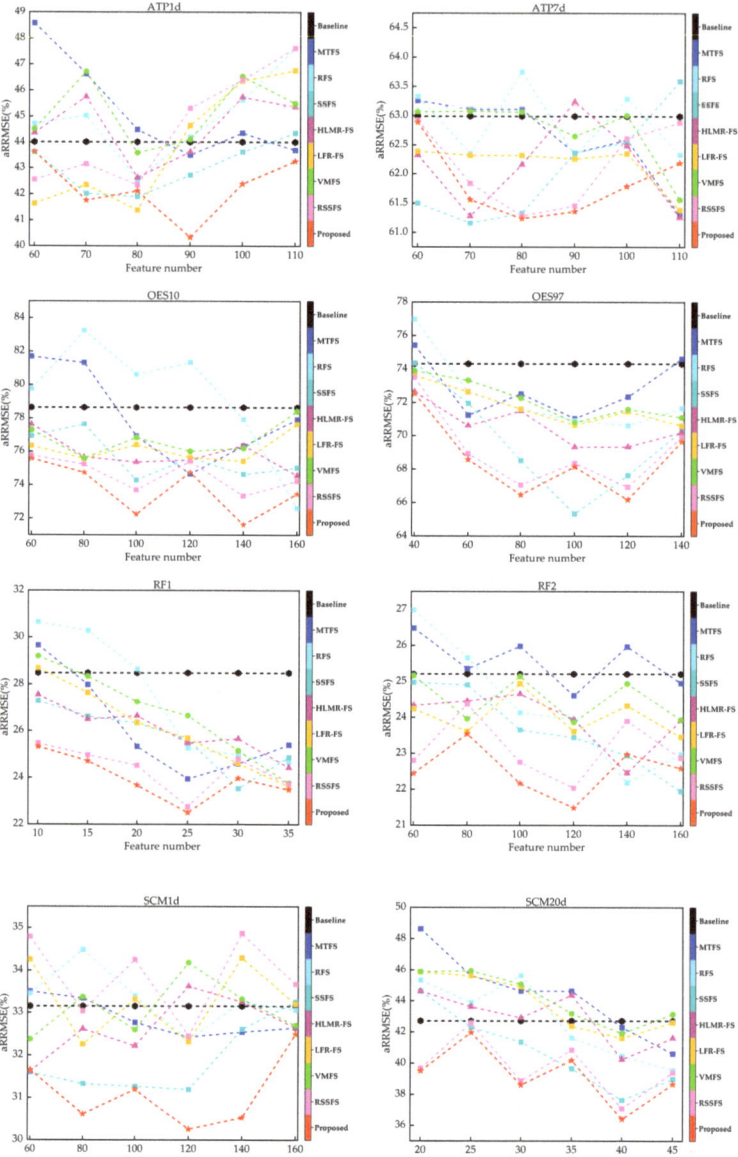

Figure 1. aRRMSE results compared with compared methods under different number of selected features.

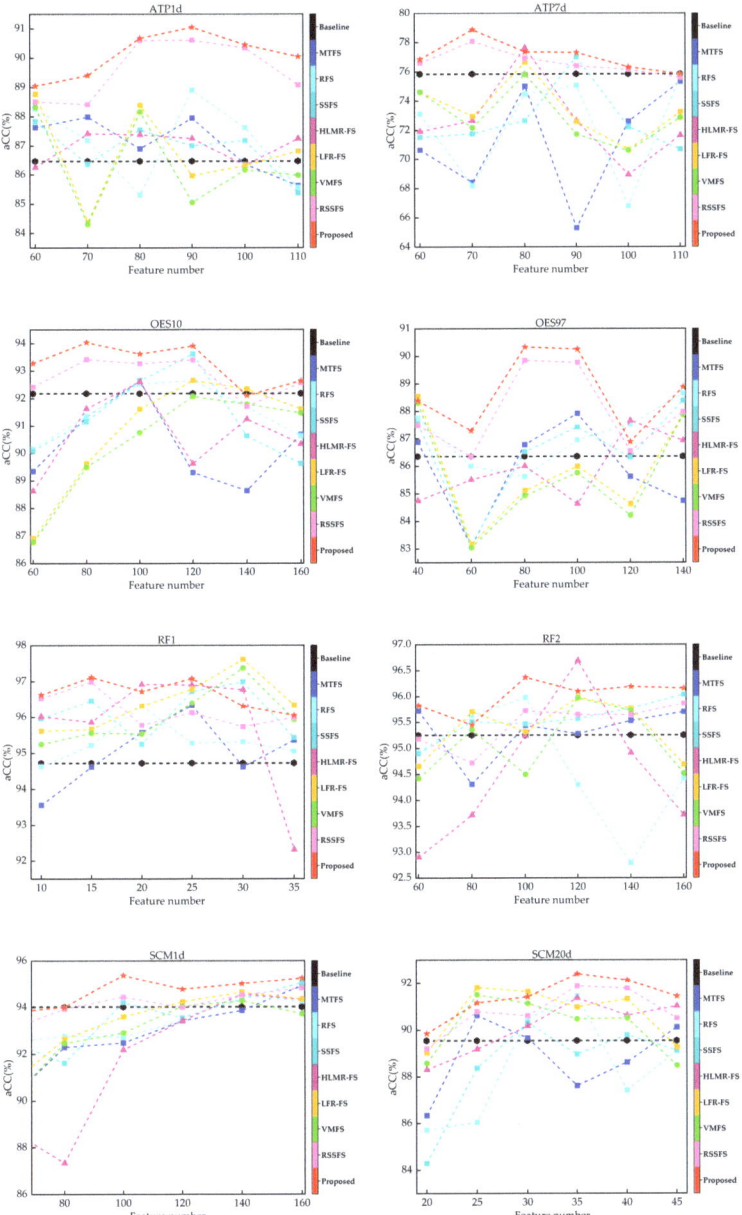

Figure 2. aCC results compared with state-of-the-art methods under different number of selected features.

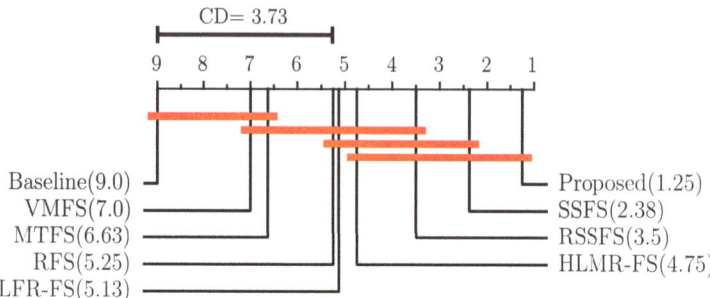

Figure 3. Average rank of different feature selection methods based on aRRMSE under Bonferroni–Dunn test.

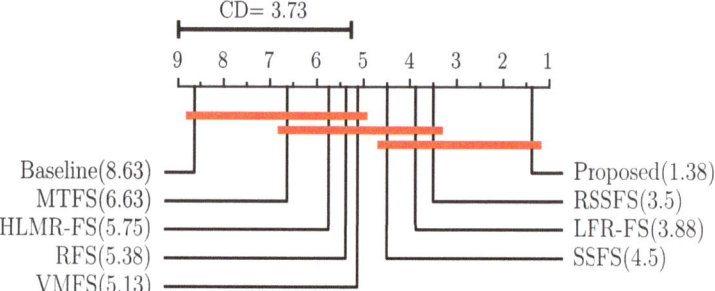

Figure 4. Average rank of feature selection methods based on aCC under Bonferroni–Dunn test.

6.5. Effect of Low-Rank Constraint

We also investigate the influence of different ranks over different data sets, set $r = 1, 2, \ldots, q$. The performance when $r = q$ is taken as the performance of the algorithm at full rank, on account of the condition $r \leq \min\{d, q\}$. The number of input features d in the adopted data set is much larger than q, so the corresponding rank value of the regression matrix at full rank is q. We set $r = \{1, 2, \ldots, 6\}$ in the ATP1d; $r = \{1, 2, \ldots, 16\}$ in the OES10; $r = \{1, 2, \ldots, 8\}$ in the RF1; $r = \{1, 2, \ldots, 16\}$ in the SCM1d. By setting different values of r to impose low-rank constraints on **A** and **B**. The fluctuations of aRRMSE and aCC values of the algorithm with α fixed are shown in Figure 5.

From Figure 5, it is evident that performance of the proposed method can be effectively improved by choosing the appropriate rank value for different data sets. In addition, most of the rank values in different data sets are better than the performance at full rank, which indicates that the regression matrix can decouple the inter-features and inter-target correlation via embedding the latent space of different dimensions, and it is beneficial to improve the regression performance and robustness of the model.

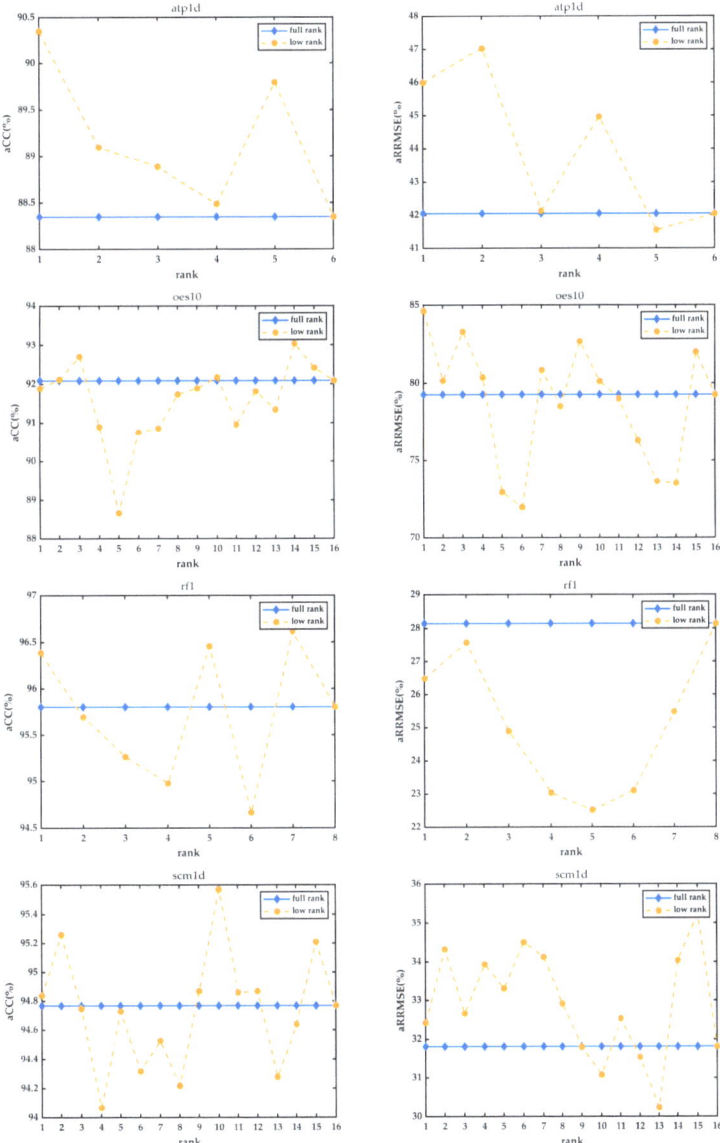

Figure 5. Performance of feature selection methods under different low-rank constraints.

6.6. Parameter Sensitivity

In this section, we further perform sensitivity analysis on different parameters in the proposed feature selection method. Since there is a closed-form solution for γ, we focus on sensitivity analysis for the regularization parameters α, λ and β. First of all, we tuned the parameter α within the range of $\{10^{-3}, 10^{-2}, \ldots, 10^3\}$ with $\lambda = 0.01$ and $\beta = 0.01$. Likewise, we tuned parameters λ and β in $\{10^{-3}, 10^{-2}, \ldots, 10^3\}$ with $\alpha = 0.1$, and the results are shown in Figures 6 and 7.

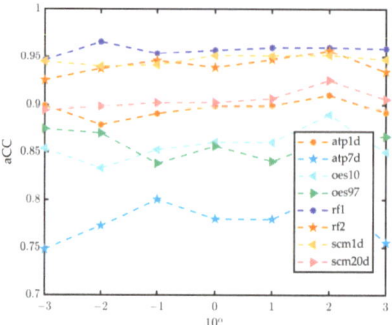

Figure 6. Sensitivity analysis of the parameter α with λ and β fixed.

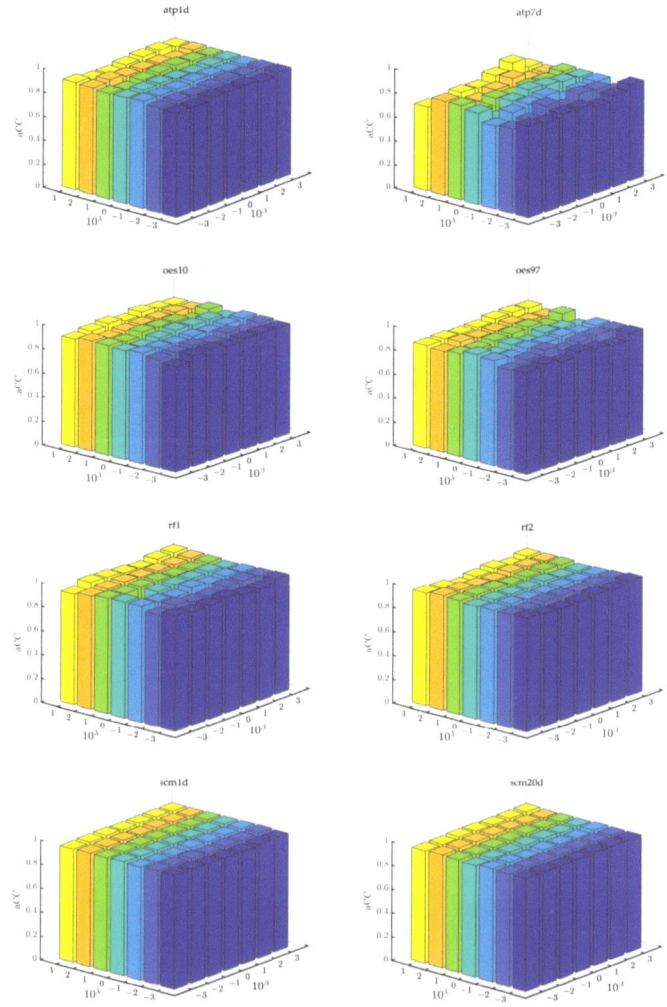

Figure 7. Sensitivity analysis of the parameter λ and β with α fixed.

In Figure 6, we can see that the variation of the parameter α will bring a certain degree of fluctuation in the model performance with λ and β fixed, which indicates that the proposed method is sensitive to α. Hence, parameter α is vital to determine the performance of the proposed method. From Figure 7, it can be seen that the changes in model performance after changes in parameters λ and β in ranges are not as significant as that of parameter α. However, properly tuning parameters λ and β can still improve the performance.

6.7. Convergence Study

We also plot the convergence curves of the objective function value of Equation (12) when the algorithm is updated iteratively on different data sets. As shown in Figure 8, it can be observed that ATP1d, ATP7d and RF1 can converge to the optimum within 20 iterations. The rest of the datasets can converge within 30 iterations, and the objective function converges quickly in the first few iterations. It indicates that the proposed alternating optimization algorithm can efficiently converge to the global optimum. Moreover, the monotone decrease of the objection function value demonstrates that the proposed problem can converge well. It confirms the effectiveness of the alternating optimization algorithm in addressing the proposed problem.

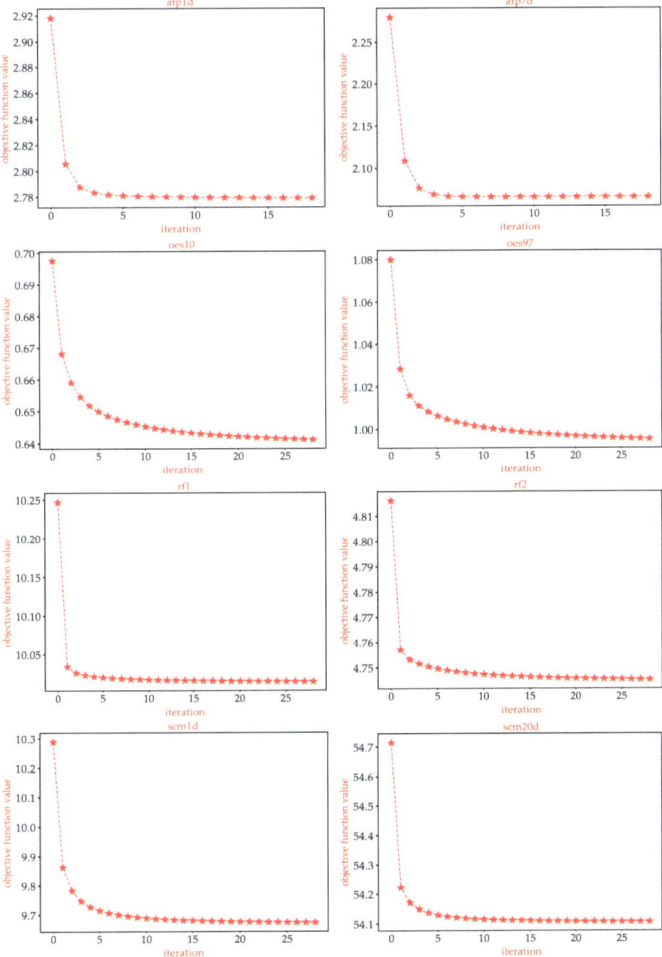

Figure 8. Convergence curves of the proposed method under different data sets.

7. Conclusions

This paper has proposed a novel MTFS method based on adaptive graph learning and global target correlations to perform feature selection in MTR problem. Considering the existence of feature redundancy and noise in the original data, adaptive graph learning based on the sample local structure is introduced. Meanwhile, a manifold regularizer based on the target correlations is constructed to explore the inter-target correlation, which enables the regression matrix to consider the correlation between targets in the sparse and low-rank learning process. Finally, an alternating optimization algorithm is proposed to solve the objective function of the MTFS problem, and the convergence of the algorithm is demonstrated both theoretically and empirically. Through extensive experiments, it is demonstrated that the proposed method has superior performance compared with other mainstream embedding MTFS algorithms. The proposed method can effectively select features for MTR data, and then improve the efficiency and accuracy of MTR modelling.

In the future, we will extend the proposed method to cope with the semi-supervised and unsupervised feature selection tasks in MTR scenarios, we will try to introduce more manifold constraints and low-rank structures to the feature selection problem of MTR and test its performance and we will also explore whether it can solve the feature selection problem in multi-task learning and MLC.

Author Contributions: Conceptualization, Y.Z. and D.H.; methodology, Y.Z.; software, D.H.; validation, Y.Z. and D.H.; formal analysis, Y.Z.; investigation, D.H.; resources, Y.Z.; data curation, D.H.; writing—original draft preparation, D.H.; writing—review and editing, D.H.; visualization, Y.Z.; supervision, Y.Z.; project administration, Y.Z.; funding acquisition, Y.Z. All authors have read and agreed to the published version of the manuscript.

Funding: This research was funded by the National Social Science Foundation of China, grant number 18BGL287, 19CGL073.

Data Availability Statement: Data are contained within the article.

Acknowledgments: The authors would like to thank Zhang Kan for his fund support.

Conflicts of Interest: The authors declare no conflicts of interest.

References

1. Li, H.; Zhang, W.; Chen, Y.; Guo, Y.; Li, G.-Z.; Zhu, X. A novel multi-target regression framework for time-series prediction of drug efficacy. *Sci. Rep.* **2017**, *7*, 40652. [CrossRef] [PubMed]
2. Kocev, D.; Džeroski, S.; White, M.D.; Newell, G.R.; Griffioen, P. Using single- and multi-target regression trees and ensembles to model a compound index of vegetation condition. *Ecol. Model.* **2009**, *220*, 1159–1168. [CrossRef]
3. Sicki, D.M. Multi-target tracking using multiple passive bearings-only asynchronous sensors. *IEEE Trans. Aerosp. Electron. Syst.* **2008**, *44*, 1151–1160.
4. He, D.; Sun, S.; Xie, L. Multi-Target Regression Based on Multi-Layer Sparse Structure and Its Application in Warships Scheduled Maintenance Cost Prediction. *Appl. Sci.* **2023**, *13*, 435. [CrossRef]
5. Zhen, X.; Islam, A.; Bhaduri, M.; Chan, I.; Li, S. Descriptor Learning via Supervised Manifold Regularization for Multi-output Regression. *IEEE Trans. Neural Netw. Learn. Syst.* **2017**, *28*, 2035–2047. [PubMed]
6. Wang, X.; Zhen, X.; Li, Q.; Shen, D.; Huang, H. Cognitive Assessment Prediction in Alzheimer's Disease by Multi-Layer Multi-Target Regression. *Neuroinformatics* **2018**, *16*, 285–294. [CrossRef] [PubMed]
7. Ghosn, J.; Bengio, Y. Multi-task learning for stock selection. In Proceedings of the 9th Advances in Neural Information Processing Systems, Denver, CO, USA, 2–5 December 1996; pp. 946–952.
8. Chen, B.J.; Chang, M.W. Load forecasting using support vector Machines: A study on EUNITE competition 2001. *IEEE Trans. Power Syst.* **2004**, *19*, 1821–1830. [CrossRef]
9. Cai, J.; Luo, J.; Wang, S.; Yang, S. Feature selection in machine learning: A new perspective. *Neurocomputing* **2018**, *300*, 70–79. [CrossRef]
10. Dinov, I.D. Variable/feature selection. In *Data Science and Predictive Analytics: Biomedical and Health Applications Using R*; Springer International Publishing: Cham, Switzerland, 2018; pp. 557–572.
11. Sechidis, K.; Spyromitros-Xioufis, E.; Vlahavas, I. Information Theoretic Multi-Target Feature Selection via Output Space Quantization. *Entropy* **2019**, *21*, 855. [CrossRef]
12. He, X.; Deng, C.; Niyogi, P. Laplacian Score for Feature Selection. In Proceedings of the Advances in Neural Information Processing Systems, Vancouver, BC, Canada, 5–8 December 2005; Volume 18.

13. Sechidis, K.; Brown, G. Simple strategies for semi-supervised feature selection. *Mach. Learn.* **2018**, *107*, 357–395. [CrossRef]
14. Kohavi, R.; John, G.H. Wrappers for feature subset selection. *Artif. Intell.* **1997**, *97*, 273–324. [CrossRef]
15. Tang, C.; Liu, X.; Li, M.; Wang, P.; Chen, J.; Wang, L.; Li, W. Robust unsupervised feature selection via dual self-representation and manifold regularization. *Knowl.-Based Syst.* **2018**, *145*, 109–120. [CrossRef]
16. Nouri-Moghaddam, B.; Ghazanfari, M.; Fathian, M. A novel multi-objective forest optimization algorithm for wrapper feature selection. *Expert Syst. Appl.* **2021**, *175*, 114737. [CrossRef]
17. Spyromitros-Xioufis, E.; Tsoumakas, G.; Groves, W.; Vlahavas, I. *Multi-Label Classification Methods for Multi-Target Regression*; Cornell University Library: Ithaca, NY, USA, 2014.
18. Spyromitros-Xioufis, E.; Tsoumakas, G.; Groves, W.; Vlahavas, I. Multi-target regression via input space expansion: treating targets as inputs. *Mach. Learn.* **2016**, *104*, 55–98. [CrossRef]
19. Tsoumakas, G.; Spyromitros-Xioufis, E.; Vrekou, A.; Vlahavas, I. *Multi-Target Regression via Random Linear Target Combinations*; Springer: Berlin/Heidelberg, Germany, 2014; pp. 225–240.
20. Zhu, Y.; Kwok, J.T.; Zhou, Z.H. Multi-Label Learning with Global and Local Label Correlation. *IEEE Trans. Knowl. Data Eng.* **2018**, *30*, 1081–1094. [CrossRef]
21. Zhu, X.; Zhang, S.; Hu, R.; Zhu, Y.; Song, J. Local and Global Structure Preservation for Robust Unsupervised Spectral Feature Selection. *IEEE Trans. Knowl. Data Eng.* **2018**, *30*, 517–529. [CrossRef]
22. Huang, Y.; Shen, Z.; Cai, F.; Li, T.; Lv, F. Adaptive graph-based generalized regression model for unsupervised feature selection. *Knowl.-Based Syst.* **2021**, *227*, 107156. [CrossRef]
23. Zhen, X.; Yu, M.; He, X.; Li, S. Multi-Target Regression via Robust Low-Rank Learning. *IEEE Trans. Pattern Anal. Mach. Intell.* **2018**, *40*, 497–504. [CrossRef]
24. Zhen, X.; Yu, M.; Zheng, F.; Nachum, I.B.; Bhaduri, M.; Laidley, D.; Li, S. Multitarget Sparse Latent Regression. *IEEE Trans. Neural Netw. Learn. Syst.* **2018**, *29*, 1575–1586. [CrossRef]
25. Yang, J.; Zhang, D.; Yang, J.Y.; Niu, B. Globally Maximizing, Locally Minimizing: Unsupervised Discriminant Projection with Applications to Face and Palm Biometrics. *IEEE Trans. Pattern Anal. Mach. Intell.* **2007**, *29*, 650–664. [CrossRef]
26. Hashemi, A.; Dowlatshahi, M.B.; Nezamabadi-pour, H. VMFS: A VIKOR-based multi-target feature selection. *Expert Syst. Appl.* **2021**, *182*, 115224. [CrossRef]
27. Petkovi, M.; Kocev, D.; Deroski, S. Feature ranking for multi-target regression. *Mach. Learn.* **2020**, *109*, 1179–1204. [CrossRef]
28. Masmoudi, S.; Elghazel, H.; Taieb, D.; Yazar, O.; Kallel, A. A machine-learning framework for predicting multiple air pollutants' concentrations via multi-target regression and feature selection. *Sci. Total. Environ.* **2020**, *715*, 136991. [CrossRef] [PubMed]
29. Yuan, H.; Zheng, J.; Lai, L.L.; Tang, Y.Y. Sparse structural feature selection for multitarget regression. *Knowl.-Based Syst.* **2018**, *160*, 200–209. [CrossRef]
30. Zhang, S.; Yang, L.; Li, Y.; Luo, Y.; Zhu, X. *Low-Rank Feature Reduction and Sample Selection for Multi-output Regression*; Springer International Publishing: Cham, Switzerland, 2016.
31. Fan, Y.; Chen, B.; Huang, W.; Liu, J.; Weng, W.; Lan, W. Multi-label feature selection based on label correlations and feature redundancy. *Knowl.-Based Syst.* **2022**, *241*, 108256. [CrossRef]
32. Xu, J.; Liu, J.; Yin, J.; Sun, C. A multi-label feature extraction algorithm via maximizing feature variance and feature-label dependence simultaneously. *Knowl.-Based Syst.* **2016**, *98*, 172–184. [CrossRef]
33. Samareh-Jahani, M.; Saberi-Movahed, F.; Eftekhari, M.; Aghamollaei, G.; Tiwari, P. Low-Redundant Unsupervised Feature Selection based on Data Structure Learning and Feature Orthogonalization. *Expert Syst. Appl.* **2024**, *240*, 122556. [CrossRef]
34. Ma, J.; Xu, F.; Rong, X. Discriminative multi-label feature selection with adaptive graph diffusion. *Pattern Recognit.* **2024**, *148*, 110154. [CrossRef]
35. Zhang, R.; Zhang, Y.; Li, X. Unsupervised feature selection via adaptive graph learning and constraint. *IEEE Trans. Neural Netw. Learn. Syst.* **2020**, *33*, 1355–1362. [CrossRef]
36. Zhu, X.; Zhang, S.; Zhu, Y.; Zhu, P.; Gao, Y. Unsupervised spectral feature selection with dynamic hyper-graph learning. *IEEE Trans. Knowl. Data Eng.* **2020**, *34*, 3016–3028. [CrossRef]
37. You, M.; Yuan, A.; He, D.; Li, X. Unsupervised feature selection via neural networks and self-expression with adaptive graph constraint. *Pattern Recognit.* **2023**, *135*, 109173. [CrossRef]
38. Acharya, D.B.; Zhang, H. Feature Selection and Extraction for Graph Neural Networks. In Proceedings of the 2020 ACM Southeast Conference (ACM SE '20), Tampa, FL, USA, 2–4 April 2020; Association for Computing Machinery: New York, NY, USA, 2020; pp. 252–255. [CrossRef]
39. Chen, L.; Huang, J.Z. Sparse Reduced-Rank Regression for Simultaneous Dimension Reduction and Variable Selection. *J. Am. Stat. Assoc.* **2012**, *107*, 1533–1545. [CrossRef]
40. Liu, G.; Lin, Z.; Yan, S.; Sun, J.; Yu, Y.; Ma, Y. Robust Recovery of Subspace Structures by Low-Rank Representation. *IEEE Trans. Pattern Anal. Mach. Intell.* **2013**, *35*, 171–184. [CrossRef] [PubMed]
41. Doquire, G.; Verleysen, M. A graph Laplacian based approach to semi-supervised feature selection for regression problems. *Neurocomputing* **2013**, *121*, 5–13. [CrossRef]
42. He, X.; Niyogi, P. Locality preserving projections. In Proceedings of the Advances in Neural Information Processing Systems, Vancouver, BC, Canada, 8–13 December 2003; Volume 16.

43. Wang, H.; Yang, Y.; Liu, B. GMC: Graph-Based Multi-View Clustering. *IEEE Trans. Knowl. Data Eng.* **2020**, *32*, 1116–1129. [CrossRef]
44. Liu, J.; Ji, S.; Ye, J. Multi-task feature learning via efficient $\ell_{2,1}$-norm minimization. In Proceedings of the Conference on Uncertainty in Artificial Intelligence, Montreal, QC, Canada, 18–21 June 2009; pp. 339–348.
45. Tsoumakas, G.; Spyromitros-Xioufis, E.; Vilcek, J. MULAN: A Java library for multi-label learning. *J. Mach. Learn. Res.* **2011**, *12*, 2411–2414.
46. Nie, F.; Huang, H.; Cai, X.; Ding, C. Efficient and Robust Feature Selection via Joint $\ell_{2,1}$-Norms Minimization. In Proceedings of the Neural Information Processing Systems (NIPS), Vancouver, BC, USA, 6–9 December 2010; pp. 1813–1821.
47. Borchani, H.; Varando, G.; Bielza, C.; Larrañaga, P. A survey on multi-output regression. *WIREs Data Min. Knowl. Discov.* **2015**, *5*, 216–233. [CrossRef]
48. Sheikhpour, R.; Gharaghani, S.; Nazarshodeh, E. Sparse feature selection in multi-target modeling of carbonic anhydrase isoforms by exploiting shared information among multiple targets. *Chemom. Intell. Lab. Syst.* **2020**, *200*, 104000. [CrossRef]
49. Shawe-Taylor, J.; Cristianini, N. *Kernel Methods for Pattern Analysis*; Cambridge University Press: Cambridge, UK, 2004.
50. Demšar, J.; Schuurmans, D. Statistical comparisons of classifiers over multiple data sets. *J. Mach. Learn. Res.* **2006**, *7*, 1–30.

Disclaimer/Publisher's Note: The statements, opinions and data contained in all publications are solely those of the individual author(s) and contributor(s) and not of MDPI and/or the editor(s). MDPI and/or the editor(s) disclaim responsibility for any injury to people or property resulting from any ideas, methods, instructions or products referred to in the content.

Article
State-Space Compression for Efficient Policy Learning in Crude Oil Scheduling

Nan Ma [1], Hongqi Li [1,*] and Hualin Liu [2,3]

1. School of Information Science and Engineering, China University of Petroleum, Beijing 102249, China; 2019310420@student.cup.edu.cn
2. Petrochina Planning and Engineering Institute, Beijing 100083, China; liuhualin08@petrochina.com.cn
3. Key Laboratory of Oil & Gas Business Chain Optimization, CNPC, Beijing 100083, China
* Correspondence: hq.li@cup.edu.cn

Abstract: The imperative for swift and intelligent decision making in production scheduling has intensified in recent years. Deep reinforcement learning, akin to human cognitive processes, has heralded advancements in complex decision making and has found applicability in the production scheduling domain. Yet, its deployment in industrial settings is marred by large state spaces, protracted training times, and challenging convergence, necessitating a more efficacious approach. Addressing these concerns, this paper introduces an innovative, accelerated deep reinforcement learning framework—VSCS (Variational Autoencoder for State Compression in Soft Actor–Critic). The framework adeptly employs a variational autoencoder (VAE) to condense the expansive high-dimensional state space into a tractable low-dimensional feature space, subsequently leveraging these features to refine policy learning and augment the policy network's performance and training efficacy. Furthermore, a novel methodology to ascertain the optimal dimensionality of these low-dimensional features is presented, integrating feature reconstruction similarity with visual analysis to facilitate informed dimensionality selection. This approach, rigorously validated within the realm of crude oil scheduling, demonstrates significant improvements over traditional methods. Notably, the convergence rate of the proposed VSCS method shows a remarkable increase of 77.5%, coupled with an 89.3% enhancement in the reward and punishment values. Furthermore, this method substantiates the robustness and appropriateness of the chosen feature dimensions.

Keywords: crude oil scheduling; efficient policy learning; state-space compression; reinforcement learning

MSC: 68T05

1. Introduction

The orchestration of crude oil storage and transportation scheduling is pivotal at the forefront of refinery operations, underpinning the safety of oil storage and transit, the stability of production, and the operational efficiency of the refinery [1]. This complex process encompasses the unloading of tankers, the coordination of terminal and factory tank storage, and the seamless transfer of resources to the processing apparatus. Effective scheduling requires intricate decision making across various operational phases, including the timely and precise movement of crude oil to designated units [2]. Objectives focus on maintaining uninterrupted processing, minimizing tanker delays, and optimizing resource allocation across storage and processing units. Operational dispatch must also navigate a myriad of practical considerations, from the punctuality of tanker arrivals to the preparedness of storage facilities and the interconnectivity of various systems. Addressing this large-scale, multiconstraint scheduling challenge is pivotal, representing a dynamic research frontier demanding innovative and efficient solutions.

Contemporary research methodologies addressing refinery crude oil scheduling predominantly draw upon operations research theory [3,4]. These approaches typically entail the formulation of the problem into a mathematical model amenable to solution [5–7]. The strength of this strategy lies in its capacity for the precise mathematical articulation of the scheduling process and production objectives, as well as in its ability to identify provably optimal solutions. However, the timeliness of these solutions poses a significant challenge. Presently, refinery crude oil scheduling is often represented and tackled as a large-scale mixed integer programming model, characterized as an NP-hard problem. Absent simplification, such models defy resolution within a practical timeframe.

Recent advancements in deep reinforcement learning have led to notable successes in tackling complex planning problems [8], prompting numerous research initiatives and applications in the realm of production resource scheduling with promising outcomes [9–12]. This methodology models business challenges as Markov decision processes and learns policies that maximize cumulative rewards through sustained interaction with the environment. Its core strengths lie in its neural-network-based approximation capabilities, rapid sequential decision making, and a degree of adaptability in addressing dynamic programming challenges [13]. Yet, when applied to actual industrial problems, these methods often grapple with expansive state spaces, extended training durations, and convergence difficulties [14], signaling the need for more efficient methods.

This study introduces a novel approach, termed Variational Autoencoder for State Compression in Soft Actor–Critic (VSCS), to model and expedite the training of deep reinforcement learning for refinery scheduling tasks. Initially, this research delineates the Markov decision process for refinery scheduling to lay the groundwork for subsequent optimization. The VSCS methodology employs a variational autoencoder to transmute the extensive, high-dimensional state space into a condensed, low-dimensional representation. Utilizing these distilled features, the VSCS algorithm learns the optimal policies in the reduced feature space, substantially enhancing both the learning efficiency and the efficacy of the derived policies. The paper's principal contributions are multifaceted, encompassing the following key dimensions:

- A novel deep reinforcement learning framework, VSCS, is presented, employing a variational autoencoder to distill the complex, high-dimensional state space of refinery crude oil scheduling into a compact, low-dimensional feature space for optimal policy identification.
- To address the challenge of selecting the dimensionality for low-dimensional features, we devised a method that rigorously evaluates the similarity of feature reconstructions. This approach, integrated with visual analytics, enables the precise determination of the optimal dimensionality for low-dimensional features.
- The VSCS approach delineated herein underwent comprehensive experiments within the crude oil scheduling problem, conclusively affirming the framework's efficacy. Experimental validation confirmed the appropriateness of the chosen low-dimensional feature dimensions, establishing a robust empirical foundation for the methodology.

The remainder of this paper is organized as follows. A brief review of related work is presented in Section 2. Section 3 shows the problem formulation. Section 4 presents the details of the VSCS method. Section 5 delineates and deliberates upon the principal experimental outcomes. Finally, some concluding remarks are given in Section 6.

2. Related Work

Crude oil storage and transportation scheduling are critically important to refinery production. This sequential decision-making process encompasses oil tanker arrival and unloading at the port, the conveyance of crude oil from terminal storage to in-plant tanks, and the subsequent delivery of crude materials to processing units. The overarching objective of scheduling is to minimize the cumulative costs, such as operational expenses, while adhering to the operational capabilities of each segment and maintaining the continuous, planned operation of processing units [15].

Production scheduling presents a multifaceted challenge extensively explored within the mathematical programming sphere, with research bifurcating into modeling methodologies and algorithmic solutions. Shah et al. pioneered a discrete-time Mixed-Integer Linear Programming (MILP) framework to navigate the intricacies of crude oil scheduling [16]. Advancing this groundwork, J.M. Pinto et al. crafted mixed-integer optimization models that capture the dichotomy of continuous and discrete temporal dynamics for refinery scheduling [17]. Jialin Xu's team leveraged continuous-time models for the simulation optimization of refinery operations, showcasing efficacy in scheduling and economic performance [1]. Further refining these approaches, Bernardo Zimberg et al. employed continuous-time models with intricate multioperation sequencing, achieving hourly resolution in their analyses [18]. Lijie Su introduced an innovative continuous–discrete-time hybrid model that stratifies refinery planning and scheduling into hierarchical levels, focusing on multiperiod crude oil scheduling with the aim of maximizing net profits, achieving solution times that range from minutes to hours [19]. Algorithmically, solutions span from MILP-NLP decomposition to solver-integrated responses [20–22] and rolling horizon strategies for time-segmented problem-solving [23]. Additionally, intelligent search mechanisms like genetic algorithms have been adopted to bolster solution throughput [24–27]. Traditional algorithms have thus concentrated on the meticulous detail of model construction and improving efficiency in confronting the complexities of refinery oil storage and transportation. Modeling has progressed from linear representations to intricate nonlinear continuous-time frameworks to mirror operational realities more closely. Nevertheless, the elevated complexity of such models demands the decomposition of problems into tractable subproblems suitable for solver optimization or the application of heuristics and genetic algorithms for more rapid approximate solutions. Consequently, advancing the performance of solutions in this domain remains an ongoing and formidable research challenge. Table 1 shows the different scales and corresponding performances of the calculation examples in the traditional method research of the crude oil scheduling problem.

Table 1. The scale and performance of traditional research methods in crude oil scheduling.

Technique	Scale	Performance
discrete-time MILP framework [16]	Four crude types, two CDUs, seven refinery tanks, and eight portside tanks; the time horizon of operation is one month, and a discretization interval of one day is used	in a few minutes
continuous and discrete temporal MILP [17]	Three CDUs, six storage tanks, and three oil pipelines; the time horizon of operation is one day, at every hour	in reasonable time
continuous-time MINLP [1]	One single docking berth, four storage tanks, four charging tanks, and two CDUs; the time horizon of operation is 15 days	25.94 s
Many-objective optimization for scheduling of crude oil operations based on NSGA-III [26]	There are three distillers with nine charging tanks and a long-distance pipeline; every time, it needs to produce a 10-day schedule	about 100 s–150 s
MILP framework with rolling horizon strategy [23]	Eight tanks, where one tank is assumed in maintenance, five crude qualities; the time horizon is 31 or 61 days (periods)	less than 5 min

Deep reinforcement learning (DRL) has emerged as a potent tool for complex decision-making challenges, with its application broadening significantly in recent years [28]. The method distinguishes itself through formidable learning and sequential decision-making capabilities, facilitating swift, dynamic scheduling decisions in diverse real-world scenarios. In the realm of manufacturing, Christian D. et al. employed DRL in the scheduling of chemical production, adeptly managing uncertainties and facilitating on-the-fly processing decisions, thereby surpassing the performance of MILP models [29]. Yong et al. pioneered a DRL-based methodology for dynamic flexible job-shop scheduling (DFJSP), focused on curtailing average delays through policy network training via the DDPG algorithm, thereby eclipsing rule-based and DQN techniques [30]. Che et al. aimed to curtail total operational expenditures to minimize energy usage and reduce the frequency of operational mode transitions, enhancing stability. For this, they utilized the PPO algorithm to train decision networks, yielding quantifiable improvements in cost-efficiency and mode-switching [31]. Lee et al. harnessed DRL to orchestrate semiconductor production line scheduling to align with production agendas, selecting DQN as the algorithm of choice and establishing strategies apt for dynamic manufacturing environments [32]. In the transportation field, Yan et al. addressed the intricacies of single-track railway scheduling, which encompasses train timetabling and station track allocation, via a sophisticated deep learning framework, securing superior results in large-scale scenarios in comparison with the commercial solver IBM CPLEX [33]. Furthermore, Pan et al. implemented hierarchical reinforcement pricing predicated on DDPG to solve the intricate distribution puzzles presented by shared bicycle resources, consequently achieving enhancements in service quality and bicycle distribution [34].

The extant research reveals that prevailing reinforcement learning methodologies face constraints in their deployment for large-scale industrial applications. These constraints arise from the considerable scale and intricacy of the scenarios, which give rise to extensive state–action spaces, thus hindering the efficiency of learning processes [14,35,36]. Within the domain of refinery crude oil scheduling, analogous challenges are encountered. To mitigate these challenges, the present study proposes the VSCS framework, which transposes the original, high-dimensional state space into a more compact, lower-dimensional feature space, thereby improving the learning process for the complexities of crude oil scheduling tasks.

3. Problem Formulation

3.1. Description of the Refinery Scheduling Problem

The refinery scheduling problem presented in this paper can be depicted as an operational process, as illustrated in Figure 1. It encompasses the arrival of crude oil tanker V_a at the port for unloading into designated port storage tanks. These tanks include owned storage vessels V_d and commercial storage vessels V_b. Following the desalting and settling operations of crude oil, the port storage tanks can transfer the oil to the in-plant tanks V_f as required via the long-distance pipeline V_p. Terrestrial crude oil V_l enters the in-plant storage tanks through the pipeline. The in-plant tank area is tasked with blending different types $m \in M$ of crude oil according to the processing schemes of the processing units V_u and transporting them to the processing units for refining.

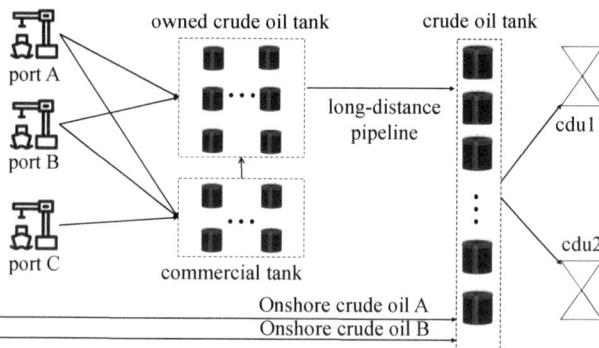

Figure 1. Schematic diagram of refinery crude oil scheduling scenario.

The initial conditions for the scheduling decision process include the anticipated arrival time of oil tankers and the storage tanks projected for unloading, the type of crude oil and the liquid level heights ($L_{vi}^{m,t0}$) stored in each tank at the outset, the upper and lower limits of tank liquid levels (C_{Ub}, C_{Lb}), the upper limit of the long-distance pipeline C_p, and the topology of the scheduling network. The operational constraints considered are as follows:

- Within a single cycle, each tank must contain only one type of oil product.
- Communal storage tanks and dock tanks can only commence oil transfer operations after completing static desalting.
- The liquid levels in all storage tanks must be maintained within the specified upper and lower capacity limits.
- The transfer rates must remain within the safe transfer speed range.
- Crude oil transported via overland pipelines enters the factory tanks at a predetermined rate.
- The processing units must operate continuously in accordance with the specified processing schemes and plans.

3.2. Markov Modeling

The scheduling objective of this study is to devise a decision-making scheme that minimizes scheduling costs within a short cycle of seven days (with each time step being four hours) while considering the operational constraints of refinery scheduling and the continuity of processing units. The decision scheme includes the oil transfer rates and target tanks for each storage unit. The refinery crude oil scheduling issue can be viewed as a sequential decision-making problem, where the operational process can be described by the fact that the state of each node in the refinery's crude oil storage and transportation operation in the next period is based on the decisions made in the current period, hence the scheduling issue can be modeled as a Markov decision process.

In the refinery scheduling Markov decision process, the type and level of materials in each storage tank are closely related to the scheduling objectives following operational execution. Moreover, the refinery's processing units require continuous feeding according to the processing plan; thus, the remaining processing volumes of various materials in the units must also be considered. Based on these considerations, the state is defined as follows, as illustrated in Equation (1).

$$S = \left\{ S^t_{va}, S^t_{vb}, S^t_{vd}, S^t_{vp}, S^t_{vf}, S^t_{vu} \right\} \tag{1}$$

where S^t_{va} includes $L^{m,t}_{va}$, which is the remaining unloading time of the tanker and other attribute information (such as node name). $S^t_{vb}, S^t_{vd}, S^t_{vf}$, respectively, represent the corresponding tank-level information $L^{m,t}_{vb}, L^{m,t}_{vd}, L^{m,t}_{vf}$, other attribute information (such as node name), etc. S^t_{vp} represents the oil head information connecting the terminal pipe area and the commercial storage pipe area, pipeline transportation volume L^t_p, etc.; S^t_{vu} includes the processing plan and the remaining processing volume of the device.

For the refinery's crude oil storage and transportation scheduling problem, the decision-making network is required to determine the appropriate scheduling actions in response to the varying states at each time period t. The action space is defined by the operational requirements of each node, with the specific action definitions provided in Equation (2).

$$A = \left\{ A^t_{V_a}, A^t_{V_b}, A^t_{V_d}, A^t_{V_p}, A^t_{V_u} \right\} \tag{2}$$

where $A^t_{V_a}$ represents the joint decision-making action of the V_a node, including the oil unloading speed. $A^t_{V_b}, A^t_{V_d}$ are the joint decision-making actions of V_b and V_d, respectively, including the oil payment speed of commercial storage tanks and terminal tank node and the oil payment target node. $A^t_{V_p}$ is the pipeline transportation speed, and $A^t_{V_u}$ includes processing speed.

In the proposed refinery crude oil scheduling model, each action executed during a scheduling step is assessed by the system through corresponding rewards, which serve to evaluate the efficacy of the action strategy. The objective of this model is to concurrently minimize operational events and maximize adherence to production constraints, according to the stipulated full-cycle processing plan. To facilitate the agent's strategy enhancement in alignment with this objective during training, the reward function is crafted to precisely guide action decisions. This function is expressed through Equations (3)–(6). Given that the algorithm aims to optimize the long-term average reward, the reward function is structured with negative values that are proportional to associated costs.

$$R = -\omega_0 R_0 - \omega_1 R_1 - \omega_2 R_2 \tag{3}$$

$$R_0 = \sum_{t \in T} \sum_{i \in \{b,d,f\}} \left(O_d \times \left(\left(C_{Ub_{vi}} - L_{vi}^{m,t} \right) + \left(L_{vi}^{m,t} - C_{Lb_{Vi}} \right) \right) \right)$$

$$+ \sum_{t \in T} O_d \times \left(L_p^t - C_p \right) + \sum_{t > T_a} O_a \times L_{v_a}^{m,t} \tag{4}$$

$$R_1 = O_p \times \left(NP_a + NP_b + NP_d + NP_f \right) + O_b \times \left(Nb_d + Nb_f + \sum_{i \in V_u} Nb_i \right) \tag{5}$$

$$R_2 = \sum_{t \in T} O_c L_{vi}^{m,t} \tag{6}$$

As shown in the above equation, R consists of three parts, where ω is the weight factor of each part; R_0 is the reward and punishment for exceeding the operation constraint, which is composed of each storage tank and the pipeline exceeding the operation constraint and the oil tanker overdue constraint; and R_1 is the speed fluctuation reward and punishment, that is, operation switching. The rewards and punishments are, respectively, composed of the oil tanker speed unloading switching, the oil payment switching of each storage tank, the processing device processing speed switching, and the reward and punishment for the oil type switching. R_2 is the reward and punishment for the inventory cost.

In our model, O_a denotes the cost coefficient associated with the delay in oil tanker unloading, with T_a representing the corresponding delay time. O_p is defined as the cost coefficient for speed fluctuations, while NP_v indicates the number of such fluctuations at each node. The term O_b refers to the cost incurred due to switching between different types of oil, with Nb_v quantifying the frequency of these oil species switches at each node. Lastly, O_d represents the cost coefficient for instances when the liquid level exceeds predetermined upper and lower limits, and O_c signifies the cost coefficient related to inventory management.

4. The Proposed VSCS Algorithm

4.1. The Framework of VSCS

The VSCS framework introduced in this study comprises two primary modules: the low-dimensional feature generation module and the policy learning module. The former autonomously extracts a condensed, low-dimensional feature representation, while the latter module leverages these features to facilitate efficient policy learning. Figure 2 delineates the structural organization and operational sequence of the VSCS framework within the context of refinery crude oil resource scheduling.

As depicted in Figure 2, the policy learning module, rooted in deep reinforcement learning, principally employs the Soft Actor–Critic (SAC) framework. This framework encompasses a policy network, a state value network, and an action value network. The objective is to deduce the appropriate reward feedback following state transitions within the refinery's crude oil storage and transportation scheduling environment. This is achieved by reconstructing the state into a lower-dimensional representation for efficient network training and subsequent action strategy formulation. The state low-dimensional feature generation module functions as a pretraining mechanism, utilizing an encoder network trained via the VAE architecture to transform the state space into a reduced feature space.

This transformation is instrumental in facilitating the strategic training of the main framework. Each module is expounded upon in the subsequent sections.

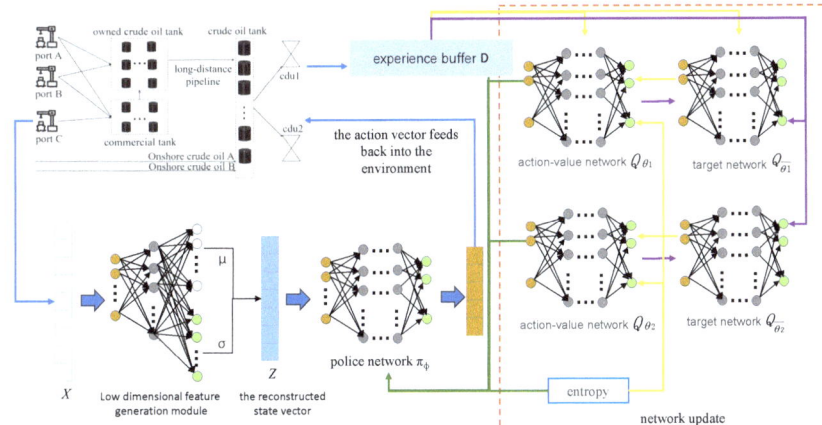

Figure 2. Framework diagram of the proposed VSCS algorithm.

4.2. Low-Dimensional Feature Generation Module

The objective of the low-dimensional feature generation module is to transmute the original, high-dimensional state space into a more tractable, low-dimensional state space while preserving the integrity of the state information to the greatest extent possible. This study employs a VAE to produce low-dimensional state features through unsupervised learning [37]. The VAE operates as a probabilistic model grounded in variational inference, comprising two primary components. The first is the encoder, which is tasked with condensing the high-dimensional state X into a compact, low-dimensional representation Z, which obeys Gaussian distribution and is composed of μ and σ generated by the encoder. The complementary component of the VAE is the decoder, which functions to regenerate the original features by reconstructing the latent variable Z back into the state transition vector X', as illustrated in Figure 3. More computation details are shown in Algorithm 1.

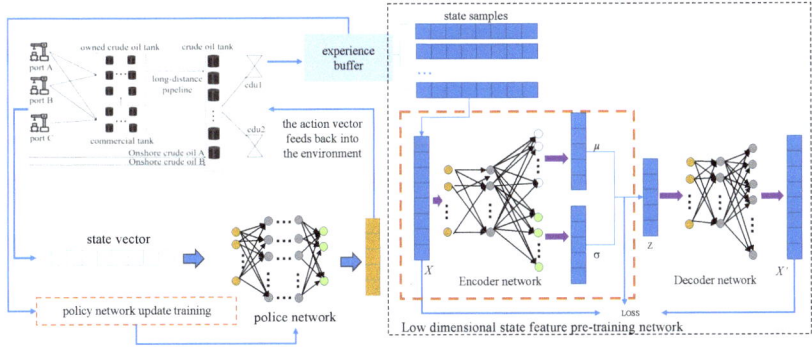

Figure 3. Framework diagram of the low-dimensional feature generation module.

In accordance with Bayesian principles, the joint probability distribution of the observed state vector X and the latent variable Z can be represented as depicted in Equation (7).

$$p(Z \mid X) = p(X \mid Z)p(Z)/p(X) \tag{7}$$

However, due to the intractability of $p(X)$, this study introduces an alternative distribution to approximate $p(Z \mid X)$. This approximative distribution, denoted as $q_\beta(Z \mid X)$, serves as an estimation of the posterior model (encoder), whereby Z is derived from X. The distribution denoted as $p_\eta(X \mid Z)p_\eta(Z)$ corresponds to the generative model (decoder). The encoder and decoder training process involves the concurrent learning of parameters β and η.

A central aspect of this work is the simultaneous training of the approximate posterior model and the generative model by maximizing the variational lower bound, which is articulated in Equation (8).

$$\zeta = -D_{KL}\big(q_\beta(Z \mid X) \| p_\beta(Z)\big) + E_{q_\beta(Z \mid X^{(i)})}\left[\log p_\eta\left(X^{(i)} \mid Z\right)\right] \tag{8}$$

The framework presumes that $p_\eta(Z)$ adheres to a Gaussian distribution, delineated in Equation (9), with Z derived through Gaussian sampling as per Equation (10). Herein, μ represents the mean, σ denotes the variance, and i is the index of the sample.

$$p_\eta(Z) \sim N(0,1) \tag{9}$$

$$q_\beta\left(Z \mid X^{(i)}\right) \sim N\left(\mu^{(i)}, \sigma^{2(i)}\right) \tag{10}$$

The loss function of this model comprises two components: the Kullback–Leibler (KL) divergence and the reconstruction loss, with the inferable outcomes delineated in Equation (11). Here, x_i signifies the encoder network's input, and x'_i denotes the output of the decoder network.

$$\zeta = \frac{1}{2n}\sum_{j=1}^{n}\left\{\sum_{j=1}^{n}\mu_j^2 + \sigma_j^2 - 1 - \log \sigma_j^2\right\} + \frac{1}{2n}\sum_{i=1}^{n}\|X_i - X'_i\|^2 \tag{11}$$

From the foregoing equation, the term $D_{KL}\big(q_\beta(Z \mid X) \| p_\eta(Z)\big)$ represents the approximation capability of the approximate posterior model, while $E_{q_\beta(Z \mid X^{(i)})}\left[\log p_\eta\left(X^{(i)} \mid Z\right)\right]$ signifies the reconstructive ability of the generative model to regenerate X' from Z. Consequently, this methodology can be employed to derive low-dimensional features from the initial state of crude oil storage and transportation dispatch, thereby attaining a reconstructed state that mirrors the description of the original state information to the greatest extent feasible.

Algorithm 1 Steps of computation in low-dimensional feature generation module

1: Initialize: $\mathcal{D}, q_\beta(Z \mid X), p_\eta(X \mid Z), \beta, \eta$
2: **while** (β, η) not convergence **do**
3:     $\mathcal{M} \sim \mathcal{D}$
4:     $Z \leftarrow$ Random sample from Gaussian distribution $\mathcal{N}(\mu, \sigma^2)$
5:     Compute ζ and its gradients
6:     Update (β, η)
7: **end while**
8: **return** β, η

4.3. Policy Learning Module

Leveraging the low-dimensional feature generation module, it is possible to produce a low-dimensional feature vector of the environment's original state, which facilitates the ensuing policy learning process. To guarantee the efficiency of policy training, the policy generation module in this study adopts the SAC framework as the principal structure for policy learning. This framework, predicated on the theory of entropy maximization, ensures that network updates equilibrate the maximization of expected returns with entropy, thereby enhancing the network's exploration capabilities and expediting the learning process. The objective function is articulated in Equation (12).

$$\pi^* = \arg\max_{\pi} E_{s_t,a_t \sim \pi}\left[\sum_{t=0}^{\infty} \gamma^t r(s_t, a_t) + \alpha H(\pi(\cdot \mid s_t))\right] \quad (12)$$

$$H(\pi(\cdot \mid s_t)) = E[-\log \pi(\cdot \mid s_t)] \quad (13)$$

In Equation (12), r denotes the reward function, and γ is the discount factor, while α signifies the entropy regularization coefficient, employed to modulate the significance of entropy in the learning process. In Equation (13), H represents the entropy value. A greater entropy value corresponds to a heightened level of exploration by the agent, promoting a more thorough investigation of the action space.

The training network within this framework comprises a policy network π_ϕ, an action value network $Q_{\theta_1,\theta_2}(a_t, s_t)$, and a target network, which are parameterized by Φ, θ_1, and θ_2, respectively. The action value network $Q_{\theta_1,\theta_2}(a_t, s_t)$ incorporates a dual Q-network structure. The soft Q-value is determined by taking the minimum value from two Q-value functions parameterized by θ_1 and θ_2. This approach is designed to mitigate the overestimation of inappropriate Q-values and to enhance the speed of training. The soft Q-value function is refined by minimizing the Bellman error, as detailed in Equation (15).

$$J_{Q(\theta)} = E_{(s_t,a_t)\sim D}\left[\frac{1}{2}\left(Q_{\theta_{i=1,2}}(s_t, a_t) - (r(s_t, a_t) + \gamma V_{\bar{\varphi}}(s_{t+1}))\right)^2\right] \quad (14)$$

$$V_{\bar{\varphi}}(s_{t+1}) = Q_{\bar{\theta}}(s_{t+1}, a_{t+1}) - \alpha \log(\pi_\phi(a_{t+1} \mid s_{t+1})) \quad (15)$$

where $V_{\bar{\varphi}}(s_{t+1})$ represents the state value of the agent at time $t+1$, and $Q_{\bar{\theta}}(s_{t+1}, a_{t+1})$ can be estimated using the target network.

Policy network π_ϕ is updated by minimizing the KL divergence, as shown in Equation (16).

$$J_{\pi(\phi)} = E_{a_t \sim \pi, s_t \sim D}\left[\log \pi_\phi(s_t, a_t) - \min_{i=1,2} Q_{\theta_i}(s_t, a_t)\right] \quad (16)$$

The proposed VSCS method is outlined in Algorithm 2.

Algorithm 2 The proposed VSCS Algorithm

1: Initialize: $N_{encoder}$ in VAE, θ_1, θ_2, ϕ in Q network and policy network.
2: $\bar{\theta}_1 = \theta_1$, $\bar{\theta}_2 = \theta_2$. Initialize experience buffer $\mathcal{D}$
3: **for** each iteration **do**
4:   **for** each environment step **do**
5:     $a_t = \pi_\phi(a_t \mid s_t)$
6:     $s_{t+1} = p(s_{t+1} \mid s_t, a_t)$
7:     $s'_t = N_{enc}(s_t)$
8:     $s'_{t+1} = N_{enc}(s_{t+1})$
9:     $\mathcal{D} = \mathcal{D} \cup \{s'_t, a_t, r_t, s'_{t+1}\}$
10:   **end for**
11:   **for** each gradient step **do**
12:     Sample from $\mathcal{D}$;
13:     Calculate the loss and update the action value network according to Equations (14) and (15)
14:     Calculate the loss and update the policy network according to Equation (16)
15:     Update the entropy regularization coefficient α
16:     Update the parameters of the target Q-network
17:   **end for**
18: **end for**

5. Experiment

To validate the efficacy of the proposed approach, this study conducts comprehensive experiments on the crude oil scheduling problem. The experiments include the following:

- Comparing the VSCS method introduced in this study with baseline algorithms using a dataset of refinery crude oil storage and transportation scheduling from an actual scenario.
- Analyzing the performance of the algorithm at various compression scales to determine the optimal low-dimensional feature dimensionality.
- Conducting a similarity analysis between low-dimensional reconstructed state features and original state samples and proposing a state reconstruction threshold for refinery crude oil scheduling problems based on reconstruction similarity.
- Evaluating the performance of the proposed algorithm by visualizing the low-dimensional features.

The goal of these experiments is to thoroughly assess the advantages and practical applicability of the proposed VSCS method in real-world crude oil scheduling tasks.

5.1. Data for Simulator

This investigation employs a dataset from a bona fide operational context within an oil company, encompassing various node types and their attributes, such as oil tankers, terminal tanks, commercial storage tanks, in-plant tanks, and processing devices, as delineated in Section 3. The dataset details encompass tanker oil load by type and volume, the initial liquid levels in storage tanks, the types of oil they house, storage capacities, transfer capabilities, and their processing apparatus' schemes and capacities. Integral to this study's reinforcement learning framework, the simulator accurately emulates the intricate and dynamic processes of crude oil storage and transportation within a refinery. The experimental setup utilizes a single oil tanker, 14 terminal storage tanks, 9 in-plant storage tanks, and 2 processing devices. This simulator facilitates an interactive learning milieu for the proposed algorithm, enabling adaptive training against the evolving dynamics of the refinery environment, providing continual feedback throughout the training phase, and assessing the algorithm's efficacy. The data input for the low-dimensional feature generation module is derived from sampling the experience pool within the aforementioned simulation environment, with a sampling scale consisting of 2048 random state samples, each with 61 dimensions.

In this study, the benchmark comparison is conducted against the SAC algorithm, a model premised on entropy maximization theory [38,39]. This approach ensures that updates to the training network balance the maximization of expected returns with entropy, thereby enhancing the algorithm's capacity for exploration and expediting the learning process.

5.2. Comparison with Baseline Algorithm

This section evaluates the enhanced performance of the proposed VSCS algorithm with respect to training convergence speed and the value of the final reward obtained post learning. To assess the stability of the algorithm following state reconstruction via VAE, the SAC algorithm is employed for baseline comparison. The experimental procedure involved multiple tests using diverse random seeds to determine the average learning efficacy of both the proposed algorithm and the baseline algorithm across ten different sets of random seeds. The learning performance is depicted through an average learning curve for clarity. Furthermore, in the experimental results, the rewards are logarithmically transformed for more coherent representation, as depicted in Figure 4. The principal parameters for the proposed VSCS algorithm is summarized in Table 2.

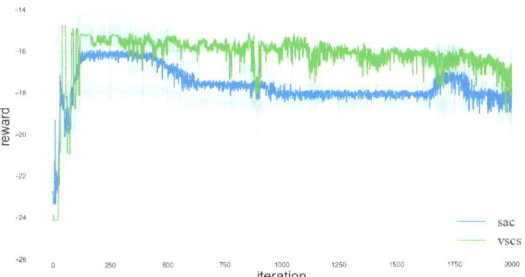

Figure 4. Learning curves of comparison methods. The solid lines show the means of 10 trials, and lighter shading shows standard errors.

Table 2. Main experimental parameters.

Model	Number of Neurons	Number of Hidden Layers	Optimizer	Discount Factor	Learning Rate	Soft Update Coefficient	Batch Size	Entropy Threshold	Experience Buffer Size
Policy learning module	512	5	Adam [40]	0.99	0.03	0.005	128	0.9	100,000
Low-dimensional feature generation module	40	1	Adam [40]						

Table 2 demonstrates that the VSCS algorithm proposed in this study markedly outperforms the baseline algorithm regarding the final reward value attained, showcasing an 89.3% enhancement in the final average reward value. In terms of training efficiency, the VSCS algorithm achieves the maximum reward in just 47 iterations. This represents a 77.5% increase in the rate at which training attains a stable state compared with the baseline algorithm. Additionally, the VSCS algorithm exhibits superior training stability relative to the baseline.

The reconstruction and compression of the state dimension prior to training the SAC network results in a significant reduction in the required sample size during the training process. This efficiency gain in sample size directly translates to enhanced network training efficiency, as the model can achieve comparable or superior learning outcomes with fewer data points.

5.3. Impact of Reconstruction with Different Compression Sizes

To assess the impact of the proposed VSCS algorithm on convergence speed and stability across varying compression scales, we conducted tests with dimensionalities set at 10, 15, 20, 25, 30, 35, 40, 45, 50, and 55. For each dimensionality, three sets of randomized trials were performed, with the average learning curves serving as the evaluative metric. The results of the learning curves are presented in Figure 5, and the algorithmic improvement rates are detailed in Table 3.

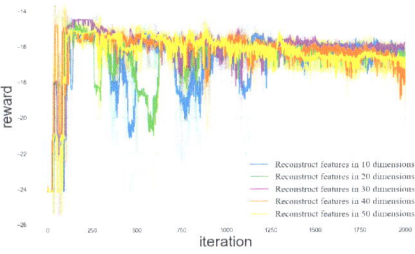

Figure 5. Comparison of low-dimensional feature reconstruction performance in different dimensions. The solid lines show the means of 3 trials, and lighter shading shows standard errors.

Table 3. Results of Comparison Methods.

	Iterations for Maximum Reward	Final Reward	Training Time to Steady State
SAC	209	−27,540,217	305
VSCS	47	−2,942,594	78
Improvement Rate (%)	77.5	89.3	74.4

Figure 5 reveals that the training process experiences increased instability when the algorithm is compressed to scales of 10 and 20, which is attributable to excessive compression that results in the loss of substantial state information. Conversely, compression scales of 30, 40, and 50 demonstrate relative stability, with the scale of 30 yielding the most effective learning strategy.

Table 4 illustrates improvements in algorithm training efficiency for the VSCS algorithm at various compression scales, with the exception of scale 15, over the baseline algorithm. Notably, at scale 40, the VSCS algorithm required only 47 rounds to achieve the cumulative maximum reward for the first time—a 77.51% increase in the rate of reaching a steady training state compared with the baseline. Furthermore, the learning performance of the VSCS algorithm was enhanced across all scales, showing an improvement rate exceeding 82%. The scales of 30 and 45 demonstrated the most significant enhancements, with an improvement rate of 92.95% in leaning performance compared with the baseline.

Table 4. The VSCS algorithm improvement rate analysis.

Feature Dimension	Iterations for Steady State	Convergence Speed Improvement Rate	Final Reward	Reward Improvement Rate
VSCS (10)	148	29.19%	−4,040,694	85.33%
VSCS (15)	215	−2.87%	−1,980,772	92.81%
VSCS (20)	158	24.40%	−2,143,448	92.22%
VSCS (25)	134	35.89%	−3,493,724	87.31%
VSCS (30)	147	29.67%	−1,940,762	92.95%
VSCS (35)	170	18.66%	−2,942,594	89.32%
VSCS (40)	47	77.51%	−2,991,348	89.14%
VSCS (45)	87	58.37%	−1,941,364	92.95%
VSCS (50)	105	49.76%	−4,876,383	82.29%

5.4. Reconstructed State Vector Similarity Analysis

In this analysis, we investigate the fidelity of state reconstruction by examining the similarity between the compressed and original states. We use the reconstruction distance to elucidate the reasons behind the enhanced training performance observed with reconstructed state vectors and introduce a threshold for reconstruction error tailored to the challenges of refinery crude oil storage and transportation scheduling. The experiment evaluates the encoder network of the VAE at compression scales of 10, 15, 20, 25, 30, 35, 40, 45, 50, and 55. We assess the congruence between 2048 original state samples and their reconstructed counterparts, which are produced by the decoder network, using Euclidean distance. The results, reflecting the similarity of output samples, are detailed in Table 5.

Table 5. Reconstruction distance analysis.

Dimensionality	55	50	45	40	35	30	25	20	15	10
Arithmetic Mean	12.66	12.72	12.66	12.61	12.67	12.47	12.52	12.55	12.53	12.54
Maximum	146.93	149.13	141.87	145.71	149.14	146.29	141.77	136.13	134.52	139.56
Minimum	0.23	0.27	0.33	0.44	0.38	0.56	0.61	1.17	1.36	0.59
Variance	608.91	620.99	617.28	608.06	619.23	606.81	611.70	614.83	614.93	611.88
Standard Deviation	24.67	24.92	24.85	24.66	24.88	24.63	24.73	24.80	24.80	24.74
Median	4.19	4.17	4.04	4.06	3.99	3.88	3.90	3.79	3.73	3.86

The encoder network with a compression scale of 30 demonstrates notable performance, yielding the highest mean similarity for reconstructed states. As detailed in Table 5, the arithmetic mean of similarity scores stands at 12.47, with a variance of 606.8.

After rigorous experimental analysis, it was determined that the reconstruction error threshold for refinery crude oil storage and transportation scheduling problems should be set at 12.47. This threshold implies that when the similarity distance falls below 12.47, the network is deemed to have achieved the standard of reconstruction.

5.5. Visual Analysis of Low-Dimensional Features

In this section, we delve into the characteristics of reconstructed states via low-dimensional visualization to elucidate the optimal effect achieved by compressing to 30 dimensions. The experiment involved reducing the dimensionality of 500 reconstructed state samples, across 10, 20, 30, 40, and 50 dimensions, down to a 2-dimensional plane using the UMAP technique [41]. We then observed the distribution of samples within this plane, employing cumulative average intracluster distance and intracluster density as metrics for quantitative analysis of the low-dimensional spatial formation. For the UMAP method, the approximate nearest-neighbor number parameter was set to 5, with the minimum interpoint distance parameter fixed at 0.3. The outcomes, displayed in Figure 6, reveal that in the two-dimensional space, the reconstructed states form clusters. Notably, the clusters at 30, 40, and 50 dimensions are more densely packed, whereas those at 10 and 20 dimensions exhibit greater dispersion.

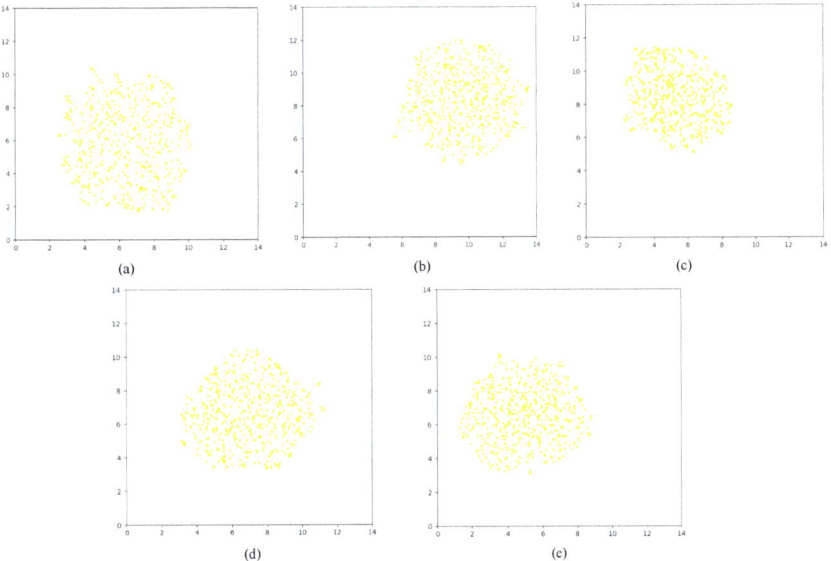

Figure 6. Results of sample dimensionality reduction visualization: (**a**) 10-dimensional sample dimensionality reduction visualization, (**b**) 20-dimensional sample dimensionality reduction visualization, (**c**) 30-dimensional sample dimensionality reduction visualization, (**d**) 40-dimensional sample dimensionality reduction visualization, (**e**) 50-dimensional sample dimensionality reduction visualization.

The quantitative analysis, utilizing the cumulative average intracluster distance (outlined in Equation (17)) and the intracluster density (specified in Equation (18)), is detailed in Table 6. Throughout the analysis, five distinct parameter configurations were employed for the assessment of means. As evidenced by Table 6, within the 30-dimensional reconstruction, the cumulative average intracluster distance is recorded at 64.10, with an average intracluster density of 0.0968—both metrics represent the most favorable values among the five parameter sets examined. These findings indicate that the 30-dimensional reconstruction yields the most cohesive cluster structure within the sample distribution.

$$d_{\text{avgdist}} = \sum_{i \in D} \sum_{j \in D} \text{dist}(x_i, x_j) / n_D \tag{17}$$

$$d_{\text{avgcent}} = \sum_{i \in D} \text{dist}(x_i, x_{\text{center}}) / n_D \tag{18}$$

Table 6. Quantitative analysis of visualization.

	50	40	30	20	10
Intracluster Cumulative Distance (5, 0.3)	75.07	73.04	71.88	79.53	90.4
Intracluster Cumulative Distance (5, 0.15)	66.32	69.14	65.7	72.67	83.5
Intracluster Cumulative Distance (10, 0.15)	57.81	57.77	57.55	61.17	70.1
Intracluster Cumulative Distance (10, 0.10)	56.38	55.4	55.14	59.02	67.3
Intracluster Cumulative Distance (10, 0.50)	71.25	71.13	70.22	75.74	86.35
Average Intracluster Cumulative Distance	65.37	65.30	64.10	69.63	79.53
Intracluster Density (10, 0.50)	0.104	0.104	0.102	0.109	0.124
Intracluster Density (10, 0.15)	0.083	0.082	0.082	0.086	0.101
Intracluster Density (5, 0.3)	0.108	0.104	0.104	0.113	0.131
Intracluster Density (5, 0.15)	0.094	0.099	0.093	0.105	0.124
Average Intracluster Density	0.0984	0.0984	0.0968	0.1042	0.1208

6. Conclusions

This study introduces the VSCS algorithm to expedite the training process of deep reinforcement learning models. The VSCS framework incorporates two key components: a low-dimensional feature generation module and a policy learning module. The former serves as a pretraining phase, leveraging a VAE to faithfully encapsulate the original state information within a reduced feature space. Upon completion of the training, the low-dimensional feature generation module integrates into the primary framework, furnishing the policy learning module with compact feature representations for policy network training. This synergistic approach facilitates end-to-end learning across both modules. A novel methodology was also developed to ascertain the optimal dimensionality for these low-dimensional features, accounting for reconstruction fidelity and visual analysis outcomes. A comprehensive experiment with the proposed method on the crude oil scheduling problem not only confirmed the efficacy of the framework but also empirically validated the optimal selection of low-dimensional feature dimensions.

The methodology presented herein primarily addresses the enhancement of performance in deep reinforcement learning when confronted with large-scale state representations. While it has yielded promising results, the prospect of its application within the industrial sector necessitates additional thorough investigation. Future research directives could include conducting generalizability studies on scheduling decisions across various refineries to solidify the method's applicability and robustness in diverse industrial contexts.

Author Contributions: N.M., conceptualization, methodology, software, formal analysis, visualization, writing—original draft, and writing—review and editing; H.L. (Hongqi Li), supervision, writing—original draft, and writing—review and editing; H.L. (Hualin Liu), formal analysis, writing—original draft, and writing—review and editing. All authors have read and agreed to the published version of the manuscript.

Funding: This research received no external funding.

Data Availability Statement: The data are not publicly available due to restrictions, their containing information that could compromise the privacy and interest of company.

Conflicts of Interest: The authors declare no conflicts of interest.

References

1. Xu, J.; Zhang, S.; Zhang, J.; Wang, S.; Xu, Q. Simultaneous scheduling of front-end crude transfer and refinery processing. *Comput. Chem. Eng.* **2017**, *96*, 212–236. [CrossRef]
2. Jia, Z.; Ierapetritou, M.; Kelly, J.D. Refinery short-term scheduling using continuous time formulation: Crude-oil operations. *Ind. Eng. Chem. Res.* **2003**, *42*, 3085–3097. [CrossRef]
3. Zheng, W.; Gao, X.; Zhu, G.; Zuo, X. Research progress on crude oil operation optimization. *CIESC J.* **2021**, *72*, 5481.
4. Hamisu, A.A.; Kabantiok, S.; Wang, M. An Improved MILP model for scheduling crude oil unloading, storage and processing. In *Computer Aided Chemical Engineering*; Elsevier: Lappeenranta, Finland, 2013; Volume 32, pp. 631–636.
5. Zhang, H.; Liang, Y.; Liao, Q.; Gao, J.; Yan, X.; Zhang, W. Mixed-time mixed-integer linear programming for optimal detailed scheduling of a crude oil port depot. *Chem. Eng. Res. Des.* **2018**, *137*, 434–451. [CrossRef]
6. Furman, K.C.; Jia, Z.; Ierapetritou, M.G. A robust event-based continuous time formulation for tank transfer scheduling. *Ind. Eng. Chem. Res.* **2007**, *46*, 9126–9136. [CrossRef]
7. Li, F.; Qian, F.; Du, W.; Yang, M.; Long, J.; Mahalec, V. Refinery production planning optimization under crude oil quality uncertainty. *Comput. Chem. Eng.* **2021**, *151*, 107361. [CrossRef]
8. Vinyals, O.; Babuschkin, I.; Czarnecki, W.M.; Mathieu, M.; Dudzik, A.; Chung, J.; Choi, D.H.; Powell, R.; Ewalds, T.; Georgiev, P.; et al. Grandmaster level in StarCraft II using multi-agent reinforcement learning. *Nature* **2019**, *575*, 350–354. [CrossRef] [PubMed]
9. Esteso, A.; Peidro, D.; Mula, J.; Díaz-Madroñero, M. Reinforcement learning applied to production planning and control. *Int. J. Prod. Res.* **2023**, *61*, 5772–5789. [CrossRef]
10. Dong, Y.; Zhang, H.; Wang, C.; Zhou, X. Soft actor-critic DRL algorithm for interval optimal dispatch of integrated energy systems with uncertainty in demand response and renewable energy. *Eng. Appl. Artif. Intell.* **2024**, *127*, 107230. [CrossRef]
11. Kuhnle, A.; Kaiser, J.P.; Theiß, F.; Stricker, N.; Lanza, G. Designing an adaptive production control system using reinforcement learning. *J. Intell. Manuf.* **2021**, *32*, 855–876. [CrossRef]
12. Park, J.; Chun, J.; Kim, S.H.; Kim, Y.; Park, J. Learning to schedule job-shop problems: representation and policy learning using graph neural network and reinforcement learning. *Int. J. Prod. Res.* **2021**, *59*, 3360–3377. [CrossRef]
13. Yang, X.; Wang, Z.; Zhang, H.; Ma, N.; Yang, N.; Liu, H.; Zhang, H.; Yang, L. A review: Machine learning for combinatorial optimization problems in energy areas. *Algorithms* **2022**, *15*, 205. [CrossRef]
14. Ogunfowora, O.; Najjaran, H. Reinforcement and deep reinforcement learning-based solutions for machine maintenance planning, scheduling policies, and optimization. *J. Manuf. Syst.* **2023**, *70*, 244–263. [CrossRef]
15. Hamisu, A.A.; Kabantiok, S.; Wang, M. Refinery scheduling of crude oil unloading with tank inventory management. *Comput. Chem. Eng.* **2013**, *55*, 134–147. [CrossRef]
16. Shah, N. Mathematical programming techniques for crude oil scheduling. *Comput. Chem. Eng.* **1996**, *20*, S1227–S1232. [CrossRef]
17. Pinto, J.M.; Joly, M.; Moro, L.F.L. Planning and scheduling models for refinery operations. *Comput. Chem. Eng.* **2000**, *24*, 2259–2276. [CrossRef]
18. Zimberg, B.; Ferreira, E.; Camponogara, E. A continuous-time formulation for scheduling crude oil operations in a terminal with a refinery pipeline. *Comput. Chem. Eng.* **2023**, *178*, 108354. [CrossRef]
19. Su, L.; Bernal, D.E.; Grossmann, I.E.; Tang, L. Modeling for integrated refinery planning with crude-oil scheduling. *Chem. Eng. Res. Des.* **2023**, *192*, 141–157. [CrossRef]
20. Castro, P.M.; Grossmann, I.E. Global optimal scheduling of crude oil blending operations with RTN continuous-time and multiparametric disaggregation. *Ind. Eng. Chem. Res.* **2014**, *53*, 15127–15145. [CrossRef]
21. Assis, L.S.; Camponogara, E.; Menezes, B.C.; Grossmann, I.E. An MINLP formulation for integrating the operational management of crude oil supply. *Comput. Chem. Eng.* **2019**, *123*, 110–125. [CrossRef]
22. Assis, L.S.; Camponogara, E.; Grossmann, I.E. A MILP-based clustering strategy for integrating the operational management of crude oil supply. *Comput. Chem. Eng.* **2021**, *145*, 107161. [CrossRef]
23. Zimberg, B.; Camponogara, E.; Ferreira, E. Reception, mixture, and transfer in a crude oil terminal. *Comput. Chem. Eng.* **2015**, *82*, 293–302. [CrossRef]
24. Ramteke, M.; Srinivasan, R. Large-scale refinery crude oil scheduling by integrating graph representation and genetic algorithm. *Ind. Eng. Chem. Res.* **2012**, *51*, 5256–5272. [CrossRef]
25. Hou, Y.; Wu, N.; Zhou, M.; Li, Z. Pareto-optimization for scheduling of crude oil operations in refinery via genetic algorithm. *IEEE Trans. Syst. Man Cybern. Syst.* **2015**, *47*, 517–530. [CrossRef]
26. Hou, Y.; Wu, N.; Li, Z.; Zhang, Y.; Qu, T.; Zhu, Q. Many-objective optimization for scheduling of crude oil operations based on NSGA-III with consideration of energy efficiency. *Swarm Evol. Comput.* **2020**, *57*, 100714. [CrossRef]
27. Ramteke, M.; Srinivasan, R. Integrating graph-based representation and genetic algorithm for large-scale optimization: Refinery crude oil scheduling. In *Computer Aided Chemical Engineering*; Elsevier: Amsterdam, The Netherlands, 2011; Volume 29, pp. 567–571.
28. Badia, A.P.; Piot, B.; Kapturowski, S.; Sprechmann, P.; Vitvitskyi, A.; Guo, Z.D.; Blundell, C. Agent57: Outperforming the atari human benchmark. In Proceedings of the International Conference on Machine Learning, PMLR, Virtual, 13–18 July 2020; pp. 507–517.
29. Hubbs, C.D.; Li, C.; Sahinidis, N.V.; Grossmann, I.E.; Wassick, J.M. A deep reinforcement learning approach for chemical production scheduling. *Comput. Chem. Eng.* **2020**, *141*, 106982. [CrossRef]

30. Gui, Y.; Tang, D.; Zhu, H.; Zhang, Y.; Zhang, Z. Dynamic scheduling for flexible job shop using a deep reinforcement learning approach. *Comput. Ind. Eng.* **2023**, *180*, 109255. [CrossRef]
31. Che, G.; Zhang, Y.; Tang, L.; Zhao, S. A deep reinforcement learning based multi-objective optimization for the scheduling of oxygen production system in integrated iron and steel plants. *Appl. Energy* **2023**, *345*, 121332. [CrossRef]
32. Lee, Y.H.; Lee, S. Deep reinforcement learning based scheduling within production plan in semiconductor fabrication. *Expert Syst. Appl.* **2022**, *191*, 116222. [CrossRef]
33. Yang, F.; Yang, Y.; Ni, S.; Liu, S.; Xu, C.; Chen, D.; Zhang, Q. Single-track railway scheduling with a novel gridworld model and scalable deep reinforcement learning. *Transp. Res. Part Emerg. Technol.* **2023**, *154*, 104237. [CrossRef]
34. Pan, L.; Cai, Q.; Fang, Z.; Tang, P.; Huang, L. A deep reinforcement learning framework for rebalancing dockless bike sharing systems. In Proceedings of the AAAI Conference on Artificial Intelligence, Hilton, HI, USA, 27 January–1 February 2019; Volume 33, pp. 1393–1400.
35. Yan, Q.; Wang, H.; Wu, F. Digital twin-enabled dynamic scheduling with preventive maintenance using a double-layer Q-learning algorithm. *Comput. Oper. Res.* **2022**, *144*, 105823. [CrossRef]
36. Chen, Y.; Liu, Y.; Xiahou, T. A deep reinforcement learning approach to dynamic loading strategy of repairable multistate systems. *IEEE Trans. Reliab.* **2021**, *71*, 484–499. [CrossRef]
37. Kingma, D.P.; Welling, M. Auto-encoding variational bayes. *arXiv* **2013**, arXiv:1312.6114.
38. Zang, W.; Song, D. Energy-saving profile optimization for underwater glider sampling: The soft actor critic method. *Measurement* **2023**, *217*, 113008. [CrossRef]
39. Hussain, A.; Bui, V.H.; Musilek, P. Local demand management of charging stations using vehicle-to-vehicle service: A welfare maximization-based soft actor-critic model. *eTransportation* **2023**, *18*, 100280. [CrossRef]
40. Kingma, D.P.; Ba, J. Adam: A method for stochastic optimization. *arXiv* **2014**, arXiv:1412.6980.
41. McInnes, L.; Healy, J.; Melville, J. Umap: Uniform manifold approximation and projection for dimension reduction. *arXiv* **2018**, arXiv:1802.03426.

Disclaimer/Publisher's Note: The statements, opinions and data contained in all publications are solely those of the individual author(s) and contributor(s) and not of MDPI and/or the editor(s). MDPI and/or the editor(s) disclaim responsibility for any injury to people or property resulting from any ideas, methods, instructions or products referred to in the content.

Article

Summary-Sentence Level Hierarchical Supervision for Re-Ranking Model of Two-Stage Abstractive Summarization Framework

Eunseok Yoo, Gyunyeop Kim and Sangwoo Kang *

School of Computing, Gachon University, 1342, Seongnam-daero, Sujeong-gu, Seongnam-si 13120, Republic of Korea; sunny8614@gachon.ac.kr (E.Y.); gyop0817@gachon.ac.kr (G.K.)
* Correspondence: swkang@gachon.ac.kr

Abstract: Fine-tuning a pre-trained sequence-to-sequence-based language model has significantly advanced the field of abstractive summarization. However, the early models of abstractive summarization were limited by the gap between training and inference, and they did not fully utilize the potential of the language model. Recent studies have introduced a two-stage framework that allows the second-stage model to re-rank the candidate summary generated by the first-stage model, to resolve these limitations. In this study, we point out that the supervision method performed in the existing re-ranking model of the two-stage abstractive summarization framework cannot learn detailed and complex information of the data. In addition, we present the problem of positional bias in the existing encoder–decoder-based re-ranking model. To address these two limitations, this study proposes a hierarchical supervision method that jointly performs summary and sentence-level supervision. For sentence-level supervision, we designed two sentence-level loss functions: intra- and inter-intra-sentence ranking losses. Compared to the existing abstractive summarization model, the proposed method exhibited a performance improvement for both the CNN/DM and XSum datasets. The proposed model outperformed the baseline model under a few-shot setting.

Keywords: abstractive summarization; text summarization; natural language processing; deep learning

MSC: 68T50

Citation: Yoo, E.; Kim, G.; Kang, S. Summary-Sentence Level Hierarchical Supervision for Re-Ranking Model of Two-Stage Abstractive Summarization Framework. *Mathematics* **2024**, *12*, 521. https://doi.org/10.3390/math12040521

Academic Editors: Florin Leon, Mircea Hulea and Marius Gavrilescu

Received: 11 January 2024
Revised: 5 February 2024
Accepted: 6 February 2024
Published: 7 February 2024

Copyright: © 2024 by the authors. Licensee MDPI, Basel, Switzerland. This article is an open access article distributed under the terms and conditions of the Creative Commons Attribution (CC BY) license (https://creativecommons.org/licenses/by/4.0/).

1. Introduction

Text summarization aims to create a concise summary containing the key information of a given document. Text summarization is divided into extractive and abstractive summarization, when generating a summary. In extractive summarization, the model extracts part of the document and then concatenates it to create a summary. An abstractive summarization model generates a summary using a combination of new words. This study focuses on abstractive summarization. Abstractive summarization has rapidly progressed through the introduction of sequence-to-sequence [1] models. A sequence-to-sequence model receives a token-level sequence as the input to an encoder and generates a token-level sequence as the output of the decoder. In the training phase, the teacher-forcing method is used to input the correct answer token into the decoder, rather than the token generated by the model, for efficient training. By contrast, in the inference phase, the tokens generated by the model are input into the decoder. Transfer learning [2], involving pre-training a language model and then fine-tuning it, is a widely used training method for abstractive summarization models. In the pre-training step, the language model learns general text generation through conducting self-supervised learning with a large unlabeled corpus. Subsequently, the pre-trained language model is fine-tuned using a human-written downstream summarization dataset.

However, the early single-stage abstractive summarization model based on a language model with a encoder–decoder structure has several limitations. The first is the training–

evaluation gap. The objective function of the generative language model is based on token-level prediction. However, the evaluation metric judges the overall similarity between the gold summary and the summary generated by the model. In addition, the sequence-to-sequence model adopts the teacher-forcing method during training, and auto-regressively generates sequences in the inference phase. Therefore, a discrepancy occurs between the training and inference phases, which is known as the exposure bias [3] problem. Second, the single-stage abstractive summarization model has an insufficient ability for selecting the optimal output summary from among candidate summaries. SimCLS [4] pointed out that current studies on abstractive summarization do not fully utilize the potential of language models. SimCLS demonstrated a significant difference in evaluation scores between the summary chosen by the model as the final output and the summary most similar to the gold summary among the candidate summaries. SimCLS revealed a difference of over 10 points in ROUGE-1 [5] score based on fine-tuned BART [6] with a CNN/DM [7] dataset.

To overcome these limitations, research on a two-stage framework for abstractive summarization is being conducted. A recent two-stage framework generated candidate summaries in the first-stage model. The second-stage model then re-ranks the candidate summaries to determine the final output summary. The two-stage framework uses the sequence-level loss to train the second-stage model. Therefore, the training–inference gap of the existing single-stage models can be resolved. This also allows the model to learn optimal summary selection from a range of candidates. In a second-stage model, either a differently structured model is introduced, or the first-stage model is reused. SimCLS and others used an encoder-only model as the second-stage model, whereas BRIO [8] and others reused the first-stage model, which is the encoder–decoder model, as the second-stage model.

In this study, we highlight two limitations of the existing second-stage re-rank model of a two-stage abstractive summarization framework and propose a novel training method to resolve them. First, the existing studies did not consider complex information in the candidate summary. The candidate summary is the result generated by the deep learning model. Therefore, as shown in Figure 1, well-generated and poorly generated sentences coexist in the candidate summary. However, the existing re-ranking models generally perform summary-level supervision, in which the loss is calculated using only one value for a single-candidate summary. If only summary-level supervision is performed during model training, it becomes difficult for the model to learn complex information from the candidate summary. In this study, we argue that using only summary-level supervision for training the re-ranking model is not an appropriate method.

The second limitation is the bias in the position of the sentence in the existing encoder–decoder-based re-ranking models. The training and inference of the encoder–decoder-based re-ranking models are executed based on a generation probability value for each token in the candidate summary. The average of the generation probability values for all the tokens constituting a single candidate summary is used as the predicted score for the corresponding candidate summary. In this study, we confirmed that the existing encoder–decoder-based re-ranking model tends to allocate lower prediction scores to sentences located toward the end of the candidate summary.

In this study, we propose a re-ranking model that uses hierarchical supervision during training to address these two limitations of the existing re-ranking model of the two-stage abstract summary framework. The proposed model jointly uses sentence and summary-level supervision during training. We designed two types of alternative sentence-level loss for sentence-level supervision. Through the joint objective function, the model learns not only the rank between the candidate summaries, but also the rank between the sentences constituting the candidate summary. Our proposed method can resolve the limitation of the existing re-ranking model, which overlooks the complex information in the candidate summary. In addition, we can alleviate the positional bias problem of the existing encoder–decoder-based re-ranking models. In experiments using two datasets, CNN/DM and XSum [9], the proposed model showed a performance improvement over the existing models in both fully supervised and few-shot settings. Through an additional analysis, we confirmed that the proposed method enables effective learning of the rank between sentences and alleviates positional bias.

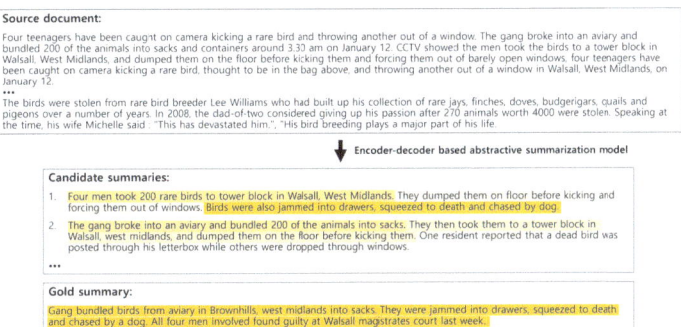

Figure 1. Example of similarity between the gold summary and each sentence in the candidate summary. The higher the ROUGE-1 recall score of the gold summary and the sentence, the darker the sentence is highlighted.

2. Related Work

2.1. Re-Ranking Model for Abstractive Summarization.

The two-stage framework for abstractive summarization has made significant progress in abstractive summarization by alleviating the train–inference gap and enhancing the potential of language models through a re-ranking model. SimCLS [4] proposes a model for re-ranking candidate summaries using RoBERTa [10], an encoder-only pre-training language model. SimCLS independently derives the representation of the source document, gold summary, and each candidate summary. The model learns that the more similar the candidate summary is to the gold summary, the closer it is to the corresponding source document. Margin ranking loss is used as the loss function. SummaReranker [11] proposed a multi-task learning model based on an encoder-only RoBERTa model, SimCLS. SummaReranker used a multi-gate mixture-of-experts [12] to jointly learn the rank of the candidate summary base on the ROUGE score [5], BART score [13], and BERT score [14]. Multi-label binary cross-entropy was used as the loss function for model training. BRIO [8] reused the first-stage model as a second-stage re-ranking model. BRIO used the encoder–decoder models BART [6] and PEGASUS [15] as re-ranking models. The model was trained to assign a higher generation probability, because the candidate summary was similar to the gold summary. A loss function based on the margin ranking loss was used for training.

2.2. Sentence-Level Supervision.

For several NLP tasks that primarily use document or passage-level supervision, studies have been conducted to perform sentence-level supervision and document/passage-level supervision. Open-domain passage retrieval aims to determine the most appropriate passage in a passage pool to respond to a given query. Document-level supervision is commonly used for training open-domain passage retrieval. DCSR [16] pointed out that using only document-level supervision for training is not the optimal method, because one passage has multiple sentences containing different information, and they suggested performing sentence-level supervision. A similar approach was studied using a document-level relation extraction task, which aimed to determine the relationship between two entities in a document with multiple sentences. In existing studies, an entire document is generally represented as a sequence or graph-based model to predict the relationship of the entity pair. SIEF [17] designed a sentence focusing loss to ensure that the document from which non-evidence sentences are removed and the original document have the same output distribution. Through sentence focusing loss, the model learned to focus on evidence sentences that are directly related to the relational information of the entity pair.

2.3. Approaches to Reflecting Detailed Information in Text Summarization

In text summarization tasks, various attempts have been made to enable models to learn detailed information contained in a text. SEASON [18] introduced a salience-aware cross-attention module to allow the model to better focus on key sentences in the source document. The model was learned by jointly performing extractive and abstractive summarization. Some studies have emphasized that the summary should not change the meaning of the source document. Thus, a model has been proposed that produces a wide range of summaries, from completely extracted to highly abstractive summaries, by allowing it control over copying [19]. There was also a study to make a more accurate and realistic summary of life events by analyzing the role of sentiment in the generated text [20].

3. Methodology

In this study, we propose a hierarchical supervision method that jointly performs sentence-level supervision and summary-level supervision to train a re-ranking model for abstractive summarization. In other words, the proposed model in this study aims to re-rank the candidate summary generated by the first-stage generation model by learning to assign higher scores to the summary or sentence most similar to the gold summary. Figure 2 illustrates the overall structure of the proposed model. The encoder takes the source document as input, and the decoder takes a single candidate summary as input. Subsequently, the decoder outputs a generation probability value for each token that constitutes a candidate summary. The average of the generation probability values of all tokens constituting the candidate summary is considered the predicted score of the corresponding candidate summary. Similarly, the predicted score of a sentence is the average of the generation probabilities of the tokens constituting the sentence. During training, summary-level supervision and sentence-level supervision are performed for the candidate summary and sentence scores predicted by the model, respectively. The model learns the ranking of the candidate summaries through summary-level supervision. The proposed method performs sentence-level supervision using two types of sentence ranking loss: (1) Intra-sentence ranking loss, which aims to learn the ranking between sentences that consist of the same candidate summary. (2) Inter-sentence ranking loss allows the model to learn the ranking between the sentences that constitute the different candidate summaries.

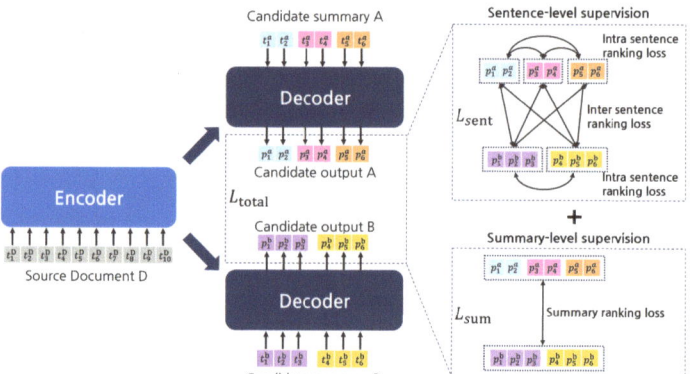

Figure 2. Overall architecture of the proposed model. The proposed model performs sentence and summary-level supervision simultaneously during training. Superscripts and subscripts associated with the elements are the source document/candidate summary index and token index, respectively. Generation probability values for tokens constituting the same sentence are expressed in uniform colors.

3.1. Problem Statement

In this study, we present two problems with the existing abstractive summarization re-ranking model. The first problem is that complex information in the candidate summary can be overlooked if the model is trained using only summary-level supervision. The existing re-ranking models are typically trained using summary-level supervision. Re-ranking models with encoder-only structures such as SimCLS [4], independently encode documents and summaries to represent an entire single document or summary as a single vector representation. In encoder–decoder re-ranking models, such as BRIO [8], the average of the generated probability values of the tokens constituting the candidate summary is used as the predicted score for the corresponding candidate summary. Therefore, model supervision is performed using only one value for a candidate summary in existing studies. However, as shown in Figure 1, well and poorly generated sentences coexist in the model-generated candidate summary. Figure 3 shows a distribution plot of the score difference between the sentence with the highest ROUGE-1 recall score and the sentence with the lowest ROUGE-1 recall score for the gold summary among all sentences constituting a single candidate summary. Candidate summaries generated for the CNN/DM [7] test dataset through fine-tuned BART [6] were used for statistical analysis. According to this distribution plot, we can confirm that the quality of sentences generated by the model was diverse, even for a single candidate summary. If the model is supervised using only summary-level supervision, it becomes difficult to learn qualitative differences between sentences. In other words, it becomes difficult to determine whether summary-level supervision is suitable for the characteristics of candidate summaries with a combination of positive (well-summarized) and negative (poorly summarized) elements.

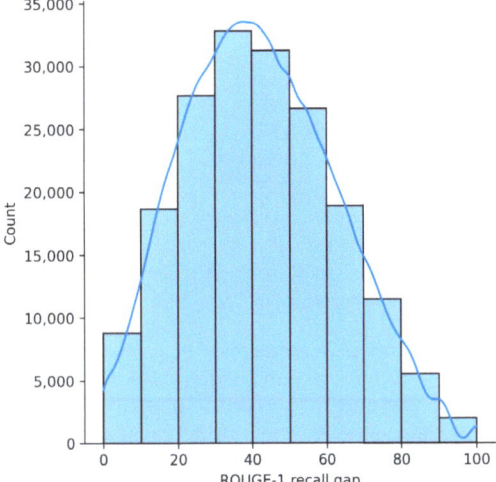

Figure 3. Distribution plot of the maximum evaluation score gap of a sentence pair in a single candidate summary. The plot shows the diversity of the quality of sentences in the single candidate summary that the model generated. For the evaluation score of each sentence, the ROUGE-1 recall score between the sentence and the gold summary was used. Candidate summaries generated for the test dataset of CNN/DM through fine-tuned BART were used.

The second limitation is the bias according to sentence position in the encoder–decoder-based abstractive summarization re-ranking model. Existing encoder–decoder re-ranking models tend to allocate a lower predicted score when the sentence is located behind the candidate summary. Figure 4 confirms the positional bias of the existing encoder–decoder re-ranking model using the CNN/DM test set. Figure 4 is a bar chart comparing the position of the sentence to which the existing model (expressed as "Baseline") assigned the lowest prediction score in one candidate summary and the position of the sentence that least resembled the gold summary (expressed as "Oracle"). "First" means the first sentence of the summary, "Last" means the last sentence, and "Intermediate" means all the sentences located between the first and last sentences. To confirm this bias, we stored the ROUGE score with a gold summary for all the sentences constituting each candidate summary. We then compared the ground-truth score of the sentence with the sentence score predicted by the model (average of the generation probability values of all tokens that made up the sentence). The analysis indicated that the probability of the last sentence of the candidate summary having the lowest ground-truth score was approximately 45%. By comparison, the rate at which the existing model (BRIO) allocated the lowest prediction score to the last sentence was approximately 76%, which is a considerable difference. The analysis results confirmed that the existing encoder–decoder re-ranking model has a bias in assigning lower prediction scores to sentences toward the end of the candidate summary.

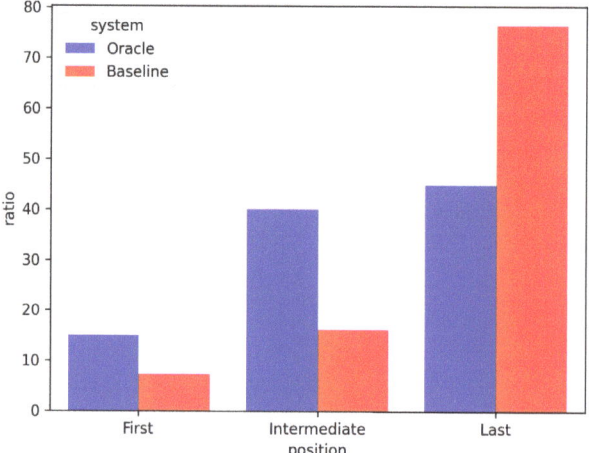

Figure 4. Bar chart of the positional bias of the existing encoder–decoder-based re-ranking model. Oracle: ground-truth, baseline: existing model. First: first sentence of summary, last: last sentence of summary, intermediate: all sentences located between first sentence and last sentence. Analysis was conducted with the test dataset from CNN/DM.

This study proposes a hierarchical supervision method that concurrently executes supervision across both narrow and wide ranges. The model learns the complex information of sentences constituting the candidate summary through sentence-level supervision. Furthermore, by independently supervising the predicted score of each sentence, we attempt to alleviate the positional bias of existing encoder–decoder-based re-ranking models.

3.2. Problem Formulation

The re-ranking model of the two-stage abstractive summarization framework aims to select the best summary among candidate summaries. Given a source document D and m candidate summaries $C = \{C^1, C^2, \ldots, C^m\}$, the model is trained to select the candidate summary that most resembles the gold summary; the proposed model aims to identify the best candidate summary $C^{b_{sum}}$, which has the highest ROUGE score for the gold summary G, based on the encoder–decoder structure. Therefore, the training objective of the model is as follows:

$$b_{sum} = \arg\max_{b_{sum}} R(C^{b_{sum}}, G) \tag{1}$$

$$\theta = \arg\max_{\theta} \log p_\theta(C^{b_{sum}}|C, D) \tag{2}$$

In Equation (1), $R(X,Y)$ is the ROUGE score of two sequences X, Y. In Equation (2), θ is a learnable model parameter.

In this study, we propose a training method that uses hierarchical supervision to simultaneously perform summary and sentence-level supervision. Therefore, a ground-truth ranking is required between all candidate summaries and between all sentences in each source document to train the model. Furthermore, we labeled the gold scores of the candidate summaries and sentences as follows and used the corresponding ground-truth ranking for training.

Summary gold score: The gold score of the candidate summary used for summary-level supervision was labeled according to BRIO. Gold scores of the candidate summaries were labeled using the mean of the ROUGE-1,2,L score or the harmonic mean of the ROUGE-1,2 score.

Sentence gold score: The ROUGE-1 recall score of the gold summary for each sentence was labeled as the gold score of the sentences used in sentence-level supervision. If the summary comprised a single sentence, it was divided into two spans. We treated the first half of the words as one sentence and the other half as another sentence.

3.3. Summary-Level Supervision

The model learns the ranks of candidate summaries by performing summary-level supervision, which is a supervisory method, over a relatively wide range. Summary-level supervision ensures that the summary score predicted by the model is consistent with the ground-truth rank. The summary score is derived using the encoder–decoder model. To obtain the summary score of the i-th candidate summary, the encoder takes the source document D as the input, and the decoder takes the i-th candidate summary $C^i = \{t_1^i, t_2^i, \ldots, t_{l^i}^i\}$ as the input (t is a token, l is the length of the candidate summary). The summary score of a specific candidate summary is the average of the generation probability values for all tokens that constitute the corresponding candidate summary. Thus, the summary score of the i-th candidate summary $S(C^i)$ is

$$S(C^i) = \frac{1}{l^{i\alpha}} \sum_{j=1}^{l^i} p_\theta(t_j^i | t_{\leq j-1}^i, D) \tag{3}$$

In Equation (3), l^i is the length of the i-th candidate summary. α is a hyperparameter that represents a penalty for the length of the candidate summary.

The summary ranking loss for summary-level supervision is defined based on the margin ranking loss. By optimizing the summary ranking loss, the model learns to allocate the summary score of the candidate summary based on the ground-truth rank. The equation for the summary ranking loss is as follows:

$$L_{sum} = \sum_i^m \sum_j^m \begin{cases} 0, & \text{if } R(C^i, G) \leq R(C^j, G) \\ \max(0, -(S(C^i) - S(C^j)) + \mu * gap_{i,j}), & \text{otherwise} \end{cases} \tag{4}$$

μ in Equation (4) is the hyperparameter that refers to the base margin for the summary ranking loss, and $gap_{i,j}$ is the gap of the ground-truth rank for the candidate summary pair C^i and C^j. The loss is calculated by assigning a larger margin to the candidate summary pair with a large rank gap and a relatively small margin to the pair with a small rank gap.

3.4. Sentence-Level Supervision

Sentence-level supervision enables the model to learn the ranking of sentences that comprise the candidate summary. Similarly to the summary score, the sentence score used in sentence-level supervision is the generation probability value of each token constituting the sentence derived using the encoder-decoder model. Here, each sentence is not input into the decoder independently; rather, the entire single candidate summary is input into the decoder. Subsequently, the average of the generation probability values of the tokens corresponding to each sentence is used as the sentence score. The sentence score of the j-th sentence in the i-th candidate summary C_j^i is

$$S'(C_j^i) = \frac{1}{l_j^{i\beta}} \sum_{k=start_j^i}^{end_j^i} p_\theta(t_k^i | t_{\leq k-1}^i, D) \quad (5)$$

In Equation (5), $start_j^i, end_j^i$ mean the position of the first token of the j-th sentence of the i-th candidate summary and the position of the last token, respectively. l_j^i is the length of the j-th sentence in the i-th candidate summary; β is a hyperparameter that represents a penalty for the length of the sentence.

In this study, two types of sentence ranking loss were designed to perform sentence-level supervision. During training, one of the two sentence ranking losses was selected and used. For each candidate summary, a set of sentences was organized based on the type of sentence ranking loss, and the loss was calculated for all sentence pairs within this set.

3.4.1. Intra-Sentence Ranking Loss

One of the losses designed for sentence-level supervision is the intra-sentence ranking loss. The intra-sentence ranking loss allows the model to learn the rank of sentences in a single candidate summary. The intra-sentence set for the i-th candidate summary is defined as $I^i = \{C_1^i, C_2^i, \ldots, C_{n^i}^i\}$. n^i refers to the number of sentences in i-th candidate summary. The model learns to assign the sentence score $S'(I^i) = \{S'(I_1^i), S'(I_2^i), \ldots, S'(I_{n^i}^i)\}$ according to the ground-truth rank by optimizing the intra-sentence ranking loss. The intra-sentence ranking loss is expressed as follows:

$$L_{intra} = \sum_i^m \sum_j^{n^i} \sum_k^{n^i} \begin{cases} 0, & \text{if } R(I_j^i, G) \leq R(I_k^i, G) \\ \max(0, -(S'(I_j^i) - S'(I_k^i)) + \mu' * gap_{j,k}), & \text{otherwise} \end{cases} \quad (6)$$

μ' in Equation (6) is a hyperparameter that signifies the base margin for the sentence ranking loss, and $gap_{j,k}$ is the gap of the ground-truth rank for the candidate sentence pair I_j^i and I_k^i. Similarly to for the summary ranking loss, the loss is calculated by assigning a larger margin to a sentence pair with a large rank gap and a relatively small margin to a pair with a small rank gap.

3.4.2. Inter-Intra-Sentence Ranking Loss

Another loss designed for sentence-level supervision is the inter-intra-sentence ranking loss. Inter-intra-sentence ranking loss allows the model to learn not only the rank between sentences in a single candidate summary, but also the rank of sentences constituting different candidate summaries. To balance the number of intra- and inter-sentence pairs, we sampled r external sentences per candidate summary. Therefore, the inter-intra-sentence set for the i-th candidate summary consists of all sentences in the corresponding candidate summary and r sentences randomly sampled from the external candidate summary. The inter-intra-sentence set of the i-th candidate summary is defined as $I'^i = \{C_1^i, C_2^i, \ldots, C_{n^i}^i, C_{y_1}^{x_1}, C_{y_2}^{x_2}, \ldots, C_{y_r}^{x_r}\}$. n^i refers to the number of sentences in i-th candidate summary. $x = \{x_1, x_2, \ldots, x_r\}$ and $y = \{y_1, y_2, \ldots, y_r\}$ are a randomly sampled candidate summary index and sentence index, respectively. Similarly to the intra-sentence ranking loss, the inter-intra-sentence ranking loss is defined based on the margin ranking loss. By optimizing the inter-intra-sentence ranking loss, the model learns to allocate the sentence score $S'(I'^i) = \{S'(I_1'^i), S'(I_2'^i), \ldots, S'(I_{n^i+r}'^i)\}$ according to the ground-truth rank. The equation for the inter-intra-sentence ranking loss is as follows:

$$L_{inter-intra} = \sum_i^m \sum_j^{n^i+r} \sum_k^{n^i+r} \begin{cases} 0, & \text{if } R(I_j^{\prime i}, G) \leq R(I_k^{\prime i}, G) \\ \max(0, -(S'(I_j^{\prime i}) - S'(I_k^{\prime i})) + \mu' * gap_{j,k}), & \text{otherwise} \end{cases} \quad (7)$$

μ' in Equation (7) is a hyperparameter that signifies the base margin for the sentence ranking loss, and $gap_{j,k}$ is the gap of the ground-truth rank for the candidate sentence pair $I_j^{\prime i}$ and $I_k^{\prime i}$. The loss calculation is also varied based on the rank gap between sentence pairs: a larger margin is assigned to pairs with a large rank gap, and a smaller margin to those with a small rank gap.

The weighted sum of the summary ranking loss and sentence ranking loss is the final loss used for training. For the sentence ranking loss, the intra-sentence ranking loss or inter-intra-sentence ranking loss is used as an alternative. The final objective function is as follows:

$$L_{total} = L_{sum} + \gamma * L_{sent} \quad (8)$$

γ in Equation (8) is the hyperparameter of the weight of the sentence ranking loss. L_{sent} is L_{intra} or $L_{inter-intra}$. As shown in the above equation, the model is trained using hierarchical supervision, which not only uses summary-level loss but also sentence-level loss. Therefore, the proposed method enables the model to learn the ranking between sentences such that complex information in the candidate summary is considered during training. In addition, because each sentence score is independently supervised, the positional bias of the existing encoder–decoder-based re-ranking model can be alleviated.

4. Experiments

4.1. Experimental Settings

4.1.1. Datasets

In this study, we used two summarization datasets with a different average number of sentences in the gold summary. We conducted experiments on a CNN/DM [7] dataset with a multi-sentence gold summary and an XSum [9] dataset with only a single-sentence gold summary. The CNN/DM and XSum datasets are some of the most commonly used datasets in summarization tasks. In addition, the CNN/DM dataset has a relatively extractive summary, and the XSum has a relatively abstractive summary, allowing experiments with various types of summary. We explored the impact of hierarchical supervision through two experimental setups: one using a dataset with multi-sentence summaries, and another where all summaries consisted of single sentences. This approach aimed to evaluate the effectiveness of hierarchical supervision with different summary structures.

CNN/DM contains news articles paired with highlights obtained from the CNN and DailyMail newspapers. The average number of sentences constituting the gold summary is approximately 3.6, which is relatively large. There are 287,227 document–summary pairs for training, 13,368 for validation, and 11,490 for testing.

XSum consists of online articles with highly abstractive summaries from the BBC. All the gold summaries are composed of a single sentence. There are 204,045 document–summary pairs for training, 11,332 for validation, and 11,334 for testing.

Data statistics are specified in Table 1.

Table 1. Statistics of the two datasets. Doc.: document, Summ.: summary.

Dataset	# Data Points			# Words		# Sentences	
	Train	Val	Test	Doc.	Summ.	Doc.	Summ.
CNN/DM	287,113	13,368	11,490	766.56	54.78	33.98	3.59
XSum	204,045	11,332	11,334	414.51	22.96	19.77	1.00

4.1.2. Implementation Details

We used the same backbone model in the first-stage generation model and the second-stage re-ranking model of the two-stage abstractive summarization framework in the experiment. The parameters of the backbone model were initialized using fine-tuned BART-large and PEGASUS for the CNN/DM and XSum datasets, respectively. Using the first-stage generation model, we generated 16 candidate summaries per source document for the training, validation, and test sets, and then used them for training and inference of the second-stage re-ranking model. A diverse beam search [21] was used as the decoding strategy for the first-stage generation model.

Adam [22] was used as the optimizer and the learning rate was tuned using the validation set. We followed BRIO for the summary length penalty and summary margin. The summary length penalty α was 2.0 and 0.6 for CNNDM and XSum, respectively. The summary margin μ was 0.001 for CNNDM and 0.1 for XSum. For both datasets, the sentence length penalty β and the sentence margin μ' used 1.0 and 0.4, respectively. γ was set to 0.007 on CNNDM and 0.01 on XSum (when γ was set like this, note that the average summary ranging loss and average sentence ranging loss had an actual quantitative ratio between 3:1 and 1:1). In the few-shot setting experiment, datasets were set to 100 and 1000 data sizes. For each size, a dataset was randomly sampled through 3 random seeds.

4.2. Main Results

In the main experiment, various abstractive summarization models were used as baselines for comparison with the proposed model. The baseline could be divided into three types. First, the single-stage models. BERTSumExtAbs [23] is a BERT [2]-based model that first fine-tunes the encoder with the extractive summarization task and then fine-tunes the decoder with the abstractive summarization task. BART [6] and PEGASUS [15] are encoder–decoder-based pre-trained language models. SEASON [18] is a model that jointly learns extractive and abstractive summarization based on BART. Second, SimCLS [4] and SummaReranker [11] are two-stage models that use encoder-only models as second-stage re-ranking models. The BRIO [8] is a two-stage model that uses a re-ranking model based on the encoder-decoder model. The performance listed in the table is the ROUGE score between the gold summary and the final output summary selected by each model. We did not compare the proposed model with ChatGPT [24], which has received a lot of attention recently. The first reason for this is that ChatGPT has not disclosed its performance. In addition, a comparison between the proposed model and ChatGPT is not suitable because of the difference in parameter size. The parameter size of the backbone model of the other baseline models and the proposed model is less than 500 million, while the parameter size of ChatGPT is about 175 billion, so a comparison with the proposed model was considered inappropriate.

The main results for the CNN/DM are listed in Table 2. In the experiment on CNN/DM, compared to the baseline models, ROUGE-1 improved by 0.07, ROUGE-2 by 0.24, and ROUGE-L by 0.14 points with the proposed model. Table 3 lists the main results for XSum. For the XSum dataset, the proposed model surpassed the baseline model in performance, achieving improvements of 0.12, 0.09, and 0.03 points for ROUGE-1, ROUGE-2, and ROUGE-L scores, respectively. The results showed that the performance of the model improved for both the experiment on CNN/DM, which has a multi-sentence gold summary, and the experiment on XSum, which only has a single-sentence gold summary. Therefore, it is effective to use hierarchical supervision to train an abstractive summarization re-ranking model. In addition, this result suggests that, not only is is effective to perform sentence-level supervision, but also to perform span-level supervision, which is a supervision method with a smaller unit. Additionally, we performed a t-test to prove the reliability of the performance improvement of the proposed model. We derived the model performance using five random seeds for the proposed model and the existing encoder–decoder-based re-ranking model(BRIO), respectively, and performed a t-test with the average values of the ROUGE-1, 2, and L scores. As the result of the t-test, the p-value was calculated as 0.004

in CNN/DM and 0.011 in XSum. As the *p*-value was lower than the alpha level $\alpha = 0.05$ in both datasets, we confirmed that the results of this experiment were statistically significant.

Table 2. Results on CNN/DM. *: outperformed the baseline model results reported in the original papers. proposed-intra: intra-sentence ranking loss used, proposed-inter + intra: inter-intra-sentence ranking loss used. The highest performance for each metric is indicated in bold text.

Model	R-1	R-2	R-L
BERTSumExtAbs	42.13	19.6	39.18
BART	44.16	21.28	40.90
PEGASUS	44.17	21.47	41.11
SEASON	46.27	22.64	43.08
SimCLS	46.67	22.15	43.54
SummaReranker	47.16	22.61	43.87
BRIO-Ctr	47.28	22.93	44.15
proposed-intra	**47.35** *	**23.17** *	**44.29** *
proposed-inter + intra	47.31 *	23.13 *	44.22 *

Table 3. Results on XSum. *: outperformed the baseline model results reported in the original papers. proposed-intra: intra-sentence ranking loss used, proposed-inter + intra: inter-intra-sentence ranking loss used. The highest performance for each metric is indicated in bold text.

Model	R-1	R-2	R-L
BERTSumExtAbs	38.81	16.50	31.27
BART	45.14	22.27	37.25
PEGASUS	47.21	24.56	39.25
SimCLS	47.61	24.57	39.44
SummaReranker	48.12	24.95	**40.00**
BRIO-Ctr	48.13	25.13	39.84
proposed-intra	**48.25** *	**25.22** *	39.99
proposed-inter + intra	48.19 *	25.13	39.87

In both datasets, the model using intra-sentence ranking loss outperformed the model using inter-intra-sentence ranking loss. This is because sentence pairs constituting different candidate summaries often contain similar meanings. It is rare for the meaning to duplicate sentences constituting a candidate summary. However, sentences containing different candidate summaries often have overlapping meanings. If the model encounters two sentences with similar meanings but different assigned gold scores, it learns to recognize a quality difference between them. This capability is crucial for nuanced understanding and ranking of a content. Therefore, these experimental results were obtained because these sentence pairs could act as noise when using the inter-intra-sentence ranking loss.

4.3. Few-Shot Results

In this study, we performed a few-shot experiment on a re-ranking model of abstractive summarization using two data sizes: 100-shot and 1000-shot. We sampled the training and validation sets thrice using three random seeds for each data size. The experiment was conducted with three sampled datasets, and we describe the average performance derived from the three experiments. We compared the proposed model with BRIO [8], which is a two-stage model that uses a re-ranking model with an encoder–decoder structure as the baseline. We also compared the proposed model to BART [6] and PEGASUS [15], which are single-step models that do not use a re-ranking model (this can be considered as a 0-shot setting because a re-ranking model does not exist). In this experiment, the few-shot setting was only applied to the second stage re-ranking model based on the first-stage generation model trained on the entire dataset.

The few-shot results for the CNN/DM, Xsum are presented in Table 4. In the experiments with 100-shot and 1000-shot settings for CNN/DM, the proposed model showed a higher performance for both settings compared with the baseline. In the experiment on XSum, the proposed model outperformed the baseline model in both the 100-shot and 1000-shot settings. The results indicated that the proposed method is effective, not only in conditions where the amount of training data is large, but also in conditions where there is a small amount of training data.

Table 4. Few-shot results on CNN/DM, XSum. proposed-intra: intra-sentence ranking loss used, proposed-inter + intra: inter-intra-sentence ranking loss used. The highest performance for each metric is indicated in bold text.

Model	100-Shot			1000-Shot		
	R-1	R-2	R-L	R-1	R-2	R-L
CNN/DM						
BART	44.16	21.28	40.90	44.16	21.28	40.90
PEGASUS	44.17	21.47	41.11	44.17	21.47	41.11
BRIO-Ctr	45.07	21.43	42.03	46.03	22.12	42.98
proposed-intra	45.51	21.78	42.45	**46.30**	**22.38**	**43.22**
proposed-inter + intra	**45.56**	**21.80**	**42.51**	46.26	22.32	43.20
XSum						
BART	45.14	22.27	37.25	45.14	22.27	37.25
PEGASUS	47.21	24.56	39.25	47.21	24.56	39.25
BRIO-Ctr	47.22	24.71	39.34	47.34	24.70	39.39
proposed-intra	**47.26**	24.74	39.36	47.40	24.73	39.40
proposed-inter + intra	**47.26**	**24.78**	**39.41**	**47.41**	**24.79**	**39.47**

In the few-shot setting, the model using inter-intra-sentence ranking loss generally showed a better performance than the model using intra-sentence ranking loss. This was because, in the few-shot setting, the gain from the additional information played a greater role than the loss from noise. Furthermore, the amount of information that could be obtained from the data was fairly small because the model was trained with a small amount of data. Therefore, because the sentence pairs used in the inter-intra-sentence ranking loss were more diverse than those in the intra-sentence ranking loss, the model using the former loss function was able to learn more information than the model using the latter loss function. The gains obtained through having more information outweighed the noise caused by the inter-sentence pairs.

In addition, when comparing the performance of the proposed model and the baseline, CNN/DM, which has multiple sentences, showed a significant performance improvement compared to XSum, where the summary consists of a single sentence. These results can also be interpreted as showing that it is effective to learn as many sentence pairs as possible using a small amount of training data.

5. Analysis

In this section, we demonstrate the effectiveness of the proposed method by performing an additional analysis using a CNN/DM [7] test dataset. Through this analysis, we check whether the proposed method resolves the two limitations of the existing re-ranking model, as pointed out in this paper.

5.1. Sentence Ranking Performance

The first limitation is that the complex information of the sentences constituting the candidate summary was overlooked in the existing studies. In previous studies that performed summary-level supervision, it was difficult to determine whether a particular sentence in a candidate summary was well-generated. To address this limitation, the proposed method uses hierarchical supervision methods that perform sentence-level and summary-level supervision together in the training of the re-ranking model. Thus, the proposed method allows the model to learn whether a particular sentence in a candidate summary contains an important part of the original document.

Table 5 lists the accuracy when distinguishing the most or least similar sentences from the gold summary among the sentences constituting the candidate summary. This study attempted to confirm whether the proposed model effectively learned the superior relationships between sentences through analysis. We compared the performance of the proposed model with that of BRIO [8], which uses a re-ranking model with the same encoder–decoder structure as the proposed model. Compared with the baseline, the proposed model showed a performance improvement of approximately 7% in both cases. The analysis results confirmed that the proposed model can learn the ranking of sentences constituting the candidate summary. Regarding the type of sentence ranking loss, the model showed a higher accuracy when using inter-intra-sentence ranking loss than when using intra-sentence ranking loss. The reason for this is that the model learns more diverse sentence pairs when using inter-intra-sentence ranking loss than when using intra-sentence ranking loss. Thus, we can assume that the inter-intra-sentence ranking loss allows the model to learn the ranking between sentences that consist of a single candidate summary more effectively.

Table 5. Analysis results for the accuracy of identifying the best-generated sentence and worst-generated sentence in a single candidate summary. Proposed-intra: intra-sentence ranking loss used, proposed-inter + intra: inter-intra-sentence ranking loss used. Analysis was conducted for CNN/DM. The highest performance for each metric is indicated in bold text.

Model	best Sentence Accuracy (%)	Worst Sentence Accuracy (%)
BRIO-Ctr	43.97	43.00
proposed-intra	49.81	50.05
proposed-inter + intra	**50.91**	**50.66**

5.2. Positional Bias

The second limitation highlighted in this study is the bias according to the position of the sentence in the existing encoder–decoder structure re-ranking model. Existing models are biased in assigning a lower prediction score because the sentence is located toward the end of the candidate summary. This study attempted to alleviate this positional bias by supervising the prediction score of a sentence to be aligned with the ground-truth ranking. Figure 5 is a bar chart comparing the position of the sentence to which the existing model BRIO [8] (expressed as "Baseline") and the proposed model (expressed as "Proposed") assigned the lowest prediction score in one candidate summary and the gold-truth (expressed as "Oracle"). "First" means the first sentence of the summary, "Last" means the last sentence, and "Intermediate" means all the sentences located between the first and last sentences. When comparing the baseline and proposed models, the probability of predicting the last sentence of the candidate summary as the most poorly-generated sentence was reduced by approximately 20%, from 76% to 57%. In addition, the probability of predicting that the first or intermediate sentence was the least similar to the gold summary increased. Through this analysis, we demonstrated that positional bias is alleviated in the proposed model.

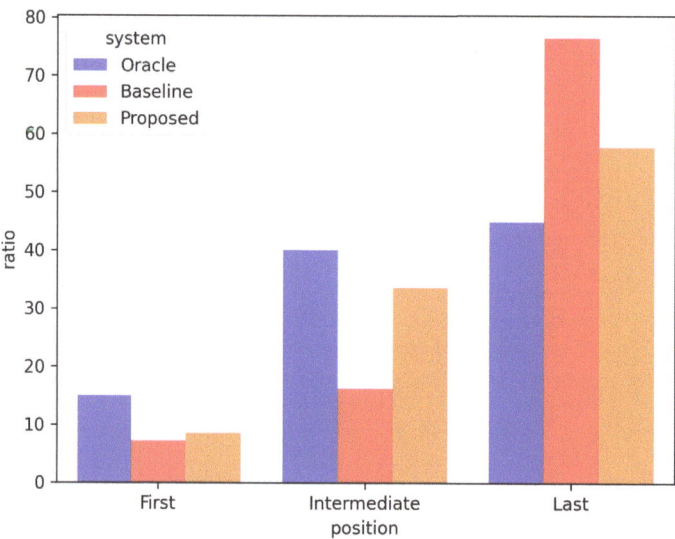

Figure 5. Analysis result of whether the positional bias of the existing encoder–decoder-based re-ranking model is alleviated. Oracle: ground-truth, baseline: existing model, proposed: proposed model. First: first sentence of summary, last: last sentence of summary, intermediate: all sentences located between first sentence and last sentence. Analysis was conducted for CNN/DM.

6. Conclusions

In this study, we proposed a re-ranking model for a two-stage abstractive summarization framework that performs hierarchical supervision. The proposed method, by concurrently implementing summary-level and sentence-level supervision, enables the model to learn not just the ranking of candidate summaries but also the ranking among sentences within each candidate summary. This dual-level approach enhances the capability of the model to discern the relative importance of both summaries and their constituent sentences. With hierarchical supervision, the model can learn complex information contained in sentences that comprise a candidate summary. The proposed method also alleviates the problem of positional bias in the existing encoder–decoder structure re-ranking model. The proposed model demonstrated the effectiveness of the hierarchical supervision method by outperforming existing studies on both the CNN/DM [7] and XSum [9] datasets. The proposed model, in the few-shot setting experiment, demonstrated improved performance over existing studies, indicating its effectiveness, even with a very small amount of training data. This suggests that the methodology introduced in this study is robust and efficient in data-constrained scenarios.

7. Limitation

The disadvantage of the proposed method is that it is difficult to tune the hyperparameters. The proposed model has various hyperparameters, such as summary sentence margin, summary sentence length penalty, sentence margin, sentence length penalty, and sentence loss function weight. Since there are many types of hyperparameters, it is a disadvantage that it takes a lot of time to adjust hyperparameters. However, the main limitation of this study is that some of the hyperparameters of the proposed model are dependent on each other. Because the sentence prediction score and summary prediction score are derived using the same model output, optimizing the summary ranking loss or sentence ranking loss affects the model's derivation of both the sentence prediction score and the summary prediction score. Therefore, the hyperparameters of the margin for the summary ranking loss and sentence ranking loss are mutually dependent. In addition, the units of value of the summary prediction score and sentence prediction score vary according to other hyperparameters, the summary length penalty, and the sentence length penalty. In addition, even if the weight of the sentence ranking loss is constant, the ratio of the loss value of the summary ranking loss to that of the sentence ranking loss varies depending on the summary or sentence margins. Table 6 shows the results of hyperparameter tuning on CNN/DM [7]. The results of this experiment show that the performance of the proposed model varies greatly depending on the combination of hyperparameters; therefore, the proposed model has a limitation in that it is very difficult to tune hyperparameters, because they are deeply dependent on each other.

Table 6. Results of hyperparameter tuning for CNN/DM. α: summary length penalty, μ: summary margin, β: sentence length penalty, μ': sentence margin, γ: sentence loss function weight. The highest performance is marked in bold text, and the lowest performance is underlined for each sentence ranking loss.

Sentence Ranking Loss	α	μ	β	μ'	γ	R-1	R-2	R-L
intra	2	0.001	1	0.02	0.007	47.16	22.97	44.08
					0.03	47.16	22.96	44.08
				0.4	0.007	**47.35**	**23.17**	**44.29**
					0.03	47.28	23.05	44.20
			2	0.02	0.007	47.20	23.03	44.16
					0.03	47.28	23.08	44.22
				0.4	0.007	47.23	22.96	44.12
					0.03	<u>47.11</u>	<u>22.94</u>	<u>44.07</u>
inter + intra	2	0.001	1	0.02	0.007	47.18	22.98	44.10
					0.03	47.14	22.90	44.05
				0.4	0.007	47.31	**23.13**	44.22
					0.03	47.22	22.97	44.13
			2	0.02	0.007	47.18	23.05	44.13
					0.03	**47.32**	23.11	**44.28**
				0.4	0.007	47.31	23.11	44.22
					0.03	<u>47.03</u>	<u>22.85</u>	<u>43.97</u>

Author Contributions: Conceptualization, E.Y. and G.K.; methodology, E.Y.; software, E.Y. and G.K.; data curation, E.Y.; writing—original draft preparation, E.Y.; writing—review and editing, E.Y. and G.K.; visualization, E.Y. and G.K.; supervision, S.K. All authors have read and agreed to the published version of the manuscript.

Funding: This work was supported in part by the National Research Foundation of Korea(NRF) grant funded by the Korea government (MSIT) (2022R1A2C1005316) and in part by Gachon University research fund of 2021 (GCU-202109980001).

Data Availability Statement: Our code is available at: https://github.com/YooEunseok/HiSumRanker, accessed on 7 January 2024. Publicly available datasets were analyzed in this study. This data can be found here: CNN/DM [7] (https://huggingface.co/datasets/cnn_dailymail, accessed on 7 January 2024), XSum [9] (https://huggingface.co/datasets/EdinburghNLP/xsum, accessed on 7 January 2024).

Conflicts of Interest: The authors declare no conflict of interest.

References

1. Sutskever, I.; Vinyals, O.; Le, Q.V. Sequence to Sequence Learning with Neural Networks. In Proceedings of the NIPS'14, 27th International Conference on Neural Information Processing Systems, Montreal, QC, Canada, 8–13 December 2014; Volume 2, pp. 3104–3112.
2. Devlin, J.; Chang, M.W.; Lee, K.; Toutanova, K. BERT: Pre-training of Deep Bidirectional Transformers for Language Understanding. In Proceedings of the 2019 Conference of the North American Chapter of the Association for Computational Linguistics: Human Language Technologies, Minneapolis, MN, USA, 2–7 June 2019; (Long and Short Papers); Burstein, J., Doran, C., Solorio, T., Eds.; Association for Computational Linguistics: Stroudsburg, PA, USA, 2019; Volume 1, pp. 4171–4186. [CrossRef]

3. Bengio, S.; Vinyals, O.; Jaitly, N.; Shazeer, N. Scheduled Sampling for Sequence Prediction with Recurrent Neural Networks. In Proceedings of the NIPS'15, 28th International Conference on Neural Information Processing Systems, Montreal, QC, Canada, 7–12 December 2015; Volume 1, pp. 1171–1179.
4. Liu, Y.; Liu, P. SimCLS: A Simple Framework for Contrastive Learning of Abstractive Summarization. In Proceedings of the 59th Annual Meeting of the Association for Computational Linguistics and the 11th International Joint Conference on Natural Language Processing, Online, 1–6 August 2021; (Short Papers); Zong, C., Xia, F., Li, W., Navigli, R., Eds.; Association for Computational Linguistics: Stroudsburg, PA, USA, 2021; Volume 2, pp. 1065–1072. [CrossRef]
5. Lin, C.Y. ROUGE: A Package for Automatic Evaluation of Summaries. In Proceedings of the Text Summarization Branches Out, Barcelona, Spain, 25–26 July 2004; pp. 74–81.
6. Lewis, M.; Liu, Y.; Goyal, N.; Ghazvininejad, M.; Mohamed, A.; Levy, O.; Stoyanov, V.; Zettlemoyer, L. BART: Denoising Sequence-to-Sequence Pre-training for Natural Language Generation, Translation, and Comprehension. In Proceedings of the 58th Annual Meeting of the Association for Computational Linguistics, Online, 5–10 July 2020; Jurafsky, D., Chai, J., Schluter, N., Tetreault, J., Eds.; Association for Computational Linguistics: Stroudsburg, PA, USA, 2020; pp. 7871–7880. [CrossRef]
7. Hermann, K.M.; Kociský, T.; Grefenstette, E.; Espeholt, L.; Kay, W.; Suleyman, M.; Blunsom, P. Teaching Machines to Read and Comprehend. In *Advances in Neural Information Processing Systems 28*; Curran Associates, Inc.: Red Hook, NY, USA, 2015; pp. 1693–1701.
8. Liu, Y.; Liu, P.; Radev, D.; Neubig, G. BRIO: Bringing Order to Abstractive Summarization. In Proceedings of the 60th Annual Meeting of the Association for Computational Linguistics, Dublin, Ireland, 22–27 May 2022; (Long Papers); Muresan, S., Nakov, P., Villavicencio, A., Eds.; Association for Computational Linguistics: Stroudsburg, PA, USA, 2022; Volume 1, pp. 2890–2903. [CrossRef]
9. Narayan, S.; Cohen, S.B.; Lapata, M. Don't Give Me the Details, Just the Summary! Topic-Aware Convolutional Neural Networks for Extreme Summarization. In Proceedings of the 2018 Conference on Empirical Methods in Natural Language Processing, Brussels, Belgium, 31 October–4 November 2018; Riloff, E., Chiang, D., Hockenmaier, J., Tsujii, J., Eds.; Association for Computational Linguistics: Stroudsburg, PA, USA, 2018; pp. 1797–1807. [CrossRef]
10. Liu, Y.; Ott, M.; Goyal, N.; Du, J.; Joshi, M.; Chen, D.; Levy, O.; Lewis, M.; Zettlemoyer, L.; Stoyanov, V. RoBERTa: A Robustly Optimized BERT Pretraining Approach. *arXiv* 2019, arXiv:1907.11692.
11. Ravaut, M.; Joty, S.; Chen, N. SummaReranker: A Multi-Task Mixture-of-Experts Re-ranking Framework for Abstractive Summarization. In Proceedings of the 60th Annual Meeting of the Association for Computational Linguistics, Dublin, Ireland, 22–27 May 2022; (Long Papers); Muresan, S., Nakov, P., Villavicencio, A., Eds.; Association for Computational Linguistics: Stroudsburg, PA, USA, 2022; Volume 1, pp. 4504–4524. [CrossRef]
12. Ma, J.; Zhao, Z.; Yi, X.; Chen, J.; Hong, L.; Chi, E.H. Modeling Task Relationships in Multi-Task Learning with Multi-Gate Mixture-of-Experts. In Proceedings of the KDD'18, 24th ACM SIGKDD International Conference on Knowledge Discovery & Data Mining, London, UK, 19–23 August 2018; pp. 1930–1939. [CrossRef]
13. Yuan, W.; Neubig, G.; Liu, P. BARTScore: Evaluating Generated Text as Text Generation. In *Advances in Neural Information Processing Systems 34*; Ranzato, M., Beygelzimer, A., Dauphin, Y., Liang, P., Vaughan, J.W., Eds.; Curran Associates, Inc.: Red Hook, NY, USA, 2021; Volume 34, pp. 27263–27277.
14. Zhang, T.; Kishore, V.; Wu, F.; Weinberger, K.Q.; Artzi, Y. BERTScore: Evaluating Text Generation with BERT. In Proceedings of the International Conference on Learning Representations, Addis Ababa, Ethiopia, 26–30 April 2020.
15. Zhang, J.; Zhao, Y.; Saleh, M.; Liu, P.J. PEGASUS: Pre-Training with Extracted Gap-Sentences for Abstractive Summarization. In Proceedings of the ICML'20, 37th International Conference on Machine Learning, Virtual, 13–18 July 2020.
16. Wu, B.; Zhang, Z.; Wang, J.; Zhao, H. Sentence-aware Contrastive Learning for Open-Domain Passage Retrieval. In Proceedings of the 60th Annual Meeting of the Association for Computational Linguistics, Dublin, Ireland, 22–27 May 2022; (Long Papers); Muresan, S., Nakov, P., Villavicencio, A., Eds.; Association for Computational Linguistics: Stroudsburg, PA, USA, 2022; Volume 1, pp. 1062–1074. [CrossRef]
17. Xu, W.; Chen, K.; Mou, L.; Zhao, T. Document-Level Relation Extraction with Sentences Importance Estimation and Focusing. In Proceedings of the 2022 Conference of the North American Chapter of the Association for Computational Linguistics: Human Language Technologies, Seattle, WA, USA, 10–15 July 2022; Carpuat, M., de Marneffe, M.C., Meza Ruiz, I.V., Eds.; Association for Computational Linguistics: Stroudsburg, PA, USA, 2022; pp. 2920–2929. [CrossRef]
18. Wang, F.; Song, K.; Zhang, H.; Jin, L.; Cho, S.; Yao, W.; Wang, X.; Chen, M.; Yu, D. Salience Allocation as Guidance for Abstractive Summarization. In Proceedings of the 2022 Conference on Empirical Methods in Natural Language Processing, Abu Dhabi, United Arab Emirates, 7–11 December 2022; Goldberg, Y., Kozareva, Z., Zhang, Y., Eds.; pp. 6094–6106. [CrossRef]
19. Song, K.; Wang, B.; Feng, Z.; Liu, R.; Liu, F. Controlling the Amount of Verbatim Copying in Abstractive Summarization. *Proc. AAAI Conf. Artif. Intell.* 2020, 34, 8902–8909. [CrossRef]
20. Lynch, C.J.; Jensen, E.J.; Zamponi, V.; O'Brien, K.; Frydenlund, E.; Gore, R. A Structured Narrative Prompt for Prompting Narratives from Large Language Models: Sentiment Assessment of ChatGPT-Generated Narratives and Real Tweets. *Future Internet* 2023, 15, 375. [CrossRef]
21. Vijayakumar, A.K.; Cogswell, M.; Selvaraju, R.R.; Sun, Q.; Lee, S.; Crandall, D.; Batra, D. Diverse Beam Search: Decoding Diverse Solutions from Neural Sequence Models. *arXiv* 2018, arXiv:1610.02424. Available online: http://arxiv.org/abs/1610.02424 (accessed on 7 October 2016).

22. Kingma, D.P.; Ba, J. Adam: A Method for Stochastic Optimization. In Proceedings of the International Conference on Learning Representations, San Diego, CA, USA, 7–9 May 2015.
23. Liu, Y.; Lapata, M. Text Summarization with Pretrained Encoders. In Proceedings of the 2019 Conference on Empirical Methods in Natural Language Processing and the 9th International Joint Conference on Natural Language Processing (EMNLP-IJCNLP), Hong Kong, China, 3–7 November 2019; Inui, K., Jiang, J., Ng, V., Wan, X., Eds.; Association for Computational Linguistics: Stroudsburg, PA, USA, 2019; pp. 3730–3740. [CrossRef]
24. Ouyang, L.; Wu, J.; Jiang, X.; Almeida, D.; Wainwright, C.L.; Mishkin, P.; Zhang, C.; Agarwal, S.; Slama, K.; Ray, A.; et al. Training language models to follow instructions with human feedback. *arXiv* **2022**, arXiv:2203.02155. Available online: http://arxiv.org/abs/2203.02155 (accessed on 4 March 2022).

Disclaimer/Publisher's Note: The statements, opinions and data contained in all publications are solely those of the individual author(s) and contributor(s) and not of MDPI and/or the editor(s). MDPI and/or the editor(s) disclaim responsibility for any injury to people or property resulting from any ideas, methods, instructions or products referred to in the content.

Article

Hybrid DE-Optimized GPR and NARX/SVR Models for Forecasting Gold Spot Prices: A Case Study of the Global Commodities Market

Esperanza García-Gonzalo [1], Paulino José García-Nieto [1,*], Gregorio Fidalgo Valverde [2], Pedro Riesgo Fernández [2], Fernando Sánchez Lasheras [1] and Sergio Luis Suárez Gómez [1]

[1] Department of Mathematics, Faculty of Sciences, University of Oviedo, 33007 Oviedo, Spain; espe@uniovi.es (E.G.-G.); sanchezfernando@uniovi.es (F.S.L.); suarezsergio@uniovi.es (S.L.S.G.)

[2] School of Mining, Energy and Materials Engineering, University of Oviedo, 33004 Oviedo, Spain; gfidalgo@uniovi.es (G.F.V.); priesgo@uniovi.es (P.R.F.)

* Correspondence: pjgarcia@uniovi.es

Abstract: In this work, we highlight three different techniques for automatically constructing the dataset for a time-series study: the direct multi-step, the recursive multi-step, and the direct–recursive hybrid scheme. The nonlinear autoregressive with exogenous variable support vector regression (NARX SVR) and the Gaussian process regression (GPR), combined with the differential evolution (DE) for parameter tuning, are the two novel hybrid methods used in this study. The hyper-parameter settings used in the GPR and SVR training processes as part of this optimization technique DE significantly affect how accurate the regression is. The accuracy in the prediction of DE/GPR and DE/SVR, with or without NARX, is examined in this article using data on spot gold prices from the New York Commodities Exchange (COMEX) that have been made publicly available. According to RMSE statistics, the numerical results obtained demonstrate that NARX DE/SVR achieved the best results.

Keywords: Gaussian process regression (GPR); time-series analysis; differential evolution (DE); support vector regression (SVR); New York Commodity Exchange; gold price forecasting

MSC: 68T20; 91B84; 62M10

1. Introduction

The global COVID-19 health crisis has caused misery and disaster ever since it started in early 2020. On 11 March 2020, the World Health Organization (WHO) declared this infectious disease to be a pandemic. As a result, several countries put in place a range of policies to try and stop the spread of the illness. Governments implemented various precautionary measures such as social distancing, workplace closures, travel limitations, and lockdowns, all to stop the disease from spreading.

This pandemic has had serious economic ramifications in addition to deaths, infections, and psychological damage. This unprecedented global health crisis has threatened the entire world and wreaked havoc on the economy by creating financial instability. The entire financial industry, including the insurance and banking sectors and the stock markets, has been impacted by COVID-19 [1]. Since the start of the pandemic, the financial markets have deteriorated and grown incredibly volatile, which has led to a drop in metal prices. The pandemic has also led to an unprecedented collapse in commodities markets, which are typically erratic. The COVID-19 outbreak caused borders to be closed and communities to be quarantined, which slowed down activity and restricted international trade in goods and commodities. In these circumstances, the supply of commodities frequently vastly outweighed their demand, leading to a decrease in commodity prices. Global investors shifted their holdings to commodities markets in the wake of the crisis and the ensuing market panic, which was accompanied by a chaotic macroeconomic and financial environment [2–7].

Gold has historically been the main commodity that best represents the commodities market [8]. According to several studies [9–11], gold is essentially the most highly valued metal. It has historically had a big impact on both politics and the economy. Therefore, the prices of gold and oil are the two most important indicators in the global markets [12]. Like gold, silver has many applications and can even be used as a hedge against inflation. According to metal experts, silver is perceived to be more volatile than gold [13]. The year 2020 saw a decline in the price of metals, something closely linked to the global economy. Due to these conditions, investors are growing more and more worried about the rise in commodity prices. Also, the price of gold increased rapidly in spite of a rise in COVID-19 cases [14]. In light of these modifications, the pandemic has promoted the buying of assets that serve as a safe haven [15]. Investor and regulatory interests in this phenomenon have caused a spike in the demand for certain commodities as investments. Therefore, understanding the relationships among the prices of gold, oil, and silver is crucial for investors, portfolio managers, and policymakers [16]. Many investors, especially novices, have traditionally placed their money in gold, which is considered a safe and trouble-free haven, to avoid complications [12]. In the years after the financial crisis, a common alternative in a variety of investment options was gold. Because it helps investors of all types manage their financial and economic concerns in times of crisis, gold is regarded as a safe-haven asset [15,17–22].

With the aforementioned points in mind, the current work attempts to explore the correlation between the price of gold and its status as a safe haven in relation to the different commodities indices under consideration. One volatility index is of particular interest to us: the gold price index [23,24]. Indeed, gold is one of the naturally occurring elements with the highest atomic number. It has the chemical symbol Au, and its atomic number is 79. In its purest form, it is reddish-yellow and bright. It is a very dense metal, ductile, malleable, and soft. Gold is a member of group 11 in the periodic table of chemical elements, and it is a transition metal [25]. Very unreactive, it is solid in normal circumstances. It usually appears as nuggets in veins, alluvial deposits, and rocks in its free elemental (native) form. It can also be found alloyed with other metals like palladium and copper, with the native element silver in solid solution series, and as mineral inclusions like those found in pyrite [25–27]. Gold is a precious metal used as a base material for coinage, jewelry, and other forms of art. It is not a common element. In the past, monetary policy used a gold standard, but after the 1930s, when gold was no longer used for coins as circulating currency, the world gold standard disappeared in favor of a flat currency system [25–28].

About 50% of the new gold produced worldwide nowadays is used for jewelry, with 40% for investments and approximately 10% in industry (see Figure 1). Due to gold's high ductility, malleability, resistance to most other chemical reactions, particularly to corrosion, and high electrical conductivity, its main industrial use, as corrosion-resistant electrical connectors in all kinds of computers, has persisted. Additionally, the production of gold leafing, colored glass, and restoration of teeth all use gold. In medicine, specific gold salts are utilized as anti-inflammatories. China is the major producer with 440 tons of gold annually as of 2017.

Raw materials are essential for taking the pulse of the global economy, and these include precious metals. Some of these resources, like fossil fuels, are scarce. The demand, supply, and prices of precious metals have a significant influence on the production of precious metals. The London Metal Exchange (LME), the New York Commodity Exchange (COMEX), and the Shanghai Futures Exchange (SHFE) are the three main physical futures trading exchanges where gold is traded as a nonferrous metal [29–31]. Prices on these exchanges are a measure of the global situation between gold demand and supply, though they may be significantly impacted by investment flows and currency exchange rates, both of which could lead to volatile price swings that are at least partially correlated with changes in the business situation [32,33].

Figure 1. Gold metallurgy factory.

Forecasting gold prices holds significant relevance within the current economic context due to the metal's multifaceted roles as a safe-haven asset, a store of value, and an indicator of market sentiment. As evidenced by numerous studies [34–36], gold prices are closely linked to geopolitical tensions, economic uncertainties, and investor risk aversion, making them invaluable indicators of market dynamics. Amidst the ongoing COVID-19 pandemic and its socio-economic ramifications, the demand for safe-haven assets like gold has surged, driving up prices and highlighting gold's importance in hedging against inflation and market volatility [37]. Additionally, with the global economy facing challenges such as inflationary pressures, geopolitical conflicts, and monetary policy shifts, forecasting gold prices has become essential for investors, financial institutions, and policymakers to make informed decisions and effectively manage risks in their portfolios [17]. In this context, the accurate forecasting of gold prices provides valuable insights into market trends, aids in risk management strategies, and facilitates better allocation of resources, thereby contributing to greater overall financial stability and resilience.

Various methods have been employed in the past to predict metal prices. Using two time-series forecasting methods, Dooley and Lenihan (2005) [38] concluded that ARIMA works slightly better than the lagged forward price modeling. Multicommodity models were proposed [39] to assist in estimating long-term silver and copper prices. Artificial neuronal networks (ANNs) for time series were promoted by Khashei et al. (2010) [40]. The consumption and import of iron ore by China was studied [41] using a grey model with the particle swarm algorithm (PSO). To capture this cyclical behavior that dominates the metal market, Kriechbaumer et al. (2014) [42] broke down time series into their time domain and frequency. Finally, Sánchez Lasheras et al. (2015) [43] used the COMEX copper spot price as an example and contrast the forecasting abilities of two different neuronal networks and an ARIMA model.

Two new techniques to predict the COMEX gold spot are used in this article. The nonlinear autoregressive with exogenous variable, in this case the non-energy index, support vector regression (NARX DE/SVR) and the Gaussian process regression hybridized with the differential evolution optimizer (DE/GPR) in time-series analysis are new methodologies that are introduced in this paper for predicting the COMEX gold spot price [44–49]. The approach suggested successfully identifies nonlinear input features, tuning the parameters of SVR with RBF kernel.

This work starts with stating the importance of gold, and then it goes on to explain the experimental dataset used in this paper. The DE/GPR and NARX DE/SVR are described in Section 2; we compare the DE/GPR and NARX DE/SVR outcomes with the experimental values, and Section 3 explains the results. Finally, Section 4 presents a summary of this paper's main findings.

2. Materials and Methods

2.1. Experimental Dataset

The monthly COMEX gold spot closing price was the primary data source for the current study, and, in fact, the dataset includes a time series of gold prices. Using the RBF kernel with the SVR method [47–49] and also with GPR along with DE for the parameter tuning [44], we estimated monthly gold prices for the years 2019 and 2020. The non-energy index was utilized to obtain a better model. The World Bank Commodity Price Data (The Pink Sheet) (2021) [50] was the source of the dataset. The goal of this project is to predict monthly gold prices for the full calendar years of 2019 and 2020.

2.2. Time-Series Analysis: Computational Procedures

2.2.1. Support Vector Machines Regression (SVR)

Here ε–SVR is presented [48,49]. If we have time-series data, we can extract a training set that consists of a predicted variable $y_i \in \mathfrak{R}, \forall i = 1, 2, \ldots, m$ that is continuous and independent variables $x_i \in \mathfrak{R}^p, \forall i = 1, 2, \ldots, m$ that can be built using p lags of y_i. As a result, the support vector regression (ε–SVR) technique creates $f(x) = w^T x + b$ where $w \in \mathfrak{R}^n$ denotes the hyperplane's perpendicular vector, also known as the director vector and $b/\|w\|$ denotes the distance between the hyperplane, with $b \in \mathfrak{R}$ and the origin of the coordinates. Additionally, for all x_i training cases, this approximation must give rise to a maximum deviation from the true value y_i of ε and at the same time, must also be as flat as possible. The problem is modeled imposing a penalty on the sum of differences that exceeds ε, and flatness is attained finding the minimal Euclidean norm $\|w\|_2$. In fact, the SVR approach aims to resolve the problem [51–53]:

$$\min_{w,b,\xi^+,\xi^-} \frac{1}{2}\|w\|_2 + C\sum_{i=1}^{m}\left(\xi_i^+ + \xi_i^-\right) \quad (1)$$

that meets the conditions

$$\begin{cases} y_i - (w^T x_i + b) \geq \varepsilon + \xi_i^+ & i = 1,\ldots,m \\ (w^T x_i + b) - y_i \geq \varepsilon + \xi_i^- & i = 1,\ldots,m \\ \xi_i^+, \xi_i^- \geq 0 & i = 1,\ldots,m \end{cases} \quad (2)$$

$\xi^+, \xi^- \in \mathfrak{R}^m$ are the slack variables, and C is the regularization constant. The penalty imposed on points that are not inside the interval ε is restrained by C in Equation (1) that is positive, which helps to prevent overfitting. This quantity measures the model complexity versus the function where we are optimizing horizontality [54–57]. For each training vector, slack variables are provided, allowing deviations that are greater than ε, while penalizing the deviations in the function. The area that $y_i \pm \varepsilon$, $\forall i$ encloses is called an ε^- insensitive tube (see Figure 2).

We employed the kernelization method to address problems like this one that are highly nonlinear. The foundation of this approach is the mapping of the initial dataset to a higher-dimensional space H, referred to as the feature space. For this, we used the kernel function $K(x_i, x_j)$ for the dot product in H. This way, we formulated the primal optimization problem given by Equation (1) in its dual form to solve it. Applying the

Karush–Kuhn–Tucker (KKT) conditions resulted in the dual formulation of the optimization problem [48,49,54–57]:

$$\max_{\alpha^+,\alpha^-} \left[\sum_{i=1}^{m} y_i (\alpha_i^+ - \alpha_i^-) - \varepsilon \sum_{i=1}^{m} (\alpha_i^+ + \alpha_i^-) - \frac{1}{2} \sum_{j=1}^{m} (\alpha_i^+ - \alpha_i^-)(\alpha_j^+ - \alpha_j^-) K(x_i, x_j) \right] \quad (3)$$

constricted to

$$\left\{ \begin{array}{l} \sum_{i=1}^{m}(\alpha_i^+ - \alpha_i^-) = 0, \\ 0 \leq \alpha_i^+ \leq C, \quad i=1,\ldots,m \\ 0 \leq \alpha_i^- \leq C, \quad i=1,\ldots,m \end{array} \right\} \quad (4)$$

We calculated the prediction for a new observation x [48,49,54–57] using:

$$f(x) = \sum_{j=1}^{m} (\alpha_i^+ - \alpha_i^-) K(x_i, x_j) + b \quad (5)$$

The radial basis function (RBF) is also called Gaussian kernel. This is one of the available kernel functions and is preferred in this study because of its better performance [48,49,54–57]:

$$K(x_i, x_j) = e^{-\sigma \|x_i - x_j\|^2} \quad (6)$$

so that the RBF kernel's typology is determined by the σ parameter.

The model was created with SVR–ε. LIBSVM [58] was used, and the tuning of the parameters was achieved with DE optimizer [44,59–61].

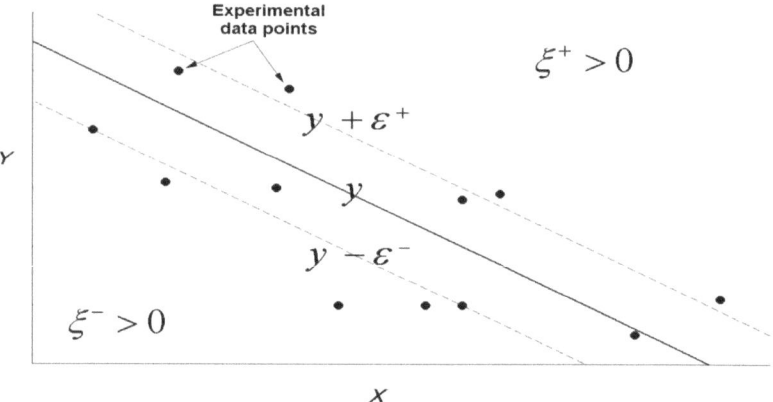

Figure 2. Illustration of the ε^- insensitive tube.

2.2.2. Gaussian Process Regression (GPR)

A Gaussian process is a stochastic process, where a set of random variables is defined with indices corresponding to time or space. For any finite linear combination, these random variables follow a multivariate normal distribution. The Gaussian process distribution, encompassing functions defined over a continuous domain such as space or time, represents the collective distribution of all these random variables [47–49].

Using lazy learning and the kernel function, the algorithm that employs a Gaussian process obtains a prediction for an unknown training data point. This estimation, which is a one-dimensional Gaussian distribution, is more than a prediction; it also provides its level of uncertainty. Multivariate Gaussian processes can be used for multi-output predictions, and the multivariate Gaussian distribution for these processes is the marginal distribution at each point [51].

Suppose that the training dataset is $D = \{(x_i, y_i) / i = 1, 2, \ldots, N\}$. The vectors $x_i \in \Re^n$ include the relevant segregation parameters as well as the extracted or combined features. The observed values give the filtered volume and outlet turbidity of the filtration process. $X = \{x_i\}_{i=1}^N$ is the matrix of the training dataset, which is used as input for obtaining the output vector $y = \{y_i\}_{i=1}^N$. Once we have some data, we can transform the prior over functions that a Gaussian process $f(x)$ converts into posterior over functions.

The mean $m(x)$ and covariance function $k(x, x')$ of a Gaussian process are the way to describe it. Then, the Gaussian process is [62,63]:

$$f(x) : GP(m(x), k(x, x')) \tag{7}$$

and

$$\begin{aligned} m(x) &= E[f(x)] \\ k(x, x') &= E\left[(f(x) - m(x))(f(x') - m(x'))^T\right] \end{aligned} \tag{8}$$

The function $m(x)$ is the predicted value of $f(x)$ for the point X. The covariance function $k(x, x')$ measures the confidence level for $m(x)$. The kernel $k(\cdot, \cdot)$ must be a positive definite. To keep things simple, the mean function is typically set to zero, but when there is no prior knowledge of the mean variable, as is the case in this work, it is also reasonable to do so.

For the Gaussian process, the covariance function selection is crucial. It also goes by the name "prior" because it contains the assumptions made about the latent regression model [64]. The RBF covariance function and the affine mean function are expressed in this study as follows [49,65]:

$$k_{SE}(x, x') = \sigma_f^2 \exp\left(-\frac{\|x - x'\|^2}{2l^2}\right) \tag{9}$$

where l is the length scale and σ_f^2 the signal variance. The performance of the Gaussian process is directly impacted by the SE covariance function parameter. In this case, l controls the function's change in horizontal scale, while σ_f^2 controls its change in vertical scale. Most applications cannot achieve the function values $f(x)$. In actual use, only the noisy inputs are provided by [62–65]:

$$y = f(x) + \varepsilon \tag{10}$$

We assumed that Gaussian noise is independent and has an identical distribution such that $\varepsilon : N(0, \sigma_n^2)$, and that σ_n is this noise's standard deviation. This will make ε the additive white noise. An individual Gaussian process can also be made up of any finite number of the input values, as shown by [62–65]:

$$y : GP\left(m(x), k(x, x') + \sigma_n^2 \delta_{ij}\right) = GP\left(0, k(x, x') + \sigma_n^2 \delta_{ij}\right) \tag{11}$$

so that δ_{ij} is the Kronecker delta function indicated below as:

$$\delta_{ij} = \begin{cases} 1 & \text{if} \quad i = j \\ 0 & \text{otherwise} \end{cases}$$

The goal is to predict, given the new point x^*, the function $\overline{f}^*$ and its variance $COV(f^*)$. In this context, X^* represents the test dataset's input matrix and N^* its size. The observed and predicted values for a new point follow a joint Gaussian previous distribution [62–65]:

$$\begin{bmatrix} y \\ f^* \end{bmatrix} : N\left(0, \begin{bmatrix} K(X, X) + \sigma_n^2 I & K(X, X^*) \\ K(X^*, X) & K(X^*, X^*) \end{bmatrix}\right) \tag{12}$$

where

- $K(X, X)$ is the training dataset covariance matrix and $K(X^*, X^*)$ is the test dataset covariance.
- $K(X, X^*)$ is the training and test dataset covariance matrix and $K(X^*, X) = K(X, X^*)^T$.

Because y and f^* are jointly distributed, it is possible to condition the prior on the inputs and investigate how likely estimations for the f^* are. That is [49,62–65]:

$$f^* | X^*, X, y : N\left(\bar{f}^*, cov\left(f^*\right)\right) \tag{13}$$

where

$$\bar{f}^* = E\left[f^* | X^*, X, y\right] = K(X^*, X)\left[K(X, X) + \sigma_n^2 I\right]^{-1} y \tag{14}$$

$$cov\left(f^*\right) = K(X^*, X^*) - K(X^*, X)\left[K(X, X) + \sigma_n^2 I\right]^{-1} K(X, X^*) \tag{15}$$

The prediction of new points can then be made using the ensuing distribution. In fact, the GPR model-predicted output value for the test point is $\bar{f}^*$. Additionally, the variance $cov\left(f^*\right)$ is used to compute the confidence interval (CI) of the predicted output value. For example, the 95% CI is $\left[\bar{f}^* - 2 \times \sqrt{cov\left(f^*\right)}, \bar{f}^* + 2 \times \sqrt{cov\left(f^*\right)}\right]$. As a result, the GPR model provides both the estimated values as well as the confidence level.

Finally, because the forecasted outputs of the GPR model only depend on the inputs x_i and the values of y, this is a nonparametric model. $\Theta = \{l, \sigma_f \sigma_n\}$ are the GPR model hyperparameters. The final regression model was constructed using the Gpy module from the Gaussian process framework in Python [66].

2.2.3. Differential Evolution (DE) Optimizer

This is an approach used to optimize problems by making multiple attempts to improve the quality of a potential solution. DE was first presented by Storn and Price in the 1990s [44]. They are metaheuristic techniques because they have the ability to explore extensive solution spaces without relying on specific assumptions about the problem [52]. In contrast to conventional optimization methods, such as gradient descent, which rely on differentiability of the optimization problem, DE utilizes multidimensional real-valued functions instead of the problem's gradient to solve it [53,54,59–61,67]. DE keeps a group of potential solutions and uses straightforward formulae to combine existing solutions to produce new ones. Subsequently, it retains the candidate solution that possesses the highest score, thus eliminating the need for a gradient. It also offers a quality estimation of the possible solution [53,54,61,67].

Differential Evolution (DE) can be employed to optimize a problem by iteratively enhancing the fitness of a possible solution. The efficiency of the Differential Evolution (DE) optimizer extends to multidimensional real-valued data, as it can successfully handle non-differentiable optimized functions. Additionally, the DE optimizer can be applied to dynamic, noisy, or non-continuous problems, showcasing its versatility across various challenging scenarios. DE optimization involves managing a potential solution population, combining it through straightforward formulae. The method optimizes by retaining the fittest solution for the given optimization problem [44]. The technique encapsulates the variables of the optimization problem, representing them as a vector. The population comprises NP vectors, representing the actual population, where the length of each vector, n, is the input variable number for the problem at hand.

If p denotes the index of a vector within the population ($p = 1, \ldots, NP$) and g represents the generation, we defined the vector as x_p^g. The components of this vector represent the input variables, denoted as $x_{p,m}^g$, and m is the index ($m = 1, \ldots, n$). The parameters in the problem are constrained within intervals limited by x_m^{min} and x_m^{max}, representing the minimum and maximum bounds, respectively. The steps of the DE algorithm are as follows [59–61,67]:

- Initialization;
- Mutation;
- Recombination;
- Selection.

After the initialization, the search begins. The mutation–recombination–selection phases conclude when a stopping criterion, such as a specified number of generations, a time threshold, or a desired level of solution attainment, is satisfied.

Initialization

During the initialization of the population in the first generation, each variable is assigned a random value within its respective minimum and maximum bounds [59–61,67]:

$$x_{p,m}^1 = x_m^{min} + rand\,(0,1) \cdot \left(x_m^{max} - x_m^{min}\right) \text{ for } p = 1,\ldots,NP \text{ and } m = 1,\ldots,n \quad (16)$$

where the random number within the interval $[0,1]$ is $rand\,(0,1)$.

Mutation

Creating the mutation involves selecting three individuals, randomly referred to as target vectors x_a, x_b, and x_c. These individuals are then used to generate NP new vectors. The process for creating the n_p^t new vectors is outlined below [59–61,67]:

$$n_p^t = x_c + F \cdot (x_a - x_b) \text{ for } p = 1,\ldots,NP \quad (17)$$

with the distinct individuals labeled as a, b, c, and p, the mutation rate is controlled by F, which falls within $[0,2]$.

Recombination

After generating the NP new vectors, we obtained the trial vectors t_m^g that are formed by applying recombination in a random way and by comparing the outcomes with the previous vectors x_p^g [59–61,67]:

$$t_{p,m}^g = \begin{cases} n_{p,m}^g & \text{if } rand\,(0,1) < GR \\ x_{p,m}^g & \text{otherwise} \end{cases} \text{ for } p = 1,\ldots,NP \text{ and } m = 1,\ldots,n \quad (18)$$

Regulated by the rate of recombination GR, the creation of trial vectors involves a combination of updated and original vectors. This is performed individually for each variable.

Selection

To select the vectors for the subsequent generation, determined by the best values obtained from the fitness function, a straightforward comparison is made between the test vectors and the original vectors [59–61,67]:

$$x_p^{g+1} = \begin{cases} t_p^g & \text{if } fit\left(t_p^g\right) > fit\left(x_p^g\right) \\ x_p^g & \text{otherwise} \end{cases} \quad (19)$$

2.3. Accuracy of This Approach

The COMEX gold spot price is the variable we tried to predict. To ensure a reliable forecast of the COMEX gold spot price using the selected input variables, we needed to find the best model. Subsequently, we compared the observed values t_i with the model-estimated values y_i. In this study, three criteria were examined to estimate fit quality: the root mean square error (RMSE) [68], the mean absolute error (MAE), and the mean absolute percentage error (MAPE) [69,70]. These statistical measures are commonly utilized to compute the accuracy of a mathematical model as well. Their expressions are [69,70]:

$$RMSE = \sqrt{\frac{\sum_{i=1}^{n}(t_i - y_i)^2}{n}} \quad (20)$$

$$MAE = \frac{\sum_{i=1}^{n}|t_i - y_i|}{n} \quad (21)$$

$$MAPE = \frac{100\%}{n}\sum_{i=1}^{n}\left|\frac{t_i - y_i}{t_i}\right| \quad (22)$$

If the RMSE is null, there is an exact match between the observed and predicted values, implying no difference between them. MAE is the average of the absolute difference between the target variable t_i and the predicted variable y_i. Finally, MAPE is frequently employed as a loss function for regression problems and in the evaluation of models. This is due to its highly intuitive interpretation in relation to relative error. Finally, R^2 was also calculated for the three models considered of the most interest [70].

2.4. Numerical Schemes

The monthly prices that were predicted began in January 2019 and ended in December 2019, and subsequently started in January 2020 and finished in December 2020. The dataset used for training included information ranging from January 1960 to March 2021. Therefore, in this specific instance, we needed to predict twelve future steps. As a result, we executed a multi-step forecast. The following three methods are used to create the training data:

1. Direct multi-step;
2. Recursive multi-step;
3. Direct–recursive hybrid.

Since the beginning, we used only one variable, namely, the gold price in the previous years. The non-energy index was added as an exogenous variable after this model was created, resulting in the NARX model. Following that, we went over the three different approaches to this multi-step forecasting problem. Here, the variables were standardized.

Direct multi-step (DM)

Under this approach, we built separate models for each prediction. If p stands for prediction, o for observation, and m for model:

$$\begin{aligned} p(t+1) &= m_1(o(t), o(t-1), \ldots, o(t-r)) \\ p(t+2) &= m_2(o(t), o(t-1), \ldots, o(t-r)) \\ &\cdots \\ p(t+12) &= m_{12}(o(t), o(t-1), \ldots, o(t-r)) \end{aligned} \quad (23)$$

The training dataset remained the same across all models, as is evident. However, twelve distinct models were created, with each model dedicated to a specific prediction. Four variables affected how these models perform. The first is the lag, or the length of time between observations. We employed $r+1$ observations for each model in this situation. One or more variables may be present in the observations at any given time. The gold price was our sole variable when we began. The final three variables were those that relate to the chosen method, SVR with an RBF kernel and/or GPR with an RBF kernel in this situation. These four parameters were optimized using the DE optimizer.

Recursive multi-step (RM)

In this instance, we created a model that is potentially identical to the first model in the previous technique. Then, we simply predicted the subsequent value at each step. We then took into account the predicted value, discarded the most recent value, and forecasted the following value. Thus, following the model construction, if p stands for prediction, o for observation, and m for model, the following prediction procedure is indicated as:

$$\begin{aligned} p(t+1) &= m(o(t), o(t-1), \ldots, o(t-r)) \\ p(t+2) &= m(p(t+1), o(t), o(t-1), \ldots, o(t-r+1)) \\ p(t+3) &= m(p(t+2), p(t+1), o(t), o(t-1), \ldots, o(t-r+2)) \\ &\ldots \\ p(t+12) &= m(p(t+11), p(t+10), \ldots, o(t-r+12)) \end{aligned} \qquad (24)$$

Indeed, we have a distinctive model, as is evident. When making predictions one step forward, we took the most recent prediction into account and discarded the earliest observation. The same factors applied as in the prior instance.

Direct–recursive hybrid (DH)

The two previous numerical systems were combined in this numerical scheme. For each prediction, we developed a unique model, but during the prediction phase, the models incorporated the forecasted values. In this instance, as we moved closer to the prediction, the lag for each model grew. In other words, if the first model started with $r + 1$ observations, the second model utilized an additional data point as it incorporated the newly predicted value during the forecasting phase. If p stands for prediction, o for observation, and m for model:

$$\begin{aligned} p(t+1) &= m_1(o(t), o(t-1), \ldots, o(t-r)) \\ p(t+2) &= m_2(p(t+1), o(t), o(t-1), \ldots, o(t-r)) \\ p(t+3) &= m_3(p(t+2), p(t+1), o(t), o(t-1), \ldots, o(t-r)) \\ &\ldots \\ p(t+12) &= m_{12}(p(t+11), p(t+10), \ldots, o(t-r)) \end{aligned} \qquad (25)$$

In this instance, we did not discard earlier observations as we moved closer to the prediction.

3. Results and Discussion

The methods for building the dataset used two distinct sets of variables: the gold price and the non-energy index that is the exogenous variable.

The first 600 months were eliminated because they did not alter the outcomes. This could be due to the fact that prices during a specific timeframe generally align with patterns observed in the preceding cycles. The price of gold is influenced by numerous political, social, and economic variables. They evolve over time, and similar situations from the past do not recur today. The dataset used for training was built from the recorded monthly gold prices spanning from January 1960 to March 2021. The lag affects how many training samples are used. A smaller lag implies a higher number of samples with identical data, as each sample encompasses a shorter time period and incorporates fewer observations. During the training phase, no data pertaining to the forecasted period (including the subsequent period) were employed. The objective was to predict monthly prices specifically for the 12 months of 2019 and the 12 months of 2020.

Tables 1 and 2 present the mean absolute percentage error (MAPE) for the four distinct models during the years 2019 and 2020.

Table 1. The year 2019 MAPE error.

Method	DH	RM	DM
DE/SVR	7.80	7.63	7.80
DE/GPR	8.06	8.69	5.06
NARX DE/SVR	7.61	6.72	5.92
NARX DE/GPR	7.51	6.72	7.48

Table 2. The year 2020 MAPE error.

Method	DH	RM	DM
DE/SVR	22.60	20.61	19.80
DE/GPR	22.82	21.82	10.12
NARX DE/SVR	20.77	20.86	22.94
NARX DE/GPR	20.23	20.44	16.16

Tables 1 and 2 show the following:

- For 2020, the year of the pandemic, the MAPEs are the worst. It seems reasonable to attribute this to the atmosphere of unpredictability brought on by the pandemic's numerous, unprecedented, and unexpected changes.
- The results obtained with only one variable are generally improved by the NARX models, though this is not always the case.
- The best models were obtained by using strategy 1.

Next, we will now choose the two best models for 2019 and the best model for 2020, and we will go into detail about their development and outcomes. The three top models are presented in Table 3 with the ideal parameters chosen by DE.

Table 3. The best models from the years 2019 and 2020.

	Type	Year	Optimal Parameters
Model 1	NARX DE/SVR	2019	$Lag = 5$, $C = 9.2785 \times 10^0$ $\varepsilon = 1.0297 \times 10^0$, $\sigma = 7.0995 \times 10^{-3}$
Model 2	DE/GPR	2019	$Lag = 4$, $\sigma_f^2 = 6.1384 \times 10^{-5}$ $l = 1.7375 \times 10^{-1}$, $\sigma_n^2 = 9.1358 \times 10^{-5}$
Model 3	DE/GPR	2020	$Lag = 5$, $\sigma_f^2 = 1.5520 \times 10^{-5}$ $l = 1.1629 \times 10^0$, $\sigma_n^2 = 3.2258 \times 10^2$

The accuracy for these models is shown in Table 4.

Table 4. Accuracy of the best models.

Model	MAE	MAPE (%)	RMSE	R^2
Model 1	83.841	5.92	92.700	0.152
Model 2	73.654	5.06	95.873	0.389
Model 3	177.32	10.12	192.68	0.301

Finally, Figure 3 displays the predicted and observed COMEX gold spot price values for the years 2019 (Model 1), 2020 (Model 3), and 2021 (Model 2) using the NARX DE/SVR, DE/GPR, and DE/GPR predictor methods, respectively.

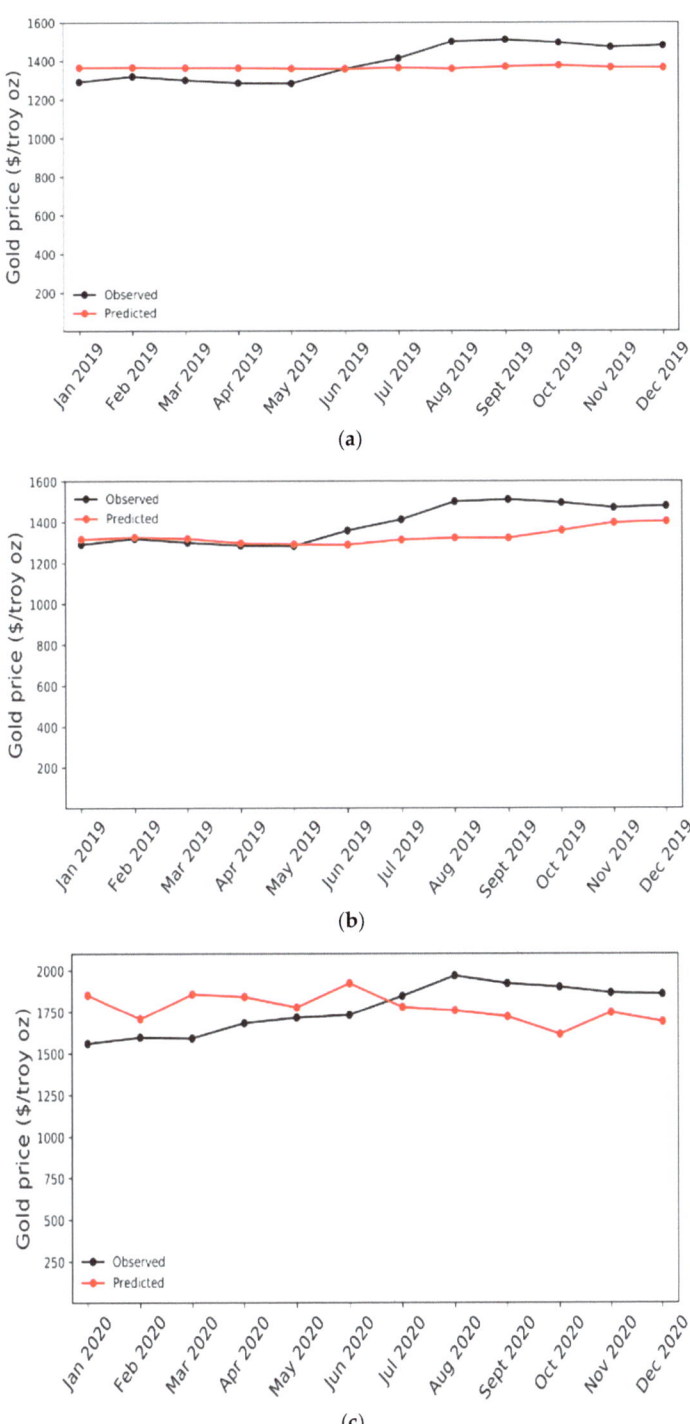

Figure 3. The COMEX gold spot price values, both observed and predicted, for three models: (**a**) Model 1 (NARX DE/SVR in the year 2019); (**b**) Model 2 (DE/GPR in the year 2019); and (**c**) Model 3 (DE/GPR in the year 2020).

The outcomes of the gold price forecasting models hold significant implications for both investors and policymakers within the realm of the gold market. For investors, the accuracy and reliability of these models can serve as invaluable tools for decision-making processes, particularly in portfolio diversification and risk management strategies. By utilizing such forecasting models, investors can gain insights into potential future movements in gold prices, enabling them to adjust their investment positions accordingly to thereby optimize returns and mitigate risks. Moreover, the ability to anticipate fluctuations in gold prices can aid investors in identifying opportune moments for buying or selling gold assets, thus enhancing their overall investment performance.

On the other hand, for policymakers, the findings from these forecasting models offer insights into the dynamics and drivers of gold price movements, which can inform policy decisions related to economic stability and monetary policy formulation. Understanding anticipated trends in gold prices can help policymakers assess their potential impact on inflation, currency valuations, and overall market sentiment. Additionally, by incorporating these forecasts into their policy frameworks, policymakers can adopt proactive measures to mitigate adverse effects stemming from volatile gold prices, thereby fostering greater economic resilience and stability. Overall, the integration of gold price forecasting models into both investment and policymaking practices represents a critical advancement in navigating the complexities of the gold market, ultimately enhancing decision-making processes and fostering more robust market outcomes.

Taking into account the results obtained in this paper, it can be said that DE/GPR leverages the robustness of GPR in handling noisy data and providing uncertainty estimates alongside predictions. Through the incorporation of DE, an optimization algorithm inspired by natural selection, DE/GPR efficiently adapts model parameters to fit complex data distributions, offering enhanced robustness and flexibility. The synergy between GPR and DE results in a computationally efficient approach with fewer hyperparameters to tune, making DE/GPR particularly appealing for tasks where accurate modeling of uncertainty and adaptability to diverse datasets are paramount.

In the case of NARX DE/SVR, this methodology combines the nonlinear modeling capabilities of SVR with the efficiency and adaptability of DE. Please also note that SVR excels in capturing intricate nonlinear relationships while maintaining robustness against overfitting by means of implicit feature selection and structural risk minimization. When coupled with Differential Evolution, NARX DE/SVR achieves superior generalization performance and tolerance to outliers, rendering it suitable for diverse applications where accurate predictions on unseen data instances are imperative. This amalgamation stands as a good example of the effectiveness of combining evolutionary optimization with robust regression techniques for addressing complex real-world problems.

But the proposed methodologies also have certain limitations that must be taken into account. These limitations can profoundly influence their outcomes in diverse applications. Firstly, DE/GPR's utilization of GPR, while advantageous for handling noisy data and providing uncertainty estimates, faces computational complexity challenges, particularly with large datasets due to its time complexity. Despite the incorporation of DE for parameter optimization, this computational burden may limit scalability. Furthermore, GPR's sensitivity to hyperparameters like kernel choice and parameters can significantly impact model performance, necessitating careful tuning. Additionally, the inherent complexity of GPR models may hinder interpretability, posing challenges in understanding the reasoning behind predictions, especially in domains where interpretability is crucial. On the other hand, NARX DE/SVR's amalgamation of SVR with DE introduces complexities in model interpretation and parameter sensitivity. SVR's tendency to produce complex models, especially with high-dimensional or nonlinear data, poses interpretability challenges, and tuning hyperparameters such as the regularization parameter and kernel parameters is crucial for optimal performance. However, these constraints can influence outcomes by necessitating trade-offs among model complexity, computational efficiency, and predictive performance. Striking the right balance requires careful consideration of hyperparameter tuning, computational resources, and interpretability needs, ultimately impacting the performance and suitability of DE/GPR and NARX DE/SVR for specific tasks and datasets.

4. Conclusions

The hybrid models constructed in this study utilized variables configured in three different ways. The output variable of this proposed hybrid models, based on support vector machines (SVM) [71] and GPR, is the COMEX gold spot price. The metaheuristic optimizer differential evolution (DE) [44,59–61,67] was employed to obtain the optimal parameters for SVM and GPR.

Based on the numerical results obtained from publicly available data on gold in the COMEX market, it can be concluded that Model 1 (NARX DE/SVR technique) is the most accurate predictor, as indicated by the RMSE statistic. Models 2 and 3 follow in terms of accuracy. However, when considering the MAPE and MAE statistics, Model 2 emerges as the best predictor, followed by Models 1 and 3. Additionally, it should be noted that the direct multi-step scheme yields the most optimal models. In the case of the R^2 metric, the most accurate model is Model 1, followed by Model 3 and Model 1. Please also note that although R^2 values are low, the good MAE, MAPE, and RMSE obtained suggest the model can make accurate predictions in terms of the magnitude and direction of the forecasted values. In such cases, the model can be considered accurate for forecasting purposes, especially if the primary goal is to minimize forecasting errors rather than explaining the variance in the data.

The forecasted gold prices generated by the DE/GPR and NARX DE/SVR models hold significant implications for all the stakeholders in the gold market. For example, investors and traders can utilize these forecasts to strategize their buying, selling, or holding decisions regarding gold assets. Through an analysis of the predicted price movements, investors can devise trading strategies, leveraging the timing of purchases or sales based on expected trends. Moreover, the forecasts empower traders to identify potential opportunities for arbitrage or speculation within the gold markets, optimizing their investment portfolios and capitalizing on market dynamics.

For gold mining companies, the forecasted gold prices offer invaluable insights for optimizing production strategies. By anticipating future price trends, mining companies can adjust production levels to maximize profitability. During periods of anticipated price increases, ramping up production can capitalize on higher prices, while during downturns, scaling back production helps minimize losses. Financial institutions, including banks and investment firms, can integrate the forecasted gold prices into their risk management and portfolio optimization strategies. By managing exposure to gold-related assets more effectively and hedging against price fluctuations, financial institutions can offer gold-linked financial products, such as exchange-traded funds (ETFs), tailored to client needs, enhancing portfolio performance and risk mitigation.

Also, central banks and governments can leverage forecasted gold prices to inform monetary policy decisions and reserve management practices. As gold prices often reflect broader economic trends and market sentiment, monitoring these forecasts enables policymakers to adjust gold reserve holdings and implement policies effectively, stabilizing economies and managing inflationary pressures. Jewelry and industrial manufacturers relying on gold as a raw material can optimize procurement and production processes through forecasted price insights. By negotiating better prices with suppliers and hedging against price fluctuations with forward contracts or options, manufacturers minimize costs and enhance operational efficiency. In essence, the forecasted gold prices derived from the DE/GPR and NARX DE/SVR models provide invaluable guidance across the gold market landscape, enabling stakeholders to make informed decisions and mitigate risks associated with gold price volatility.

In conclusion, we hold the belief that there is a bright outlook for research endeavors that merge hybrid models capable of harnessing the full potential of SVR and GPR models. Such models have the potential to combine various machine learning techniques, paving the way for innovative advancements in the field. Furthermore, these innovative techniques based on statistical machine learning have proven to be better than classical time-series techniques such as the ARIMA model at foretelling the price of other metals such as copper [43] and thermal coal [72] or even the forecasting of pollution incidents [73].

Finally, it can be said that researchers can explore various methodologies to develop more accurate and reliable forecasting models for gold prices, including long short-term memory (LSTM) [74], Prophet [75], ensemble methods, hybrid models, deep learning architectures [76], etc. LSTM is a type of recurrent neural network and is effective at capturing long-term dependencies in sequential data, making it promising for forecasting tasks in financial markets. Prophet, developed by Facebook, is tailored to handle time-series data with strong seasonal patterns, making it suitable for forecasting gold prices, which exhibit complex seasonal and cyclical patterns. Ensemble methods combine multiple models to improve predictive performance, while hybrid models integrate different techniques to leverage their complementary strengths. Deep learning architectures like convolutional neural networks [77] and transformer-based models [78], offer additional avenues for exploring and understanding gold price dynamics, enabling researchers to develop more informed decision-making tools for the gold market.

Author Contributions: E.G.-G.: Formal analysis, Data curation, Investigation, Writing—original draft, Visualization, Conceptualization, Methodology, and Software. P.J.G.-N.: Formal analysis, Data curation, Investigation, Visualization, Writing—original draft, Supervision, Conceptualization, Methodology, and Software. G.F.V.: Formal analysis, Investigation, Data curation, Writing—original draft, Conceptualization, and Methodology. P.R.F.: Formal analysis, Data curation, Investigation, Writing—original draft, Conceptualization, Visualization, Methodology, and Software. F.S.L.: Methodology, Investigation, Formal analysis, Data curation, Visualization, and Writing—original draft. S.L.S.G.: Methodology, Validation, and Writing—review and editing. All authors have read and agreed to the published version of the manuscript.

Funding: This research was funded by Plan Nacional by Ministerio de Ciencia, Innovación y Universidades, Spain, grant number MCINN-23-pID2022-139198NB-100.

Data Availability Statement: Data and source code will be made available on request.

Acknowledgments: We would like to acknowledge the Oviedo University Mathematics Department for providing computational support. We would also like to acknowledge the funding from Plan Nacional by Ministerio de Ciencia, Innovación y Universidades, Spain, grant number MCINN-23-pID2022-139198NB-100. Additionally, we are grateful to Anthony Ashworth for correcting the English spelling and grammar in this study.

Conflicts of Interest: The authors declare no conflict of interest.

References

1. Goodell, J.W.; Huynh, T.L.D. Did Congress trade ahead? Considering the reaction of US industries to COVID-19. *Financ. Res. Lett.* **2020**, *36*, 101578. [CrossRef]
2. Bampinas, G.; Panagiotidis, T. On the relationship between oil and gold before and after financial crisis: Linear, nonlinear and time-varying causality testing. *Stud. Nonlinear Dyn. Econom.* **2015**, *19*, 657–668. [CrossRef]
3. Chaya, J.; Azar, S.A.; Khakhar, P. Financial non-neutrality; A link between income inequality and aggregated debt characteristics in the United-States. *Int. J. Soc. Sci. Humanit. Stud.* **2021**, *13*, 29–54.
4. Haaskjold, H.; Aarseth, W.K.; Røkke, T.A.; Ivarson, M. Spinning the IPD Wheels- Moving towards frictionless project delivery. *J. Mod. Proj. Manag.* **2021**, *9*, 70–87.
5. Rodríguez, A.C.; Aguilar, J.L.; Arbiol, I.A. Relationship between physical physiological and psychological responses in amateur soccer referees. *Rev. Psicol. Deporte* **2021**, *30*, 26–37.
6. Iglesias García, C.; Saiz Matinez, P.; García-Portilla González, M.P.; Bousoño García, M.; Jiménez Treviño, L.; Sánchez Lasheras, F.; Bobes, J. Effects of the economic crisis on demand due to mental disorders in Asturias: Data from the Asturias Cumulative Psychiatric Case Register (2000–2010). *Actas Españolas Psiquiatr.* **2014**, *42*, 108–115.
7. Iglesias-García, C.; Sáiz, P.A.; Burón, P.; Sánchez-Lasheras, F.; Jiménez-Treviño, L.; Fernández-Artamendi, S.; Bobes, J. Suicidio, desempleo y recesión económica en España. *Rev. De Psiquiatr. Y Salud Ment.* **2017**, *10*, 70–77. [CrossRef]
8. Tuan, B.A.; Pho, K.H.; Pan, S.H.; Wong, W.K. Applications in sciences in the prevention of COVID-19. *Adv. Decis. Sci.* **2022**, *26*, 1–16.

9. Hoang, V.T.H.; Wong, W.K.; Zhu, Z.Z. Is gold different for risk-averse and risk seeking investors? An empirical analysis of the Shanghai Gold Exchange. *Econ. Model.* **2015**, *50*, 200–211. [CrossRef]
10. Hoang, V.T.H.; Zhu, Z.Z.; Xiao, B.; Wong, W.K. The seasonality of gold prices in China: Does the risk-aversion level matter? *Account. Financ.* **2018**, *60*, 2617–2664. [CrossRef]
11. Hoang, V.T.H.; Zhu, Z.Z.; Khamlichi, A.E.; Wong, W.K. Does the Shari'ah screening impact the gold-stock nexus? A sectorial analysis. *Resour. Policy* **2019**, *61*, 617–626. [CrossRef]
12. Eryigit, M. Short-term and long-term relationships between gold prices and precious metal (palladium, silver and platinum) and energy (crude oil and gasoline) prices. *Econ. Res. Ekon. Istraživanja* **2017**, *30*, 499–510. [CrossRef]
13. Yaya, O.S.; Vo, X.V.; Olayinka, H.A. Gold and silver prices, their stocks and market fear gauges: Testing fractional cointegration using a robust approach. *Resour. Policy* **2021**, *72*, 102045. [CrossRef]
14. Atri, H.; Kouki, S.; imen Gallali, M. The impact of COVID-19 news, panic and media coverage on the oil and gold prices: An ARDL approach. *Resour. Policy* **2021**, *72*, 102061. [CrossRef] [PubMed]
15. Tanin, T.I.; Sarker, A.; Hammoudeh, S.; Shahbaz, M. Do volatility indices diminish gold's appeal as a safe haven to investors before and during the COVID-19 pandemic? *J. Econ. Behav. Organ.* **2021**, *191*, 214–235. [CrossRef] [PubMed]
16. Alawi, A.H. Media and intercultural communication shifts: A semiotic analysis of the cultural identity in two international films. *Croat. Int. Relat. Rev.* **2021**, *27*, 1–13.
17. Agyei-Ampomah, S.; Gounopoulos, D.; Mazouz, K. Does gold offer a better protection against losses in sovereign debt bonds than other metals? *J. Bank. Financ.* **2014**, *40*, 507–521. [CrossRef]
18. Balcilar, M.; Gupta, R.; Pierdzioch, C. Does uncertainty move the gold price? New evidence from a nonparametric causality-in-quantiles test. *Resour. Policy* **2016**, *49*, 74–80. [CrossRef]
19. Baur, D.G.; McDermott, T.K. Is gold a safe haven? International evidence. *J. Bank. Financ.* **2010**, *34*, 1886–1898. [CrossRef]
20. Bilgin, M.H.; Gozgor, G.; Lau, C.K.M.; Sheng, X. The effects of uncertainty measures on the price of gold. *Int. Rev. Financ. Anal.* **2018**, *58*, 1–7. [CrossRef]
21. Bouoiyour, J.; Selmi, R.; Wohar, M.E. Measuring the response of gold prices to muncertainty: An analysis beyond the mean. *Econ. Model.* **2018**, *75*, 105–116. [CrossRef]
22. Beckmann, J.; Berger, T.; Czudaj, R. Gold price dynamics and the role of uncertainty. *Quant. Financ.* **2019**, *19*, 663–681. [CrossRef]
23. Maghyereh, A.I.; Abdoh, H. Connectedness between crude oil and US equities: The impact of COVID-19 pandemic. *Annu. Rev. Econ.* **2022**, *17*, 2250029. [CrossRef]
24. Arfaoui, M.; Rejeb, A.B. Oil, gold, US dollar and stock market interdependencies: A global analytical insight. *Eur. J. Manag. Bus. Econ.* **2017**, *26*, 278–293. [CrossRef]
25. Macdonald, E. *Handbook of Gold Exploration and Evaluation*; Woodhead Publishing: New York, NY, USA, 2007.
26. Stevens, R. *Mineral Exploration and Mining Essentials*; Robert Stevens Publishing: London, UK, 2011.
27. Skonieczny, M. *Gold Production from Beginning to End: What Gold Companies Do to Get the Shiny Metal into Our Hands*; Investment Publishing: New York, NY, USA, 2015.
28. U.S. Geological Survey. Gold, Mineral Commodity Summaries. 2018. Available online: https://www.usgs.gov/centers/nmic/gold-statistics-and-information (accessed on 10 March 2024).
29. Streifel, S. Impact of China and India on Global Commodity Markets Focus on Metals & Minerals and Petroleum, Report. 2006. Available online: http://www.tos.camcom.it/Portals/_UTC/Studi/ScenariEconomici/39746563551035393/ChinaIndiaCommodityImpact.pdf (accessed on 10 March 2024).
30. Cuddington, J.T.; Jerrett, D. Super Cycles in Real Metals Prices? *IMF Econ. Rev.* **2008**, *55*, 541–565. [CrossRef]
31. Roache, S.K. China's Impact on World Commodity Markets. IMF Working Paper No. 12/115. 2012. Available online: https://ssrn.com/abstract=2127010 (accessed on 10 March 2024).
32. Gordon, R.B.; Bertram, M.; Graedel, T.E. Metal stocks and sustainability. *Proc. Natl. Acad. Sci. USA* **2006**, *103*, 1209–1214. [CrossRef] [PubMed]
33. Tilton, J.E.; Lagos, G. Assessing the long-run availability of copper. *Resour. Policy* **2007**, *32*, 19–23. [CrossRef]
34. Li, J.; Wang, R.; Aizhan, D.; Karimzade, M. Assessing the impacts of COVID-19 on stock exchange, gold prices, and financial markets: Fresh evidences from econometric analysis. *Resour. Policy* **2023**, *83*, 103617. [CrossRef]
35. Baur, D.G.; Lucey, B.M. Is Gold a Hedge or a Safe Haven? An Analysis of Stocks, Bonds and Gold. *Financ. Rev.* **2010**, *45*, 217–229. [CrossRef]
36. Corbet, S.; Larkin, C.; Lucey, B. The contagion effects of the COVID-19 pandemic: Evidence from gold and cryptocurrencies. *Financ. Res. Lett.* **2020**, *35*, 101554. [CrossRef]
37. Ji, Q.; Zhang, D.; Zhao, Y. Searching for safe-haven assets during the COVID-19 pandemic. *Int. Rev. Financ. Anal.* **2020**, *71*, 101526. [CrossRef]
38. Dooley, G.; Lenihan, H. An assessment of time series methods in metal price forecasting. *Resour. Policy* **2005**, *30*, 208–217. [CrossRef]
39. Cortazar, G.; Eterovic, F. Can oil prices help estimate commodity futures prices? The cases of copper and silver. *Resour. Policy* **2010**, *35*, 283–291. [CrossRef]
40. Khashei, M.; Bijari, M. An artificial neural network (p,d,q) model for time series forecasting. *Expert. Syst. Appl.* **2010**, *37*, 479–489. [CrossRef]

41. Ma, W.; Zhu, X.; Wang, M. Forecasting iron ore import and consumption of China using grey model optimized by particle swarm optimization algorithm. *Resour. Policy* **2013**, *38*, 613–620. [CrossRef]
42. Kriechbaumer, T.; Angus, A.; Parsons, D.; Rivas Casado, M. An improved wavelet–ARIMA approach for forecasting metal prices. *Resour. Policy* **2014**, *39*, 32–41. [CrossRef]
43. Sánchez Lasheras, F.; de Cos Juez, F.J.; Suárez Sánchez, A.; Krzemień, A.; Riesgo Fernández, P. Forecasting the COMEX copper spot price by means of neural networks and ARIMA models. *Resour. Policy* **2015**, *45*, 37–43. [CrossRef]
44. Storn, R.M.; Price, K. Differential evolution—A simple and efficient heuristic for global optimization over continuous spaces. *J. Glob. Optim.* **1997**, *11*, 341–359. [CrossRef]
45. Brockwell, P.J.; Davis, R.A. *Introduction to Time Series and Forecasting*; Springer: New York, NY, USA, 2016.
46. Shumway, R.H.; Stoffer, D.S. *Time Series Analysis and Its Applications: With R Examples*; Springer: New York, NY, USA, 2017.
47. Rasmussen, C.E. *Gaussian Processes in Machine Learning: Summer School on Machine Learning*; Springer: Berlin/Heidelberg, Germany, 2003.
48. Hastie, T.; Tibshirani, R.; Friedman, J. *The Elements of Statistical Learning: Data Mining, Inference, and Prediction*; Springer: New York, NY, USA, 2016.
49. Kuhn, M.; Johnson, K. *Applied Predictive Modeling*; Springer: New York, NY, USA, 2018.
50. World Bank Commodity Price Data (The Pink Sheet). Bloomberg, Engineering and Mining Journal; Platts Metals Week; and Thomson Reuters Datastream; World Bank. 2021. Available online: http://pubdocs.worldbank.org/en/561011486076393416/CMO-Historical-Data-Monthly.xlsx (accessed on 10 March 2024).
51. Vapnik, V. *Statistical Learning Theory*; Wiley–Interscience: New York, NY, USA, 1998.
52. Cristianini, N.; Shawe-Taylor, J. *An Introduction to Support Vector Machines and Other Kernel–Based Learning Methods*; Cambridge University Press: New York, NY, USA, 2000.
53. Schölkopf, B.; Smola, A.J.; Williamson, R.C.; Bartlett, P.L. New support vector algorithms. *Neural Comput.* **2000**, *12*, 1207–1245. [CrossRef]
54. Hansen, T.; Wang, C.J. Support vector based battery state of charge estimator. *J. Power Sources* **2005**, *141*, 351–358. [CrossRef]
55. Li, X.; Lord, D.; Zhang, Y.; Xie, Y. Predicting motor vehicle crashes using Support Vector Machine models. *Accid. Anal. Prev.* **2008**, *40*, 1611–1618. [CrossRef] [PubMed]
56. Steinwart, I.; Christmann, A. *Support Vector Machines*; Springer: New York, NY, USA, 2008.
57. Hamel, L.H. *Knowledge Discovery with Support Vector Machines*; Wiley-Interscience: New York, NY, USA, 2011.
58. Chang, C.-C.; Lin, C.-J. LIBSVM: A library for support vector machines. *ACM Trans. Intell. Syst. Technol.* **2011**, *2*, 1–27. [CrossRef]
59. Price, K.; Storn, R.M.; Lampinen, J.A. *Differential Evolution: A Practical Approach to Global Optimization*; Springer: Berlin/Heidelberg, Germany, 2005.
60. Feoktistov, V. *Differential Evolution: In Search of Solutions*; Springer: New York, NY, USA, 2006.
61. Rocca, P.; Oliveri, G.; Massa, A. Differential evolution as applied to electromagnetics. *IEEE Trans. Antennas Propag.* **2011**, *53*, 38–49. [CrossRef]
62. Rasmussen, C.E.; Williams, C.K.I. *Gaussian Processes for Machine Learning*; MIT Press: Cambridge, MA, USA, 2006.
63. Marsland, S. *Machine Learning: An Algorithmic Perspective*; Chapman and Hall/CRC Press: Boca Raton, FL, USA, 2014.
64. Schneider, M.; Ertel, W. Robot learning by demonstration with local Gaussian process regression. In Proceedings of the IEEE/RSJ International Conference on Intelligent Robots and Systems, Taipei, Taiwan, 18–22 October 2010; pp. 255–260.
65. Shi, J.Q.; Choi, T. *Gaussian Process Regression Analysis for Functional Data*; Chapman and Hall/CRC Press: Boca Raton, FL, USA, 2011.
66. GPy: A Gaussian process framework in Python. Available online: http://sheffieldml.github.io/GPy/ (accessed on 23 June 2023).
67. Chakraborty, U.K. *Advances in Differential Evolution*; Springer: Berlin/Heidelberg, Germany, 2008.
68. Artime Ríos, E.M.; Sánchez Lasheras, F.; Suarez Sánchez, A.; Iglesias-Rodríguez, F.J.; Seguí Crespo, M.M. Prediction of Computer Vision Syndrome in Health Personnel by Means of Genetic Algorithms and Binary Regression Trees. *Sensors* **2019**, *19*, 2800. [CrossRef] [PubMed]
69. Wasserman, L. *All of Statistics: A Concise Course in Statistical Inference*; Springer: New York, NY, USA, 2003.
70. Freedman, D.; Pisani, R.; Purves, R. *Statistics*; WW Norton & Company: New York, NY, USA, 2007.
71. Casteleiro-Roca, J.L.; Jove, E.; Sánchez-Lasheras, F.; Méndez-Pérez, J.A.; Calvo-Rolle, J.L.; de Cos Juez, F.J. Power Cell SOC Modelling for Intelligent Virtual Sensor Implementation. *J. Sens.* **2017**, *2017*, 9640546. [CrossRef]
72. Krzemień, A.; Riesgo Fernández, P.; Suárez Sánchez, A.; Sánchez Lasheras, F. Forecasting European thermal coal spot prices. *J. Sustain. Min.* **2015**, *14*, 203–210. [CrossRef]
73. Sánchez, A.B.; Ordóñez, C.; Sánchez Lasheras, F.; de Cos Juez, F.J.; Roca-Pardiñas, J. Forecasting SO2 Pollution Incidents by means of Elman Artificial Neural Networks and ARIMA Models. *Abstr. Appl. Anal.* **2013**, *2013*, 238259. [CrossRef]
74. Liu, K.; Cheng, J.; Yi, J. Copper price forecasted by hybrid neural network with Bayesian Optimization and wavelet transform. *Resour. Policy* **2022**, *75*, 102520. [CrossRef]
75. Ghosh, I.; Jana, R.K. Clean energy stock price forecasting and response to macroeconomic variables: A novel framework using Facebook's Prophet, NeuralProphet and explainable AI. *Technol. Forecast. Soc.* **2024**, *200*, 123148. [CrossRef]

76. Suárez Gómez, S.L.; García Riesgo, F.; Pérez Fernández, S.; Iglesias Rodríguez, F.J.; Díez Alonso, E.; Santos Rodríguez, J.D.; De Cos Juez, F.J. Wavefront Recovery for Multiple Sun Regions in Solar SCAO Scenarios with Deep Learning Techniques. *Mathematics* **2023**, *11*, 1561. [CrossRef]
77. Sanchez Lasheras, F.; Ordóñez, C.; Roca-Pardiñas, J.; de Cos Juez, F.J. Real-time tomographic reconstructor based on convolutional neural networks for solar observation. *Math. Methods Appl. Sci.* **2019**, *43*, 8032–8041. [CrossRef]
78. Liu, Z.; Qian, S.; Xia, C.; Wang, C. Are transformer-based models more robust than CNN-based models? *Neural Netw.* **2024**, *172*, 106091. [CrossRef] [PubMed]

Disclaimer/Publisher's Note: The statements, opinions and data contained in all publications are solely those of the individual author(s) and contributor(s) and not of MDPI and/or the editor(s). MDPI and/or the editor(s) disclaim responsibility for any injury to people or property resulting from any ideas, methods, instructions or products referred to in the content.

Article

Graph Information Vanishing Phenomenon in Implicit Graph Neural Networks

Silu He [1], Jun Cao [1], Hongyuan Yuan [1], Zhe Chen [1], Shijuan Gao [1,2,*] and Haifeng Li [1]

[1] School of Geosciences and Info-Physics, Central South University, Changsha 410083, China; hesilu@csu.edu.cn (S.H.); 195011042@csu.edu.cn (J.C.); 235011057@csu.edu.cn (H.Y.); 235011047@csu.edu.cn (Z.C.); lihaifeng@csu.edu.cn (H.L.)
[2] Information & Network Center, Central South University, Changsha 410083, China
* Correspondence: gaoshijuan@csu.edu.cn

Abstract: Graph neural networks (GNNs) have been highly successful in graph representation learning. The goal of GNNs is to enrich node representations by aggregating information from neighboring nodes. Much work has attempted to improve the quality of aggregation by introducing a variety of graph information with representational capabilities. The class of GNNs that improves the quality of aggregation by encoding graph information with representational capabilities into the weights of neighboring nodes through different learnable transformation structures (LTSs) are referred to as implicit GNNs. However, we argue that LTSs only transform graph information into the weights of neighboring nodes in the direction that minimizes the loss function during the learning process and does not actually utilize the effective properties of graph information, a phenomenon that we refer to as graph information vanishing (GIV). To validate this point, we perform thousands of experiments on seven node classification benchmark datasets. We first replace the graph information utilized by five implicit GNNs with random values and surprisingly observe that the variation range of accuracies is less than ± 0.3%. Then, we quantitatively characterize the similarity of the weights generated from graph information and random values by cosine similarity, and the cosine similarities are greater than 0.99. The empirical experiments show that graph information is equivalent to initializing the input of LTSs. We believe that graph information as an additional supervised signal to constrain the training of GNNs can effectively solve GIV. Here, we propose GinfoNN, which utilizes both labels and discrete graph curvature as supervised signals to jointly constrain the training of the model. The experimental results show that the classification accuracies of GinfoNN improve by two percentage points over baselines on large and dense datasets.

Keywords: graph neural network; graph information; joint training; graph curvature

MSC: 68-XX

Citation: He, S.; Cao, J.; Yuan, H.; Chen, Z.; Gao, S.; Li, H. Graph Information Vanishing Phenomenon in Implicit Graph Neural Networks. *Mathematics* 2024, 12, 2659. https://doi.org/10.3390/math12172659

Academic Editor: Alessandro Niccolai

Received: 30 July 2024
Revised: 23 August 2024
Accepted: 26 August 2024
Published: 27 August 2024

Copyright: © 2024 by the authors. Licensee MDPI, Basel, Switzerland. This article is an open access article distributed under the terms and conditions of the Creative Commons Attribution (CC BY) license (https://creativecommons.org/licenses/by/4.0/).

1. Introduction

Graph neural networks (GNNs) have achieved great success on a wide range of graph analysis tasks, such as recommender systems [1,2], traffic flow prediction [3,4], and biochemistry research [5,6]. The success of GNNs is mainly attributed to adaptively enriching the representations of target nodes by aggregating the features of neighboring nodes in a supervised learning paradigm, which can be summarized as the message-passing neural network framework (MPNN) [7]. The MPNN generates node representations by iteratively transforming, aggregating, and updating the features of neighboring nodes. The transformation and update operations usually correspond to linear transformations and nonlinear activation functions, respectively, while the aggregation operation is more complex and valuable. The aggregation operation involves two main aspects: defining the neighboring nodes and measuring the importance of the neighboring nodes. Many works designed GNNs that simply utilized the nodes directly connected to the target node as the neighboring nodes [8–10], and other designs employed the acquisition of neighboring nodes by random walk in order to explore rich and diverse local topologies [11,12]. There are usually three ways to define the weights of neighboring nodes: (1) consider the importance of all neighboring nodes as equal [5,10,13], (2) use node degree to assign the importance of neighboring nodes [8], and (3) assign the importance of neighboring nodes implicitly in a data-driven manner [9,14].

The weights of neighboring nodes that are implicitly generated can adapt datasets automatically. We refer to GNNs adopting this scheme as implicit GNNs. We reorganize the pipeline of generating the weights of implicit GNNs into three parts: (1) the graph information, (2) the learnable transformation structures (LTSs), and (3) the weights of neighboring nodes, as shown in Figure 1. The graph information is the input of the LTS, and the weights of neighboring nodes are the output. For example, CurvGN [14] takes advantage of the Ricci curvature [15] and the multilayer perceptron (MLP) to generate the weights.

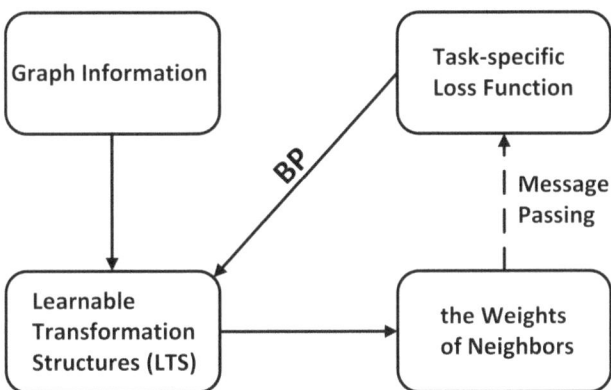

Figure 1. An illustration of the forward propagation pipeline of LTSs in implicit GNNs. BP means backward gradient propagation.

In general, the weights generated by implicit GNNs are not only adaptive to datasets but also take advantage of the valuable properties of graph information to enhance the quality of node representations. However, we argue that the LTSs only transform graph information into the weights of neighboring nodes in the direction that minimizes the loss function during training and does not utilize the unique properties of graph information, a phenomenon that we refer to as graph information vanishing (GIV). To validate this point, we select five implicit GNNs, CurvGN, PEGN [16], GAT, HGCN [17] and AGNN [18], and conduct thousands of experiments on 7 node classification datasets. First, we replace the graph information with the random values obtained by sampling from a 0–1 uniform distribution. Surprisingly, we observe that the variation range of classification accuracies is less than ± 0.3%. Then, we visualize these two types of weights, the difference between which is difficult to visually perceive. Moreover, we quantitatively characterize the similarity of the weights generated from graph information and random values by cosine similarity. The cosine similarities are greater than 0.99 under most conditions. The experimental results indicate that the weights generated by the LTSs do not retain the valuable properties of graph information, i.e., the mechanism of implicit GNNs cannot properly utilize graph information.

We argue that GIV is triggered by the fact that the loss function is task-specific and not associated with graph information. Assuming the existence of latent optimal weights that minimize the task-specific loss, the goal of the LTSs is simply to update the learnable parameters by back propagation so that the learned weights are as close to the latent optimal weights as possible. If the fitting ability of the LTSs is strong enough, the input can be arbitrary in theory. Since the loss function is independent of the graph information, the weights generated by the LTSs naturally do not retain the properties of graph information.

We also believe that graph information characterizing datasets is essential to improve the performance of GNNs. According to the above analysis, GIV is caused by the lack of connection between the loss function and graph information. Intuitively, graph information can also be used as an auxiliary supervised signal to constrain the training of GNNs, thus effectively utilizing graph information to enrich the knowledge of GNNs. Inspired by joint learning [6], we propose GinfoNN, which is able to utilize both supervised signals provided by labels and auxiliary supervised signals provided by graph information. GinfoNN decomposes GNNs into two parts, a feature extractor and a task-specific head, while adding a task–auxiliary head. The task-specific head and task–auxiliary head correspond to task-specific loss based on the labels and task–auxiliary loss based on graph information, respectively. In particular, we take the discrete graph curvature [14,19] as an auxiliary supervised signal that quantifies the structural connectivity of node pairs. Experimental results show that GinfoNN outperforms the baselines on large and dense datasets. The ablation experiments also demonstrate the necessity of the discrete graph curvature for improving the performance of GNNs.

The remainder of this paper is organized as follows. In Section 3, we review the pipeline of implicit GNNs for computing the weights of neighboring nodes, rederive five implicit GNNs, and illustrate GIV through empirical experiments. In Section 4, we describe the framework GinfoNN and the discrete graph curvature in detail. In Section 5, we evaluate the performance of GinfoNN on node classification benchmark datasets. In Section 2, we briefly review the related work. Finally, Section 6 discusses several inspiring issues related to this work, and Section 7 concludes the paper.

2. Related Work

GNNs. GNNs can be divided into spectral GNNs and spatial GNNs. The initial concept of convolution on the graph [20] is defined based on the spectral graph theory. This method cannot design spatially localized filters and needs intense computations due to the matrix eigendecomposition. In order to avoid computing the eigendecomposition of the graph Laplacian matrix, a truncated expansion of Chebyshev polynomials is employed to approximate the filter [21]. GCN [8] further simplifies the filter by fixing the polynomials to 1 and using a renormalization trick. Since spectral GNNs focus on specific graphs, they face many insurmountable limitations, such as the inability of trained models to generalize to other graphs, which can be handled well by spatial GNNs. Spatial filters can directly work on the local structure of graphs, and different filters can be designed for nodes with different-sized neighbors [5]. MoNet [22] proposes a mixture model to successfully adapt CNN for the non-Euclidean domain and generalize some previous models. GraphSAGE [10] samples fixed-size neighbors as receptive fields and uses different methods to aggregate their representations. To assign specific weights for neighborhood nodes, GAT [9] incorporates the self-attention mechanism into graph convolution. CurvGN [14] and PEGN [16] introduced the Ricci curvature and persistence images as additional knowledge to assign specific weights to channels of node features, respectively. With the exploration of the connection between GNN and the diffusion model, diffusion-based GNNs open a new path to improving GNNs. HiD-Net [23] proposes a new general diffusion framework for unifying GNNs and shows effectiveness on both homophily and heterophily graphs.

Theoretical analysis. GNNs, as black-box models, arouse wide concern about their power and limits. The mechanism and oversmoothing problem of GCN are explored and explained by considering the convolution layer as symmetric Laplacian smoothing [24]. A theoretical framework is proposed for analyzing the discriminative power of GNNs to distinguish different graph structures [13]. The expressive power of GCNs with deeper layers is investigated, and a weight normalization strategy is proposed to improve their expressive power [25]. The expressive power of GNNs for Boolean node classification is further analyzed, and adding readout functions acts as an efficient way to increase logical expressiveness [26]. The explanation of GNNs is also investigated systematically [27]. Besides, some methods contribute to modifying network architectures to improve the performance of GNNs. SGC [28] simplifies graph convolutional networks to adapt large-scale graphs by removing nonlinearities weight matrices. Deepgcns [29] expands the layers of GCN from 2 to 56 layers by referring to the concept of residual/dense connections in CNN. For the graph classification task, the effect of attention on the readout phase is analyzed, and a weakly supervised method is proposed to train attention [30]. Note that the most of analysis works focus on GCN and its variants, which are regarded as explicit GNNs in this paper. By contrast, the analysis of implicit GNNs is not nearly enough.

Joint learning. Joint learning aims at enriching the supervision signals by utilizing various attributive and topological graph information. Utilizing attributive information to generate pseudo labels can boost the adversarial robustness of GNNs [31]. M3S [32] proposes a multistage joint-training mechanism by using the K-means clustering algorithm. PairwiseDistance [33] regards the shortest distance between two nodes as the auxiliary supervision signal. Centrality Score Ranking [34] recovers the relative order of centrality scores between pairwise nodes as the auxiliary task. GPN [35] develops a bilevel optimization framework to simultaneously optimize the graph generator and the downstream predictor. Implementing an adversarial solution in the joint learning paradigm can learn causal independence and achieve graph out-of-distribution generalization [36]. Joint learning has been shown to improve the performance and adversarial robustness of GNNs by exploiting valuable graph information, which can actually utilize graph information and solve GIV naturally.

3. Implicit GNNs

3.1. Implicit GNNs: A Unified View

In this section, we first summarize several key components of GNNs and further sort out the pipeline for implicit GNNs to compute the weights of neighboring nodes.

Key components of GNNs. GNNs consist of a message-passing phase and a readout phase in the message-passing neural network framework (MPNN) [7]. The message-passing phase is on the node level, while the readout phase is on the graph level. We only focus on the message-passing phase, on which the weights of neighboring nodes have a significant effect. In general, the forward propagation formula for message passing can be summarized as

$$h_i^l = Y^l\left(h_i^{l-1}, \square_{j \in \mathcal{N}(i)} \Phi^l\left(h_i^{l-1}, h_j^{l-1}, e_{i,j}^{l-1}\right)\right) \tag{1}$$

where $h_i^{l-1} \in \mathbb{R}^F$ is the representation of the node i on the $l-1$ layer, F indicates the dimension of the node feature, $e_{i,j} \in \mathbb{R}^D$ is the feature of the edge from node i to node j, D indicates the dimension of the edge feature, $\mathcal{N}(i)$ is the neighboring nodes of node i, Y and Φ are differentiable functions, and $\square$ is a differentiable, permutation-invariant aggregation function, e.g., sum, mean, or max.

$$h_i^l = \sigma^l\left(\square_{j \in \mathcal{N}(i)}\left(\tau_{i,j}^l W^l h_j^{l-1}\right)\right), \tag{2}$$

$$\tau_{i,j}^l = \Delta^{l-1}\left(e_{i,j}^{l-1}\right) \tag{3}$$

where σ is the activation function, W is a matrix of filter parameters, $\tau_{i,j}$ is the weight of the node feature from node j to node i, and Δ is a transformation function.

The forward propagation formulas of mostly spatial GNNs can be simplified for the aggregation part and the reweight part. The corresponding formulas are Equation (2) and Equation (3), respectively. If Δ needs to be learned, such as MLP, the GNN is referred to as an implicit GNN; otherwise, it is referred to as an explicit GNN. In other words, we classify

GNNs as explicit GNNs or implicit GNNs according to whether the weights of neighbors need to be learned.

The pipeline of generating the weights for implicit GNNs. For implicit GNNs, edge feature $e_{i,j}$ is interpreted as graph information, which helps to assign the weights of neighbors in aggregation, and Δ is referred to as the learnable transformation structure (LTS). A common assumption behind implicit GNNs is that $e_{i,j}$ can help GNNs by learning more knowledge about datasets, and the LTS ensures that $\tau_{i,j}$ automatically adapts datasets in a data-driven manner. The pipeline of implicit GNNs is shown in Figure 2, and the role of LTS is illustrated at the bottom of Figure 2. Some popular GNNs, such as CurvGN, PEGN, GAT, HGCN, and AGNN, can be rederived into the pipeline. The benefit of this protocol is to help us unify the analysis and the understanding of GIV for implicit GNNs. The graph information $e_{i,j}$ and the corresponding LTSs utilized by these five models are shown in Table 1.

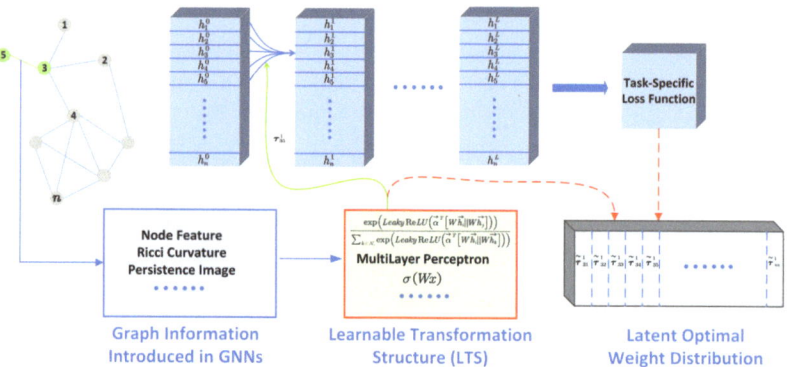

Figure 2. A pipeline of implicit GNNs. The top part of the figure is the aggregation of GNNs, while the bottom part of the figure is the reweight part. Given the dataset and the network architecture, we assume the task-specific loss function forces the LTSs to learn the latently optimal weight distribution during training.

Table 1. Summary of graph information and LTS for the five implicit GNNs.

Model	Graph Information ($e_{i,j}$)	LTS (Δ)
CurvGN	Ricci curvature	MLP
PEGN	Persistence image	MLP
GAT	$\left(h_i \| h_j\right)$	Attention mechanism
HGCN	$\left(\log^K(h_i) \| \log^K(h_j)\right)$	MLP
AGNN	$\cos\left(h_i \cdot h_j\right)$	A learnable parameter

3.1.1. Special Case 1

When utilizing the CurvGN model, it is assumed that the Ricci curvature can endow GNNs with more discriminative power. The Ricci curvature is a measure whose result indicates whether the structural relationship between a pair of nodes is tight or alienated. The neighbors of pairwise nodes in the same community often have many shortcuts and largely overlap. If the Ricci curvature of edges connecting two communities is positive, then information should be easily exchanged between the corresponding nodes, and if this is negative, then information is not easily exchanged between the corresponding nodes.

The Ricci curvature is the graph information of CurvGN, and the two-layer MLP is the LTS. The formula of the reweight part is

$$\tau_{i,j}^l = \text{SOFTMAX}_{j \in \mathcal{N}(i)} \left(\text{MLP}^l \left(e_{i,j} \right) \right) \tag{4}$$

where $\text{SOFTMAX}_{j \in \mathcal{N}_i}$ represents an individual normalization for each channel of the node features. The dimension of τ^l is set to the same as h^l. Therefore, τ^l can give separate weights to each channel of the node features to make the model more discriminative. The aggregation part of CurvGN is formulated as

$$h_i^l = \sigma \left(\sum_{j \in \mathcal{N}(i)} \text{diag} \left(\tau_{i,j}^l \right) W^l h_j^{l-1} \right) \tag{5}$$

3.1.2. Special Case 2

PEGN argues that local structural information of graphs can improve the adaptability of GNNs to large graphs with heterogeneous topology. PEGN uses persistence homology, a principled mathematical tool, to describe the loopiness of nodes' neighbors, which measures the information transmission efficiency of each node. PEGN utilizes persistence images to quantitatively characterize the persistence homology of each edge.

PEGN refers to persistent images of graphs as graph information. The reweight part and aggregation part of PEGN is the same as that of CurvGN. PEGN also selects a two-layer MLP as the LTS of the model.

3.1.3. Special Case 3

GAT aims to address the limitations of spectral GNNs by implicitly computing the weights of neighboring nodes. GAT introduces the self-attention mechanism to automatically transform the hidden representation of nodes into the attention coefficients which are treated as weights of neighbors.

The graph information introduced by GAT is the vector that concatenates the hidden features of pair-wise nodes $e_{i,j} = \left(h_i \| h_j \right), e_{i,j} \in \mathbb{R}^{2F'}$, and $\|$ represents the concatenation operation. The formula of GAT's reweight part is

$$\tau_{i,j} = \text{SOFTMAX}_{j \in \mathcal{N}(i)} \left(\vec{a}^T W e_{i,j} \right) \tag{6}$$

where the weight matrix $W \in \mathbb{R}^{2F' \times 2F'}$ and the weight vector $\vec{a} \in \mathbb{R}^{2F'}$ are shared by all information. The LTS of GAT is $\vec{a}^T W$. To ensure the stability of training, GAT also utilizes a K-head attention mechanism. The formula of the aggregation part is given by

$$h_i^l = \sigma \left(\sum_{j \in \mathcal{N}(i)} \prod_{k=1}^{K} \left(\tau_{i,j}^k W^k h_j^{l-1} \right) \right) \tag{7}$$

3.1.4. Special Case 4

HGCN extends GNNs from Euclidean space to hyperbolic space and aims to solve the distorted deformation when graphs are hierarchical or scale-independent in Euclidean space. HGCN first maps node features to the hyperboloid manifold by exponential mapping and then maps node features in the hyperboloid space to the tangent space by logarithmic mapping. Since the tangent space is Euclidean and isomorphic to $\mathcal{R}^d$, the whole computation of the aggregation part is in the tangent space. The output generated by aggregation is then mapped to the hyperbolic space by an exponential mapping. Finally, HGCN implements GNN in hyperbolic space.

HGCN takes the concatenated vector of hidden features of two nodes on the edge in the tangent space as graph information $e_{i,j} = \left(\log^K(h_i) \| \log^K(h_j) \right)$, where K denotes the hyperbolic curvature. To transform graph information as the weight of node features, MLP is used as the LTS. So, the formula of the reweight part is

$$\tau_{i,j}^l = \text{SOFTMAX}_{j \in \mathcal{N}(i)}\left(\text{MLP}^l(e_{i,j})\right) \quad (8)$$

where $\tau \in \mathbb{R}$ is the weight of node j to node i. The formula of the aggregation part is

$$h_i^l = \exp^K\left(\sum_{j \in \mathcal{N}(i)} \tau_{i,j}^l \log^K\left(h_j^{l-1}\right)\right) \quad (9)$$

Note that some operations, such as the activation function in hyperbolic space, are omitted to highlight the core of HGCN. For more details, please see [17].

3.1.5. Special Case 5

AGNN is a special kind of GNN, which does not use the weight matrix to transform the node features in the aggregation process but only uses the attention propagation matrix to aggregate the node features. The attention propagation matrix is generated by a special attention mechanism in a data-driven mode. AGNNs argue that the mechanism is able to gain more accurate predictions by learning the dynamic and adaptive weights of neighbors.

The AGNN uses the cosine of the hidden features of the two nodes on the edge as graph information $e_{i,j} = \cos(h_i \cdot h_j) \in \mathbb{R}$, and $\cos(h_i \cdot h_j) = h_i^T h_j / \|h_i\| \|h_j\|$. Then, the attention mechanism of AGNN is the reweight part, which is calculated as

$$\tau_{i,j}^l = \text{SOFTMAX}_{j \in \mathcal{N}(i)}\left(\beta^l e_{i,j}\right) \quad (10)$$

where β^l is a learnable scalar, which is the TLS of the AGNN. If node i and node j are not connected, the corresponding value of the attention propagation matrix is 0. Therefore, the formula of the aggregation can be rewritten as

$$h_i^l = \sum_{j \in \mathcal{N}(i)} \tau_{i,j}^l h_j^{l-1} \quad (11)$$

3.2. Graph Information Vanishing of Implicit GNNs

3.2.1. The Effect of Random Values Substituting Graph Information

We explore the impact of replacing graph information with random values on implicit GNNs. See Section 5.1 for more information on the datasets. To avoid randomness and ensure reproducibility, we select three random seeds, which are 0, 10, 100. Then, we randomly sample from a 0–1 uniform distribution and replace the generated random values with graph information, with the corresponding models being model_0, model_10, and model_100, respectively. We compare the classification accuracies of the five implicit GNNs and their corresponding random-value substituting models on seven benchmark datasets, as shown in Table 2. Experimental results suggest that replacing graph information with random values causes almost no performance degradation of implicit GNNs. The best results on different datasets are distributed between implicit GNNs and implicit GNNs with random values among the five sets of models. Note that the difference in accuracies between implicit GNNs and implicit GNNs with random values is small and less than 0.3 percent on most datasets. It illustrates that replacing the graph information with random values has almost no impact on the performance of implicit GNNs. For the LTS, the roles of graph information and random values appear to be equivalent, i.e., to provide the initialization input of the LTS.

On large and dense datasets, the accuracies of the AGNN are slightly better than that of AGNN_*. The reason is that the LTS of the AGNN is a learnable parameter that only exponentially scales up or down the cosine values between neighboring nodes. Due to the smoothing capability of GNNs, the node features tend to be similar and their corresponding cosine values are relatively large when a pair of nodes shares more neighboring nodes.

The cosine operation slightly enhances the discriminative power of the model when the transformation power of LTS is insufficient. However, we also notice that the transformation ability of LTS of AGNN is too weak, resulting in the accuracies on large and dense datasets being much lower than that of other models with strong transformation ability of LTS. If we change the LTS to a self-attention mechanism, i.e., change the AGNN to GAT, replacing graph information with random values will have almost no impact on the performance of implicit GNNs.

We note that no particular implicit GNNs perform optimally on all datasets. It suggests that the possible direction to improve the performance of the GNN models may be to explore novel network architecture with better generalization capability rather than introducing different types of graph information as the input of LTS.

Table 2. Summary of statistic results in terms of comparing different implicit GNNs with the corresponding GNNs with random values on seven benchmark datasets. OOM means out of memory.

Methods	Cora	CiteSeer	PubMed	Coauthor CS	Coauthor Physics	Amazon Computers	Amazon Photo
CurvGN	82.1 ± 0.6	**71.8 ± 0.6**	**79.0 ± 0.4**	92.3 ± 0.3	93.3 ± 0.3	84.0 ± 0.6	91.2 ± 0.6
CurvGN_0	**82.2 ± 0.4**	71.5 ± 0.5	78.9 ± 0.4	92.3 ± 0.4	**93.4 ± 0.2**	**84.1 ± 0.6**	91.1 ± 0.6
CurvGN_10	82.1 ± 0.5	71.6 ± 0.5	78.9 ± 0.4	**92.5 ± 0.3**	**93.4 ± 0.2**	83.9 ± 0.6	**91.2 ± 0.5**
CurvGN_100	81.9 ± 0.5	71.6 ± 0.7	78.9 ± 0.3	92.4 ± 0.4	93.4 ± 0.3	83.8 ± 0.6	91.2 ± 0.6
PEGN	82.1 ± 0.6	**71.7 ± 0.6**	**79.0 ± 0.3**	92.5 ± 0.4	93.3 ± 0.3	82.3 ± 0.8	91.7 ± 0.6
PEGN_0	82.1 ± 0.6	71.6 ± 0.6	78.9 ± 0.3	92.3 ± 0.4	**93.4 ± 0.3**	83.6 ± 0.7	91.8 ± 0.5
PEGN_10	82.2 ± 0.7	71.6 ± 0.7	78.9 ± 0.3	**92.5 ± 0.3**	**93.4 ± 0.3**	83.2 ± 0.7	91.7 ± 0.5
PEGN_100	**82.3 ± 0.5**	**71.7 ± 0.6**	78.9 ± 0.4	92.3 ± 0.3	93.3 ± 0.3	83.3 ± 0.6	**91.9 ± 0.6**
GAT	82.7 ± 0.7	71.6 ± 0.8	77.7 ± 0.5	**91.2 ± 0.4**	92.5 ± 0.6	83.2 ± 1.0	**91.9 ± 0.8**
GAT_0	82.5 ± 0.7	71.6 ± 0.8	**77.7 ± 0.4**	**91.2 ± 0.4**	92.4 ± 0.3	**83.3 ± 0.7**	91.7 ± 0.4
GAT_10	82.6 ± 0.6	**71.7 ± 0.7**	77.7 ± 0.4	**91.2 ± 0.4**	**92.5 ± 0.4**	83.2 ± 0.8	91.7 ± 0.5
GAT_100	82.5 ± 0.7	71.5 ± 1.0	77.6 ± 0.4	**91.2 ± 0.5**	92.4 ± 0.4	83.3 ± 0.8	91.6 ± 0.6
HGCN	81.2 ± 1.5	67.8 ± 1.3	76.9 ± 0.7	91.3 ± 0.6	OOM	**81.7 ± 1.2**	**91.2 ± 0.8**
HGCN_0	**81.4 ± 1.2**	67.8 ± 1.6	**77.2 ± 0.6**	91.4 ± 0.6	OOM	81.3 ± 1.2	90.5 ± 0.8
HGCN_10	81.1 ± 1.3	**68.1 ± 1.3**	77.2 ± 0.8	**91.5 ± 0.6**	OOM	81.3 ± 1.3	90.4 ± 0.9
HGCN_100	81.2 ± 1.3	68.0 ± 1.3	77.0 ± 0.8	**91.5 ± 0.5**	OOM	81.2 ± 1.2	90.6 ± 0.8
AGNN	82.2 ± 0.6	71.0 ± 0.7	**78.6 ± 0.3**	**90.5 ± 0.4**	**92.0 ± 0.2**	**77.4 ± 1.1**	**90.1 ± 0.8**
AGNN_0	**82.6 ± 0.6**	**71.5 ± 0.6**	77.3 ± 0.4	89.6 ± 0.4	91.8 ± 0.3	76.6 ± 0.8	87.8 ± 0.8
AGNN_10	82.0 ± 0.6	70.7 ± 1.0	77.4 ± 0.2	89.7 ± 0.3	91.6 ± 0.3	76.5 ± 0.9	87.8 ± 0.7
AGNN_100	81.5 ± 0.8	**71.5 ± 0.7**	78.2 ± 0.3	89.9 ± 0.4	91.8 ± 0.3	76.1 ± 1.0	87.9 ± 0.7

3.2.2. Similarity of Weights of Neighbors

We qualitatively and quantitatively show that the weights of neighboring nodes obtained from the random values models are highly similar to those obtained from the original models. Without loss of generality, we select GATs and CurvGNs for detailed analysis. Figure 3 visualizes the weights of neighbors of GAT, GAT_0, CurvGN, and CurvGN_0 in the first layer on different datasets. Note that Citeseer is a relatively sparse and small dataset, and Computer is a relatively dense and large dataset. Regardless of the structure of the graphs, we hardly perceive the difference in the weights of neighbors between GAT and GAT_0 with our eyes. The phenomenon is also present on CurvGN. Due to the different network architectures between GAT and CurvGN, there are some small observable differences in their weights of neighbors. It qualitatively illustrates that even taking completely different graph information, LTS has the ability to transform it into highly similar weights of neighboring nodes.

We quantitatively characterize the similarity of weights of neighbors through the cosine similarity. Since the weights of neighboring nodes may be a matrix, we first need to reduce the dimensionality from matrix form to vector form. We observe that there is almost no difference in the colors of the same column of Figure 3, which indicates that the difference in the values of the weights in different channels is very small. Further, we quantitatively measure the average variation in the weights across channels using

$$C(A_{m \times n}) = \frac{\sum_j^n \sum_i^m \left| a_{i,j} - \frac{\sum_k^m a_{k,j}}{m} \right|}{m \times n} \qquad (12)$$

where A indicates the weights of neighboring nodes, m is the dimension of A, n is the number of edges. The above formula actually measures the average absolute difference between the values of different channels compared with the mean values. The average absolute difference in hidden layers' weights for different models on benchmark datasets is shown in Table 3. We found that the average absolute difference in weights of different channels is quite small and can be negligible. Therefore, we use averaging over channels to reduce the weights of neighbors in matrix form to vector form $\vec{A}$ and then compute the cosine similarity to compare the similarity of different weights. The formula of the cosine similarity is shown as

$$\text{cosineSIM}(\vec{\tau_1}, \vec{\tau_2}) = 0.5 \frac{\vec{\tau_1} \cdot \vec{\tau_2}}{|\vec{\tau_1}| \times |\vec{\tau_2}|} + 0.5. \qquad (13)$$

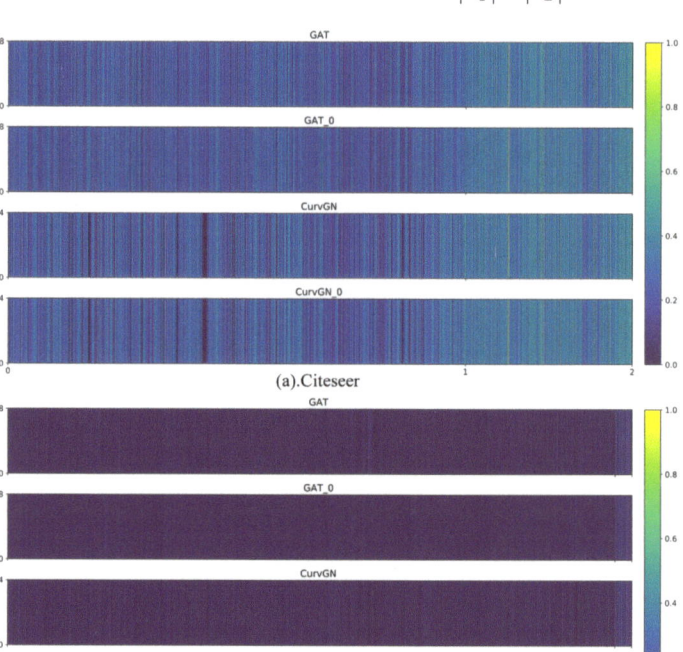

Figure 3. An illustration of visualization of hidden layer's weights of neighbors for different models on different datasets: (**a**) Weights of neighbors on Citeseer and (**b**) weights of neighbors on Amazon Computers. The vertical axis of each subgraph represents the dimension of the weights of neighbors. The horizontal axis of the subgraph is divided into two parts, where 0 to 1 represents the weights of edges, and 1 to 2 represents the weights of self-loops.

We select cosine similarity to quantify the high similarity of the weights of neighboring nodes generated by graph information and random values, as shown in Table 4. For GAT, CurvGN, and PEGN, Table 4 shows that the cosine similarity of the weights exceeds

0.99 in most cases. We notice a small decrease in the similarity of the weights for GAT on Coauthor CS and Coauthor Physics. The reason is that GAT uses 128-dimensional vectors as graph information and the LTS has insufficient learning ability on relatively large and dense datasets. Highly similar weights of neighbors illustrate that replacing graph information with random values has almost no effect on implicit and also explains the results of Table 2 and Figure 3. A large number of experiments confirm the existence of GIV for implicit GNNs.

Table 3. Summary of consistency of hidden layers' weights of neighbors for different models.

Methods	Cora	CiteSeer	PubMed
GAT	6.7×10^4	1.6×10^4	5.9×10^4
GAT_0	9.8×10^3	7.6×10^3	9.1×10^3
CurvGN	1.2×10^4	1.6×10^4	8.7×10^6
CurvGN_0	1.5×10^4	1.5×10^4	6.9×10^5

Table 4. Summary of cosine similarity of hidden layer's weights of neighbors for LTS with different graph information. Keep 4 decimal places and round off the rest.

Methods	Cora	CiteSeer	PubMed	CS	Physics
GAT, GAT_0	0.9998	1.0	0.9998	0.9972	0.9984
CurvGN, CurvGN_0	1.0	1.0	1.0	1.0	1.0
PEGN, PEGN_0	1.0	1.0	1.0	1.0	1.0

4. Ginfonn: Graph Curvature Boosts GNNs

In this section, we first detail a kind of graph information that characterizes the structural relationship of pairwise nodes, the Ricci curvature, which is the same as the graph information utilized by CurvGN. Inspired by Joint Training [33], we develop GinfoNN, which effectively exploits the Ricci curvature by treating it as an auxiliary supervised signal. This way inherently solves GIV, which means that GinfoNN exactly makes use of graph information.

4.1. The Ricci Curvature

Curvature is able to qualitatively measure the degree of curvature in space. In Euclidean space, curvature measures the degree to which a curve deviates from a straight line, or a surface deviates from a plane. In Riemannian geometry, curvature measures the degree to which a local manifold deviates from Euclidean space, and Ricci curvature portrays its deviation in the orthogonal direction. Ollivier et al. [19] generalize the Ricci curvature from continuous space to discrete space by means of optimal transport theory, e.g., graph.

The Ricci curvature on the graph measures the extent of overlap or connection of pairwise nodes to neighboring nodes. The Ricci curvature treats the target node i and its neighboring nodes as a kind of probability distribution m_i. We consider any probability distribution as an object of mass 1. Now, we want to know the minimum average mass-preserving transportation plan for transferring the mass of m_i to m_j, known as the Wasserstein distance $W(m_i, m_j)$. Naturally, the larger the Wasserstein distance of a pair of nodes, the weaker the connection between the two nodes, and vice versa. Besides, the Ricci curvature also takes the shortest distance between two nodes $d(i, j)$ into account. The Ricci curvature of an edge e_{ij} can be formulated as

$$c_{ij} = 1 - \frac{W(m_i, m_j)}{d(i, j)} \tag{14}$$

We choose a simple and effective probability distribution with a hyperparameter α, as in [15]. Following the existing work [37], we set $\alpha = 0.5$. For an undirected and unweighted graph $\mathcal{G} = (\mathcal{V}, \mathcal{E})$, the probability distribution of the node j with degree k can be

$$m_i(j) = \begin{cases} \alpha & \text{if } j = i \\ (1-\alpha)/k & \text{if } j \in \mathcal{N}(i) \\ 0 & \text{otherwise} \end{cases} \quad (15)$$

The Ricci curvature contains a wealth of local structural information from the perspective of graph theory. In general, we consider the (infinitely extended) grid as a plane on the graph, and all its nodes are structurally equivalent. The Ricci curvature, on the other hand, portrays the direction and degree of deviation of the local structure with respect to the grid. If the curvature is negative, the neighboring nodes of these two nodes tend to be separated. If the curvature on the edges is positive, it indicates that these two nodes are relatively closely connected structurally, as their neighboring nodes tend to converge. Furthermore, a subgraph constitutes a community structure if the curvature of most of its edges is positive [38]. Since the Ricci curvature can appropriately characterize the relationship of pairwise nodes on the local structure, we choose the Ricci curvature as the auxiliary supervision signal.

4.2. The Framework of GinfoNN

Inspired by joint learning, we developed GinfoNN, which can effectively exploit the properties of graph information. The goal of joint learning is to improve the generalization of the model by simultaneously minimizing the objective function of the downstream task and the auxiliary task. We briefly introduce the workflow of joint learning on GNNs, as shown in Figure 4. Joint learning can be divided into three parts: (1) a feature extractor; (2) a downstream task head and (3) an auxiliary task head. First, we need a feature extractor to transform node features into node representations, which can be arbitrary types and numbers of layers of GNNs. Based on the extracted node representations, the downstream task head transforms the features into prediction results and the auxiliary task head transforms the features into the corresponding output. Both the downstream task head and the auxiliary task head can be either a GNN or a linear transformation layer. Finally, we jointly optimize the objective functions of the downstream and auxiliary tasks.

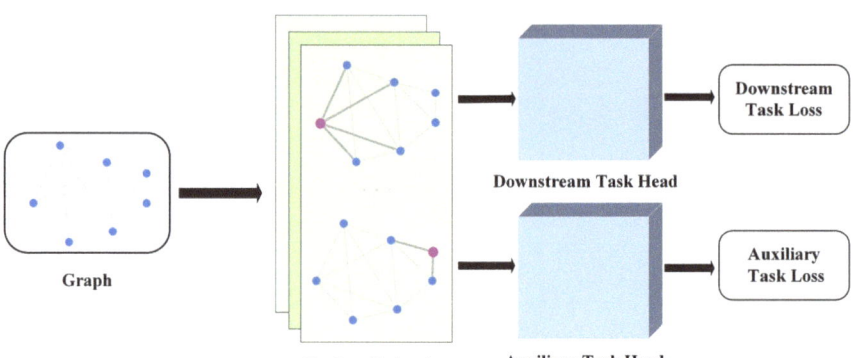

Figure 4. An overview of the GinfoNN framework.

Feature Extractor. The Feature extractor is a layer of spatial GNNs that learns the weights of neighboring nodes and aggregates the node features of neighboring nodes according to the weights. According to the experimental results of AGNN on large and dense datasets, we want to utilize the node features as much as possible. Therefore, we choose the 2-layer MLP as the LTS to convert the concatenated node features into weights. The calculation formula is shown as

$$\tau_{i,j} = \text{Softmax}\left(\text{MLP}\left(Wh_i^0 \| Wh_j^0\right)\right) \quad (16)$$

where $\|$ means the concatenation operator. The forward propagation formula of the feature extractor is

$$h_i^1 = \sigma\left(\sum_{j \in \mathcal{N}(i)} \tau_{i,j} W h_j^0\right) \quad (17)$$

where $\sigma()$ means the activation function, which is the ReLU function.

Downstream Task Head. The downstream task head is a layer of spatial GNNs, which transforms the latent node representations generated by the feature extractor into the target node representations for a specific task. To improve the computational efficiency, we do not calculate the weights of neighboring nodes in this layer, instead, use the weights obtained by the feature extractor directly. The forward propagation formula of the downstream task head is

$$h_i^2 = \sum_{j \in \mathcal{N}(i)} \tau_{i,j} W h_j^1 \quad (18)$$

Auxiliary Task Head. The auxiliary task head is a transformation function, which transforms the latent node representations generated by the feature extractor into the Ricci curvature. Then, we choose a two-layer MLP as the auxiliary task head. Note that the Ricci curvature is edge-specific. We need to use the cosine function to transform the outputs of those two nodes of an edge into a scalar. The forward propagation formula of the auxiliary task head is shown as

$$g_{i,j} = \cos\left(\text{MLP}\left(h_i^1\right), \text{MLP}\left(h_j^1\right)\right) \quad (19)$$

where cos indicates the cosine function.

Loss Function. The loss function of GinfoNN consists of the downstream task loss and the auxiliary task loss. Since the benchmark datasets are for node classification, we select the cross entropy as the downstream task loss. For the auxiliary task, we notice that the Ricci curvature is continuous and is distributed in $[-1,1]$. We select the mean squared error (MSE) as the auxiliary loss function. Besides, we also adjust the importance of task–auxiliary loss through the hyperparameter α. The loss function of GinfoNN is

$$\text{Loss} = \text{CrossEntropy}\left(h_i^2, y_i\right) + \alpha \|g_{i,j} - c_{i,j}\|_2 \quad (20)$$

where y_i is the one-hot encoding of node labels, and $c_{i,j}$ is the Ricci curvature of edge $e_{i,j}$.

GinfoNN utilizes both label information and the Ricci Curvature to improve the generalization of GNNs. Unlike CurvGN which uses the Ricci Curvature as the input of LTS, GinfoNN uses it as the supervision signal of the auxiliary task head. GinfoNN effectively solves GIV and improves the performance of the model by exploiting the Ricci Curvature. In this way, we can easily and effectively take advantage of various graph information to enrich and improve the performance and knowledge of GNNs.

5. Experiments and Results

5.1. Databases

We select seven node classification benchmark datasets: Cora, Citeseer, PubMed, Coauthor CS, Coauthor Physics, Amazon Computers, and Amazon Photos. The detailed statistics of these seven datasets are shown in Table 5. For all datasets, the training set consists of 20 nodes per class, the validation set has 500 nodes, and the test set has 1000 nodes. Cora, Citeseer, and PubMed [39] have been widely used to evaluate the performance of GNNs, while these three benchmark datasets suffer from the disadvantages of a small total number of nodes and sparse connections. We added four more datasets, Coauthor

CS, Coauthor Physics, Amazon Computers, and Amazon Photos, with a relatively larger number of nodes, number of edges, and average node degree. Coauthor CS and Coauthor Physics are used in the KDD Cup 2016 challenge and are based on the co-authorship graphs obtained from the Microsoft Academic Graph. The node features are word vectors extracted from the keywords of all papers of each author, and the classes represent the most active research areas of the authors. Amazon Computers and Amazon Photo are subgraphs of the Amazon co-purchase graph [40] with nodes representing items, edges representing two items often purchased at the same time, node features extracted from product reviews as word vectors, and classes representing product categories. We use pytorch_geometric [41] for the graph data loading and construction. In order to achieve better training for all models, we adopt feature normalization. All datasets are partitioned in the same way as in [42].

Table 5. Statistic details of the benchmark datasets used in the experiments.

Datasets	Nodes	Edges	Features	Classes	Training Nodes	Avg. Degree
Cora	2708	5429	1433	7	140	3.90
CiteSeer	3327	4732	3703	6	120	2.74
PubMed	19,717	44,338	500	3	60	4.50
CS	18,333	100,227	6805	15	300	8.93
Physics	34,493	282,455	8415	5	100	14.38
Computers	13,381	259,159	767	10	200	35.76
Photos	7487	126,530	745	8	160	31.13

5.2. Experimental Setup

5.2.1. Baselines

To fairly evaluate the performance of GinfoNN, we chose some other important GNNs as baselines, in addition to the above five implicit GNNs: CurvGN, PEGN, GAT, HGCN, and AGNN. These baselines include spectral GNNs and spatial GNNs. GCN uses node degree to evaluate the importance of neighboring nodes. MoNet [22] not only proposes a unified framework for GNNs but also generalizes CNNs to non-Euclidean data, such as graphs and manifolds. GraphSAGE [10] proposed a neighboring sampling technique and three ways to aggregate neighboring node features and generalize GNNs from transductive learning to inductive learning. APPNP [11] introduces PageRank into GNNs and constructs a high-level node propagation mechanism. CGNN [43] explicitly transforms the Ricci curvature into weights in the aggregation process through the negative curvature transformation module and the curvature normalization module.

5.2.2. Set-Up

To enhance the reproducibility of the experiments, we choose 2021 as the random seed. We utilize the Adam stochastic gradient descent optimizer with a learning rate of 0.005 and L2 regularization of 0.0005 for training. We initialize the weight matrix with Glorot initialization. We use an early stopping strategy based on the validation set's accuracies with a patience of 100 epochs. In this paper, for all statistic results (Tables 2 and 6), we repeat 50 experiments (runs) for each model and use the average classification accuracy of the test set and its standard deviation as the main evaluation metric. For GinfoNN, we only adjust the hyperparameter α, which represents the importance of the auxiliary task loss. We train all models on a single Nvidia 2080Ti, and the code for the models is built on pytorch_geometric [41].

Table 6. Summary of statistical results in terms of mean test set classification accuracies (in percent) and standard deviation on seven node classification benchmark datasets. Red numbers mean the best accuracies, and **bolded** numbers mean the second-best performance. OOM means out of memory.

Methods	Cora	CiteSeer	PubMed	Coauthor CS	Coauthor Physics	Amazon Computers	Amazon Photo
GCN	81.5 ± 1.3	71.9 ± 0.9	77.8 ± 2.9	91.1 ± 0.5	92.8 ± 1.0	82.6 ± 2.4	91.2 ± 1.2
MoNet	81.3 ± 1.3	71.2 ± 2.0	78.6 ± 2.3	90.8 ± 0.6	92.5 ± 0.9	83.5 ± 2.2	91.2 ± 1.3
GraphSAGE	79.2 ± 7.7	71.6 ± 1.9	77.4 ± 2.2	91.3 ± 2.8	93.0 ± 0.8	82.4 ± 1.8	91.4 ± 1.4
GAT	82.7 ± 0.7	71.6 ± 0.8	77.7 ± 0.5	91.2 ± 0.4	92.5 ± 0.6	83.2 ± 1.0	**91.9 ± 0.8**
AGNN	82.2 ± 0.6	71.0 ± 0.7	78.6 ± 0.3	90.5 ± 0.4	92.0 ± 0.2	77.4 ± 1.1	90.1 ± 0.8
APPNP	83.3 ± 0.7	72.3 ± 0.4	80.2 ± 0.2	**92.5 ± 0.2**	93.3 ± 0.2	83.2 ± 0.7	91.7 ± 0.7
HGCN	81.2 ± 1.5	67.8 ± 1.3	76.9 ± 0.7	91.3 ± 0.6	OOM	81.7 ± 1.2	91.2 ± 0.8
CurvGN	82.1 ± 0.6	71.8 ± 0.6	79.0 ± 0.4	92.3 ± 0.3	93.3 ± 0.3	**84.0 ± 0.6**	91.2 ± 0.6
PEGN	82.1 ± 0.6	71.7 ± 0.6	**79.0 ± 0.3**	92.5 ± 0.4	93.3 ± 0.3	82.3 ± 0.8	91.7 ± 0.6
CGNN	81.6 ± 0.6	71.6 ± 0.6	78.2 ± 0.4	93.0 ± 0.3	**93.5 ± 0.4**	83.5 ± 0.6	91.6 ± 0.4
GinfoNN	**83.2 ± 0.7**	**71.9 ± 0.5**	79.0 ± 0.7	92.3 ± 0.5	93.7 ± 0.5	85.0 ± 0.7	93.1 ± 0.6

5.3. Curvature Boosts Generalization

The mechanism of GinfoNN and the structural property of the Ricci curvature improve the generalization of GNNs together. The classification accuracies and F1-score of GinfoNN and the baselines on the seven node classification benchmark datasets are shown in Table 6 and Table 7, respectively. Experimental results evaluated by both accuracy and weighted F1-score indicate that GinfoNN outperforms the baselines on large and dense datasets. The reason is that Ricci curvature effectively describes the interactions between neighboring nodes within the local topological structure, serving as a kind of unique and valuable graph information. Preserving this information promotes the model to distinguish the categorical properties of nodes and edges. Explicitly leveraging the learning of Ricci curvature as an auxiliary task not only prevents the vanishing of graph information represented by Ricci curvature but also acts as a supervision signal as a constraint of learning node representations. Therefore, GinfoNN provides GNNs with the Ricci curvature as an auxiliary but valuable supervision signal, effectively compensating for the shortcomings. It enables GinfoNN to perform the best classification on large and dense datasets. As shown in Figure 5, it can be observed that the four added datasets exhibit a significant imbalance of categorical distribution, which affects the propagation of label information across the whole graph. Due to the small proportion of labeled nodes (20 nodes per class), the supervision signal provided by labels on large-scale datasets is insufficient to transmit to the full graph. This imbalance of global spatial distribution makes it even more challenging for the signal to transmit effectively.

Table 7. Summary of statistical results in terms of mean test set classification F1-score (in percent) and standard deviation on seven node classification benchmark datasets. We adopted the weighted form of the F1-score. Red numbers mean the best accuracies, and **bolded** numbers mean the second-best performance. OOM means out of memory.

Methods	Cora	CiteSeer	PubMed	Coauthor CS	Coauthor Physics	Amazon Computers	Amazon Photo
GCN	79.2 ± 1.8	70.2 ± 1.4	76.6 ± 3.2	89.9 ± 0.6	91.3 ± 1.4	82.2 ± 3.0	90.3 ± 2.6
MoNet	79.2 ± 2.0	69.4 ± 2.8	78.0 ± 3.3	90.6 ± 1.3	91.1 ± 0.9	82.8 ± 3.2	90.2 ± 2.8
GraphSAGE	77.5 ± 6.8	**70.7 ± 2.3**	76.2 ± 2.6	91.1 ± 2.4	90.9 ± 1.2	81.9 ± 2.8	90.5 ± 2.0
GAT	81.9 ± 0.7	69.5 ± 1.1	77.6 ± 0.4	91.0 ± 0.5	91.1 ± 0.6	81.5 ± 2.1	91.0 ± 1.5
AGNN	81.6 ± 1.7	69.6 ± 1.7	75.9 ± 0.8	90.3 ± 0.4	91.0 ± 0.9	76.8 ± 2.7	89.6 ± 1.1
APPNP	82.5 ± 1.1	71.0 ± 1.6	79.0 ± 0.8	**91.5 ± 0.4**	91.2 ± 1.9	81.7 ± 1.4	91.3 ± 2.2
HGCN	78.9 ± 2.6	67.5 ± 1.6	76.0 ± 0.9	90.8 ± 1.6	OOM	80.9 ± 2.3	90.1 ± 1.4
CurvGN	81.6 ± 2.0	70.3 ± 1.4	78.5 ± 0.9	91.2 ± 1.4	90.8 ± 0.6	**83.0 ± 1.4**	90.1 ± 1.2
PEGN	81.4 ± 1.5	70.2 ± 1.5	78.7 ± 2.0	91.3 ± 0.8	91.1 ± 0.8	81.6 ± 2.2	90.9 ± 0.9
CGNN	79.8 ± 1.2	70.2 ± 1.4	77.4 ± 1.3	92.4 ± 1.0	92.0 ± 1.4	82.6 ± 1.7	90.6 ± 1.6
GinfoNN	**82.0 ± 1.0**	70.4 ± 1.3	78.7 ± 1.1	91.4 ± 0.9	**91.5 ± 1.1**	83.1 ± 1.6	91.9 ± 1.3

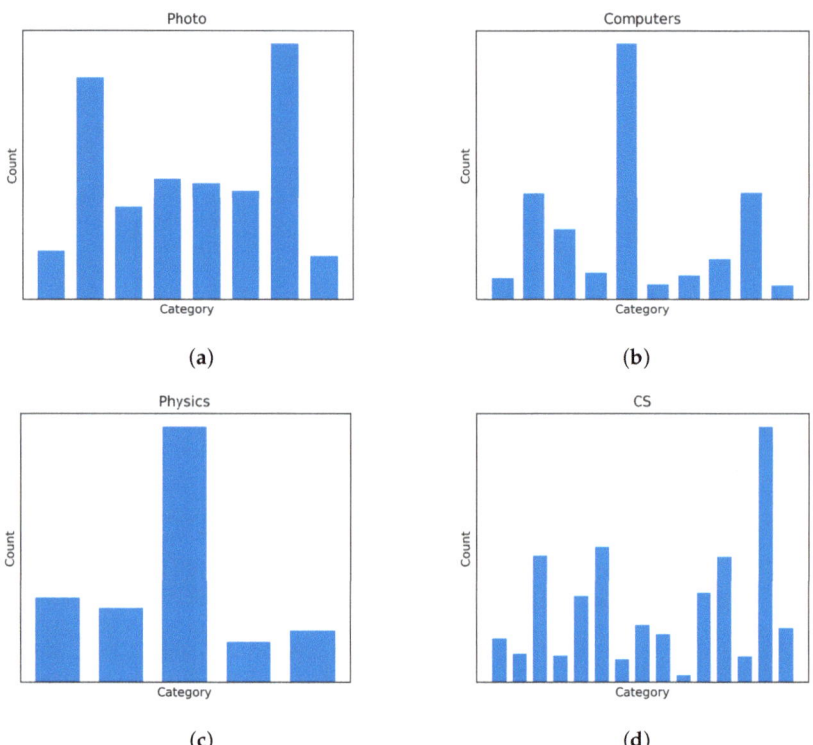

Figure 5. The categorical distribution of four added datasets. The horizontal axis represents different node categories, and the vertical axis indicates the number of nodes in each category: (**a**) Photos; (**b**) Computers; (**c**) Physics; (**d**) CS.

Meanwhile, we find that the performance of APPNP is optimal on small datasets. This is because APPNP improves the propagation mechanism of node features based on PageRank, which gives the target node a larger perceptive field. However, GinfoNN still achieves comparable classification accuracies compared with the baselines. This indicates that the Ricci curvature as an auxiliary supervision signal does not interfere with the supervision signal provided by the label and impairs the performance of GNNs. The experimental results illustrate that auxiliary supervision signals are crucial for improving the performance of GNNs when the dataset is large, dense, and relatively underlabeled.

5.4. Ablation Experiment

In this subsection, we design the ablation experiment to illustrate the necessity of the auxiliary task head. If the auxiliary task head is removed, it would impair the generalization of GinfoNN. Figure 6 shows the classification accuracies of GinfoNN with the auxiliary task head and GinfoNN with the auxiliary task head removed on the seven benchmark datasets. We find that the classification accuracies of GinfoNN and GinfoNN_Non are close on relatively small and sparse datasets. Nevertheless, the classification accuracies of GinfoNN are significantly better than GinfoNN_Non on the large and dense datasets. In particular, on the Photo dataset, GinfoNN improves by 1.5 percentage points. This ablation experiment illustrates that the auxiliary task head effectively improves the generalizability of GNNs.

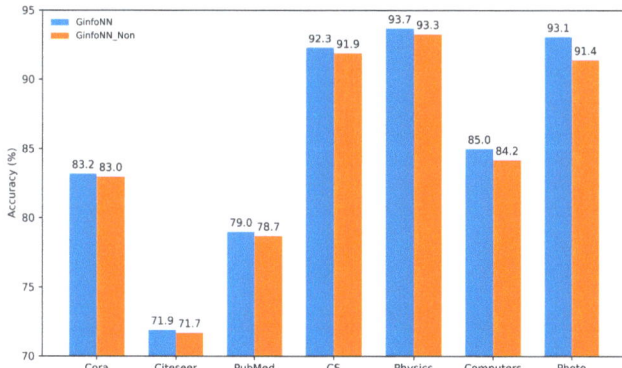

Figure 6. Comparison of predicted accuracies of GinfoNN with and without the auxiliary task head. GinfoNN_Non means GinfoNN without the auxiliary task head.

6. Discussion

Applications on real-world task scenarios. A graph is a crucial data type widely present in various fields. Graph representation learning also holds significant practical value, such as user classification in social networks, risk assessment in financial systems, recommendation systems, etc. GinfoNN is a general graph representation learner, making it applicable to various tasks across different domains. Additionally, Ricci curvature represents different physical meanings in different fields. For example, in transportation networks, Ricci curvature can be used to identify bottleneck segments [44]. Therefore, understanding graph data and graph information in real-world applications enables better adaptation of GinfoNN to practical applications while providing interpretable insights.

Extentions to more learning paradigms and other types of graph information. Explicitly incorporating the learning of Ricci curvature as a constraint during the model's representation learning process can help prevent the model from falling into the GIV dilemma. In this paper, Ricci curvature is selected as a form of effective graph information, and joint learning is chosen as the learning method, providing a preferable way for addressing the GIV issue. In the future, new learning paradigms such as self-supervised learning [45,46] and zero-shot learning, as well as the introduction of other types of graph information, can be further explored.

Generalizations on heterophilic graphs. The selected datasets are all high-homophily, which is also the main type in graph benchmark datasets. However, there exists a type of high-heterophily dataset [47], where the interactions between neighboring nodes show entirely different meanings. Whether Ricci curvature in heterophilic datasets will exhibit different properties, and whether it can provide equally effective information are questions that can be explored in the future.

7. Conclusions

In this paper, we find the existence of GIV for implicit GNNs, which leads to that GNNs do not exploit the property of graph information. We first show that random value substitution does not significantly affect the performance of implicit GNNs through extensive experiments. Then, we find that the weights of neighbors generated by the LTS using different graph information have high similarity from both qualitative and quantitative perspectives. Empirical experiments suggest that GIV does exist for implicit GNNs. Inspired by joint learning, we propose GinfoNN, which uses the Ricci curvature as an auxiliary supervision signal to constrain the training of the feature extractor. The experimental results show that GinfoNN outperforms baselines on heterogeneously large and dense datasets. GinfoNN provides new insights into how GNNs can utilize various valuable graph information.

Author Contributions: Conceptualization, J.C. and S.H.; methodology, J.C. and S.H.; software, H.Y. and Z.C.; validation, H.Y. and Z.C.; formal analysis, S.H.; investigation, H.Y. and Z.C.; resources, H.L.; data curation, H.Y.; writing—original draft preparation, J.C. and S.H.; writing—review and editing, J.C. and S.H.; visualization, J.C.; supervision, H.L.; project administration, S.G.; funding acquisition, S.G. All authors have read and agreed to the published version of the manuscript.

Funding: This research was funded by the National Natural Science Foundation of China, Grant Numbers: 62207032; Research Foundation of the Department of Natural Resources of Hunan Province, Grant Numbers: HBZ20240101; Scientific Research Project of the Department of Education of Hunan Province, Grant Numbers: 22B0014.

Institutional Review Board Statement: Not applicable.

Informed Consent Statement: Not applicable.

Data Availability Statement: No new data were created or analyzed in this study. Data sharing is not applicable to this article.

Acknowledgments: We acknowledge the High-Performance Computing Platform of Central South University and HPC Central of the Department of GIS for providing HPC resources.

Conflicts of Interest: The authors declare no conflicts of interest.

Abbreviations

The following abbreviations are used in this manuscript:

GNN   Graph Neural Network
LTS   Learnable Transformation Structure
GIV   Graph Information Vanishing

References

1. Zhang, M.; Chen, Y. Link prediction based on graph neural networks. In Proceedings of the 32nd International Conference on Neural Information Processing Systems, Red Hook, NY, USA, 3–8 December 2018; pp. 5171–5181.
2. Bian, T.; Xiao, X.; Xu, T.; Zhao, P.; Huang, W.; Rong, Y.; Huang, J. Rumor detection on social media with bi-directional graph convolutional networks. In Proceedings of the AAAI Conference on Artificial Intelligence, New York, NY, USA, 7–12 February 2020; Volume 34, pp. 549–556.
3. Yu, B.; Yin, H.; Zhu, Z. Spatio-temporal graph convolutional networks: A deep learning framework for traffic forecasting. In Proceedings of the 27th International Joint Conference on Artificial Intelligence, Stockholm, Sweden, 13–19 July 2018; pp. 3634–3640.
4. Kosaraju, V.; Sadeghian, A.; Martín-Martín, R.; Reid, I.D.; Rezatofighi, H.; Savarese, S. Social-BiGAT: Multimodal trajectory forecasting using Bicycle-GAN and graph attention networks. In Proceedings of the Advances in Neural Information Processing Systems, Neural Information Processing Systems (NIPS), Vancouver, BC, Canada, 8–14 December 2019.
5. Duvenaud, D.; Maclaurin, D.; Aguilera-Iparraguirre, J.; Gómez-Bombarelli, R.; Hirzel, T.; Aspuru-Guzik, A.; Adams, R.P. Convolutional networks on graphs for learning molecular fingerprints. In Proceedings of the 28th International Conference on Neural Information Processing Systems, Cambridge, MA, USA, 7–12 December 2015; Volume 2, pp. 2224–2232.
6. Jin, W.; Yang, K.; Barzilay, R.; Jaakkola, T. Learning Multimodal Graph-to-Graph Translation for Molecule Optimization. In Proceedings of the International Conference on Learning Representations, Vancouver, BC, Canada, 30 April–3 May 2018.
7. Gilmer, J.; Schoenholz, S.S.; Riley, P.F.; Vinyals, O.; Dahl, G.E. Neural message passing for quantum chemistry. In Proceedings of the International Conference on Machine Learning, Sydney, NSW, Australia, 6–11 August 2017; pp. 1263–1272.
8. Kipf, T.N.; Welling, M. Semi-supervised classification with graph convolutional networks. *arXiv* **2016**, arXiv:1609.02907.
9. Veličković, P.; Cucurull, G.; Casanova, A.; Romero, A.; Lio, P.; Bengio, Y. Graph attention networks. *arXiv* **2017**, arXiv:1710.10903.
10. Hamilton, W.L.; Ying, R.; Leskovec, J. Inductive representation learning on large graphs. In Proceedings of the 31st International Conference on Neural Information Processing Systems, Red Hook, NY, USA, 4–9 December 2017; pp. 1025–1035.
11. Klicpera, J.; Bojchevski, A.; Günnemann, S. Predict then propagate: Graph neural networks meet personalized pagerank. *arXiv* **2018**, arXiv:1810.05997.
12. Zhang, K.; Zhu, Y.; Wang, J.; Zhang, J. Adaptive structural fingerprints for graph attention networks. In Proceedings of the International Conference on Learning Representations, New Orleans, LA, USA, 6–9 May 2019.
13. Xu, K.; Hu, W.; Leskovec, J.; Jegelka, S. How powerful are graph neural networks? *arXiv* **2018**, arXiv:1810.00826.
14. Ye, Z.; Liu, K.S.; Ma, T.; Gao, J.; Chen, C. Curvature graph network. In Proceedings of the International Conference on Learning Representations, New Orleans, LA, USA, 6–9 May 2019.
15. Lin, Y.; Lu, L.; Yau, S.T. Ricci curvature of graphs. *Tohoku Math. J. Second Ser.* **2011**, *63*, 605–627. [CrossRef]

16. Zhao, Q.; Ye, Z.; Chen, C.; Wang, Y. Persistence enhanced graph neural network. In Proceedings of the International Conference on Artificial Intelligence and Statistics, Online, 26–28 August 2020; pp. 2896–2906.
17. Chami, I.; Ying, R.; Ré, C.; Leskovec, J. Hyperbolic graph convolutional neural networks. *Adv. Neural Inf. Process. Syst.* **2019**, *32*, 4869.
18. Thekumparampil, K.K.; Wang, C.; Oh, S.; Li, L.J. Attention-based graph neural network for semi-supervised learning. *arXiv* **2018**, arXiv:1803.03735.
19. Ollivier, Y. Ricci curvature of metric spaces. *C. R. Math.* **2007**, *345*, 643–646. [CrossRef]
20. Bruna, J.; Zaremba, W.; Szlam, A.; LeCun, Y. Spectral networks and locally connected networks on graphs. *arXiv* **2013**, arXiv:1312.6203.
21. Defferrard, M.; Bresson, X.; Vandergheynst, P. Convolutional neural networks on graphs with fast localized spectral filtering. In Proceedings of the 30th International Conference on Neural Information Processing Systems, Barcelona, Spain, 5–10 December 2016; pp. 3844–3852.
22. Monti, F.; Boscaini, D.; Masci, J.; Rodola, E.; Svoboda, J.; Bronstein, M.M. Geometric deep learning on graphs and manifolds using mixture model cnns. In Proceedings of the IEEE Conference on Computer Vision and Pattern Recognition, Honolulu, HI, USA, 21–26 July 2017; pp. 5115–5124.
23. Li, Y.; Wang, X.; Liu, H.; Shi, C. A generalized neural diffusion framework on graphs. In Proceedings of the AAAI Conference on Artificial Intelligence, Vancouver, BC, Canada, 20–27 February 2024; Volume 38, pp. 8707–8715.
24. Li, Q.; Han, Z.; Wu, X.M. Deeper insights into graph convolutional networks for semi-supervised learning. In Proceedings of the AAAI Conference on Artificial Intelligence, New Orleans, LA, USA, 2–7 February 2018; Volume 32.
25. Oono, K.; Suzuki, T. Graph Neural Networks Exponentially Lose Expressive Power for Node Classification. In Proceedings of the International Conference on Learning Representations, New Orleans, LA, USA, 6–9 May 2019.
26. Barceló, P.; Kostylev, E.; Monet, M.; Pérez, J.; Reutter, J.; Silva, J.P. The logical expressiveness of graph neural networks. In Proceedings of the 8th International Conference on Learning Representations (ICLR 2020), Addis Ababa, Ethiopia, 26–30 April 2020.
27. Agarwal, C.; Zitnik, M.; Lakkaraju, H. Probing gnn explainers: A rigorous theoretical and empirical analysis of gnn explanation methods. In Proceedings of the International Conference on Artificial Intelligence and Statistics, Virtual, 28–30 March 2022; pp. 8969–8996.
28. Wu, F.; Souza, A.; Zhang, T.; Fifty, C.; Yu, T.; Weinberger, K. Simplifying graph convolutional networks. In Proceedings of the International Conference on Machine Learning, Long Beach, CA, USA, 9–15 June 2019; pp. 6861–6871.
29. Li, G.; Muller, M.; Thabet, A.; Ghanem, B. Deepgcns: Can gcns go as deep as cnns? In Proceedings of the IEEE/CVF International Conference on Computer Vision, Seoul, Republic of Korea, 27 October–2 November 2019; pp. 9267–9276.
30. Knyazev, B.; Taylor, G.W.; Amer, M. Understanding Attention and Generalization in Graph Neural Networks. *Adv. Neural Inf. Process. Syst.* **2019**, *32*, 4202–4212.
31. You, Y.; Chen, T.; Wang, Z.; Shen, Y. When does self-supervision help graph convolutional networks? In Proceedings of the International Conference on Machine Learning, Online, 26–28 August 2020; pp. 10871–10880.
32. Sun, K.; Lin, Z.; Zhu, Z. Multi-stage self-supervised learning for graph convolutional networks on graphs with few labeled nodes. In Proceedings of the AAAI Conference on Artificial Intelligence, New York, NY, USA, 7–12 February 2020; Volume 34, pp. 5892–5899.
33. Jin, W.; Derr, T.; Liu, H.; Wang, Y.; Wang, S.; Liu, Z.; Tang, J. Self-supervised learning on graphs: Deep insights and new direction. *arXiv* **2020**, arXiv:2006.10141.
34. Hu, Z.; Fan, C.; Chen, T.; Chang, K.W.; Sun, Y. Pre-training graph neural networks for generic structural feature extraction. *arXiv* **2019**, arXiv:1905.13728.
35. Ding, Q.; Ye, D.; Xu, T.; Zhao, P. GPN: A Joint Structural Learning Framework for Graph Neural Networks. *arXiv* **2022**, arXiv:2205.05964.
36. Gui, S.; Liu, M.; Li, X.; Luo, Y.; Ji, S. Joint Learning of Label and Environment Causal Independence for Graph Out-of-Distribution Generalization. In Proceedings of the Thirty-Seventh Conference on Neural Information Processing Systems, New Orleans, LA, USA, 10–16 December 2023.
37. Ni, C.C.; Lin, Y.Y.; Gao, J.; Gu, X.D.; Saucan, E. Ricci curvature of the internet topology. In Proceedings of the 2015 IEEE Conference on Computer Communications (INFOCOM), Kowloon, Hong Kong, 26 April–1 May 2015; pp. 2758–2766.
38. Sia, J.; Jonckheere, E.; Bogdan, P. Ollivier-ricci curvature-based method to community detection in complex networks. *Sci. Rep.* **2019**, *9*, 9800. [CrossRef] [PubMed]
39. Sen, P.; Namata, G.; Bilgic, M.; Getoor, L.; Galligher, B.; Eliassi-Rad, T. Collective classification in network data. *AI Mag.* **2008**, *29*, 93. [CrossRef]
40. McAuley, J.; Targett, C.; Shi, Q.; Van Den Hengel, A. Image-based recommendations on styles and substitutes. In Proceedings of the 38th International ACM SIGIR Conference on Research and Development in Information Retrieval, Santiago, Chile, 9–13 August 2015; pp. 43–52.
41. Fey, M.; Lenssen, J.E. Fast graph representation learning with PyTorch Geometric. *arXiv* **2019**, arXiv:1903.02428.
42. Shchur, O.; Mumme, M.; Bojchevski, A.; Günnemann, S. Pitfalls of graph neural network evaluation. *arXiv* **2018**, arXiv:1811.05868.

43. Li, H.; Cao, J.; Zhu, J.; Liu, Y.; Zhu, Q.; Wu, G. Curvature Graph Neural Network. *arXiv* **2021**, arXiv:2106.15762.
44. Han, X.; Zhu, G.; Zhao, L.; Du, R.; Wang, Y.; Chen, Z.; Liu, Y.; He, S. Ollivier–Ricci Curvature Based Spatio-Temporal Graph Neural Networks for Traffic Flow Forecasting. *Symmetry* **2023**, *15*, 995. [CrossRef]
45. Li, H.; Cao, J.; Zhu, J.; Luo, Q.; He, S.; Wang, X. Augmentation-free graph contrastive learning of invariant-discriminative representations. *IEEE Trans. Neural Netw. Learn. Syst.* **2024**, *35*, 11157–11167. [CrossRef]
46. Zhang, Z.; Ren, Z.; Tao, C.; Zhang, Y.; Peng, C.; Li, H. Grass: Contrastive learning with gradient guided sampling strategy for remote sensing image semantic segmentation. *IEEE Trans. Geosci. Remote. Sens.* **2023**, *61*, 5626814. [CrossRef]
47. He, S.; Luo, Q.; Fu, X.; Zhao, L.; Du, R.; Li, H. Cat: A causal graph attention network for trimming heterophilic graphs. *Inf. Sci.* **2024**, *677*, 120916. [CrossRef]

Disclaimer/Publisher's Note: The statements, opinions and data contained in all publications are solely those of the individual author(s) and contributor(s) and not of MDPI and/or the editor(s). MDPI and/or the editor(s) disclaim responsibility for any injury to people or property resulting from any ideas, methods, instructions or products referred to in the content.

MDPI AG
Grosspeteranlage 5
4052 Basel
Switzerland
Tel.: +41 61 683 77 34

Mathematics Editorial Office
E-mail: mathematics@mdpi.com
www.mdpi.com/journal/mathematics

Disclaimer/Publisher's Note: The title and front matter of this reprint are at the discretion of the Guest Editors. The publisher is not responsible for their content or any associated concerns. The statements, opinions and data contained in all individual articles are solely those of the individual Editors and contributors and not of MDPI. MDPI disclaims responsibility for any injury to people or property resulting from any ideas, methods, instructions or products referred to in the content.

www.ingramcontent.com/pod-product-compliance
Lightning Source LLC
LaVergne TN
LVHW072314090526
838202LV00019B/2279